A Passion for Purses
1600-2005

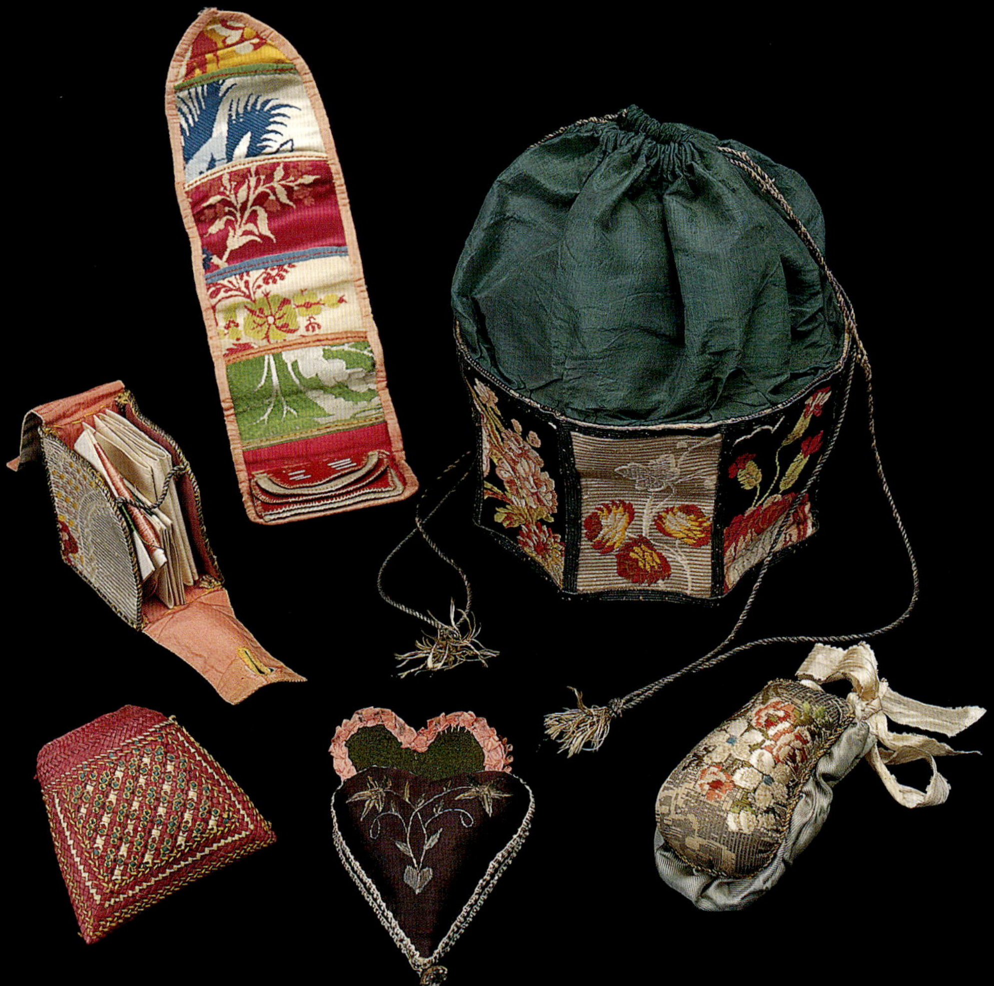

Paula Higgins and Lori Blaser

Schiffer Publishing Ltd
4880 Lower Valley Road Atglen, Pennsylvania 19310

Published by Schiffer Publishing Ltd.
4880 Lower Valley Road
Atglen, PA 19310
Phone: (610) 593-1777; Fax: (610) 593-2002
E-mail: Info@schifferbooks.com

For the largest selection of fine reference books on this and related subjects, please visit our web site at **www.schifferbooks.com**
We are always looking for people to write books on new and related subjects. If you have an idea for a book please contact us at the above address.

This book may be purchased from the publisher.
Include $3.95 for shipping.
Please try your bookstore first.
You may write for a free catalog.

In Europe, Schiffer books are distributed by
Bushwood Books
6 Marksbury Ave.
Kew Gardens
Surrey TW9 4JF England
Phone: 44 (0) 20 8392-8585; Fax: 44 (0) 20 8392-9876
E-mail: info@bushwoodbooks.co.uk
Website: www.bushwoodbooks.co.uk
Free postage in the U.K., Europe; air mail at cost.

Library of Congress Control Number: 2006937730

Covers and book designed by: Bruce Waters
Type set in Snell Roundhand heading font/text font Aldine 721

ISBN: 978-0-7643-2617-2
Printed in China

Dedication

To our husbands,
William J. Higgins and Cary Michael Blaser,
this work is dedicated with love and appreciation
for their unwavering support for us
as collectors and authors.

Acknowledgments

We sincerely thank Laura Brown of Granite Pail Collectibles. Laura's role in the beginning was key to promoting the idea for this book, and without her help it would not have been realized. Terri Lykins contributed her vast knowledge and expertise on beaded purse restoration, adding an extra bonus for the readers. We are indebted to our contributors Ellen Foster of Vanity Lady, Sharon Lu Visi, Terri Lykins, Linda Marshall, Katerina Musetti, Melissa Overdorf, Lee Ann Papale, Ruth Penson, Alan SW Reed, Marcy Rick, Shara Stewart, and Kim Stonecipher for their friendship, support, time, and beautiful purses.

A special thanks goes to the staff at Cora Ginsburg LLC in New York, New York. Their advice and knowledge is always greatly appreciated, and their photographs invaluable to this work. Our photographers, Photography by Arlene, Cindy Batten, Tom Ferguson of Ferguson Photography and Design, Virgil C. Henle, Steve Marshall, Elyn F. Marton, and Joel Sano were crucial to the completion of this book, and to them we extend our sincere gratitude.

To our families, William J. Higgins, Cary Michael Blaser, Jeff Blaser, Adam Blaser, Brian Blaser, and Sharleen Bergman, we offer thanks for their patience, encouragement, and support. We also thank Nancy and Peter Schiffer for their untiring support, advice, and kindness. This book would not have been possible without their considerable assistance and commitment to the project.

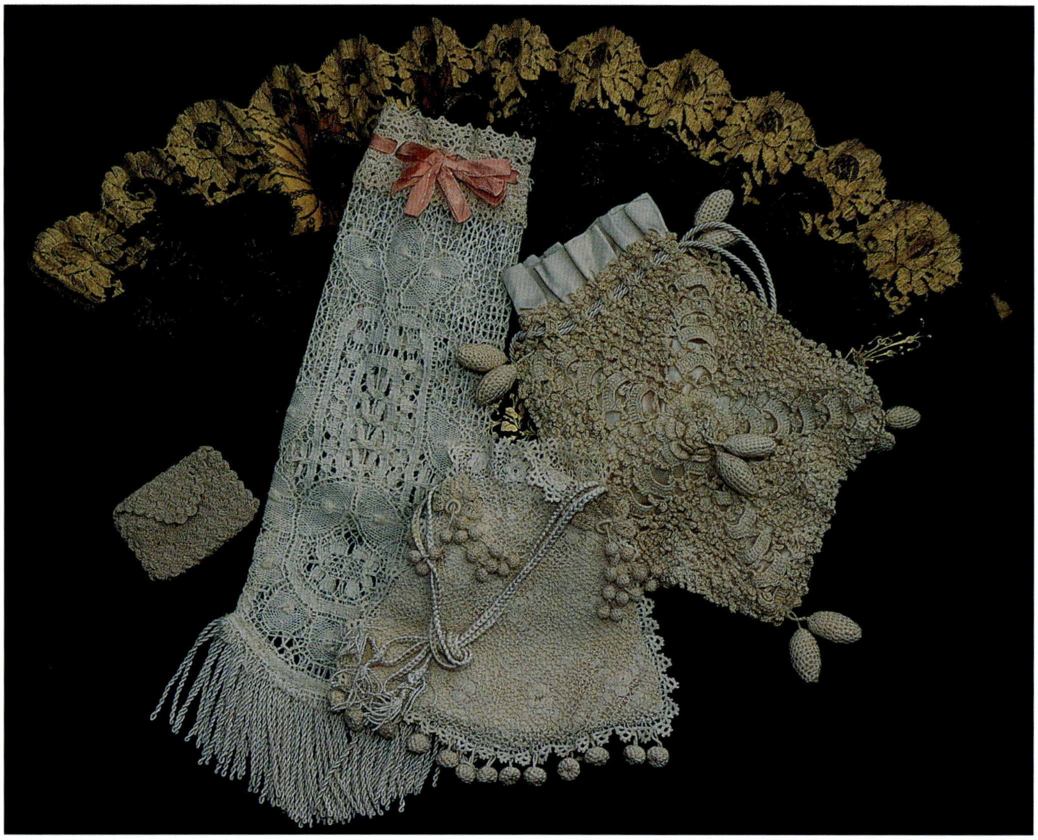

Contents

Introduction

Collecting purses is a passion some people might find mystifying. But for those of us who love them, the reasons are obvious. We value them as pieces of textile art, often handmade and usually designed by women, representing a design aesthetic that is distinctly feminine. They are prized for their beauty and for their connection to women of other times and other centuries. Because many purses were personally designed by women from our historic past, they are preserved items of our social history. Most antique purses were handmade, and now are a testimony to what could be accomplished when material resources were not readily available: light came from a candle or an oil lamp and heat from a fireplace. Imagine trying to bead knit a purse with beads of sizes 18 or 20 under these conditions. The fact is that some of the embroidery techniques were so complex they are no longer in use today, and this makes us admire them even more. These antique purses are unique works of art, created from their makers' own personal visions and perspectives.

Like all forms of art, some of the purses included here were made with more skill than others. Therefore, some purses have more appeal by virtue of their superior design, materials, or craftsmanship. Individual purses evoke emotions based on the brilliance of their form or design, and the beauty of their decoration. Art inspires the imagination, and purses do as well. Today, we are left wondering about the lives and hopes of the women who made these purses, why they chose certain colors and designs, and how they communicate about themselves with us through these small items they left behind.

Women's purses are highly personal items reflecting the owner's sense of style, social status, and relative wealth. This is true for a purse made 400 years ago or a purse made yesterday. Yet, the contents of a purse varied, not only from century to century but from decade to decade, as well. A purse made c.1600 may have held sweet herbs or a sachet to ward off unpleasant body odors, since people seldom bathed; a purse carried today might hold a cell phone or a palm pilot. Besides being decorative, purses have become highly functional. It is hard to imagine a woman of the 21st century without a purse or a bag to hold the necessities of her daily life.

As you page through this book, you will see pictures that relate how purse designs reflect the periods in which they were made. Their forms and styles of decoration echo other decorative arts from the same eras. For example, eighteenth century embroidered purses and wallets are as exquisitely worked as a court dress from the same time. Designs stenciled on theorem purses from the 1820s to 1830s resemble designs on stenciled furniture from the same period. The bombé-shaped purse with a faux ivory body made c.1830 imitates furniture from the Biedermeier era. In other words, purse designs were not made in a vacuum, but are a reflection of designs in other decorative arts.

As antiques, purses enjoy the respect they deserve. Some purses currently have only collectible status because of their recent vintage, but they are worth buying as antiques of the future. A purse's value probably will be maintained and enhanced if it is a quality item that reflects the design aesthetic of its period.

The field of purse collecting has grown dramatically, as evidenced by a declining availability. Many wonderful purses are in private collections, where they will not be seen by the public. As with antiques such as furniture, museums have been acquiring purses, from the truly aged to those more recent. Also, literature on purses is increasing annually, indicating a high degree of interest held by serious collectors. Their value in the marketplace also has risen consistently over the past twenty years. While prices vary throughout the United States and internationally, purses have generally maintained their values and have been good investments.

Most collectors today acknowledge that the thrill of hunting for fine purses is a motivating factor in their pursuit. Purses can be found at antiques shows, antiques shops, in monthly antiques newspapers, at auctions, and in vintage textile and clothing shops. With the advent of the internet, purse buying has been transformed. Besides numerous internet purse dealers, collectors now have access to Ebay, the internet auction site which enables everyone with access to a computer to bid on objects of their choice. Because some sellers are unknowledgeable about their merchandise, rare and lovely purses still can be found for relatively small prices. A purse from c.1630 described in this book was won on Ebay for nine dollars plus shipping. The message is, if you know what you are seeking you may find a treasure.

Many of the purses described in this book have been contributed by members of the Antique Purse Collector's Society, as well as numerous artists and antiques dealer Cora Ginsburg LLC. The intent here is to present a timeline of purses from c.1600 to 2005. Because many purse and textile historians feel that purse design and beadwork was at its peak during the first half of the 19th century, representative pieces from that period are especially featured. Also, many purses from the mid-nineteenth through the twentieth centuries were selected for their exceptional historic merit, rarity, beauty, and design.

The values placed here on each purse reflect the current market trend. It is important to note that prices vary from location to location, and venue to venue. The values used here are also based on purses in very good to excellent condition and some purses are described as rare or very rare.

It is our hope that readers will find here interesting and beautiful purses that have not been seen in print before, and therefore advance their appreciation of purses as an art form.

The Antique Purse Collector's Society

Melissa Overdorf founded the first internet antique purse society on December 1, 2003. Her goals were to form a society that functioned as a resource for antique purse collectors and to provide a network for them to share their passion for purses. The Antique Purse Collector's Society (APCS) currently has over 250 enthusiastic members from America, Australia, Canada, England, Germany, Japan, and The Netherlands. Her goals seem to have been met.

Categories on the APCS site include: a discussion board, display ideas, member profiles, a member museum, purse repair resources, cleaning tips, links to museums with internet capabilities, links to purse dealers, a classified section, book reviews, and more. The discussion board is a place where information and ideas are exchanged, making it especially valuable. Melissa also holds purse society gatherings; the second meeting was in Los Angeles in August of 2005. The next meeting is planned for Washington, D.C., in 2007. Each gathering's attendance has doubled.

As members of the Antique Purse Collector's Society, the authors attest to its many benefits, especially the opportunity to meet other collectors. All are welcomed, whether their collection is great or small, and for this opportunity we are indebted to Melissa. Anyone who is interested in joining the society may do so for a nominal fee. Please contact www.antiquepursesociety.com.

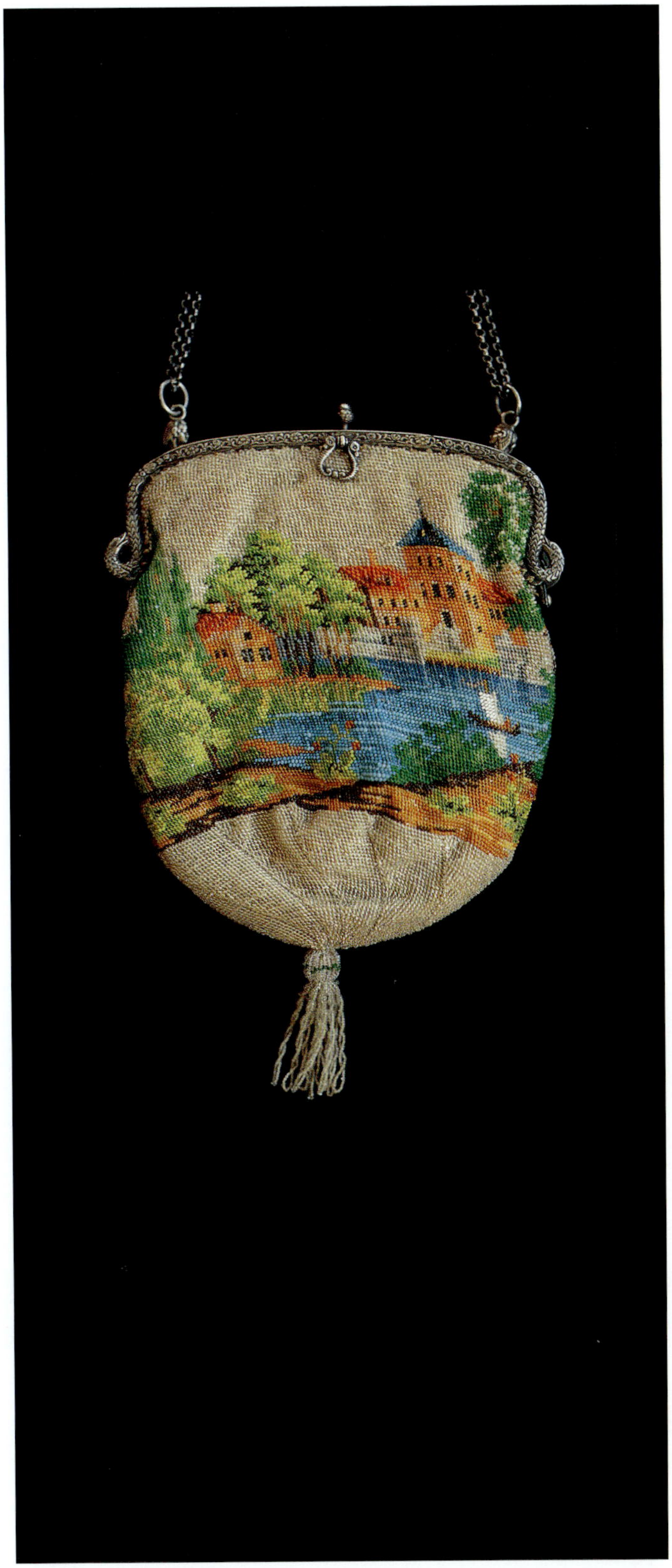

Chapter 1
An Overview of Purses, 1600 to 2005

Two hikers found the body of a frozen man in the Tyrolean Alps in 1991. It was discovered that the man was 5,300 years old, having lived during the Ice Age. Along with his amazingly well preserved body, 70 objects were also found. Among them were a leather pouch filled with herbs and a belt pouch. A bone awl, a piece of tinder, and three flint implements were found inside the leather pouch. The fact is that leather bags or purses were carried by people during the Ice Age.

Other very early known purses include a 5th century Scythian pouch made from leather and a 12th century purse, both now residing in the Museen fur Kunst unde Gewerbe, in Hamburg, Germany. The exhibition at the Musée de la Mode et du Textile, in Paris, (October 6, 2004 - February 2, 2005) and its accompanying book, *Carried Away—All About Bags,* showed several examples of 12th through 15th century bags from museum and cathedral collections. Especially notable are two very beautiful bags embroidered with courting scenes in silk and gold threads. Brass rubbings and tomb figures from that time occasionally show women with tasseled pouches hanging from their girdles. Purses were also known as *burses*, *tasques*, and *escarcelles*. Another type of bag known as the *charniere* was used to hold food for pet birds and as a game bag. But, since these are bags we will most likely see only in museums, we have chosen to start the history of purses for this book in the 17th century.

Seventeenth Century Purses

Most purse collectors are unfamiliar with 17th century purses that populate museums around the world, but it is accurate to say that they vary considerably in style and design. Styles ranged from tiny pouches made in the shape of a frog, worked in buttonhole stitches, to large seal bags made of velvet and gold embroidery. Embroidery was a skill practiced by professionals in shops and by women in their homes. Many of the women were highly skilled, and their embroidery was comparable to the professionally worked pieces, often making it difficult to distinguish them. Designs from the early 17th century were stylized and somewhat angular. They were found in pattern books of the period and sold to both professional and home embroiderers. Late 17th century embroidered purses reflected a more Baroque design influence, featuring heavily embroidered silks and velvets. ("Baroque" is from the Portuguese word *Barocco*, meaning art that is flamboyant, bizarre, or highly ornamental.)

The 17th century is famous for its *swete*, or sweetmeat bags, which were usually no bigger than 5 by 4 inches in size. These beautifully embroidered sachets were often filled with sweet herbs, which hid unpleasant body odors. Sweet bags also held money, papers, and small sewing items. They were made from embroidered silk and velvet, and fine canvas embroidered in tent stitch. Their designs included exquisitely worked florals and extraordinary animals and wildlife. Occasionally, a pin-pillow or a knife case was attached. Plaited drawstrings, typically ended with bulbous acorn-style tassels, and three more tassels hung across the bottom for decoration.

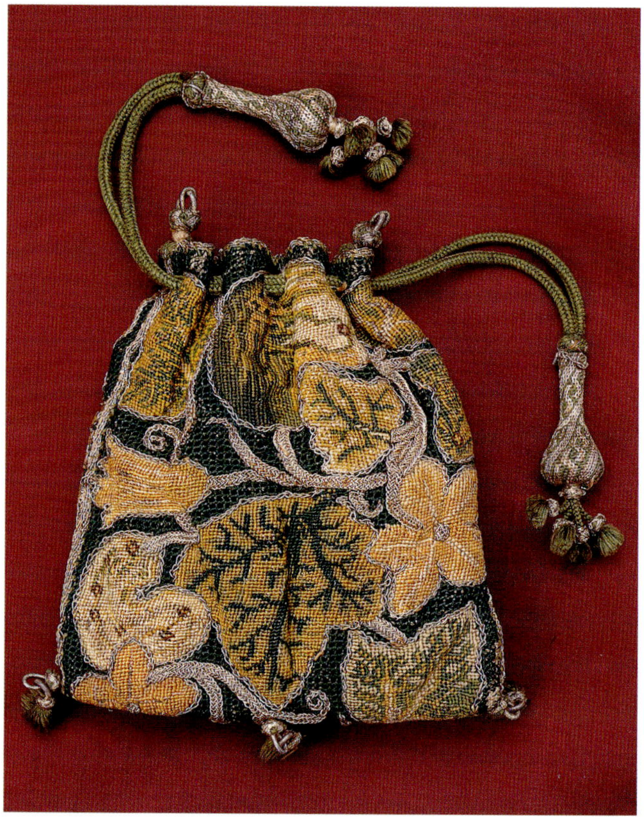

17th century sweet meat purse made from a background of green filet needlework with tent stitch depictions of gourds, blossoms, and veined leaves on silver metallic braid vines. Lined in white leather. 5.5 x 5 in. *Courtesy of Cora Ginsburg LLC.* Very rare.

Other surviving 17th century purses include a bag made in the shape of a bunch of grapes, decorated with pearls, and a large nut cut in half, which was sewn to a gusset. This certainly has to be one of the oddest and most charming uses of a nut in recorded history. The little frog purse, also worked in buttonhole stitches, is so tiny that it is hard to imagine what it could have held. Perhaps it was purely decorative. Whatever the case, it can be safely said that purse makers in the 17th century did not lack for imagination.

Pocketbooks, or wallets, were also carried during the late 17th century. Although some were beaded, most were embroidered on fine canvas, silk, or velvet. Designs included mythological figures and creatures, hearts, stylized florals, and stags. Another purse form that enjoyed popularity was the "snap-hance" purse. The name came from their curved brass frames, closed with a latch, which had to be pried apart. The bodies of these purses were usually made from velvet, which were embroidered with gold or silver thread. These purses were quite small and could hold little more than a few coins.

Gaming bags, made from velvet and leather, had flat bottoms with short sides and were designed specifically for card playing and gambling. They were beautifully embroidered with silver and gold threads, with the owner's family crest or monogram often worked onto the bottom. Smooth, cream colored leather lined these beautifully needleworked purses. Women also carried rectangular workbags made from cotton or linen, which were decorated with crewelwork designs of coiling stems and wildlife.

Around 1630, completely beaded bags made their appearance. They were fashioned from a network of beads on linen or silk threads, or they were bead embroidered on leather. They were not large and usually square or slightly rectangular in shape. Diaper designs (repetitive geometric patterns), were popular, as were designs featuring acorns. Early beaded designs were quite unsophisticated and angular because of their method of construction, giving them a distinctive look. Some early beaded purses had mottos embroidered on them, such as "Remember the Pore," "Here it is Hit or Miss," and "The Gift of a Friend."

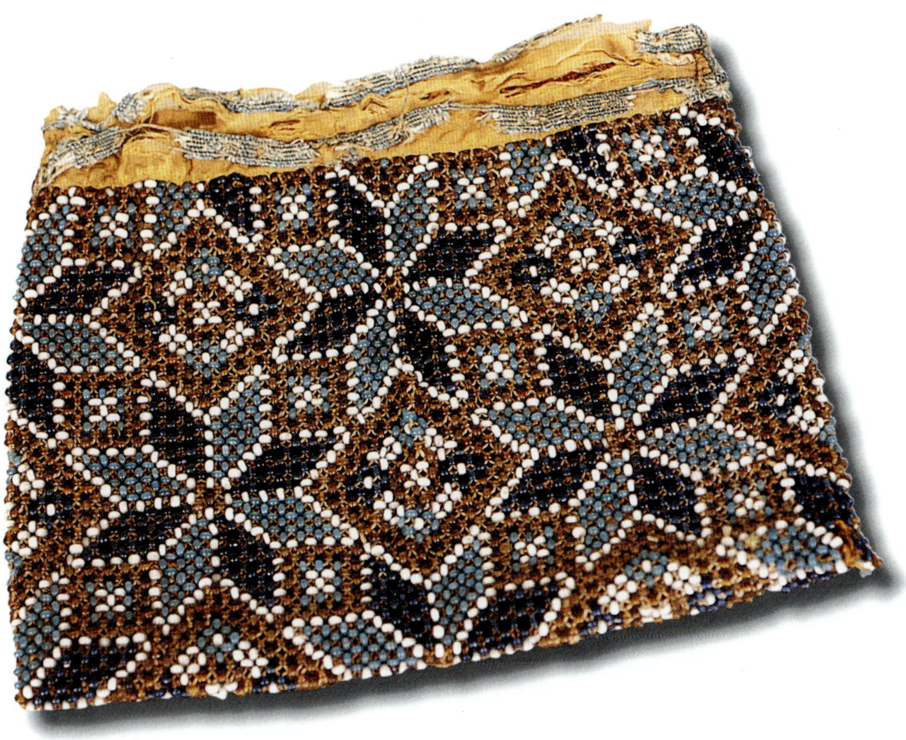

C.1630 purse made from a network of beads, in a stylized floral and geometric design. Simple, repetitive angular designs were easily made using this network technique. 5.5 x 4.5 in. *Collection of Lori Blaser.* Very rare.

Another type of purse specific to the 17th century was the Limoges Marriage Purse. Made to commemorate a marriage, they were made from enameled plaques, which were painted with pictures of the bride and groom. The plaques were sewn together with colorful silk gussets and finished with silk cord drawstrings and ribbons.

Tapestry purses were also made during this period. Woven with metal and silk threads, they were pouch-shaped or made from four, shield-shaped panels and decorated with knotted tassels. One exceptional example depicts a galleon. Late 17th century tapestry purses also featured bulbous, Baroque-inspired floral designs.

According to some textile experts, in the 17th century pockets made their first appearance. Pockets were a style that lasted for centuries, even into the early 20th century, as travel accessories. Pockets of the 17th century were made singly and in pairs, and tied around the waist. They usually resembled saddlebags and hung at the sides, typically under the woman's skirt. Occasionally, a beautifully embroidered pocket would be worn over the outside skirt. Pockets had vertical slits, allowing for easy access to their contents by owners and thieves alike. Pockets were usually embroidered, but occasionally they were made from plain cloth, such as linen.

The first miser purses also are believed to have appeared in the 17th century. It probably did not look exactly like the misers of the late 18th and 19th centuries (see Chapter Three), but it was similar in appearance and function. Instead of the modified barbell shape we have become familiar with, it more closely resembled a long tube of material or knitting.

Seventeenth century purses can be purchased today from specialty dealers of antique textiles and costumes, and every once in a while one will appear on Ebay. Most likely of European origin, they are historically important examples well worth acquiring. The collector has only to know what to look for to be able to add a rare purse to a collection.

Eighteenth Century Purses

The textiles artists of the 18th century produced some of the most beautiful bags and purses ever made. Exquisite quality in 18th century embroidery distinguishes these purses from those made in other centuries. Polychrome silk and metal threads and rich crewel yarns decorated home- and professionally-made bags, pocketbooks, misers, pouches, and reticules. Some embroidery techniques found on them, such as the complex Queen's or Rococo stitch, have not been in use for over 150 years because they are so difficult to execute. Despite its complexity, the Queen's stitch was popular during the 18th century and it is frequently seen on pocketbooks from that time. Other stitches in use were the tent, Romanian, whip, buttonhole, satin, backstitch, herringbone, and cross-stitch. Probably the most well-known stitch of the 18th century was the Irish stitch, which produced a vibrant geometric pattern. (In the late 19th century the Irish stitch was renamed the Florentine stitch, and then it was renamed again in the 20th century as the Flame stitch.) Popular 18th century designs included strawberries, insects, birds, stags, trees, flowers, mythological creatures, and figures.

Towards the end of the 18th century, many workbags, pocketbooks, and purses were embellished with tambour work. This finely executed chain stitch originated in India or China, and had the advantage of being worked very quickly. There exist 18th century portraits of young girls working with tambour hooks on fabric stretched over tambour hoops. Tambour work saw a resurgence in popularity in the first half of the 20th century, but usually the quality was inferior to 18th century examples.

Small, shield-shaped purses, embroidered with silk and sewn to straight pinchbeck frames, were popular during the mid-eighteenth century. Pinchbeck metal was developed in the early 18th century by Christopher Pinchbeck and can resemble gold quite convincingly. It is much lighter in weight than other metals, and made from an alloy of zinc and copper. Pinchbeck was used into the first half of the 19th century for English and European purse frames, sliders, and jewelry.

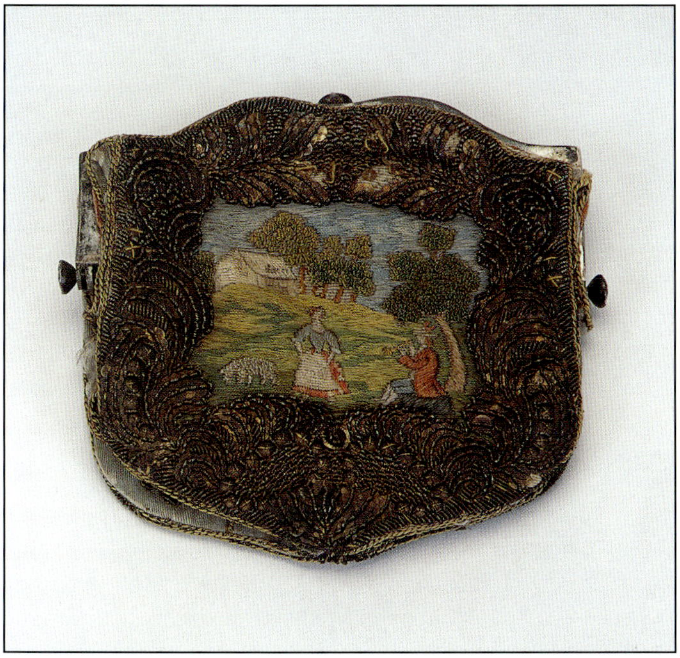

C.1730 shield shaped purse featuring 18th century pastoral scene with figures. Embroidered in silk, gilt threads, and paillettes. The frame has three red jewels, one at the top and one at the end of each hinge. It was also called a "snap-hance" frame because it had to be pried open. The original, pink silk lining is intact. 4.25 x 4 in. *Collection of Lori Blaser.* Very rare.

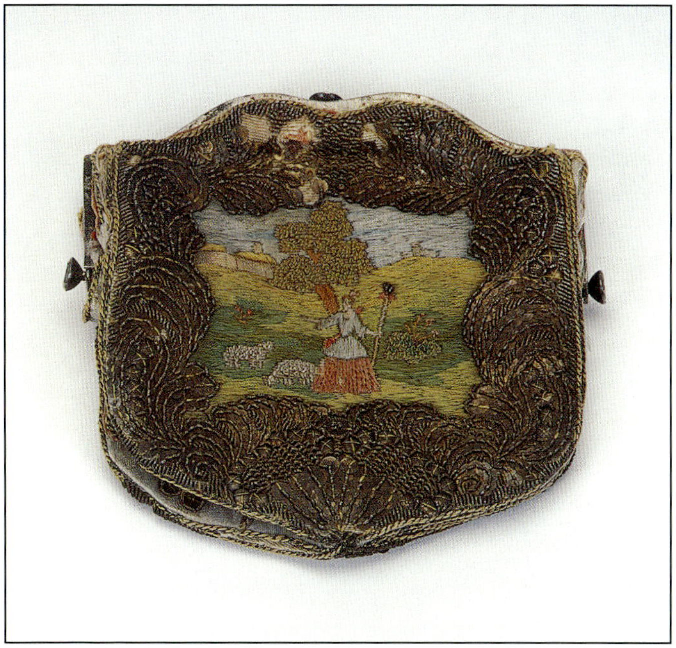

The reverse side of the shield shaped purse with a different scene and figural.

Early American pocketbooks from the 18th century have a naïve, unsophisticated quality, but a liveliness in design that their European counterparts do not have. They used stitches, such as the Romanian stitch, that enabled them to use less of their costly silk and crewel yarns. This stitch showed very little of the thread on the back of the material, the side that no one would see, while producing a perfectly finished surface. The majority of 18th century American pocketbooks were worked in Irish stitch (flame stitch), Queen's stitch, or tent stitch. Occasionally, the name of the owner and/or the year the purse was made was embroidered opposite the flap. Any 18th century American purse is rare and desirable, especially with a known provenance. These purses typically sell for thousands of dollars.

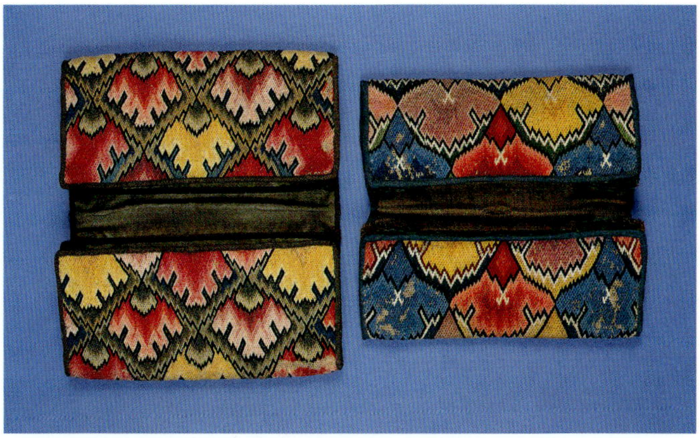

18th century American flamepoint (also known as flamestitch) pocketbooks in shades of pink, green, yellow, and blue. *Courtesy of Cora Ginsburg LLC.* Rare.

Morocco leather (embroidered with metal threads) and silk embroidered purses were made in Constantinople and exported to Europe during the 18th century. Turkey had a thriving export economy, much of it based on textiles. Many of these purses were embroidered with the word *Constantinople*, which clearly indicates their place of origin. French and English embroiderers also produced some beautifully worked pocketbooks. They were embroidered with delicate designs of swags, flowers, urns, and initials, and then further embellished with *paillettes*. These purses were multi-functional, holding letters, documents, bits of fabric, penwipes, bank bills, obituaries, newspaper clippings, pieces of hair, and small booklets.

Another type of purse associated with the 18th century is the pocket (see also Chapter Two). Like earlier 17th century versions, they often were made in pairs, as pear or saddlebag shapes, and with vertical slits for accessing their contents. Many surviving examples are beautifully embroidered in crewels and silk threads. Some were made from patterned whole cloth, patchwork, or plain linen and cotton. Others derive from appliquéd and quilted fabric. They were popular in America and England, but less so in France. Interestingly, pockets were considered somewhat vulgar by fashionable French women of the time. Early American pockets are very hard to find today in their original pair form, and often only one of the pair survives. Pockets were used like any purse, holding whatever the wearer needed for her activities of daily living. Because they were highly valued by their 18th century owners, they generally were preserved and passed down to the next generation. Early American crewel-worked pockets sell for thousands of dollars, even in less-than-perfect condition.

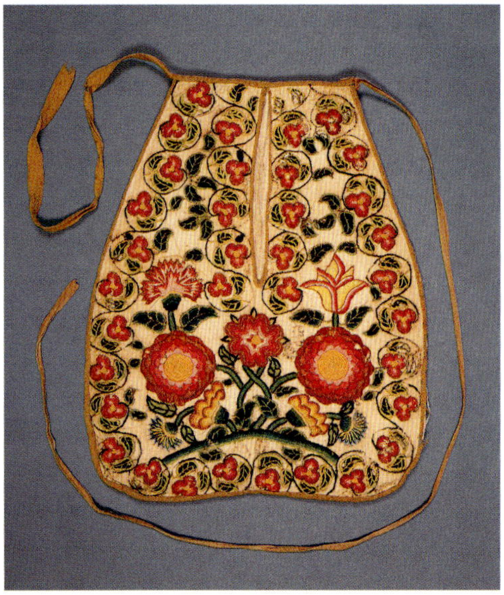

Late 18th century American pocket from Chester County, Pennsylvania. The colorful and lively design is characteristic of early American embroidery. Pockets of this quality, and with an American provenance, are especially desirable. It is even more rare to find them in pair form. *Courtesy of Cora Ginsburg LLC.* Very rare.

Misers from the 18th century are among the most charming and beautifully made of the genre (see also Chapter Three). The earliest versions were shaped like a sock and were finely knitted. Towards the end of the 18th century, they more closely resembled a barbell shape. Netting was a very popular pastime in the late 18th century and misers directly benefited from this new technique. Professionally made misers were very finely netted. Home-made misers were also beautiful, but the netting was usually less fine. Metal sliders slid to either end to close of the purse. Shops carried pinchbeck, gilt, silver, and steel sliders, which women bought to decorate their homemade misers and purses. Many 18th century misers were finished with thick, short silk tassels at either end of the purse, or long silk tassels with glass pearls, instead of metal charms (fishes). Another miser characteristic typical of the 18th century was their long length; usually 19 inches to 24 inches. By 1800 to 1810, they had shortened considerably. Later 19th century versions were crocheted and less unique in their designs. Because so many misers were made, they have survived not only from the 19th century, but also from the 18th century.

Chatelaines (see also Chapter Four) from the 18th century were not called chatelaines, but rather "waist bags." Their scrolling metal frames and hooks were all one piece, and attached to bags made from velvet or leather. The back of the hook was long to support the bag. 18th century waist bags should be considered rare. Beautiful chatelaines made with hooks, chains, and attached appendages also were worn in the 18th century. Some of the examples seen in the book, *Chatelaines—Utility to Glorious Extravagance*, by Cummins and Taunton, are literally works of art. They were made in a beautiful Rococo style from gold, gilt, and pinchbeck, and decorated with enamel, rock crystal, and mother-of-pearl. Watches, scent bottles, thimbles, vinaigrettes, scissors, and watch fobs hung from chatelaine chains. 18th century chatelaines are quite expensive today.

Reticules made from plant fibers, or *bast*, are another style unique to the late 18th and early 19th centuries. These purses were often made from pear or pineapple fibers, although other plant fibers could be used. It is believed by textile historians that they were made in the Philippines, and exported from Manila to Europe and the United States (see an example on page 253 of one imported to the United States). A few textile authorities also believe they were made in Spain as well. Trade with China and the Philippines had been thriving for some time, and items were made to cater to the European sensibility. These bags were either knitted or netted in an openwork design, and then decorated with linear, vertical floral designs. Flower designs were embroidered over paper forms onto the purses. Another distinguishing feature were their basket bottoms. Four different examples of this type of purse have been seen, and each of the four bottoms were designed differently. Recently, one has been offered for sale that was finished with three plant fiber tassels across the bottom, and not with a basket. They are remarkable and rare purses, and they would make a wonderful addition to any collection.

Bead decorated purses were also emerging as a favorite type of purse during the 18th century. In the early years of the century, pocketbooks were bead embroidered on fine canvas or made with a network technique. Designs included stags, stylized carnations, birds, and figures. This early method of beading did not lend itself to shading techniques, and the designs were quite angular and primitive in appearance.

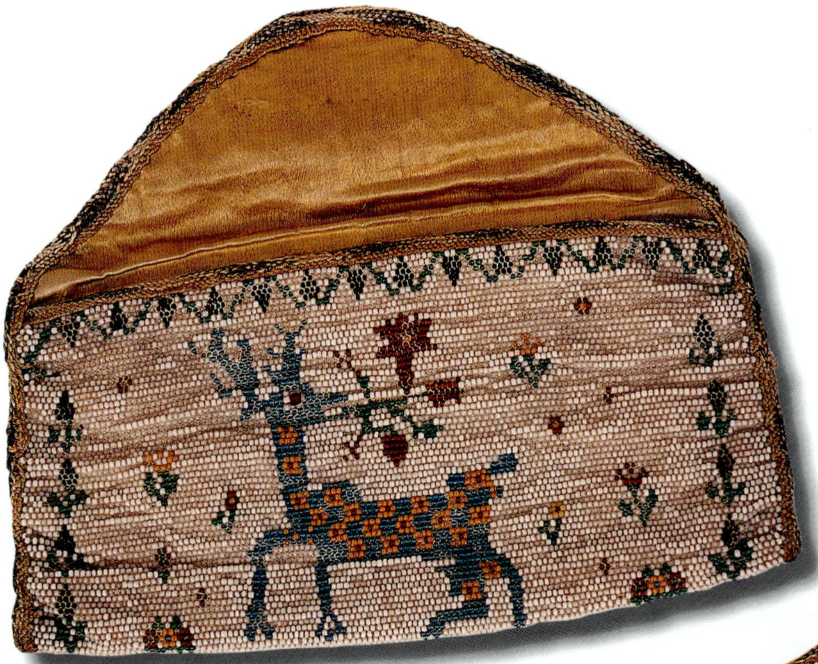

Early eighteenth century pocketbook with a design of a stag and small flowers. The angularity of the design is typical of early beadwork. The original lining is present. 6 x 3.75 in. *Collection of Lori Blaser.* Very rare.

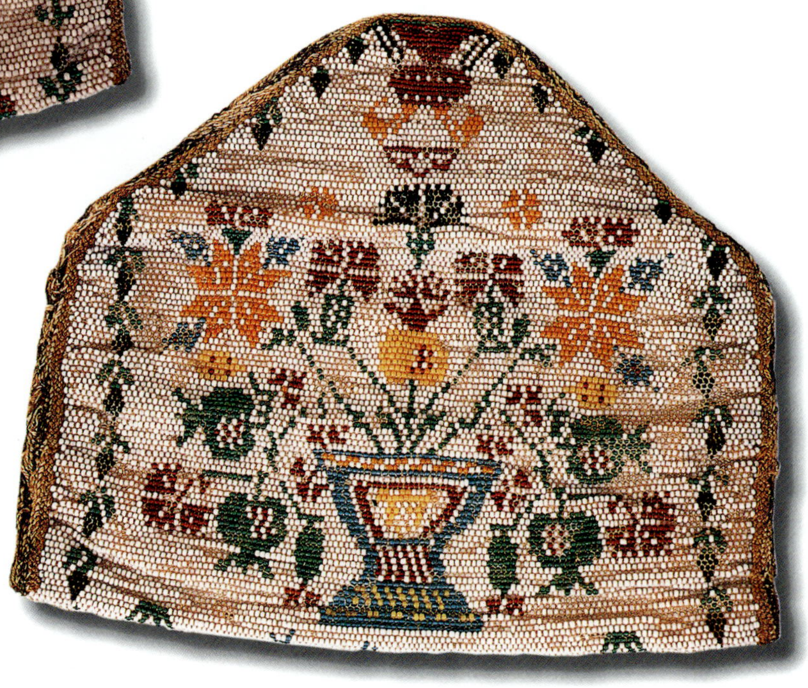

The reverse side of the pocketbook featuring a vase of flowers. This was a popular early beadwork design.

During the early 18th century, the famous sablé beaded purses appear. Sablé means "grain of sand" in French. Extremely small glass beads (size 22-30), with tiny center holes, were used to make these beautiful beadwork masterpieces. Because the beads were so tiny, it was impossible to insert a needle through their center holes. Ingenious methods were utilized to thread the beads onto the silk. One method was to tie a human hair or horsehair to a silk thread, and then string the beads on, one by one. Sometimes the threads were pointed with shellac. The design was then beaded with a horizontal and vertical looping method, which resembled a buttonhole or basket stitch when completed. Once finished, the beadwork hung loose from its lining or backing, giving it a distinctive feel when it is held in the hand. It is believed that Charles Germain de Saint-Aubin set up the first workrooms in Paris for sablé beadwork. He was the chief clothing designer to Louis XV and a friend of Madame de Pompadour. These wonderful beadwork purses were very difficult and time consuming to make, so only the wealthy could afford them. Designs included florals, scrolling Rococo borders, nymphs, the Phoenix, mottos, and mythological figures. Sablé pouches were also made, but they are a truly rare type of purse—usually found only in museums. Unfortunately, sable beadwork is very fragile, so many surviving examples have sustained damage. To our knowledge, there is no one alive who can repair this type of beadwork. They are a truly rare type of beaded purse and sell for several thousand dollars when bought from a specialty dealer.

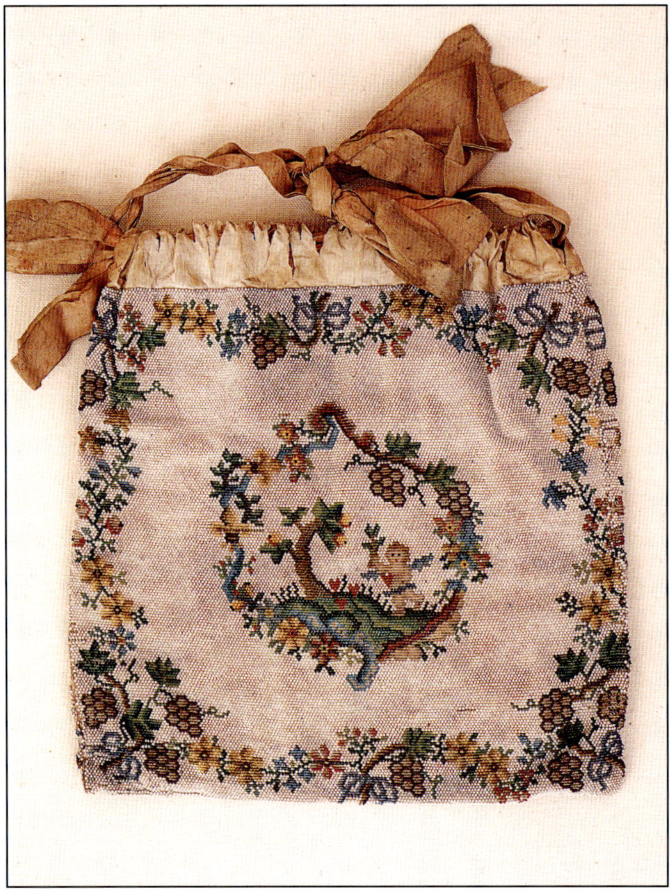

Mid-eighteenth century French sablé beaded bag showing a cherub, hearts, garland, grapes, and flowers. Sablé means "grain of sand" in French and refers to the size of the tiny beads. Made from a horizontal and vertical looping technique, these bags were quite costly even in the 18th century. The drawstring and top are original to the bag. 8.5 x 8 in. *Collection of Lori Blaser.* Very rare.

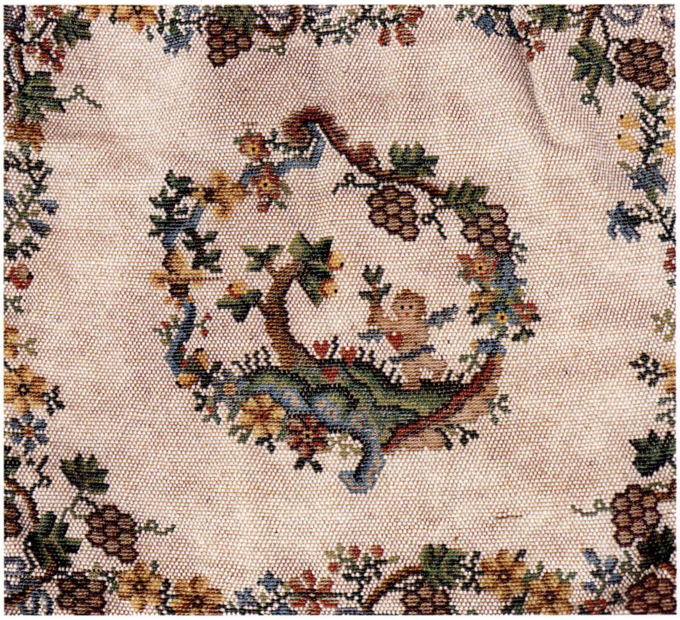

Close-up of cherub.

The reticule makes its appearance towards the last decade of the 18th century. The forerunner of the reticule was the workbag, knotting bag, and sewing bag. Women used these bags to carry sewing equipment, knotting shuttles, threads, crewels, and fabric. Occasionally, they had basket bottoms made from silk covered card. It is only natural that they evolved into general carryalls to hold whatever was needed. Bags and reticules were made from netting, patterned fabrics, and embroidered silks. By the end of the century, shapes varied from rectangle to round. Sizes might be large or small, and they were decorated with metal laces, fly fringe, and paillettes. In France they were known as "ridicules," which is where the term reticule is derived from, and in England they were known as "indispensibles."

A group worthy of mention are printed purses. Very few of these purses have survived, unfortunately. Made from white silk, they were printed with brown ink, in a design commemorating a significant event. For example, there is a surviving purse printed with a picture of King George III, who had recovered from a life-threatening illness. England rejoiced over his recovery and purses were printed to commemorate the event. In the early 19th century, printed purses were made as a type of social commentary against the institution of slavery. Typically, these purses showed black slaves in chains, and it was accompanied by a short text, which condemned this injustice. Nineteenth century printed purses were usually mounted on steel frames. Anti-slavery printed purses are a very rare type of purse. One example was offered several years ago in the *Maine Antiques Digest* for $3,025.

Purse frames were not used as frequently in the 18th century as they were in the 19th century. The drawstring and pocketbook forms were more popular, easier to use, and they could be made at home. Some early frames were very unsophisticated and simple, requiring the owner to pry open the frame to reach the purse's contents. Others had pushbuttons and latches to open the frame. Frame shapes varied in style and they could be highly decorative, as in the case of chatelaine frames, or simply designed, as in the case of the straight pinchbeck frames. Towards the end of the 18th century, engraved, curved frames were made for coin purses. These frames did not have carry chains. It is not unusual to see an early beaded coin purse made with a netted header, which was also attached to a frame.

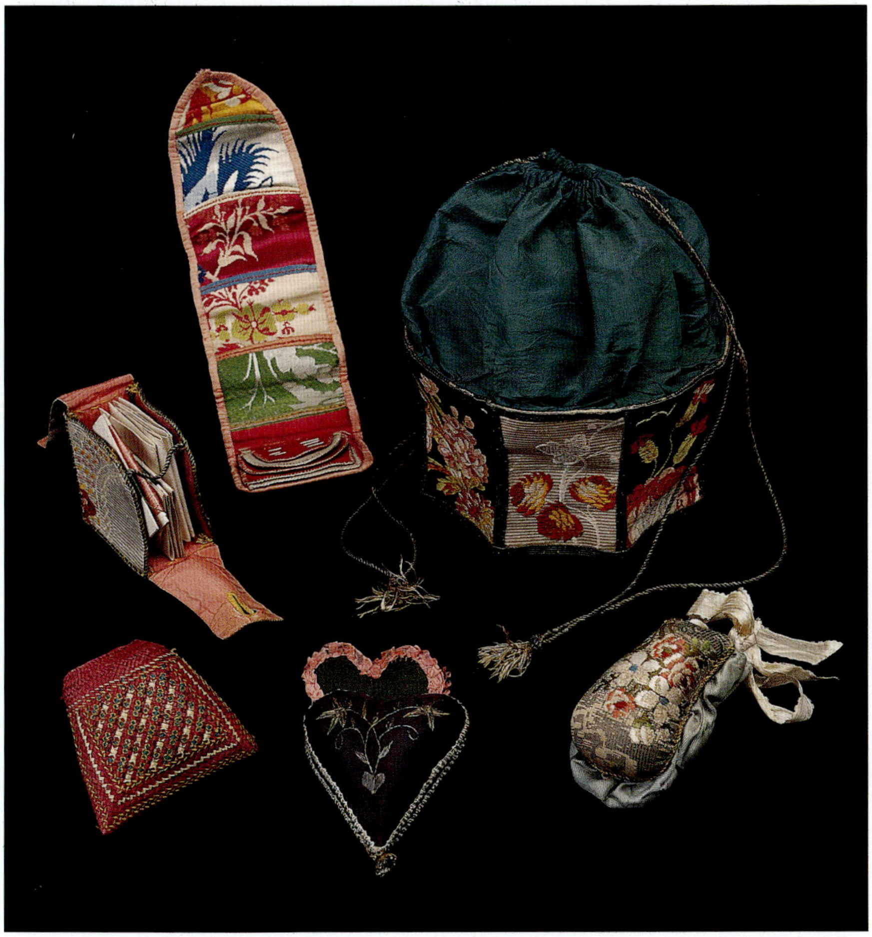

C.1780 octagon, silk brocade sewing purse with green silk drawstring pouch. The original sewing accessories remain with the purse and include a heart-shaped needlecase, ivory threadcase, pin cushion, red straw threadcase, and a brocaded housewife. Made in England. *Courtesy of Cora Ginsburg LLC.* Very rare.

Nineteenth Century Purses

The first half of the 19th century is considered by many textile historians to be an important period in the history of purse design. Featuring unique styles and unusual shapes, they represent a high point in creativity. Diverse materials were also used during this period. Fabrics, paper, wax, feathers, steel, tortoiseshell, beads, ivory, wood, and straw were all possibilities. Although beaded purses were made prior to the 19th century, many experts believe that beadwork was at its finest in terms of execution and quality during this period (the exception being the sablé beadwork purses from the 18th century). Some of the credit may go to France's Empress Josephine, who was obsessive in the area of clothing and a particular fan of purses. Some of the most beautifully designed and executed purses came from France, thanks to designers who pleased Empress Josephine and her court.

Fabric reticules were very popular during the first 30 years of the 19th century. Fabric purses were made to coordinate with dresses of silk, satin, and velvet. Feathers, bullion, lace, *paillettes*, hand painting, fringe, feathers, tassels, buttons, and ribbons were all used to decorate early 19th century purses. The *sabretache* (hexagonal) shape was a popular form, featuring four tassels along the sides and bottom. Another admired shape was the circular purse. It was made drawstring style the majority of the time, but another variation was to attach the round bag to the inside of metal hoops, forming a wheel shape. Purses were innovative and charming, and one very lovely example had a gold paper lyre attached to the front and back of the bag.

White work purses were another favored style. All things Neo-Classical were the height of fashion during the first two decades of the 19th century. Diaphanous columns of white fabric passed for dresses, and purses were needed to complete the look. So white work purses were made from white cotton, and embroidered with white threads in Neo-Classical designs. Designs of wreaths, garlands, initials, names, dates, weeping willow trees, ivy, and medallions were popular. Some bags were multi-tasseled, in the *sabretache* form, and others had only one tassel. These purses were made in great quantities in America and especially in New England. However, they are fairly hard to find because many deteriorated due to poor storage conditions. Finding one with a known provenance is a true find for any purse collector. Another version of this style is the pen and ink purse. Schoolgirls would decorate plain white bags with pen and ink floral designs and poems. Some were dated and embroidered with the name of the owner. These are even more difficult to find and seldom survive in good condition. Many of the pen and ink purses that have survived now reside in museums in New England.

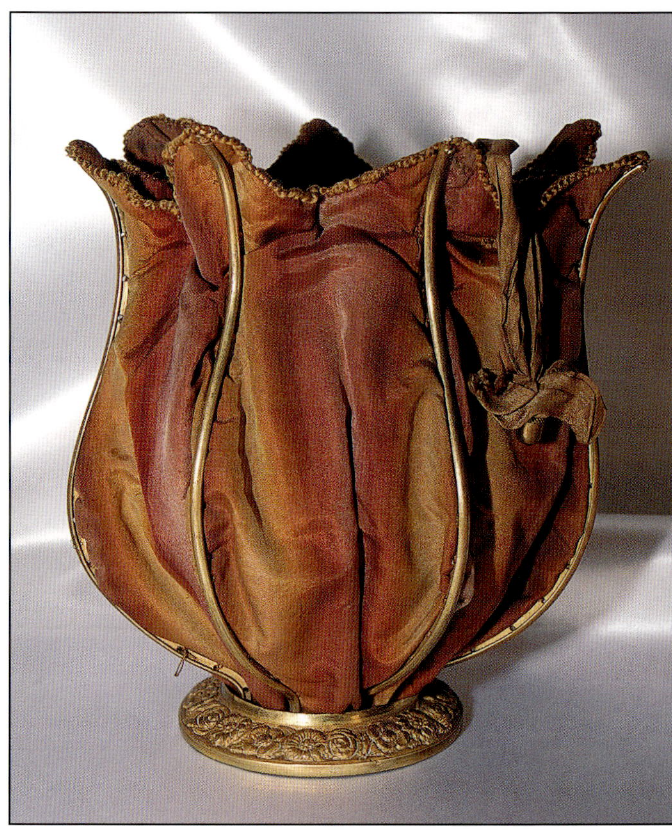

Early 19th century French purses were known for their unique and innovative designs as represented by this purse. The tulip shaped reticule with the repoussé base would have been the height of fashion during the French Empire Period. The purple and gold ombré silk changes color as it moves. Tiny brass acorns decorate the silk drawstrings. 6 x 5.5 in. *Collection of Paula Higgins.* Very rare.

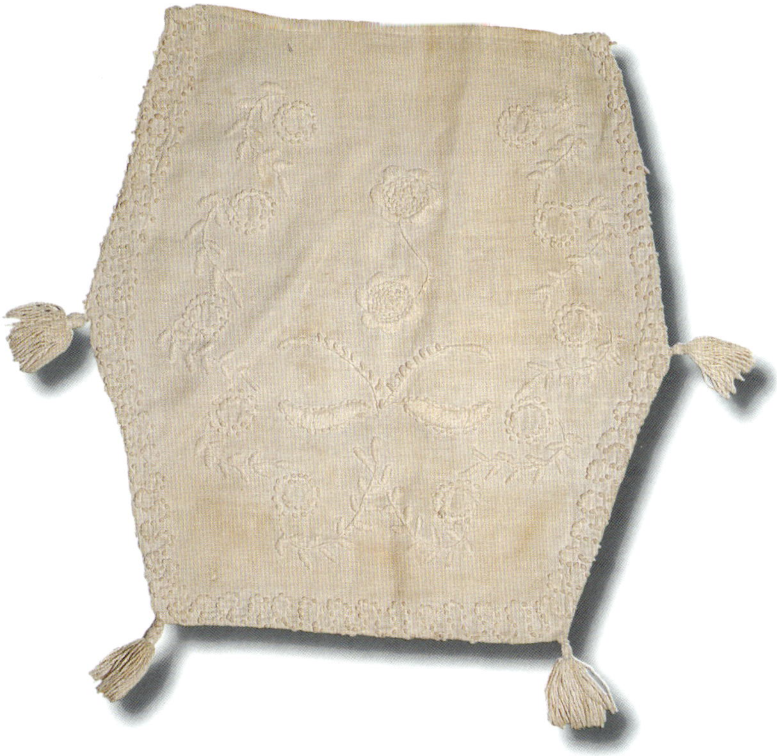

Early 19th century, American white work bag originally made by Sarah Clement Whittier. Sarah was born in Hopkinton, New Hampshire in 1782. She married Nathaniel Whittier in 1803. It is believed she used this bag to hold her day cap. This side features a floral spray, and the reverse side, a garland of flowers. The bag is embroidered with French knots. Sarah made a companion bag, which also descended down through her family. 9 x 9.5 in. *Collection of Paula Higgins*. Rare.

Berlin iron work purses, also known as Silesian wirework purses (and as spun steel purses in some museums), were specific to the 19th century. They are known in Europe as *Fer de Berlin* purses. These rare, early mesh purses were made from fine wirework in several shapes and designs. The early, 19th century envelope style is the most familiar form, but a half moon, *sabretache*, and pouch shape were also made. Steel *paillettes* decorated the outside of the purse, and they were closed with steel keys. Originally, the designs for the iron mesh came from ironwork foundries in Silesia. The foundries were moved to Berlin, but they were eventually taken over by the French in 1806 during wartime. Many design patterns were taken to France at this time. It is believed that most surviving, early 19th century wirework examples were made in France. There are two examples of this type of purse in Chapter 8 (see page 146). In the middle of the nineteenth century, small, palm-sized wirework coin purses were made. They were much smaller than the earlier 19th century versions, Unfortunately, they had a tendency to rust and now are hard to find in good to excellent condition. In Chapter 8, an example in mint condition with its original cardboard box is shown on page 146.

During the early 19th century, German, French, and English makers produced tortoiseshell and leather purses of uncommon beauty. Large panels of polished tortoiseshell were trimmed and gusseted with gold embossed leather, and they were attached to metal chains or leather carry cords. The French examples usually had an elliptical plaque on the back inscribed with the word *Souvenir*. The German tortoiseshell purses were often inlaid with beautiful mother-of-pearl floral designs, adding a lovely touch. A common design feature was their steel lock, often made in a lovely lyre shape. An example pictured on page 236 retains its original key, which still works the lock. A tortoiseshell and leather purse once owned by Pauline Bonaparte, which has her name embossed under the flap, is pictured in the book *Carried Away-All About Bags*. Pauline Bonaparte was Napoleon's beautiful and charismatic sister. On page 236 is shown its twin, purchased from Cora Ginsburg LLC. Tortoiseshell purses became much smaller after 1830 and were used for carrying a few coins. These small confections were made throughout the rest of the 19th century. Beautifully inlaid with gold and mother-of-pearl, or inset with paintings under glass, they are also lovely and worth adding to any collection. Inside, the coin purses were two sections and usually a middle section with a clip to close it. It has been suggested that the coin purses lined with blue or red silks are earlier than those lined with lighter colored silks.

Netting was a common woman's pastime in the early 19th century. Netted purses of all kinds were made at home. One type specific to the first two decades of the 19th century is a purse netted with two round hoops, one at the top and one at the bottom. It formed a double cone shape and closed with a drawstring. Some were made with cut steel beads interspersed, and others were made with ribbons wound around the hoops. They all had tassels at the bottom and today they are a rare type of purse. When *The New York Times* published an article on April 6, 1997, on a museum show of antique purses at the Brooklyn Museum of Art, one of these purses was pictured.

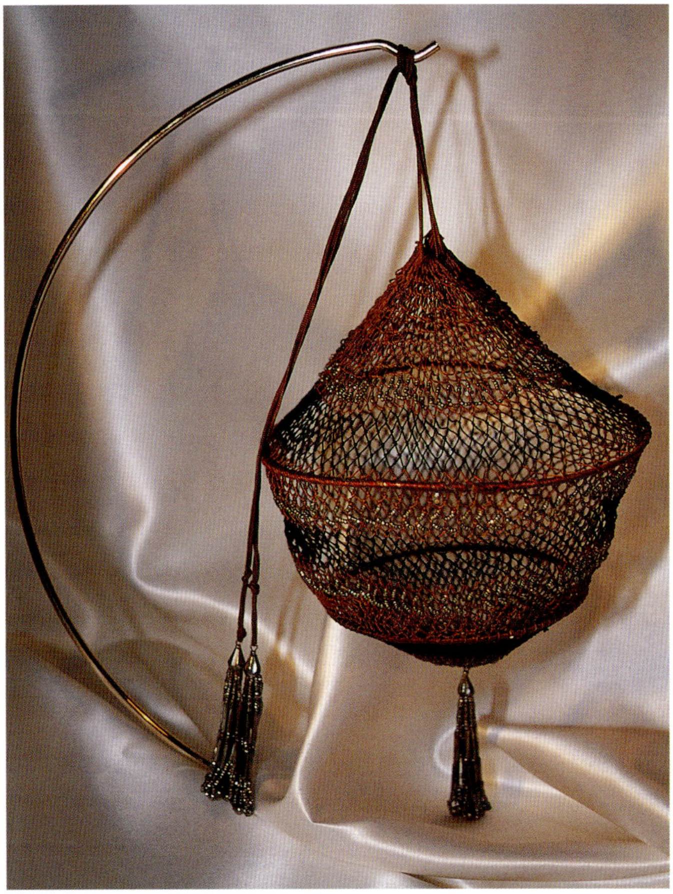

Early 19th century netted reticule, made with two metal hoops inserted to create a modified cone shape. Tiny cut steel beads are interspersed throughout the netting. Other examples have been seen with ribbons wound around the metal hoops. Made in England. 9 x 5.5 in. *Collection of Paula Higgins.* Rare.

chatelaine design elements, such as ring attachments. Textile historians believe pockets were used as late as 1910, especially for traveling.

Misers were very popular in the 19th century and continued in use into the early 20th century. Carried by both men and women, they were made to hold coins or gaming chips. Early 19th century misers were often netted like the late 18th century versions, but they were shorter in length. Gilt fish and sliders were bought at dry goods stores to decorate them. The earliest cut steel decorated misers were made from very fine cut steel beads, and they were finely knitted or netted in delicate and feminine designs. Early misers were also made from fabric, plain and embroidered. The Museum of Fine Arts in Boston, Massachusetts, has an excellent collection of early 19th century misers.

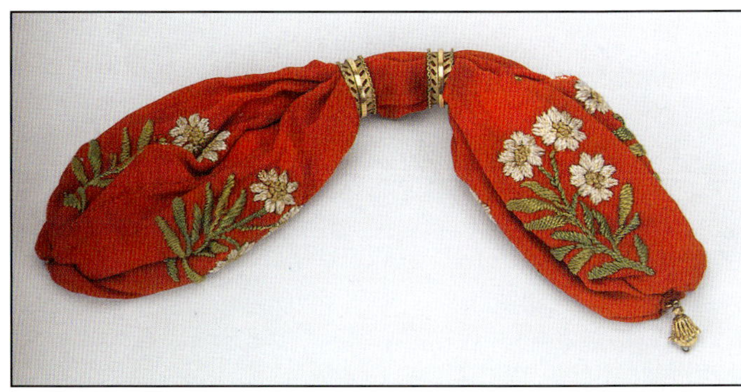

C.1830 red wool and embroidered miser with original sliders and fish/tassel. Made in England. 8 x 2.5 in. *Collection of Lori Blaser.* $300-350.

Pockets continued to be made and used by women, particularly in rural areas, although they were considerably less refined than their 18th century counterparts. Patchwork pockets were made from leftover scraps of material, and plain white pockets were popular as well. Although pockets continued to be used throughout the 19th century until about 1910, they declined somewhat in popularity. In the second half of the 19th century, pockets were used for sewing needs and for traveling. Occasionally, they were hung from rings, rather than tied on at the waist. One woman from the late 19th century noted that pockets were hung from their rings on bedsteads when not being worn. There is a pocket on page 35 that was made in a crazy quilt design and embroidered and appliquéd. It also hung from a ring. Because chatelaines were popular during the late 19th century, it is easy to see how later pockets acquired

By 1830, bead knitted misers were made in colorful patterns. As the 19th century progressed, embroidery and handwork became less refined. Priorities were changing, the sewing machine had been invented, and the industrial age had arrived. Later examples were crocheted with larger cut steel beads in simple geometric designs. During the last half of the 19th century, fabric travel bags, which were really large misers, were carried over the arm. By the late 19th century, misers were losing favor with the arrival of the roomier leather handbag. However, it is believed that misers were being used as late as the early 20th century, especially to hold gaming chips. Misers remain readily available, but the earlier and more unusual misers generally appeal to collectors today.

A rare type of purse dating to the 1820s and the 1830s is the Theorem purse. Theorem purses are a true

American folk art form, featuring stenciled designs painted on velvet or cotton purses. Floral and fruit designs were the most popular. Their representations were one dimensional, giving them a primitive appearance. After the bag was painted, spirit gum was used to set the colors. Typically they were made in a drawstring reticule style, but framed examples have also survived. Although they are primarily seen as an American folk art form, they were also made in Europe. One purse from Europe had a castle painted in the middle of a stenciled design, and it was mounted on a pinchbeck frame. When Theorem purses are offered for sale today, they can reach very high prices. A Theorem purse on Ebay sold several years ago for over $3,500, and one was offered in *The Maine Antique Digest* and sold for $2,450 in August, 1998.

Pocketbooks or wallets also continued to be used during the first half of the 19th century. Although they were still made in the rectangular shape during the early 19th century, they also took on a slightly squarer shape c.1800. Designs were a little lighter, reflecting the Neo-Classical design influence. Some wallets were hand painted, while others were embroidered with the complex Queen's stitch. This stitch was in use as late as the 1830s. The flame stitch was still seen on very early 19th century wallets, and again on Berlin wool work reticules 30 years later. Men's wallets and pocketbooks took on a more masculine style and were typically made of leather. Some rare, European leather examples were made with printed-paper liners featuring pictures of towns or rural scenes.

The beaded purse was among the most popular purse style in the 19th century. Besides the fact that they could be made easily at home, they were often pieces of wearable art with their jewel-like beads. During the early years of the 19th century, purses were very finely knitted with cotton or silk thread. Beaded floral designs were interspersed throughout the knitted purse, leaving large areas of plain knit. Silk acorn tassels or silk thread tassels hung from the bottom of these early knitted and beaded purses. Other purses, particularly small coin purses, were completely beaded. By 1830, almost all beaded purses were covered with beads. The majority of early beaded purses were knitted, but by thc 1830s some were crocheted. True crochet makes its appearance by the very early 19th century. Beaded crochet work appears slightly later.

Early beaded purse designs included:
three sectional, primitive florals
primitive scenics and figurals
Arabic and Oriental figurals
Wreaths
Garlands
Ivy
Deer
Dogs
Birds
hunting scenes
funereal designs with tombs and weeping willow trees

Other designs favored by early beaders included:
Venetian scenics
souvenir designs
detailed scenics of European towns
butterflies
dates
names
mottos
the anchor, cross, and heart motif
the lyre and rose design
sheep
shepherds
chalets
baskets of flowers
interior scenes
Indian figurals
German figurals

Their shapes included:
lozenge
pouch
round
rectangular
square
an early bucket bottom style

Linings were made from:
Chinese silk
Leather
Linen
Cotton
old dress fabrics

Purses were fringed or finished with a simple ball and tassel. Drawstrings were made from silk cords, silk ribbons, and metal chains. Some early purses were mounted on frames of gilt, iron, silver, cut steel, brass, or pinchbeck.

Beaded basket purses from the early Biedermeier Era (1815-1835) are a rare type of purse today, and they can be very costly. Usually, they were made from fine gauge cotton knit, which was interspersed with a beaded floral design. A rare exception, pictured on page 173, was completely beaded. Their distinguishing feature was their shape, which resembled a footed basket. Interior hoops made from baleen or wood provided support for their shape. On the bottom, round card was inserted to stiffen the base. This style was especially popular in Germany.

The distinctive piecrust beaded purse dates to the 1820s to 1830s. This style of purse was made from pie-shaped beaded wedges, which were sewn together to form a circle. It was usually fringed from end to end, although there are examples that were never fringed. Most piecrust purses were mounted on frames. Occasionally, a piecrust purse appears that was attached to a header with a drawstring that is original to the purse. Piecrust purses often date to the first part of the 19th century, but it is worth noting that they were still being made into the 20th century.

Another beaded purse style unique to the 19th century is the cut steel, embroidered paisley purse. Kashmir shawls, woven in paisley designs, were very popular during the first half of the 19th century. Kashmir wool comes from the underbelly of the mountain goat in Kashmir and has a silk-like quality that is unmistakable, never to be confused with coarser wools. Most likely, the majority of the paisley fabrics used to make these shawls and purses came from France or Scotland. In both countries a high quality paisley wool fabric was produced. When the shawls were no longer useable because of wear, their fabric was used to make purses. The paisley design was embroidered with small cut steel beads, producing a very rich effect. High quality paisley fabrics had lovely color schemes and texture, and the purses were mounted on beautiful sterling frames. Machine-made paisley fabrics were being produced by 1874, and they were also used to make purses. Their color schemes were less subtle and their textures less refined. High quality, cut steel embroidered paisley purses are very elegant and undervalued, because they lack the flash of the completely beaded purse.

One of the most frequently asked questions is whether a frame is original to the purse. If the purse is clearly pre-Civil War era, but the frame has a twist clasp, then the frame is not original. It is believed that twist clasps were first made in the 1870s. Pushbutton clasps and ball-push-through clasps (not commonly seen) pre-date the 1870s. To confuse the issue even more, many early purse designs were still being made into the late 19th and early 20th centuries and early 19th century frame designs were being remade in the early 20th century. Add to that the accepted practice during the early 20th century of taking great-grandmother's purse out of the trunk and adding a frame to it, and you will be completely confused. So, dating purses can be problematic, especially because so many purses have been reframed. Many collectors reframe purses for aesthetic reasons and to increase their re-sale values. As purse restoration becomes more authentic (using antique trims, fabric linings, and beads), it may become impossible to determine what is original and what is not, without having the threads analyzed.

Beaded purses continued to be used for most of the 19th century, although other styles, such as leather handbags and chatelaines, gave them direct competition. Later 19th and early 20th century beaded purses were more likely to be mounted on frames, and they were larger than the beaded reticules from the first half of the 19th century. Later purse designs were more sophisticated and detailed, and frames were jewel studded, enameled, and ornate.

Another purse style specific to the 19th century is the China ribbon, chenille, and aerophane-decorated reticule. Silk and satin purses were embroidered with silk ribbons, chenille thread, and fine gauze (aerophane) in floral designs. The total effect was feminine and lovely. These homemade purses date to the 1830s and 1840s and were popular in England. They are not commonly found today.

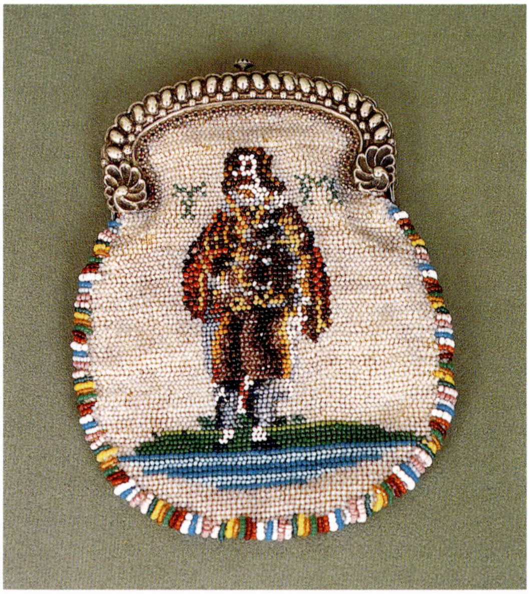

Early 19th century beaded coin purse with an imaginative representation of a 17th century cavalier. The initials T and M flank the cavalier. An unusual looped fringe encircles the purse. The silver frame is typical of early 19th century design. 5 x 3.75 in. *Collection of Lori Blaser.* $550-650.

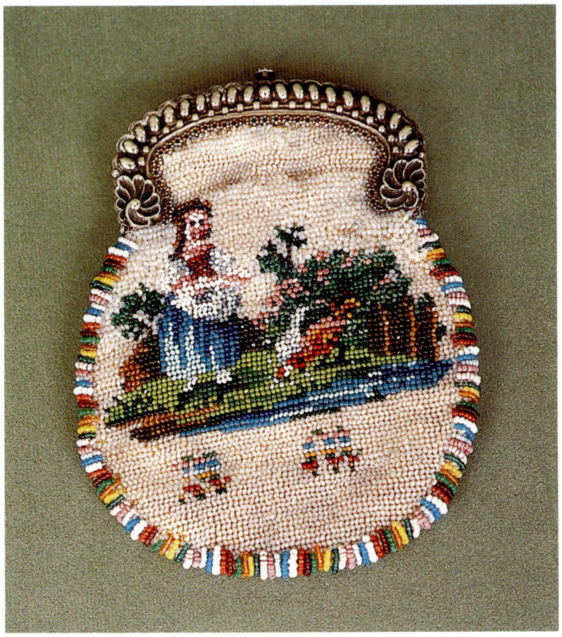

Reverse of beaded coin purse with feminine figure in a pastoral setting. These early figural coin purses have considerable charm.

The 19th century was a sentimental time and a time of travel for the wealthy and the middle classes. Women collected souvenirs while traveling and purses were created especially for this purpose. Among the most charming and beautiful antique purses are souvenir purses from the 19th century. Oval ivory plaques were hand painted with scenes of Paris, China, Venice, and other tourist sites, and then set into gilt coin purses. In some cases, the ivory plaques were set into pierced gilt baskets, which held embroidered velvet or knitted reticules. The Paris Exhibitions were a popular subject for these purses. In their highest incarnation they are breathtaking. Less expensive versions used lithographed papers instead of ivory plaques, but the effect was similar. Some of the smaller reticule styles had tops fitted with vinaigrettes, metal calendars, and chains with finger rings. This style was popular around 1840. Beaded purses with scenes of Venetian gondolas from the middle of the 19th century are another type of souvenir purse. Covered gondolas indicate a 19th century date. It is important to note that the word "souvenir" means "remember me." However, when "souvenir" was used on early 19th century tortoiseshell and leather handbags and on early beaded purses, it was meant to express a sentiment, not to represent a keepsake from a particular city or country.

Straw purses were made throughout the 19th century. Early straw purses are uncommon and somewhat hard to identify. One early style was braided in a round or oval shape, in two halves, and closed with a loop. Some textile experts believe they came from Italy, although an example pictured on page 22 was bought in England and dates to around 1830. Other early styles were made in a heavily decorated basket style, and were carried over the arm. An interesting example dating to about 1840 is pictured in Desire Smith's book, *Handbag Chic-200 Years of Designer Fashion.* Made of natural straw, it is decorated with an embroidered floral design. Pocketbooks or wallets, beautifully made from very fine pieces of straw, are another rare type of purse made during the late 18th and early 19th centuries.

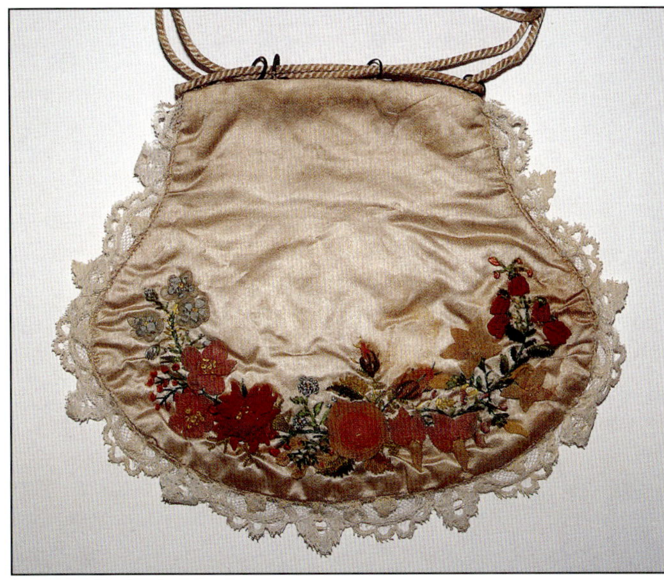

This c.1830 purse was made from aerophane gauze (crepe work), chenille embroidery, and ribbon work. Floral designs were a form of coded language, with each flower having a special meaning. The half wreath design was typical of the first half of the 19th century. Purses like this one were especially popular in England. 8 x 6 in. *Collection of Paula Higgins.* $350-450.

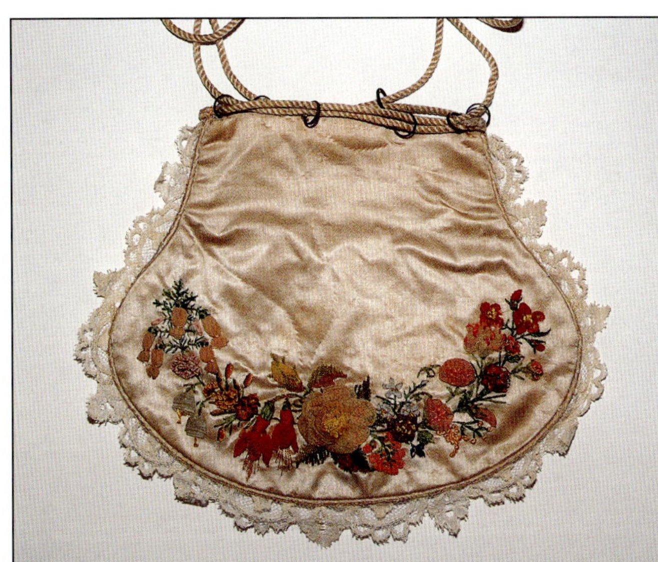

Reverse side of aerophane gauze, chenille embroidery, and ribbon work purse.

Coin purses of the 19th century are notable for their variety and charm. Beautifully decorated with medallions, portraits, reverse paintings on glass, enameling, embossing, engraving, gold leaf, inset metals, cameos, and mother of pearl, they were expensive and impressive considering their small size. These lovely palm-sized purses were made from many different materials, including: beadwork, tortoiseshell, leather, ivory, bone, mother of pearl, malachite, *papier mache*, shells, and metals. Coin purses were used throughout the 19th century and many of the most exquisite examples came from France.

The shell shape was considered stylish during the first half of the 19th century. Purses shaped like clamshells and mounted on steel frames are occasionally seen in museum collections. They were made from card that was covered with velvet. It is a very rare type of purse today, but occasionally you will see one pictured in an early 19th century fashion print. A sterling silver, clamshell shaped, coin purse from the mid-nineteenth century is shown on page 131. 20th century brass versions are often mistakenly identified as 19th century.

Berlin work purses are easily identified by their colorful geometric or floral designs. Merino wools were embroidered onto canvas or fabric, and then decorated with cording and chenille tassels. In the first decade of the 19th century, a Berlin publisher by the name of Phillison made the first Berlin work patterns. Eventually, other Berlin publishers printed more patterns, which they exported to the rest of Europe, England, and America. By 1830, Berlin work was thriving and continued to be popular through the 1860s. It was not nearly as fine as 18th or early 19th century embroidery, but it was relatively simple, colorful, and it worked up quickly. While some Berlin work purses are mundane and lacking in personality, there are examples worth acquiring because of their fine workmanship, complex designs, and beautiful color schemes.

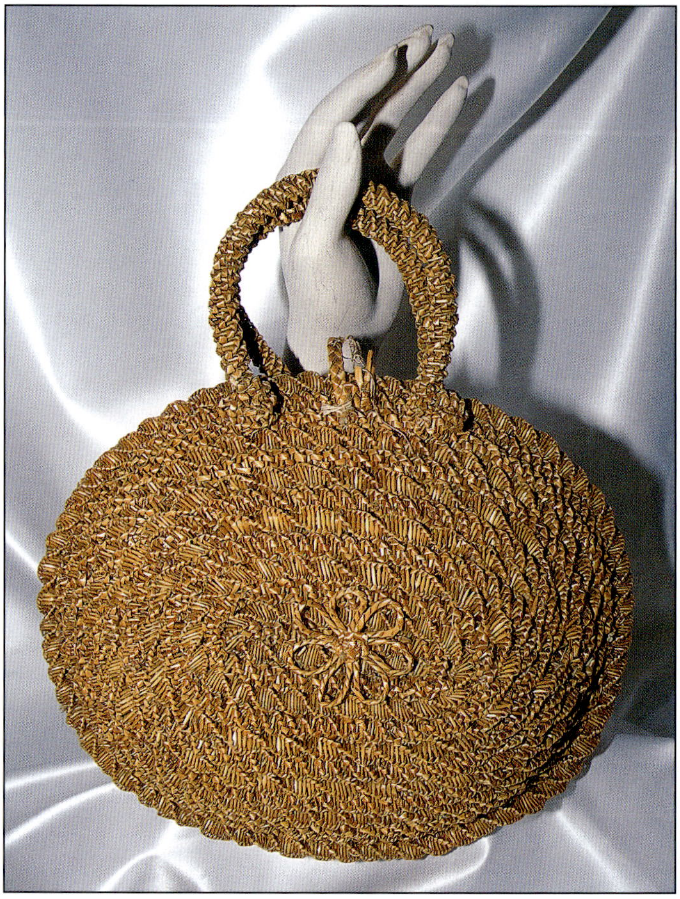

C.1830 purse made from twisted and coiled straw with a double handle. This purse originally came from England but it may have been made elsewhere in Europe, possibly Italy. 13 x 8 in. *Collection of Paula Higgins.* Rare.

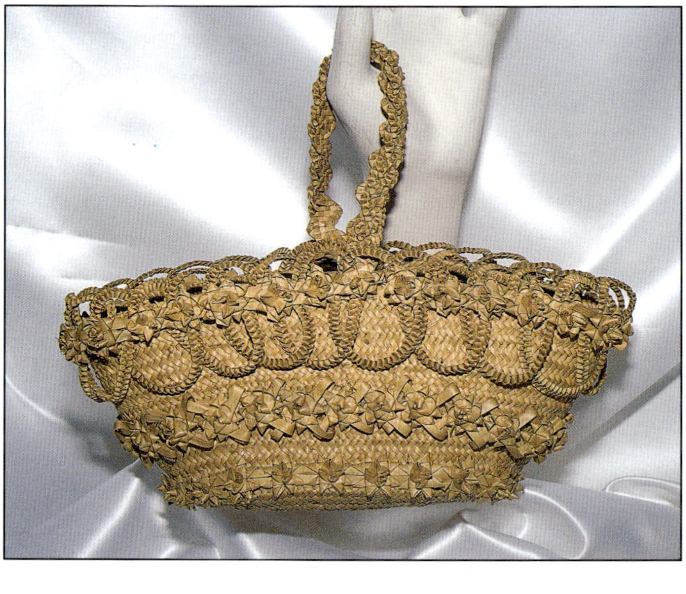

C.1830 basket style straw purse decorated with braided loops and straw flowers. Straw work purses were popular in Europe during the first half of the 19th century but they have not survived in great numbers. 10 x 7 in. *Collection of Paula Higgins.* Rare.

Knitted reticules made their appearance around 1800. Very fine gauge knitted purses were made from metallic, silk, and cotton threads. Three-section designs were favored and echoed the beaded designs from the same period. Crocheted purses were also seen during the first half of the 19th century, but they became truly popular later in the 19th century. During the mid-nineteenth century, colorful knitted and crocheted purses were made in paisley and linear Zouave designs, imitating the silk sashes of Algerian soldiers. Colors of rust-red, blue, and tan are commonly seen on these mid-nineteenth century purses. One of their finer features was a tassel made from multiple knots and smaller tassels, which hung like a chandelier. Towards the end of the 19th century and into the early 20th century, white crocheted reticules were the height of fashion. Some of them were very plain and uninspired, while other examples were exquisitely worked, almost like lace. They were made to be worn with the lovely, high-necked, tea gowns of the late Victorian Period.

Carpetbags are a type of purse specific to the mid- and late-19th century. Fairly large and strong, they were made from pieces of floral or geometric patterned carpets or Berlin work. They were particularly used as travel bags, especially for train travel. Leather handles were common, and unfortunately the handles rarely survive in good condition. Another rarely surviving carpetbag feature is the key. Most carpetbags had keys to lock their contents. The Berlin work examples are very desirable and uncommon, especially in good condition, making one in good condition a true find. They fail to appeal to many collectors, perhaps because of their large size.

The chatelaine is a purse style that we most commonly associate with the 19th century. Chatelaine means "mistress of the house or castle." Keys on rings were carried by the head of the household to gain access to all parts of the house or castle. It was a natural evolution for the ring or hook to be attached to other necessary items as well. Although chatelaines had been in use prior to the 19th century, and were known as waist bags in the 18th century, they evolved into a more widely used fashion accessory by 1870. Early 19th century chatelaines are rarely seen, but they were worn under the high empire waists of the day. Chatelaines came in a variety of shapes: flared, round, triangular, egg shaped, and pouch. Leather was a popular material for chatelaines, but fabric, metals, jet, beadwork, enamel, and sweetgrass were also used. Finger ring chatelaines were seen around 1840, in the small souvenir and coin purse forms. Their tops were decorated with cameos, enamel work, hand painting, and lithographed scenes. The ring would slip over the finger, and the purse would dangle from the finely worked chains. Wrist chatelaines were worn in the late 19th century and into the 20th century. Small leather or mesh bags hung from large wrist rings, which freed the hand for other uses (and for dancing). The classic chatelaine style required a hook, which was worn over a belt or waistband. From the hook hung chains attached to several appendages such as scissors, coin purses, tape measures, spectacle cases, and pen wipes. Chatelaines were made from cut steel, silver, gold, and German silver. Bags made from leather, fabrics, or beadwork, were suspended from hooks as another fashionable alternative. Fully beaded, all original chatelaine bags are rare and they can be expensive when offered for sale.

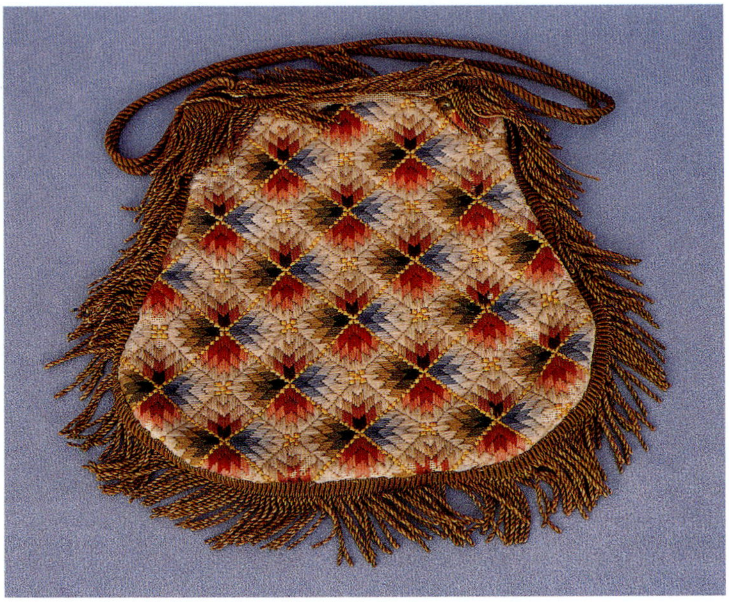

Lovely Berlin wool work purse with gold colored, twisted fringe. 8 x 8 in. *Collection of Lori Blaser.* $350-400.

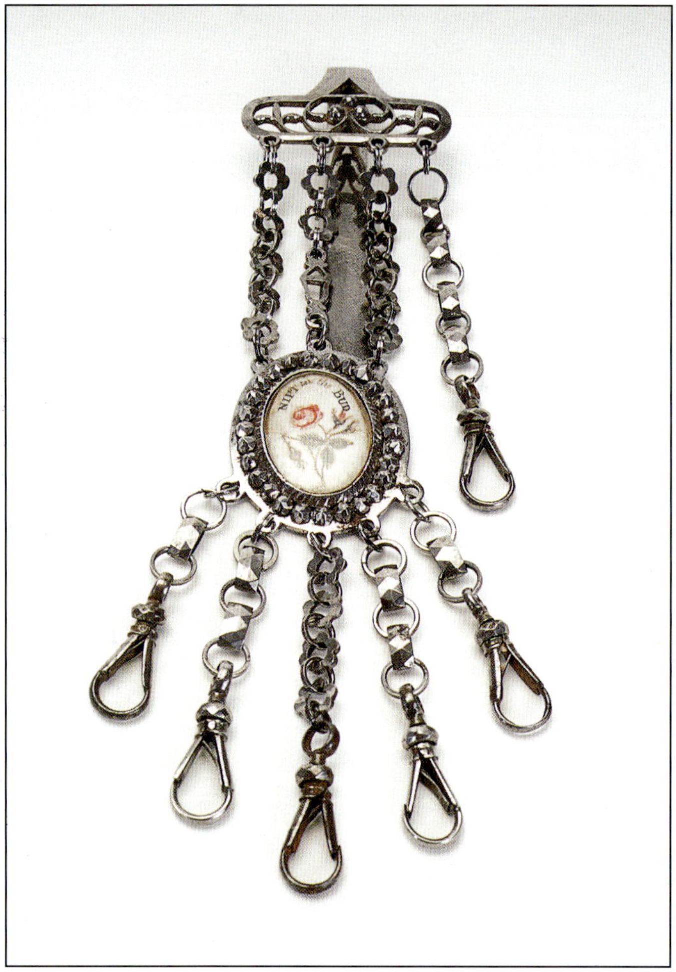

Late 18th century faceted, cut steel chatelaine with a hand painted rose on an ivory plaque. "Nipt in the bud" is inscribed on the plaque. Cut steel was a popular medium for jewelry, shoe clips, and chatelaines during the late 18th century. This chatelaine was a gift to the author from her husband, who chose this gift on his own. 6 x 1.5 in. *Collection of Lori Blaser.* Rare.

The 1870s brought the arrival of the leather handbag, which looked very much like the mid-twentieth century version. Besides the color brown, they came in dark red, green, and blue leather. Mounted on silver colored frames, they closed with twist or slide clasps. Their handles were made from leather or plush. Resembling thick velour, plush also covered these modern-looking handbags. Smaller plush handbags were also made to hold coins. The handbag was a trend that carried over into the twentieth century, where it gained prominence.

Twentieth Century Purses

Prior to 1920, most leather handbags were made in Germany, because of German superiority in dyeing and manufacturing capabilities. New dye colors of white, pink, and mauve were popular, and skins of all types were used. For cheaper bags, a pattern could be stamped onto less costly leathers. Bags came with fitted pockets, mirrors, and change purses. By 1910 they had reached a very large size, but smaller, leather opera bags were also made to house beautifully decorated opera glasses.

Early 20th century leather bags could be ordered from mail order catalogs, making them accessible to women in rural areas. Ostrich, alligator, seal, antelope, kid, and goatskin were paired with Bakelite, nickel, copper, and brass frames. Jemco produced many of these frames and advanced collectors are familiar with their stamp. The Meeker, Bosca, Cameo, and Roycroft Companies made bags that went with the frames. Designs included Art Nouveau styled florals, medallions, initials, and geometric designs. Bird and animal designs were also used but they are relatively rare. Roycroft purses were made in the Arts and Crafts style by a group of artists working in shops in New York City. They are among the most desirable and beautifully designed of all the leather purses made during this period.

By the late 1920s and 1930s, leather bags were made in a pouch or envelope shape and were carried under the arm. Many of the streamlined Art Deco designs were so timeless they could be carried today. Suede was popular and so were zippers. White leather purses embossed with linear designs and bags with pleats and matching shoes were seen in all the catalogs. Unusually shaped leather purses, in round and triangular forms, were decorated with Surrealist designs. Metallic colored leathers in gold and copper were made for eveningwear.

As a consequence of World War II, certain materials, such as metals, became in short supply. Therefore, many purses of that time were made without metal closures or zippers, and they became chunkier and large. The envelope and pouch shape remained widely used. During World War II, leather shoulder bags gained prominence; even the women's armed services appropriated the style. The shoulder bag worked especially well with the tailored suits and dresses from that period. By the late 1940s and early 1950s, leather bags took on boxier and slightly smaller shapes. Snakeskin, made in box designs, and alligator bags were also popular styles. The round leather box purse, the leather bucket bag, and the long, patent leather clutch are classic designs from around 1950. The greatest icon of all purses, the

Kelly bag, made by Hermes and named after Grace Kelly, became the highest of all status symbols. A Kelly bag made in 1994 recently sold in London for $19,115. In Anna Johnson's book, *Handbags-The Power of the Purse,* the whole process of making one of these impeccably designed bags is outlined. They now sell for thousands of dollars, both new and used.

The 1960s brought a softer look to leather bags, with cut-out handles and curved shapes. A style particularly associated with the 1960s was the brown leather pouch with a round wooden handle, which opened by sliding the rings around the handle. Its design was quite ingenious and functional. By the end of the 1960s, the large soft suede and leather bags inspired by the free spirit and back-to-nature movements had arrived. Some of these purses were handmade with considerable skill and artistry. Although they currently qualify as vintage and not antique, a well-done example is worth adding to any collection.

Towards the late 20th century, leather was worked in many different forms, from soft to structured. Designer-made leather bags gained prominence during the late 20th century, especially those by Judith Leiber, Christian Dior, Coco Chanel, Louis Vuitton, Gucci, Hermes, Fendi, Prada, Ferragamo, Lana Marks, Barry Kieselstein-Cord, Jamin Puech, Moschino, Bottega Veneta, Rodo, and Jean Paul Gaultier. These designers' purses were all avidly collected. Designer logos on handbags became status symbols coveted by all levels of society. To fill a less wealthy niche, knock-off designer bags were sold around the world for a fraction of the genuine articles' prices. Authentic versions are the antiques of tomorrow and will require a knowledgeable eye to differentiate the real from the knock-offs.

At the beginning of the 20th century, fabric bags were still in style and were mounted on frames or carried on long drawstrings. Directoire style dresses, with high waists and slim silhouettes, were accessorized with feminine reticules to complete the look. Large oval shaped bags were popular, and home embroidery was still practiced widely. Others were professionally made with antique style embroidery, applied ribbon rosettes, gold bullion, and metallic laces in the romantic style during the Belle Epoque Period. It is at this time, that we also see genuine antique (18th century) textiles used to make early 20th century purses. This can be confusing when trying to date a purse. These purses were usually small, and they were typically attached to expensive frames. Some dresses had fabric bags made especially to match, and featured caped or petal shaped tops. French designers used exotic patterned purse fabrics to go with their high-end dresses. During World War I, textile souvenir purses were made to sell to American soldiers, who would send them back to their wives at home. These purses may be dated, or in some cases, embroidered with the flags of the allied countries. Black velvet and black silk pouch shaped bags were attached to 800 silver and sterling silver frames to create a rich look. Many of these frames were ornately designed with cherubs, flowers, scrollwork, and gemstones. If a frame is marked "800" it is European in origin. Occasionally, a frame is marked 925, which is the European equivalent of sterling.

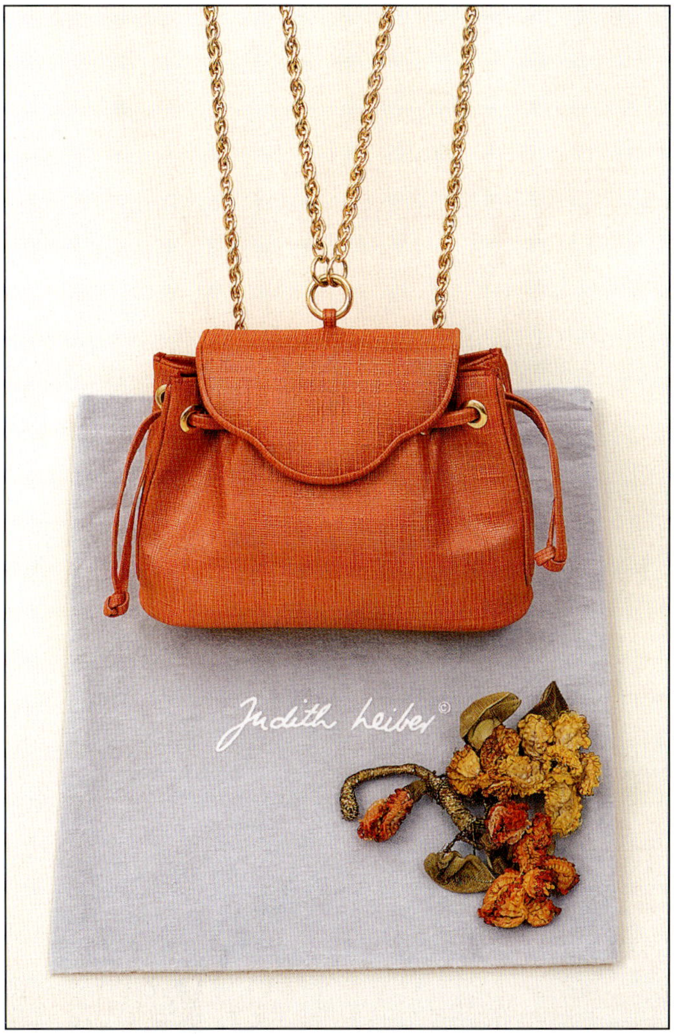

Made by Judith Leiber, this coral colored leather backpack purse dates to the 1990s. 8 x 6 in. *Collection of Lori Blaser.* Rare.

During the 1920s, and until 1932, a small group of fabric and beaded purses were made in the modernist style of the Wiener Werkstatte in Vienna. Their rectilinear designs, refinement, and simplicity make them distinctive and rare today. Strong blocks of color were another hallmark of these highly desirable purses. Although they are often overlooked as bags with abstract designs and limited visual appeal, they actually require a sophisticated sensibility to appreciate their bold and unique designs.

Large, pouch-shaped bags made from grosgrain, wool, and broadcloth were fashionable during the 1930s and 1940s. At this time the gimp or cordé bag made its appearance. These crocheted purses were made at home and professionally. Although many were mediocre in design and execution, some of the professionally made examples featured Bakelite or Prystal handles, which added to their appeal.

Glass beaded purses maintained their popularity into the 20th century, especially during the 1920s. Many very old beaded purses were brought out of storage for further use. Because re-cycling was acceptable, it is not uncommon to see a 19th century beaded purse remounted on an early 20th century frame. But the German beaded purse industry was still thriving and producing old and new designs for buyers worldwide. So it is probably accurate to say that many of the beaded florals, figural, and scenic purses in private collections today date to the early 20th century. Geometric, abstract, and Egyptian themed beaded purses definitely date to the early 20th century. After Egyptian King Tutankhamen's tomb was opened in 1922, beaded purses were designed with scenes of sphinxes and pyramids. Italy, France, and Czechoslovakia were also exporting beaded bags. Loomed, cut steel beaded purses were imported from France and Austria in large numbers, and although they were less likely to rust, many of them have experienced color fading. Purse frames were decorated with cameos, faux and real jewels, enamel, and micro-mosaics. Beaded purses could be bought from catalogs for as little as a few dollars or as much as one hundred dollars. Surprisingly, there are very few pictures from the 1920s showing a woman holding one of these treasures.

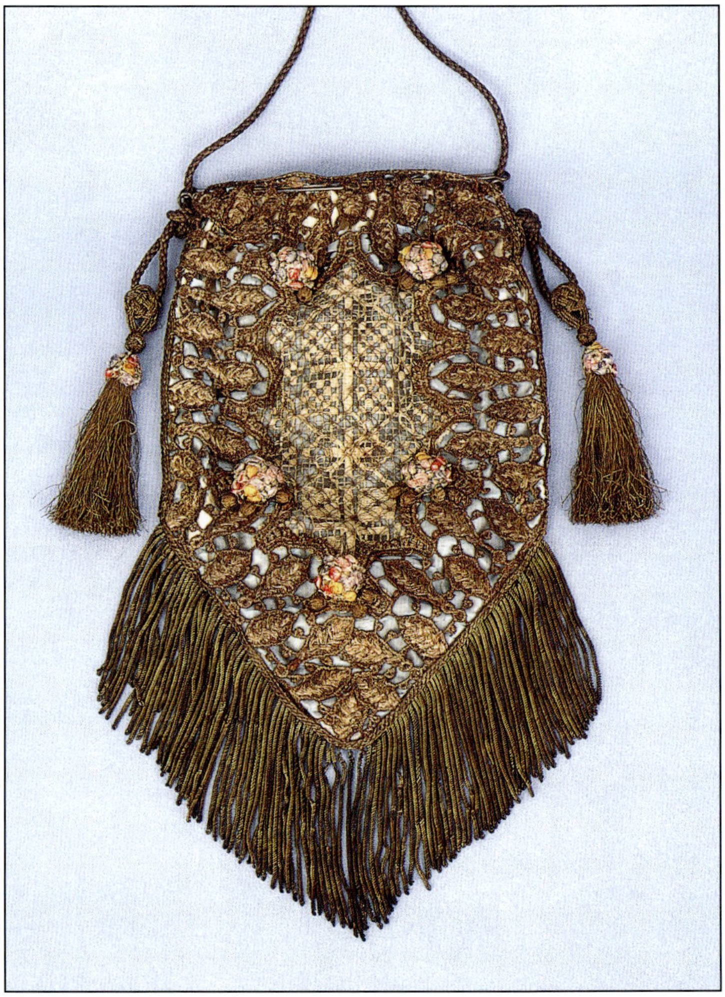

Purses made in an earlier romantic style were popular during the turn of the century. Made from layers of silk and gold metallic lace, gold bullion, gold lace trim, and silk rosettes, this purse is the epitome of richness and romanticism. 16.5 x 8.5 in. *Collection of Lori Blaser.* $300-350.

By the 1940s beaded purses were being made in solid colors and in box-like shapes. They paled in comparison to earlier versions, but had the advantage of being roomier and sturdier. Sometimes, beaded shoes were made to go with them. Beaded purses continued to be made until the end of the 20th century by companies in Belgium, Japan, China, India, and France. The finest late 20th century examples were made in France.

The 1920s also saw the arrival of the dance and vanity purse. Small, beautifully designed and decorated, these mesh and hard cased purses dangled from silk cords. They contained compartments for powder, rouge, lipstick, and coins. Many of them had silk tassels hanging from the bottom, which hid cylindrical lipstick holders. Cases were round, bolster shaped, rectangular, square, triangular, figural, and egg shaped. Their bodies were made from plastics, mesh, gold, silver, fabric, bone, ivory, and metal. Decorative touches included: beads, enamel, rhinestones, feathers, gems, watches, petit point, and paint. They are among the most charming of all vintage purses because of their small size and visually appealing designs.

No purse is more associated with the 1920s and 1930s than the mesh purse. Handmade, ring mesh purses had been made as early as 1892 in America, but the mesh purse didn't truly develop as an art form until the early 1920s. Two manufacturers, Mandalian and Whiting & Davis, made fine mesh purses. The Mandalian purses are considered to be the finest, in terms of their workmanship and aesthetics. Mandalian was eventually bought by Whiting & Davis in 1944. The Whiting & Davis *El-Sah*, topaz bezel-set purse, and "The Stars" series, produced many decades later, are among the costliest of all mesh purses. "The Stars" series of four bags featured mesh that was cleverly enameled with the faces of movie actors Clark Gable, Charlie Chaplin, Marion Davies, and Renee Adoreé. Few were made, and for only a very short period of time, before the company withdrew them, fearing royalty reprisals from members of the stars' families.

Two other types of mesh also were made: fine ring mesh and flat armor, or "spider," mesh. A popular finish for the fine ring mesh was stenciling with multiple colors to produce an impressionistic design. These purses were known as Dresden mesh. The flat mesh purses were also painted with a stenciling method and each color was baked on before another one was applied. Various finishes could be applied such as beadlite, pearl, and ivory tone. German and French makers also produced mesh purses, but some were of inferior quality, particularly the Dresden mesh, which were coarser. However, there are some wonderful French-made mesh purses, which are distinguished by their unique designs. Mesh purses were decorated with watches, enameling, drop fringe, real and faux jewels, and compacts. By the late 1930s, the Whiting & Davis mesh purse had grown larger, and was made in solid colors of gold, silver, white, and black.

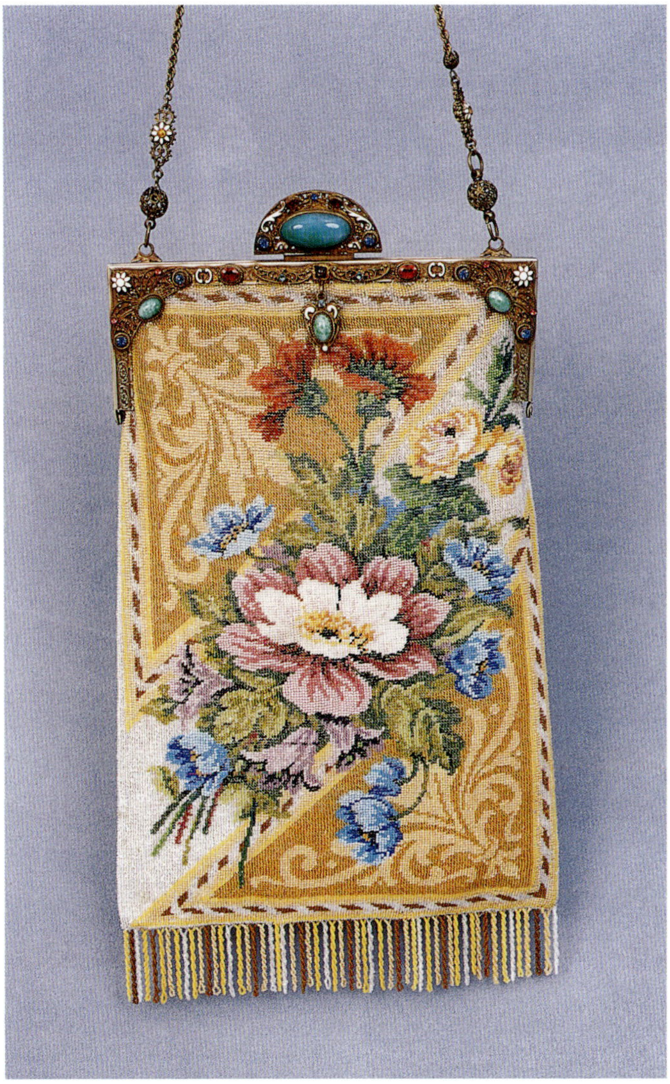

Fine bead knitted purse, with a jeweled frame and stand-up clasp. The unusual color combination and the floral-geometric pattern make it appealing even to advanced collectors. 14.5 x 8.25 in. *Collection of Lori Blaser.* $1,200-1,400.

Petit point purses from Austria and France were carried by fashionable women during the first half of the 20th century. Austria was the leading exporter of petit point purses to Europe and America. Heinrich Muller, a Viennese art dealer, was the major seller of petit point patterns to Europe and Russia during the early 20th century. Patterns dating as far back as the 16th century were used to create beautiful purse designs, and Biedermeier themes such as temples, ruins, and mythological figures were also used. Biblical figures, 18th century courting scenes, pastoral landscapes, scenes depicting famous musicians, and the famous LeViste family tapestries were all possible design sources. Fine petit point purses had 900 to 3,000 stitches per square inch. Their color schemes were soft and pleasing, unlike the harsh colors of machine made petit points. They were mounted on silver and gilt frames, decorated with pearls, enameling, and jewels. Petit point purses were still being made in Austria into the late 20th century, and although later in date, they are well worth collecting. Their pierced, sterling clasps help to date these later purses. Some collectors prefer the more ornate earlier frames, but much of the value is in the petit point itself, and it should be evaluated on the merits of the workmanship and its overall aesthetics.

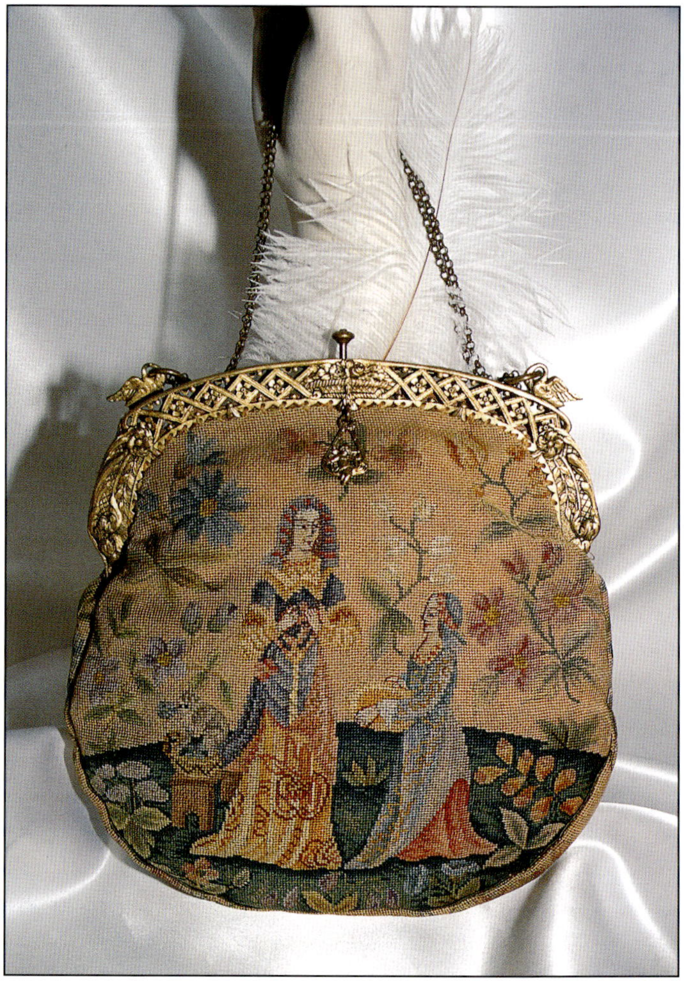

This petit point design, known as the Lady, Lion, and the Unicorn design, was taken from a series of tapestry wall hangings made to commemorate the marriage of Jean LeViste of Brossac Castle in the 15th century. The tapestries represent the five senses of hearing, taste, smell, touch, and sight. The 6th tapestry represents the renunciation of the five senses. 9 x 8 in. *Collection of Paula Higgins.* $650-750.

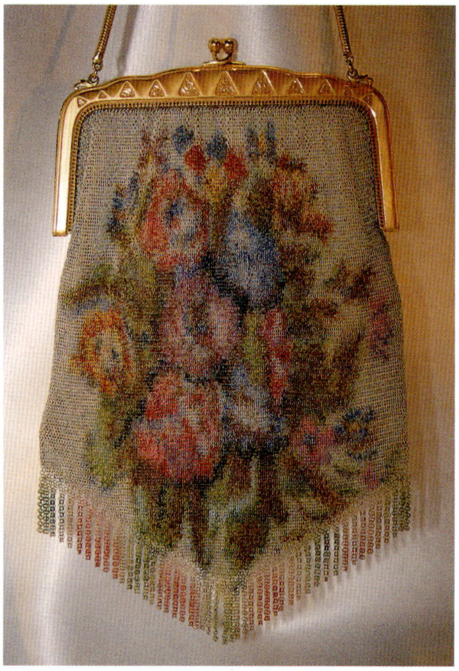

Colorful floral designed Dresden Mesh with a gold plated frame, made by Whiting & Davis. Dresden mesh are attractive to many collectors because of their impressionistic quality. Whiting & Davis produced the finest ring mesh available, specifically for their Dresden mesh purses. 9 x 6 in. *Collection of Paula Higgins.* $300-$350.

Tapestry purses, sometimes known as Aubusson tapestry purses, were also carried by women during the early 20th century. Handmade tapestries were woven on looms, and made with silk, wool, metallic, and linen threads. Designs were created by weaving the weft threads (which run side-to-side) into the warp threads with fingers or a bobbin. The weaver would not see the completed surface while she was working unless she had a mirror. As different colors were woven into the tapestry, slits were left, which were sewn together before the piece was finished. Tapestry weaving started in Aubusson, France during the 16th century, and continued into the 20th century. Designs came from "cartoons" patterned after the paintings of Boucher,

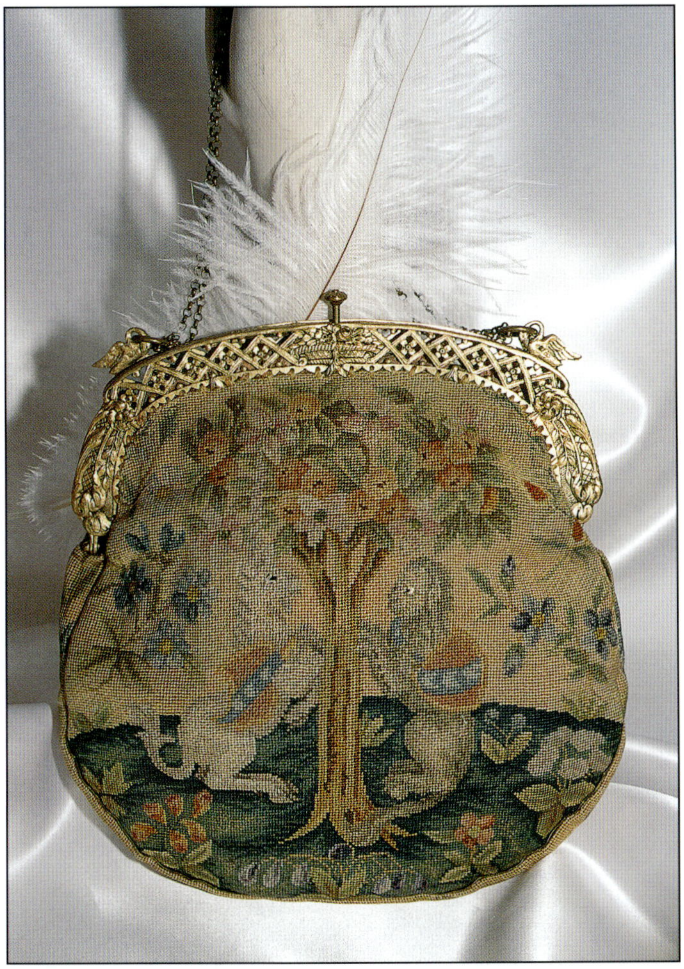

The reverse of the petit point showing the lion and the unicorn.

Watteau, and Fragonard. Once the bodies of the purses were completed, they were attached to beautiful silver and jeweled frames. Modern tapestries are made by jacquard weaving machines, and while costly, they lack the beauty of the handmade tapestries.

A less common type of embroidered purse, from the same period, is the silk stitched purse. These French-made evening bags were worked in tiny silk stitches, which blend into each other and cover the entire surface. The effect was soft, silky, and lovely. Although the majority of these purses were mounted on beautiful frames, some were mounted on silk stitched covered frames, or they were made without a frame, in a clutch style. Favored designs included courting scenes, but occasionally a less common design is encountered, which brings a higher price.

Plastic purses are true 20th century icons. Sculptured shapes, worked in plastics, transformed purse design. Twentieth century plastics allowed for almost any kind of shape and decoration the imagination could conceive. There are collectors who buy only plastic purses, and a wall display of them is imposing; their visual impact is impressive.

Celluloid was a synthetic material first developed in 1863, but did not become widely used until 1910. It imitated the more costly natural materials of ivory and tortoiseshell. As a cheaper alternative, celluloid was used to make purses and especially purse fittings, such as clasps and frames. Unfortunately, it was flammable and it gradually deteriorated, shrunk, crazed, and buckled. To test for celluloid, heat a pin and insert it in an inconspicuous area of the material. If it is celluloid, it will smell like camphor.

Bakelite was another synthetic plastic first manufactured in 1907 from phenol, carbolic acid, and formaldehyde. It is heavier than other plastics and originally came in five colors. When the Union Carbide Company bought the Bakelite Company in 1938, 15 new colors were added. To test for Bakelite, you can rub it until it is warm and it will smell of formaldehyde. This test can also be done with a hot pin. Another test for Bakelite is to use a small amount of Formula 409 on the surface. Wipe it with a white cloth. If it is Bakelite, the cloth should turn yellow.

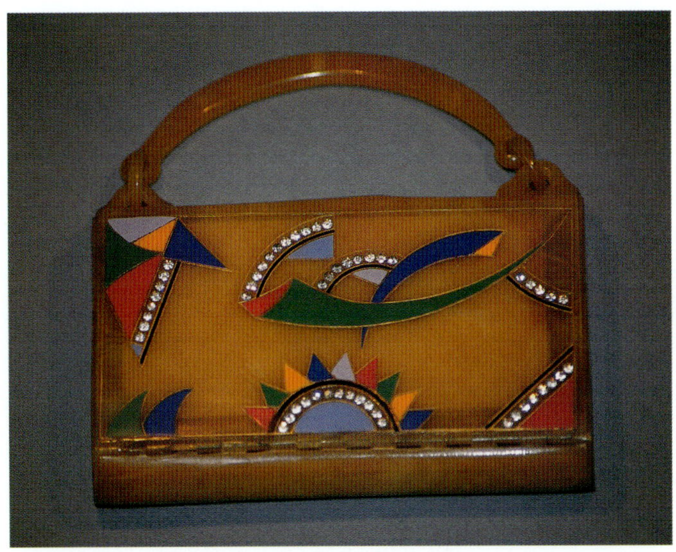

A colorful, rhinestone set Bakelite purse from the Art Deco Period, which was made for a child. Like the larger, adult versions, this purse is fitted with a pocket and mirror. 5 x 3 in. *Collection of Paula Higgins.* $400-500.

Lucite, a trade name for an acrylic synthetic plastic, was first produced in 1931, but it was not used significantly in the general population until the 1950s. Its strength and crystalline appearance appealed to the post-war woman, and the Lucite purse itself functioned as a piece of wearable sculpture. Lucite bags were made by manufacturers such as: Wilardy, Llewellyn, Rialto, Kahn, Florida, Dorset Rex, Tyrolean, Myles, and Patricia of Miami. Usually they were stamped or labeled, but an unsigned piece is not uncommon as many of the labels were lost. Collectors today look for the rare shades of red, pink, or blue. For even more variety, Lucite was made in both translucent and opaque forms.

The not insignificant problem with plastic purses is that they can deteriorate if stored improperly in high humidity or high temperatures. If they develop "plastic disease," they should be discarded. In fact, a purse that develops plastic disease must be removed from any contact with other plastic purses, since the disease can spread. Plastic disease presents as brittleness, crazing, corrosion, a vinegar odor, and weeping (a sticky or oily substance on the surface). Other problems include cracking, warping, and color loss. Some collectors use Novus polish to repair scratches, with varying degrees of success. If you collect plastic purses, avoid storage in contact with metals. Also, avoid water, detergent, and solvents, which can cause swelling and remove the finish.

The jewelry company of Van Cleef and Arpels designed the first minaudiere. Unlike the dance purse, these slender, hard cased containers were held in the palm of the hand. They were designed to hold make-up, coins, powder, puffs, combs, lighters, and cigarettes. Early ones from the 1930s were usually rectangular or square and had fitted compartments. They were embroidered, covered with leather, embossed, and decorated with jewels, both real and faux. Later 20th century versions by Judith Leiber were made in a variety of shapes, including figural. Judith Leiber's minaudieres were hand decorated with beautiful Swarovski crystals. They are still being made to this day, and as handmade pieces they are priced accordingly. Occasionally, auction houses will offer beautiful gem encrusted minaudieres made by famous jewelry houses, and they bring substantial prices.

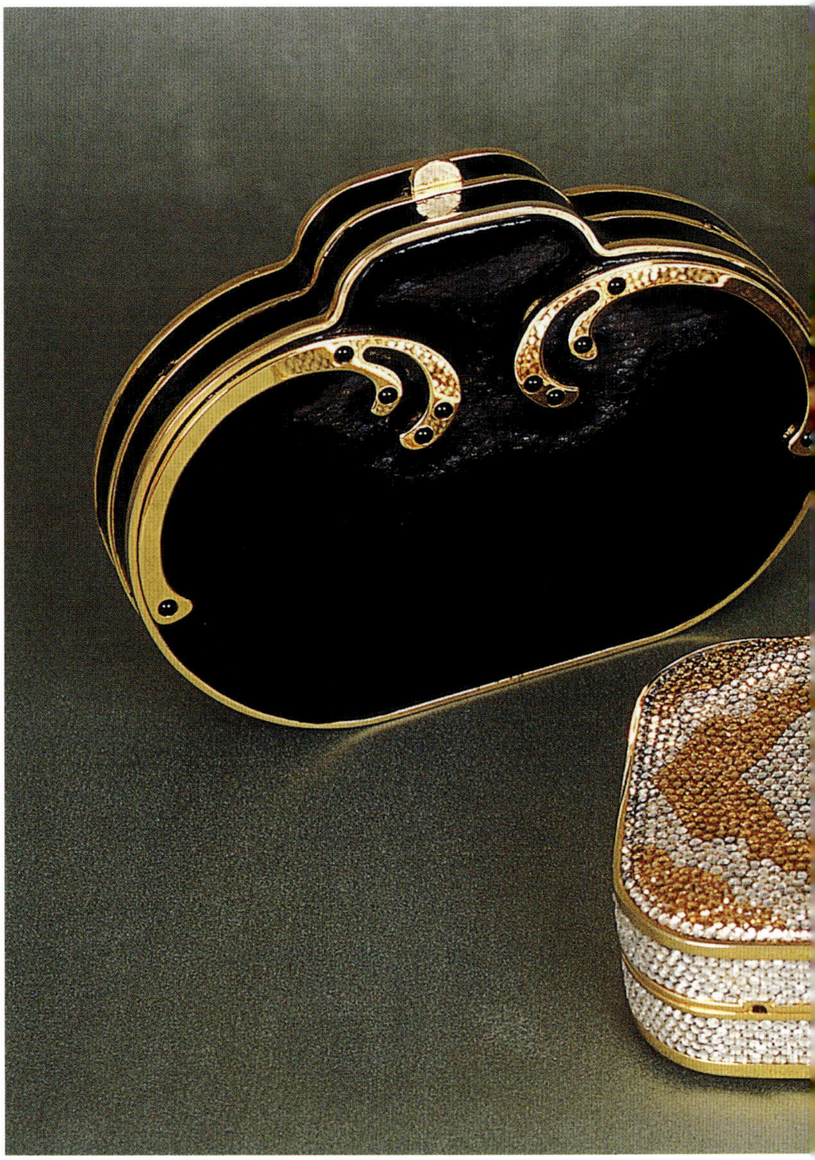

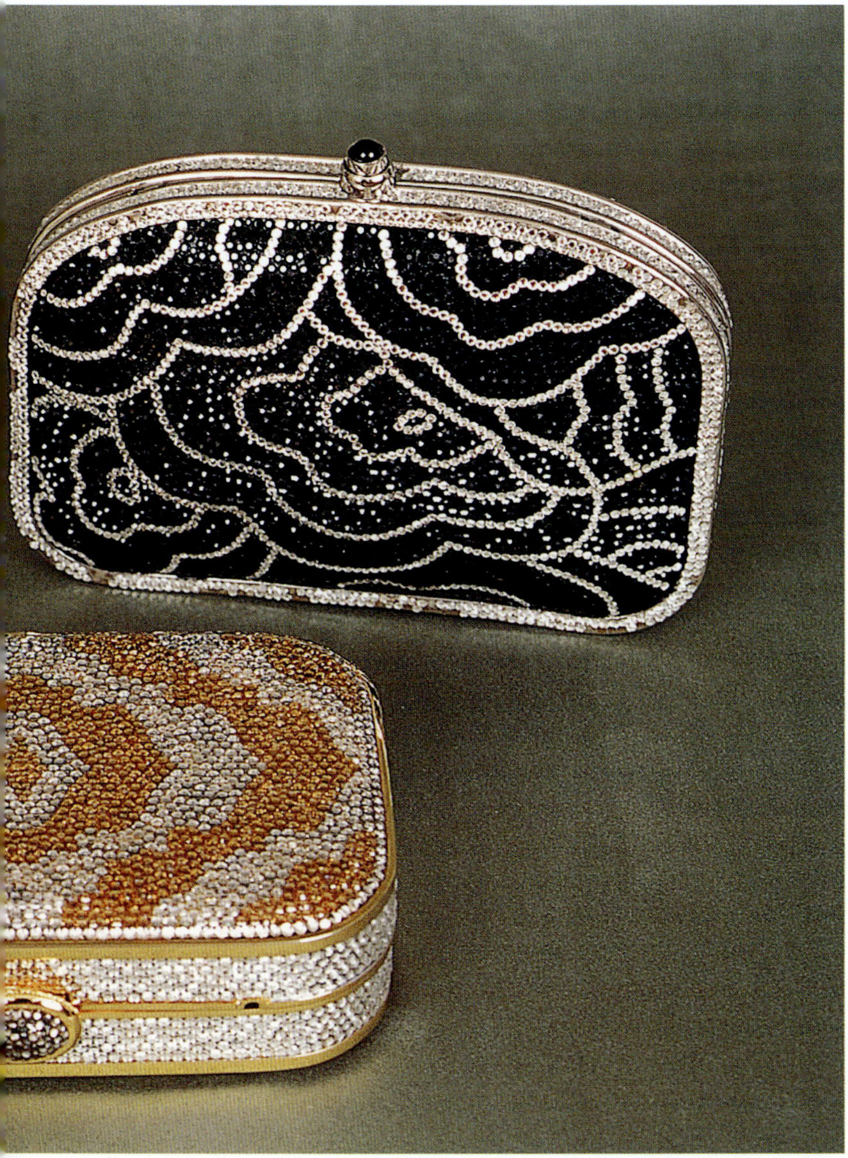

A trio of beautiful evening bags. Left: Black Karung snakeskin purse with gold trim and black cabochon stones by Finesse La Model 1980s. 6.5 x 5 in. Right: Judith Leiber black and white crystal set purse from the 1980s. 6 x 4 in. Center: Gold and white crystal set purse by Finesse La Model from the 1980s. 6 x 4 in. All purses from the *Collection of Ruth Penson.* Rare.

A uniquely American purse type is the Nantucket Lightship Basket purse. In its finest form, it is a masterpiece of craftsmanship and beauty. They were first made by 19th century sailors as simple, but beautifully constructed baskets, while working off Nantucket on lightships. Because sailors were out at sea for extended periods of time, this craft was a way to occupy their free time, as well as an opportunity to earn more money. After World War II, José Formoso Reyes, a native of the Philippines, settled with his wife on Nantucket Island and started to make baskets in the old Nantucket tradition. In this effort, he was mentored by Mitchell Ray, a noted basketmaker. Before long, Reyes was covering his baskets with lids, and then decorating the basket tops with scrimshawed whales and seagulls. By the time of his death in 1980, he had made over 5,000 baskets. Queen Elizabeth II was presented with one at the time of her coronation in 1953. His baskets sell in the thousands when they come up for auction. Present-day Nantucket Lightship Basket purses are very refined and beautifully constructed, from either oak or cane staves, and many are decorated with scrimshawed plaques. There is an exquisite example on page 255, made by Alan S W Reed and Lee Ann Papale. It is important to know that there are some very convincing reproductions and knock-offs of Nantucket basket purses, which have been made overseas. Some of these knock-off baskets have real scrimshaw plaques applied, to lend an air of authenticity. One indication of their knock-off status is that their hinges are made from plastic, not leather. An excellent resource to learn more about these special purses is Martha Lawrence's book, *Lightship Baskets of Nantucket*.

Chapter 2
Pockets

Antique tie-on pockets functioned as a type of purse for women from our historic past. It is believed they were in use as early as the middle 17th century. They tied around the waist until the late 19th century, at which time they were also hung from rings, chatelaine style. Pocket contents changed from century to century, and place to place (rural vs. town). But at one point or another, pockets held keys, money, watches, recipes, cups, cosmetics (powder), and sewing accessories. Until recently, it was thought that pockets remained in use only until the 1840s when pockets were first sewn into dresses. However, recent research by Barbara Burman, from the Winchester School of Art in England, has shown that pockets were actually in use as late as 1910. Her "Pockets of History" project is the most in-depth review of antique pockets, their physical characteristics, and how they relate to women and social change that has ever been published. In the United States, Yolanda Van Der Krol contributed an excellent article on pockets to *The Magazine ANTIQUES*, in the March, 1996 issue.

Although pockets were often made in pairs, to be worn on both hips, they were also made as a single pocket. Women accessed their pockets through slits in their dresses or through opened seams. Occasionally, they were worn over a dress or skirt, and under an apron. Previous literature had them being worn exclusively under the skirt, but more recent research has shown this was not always the case. Most pockets were made with vertical slits in order to access their contents, but there are 19th century examples, which were made with horizontal openings. Shaped like saddlebags, they were flared at the bottom, until the early 19th century, when some examples became slightly narrower at the bottom. Many pockets were angled at the top, allowing them to settle on the wearer's hips more comfortably. Pockets also had extensions added to their tops because they were passed on to the next, taller generation. Van Der Krol notes that their design falls into four categories: embroidered, whole cloth, appliquéd, and pieced. Pockets were made at home, and they were also ready made and sold from shops. The earliest surviving pockets were beautifully embroidered on linen and silk, with figures, small animals, and flowers. These very early examples usually present as single pockets, and not in pair form like the later versions. Seventeenth and early 18th century pockets are museum items and are rarely offered for sale.

Eighteenth century American crewel worked pockets are highly desirable and very expensive when offered for sale. Crewelwork designs included figures, vines, vases, flowers, small geometric designs, and animals. Occasionally, an American crewel worked pocket can be found on Ebay and although it may sell for less than retail, it will still command a very high price. Early American Irish stitched examples have also survived, but these are quite rare. British embroidered pockets have more refined and balanced designs than their American counterparts, but American pockets have more originality. Fashionable 18th century French women considered pockets somewhat déclassé so fewer French pockets survive from this period.

Whole cloth pockets made from printed fabrics (wood block printing, copperplate printing, and roller printing) were also popular during the 18th century. But the most common whole cloth pocket was made from white fabric. A pocket in the Victoria and Albert Museum in London is made from white matelassé, which is a type of woven quilting (an extra weft is added to the fabric).

After the American Revolution, c.1780, patchwork pockets became popular in America because printed cotton fabrics were more widely available once normal trade resumed. However, dating them can be problematic. Women recycled fabrics, and some patchwork pockets date into the early 19th century, even though they were made with 18th century fabrics. Dating is more accurate if there is a known provenance that comes with the pocket. Earlier patchwork pockets incorporated patches of white, whereas later examples typically used all patterned cottons.

In the Victoria and Albert Museum there are two examples of pieced pockets made c.1830 from 18th century, gold embroidered fabrics. Once the pockets were examined as a whole, their latest fabrics (19th century) determined their age. Appliqued pockets are very rare and in the following chapter is an example, which was de-accessioned from the Sturbridge Village Museum. It dates to c.1880 and it is American. Later 19th century pockets were sometimes hung from rings, like chatelaines. One 19th century writer noted that after she took it off at the end of the day, she hung it on her bedpost from its ring. Recent research has established that pockets were used as travel accessories as late as 1910, especially in rural areas. In the 20th century, white, whole cloth pockets were the most common and they were machine stitched.

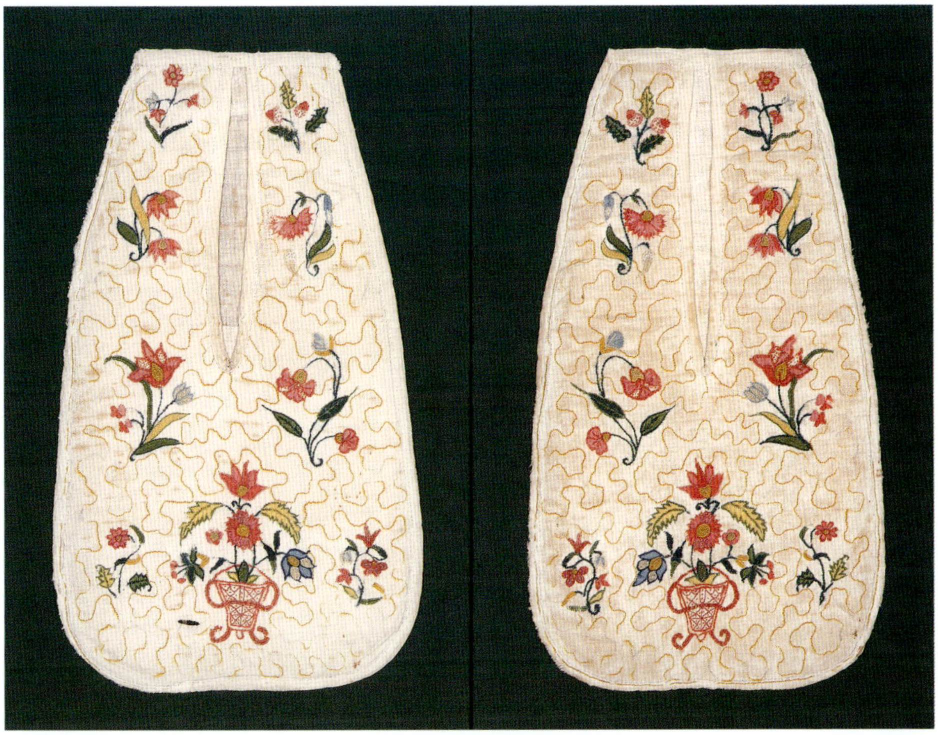

Pair of crewel work pockets with pink urns filled with blue and pink flowers, and floral and acorn sprigs. The background is made of fustian, which is embroidered with a yellow vermicelli pattern. The name of *Mary Measure* is on the back of both pockets. She lived in Lincolnshire, England c.1740. *Courtesy of Cora Ginsburg LLC.* Very rare.

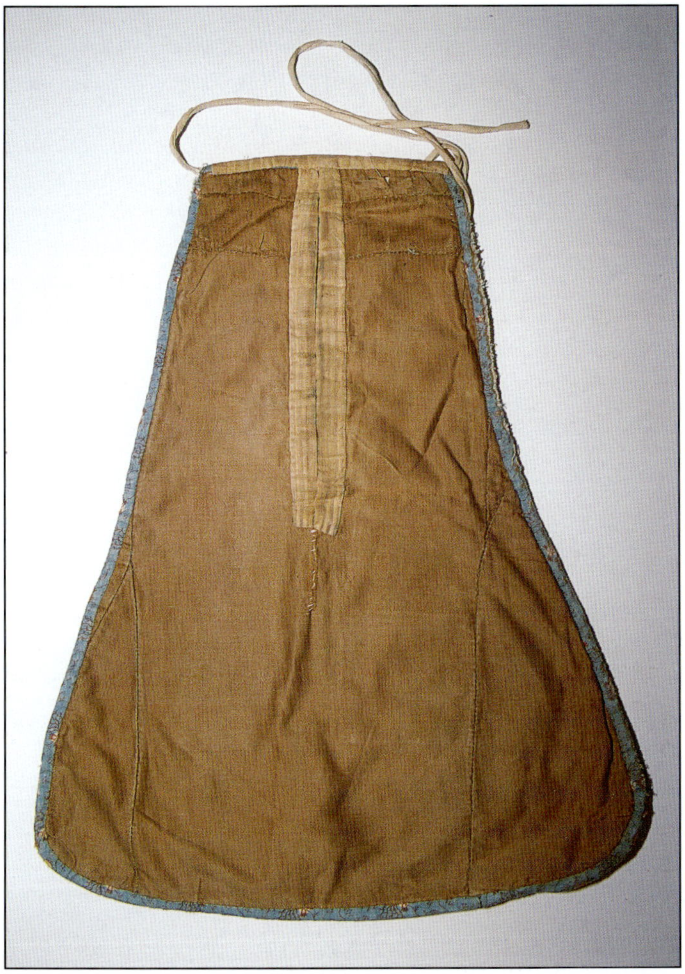

Early American, brown pocket from New York state. Pieced together from leftover material and trimmed with blue sprigged cotton, it is a rare survival because it was made for everyday use. Usually, the finer embroidered pockets from the late 18th century survived, and were then passed onto family members. 15 x 12 in. *Collection of Paula Higgins.* Rare.

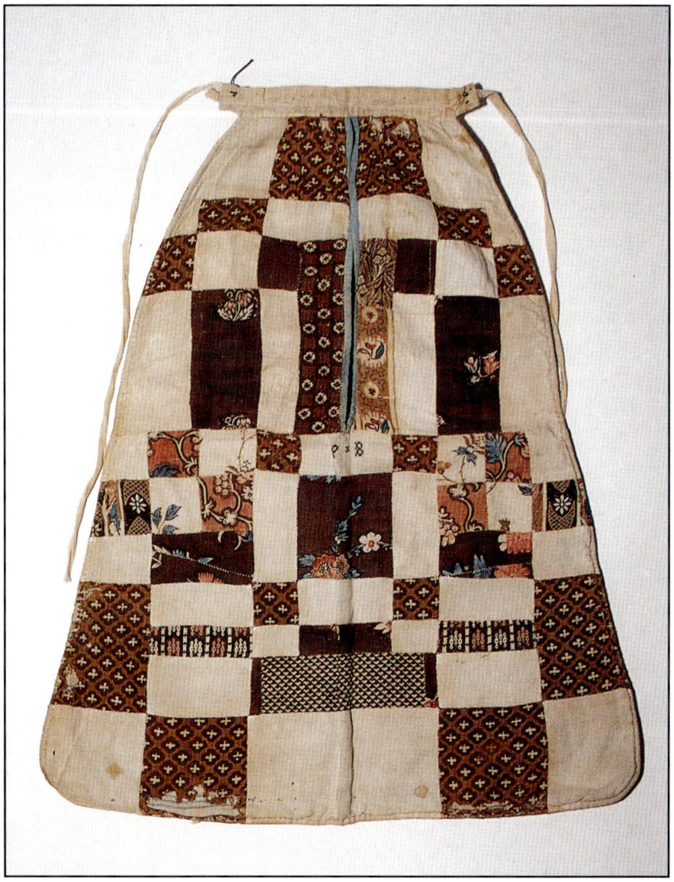

Late 18th century American patchwork pocket originally owned by Phoebe Boss of Rhode Island. Her initials were cross-stitched in the center of the pocket. Earlier patchwork pockets were made with patches of white or cream, interspersed with patterned calicos. Cotton calicos became more widely available after the Revolutionary War when normal trade resumed. 16 x 14 in. *Collection of Paula Higgins.* Rare.

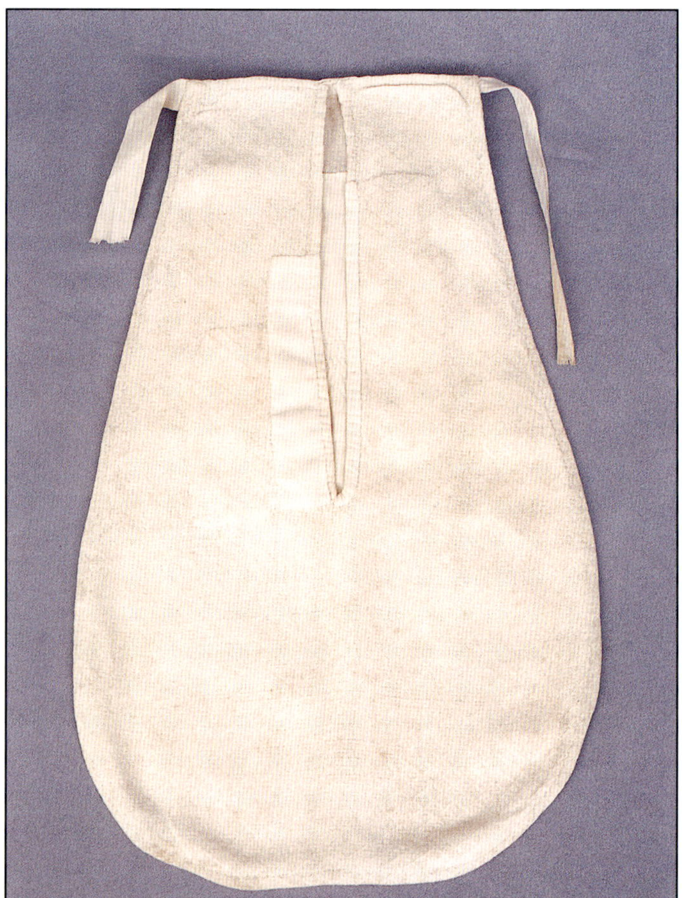

C.1800 American white linen pocket. White was a popular color for pockets from the 18th century to the early 20th century. Some early white pockets were quilted. 17.5 x 11 in. *Collection of Lori Blaser.* $350-450.

C.1810 American patchwork pocket from the Vosberg family of Georgetown, Maryland. The Vosgbergs owned a dry goods store in the 19th century. The store was closed in the 1920s, so the remaining contents, along with other family household items were stored in an attic. The attic contents were auctioned off when the family home was sold. 15 x 11 in. *Collection of Paula Higgins.* $800-1,000.

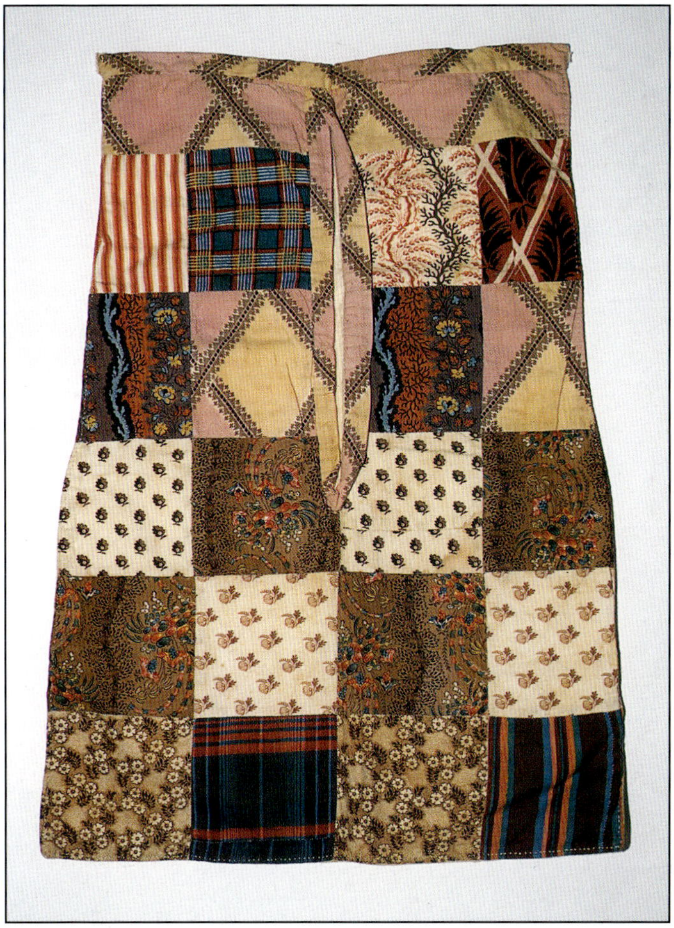

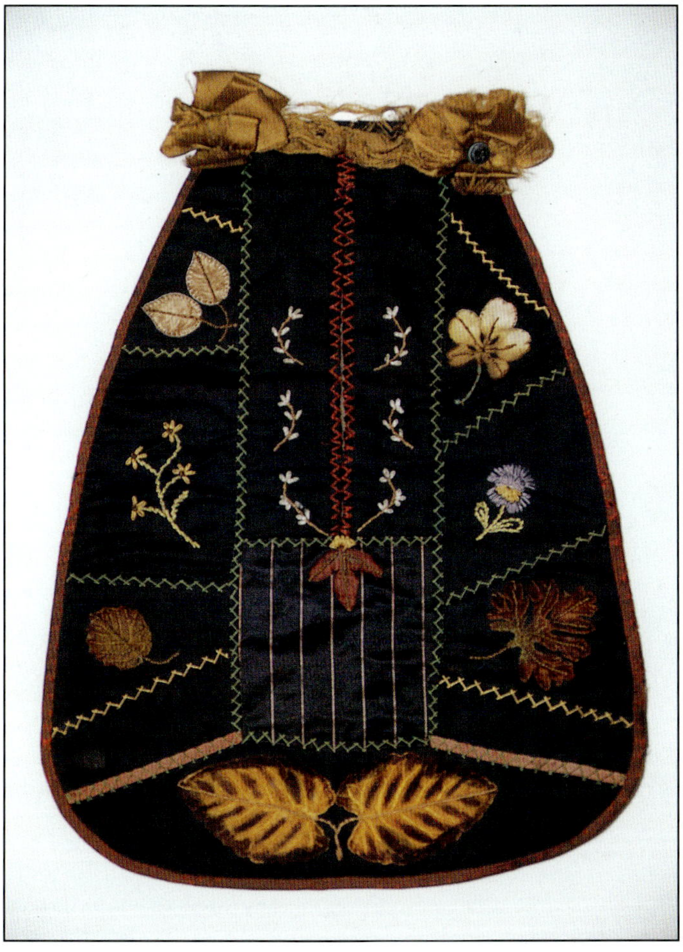

This c.1870s pocket was formerly in the collection of Sturbridge Village Museum in Massachusetts. It is appliquéd with leaves, and embroidered with flowers and featherstitching. Appliqued pockets are rare. This purse also had a ring attachment, a feature seen on a few late 19th century pockets. One writer from the late 19th century said that rings were used to hang the pockets on bedsteads. 14 x 12 in. *Collection of Paula Higgins.* Rare.

Chapter 3
Misers

Women and men were carrying misers, also known as stocking purses, by the late 17th century. In their earliest form, they were shaped like a long stocking, and knitted in colorful silks. Designed specifically to hold coins, access was gained by a vertical opening in the middle of the purse. If the miser had sliders (rings to close off the purse), they were slid to each end to prevent the coins from falling out.

By the 18th century, misers were being netted professionally and sold from dry goods shops. Netting was also a popular past time enjoyed by women in their homes in the 18th and early 19th centuries. Consequently, many early, homemade netted misers have survived. Professionally netted misers can be distinguished from homemade examples by their fine and delicate network. This network was occasionally embroidered with small flowers, creating a very feminine look. Homemade misers were not as finely executed, usually having larger spaces in the network. Women bought sliders, fishes (metal charms), and professionally made tassels from shops to complete their misers. By the late 18th century, many misers were rounded on both ends, for a more balanced design. Eighteenth century misers were also longer than 19th century misers, averaging nineteen to twenty-four inches in length. Misers from this period typically had silk tassels, which were occasionally decorated with glass pearls or beautifully worked knots. Sliders used on 18th century misers were occasionally made from pinchbeck, an alloy of zinc and copper. Pinchbeck resembles gold, but it is very lightweight in comparison.

In the early years of the 19th century, misers were still netted and knitted, but their size decreased by about half. Misers were also made from silk fabric, some featuring vandyked ends, but this type of miser is quite rare. Early 19th century sliders were made from a variety of materials. Many were finely detailed with engraving, embossing, damascene work, and carving. Knitted silk misers with cut steel beads date to this period also (late 18th to early 19th centuries). Early knitted misers were long, made with very fine cut steel beads, and embellished with names, dates, or unusual designs. The Museum of Fine Arts in Boston, Massachusetts has an excellent collection of early misers, which can be seen by appointment.

Crocheted misers, made with larger cut steel beads, also make their appearance in the first half of the 19th century. Finished with cut steel tassels, they survive by the hundreds and are less desirable than the knitted and netted examples. However, they are not necessarily undistinguished, and many collectors have at least one. Completely knitted misers, with paisley designs and chandelier silk tassels, date to the mid-nineteenth century. Glass bead knitted misers dating to c.1830 are very collectible. Typically decorated with floral designs, they are much less common than the crocheted cut steel examples.

Misers continued to be made throughout the 19th century, and into the early 20th century to hold gaming chips. As a general rule, they lack the refinement and beauty of the earlier misers, but every now and then, one will appear with considerable eye appeal. Turkish makers produced colorful, glass-beaded misers featuring birds and diamond-shaped designs. They finished their misers with lovely silk and bead tassels, which have a very unique appearance. A Turkish miser is pictured in this chapter. These misers were exported to Europe and appear occasionally on Ebay.

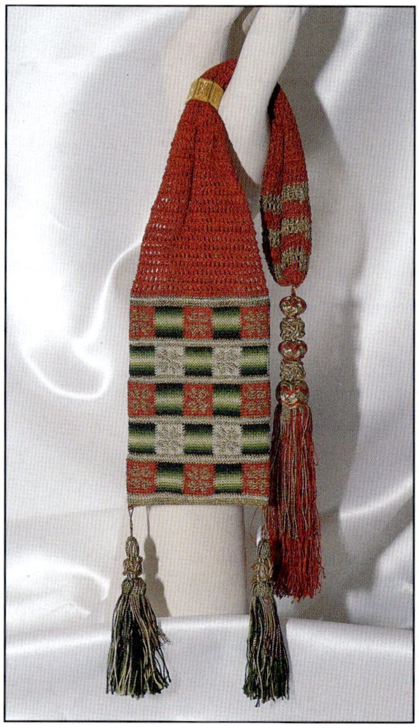

An 18th century miser formerly in the collection of the noted Austrian textile collector, Emma Henriette Schiff von Suvero. Knitted with silk and silver threads, and decorated with knotted tassels, a pinchbeck slider, and glass pearls (set in the gold wire/green tassels). Emma von Suvero's collection was confiscated by the Nazis during World War II. It was subsequently returned to her family many years later by the Austrian government and then auctioned by her descendents. 20 x 2 in. *Collection of Paula Higgins.* $1,000-1,200.

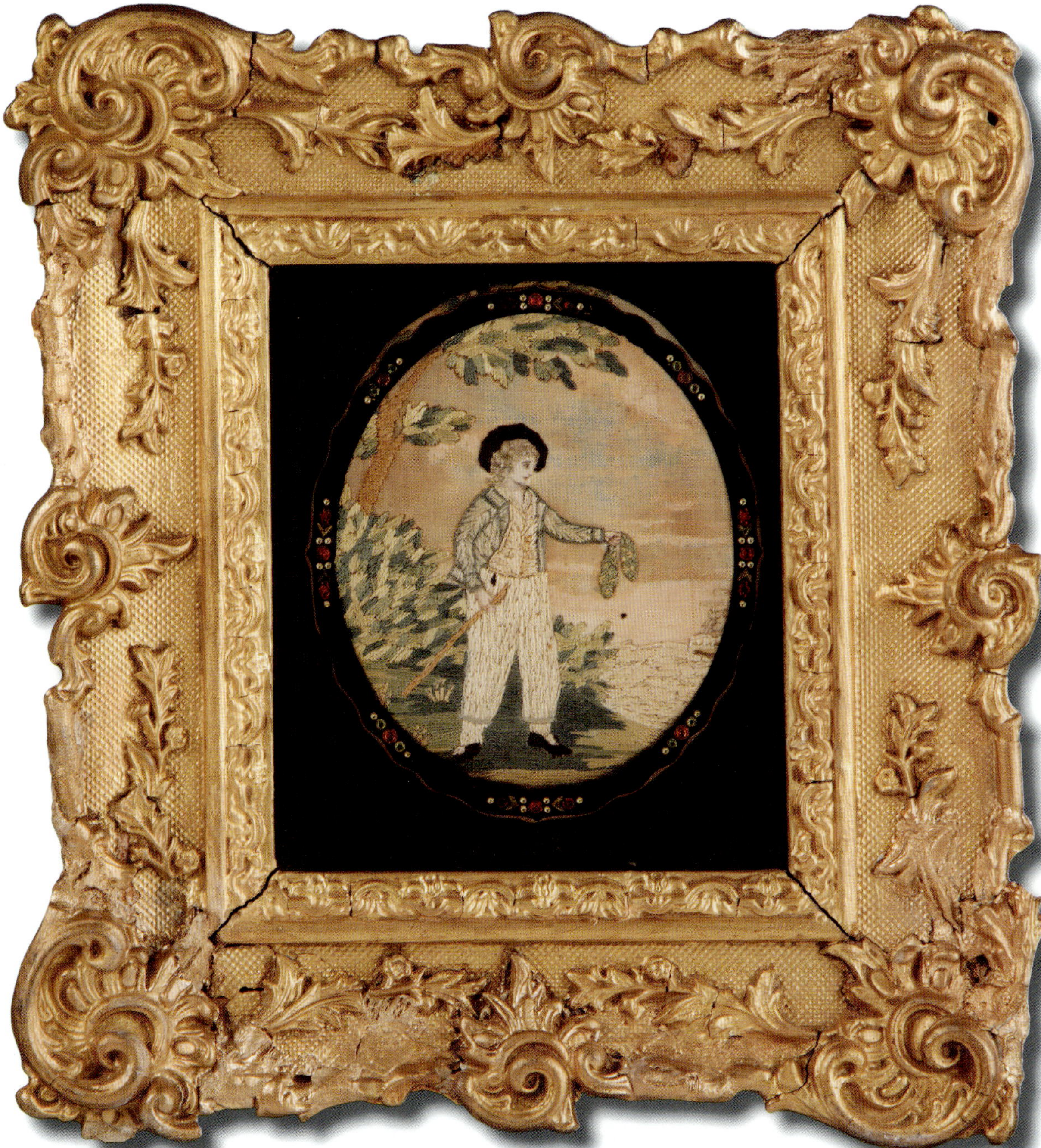

Early 19th century silk stitched picture of a young man looking out to sea, while holding a walking stick in one hand, and a miser in the other. Painted or embroidered pictures showing people holding misers are seldom ever seen, making this a true treasure. Misers were used by both women and men. *Collection of Sharon LuVisi.* Very rare.

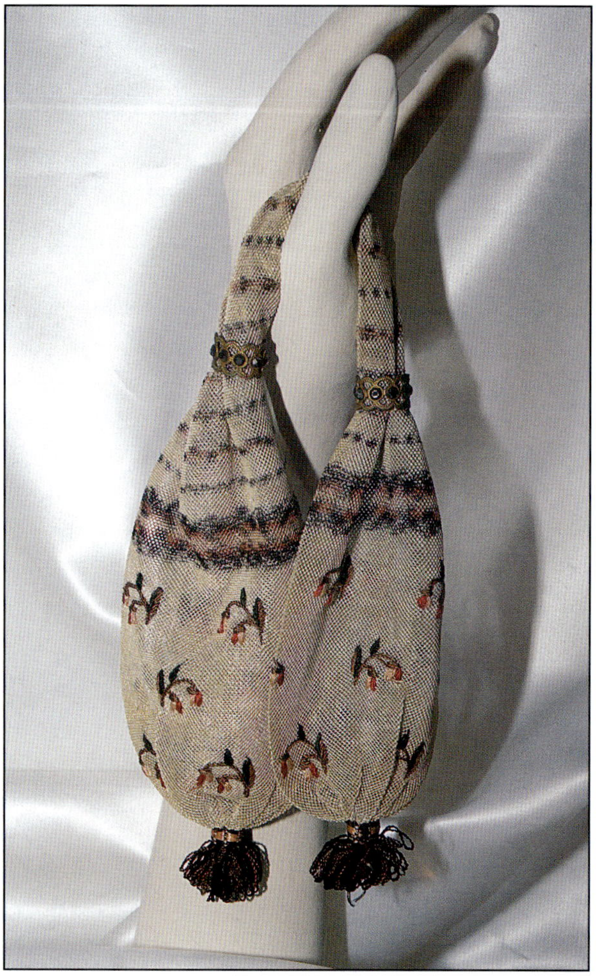

Netted and embroidered late 18th century miser. The fineness of the network indicates that it was probably made by a professional, rather than at home. Short silk tassels are a typical feature of early misers. Made in England. 19 x 3 in. *Collection of Paula Higgins*. $800-1,000.

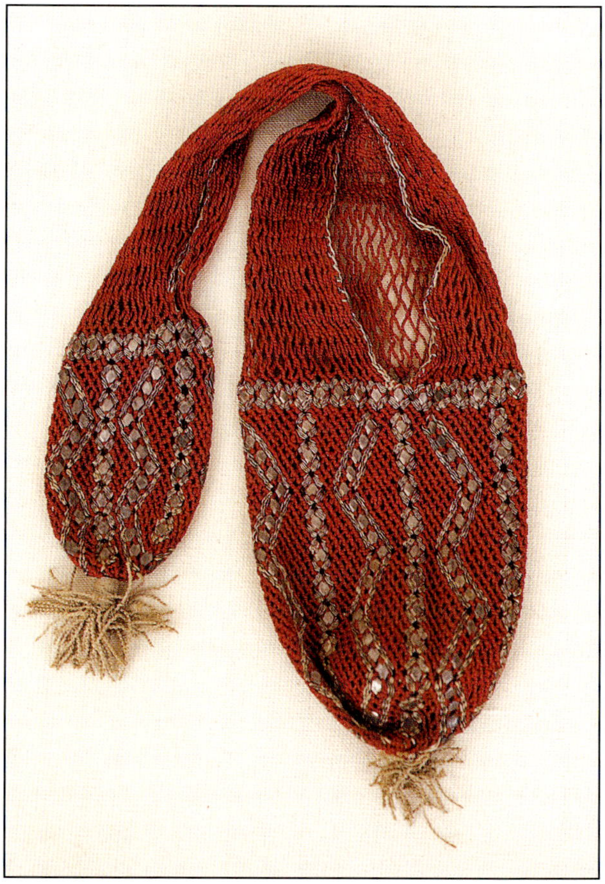

Red silk, netted miser decorated with silver strips. This is a very unusual and effective decorative technique. It dates to the 18th century. The ends are finished with short silk tassels. The long length is another 18th century miser characteristic. 16 x 3.5 in. *Collection of Lori Blaser.* $800-1,000.

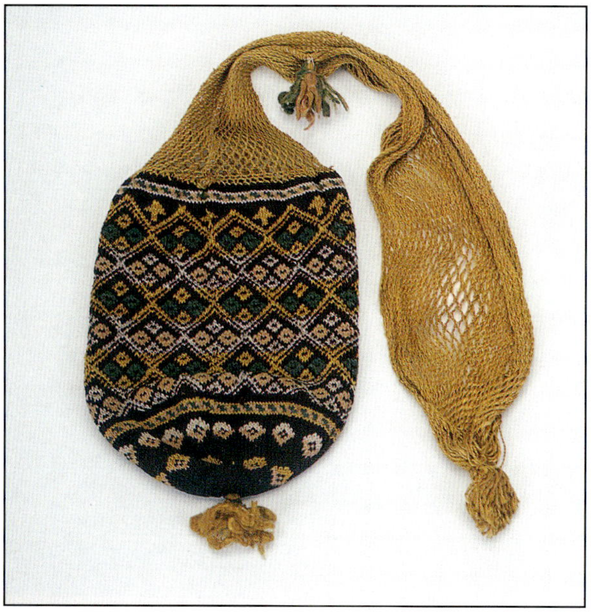

Late 18th century netted and knitted, green and gold silk miser. This purse was found under some floorboards in an old house in London, not far from Buckingham Palace. 23 x 4.75 in. *Collection of Lori Blaser.* $800-1,000.

Late 18th century American miser. Finely knitted with silk thread in a flamepoint pattern. Decorated with silk tassels and steel sliders. This piece was deaccessioned from a museum. 21 x 3 in. *Collection of Paula Higgins.* Rare.

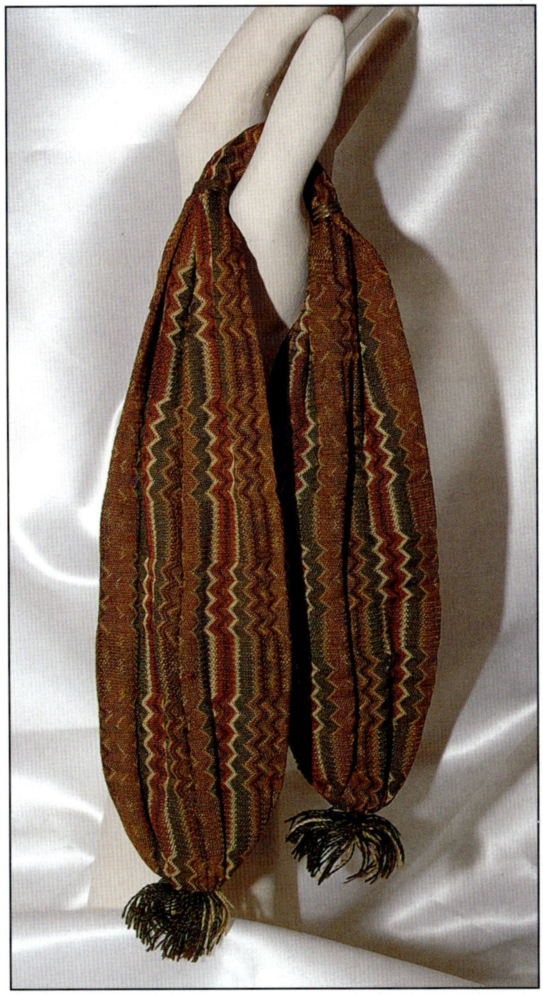

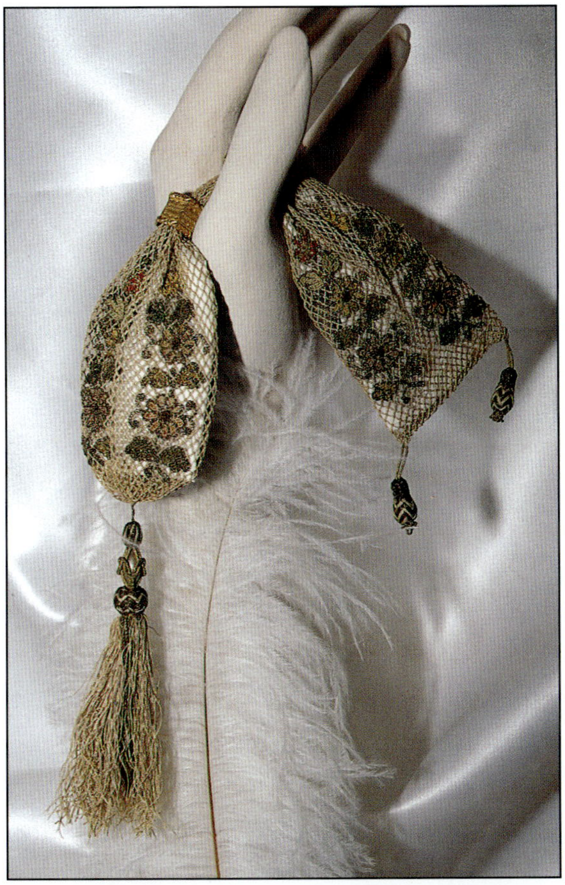

Late 18th century netted and embroidered miser, decorated with knotted tassels, a pearl set in gold wire, and pinchbeck sliders. Although this miser was professionally made, the netting is less fine, which can be an indication that the miser was homemade. Ready-made sliders and tassels could be purchased at dry goods stores to finish the completed miser. Made in England. 13 x 3 in. *Collection of Paula Higgins.* $800-1,000.

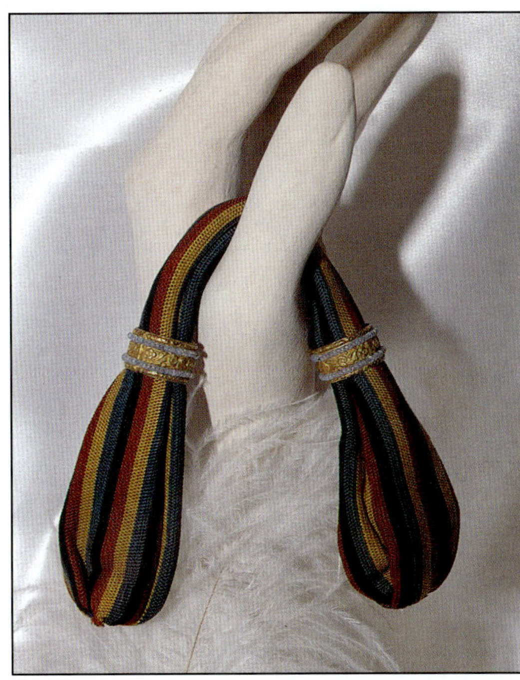

C.1795-1810 miser formerly in the collection of Emma Henriette Schiff von Suvero, a famous collector of early textiles. Made from finely knitted silk and finished with pinchbeck and blue opalescent glass sliders. Blue opalescent glass was used on jewelry items in the late 18th and early 19th centuries. 8 x 1.5 in. *Collection of Paula Higgins.* $650-$750.

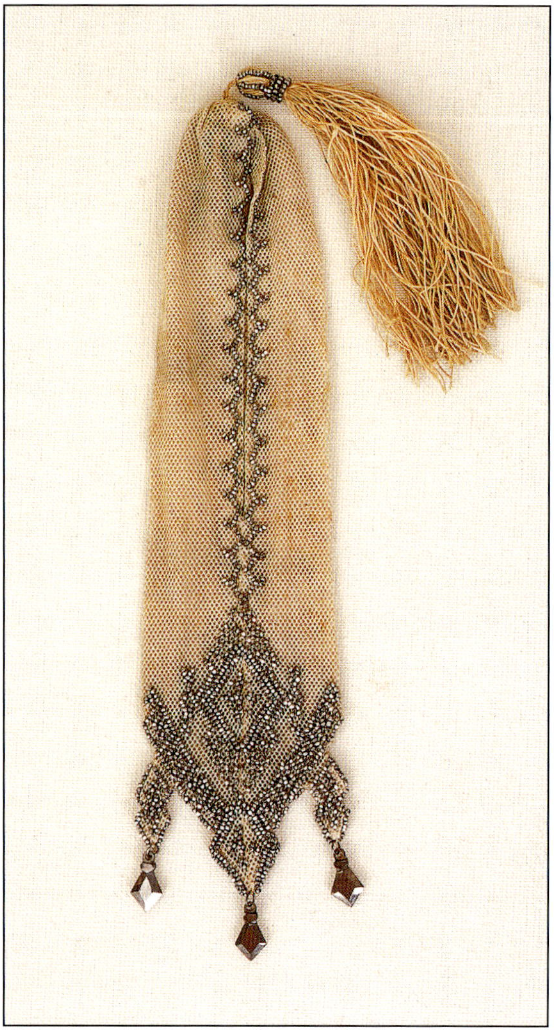

C.1800 finely netted miser made with cut steel beads, faceted tassels, and a long tassel on the opposite end. Fine, cut steel beads were often used on netted misers during the late 18th and early 19th centuries. 13 x 2. *Collection of Lori Blaser.* $600-800.

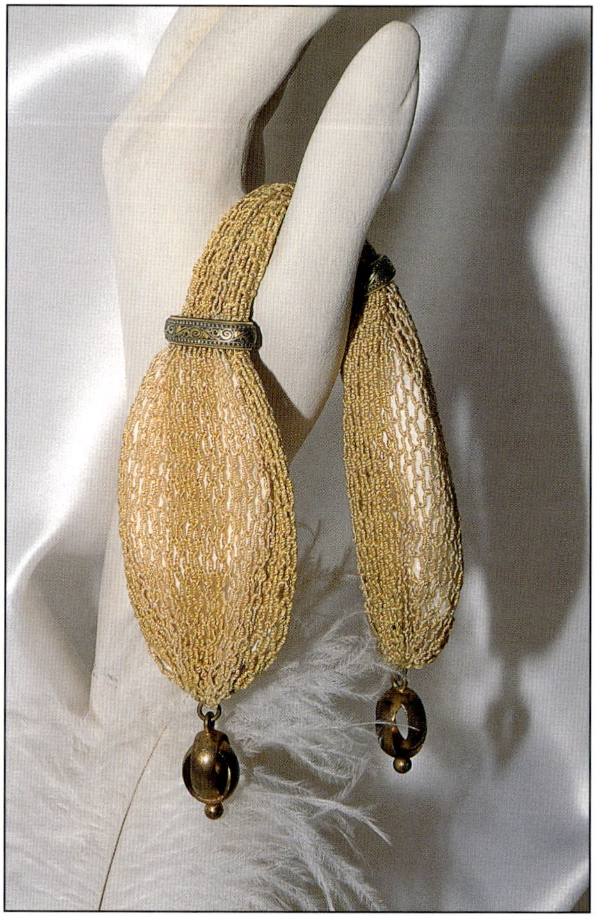

Early 19th century, gold colored netted miser with Damascene sliders and brass tassels. The sliders are marked with the name *Luis Galan.* 8 x 2. *Collection of Paula Higgins.* $300-350.

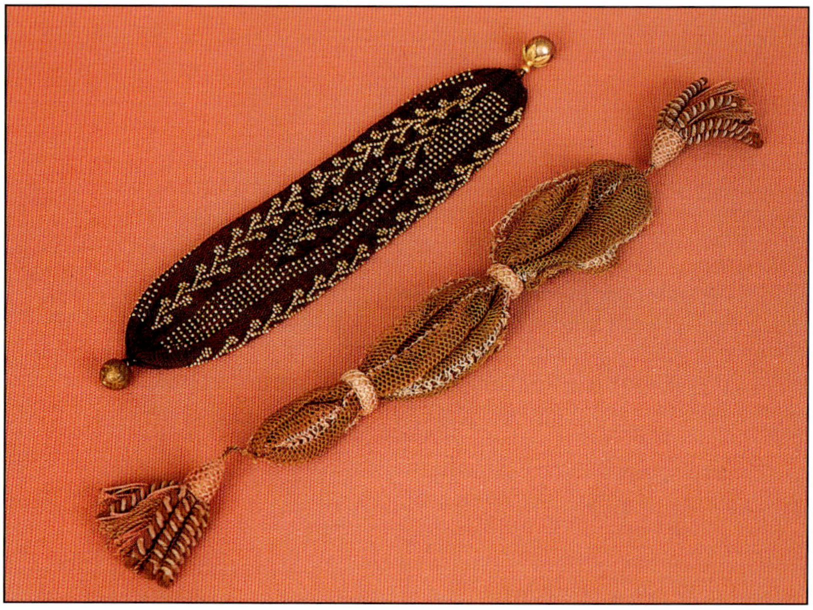

Two early 19th century misers. Left: Knitted miser decorated with gold beads. 8 x 1.5 in. Right: Netted miser finished with thick, twisted tassels. 10.5 x 1.5 in. *Collection of Lori Blaser.* $350-450.

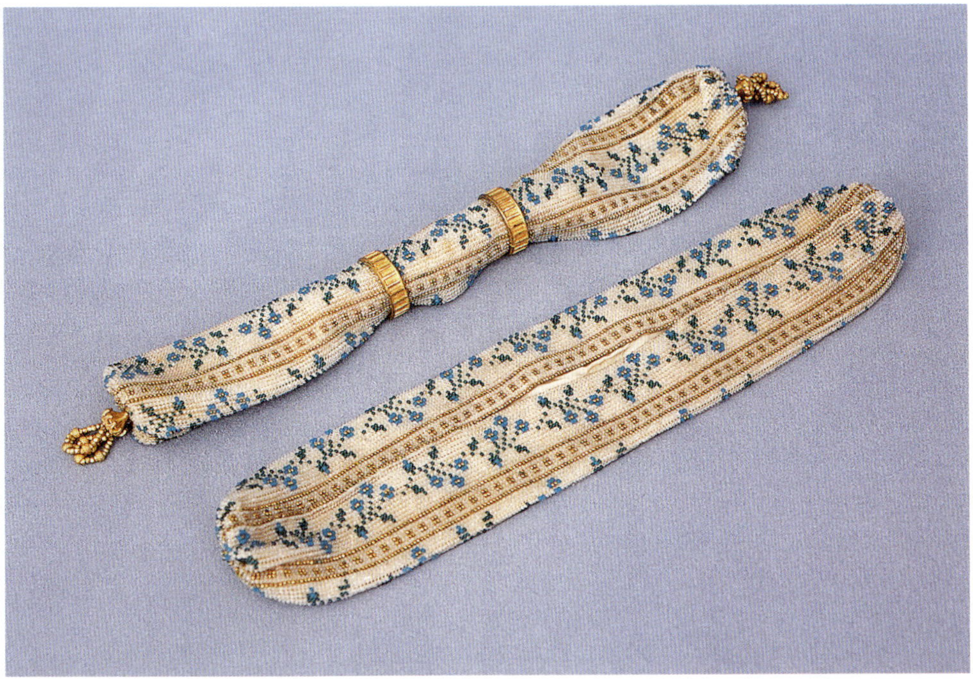

C.1820 matching pair of beaded misers. One of the pair was never fitted with sliders and tassels. Pairs of misers are rare, especially a pair of early beaded misers. 10 x 2. *Collection of Lori Blaser.* $750-850.

C.1820-1830 silk miser with an exceptional network of cut steel and floral wire work decoration on one end, and coiled wire work on the other. This type of wire work was typical of the early 19th century and helps to date the purse. 8 x 3 in. *Collection of Sharon Lu Visi.* $450-500.

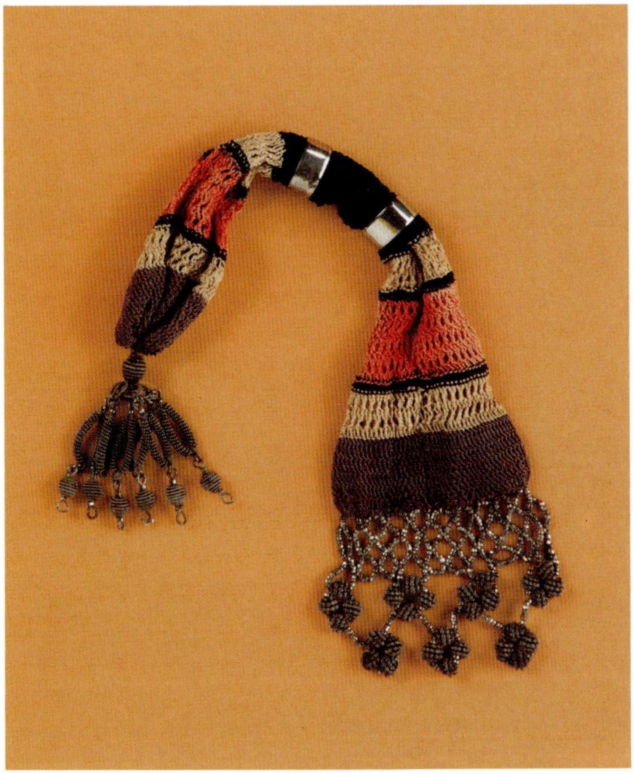

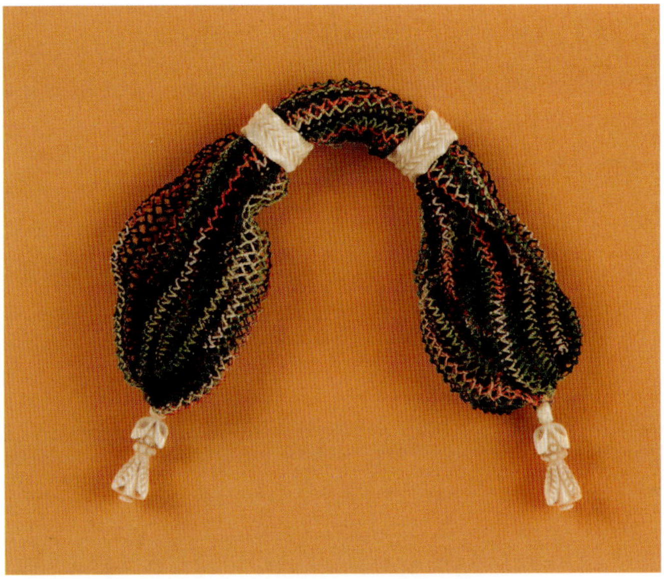

Early 19th century netted and striped miser. Lovely carved ivory tassels, worked in a leaf design, are attached at either end. Matching ivory sliders are carved in an arrow design. 6 x 3 in. *Collection of Sharon Lu Visi.* $350-400.

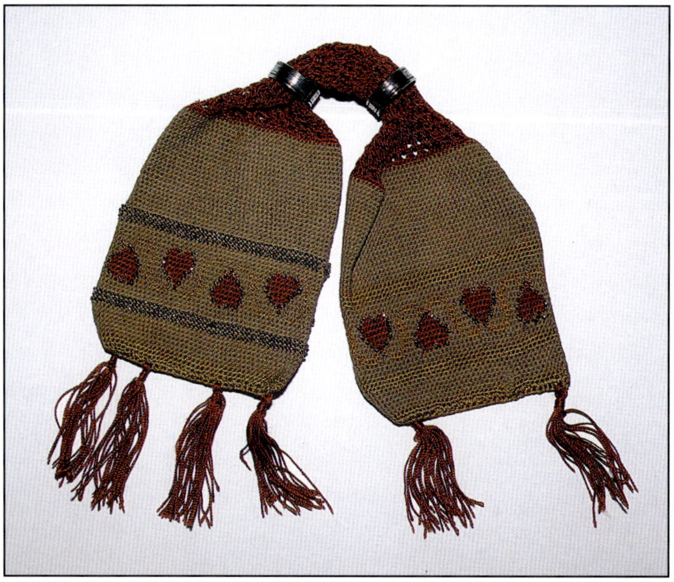

C.1830 silk miser designed with hearts, tiny cut steel beads, silk tassels, and steel sliders. Originally purchased in Austria. 8 x 2 in. *Collection of Paula Higgins.* $200-250.

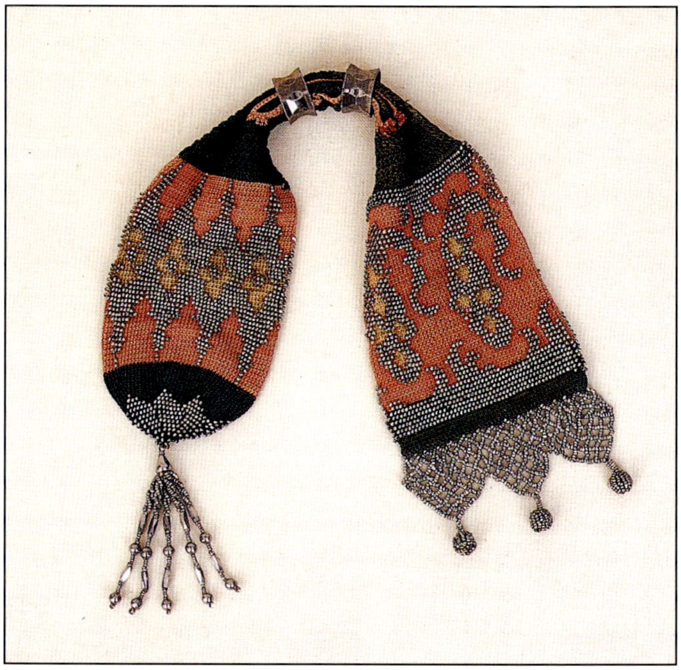

Beautiful, knitted silk miser decorated with fine cut steel beadwork in a diamond and paisley design. The steel mesh with the tiny ball tassels is exceptional. 17 x 3 in. *Collection of Melissa Overdorf.* $350-400.

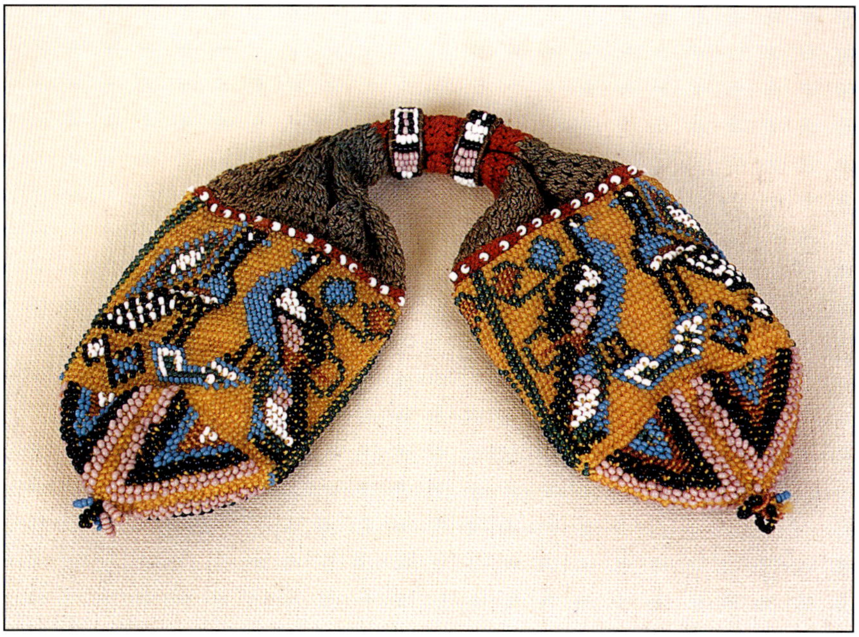

Turkish or Eastern Mediterranean bead crocheted miser. The angular bird design and the half diamond or diamond shapes are typical of Turkish beadwork. Turkey exported many purses in the 18th and 19th centuries. The rings are also beaded on this miser, adding a nice touch. 10.5 x 2.5 in. *Collection of Lori Blaser.* $300-350.

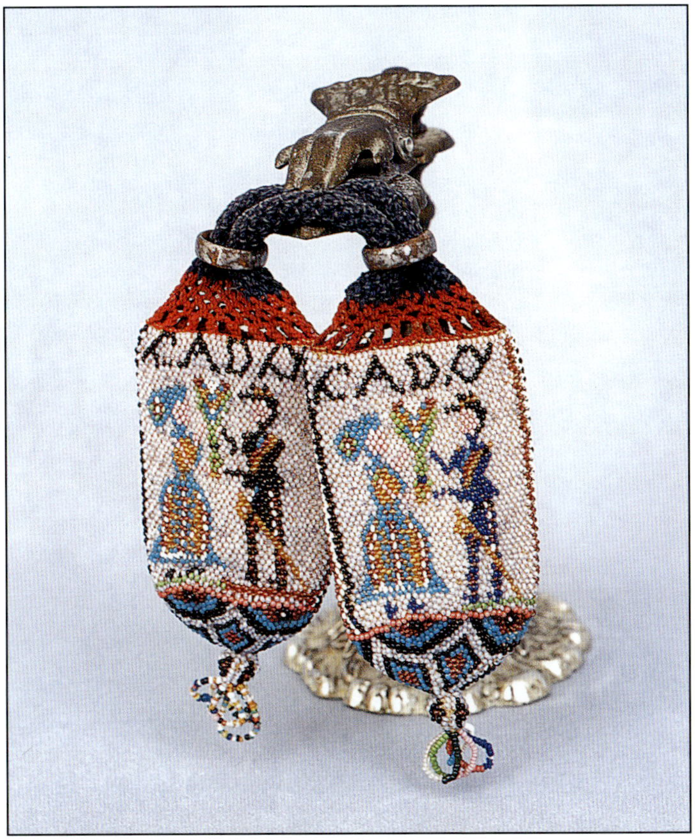

Turkish or Eastern Mediterranean, figural beaded miser. The angularity of the design and the tight crocheted beading is typical of Turkish beadwork. Figural misers are uncommon and desirable. 12 x 2 in. *Collection of Lori Blaser.* $400-500.

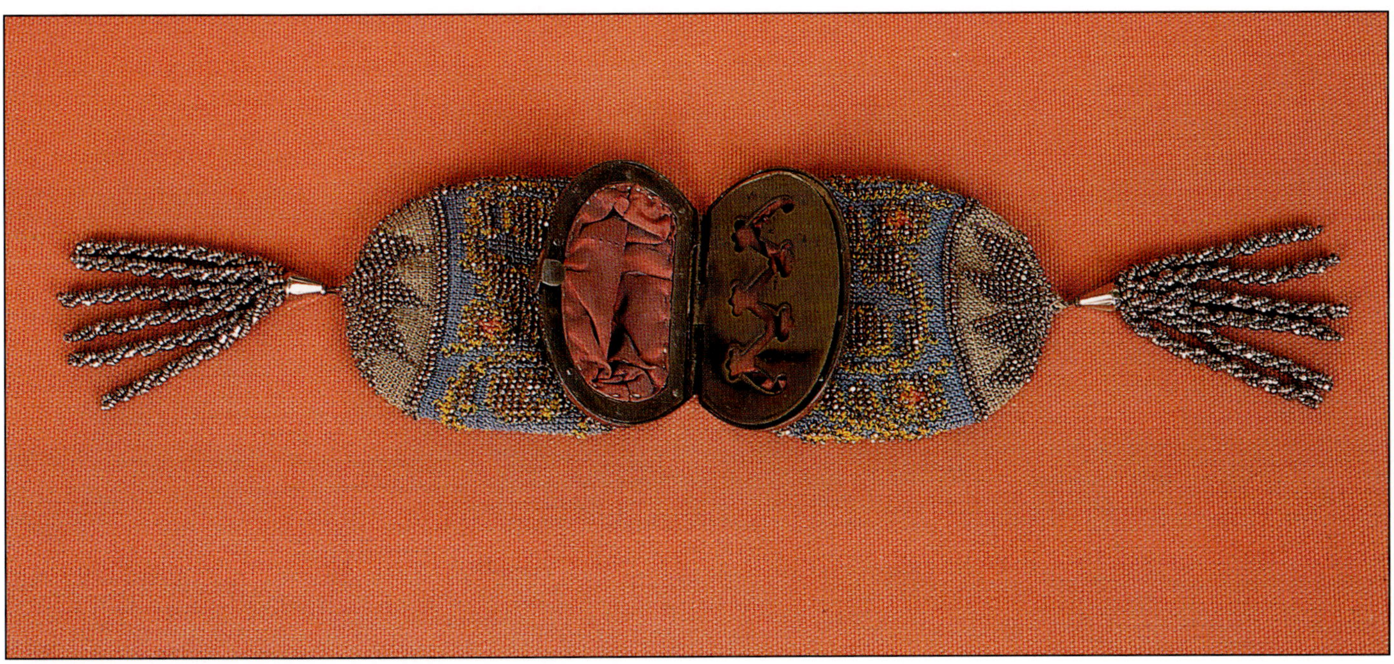

This double sided purse with a steel frame functions as a type of miser. Besides having an attractive color scheme and nice beading, it retains its original lining. 11 x 2.25 in. *Collection of Lori Blaser.* $350-450.

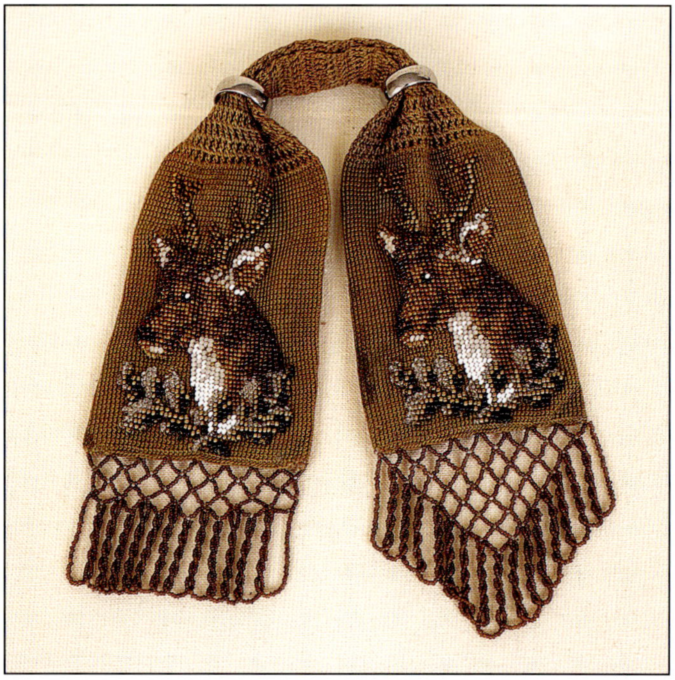

Glass beaded figural miser. Deer misers are charming and a wonderful addition to any miser collection. This one is in excellent condition. 16 x 2.5 in. *Collection of Lori Blaser.* $350-450.

This miser purse is in mint condition. It is made from wine red and gold colored crochet, and decorated with cut steel beads. The sliders are covered in the same red thread. 16 x 3 in. *Collection of Linda Marshall.* $300-350.

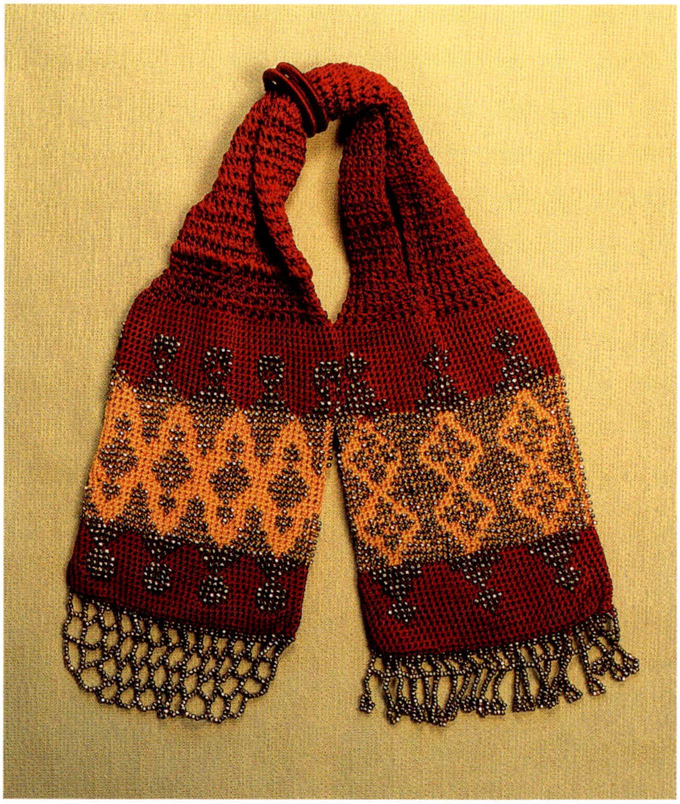

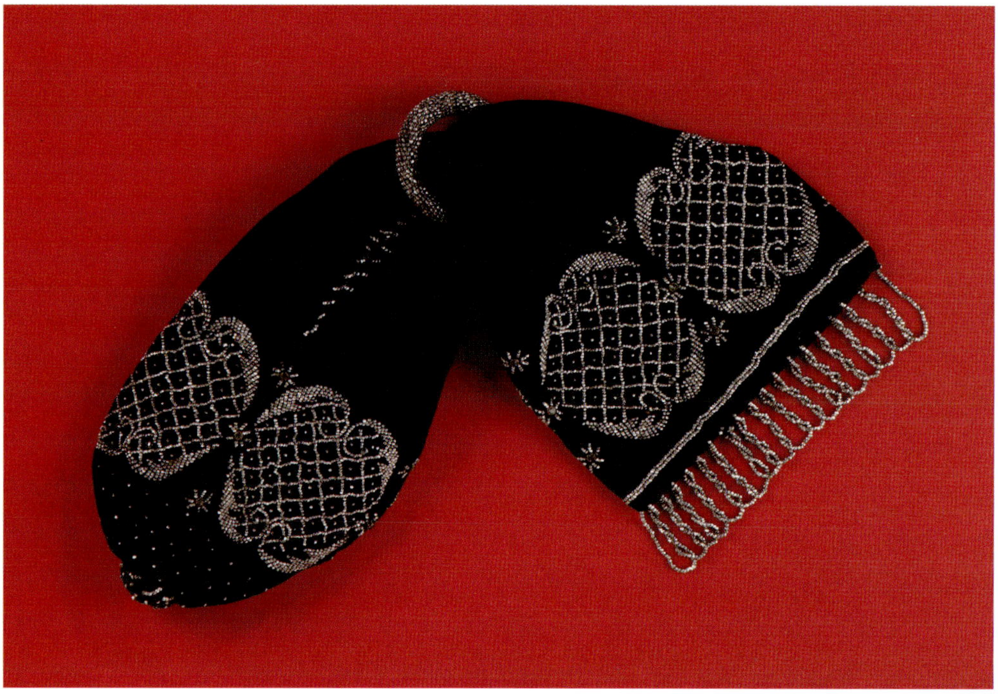

Large black velvet and cut steel beaded miser. This extra large size may have been used for traveling. Large miser bags were used for traveling in the mid-late 19th century. The black background with the cut steel beads creates an elegant and rich impression. 20 x 5 in. *Collection of Sharon LuVisi.* $350-450.

Another large velvet miser decorated with cut steel beads in a delicate and lovely design. The sliders are also covered with cut steel beads and the tassels are finished in star shapes. 20.5 x 4.5 in. *Collection of Lori Blaser.* $350-450.

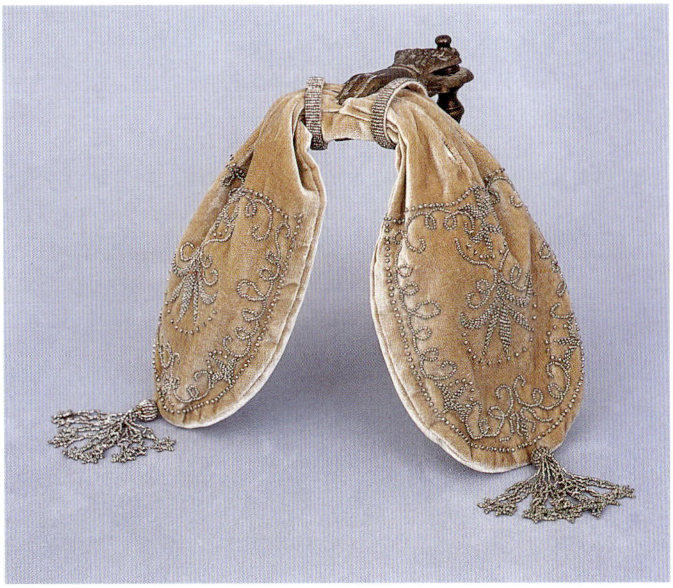

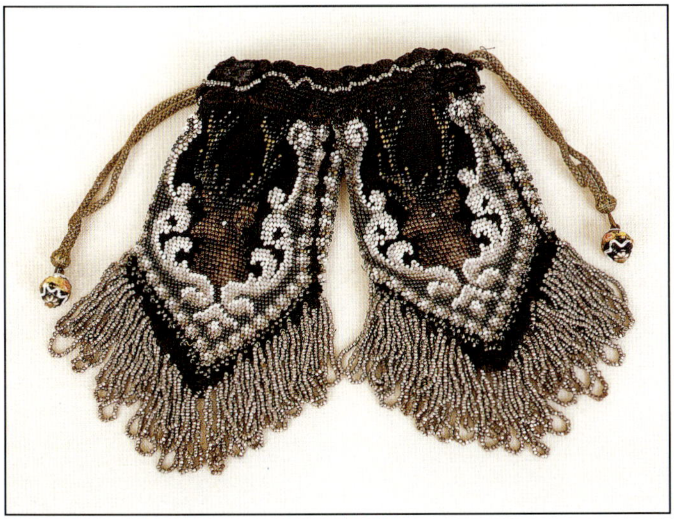

Although not technically a miser, it fits into this category well because of its ingenious double pouches. Closed with a drawstring, coins were dropped in either end. Deer heads were a popular Victorian design. 6.75 x 5.5 in. *Collection of Lori Blaser.* $300-350.

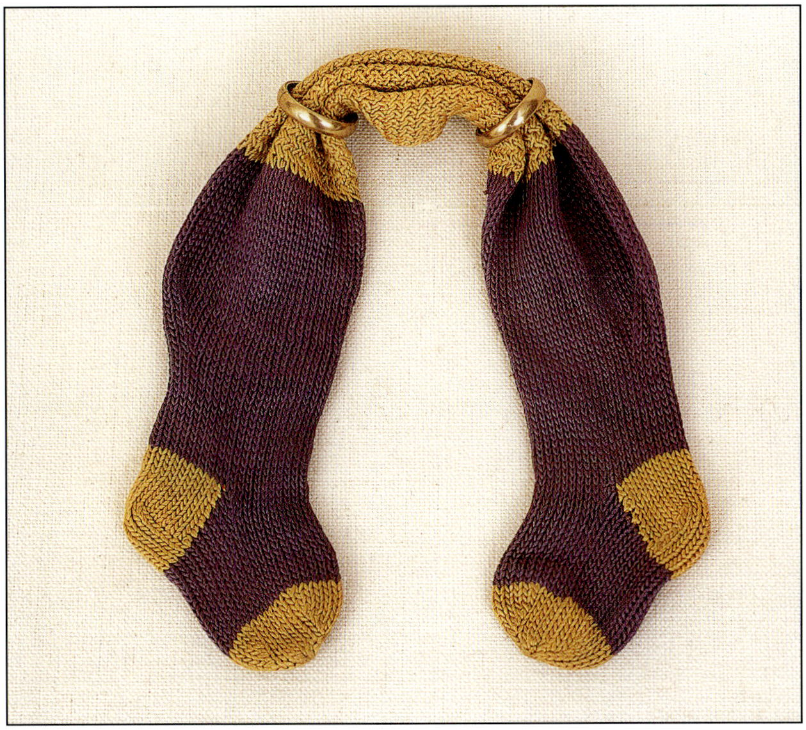

This sock miser is both clever and humorous. Knitted from purple and gold silk, it closes with gold sliders. Although they appear on Ebay occasionally, they are seldom of this quality. 11 x 1.5 in. *Collection of Lori Blaser.* $200-250.

Chapter 4
Chatelaines

Genevieve Cummins and Nerylla D.Taunton note in their book, *Chatelaines —Utility to Glorious Extravagance*, that the first use of the word "chatelaine" in reference to waist-hung items was in 1828. Prior to that, chatelaine bags in the 18th century were known as "waist bags" and "equipages." The word "chatelaine" means "mistress of the castle and keeper of the keys."

Leather bags were hung from the waist as far back as the 15th century. Some of these bags still survive and can be seen in major museums around the world. But as collectors, the earliest we see them from is the late 18th century. Leather and velvet bags were hung from scrolling Rococo gilt frames and hooks, which were all one piece. Eighteenth century waist bags were embroidered with metal threads, bullion, and *paillettes*. The chatelaine and equipage from the 18th century was a work of art. Beautiful repoussé hooks and chains were attached to watches, etuis, thimble and scissor cases, perfume bottles, watch keys, vinaigrettes, and seals. They were made in the Rococo style in pinchbeck, gold, and gilt. These 18th century versions are among the most costly and desirable of all chatelaines. Cut steel chatelaines were also popular during the 18th century, and the more expensive models were inset with Wedgwood plaques. These early chatelaines are relatively rare.

Early 19th century chatelaines are also rare, and typically of European origin. They were worn under the high empire waists favored by fashionable women of the time. Paintings and prints from the early 19th century will sometimes show a Regency or Empire chatelaine. Many were set with jewels, agate, or hand painted medallions. Needless to say, these exquisitely decorated chatelaines bring high prices at auction. Finger ring chatelaines, suspending small perfume bottles, were also worn during the first two decades of the 19th century. Early 19th century fabric chatelaines are a rare find because they were made from less sturdy materials, so relatively few have survived. By 1829 the waistline was dropping to a more normal position so the chatelaine was again seen at the waist. Circa 1840, finger ring chatelaines were attached to small reticules. Inside their tops, were small metal calendars or vinaigrettes. This type of chatelaine is very popular with collectors.

During the 1860s leather and fabric chatelaine bags hung from leather belts. They were especially useful when traveling or visiting, and they were sometimes worn over a light coat. Advertisements from this period indicate that some chatelaine frames and bags were made to match. Another style was made with a belt, hung with chains and appendages. These are rare types of chatelaines and usually seen only in museum costume collections.

In the 1870s chatelaines came into their prime and remained popular until the second decade of the 1900s. Chatelaines were worn from the waist, fingers, and also from the wrist, bracelet style. As useful accessories, they were modified for specific functions, and worn by nurses, actresses, seamstresses, housewives, and sportswomen. They were also worn as part of national costumes. Materials included: cut steel, jet, fabric, straw, enamel, jewels, metals, Irish bog, leather, and beadwork. Complete, all original sterling chatelaines bring high prices. To determine if all the pieces are original, it is helpful if they are all marked with the same trademark or maker's mark. However, that isn't always the case and yet all the pieces may still be original. Occasionally, the hook and attachments will all display the same design, jewelling, or enameling, which indicates that they are all original to the chatelaine. A beaded chatelaine bag with its original frame and hook is very collectible. In the 1870s, beaded bags with earlier designs were attached to German silver chatelaine frames. Late 19th and early 20th century beaded chatelaine bags are often seen in pictures of European women dressed in their national or native costumes. These bags were typically decorated with a floral beadwork design, and mounted on heavy silver frames attached to a hook. Sometimes, as an alternative, they were embroidered with floral embroidery like rosesaum. Decorated leather chatelaine bags surviving in good condition are a worthy addition to any purse collection. Plain black velvet or suede bags attached to ornate sterling or 800 silver chatelaine frames are elegant and sophisticated.

Finger and wrist chatelaines were popular from 1890-1920. Small silver coin purses, pencils, perfume bottles, mirrors, card cases, and compacts were among the many accessories attached to finger and wrist chatelaines. It would not have been unusual to see six chains with attachments hanging from a single finger ring. By the 1920s, accessories and clothing were undergoing a transformation from the heavily decorated to the streamlined. Chatelaines went out of style, to be replaced by the *pochette*, mesh bag, and the handbag.

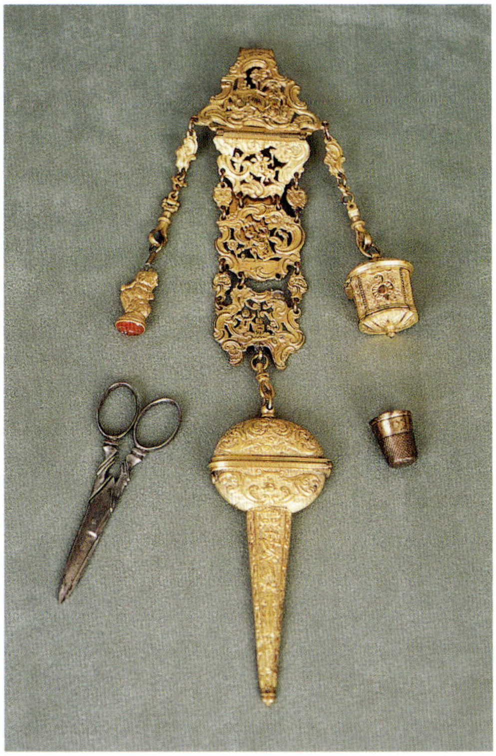

Beautiful, 18th century gilt metal chatelaine with thimble case, scissor case, and carnelian wax seal. Rococo designed chatelaines are lovely and rare. Made in England. 9.5 x 2.5 in. *Collection of Lori Blaser.* Rare.

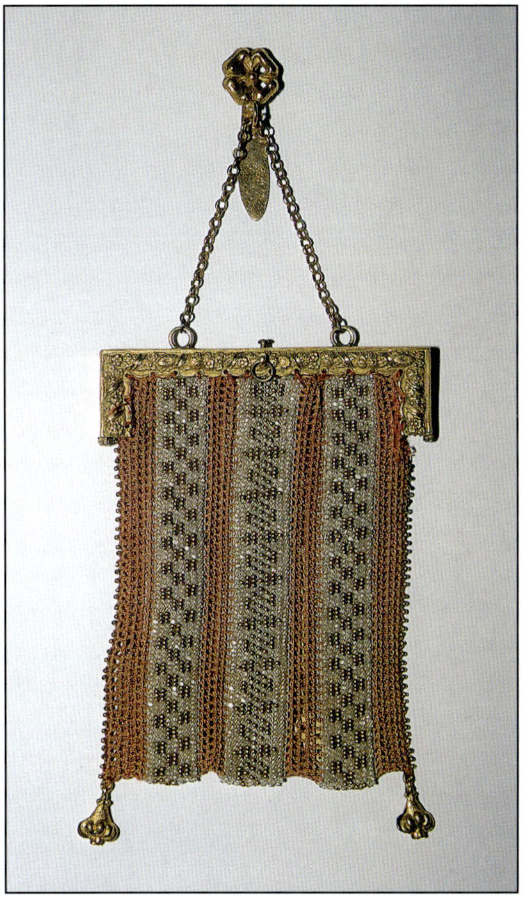

C.1810 chatelaine made from coral silk, gold beads, and clear glass beads in a striped pattern. The gilt frame is embossed in a floral and ribbon neo-classical design. Two tiny "fishes" are attached at either end on the bottom. This tiny chatelaine would have been worn under the high waists of the Empire Period. 8 x 2.5 in. *Collection of Paula Higgins.* Rare.

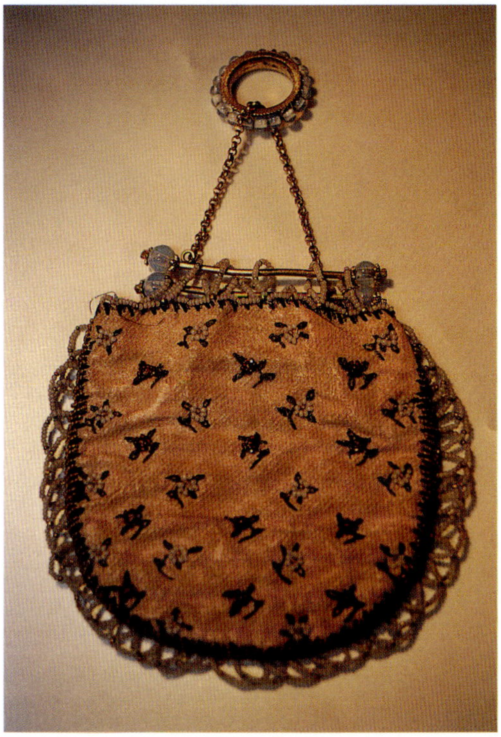

A c.1830 purse made in the "en diablé" fashion. In English this means "the devil's purse" and it was given this name because it was so difficult to open and close the purse when attached to this type of stick closure. The two gold sticks were meant to slide through the ring, then the ring would slide over silk loops, closing off the purse. Normally, tiny crocheted or knitted purses were mounted on this type of closure. However, this purse is wider, made from stiffer material, and the loops are beaded, making it impossible to close it in this manner. The loops simply hang on the bars, and then the bars cross at either end to close off the purse. The ring was probably used in the chatelaine fashion, which is why it is placed in this category. Attached to the ring and the sticks are opalescent blue beads, which were popular during the late 18th and early 19th centuries. 5 x 3.5 in. *Collection of Paula Higgins.* $300-$400.

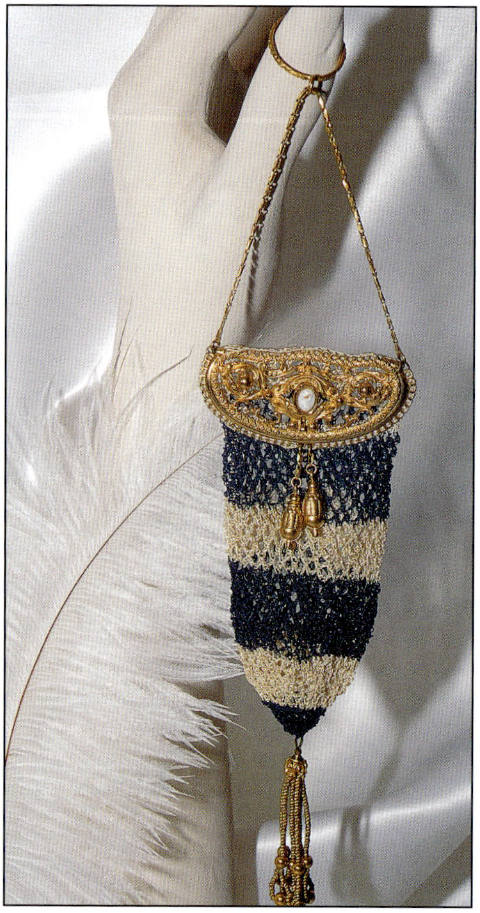

C.1840 Netted finger ring chatelaine decorated with a gilt frame set with a small shell cameo, embossed finger ring, and gold beaded tassels. These charming, but small and insubstantial chatelaines, could hold little more than a few coins. 6 x 2.5 in. *Collection of Paula Higgins.* $300-350.

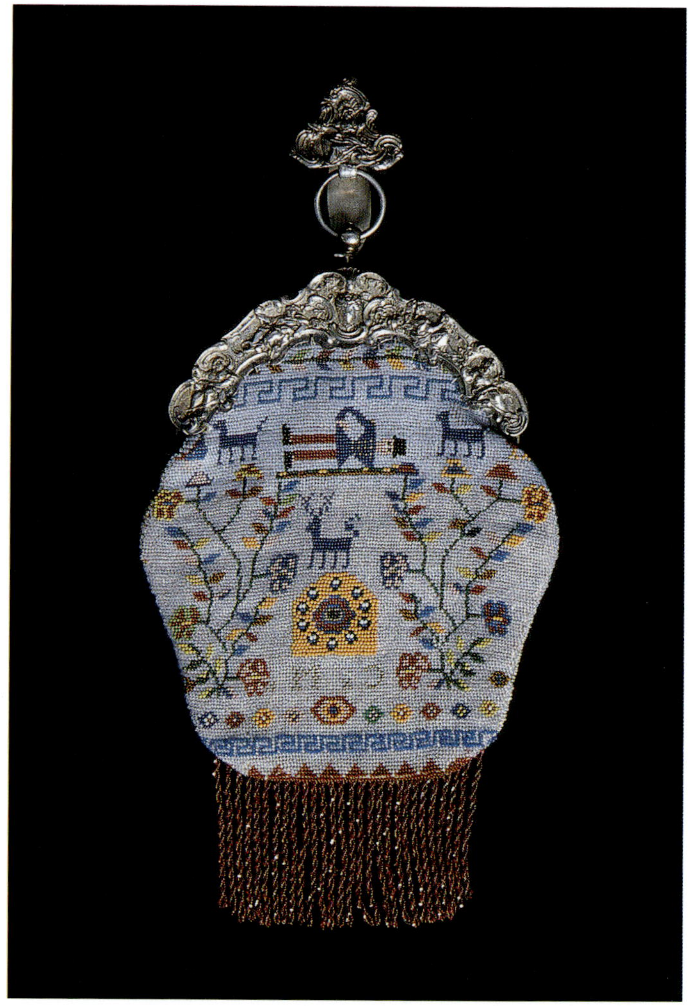

Wonderful beaded chatelaine with attached silver frame and hook. Fully beaded chatelaine purses are rare, especially when the frame is original to the purse. This purse features a figural design with a man positioned horizontally at the top, two dogs, and a stag. Made in Europe. 10 x 8 in. *Collection of Terri Lykins.* $800-1,000.

Late 19th century silver plated chatelaine with attached notebook tablet, perfume bottle, mirror, and pencil. 9.5 x 2.5 in. *Collection of Lori Blaser.* $1,000-1,200.

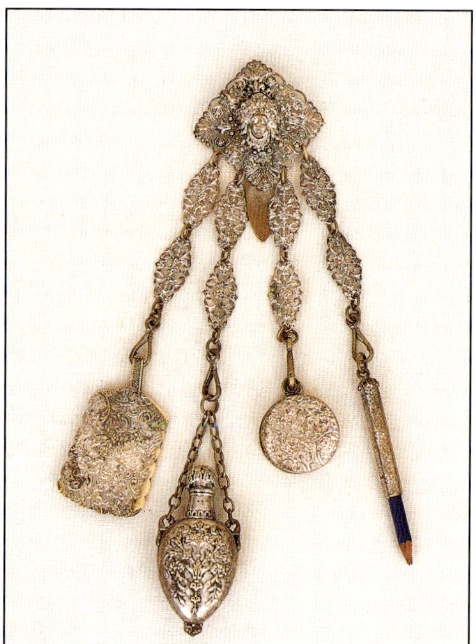

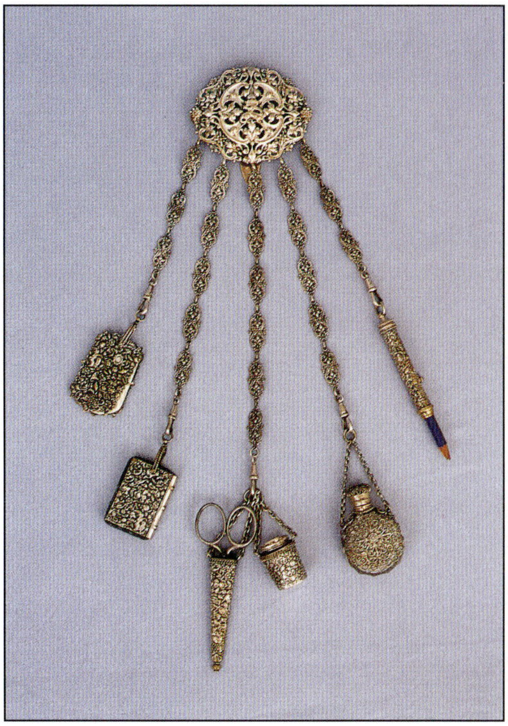

Late 19th century silver plated chatelaine with attached notebook tablet, pincushion, scissors in a sheath, thimble and thimble holder, perfume bottle, and pencil. These chatelaines are becoming very difficult to find with all original attachments. 13 x 4.5 in. *Collection of Lori Blaser.* $1,200-1,500.

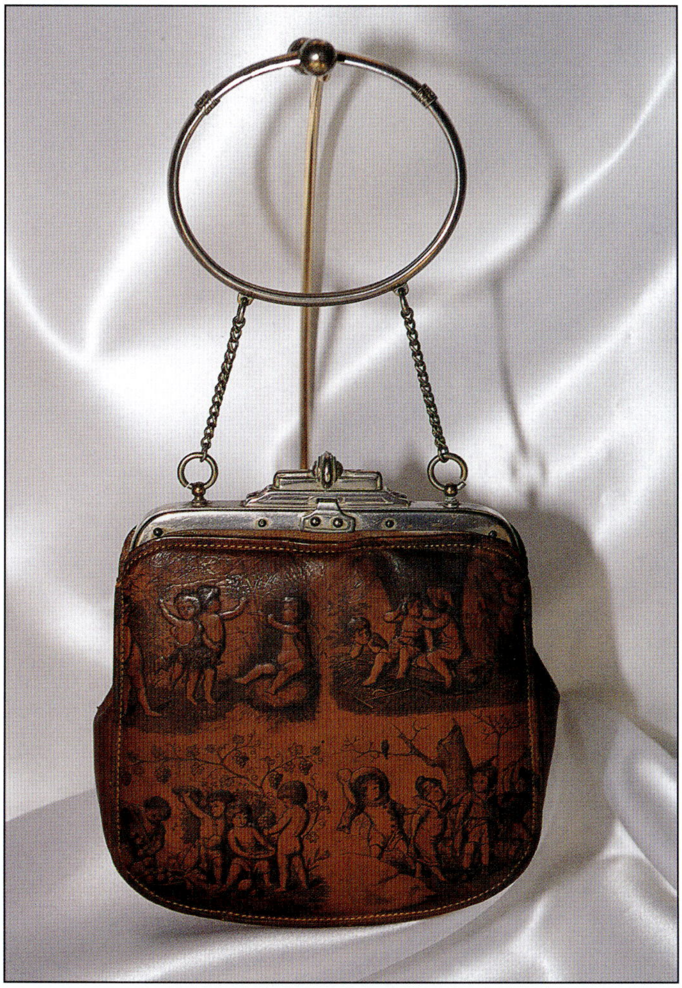

Dated 1889 leather wrist chatelaine with embossed scenes of children at play. The frame resembles luggage hardware from the same period. Inside is a blue silk lining with a pocket. The combination of features is unusual and desirable. Made in England. 10.5 x 5.5 in. *Collection of Paula Higgins.* Rare.

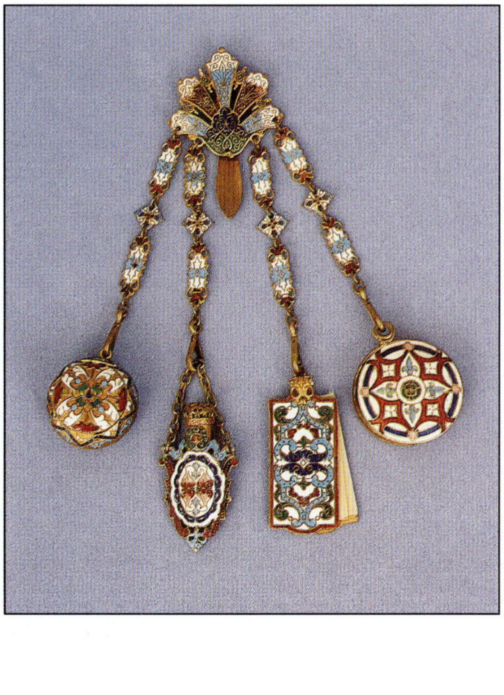

Late 19th century enameled chatelaine with attached mirror, dance card, perfume bottle, and powder compact. Enameled chatelaines are among the most sought after in the chatelaine category. Beautifully decorated with bright enamels, they also functioned as pieces of jewelry. 8.5 x 3.5 in. *Collection of Lori Blaser.* $1,200-1,500.

C.1900 filigree metal chatelaine with colored paste stones. Attachments include a pillbox, scissors, thimble case, scent bottle, and perfume funnel. Unusual chatelaines with their original attachments are always worth adding to a collection. 10 x 3 in. *Collection of Lori Blaser.* $800-1,000.

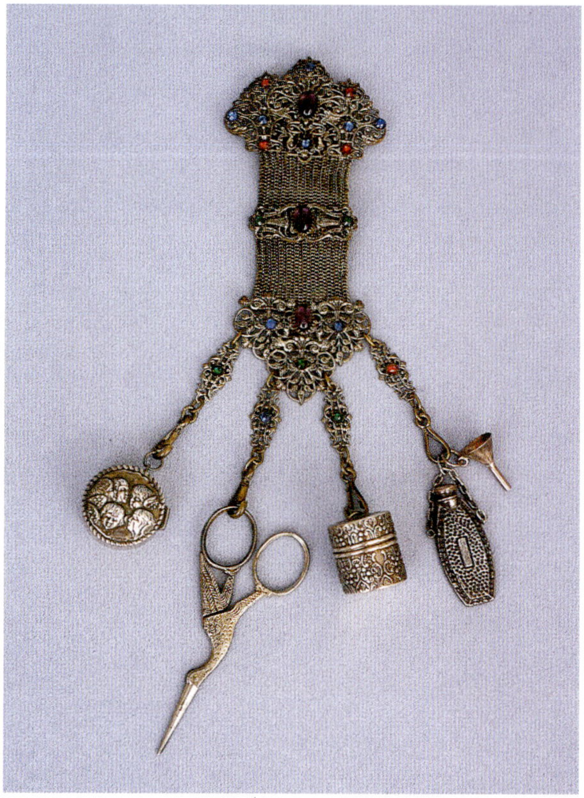

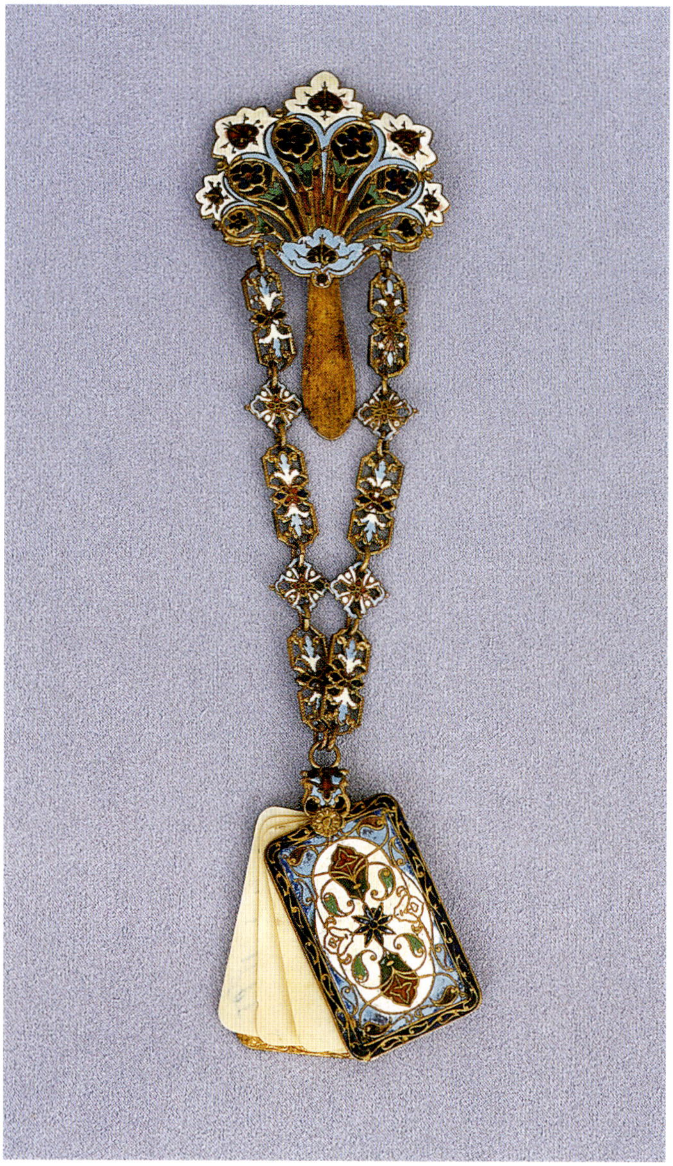

Late 19th century dance card chatelaine with beautiful enamel work in excellent condition. 8 x 2 in. *Collection of Lori Blaser.* $650-750.

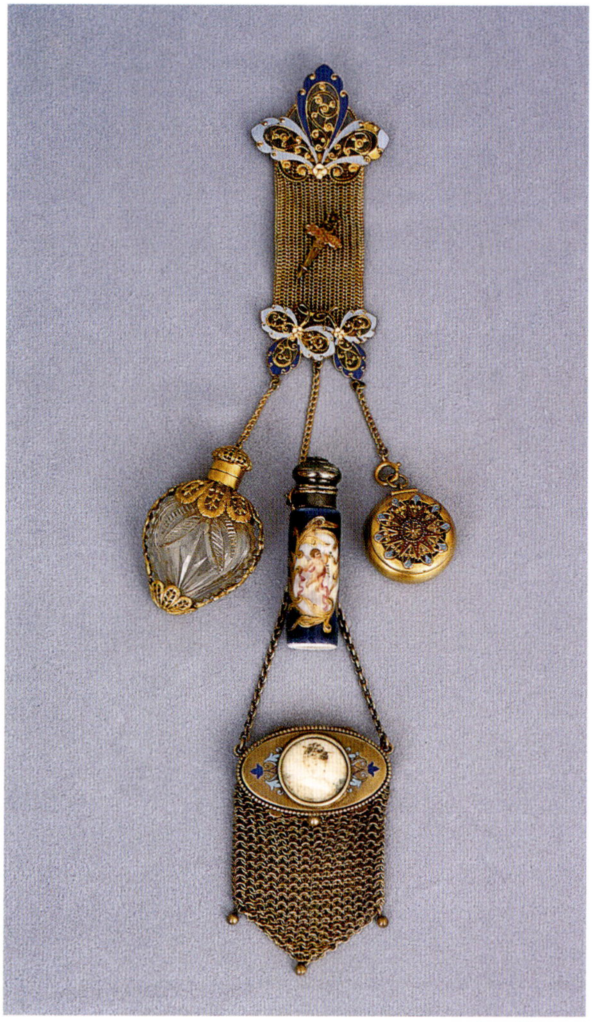

C.1900 stunning gold mesh, pin back chatelaine with four appendages. Attached are a cut crystal, perfume bottle, an enameled scent bottle, a coin purse with a hand painted ivory medallion, and a powder compact. 13 x 3 in. *Collection of Lori Blaser.* Rare.

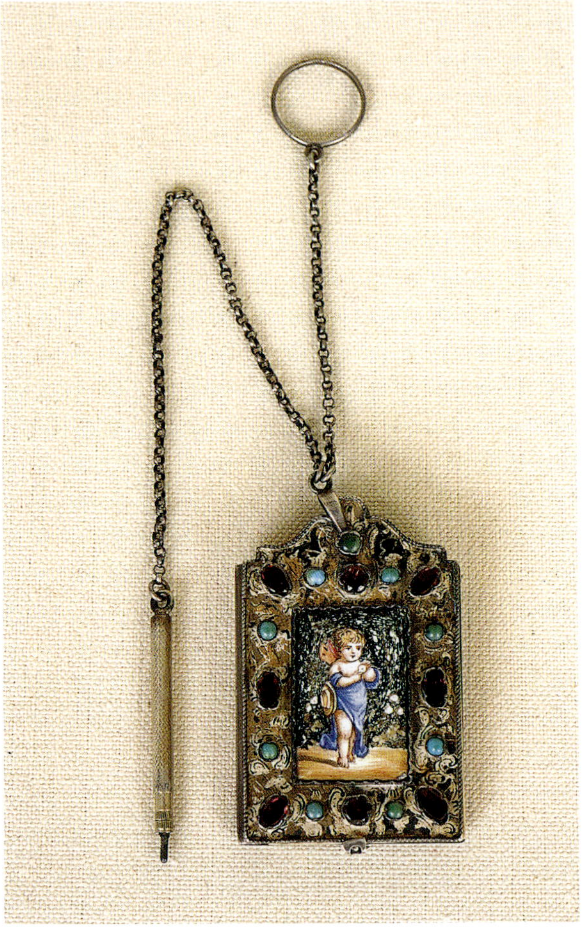

C.1890 dance card chatelaine with an enameled cherub/putti in the center, surrounded by bezel set garnets and turquoise stones. The finger ring and pencil are made from sterling silver. This Renaissance Revival chatelaine is richly decorated, and despite its small size, impressive. 2.5 x 1.5 in. *Collection of Lori Blaser.* Rare.

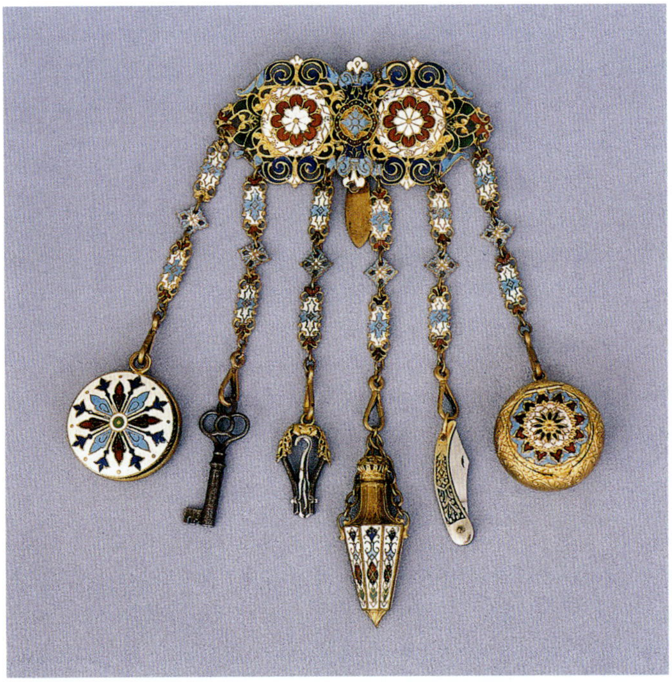

C.1900 large enameled chatelaine with powder compact, knife, perfume bottle, folding button hook, key, and mirror. Early 20th century exoticism is reflected in the enamel design and shape of the chatelaine hook. 8.5 x 5.75 in. *Collection of Lori Blaser.* Rare.

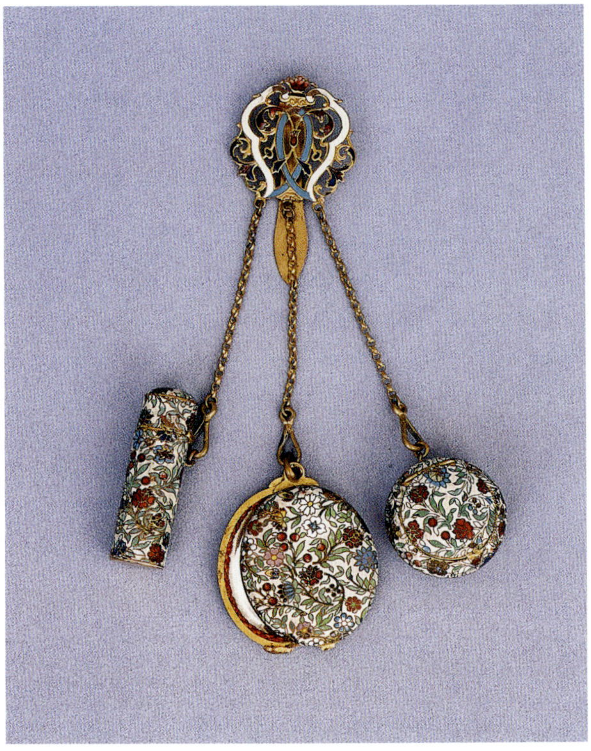

Beautiful enameled chatelaine with perfume bottle, mirror, and powder compact. The enamel work on the attachments is exceptional. 8.5 x 3 in. *Collection of Lori Blaser.* $800-1,000.

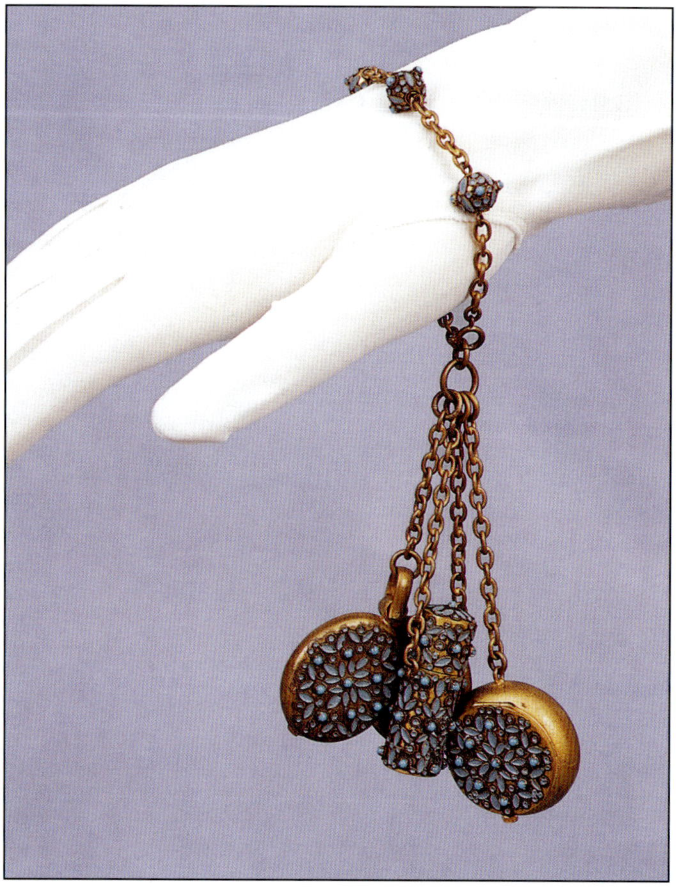

Wrist chatelaine decorated with enameling and turquoise stones. The mirror, perfume bottle, and powder compact are attached to a jeweled bracelet. 8.5 x 3.25 in. *Collection of Lori Blaser.* $600-700.

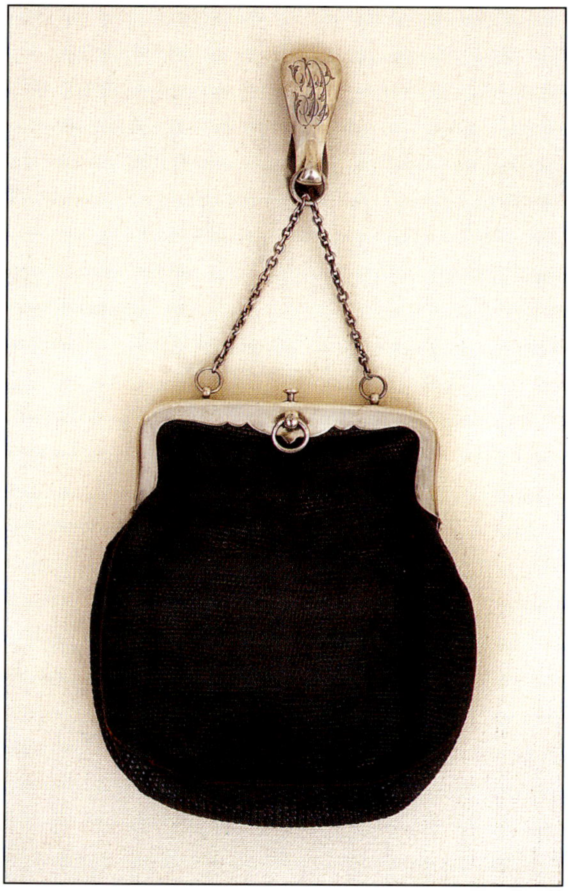

Rare Tiffany & Co. chatelaine made from an exotic skin, and attached to a sterling silver frame and hook. A Tiffany & Co. chatelaine bag is a true prize for any purse collector. The refined styling is a Tiffany & Co. hallmark. 6 x 5 in. *Collection of Melissa Overdorf.* Rare.

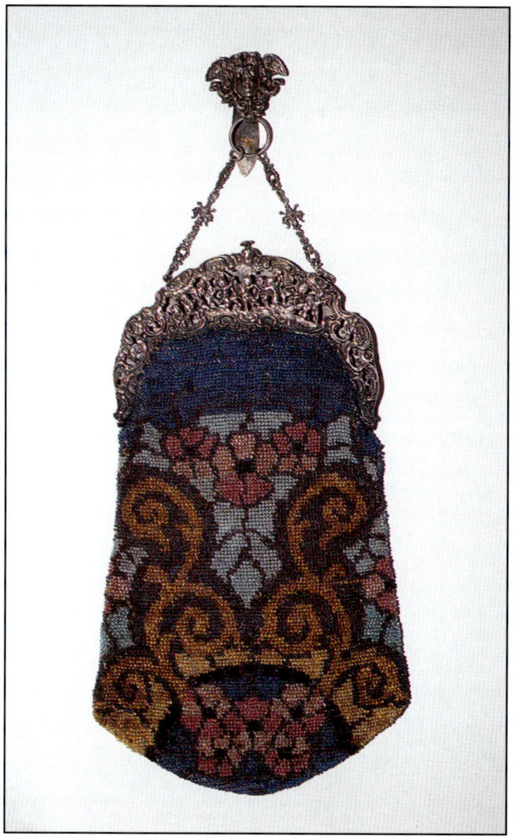

Art Nouveau beaded chatelaine purse with 800 silver frame. The frame is decorated with putti, pierced work, and a Medusa head hook. The silk lining was made to match the exterior beadwork. Made in France at the turn of the 20th century. 15.5 x 6.5 in. *Collection of Paula Higgins.* $1,000-1,200.

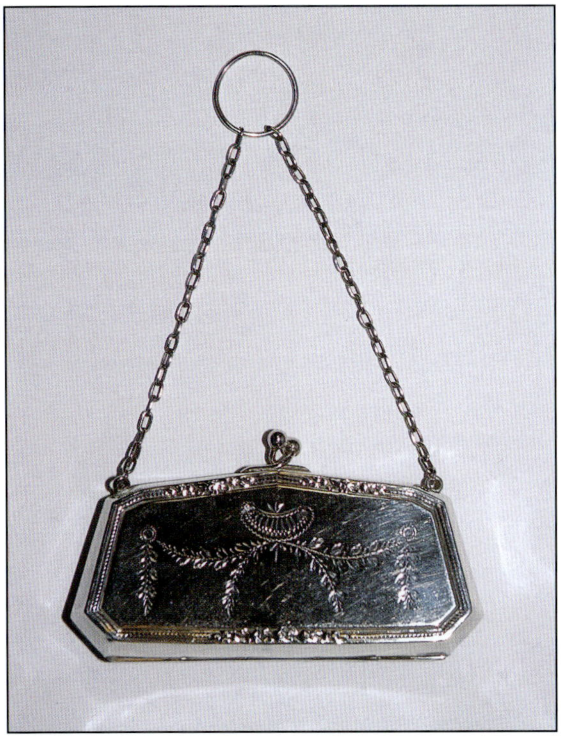

Sterling silver, finger ring chatelaine. The engraved, floral swag is typical of Edwardian design. Made to hold only coins, it was an elegant evening accessory. 4.5 x 2.5 in. *Collection of Paula Higgins.* $300-350.

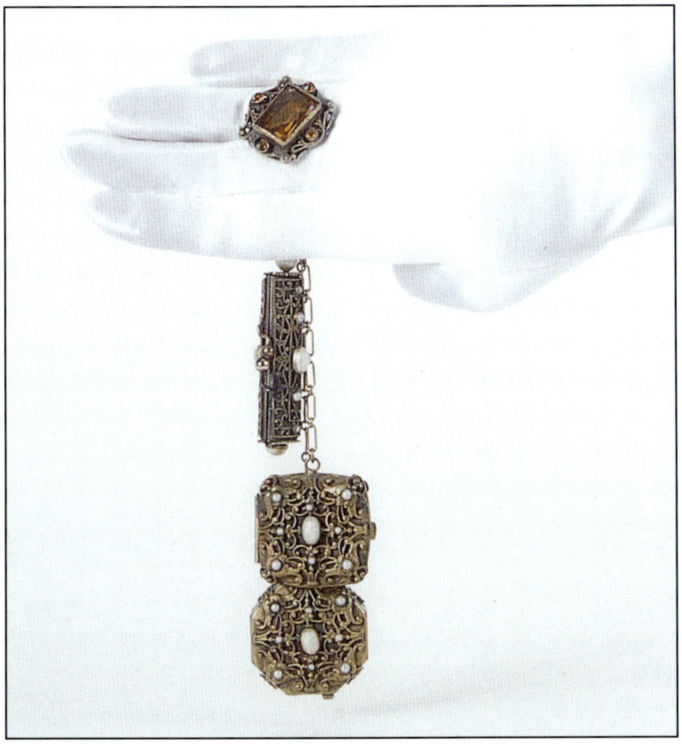

Early 20th century dance chatelaine with lipstick holder, powder container, and coin purse. The finger attachment is set with a large stone. 8 x 1.75 in. *Collection of Lori Blaser.* $600-750.

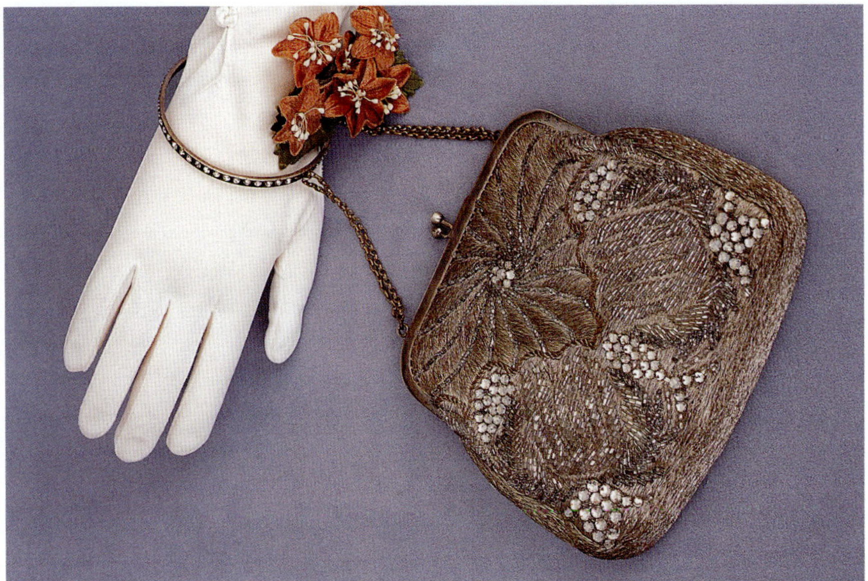

Rare wrist chatelaine made for evening wear. The bag is made from silver thread, clear glass beads, and prong set rhinestones. The wrist bracelet has channel set rhinestones. 6.75 x 6.75 in. *Collection of Lori Blaser.* Rare.

Chapter 5
Fabric, Tapestry, and Needleworked Purses

Purses in this category are often true works of art, requiring countless hours of work to design and complete. They are undervalued in the United States, but less so in Europe, where the skill needed to create these textile treasures is highly esteemed. Many books on antique and vintage purses typically relegate the textile purse to secondary status, after beaded purses. Hopefully, readers will gain an appreciation of the historical importance, artistic merit, and value of textile purses.

Most early textile purses were embroidered with linen, silk, or metal threads. Favored embroidery stitches included: the tent stitch, Gobelin stitch, satin stitch, and the chain stitch. Finely woven and embroidered purses dating to the 12th, 13th, and 14th centuries still survive in European museums. Decorated with medieval figures, obelisks, shield designs, and geometric shapes, they featured multiple tassels and drawstrings. Besides functioning as purses or money bags, they also held the remains of saints and were known as "relic bags."

The sweet meat bags of the late 16th and early 17th centuries (1575-1630) are the earliest bags most collectors are familiar with. Made in Europe, they were beautifully embroidered in tent and Gobelin stitches with silk and metal threads. Figural, animal, insect, and floral designs were the most popular. The Tudor Rose, emblematic of the Tudor Dynasty and Elizabethan England, was also a very popular design for sweet meat purses. These bags were small in size, and they often contained sweet smelling herbs to cover up body odors, which is why they acquired the name "swete purses" in the literature of the period. Plaited drawstrings with bulbous knob ends, and knotted tassels hanging from the bottom were characteristic features. Sweet meat purses are very rare, but periodically they appear at auction or for sale from specialty dealers. Embroidered pocketbooks, bordered with metallic laces, and small tapestry purses, made with four sides were also made in the 17th century. Understandably, seventeenth century purses are generally expensive when offered for sale.

Charles Germain de Saint-Aubin discusses the most important embroidery techniques of the period in his 18th century work on embroidery, *Art of the Embroiderer*. They included: embroidery in high and low relief, *nué* (shaded gold embroidery), satin stitch, *guipure* (gold thread over vellum/paper), rapport embroidery (separate pieces of embroidery applied to fabric to create a design), couching, *gaufrure* (a waffle design with gold thread), chenille work, silk thread, white work, *tapisserie* (needlework on canvas), embroidery with *paillettes*, and appliqué. Needless to say, many of these techniques are no longer used today because of their cost.

Eighteenth century purses and pocketbooks were embroidered with costly silks and metal threads in chain, silk, and satin stitches. The British also used the complex Queen's stitch or Rococo stitch on small pocketbooks. In America, the Roumanian stitch, Queen's stitch, tent stitch, and Irish stitch were popular. American embroidery designs were often lively, colorful, and less rigid than their European counterparts. French and British embroideries were balanced and beautifully executed, sometimes sacrificing charm for symmetry and perfection. Examples of both can be seen in the following pages.

Tambour work, which originated in either China or India, was practiced in Europe and America during the later years of the 18th century. Worked on fabric stretched over a tambour hoop, very fine chain stitches were produced with a hook. This stitch worked up very quickly in comparison to other needlework methods, which explained its popularity. Many workbags and pocketbooks from the late 18th century were decorated with tambour worked floral designs.

White work is another embroidery method dating to the late 18th century, which carried over into the early 19th century. In white work, white thread is embroidered onto white fabric, usually cotton. Early American white work reticules are highly prized and rare. Most white work reticules came from New England, but examples have been seen from Europe also. Some are dated or embroidered with the owner's name or initials, making them even more desirable. Another variation of this type of purse is the pen and ink reticule. Poems, sentimental expressions, names, and dates were inked onto plain white cotton bags. This is a very rare type of purse and a true find. Pen and ink purses typically came from New England and date to the early 19th century.

Another very rare style is the printed purse. Plain white silk purses were printed with commemorative designs or anti-slavery designs. Most of these bags were made in England, including the anti-slavery purses. They are among the most rare of all textile purses, usually only found in museums.

It is accepted by textile historians that crochet had its beginnings in tambour work. Loops could be formed in the air with a hook, and it is believed that some enterprising woman developed the crochet technique while experimenting with a tambour hook and thread. Prior to c.1800, no true crochet work has been found, although very old examples of *naalbinding* have been confused with crochet. It is believed that the oldest crocheted purse dates to no earlier than c.1800. Most crocheted purses date to the mid-nineteenth century or later.

Examples of completely knitted, early 19th century purses are uncommon. Surviving examples are usually of the small coin purse variety, attached to pinchbeck or silver frames. But larger knitted reticules were also made with cotton, silk, or metal threads in a very fine gauge knit. By 1820, bead knitted purses had eclipsed the plain knitted reticule in popularity.

Hand painted purses from the 19th century are very desirable. Both the free hand painted and the stenciled purses, known as Theorem purses, qualify as schoolgirl art. Young women in the early 19th century were taught painting and needlework skills as part of their formal education. It was only natural they would apply them to small items like reticules. Early American, free hand-painted purses are exceptionally rare. Theorem purses, which are stenciled (they may have some free hand-painted details), are also rare. The last example offered in *The Maine Antique Digest*, sold for $2,450 in August, 1998. Most Theorem purses were painted on velvet and the design was set with spirit gum. Some were made reticule style, with a drawstring, and others were mounted on gilt frames. Floral and fruit scenes were the most popular, and the finished result was directly related to the merits of the individual artist. Stenciled purses were usually American in origin but a European example has been seen.

Chenille, aerophane gauze, and silk ribbon worked purses also date to before the Civil War. Many purses embroidered with these techniques came from England where they were especially popular. Beautiful floral designs, often in a wreath design, were embroidered on silk or velvet backgrounds. Usually, the design was different on the front and back. There are two examples in the following chapter, one, which has been completely covered with embroidery on a black background. A white background is more common, but the black background is especially effective.

Berlin work purses, made from patterns imported from Germany, date to the mid-nineteenth century. L. Wittich and Phillison sold the first patterns from Berlin, which is why they were called Berlin work. These patterns were cheap and the designs worked up quickly. Merino wool was embroidered on canvas, and the canvas was made into a purse. It was finished with tassels hung from the sides, and a corded border around the purse. Aniline dyes, invented in 1858, produced a wide array of bright colors to dye the wools. Wool loss can be a problem with these bags, but an attractive example in good condition is worthy of any collection. Another type of Berlin work included braid work applied in a Turkish design to fabric reticules. The British were highly inventive during the mid-nineteenth century, using fish scales and beetle wings to embellish purses and other clothing items. In this chapter there is a velvet purse decorated with fish scales in a floral design.

Ribbon work was another popular embroidery technique used to decorate purses from the late 18th century to the early 20th century. The 18th and early 19th century ribbon worked purses were beautifully decorated with floral designs, and made with finely shaded China ribbons. The later 19th and 20th century examples, while lovely, lack the intricate workmanship of earlier ribbon work, and the ribbons were not as refined, lacking the shading of the earlier ribbons.

Carpetbags fail to appeal to many collectors because of their chunky appearance and darker color schemes. But a nice example, in good condition, is worth adding to a collection for its historic merit alone. They were made for train travel, usually with locks and keys. Designs resembled Wilton carpet patterns, although some were needle worked with Berlin work designs. Many were made with rolled leather or carpet handles, which have deteriorated over time. A carpetbag in very good to excellent condition is a true find.

Black velvet bags attached to ornate sterling or 800 silver frames are familiar to all antique purse collectors. Dating to c.1900, the frames were the focal point of the bag. Frames were decorated with *putti* (cherubs), scrolling lines, animals, birds, vines, and flowers. The plain velvet bag was a sophisticated and perfect match for these elegantly designed frames. Expensive versions had jeweled set frames, and some examples were attached to ornate chatelaine frames as an alternative.

Turkish silk and metal thread embroidered reticules, from the mid-nineteenth to the early twentieth centuries, are distinguished by their lovely gold, silver, and silk embroidery. Turkish half-moons, letters, and stylized floral designs were used for decoration. They were exported all over Europe, especially to England. Some examples were completely worked in gold thread, creating a rich effect. The perimeter of the purse was often edged with metal threadwork. These purses bring fairly strong prices in Europe, but less so in America.

A particularly charming type of purse from the early 20th century is the rosette and lace decorated fabric reticule. Designers were trying to recreate an earlier 19th century romantic style, which resulted in these extremely feminine reticules. A common design feature seen on the bottom was a mirror, which formed a base. Another variation, also reflecting a return to an earlier style, was the more heavily decorated silk brocade purse. Also made in the reticule style, it was decorated with gold bullion fringe, gold tassels, and gold and silver braid. Dating these purses can be confusing because they have a genuinely old appearance, and may in fact, be decorated with 19th century materials. They appear occasionally on Ebay and they can inspire heavy bidding because of their visual appeal. The high-end version of this romantic style was made with authentic 18th century embroidered fabric. Quite small in size, they were mounted on early 20th century enameled frames. Being familiar with 18th century textiles, enables a collector to recognize these very fine evening purses.

Tapestry purses, often called Aubusson tapestry purses, were woven not embroidered. The finished work is a whole piece of cloth, made with a weft and a warp. Worked on a frame with a shuttle, the finest examples are handmade and not machine made. The most common designs feature bucolic scenes with 18th century figures and farm animals. Sometimes they were literally copied from 18th century tapestries by Watteau, Boucher, and Fragonard. Tapestry purses, which have retained their original vivid colors, bring higher prices. A common tapestry and petit point design is The Lady, Lion, and Unicorn motif. The history of this design dates back to the 15th century when Jean LeViste of Brossac Castle in France had a series of tapestries made to commemorate his marriage. Five tapestries were made representing the senses of hearing, taste, smell, touch, and sight. A sixth tapestry, called "*A Mon Seul Desir*," represents the renunciation of the preceding five senses, in essence purity. These tapestries still survive, and now hang in the Cluny Museum in Paris, a major repository of medieval art. Tapestry and petit point purses were made with many variations of the Lady, Lion, and Unicorn designs, but they all originate from the LeViste family tapestries. Tapestry purses were mounted on ornate silver, gilt, brass, and enameled frames, set with faux jewels and cameos. A beautiful, handmade tapestry purse should hold its value because they are no longer being made today.

Chinese embroidered purses, made for export, are another type of textile purse dating to the early 20th century. Large, rectangular pouches were attached to round glass or jade handles. These purses were often made from rank badges worn by Chinese civil servants. The Chinese embroiderer used the long and short stitches, seed stitch, Pekinese stitch, satin stitch, and couching stitch. Chi-Lin a Chinese mythical beast, the Phoenix, dragons, butterflies, peonies, and plums were all popular and symbolic designs. For example, the peony signified good luck and wealth. Long silk tassels hung from either side adding balance to the design. Beautiful color combinations, worked on a silk background, created stunning oriental designs reflecting the exoticism of early 20th century design. More traditional Chinese purses from the Chi'ing Dynasty are also collected. Typically smaller, they came in a variety of shapes including: gourd, heart, envelope, square, and the closed fan shape. Early 20th century Chinese embroidery is usually of a very high quality. Unfortunately, it is often under valued in comparison to European embroidery because it fails to appeal to our western sensibilities.

French-made, silk-stitched purses are among the most beautiful of all textile purses. The surface of the bag was entirely covered with fine, silk stitches, making it a labor-intensive process. The total effect was silky, shimmering, and rich. Designs included courting scenes, carriage scenes, bucolic country scenes, and medieval hunt scenes. A recent example was embroidered with a scene of George Washington on one side, and the signing of the Declaration of Independence on the other side. This purse can be seen in Chapter 13. It sold at auction in 2006 for over $4,000. Beautifully framed, these silk stitched purses were expensive then, and they remain so today.

Petit point purses vary in quality, the finest having 3,000 stitches to the square inch. A gros-point stitch, sometimes referred to as needlepoint, covers twice the area of a petit point stitch. The majority of petit point was made in Austria, and it was a state-supported industry. The French also produced petit point purses of a very high quality. Mythological scenes and figures, 18th century courting scenes, garden scenes, cherubs, and religious themes were all used to create lovely petit point designs. Collectors look for the jeweled and enameled framed petit points from the first half of the 20th century, but many later petit points with the sterling stand-up clasps are also beautifully worked and worth adding to a collection. Less common and more valuable are the rare 18th century scenes of Mozart. These petit point purses can sell in the thousands. Tiffany & Company also sold a special type of petit point purse, which was finished with a twisted, interlocking beaded fringe. The Tiffany & Company petit points usually feature a floral design or basket of flowers, worked against a cream or brown background. Simple, narrow sterling frames with slide and twist clasps were attached, and the linings were stamped with the name "Tiffany & Co." The stamped name sometimes wore off, so it is important to know the characteristics of a Tiffany & Company purse. In this chapter there is another purse sold by Tiffany & Company, which was needle worked in an Art Deco design. It also has a beaded fringe in corresponding colors, and a narrow sterling frame with a slide clasp.

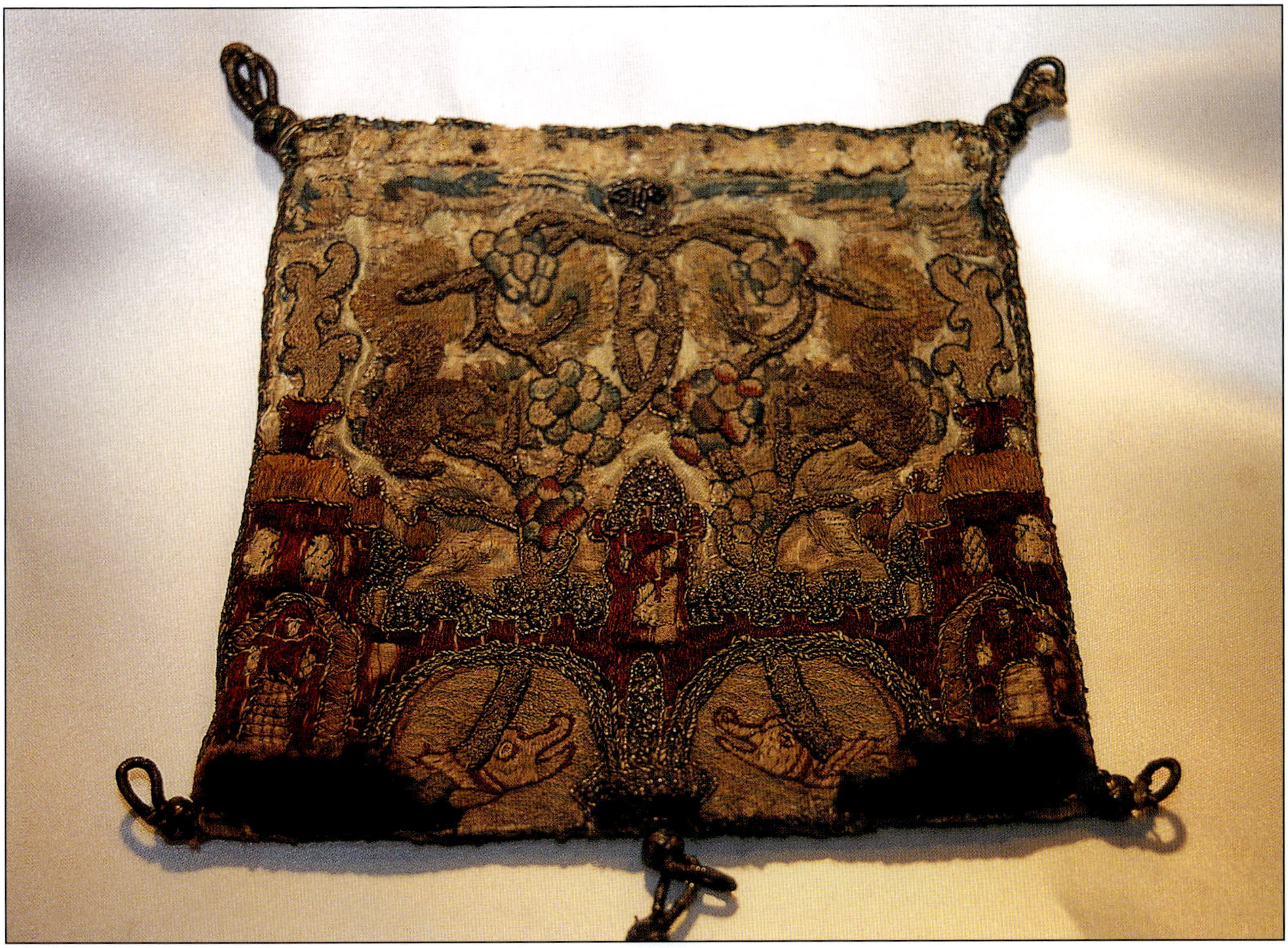

C.1600 scenic and figural "sweet meat" purse. They were called "sweet meat" purses because they held aromatic herbs and spices to ward off unpleasant body odors (people seldom bathed in the 16th and 17th centuries). This side shows a castle worked in red silk, a moat with furry beasts, and two squirrels sitting on boughs in the center. These designs were all symbolic. The background is made from cream silk. Tassels once hung from loops at the top and bottom. British. 5 x 5 in. *Collection of Paula Higgins.* Very rare.

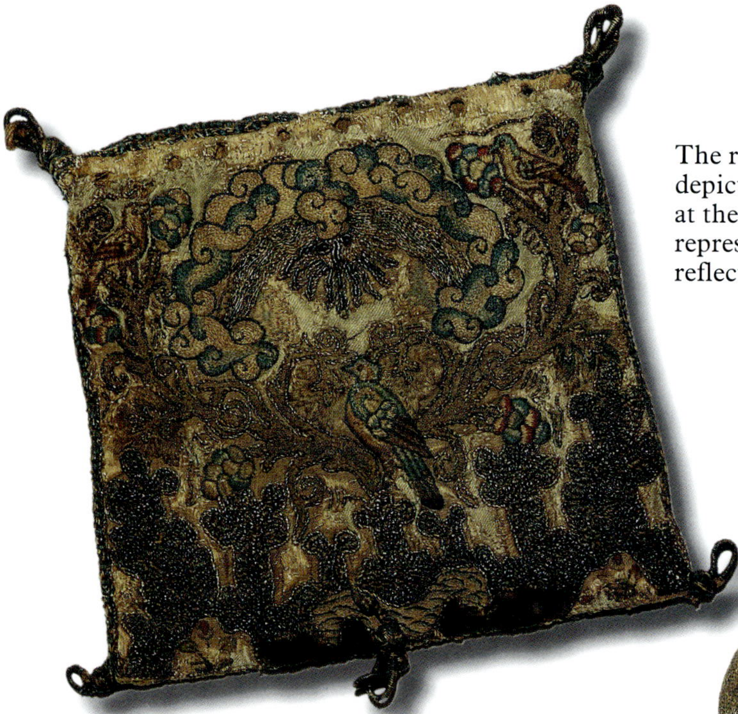

The reverse side of the sweet meat purse on page 57 depicting birds at the top and bottom. A bearded head at the top center, worked in silver metal threads, may represent God or a mythical god. The clouds at the top reflect a Chinese influence.

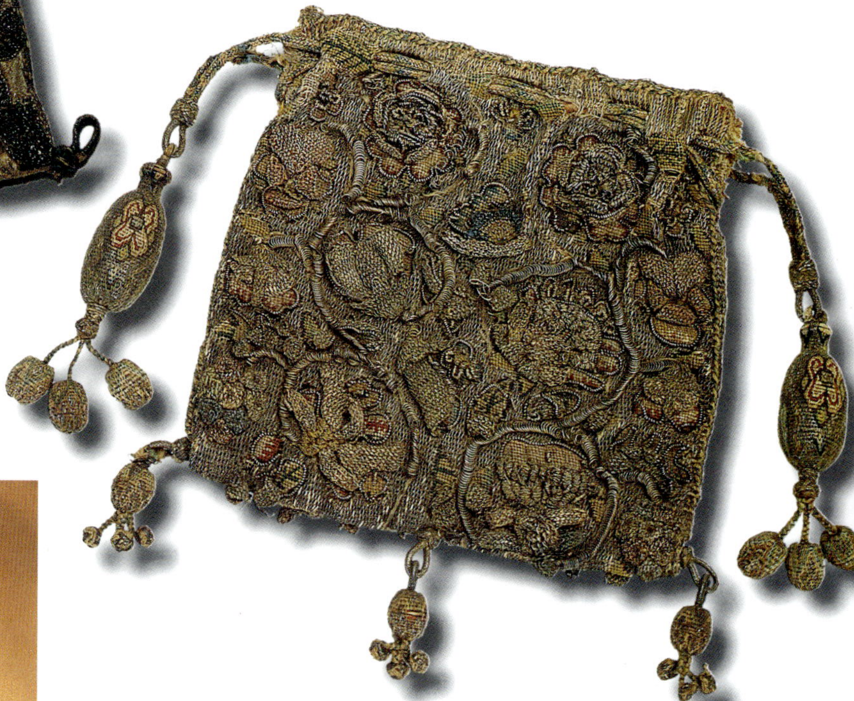

C.1600 sweet meat purse with all of its original tassels. This sweet meat purse is embroidered with metal and colored silk threads in three-dimensional floral designs, including the Tudor Rose. The Tudor Rose was the symbol of the Tudor dynasty, most notably Henry VIII and Elizabeth I. British. 5 x 5 in. *Collection of Lori Blaser.* Very rare.

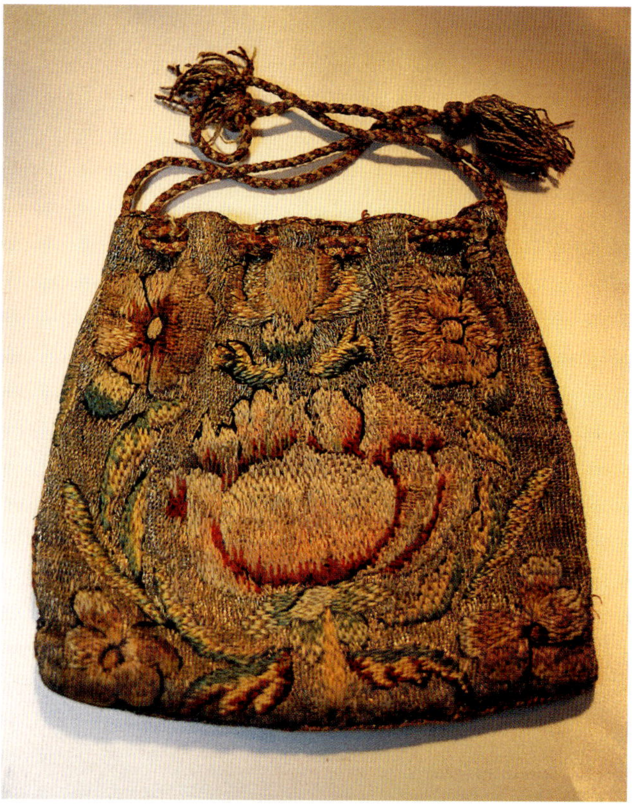

C.1650 embroidered sweet meat purse with original plaited drawstring. Made from polychrome silk and gold threads, a large blossom dominates the design. The inside is lined in cream leather. 5.5 x 5 in. *Collection of Paula Higgins.* Very rare.

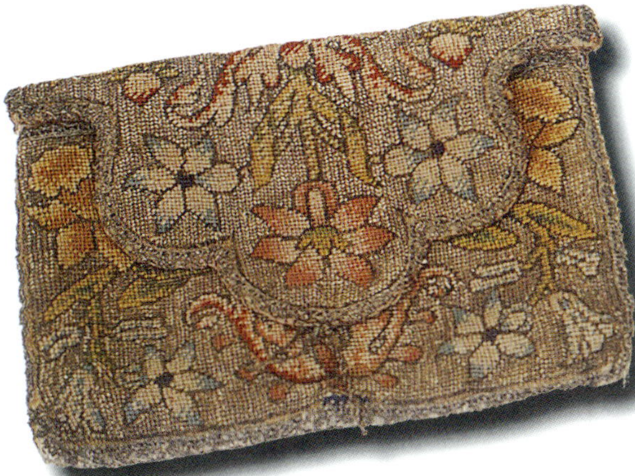

Mid-seventeenth century pocketbook, needleworked in a floral design with polychrome silk threads, against a background of silver threads. The lace edging has flat pieces of silver worked into the lace. Inside is the original, pink silk lining. When this piece was made, sumptuary laws in England prohibited the use of gilt thread to anyone outside the court. 8 x 5.5 in. *Collection of Lori Blaser.* Very rare.

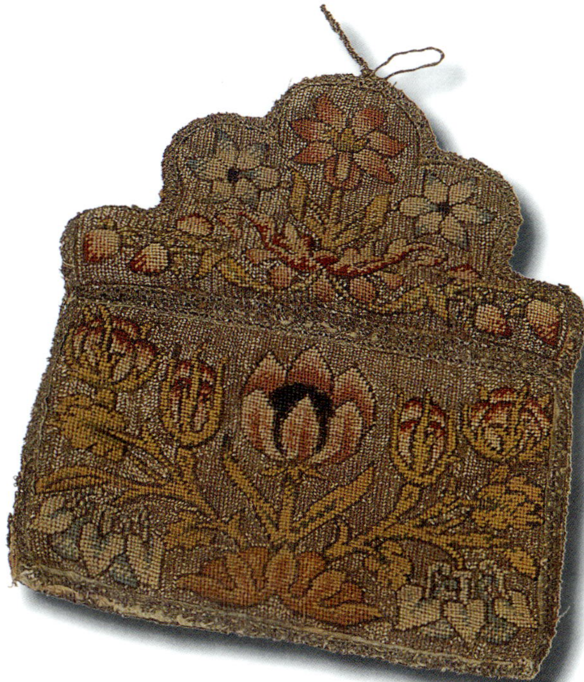

The reverse side of the mid-seventeenth century pocketbook opened.

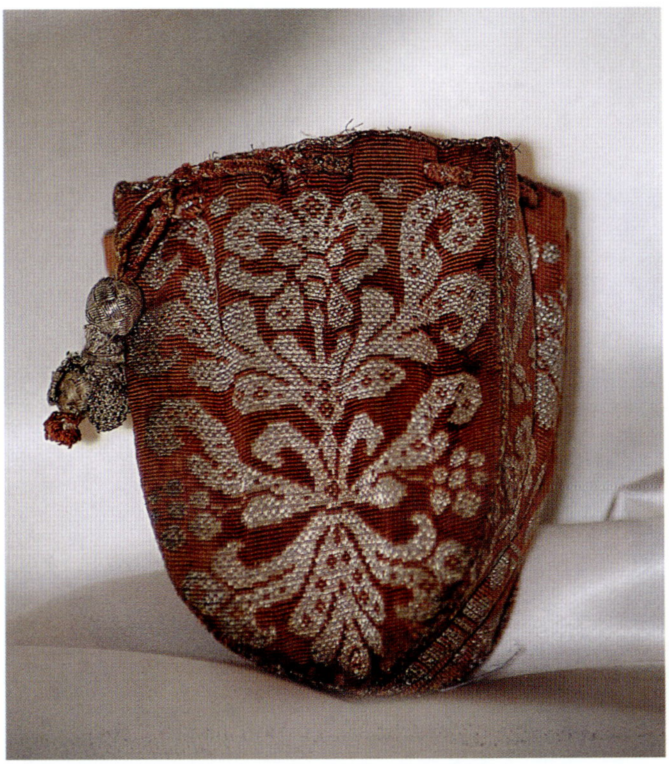

Late 17th century tapestry purse made from coral silk and metal threads with a high silver content. The scrolling, bulbous floral design is typical of the late 17th century. It retains its original, lime green silk lining. 3.5 x 2.5 in. *Collection of Paula Higgins.* Very rare.

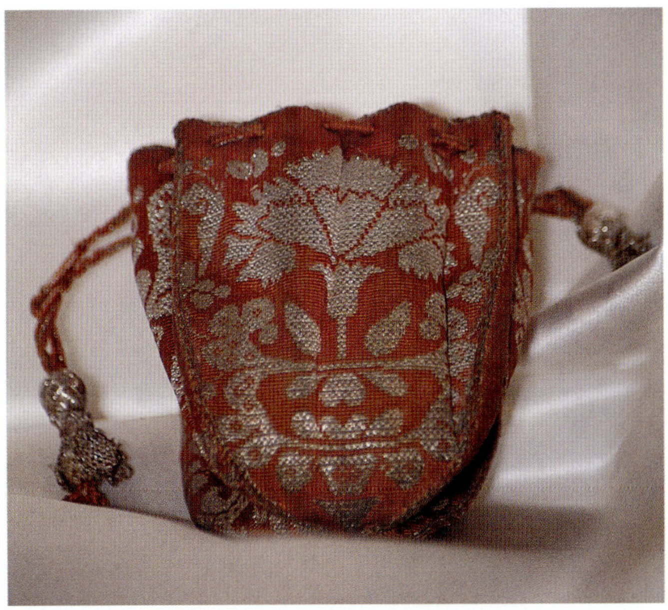

The reverse side of the 17th century tapestry purse. This purse has four sides, with two different floral designs. The splayed carnation is a classic 17th century design. Two tassels are finished with intricate silver knots, surrounded by petals made from silver metal thread and wire.

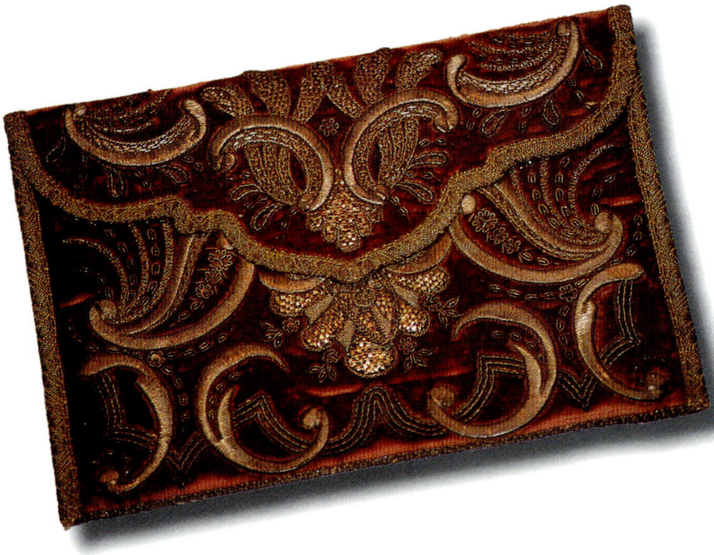

C.1700 crimson velvet pocketbook embroidered in a Baroque design with gilt threads and paillettes. European, possibly Italian. Lined in cream silk. 7 x 5 in. *Collection of Paula Higgins.* Rare.

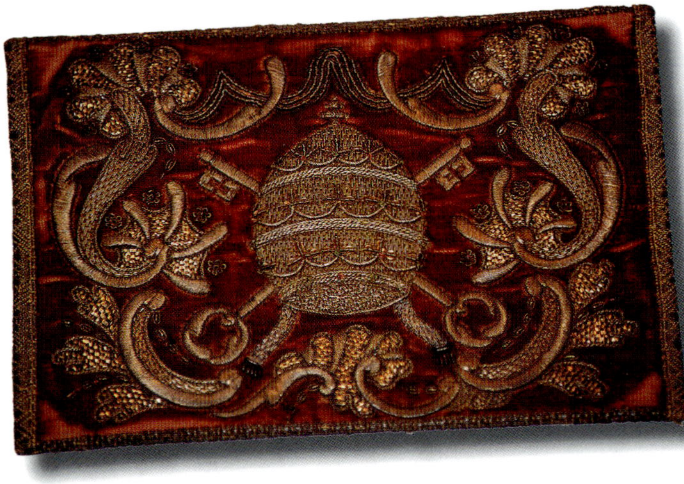

The reverse of the pocketbook. A miter or crown, topped with a cross, is intersected by two keys. Early purse designers often incorporated "plays on words" into their symbolic designs.

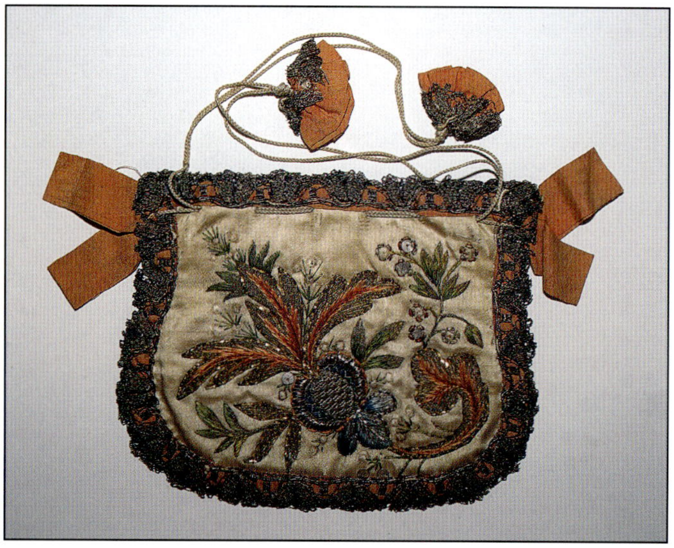

18th century purse embroidered with a pomegranate design in polychrome silk and gilt metal threads. The pomegranate was a popular design from the 16th century through the 18th century. Gilt lace edges the purse. The ribbons are original. European. 5.75 x 4.75 in. *Collection of Paula Higgins.* Rare.

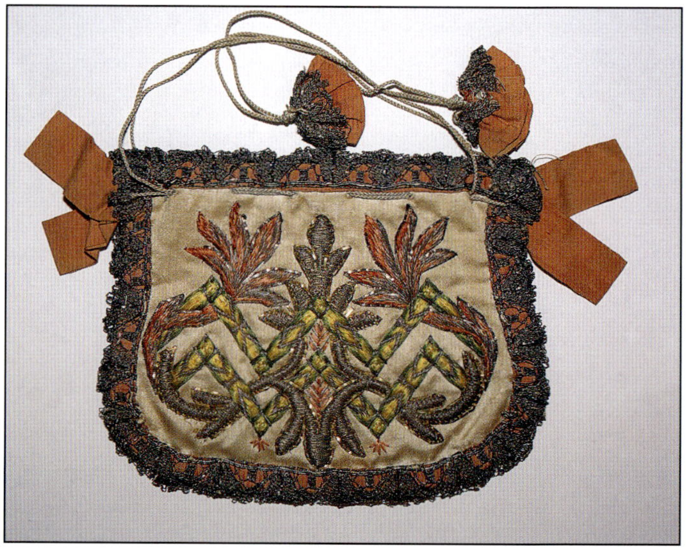

Reverse of the 18th century purse.

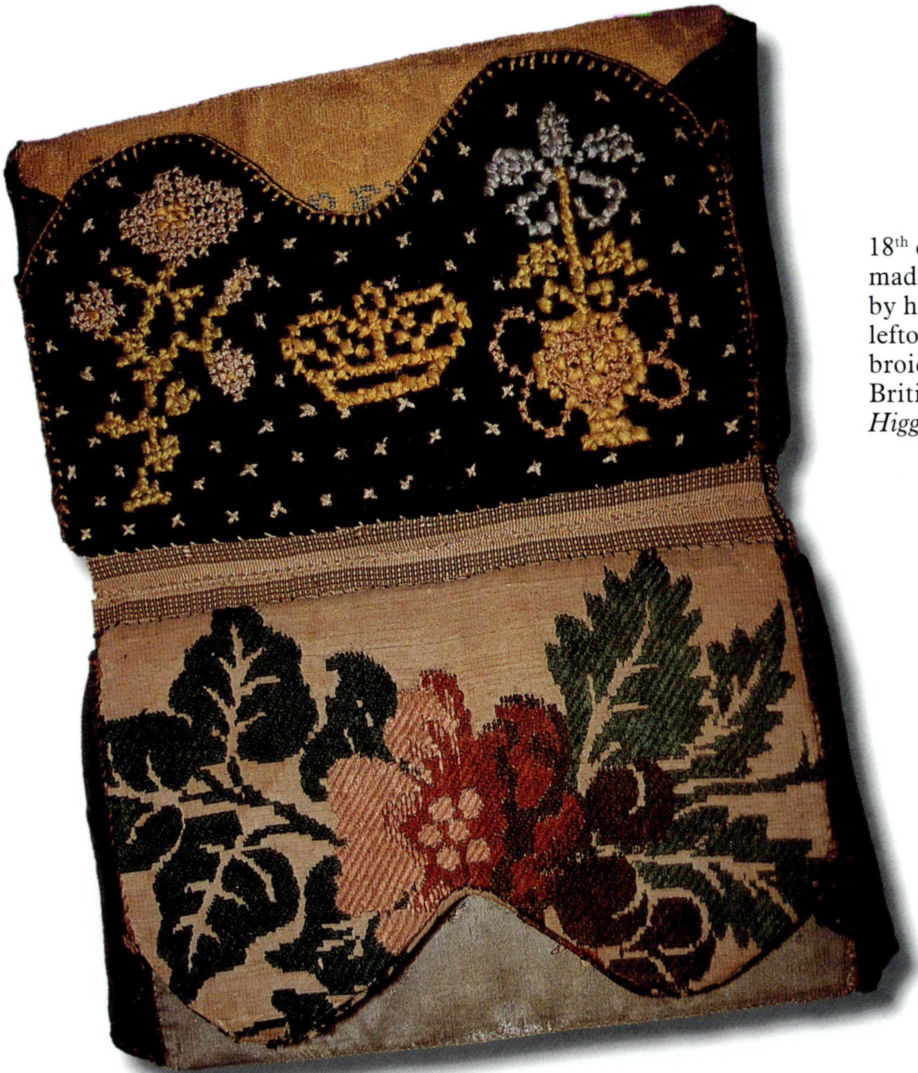

18th century homemade pocketbook made for *Andrew Duncan,* probably by his wife. This purse is made from leftover materials and partially embroidered with a crown and flowers. British. 7 x 5 in. *Collection of Paula Higgins.* $600-800.

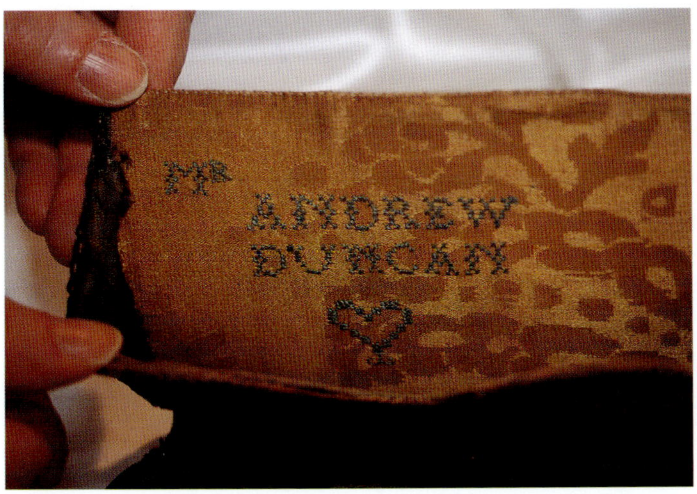

The inside of the purse with Andrew Duncan's name cross-stitched with a heart.

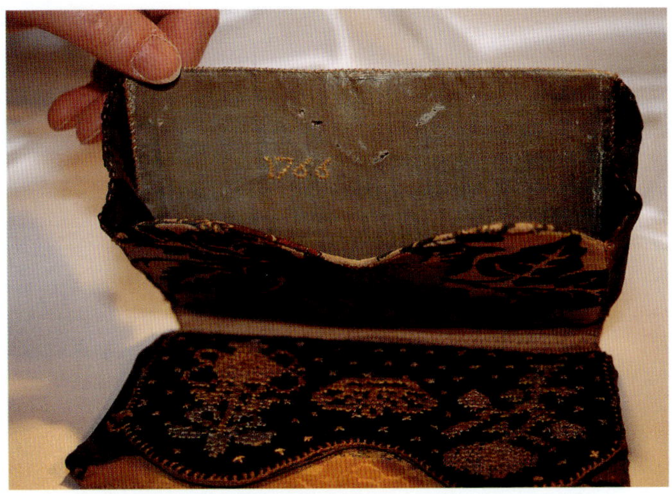

The date *1766* cross-stitched on the other side of the Andrew Duncan pocketbook.

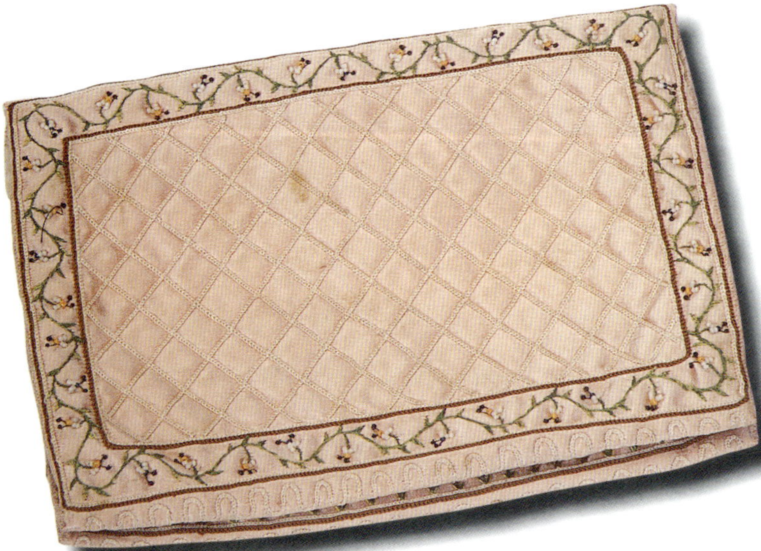

Late 18th century pink quilted pocketbook, which is embroidered and beaded in a flower and vine pattern. The combination of embroidery and beadwork on an 18th century pocketbook is unusual and lovely. 5.5 x 4 in. *Collection of Lori Blaser.* $1,200-1,500.

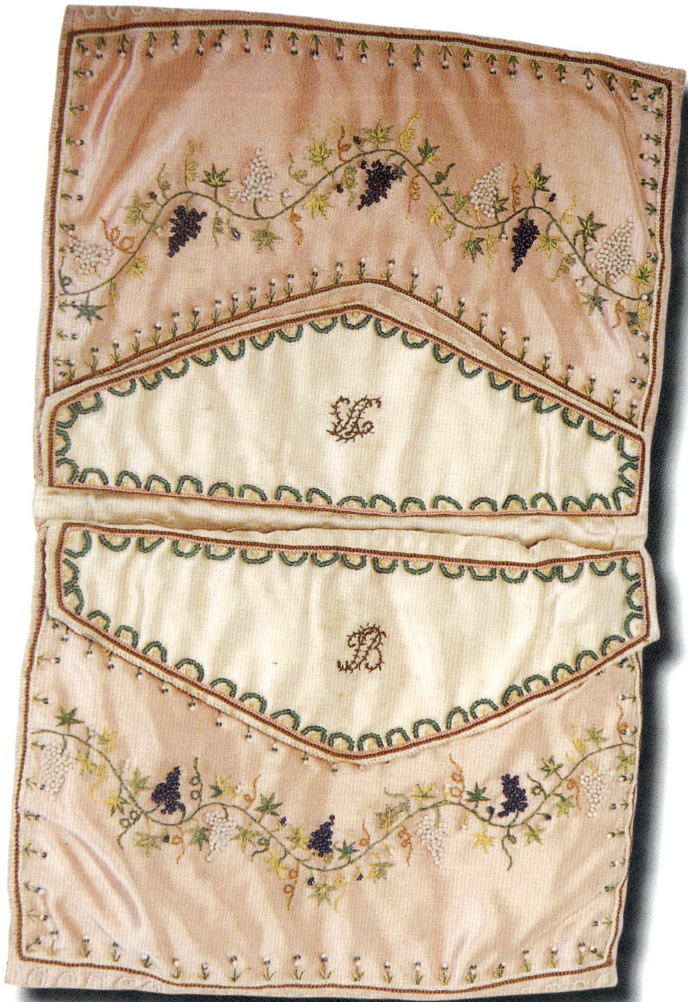

The inside of the late 18th century pocketbook. A grape and leaf design, with the letters *J* and *B*, are embroidered on the interior. The grapes are beaded.

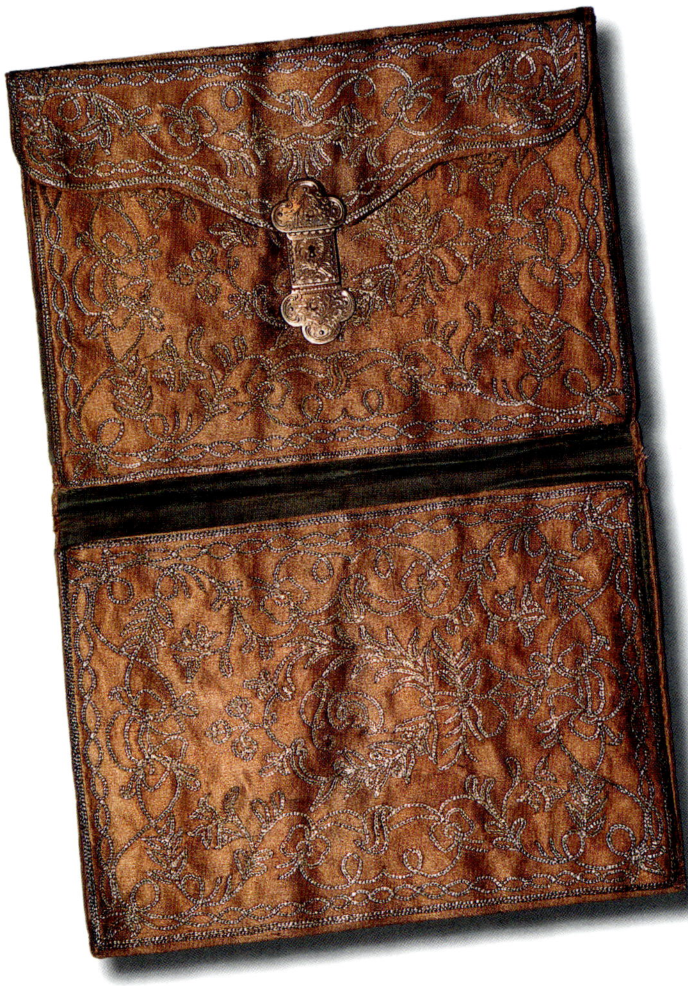

Late 18th century, copper silk pocketbook embroidered with gold thread and lined with green silk. A pinchbeck clasp locks an interior pocket. 7.5 x 6 in. *Collection of Paula Higgins.* $800-1,000.

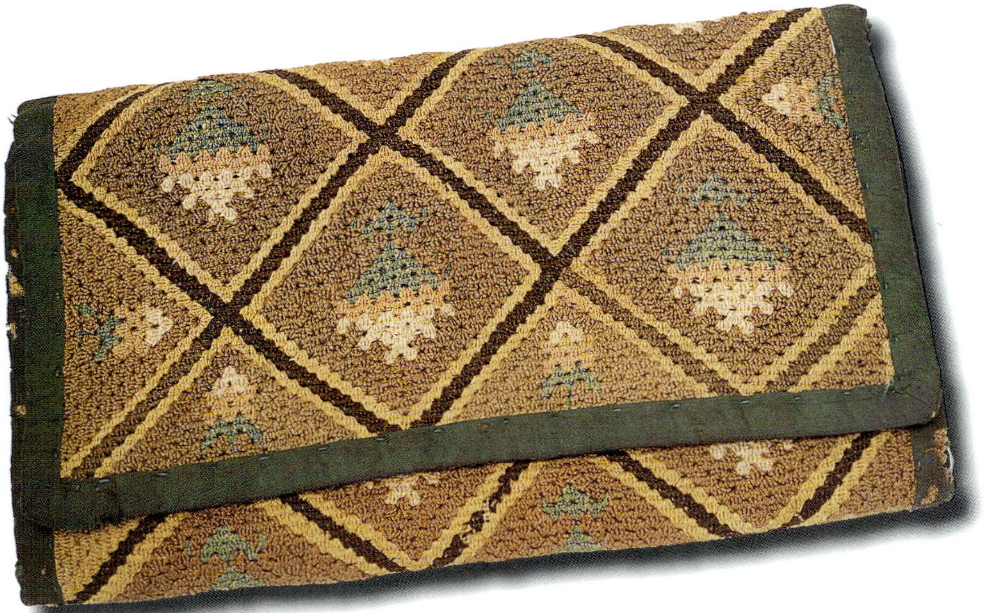

Late 18th century, American Queen's stitched pocketbook worked in the strawberry design. American Queen's stitched pocketbooks are rare, especially in this larger size. Queen's stitch is among the most complex of all needlework stitches. Because it was so difficult to work, it hasn't been used since the 1830s. 8.5 x 6 in. *Collection of Lori Blaser.* Rare.

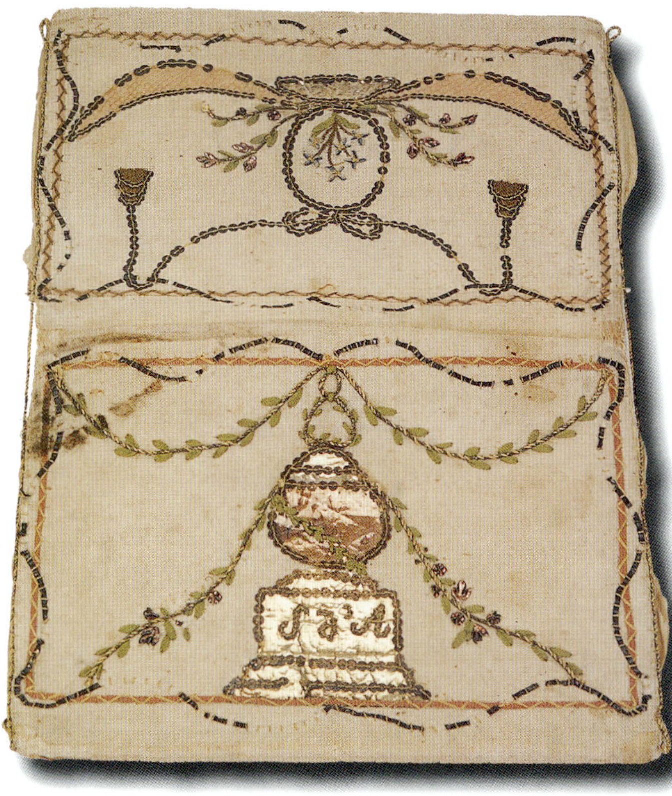

18th century, cream silk memorial pocketbook, embroidered with pink and green silk, pink and gold foil appliqué, and paillettes. The urn is draped with vines, and the base is initialed with the letters *S* and *A*. Foil work is rarely seen on purses of any kind. 7 x 5 in. *Collection of Lori Blaser.* Rare.

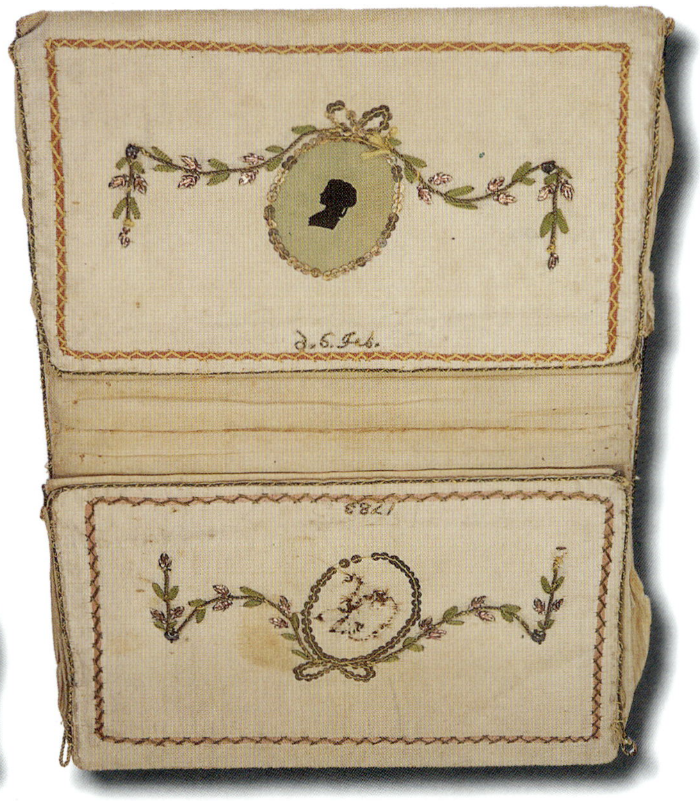

The inside of the pocketbook has a silhouette of a woman on one side. On the other side is a bow with the initials *C* and *K*, and the inscription *d. Feb. 1783.*

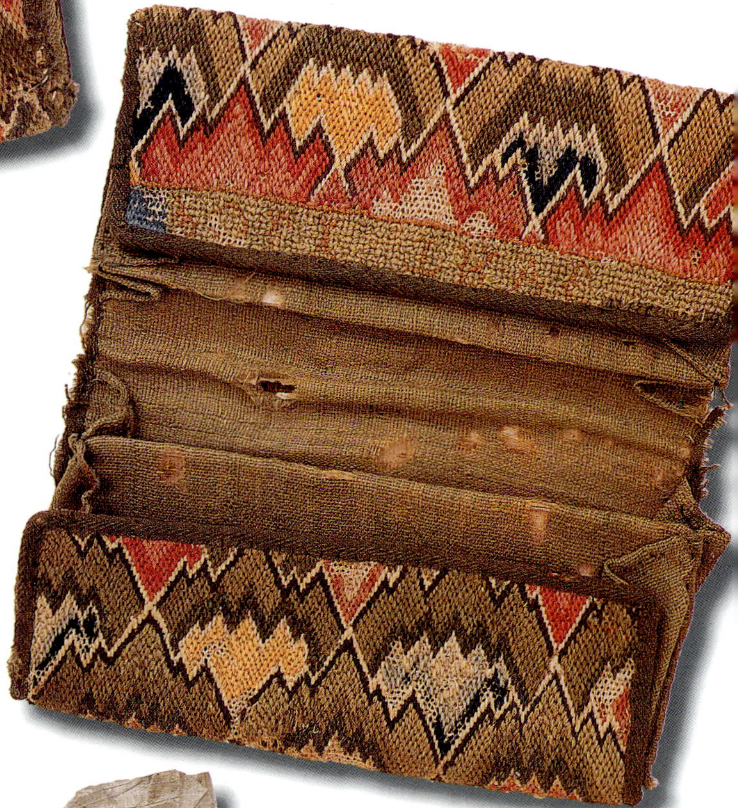

The inside of the Irish stitched pocketbook embroidered with the name *Poly True*. The colors used on this purse are typical of 18th century American embroidered purses.

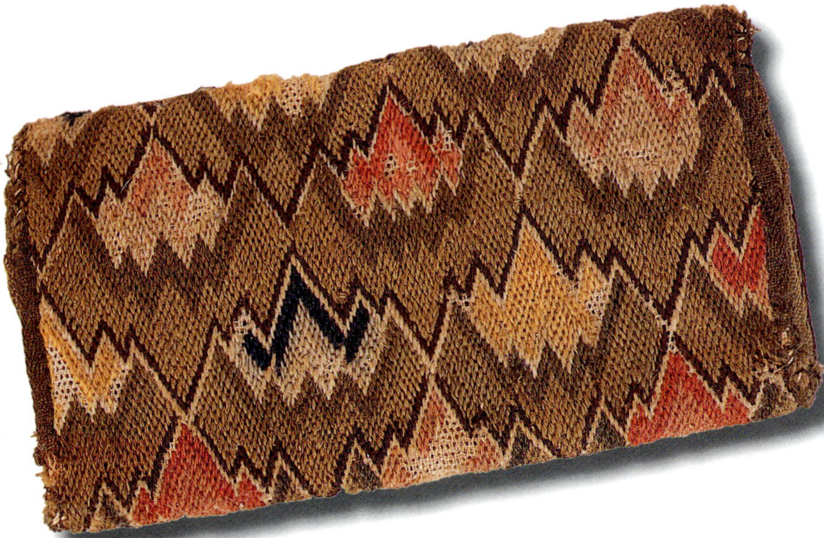

Irish stitched pocketbook worked in a flamepoint design. This purse is American and dates to the 18th century. 7.25 x 4.5 in. *Collection of Lori Blaser.* $1,200-1,500.

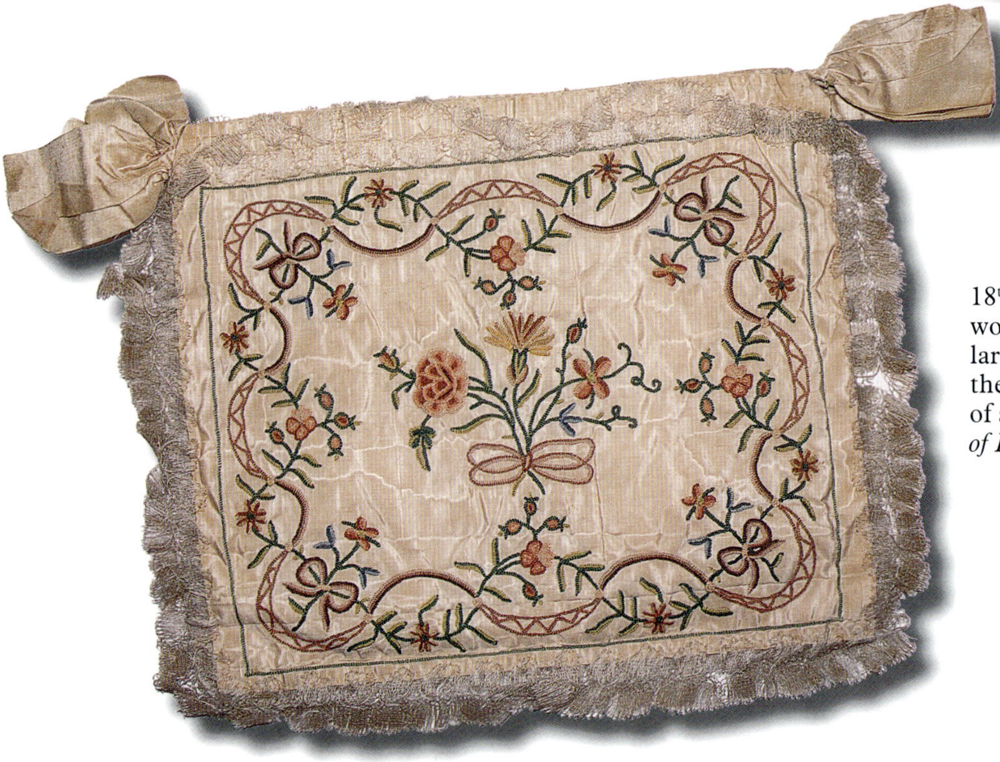

18th century, French workbag tambour worked in a scrolling floral design. These large workbags evolved into the reticule by the late 18th century. The tambour work is of a very fine quality. 11.25 x 9 in. *Collection of Paula Higgins.* $1,200-1,500.

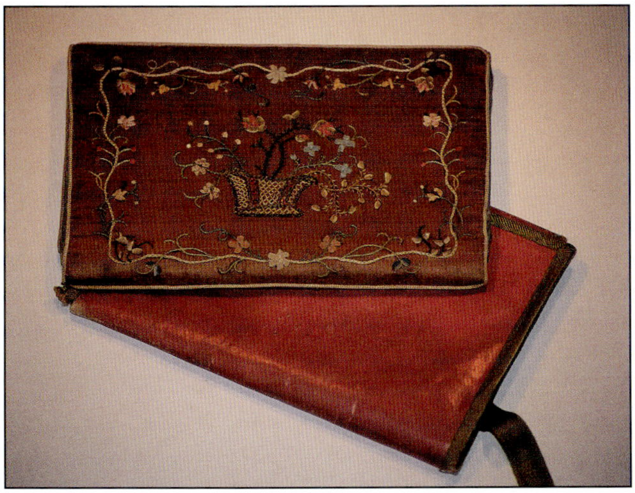

Late 18th century pocketbook embroidered with silk, paillettes, and ribbons. The central basket of flowers is a classic 18th century design. Under the purse is the outer, glazed cover, which is original to the purse. 7 x 5 in. *Collection of Paula Higgins.* Rare.

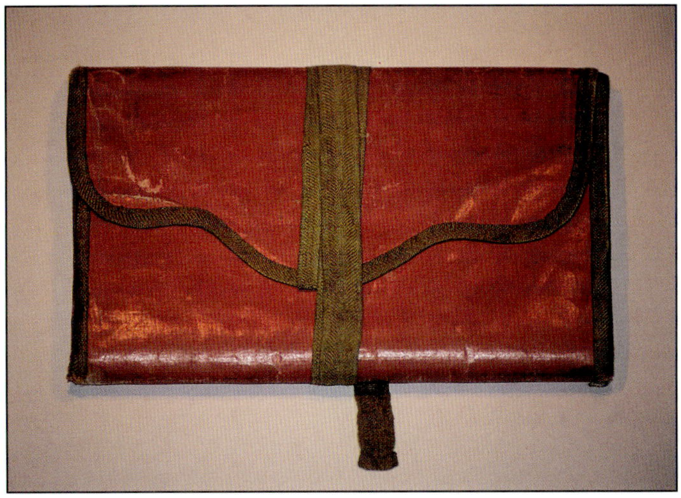

The original, outer glazed cover of the embroidered 18th century purse. Glazing was a popular finish for textiles in the late 18th century. The green silk ribbon is original to the purse also.

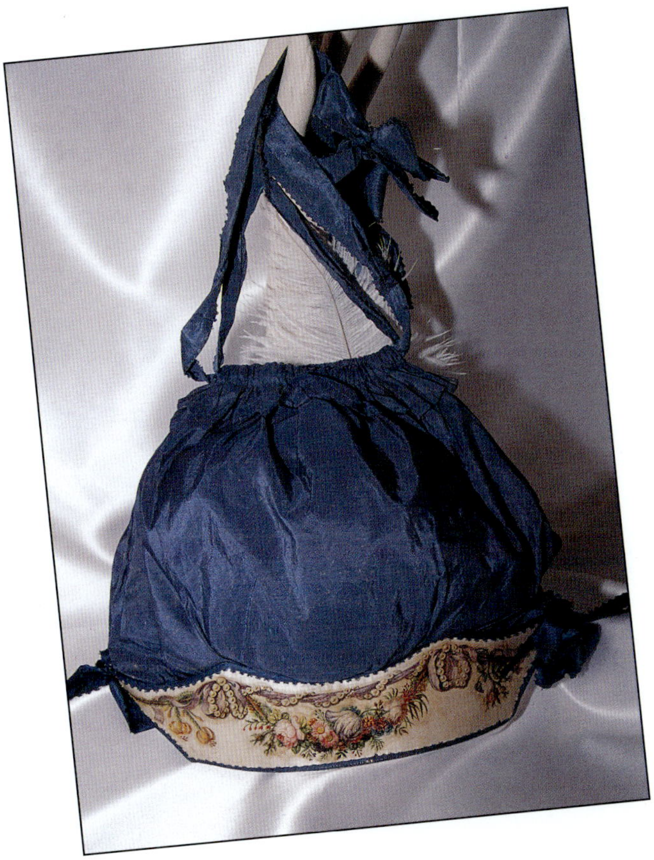

Late 18th century basket purse painted and owned by Mary Knowles, a famous 18th century British embroiderer, friend of Samuel Johnson, and woman of letters. She was also a close friend of Queen Charlotte. Mary embroidered an extraordinary portrait of King George III, which was as lifelike as a painted portrait. 9.5 x 9 in. *Collection of Paula Higgins.* Rare.

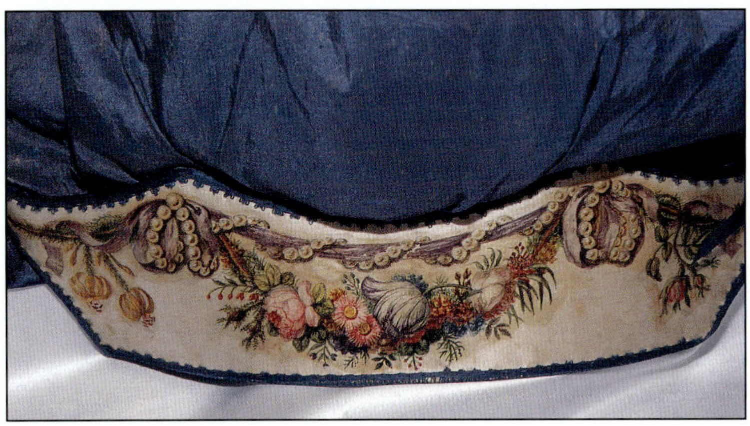

Close-up of the basket painted by Mary Knowles. The twisted rope of pearls, entwined with ribbons and flowers is typical of Georgian design.

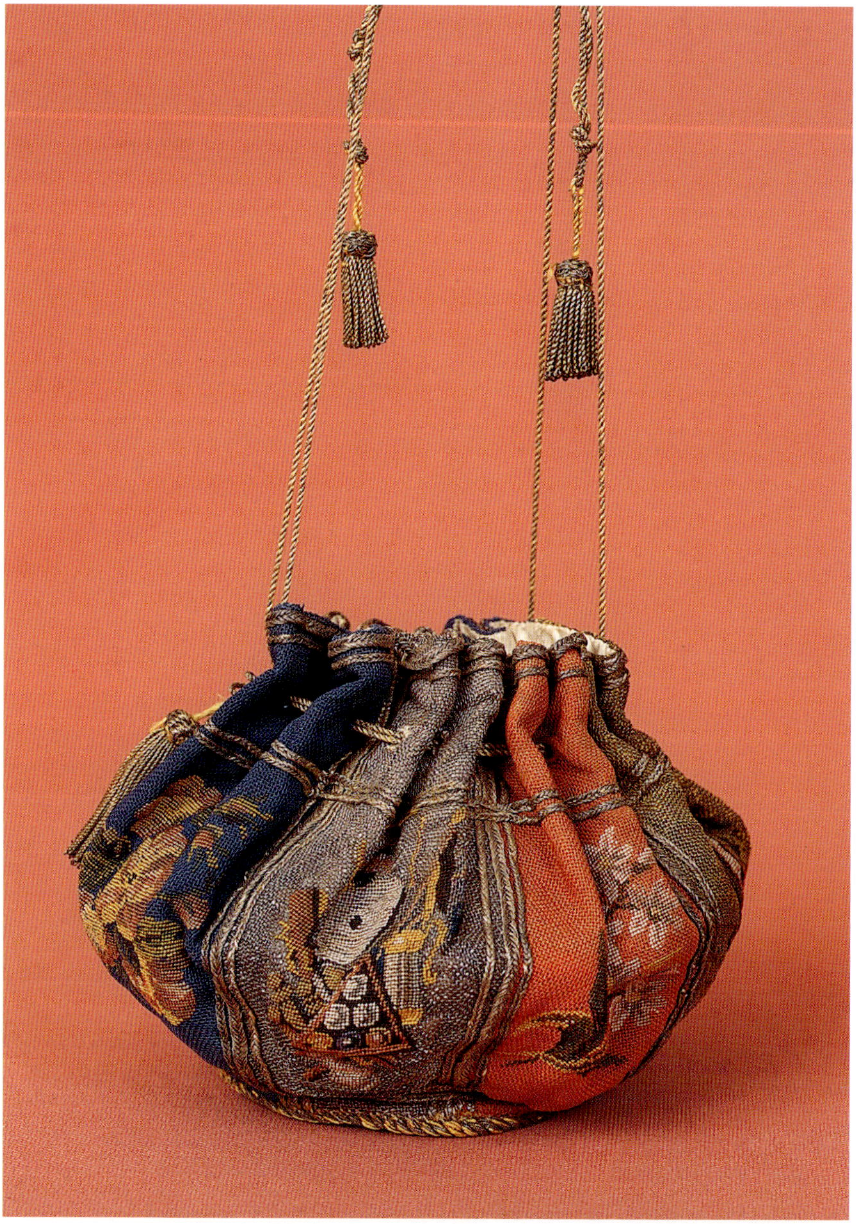

Beautiful c.1800 embroidered gaming purse. Nine different scenic or figural designs decorate the sides and bottom of this purse. Made with silk, gold, and silver threads, the workmanship is extraordinary. 6.5 x 4.5 in. *Collection of Lori Blaser.* Very rare.

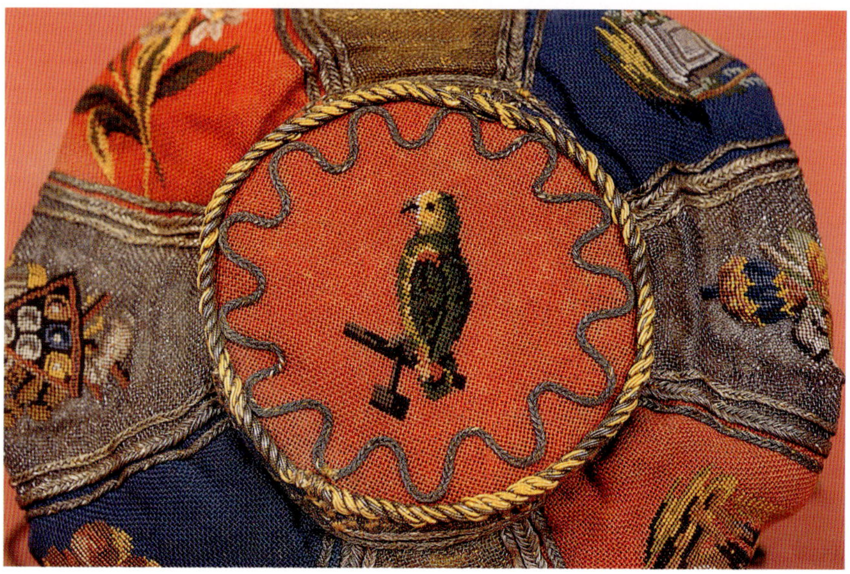

The bottom of the purse is embroidered with the figure of a bird on a stand.

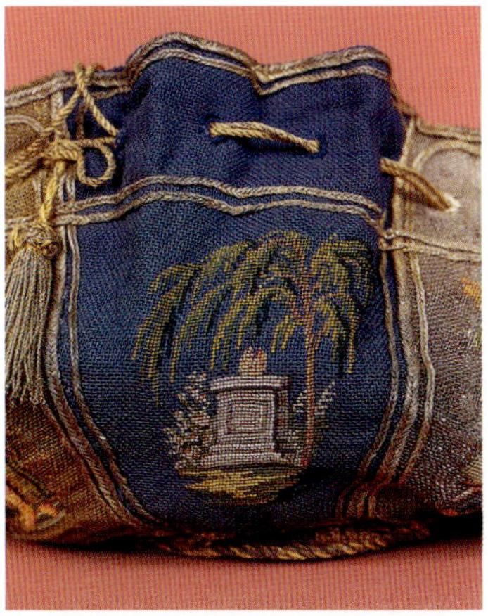

A memorial scene with a monument and weeping willow are embroidered on another panel. Memorial scenes became very popular after Washington died.

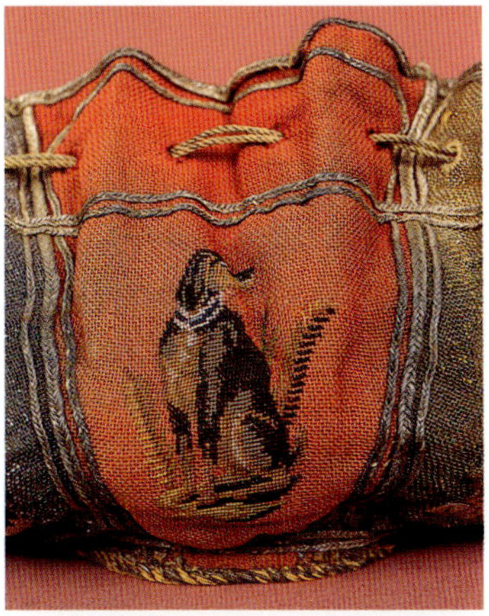

Man's best friend also earned a spot on this purse. Dogs were popular embroidery subjects during the 19th century.

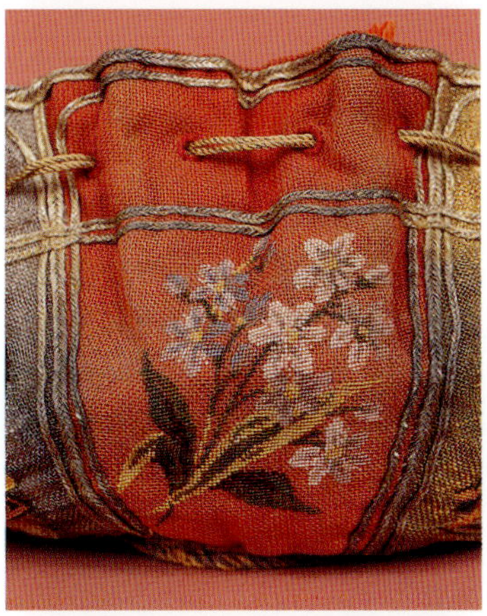

A lovely spray of flowers against a coral background.

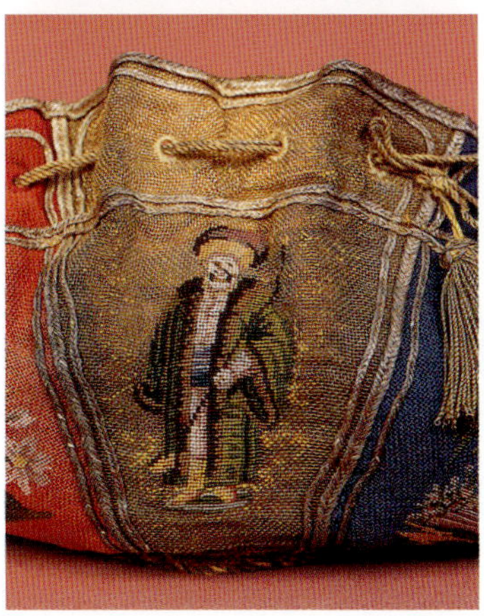

Oriental and Arabic figures were often incorporated into purse designs during this period.

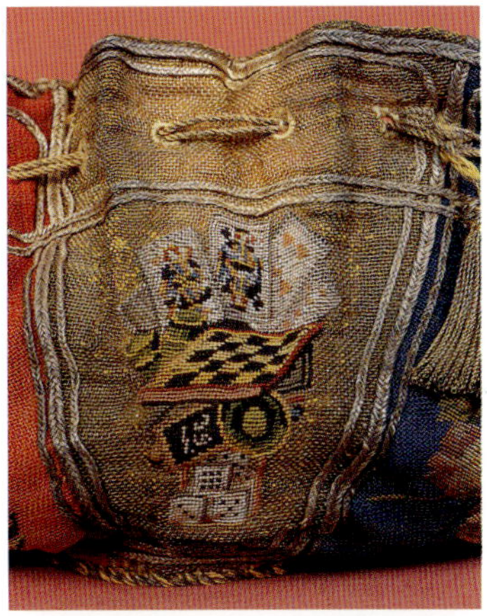

A wonderful panel depicting different types of games such as dice, checkers, and cards.

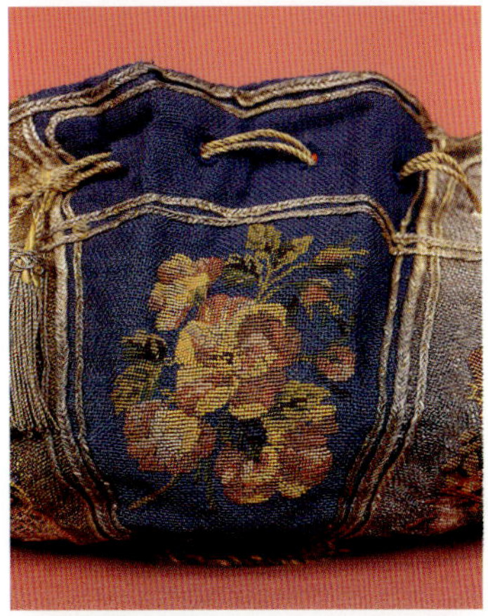

Another floral design of pansies.

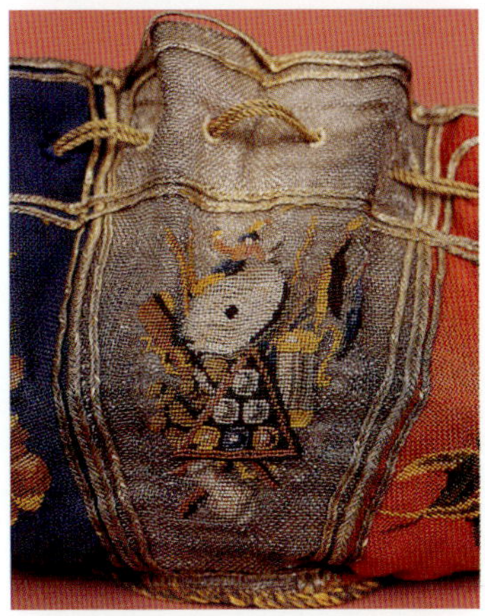

A panel decorated with a rack and billiard balls.

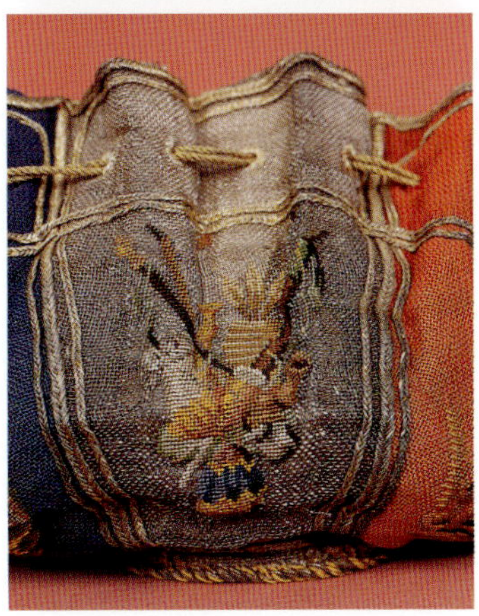

An embroidery of pipes, and possibly a sword, set against a silver background.

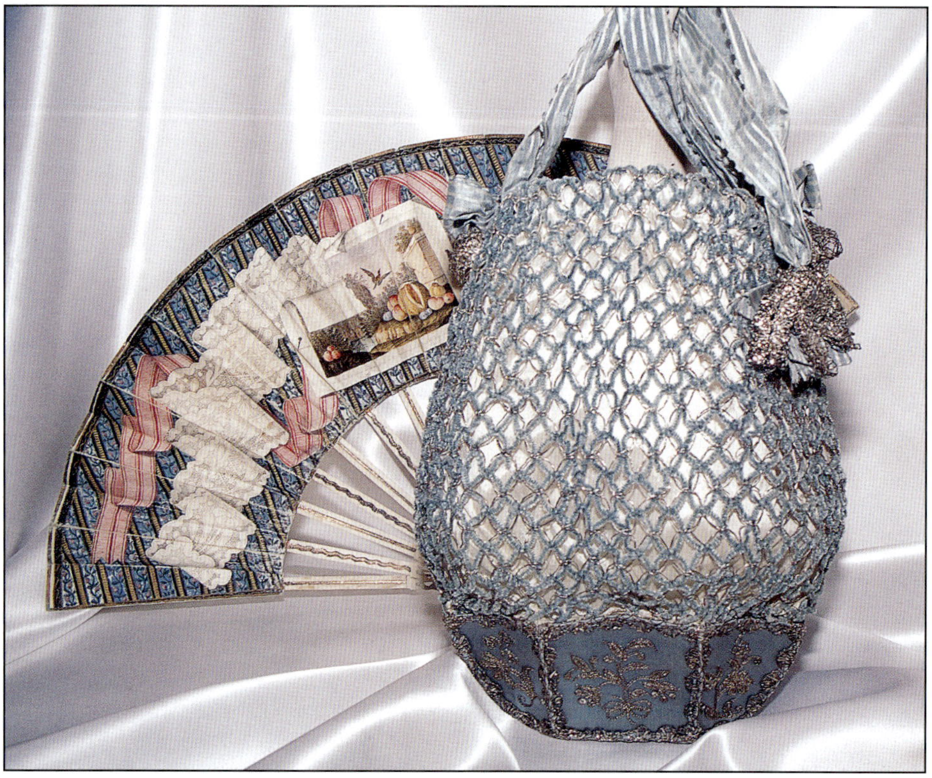

Late 18th century basket purse bought by Jane Austen's brother, Edward Austen-Knight (he took the name of the extended family member who adopted him) for his wife, Elizabeth. Made from chenille and silver metal threads in a network design, with a cream silk lining. The basket is tambour worked in different floral designs. Behind the basket is an 18th century fan. 11 x 8 in. *Collection of Paula Higgins.* Very rare.

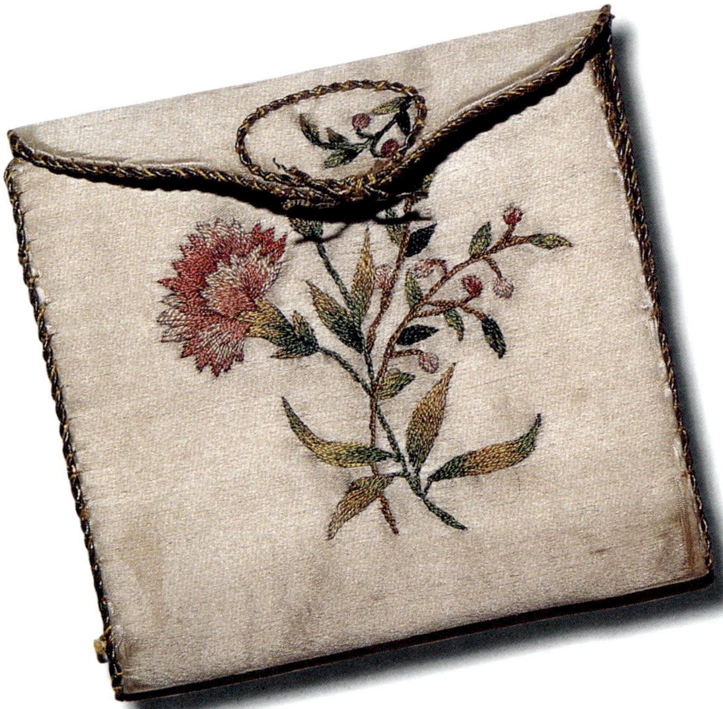

Late 18th century, American embroidered purse. The carnation was a popular 18th century embroidery subject. The silk background is mounted over card. 4.5 x 4. *Collection Of Paula Higgins.* $650-750.

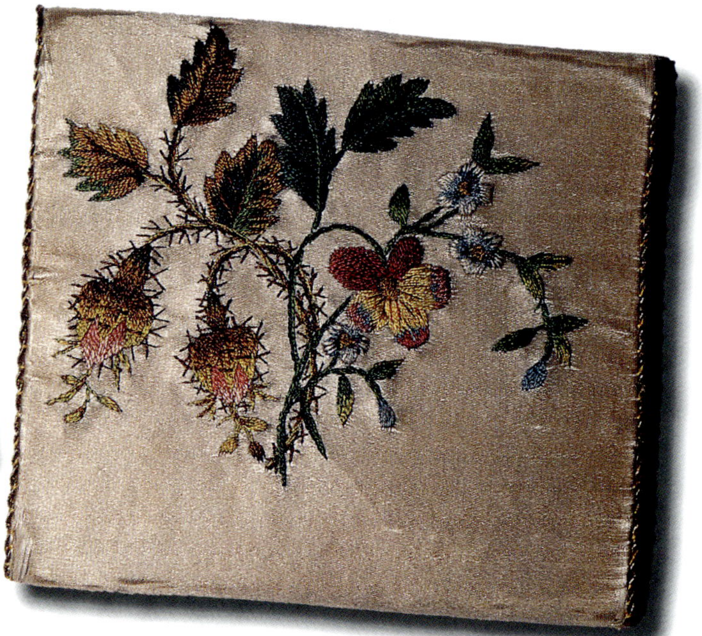

The reverse side of the late 18th century, American embroidered purse.

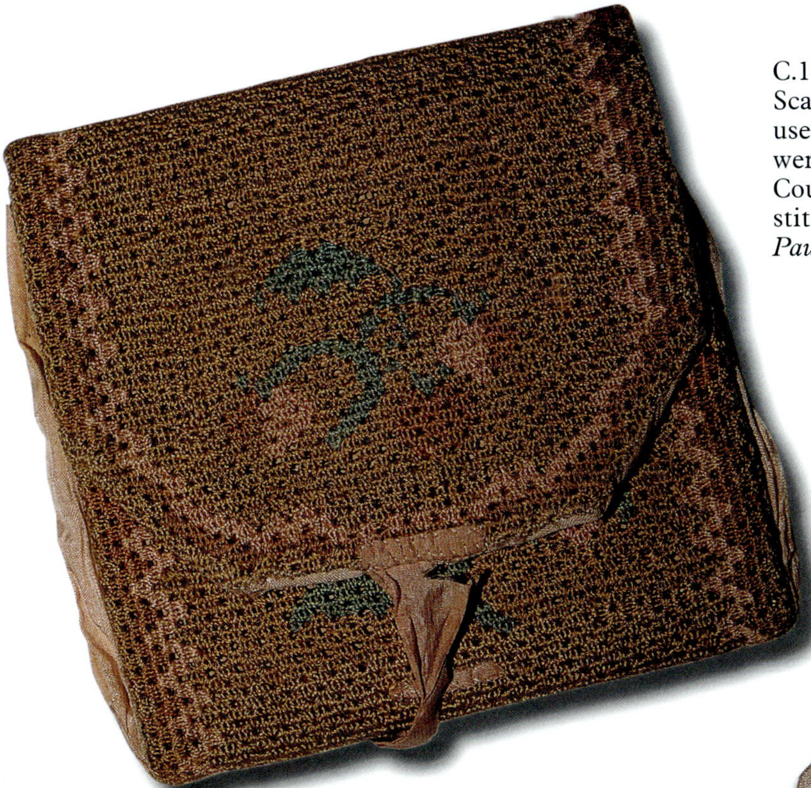

C.1800-1810 American purse once owned by Hannah Scattergood, a Quaker. The name Hannah Scattergood was used in the 18th and early 19th centuries. Presumably, they were related to one another. This purse came from Bucks County, Pennsylvania. Made from the complex Queen's stitch in a strawberry design. 4.25 x 4.25 in. *Collection of Paula Higgins.* Rare.

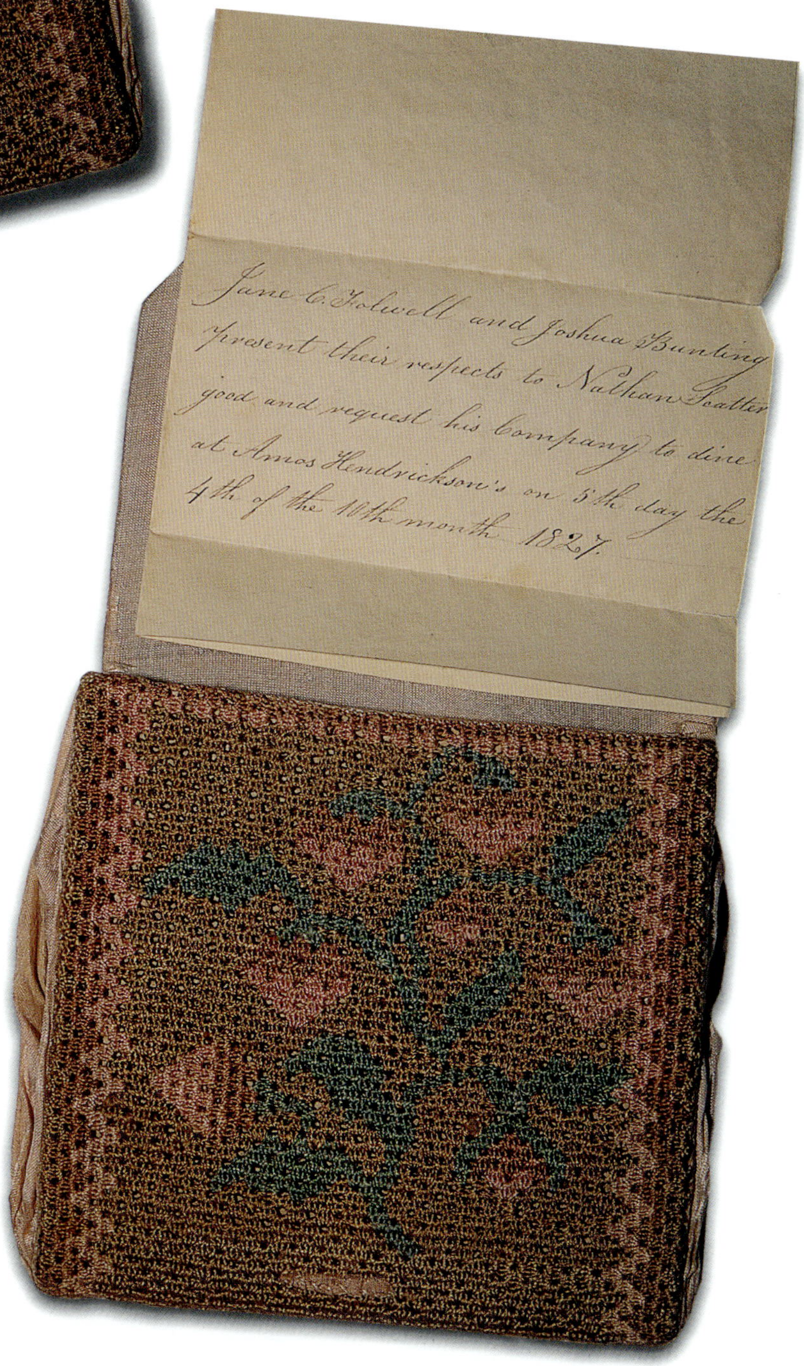

The inside of the Hannah Scattergood purse. Early papers from the Scattergood family came inside the purse. This is an invitation requesting Nathan Scattergood to dine at Amos Hendrickson's in 1827. Obituaries and marriage announcements were also included.

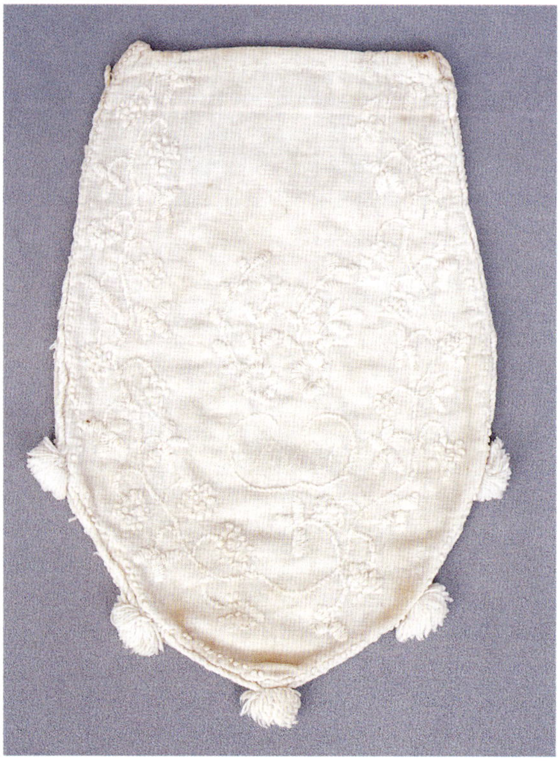

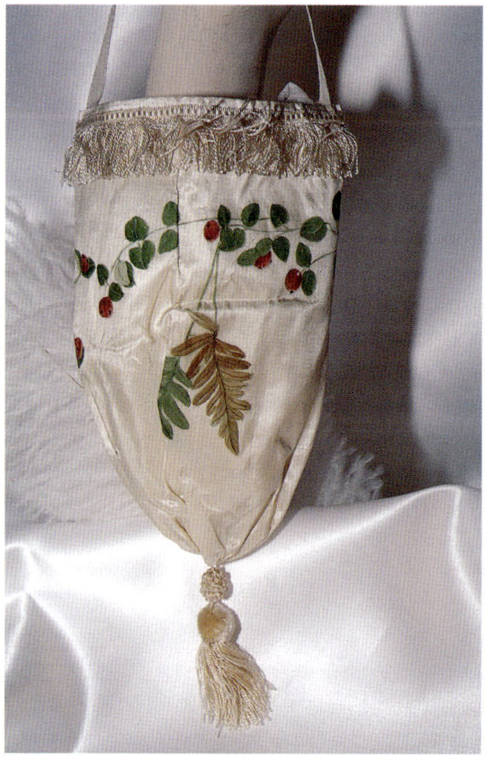

Early 19th century, American silk reticule. A design of checkerberries was free hand painted around the purse. This purse came from an estate in New Hampshire. A fine silk fringe encircles the top, and a chenille and silk tassel hangs from the bottom. 9 x 3.5 in. *Collection of Paula Higgins.* Very rare.

Early 19th century, American white work bag (one of two) once owned by Sarah Clements. Born in 1782 in New Hampshire, she married Nathaniel Whittier in 1803. Embroidered with French knots in a scrolling grape and vine design. 10.5 x 7.25 in. *Collection of Lori Blaser.* Rare.

A close-up of the bow on the white work purse. The name *Louisa Fay* is embroidered inside the bow.

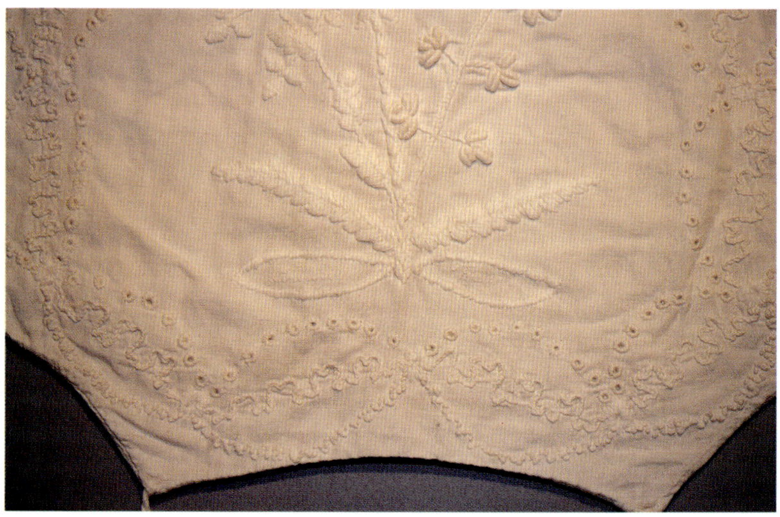

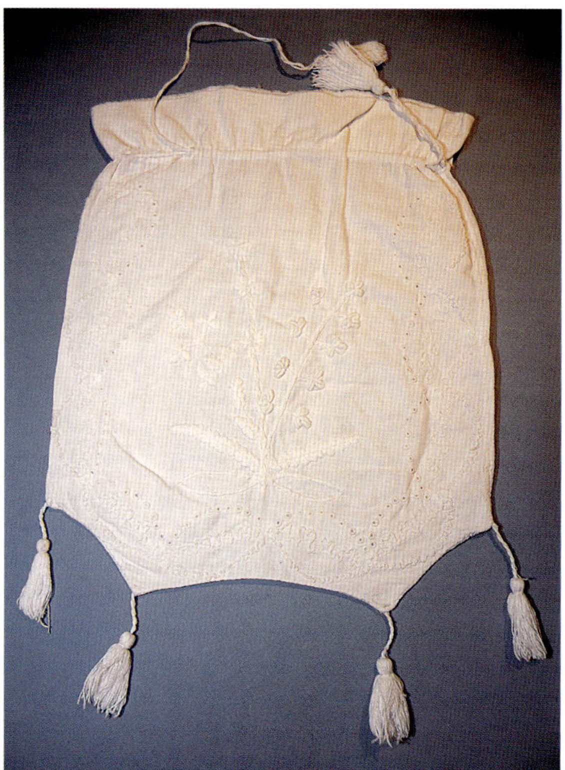

Early 19th century, American white work purse made by Louisa Fay. The classic floral spray is embroidered on one side, and a medallion encircling the initials *L* and *F* is on the reverse. 10 x 8.5 in. *Collection of Paula Higgins.* Rare.

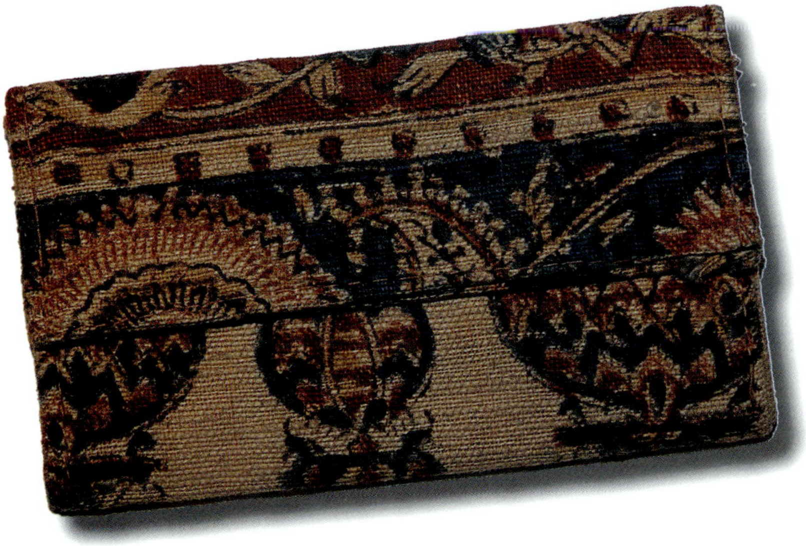

C.1800 block printed pocketbook. French or American. 6 x 4 in. *Collection of Paula Higgins*. $300-350.

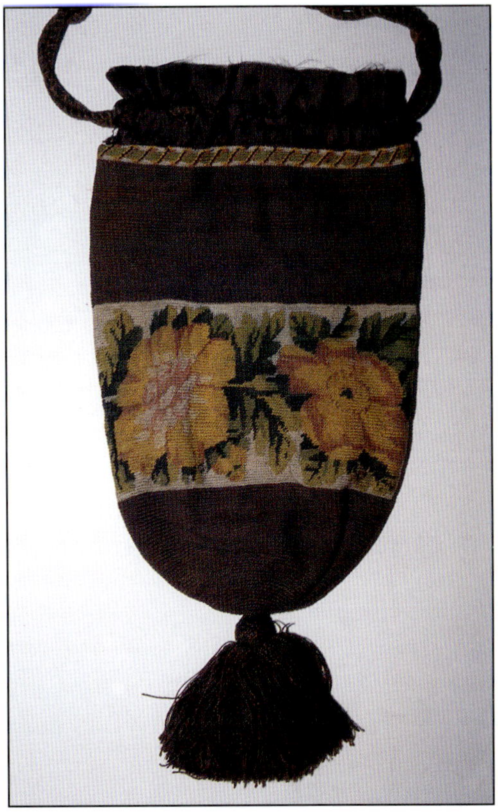

C.1800 finely knitted reticule. British. 9 x 6 in. *Collection of Paula Higgins*. $300-350.

Early 19th century Syrian tapestry purse made from silk and silver threads. The stylized floral design is typical of Syrian purses. They were exported to Europe in the 19th century, especially to England. Exotic textiles were highly valued by Europeans. 8 x 5 in. *Collection of Paula Higgins*. $400-500.

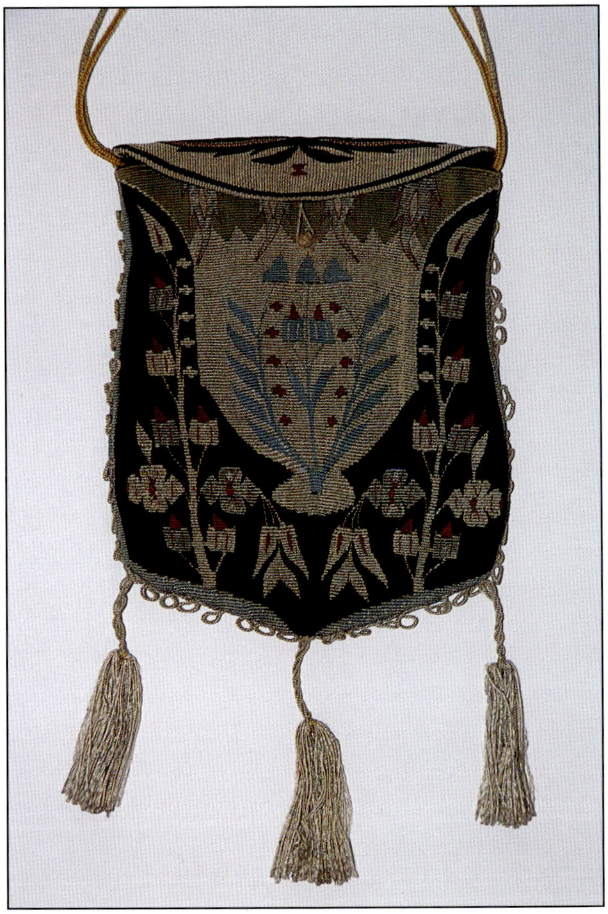

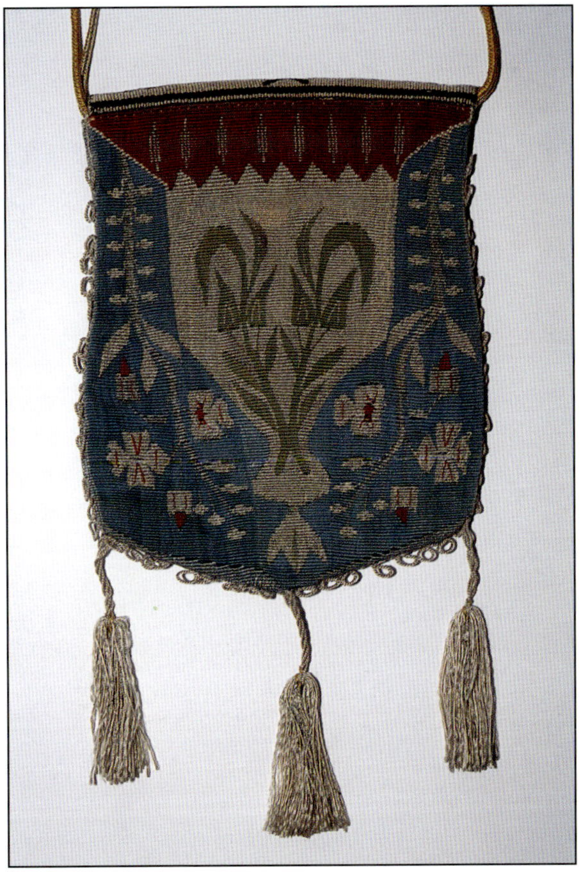

The reverse of the Syrian export purse.

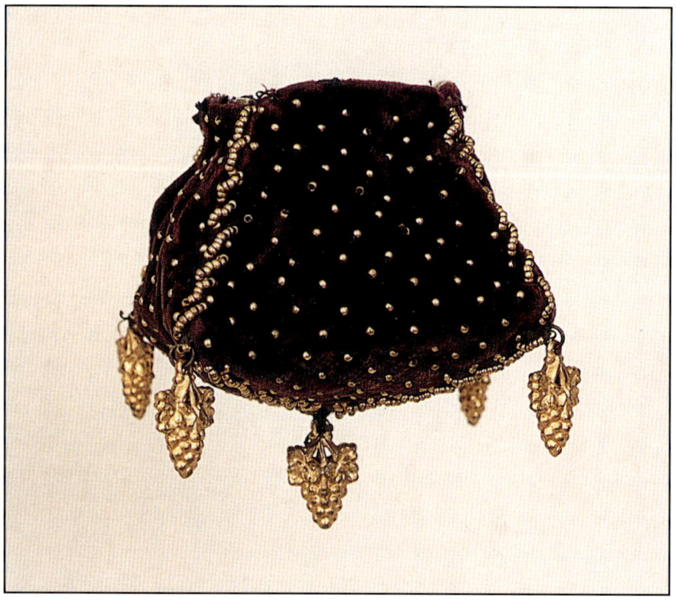

Early 19th century, French purple velvet reticule with gilt tassels made in the shape of a bunch of grapes. The French made some unusual and stylish purses in the early years of the 19th century thanks to the influence of Empress Josephine. 2.5 x 2.5 in. *Collection of Lori Blaser.* Rare.

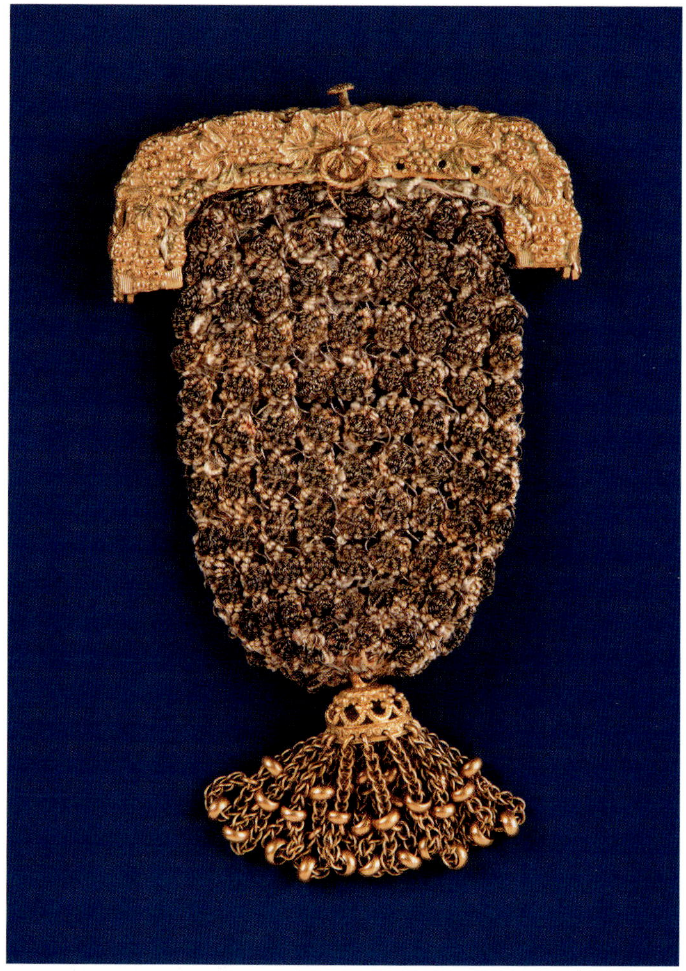

This is a wonderful example of an early 19th century coin purse. The "spider web' design is sometimes seen on these early needleworked purses. It is mounted on a gilt, grape and leaf designed frame, and a chain and ring tassel hangs from the bottom. 4 x 2.5 in. *Collection of Sharon LuVisi.* $300-350.

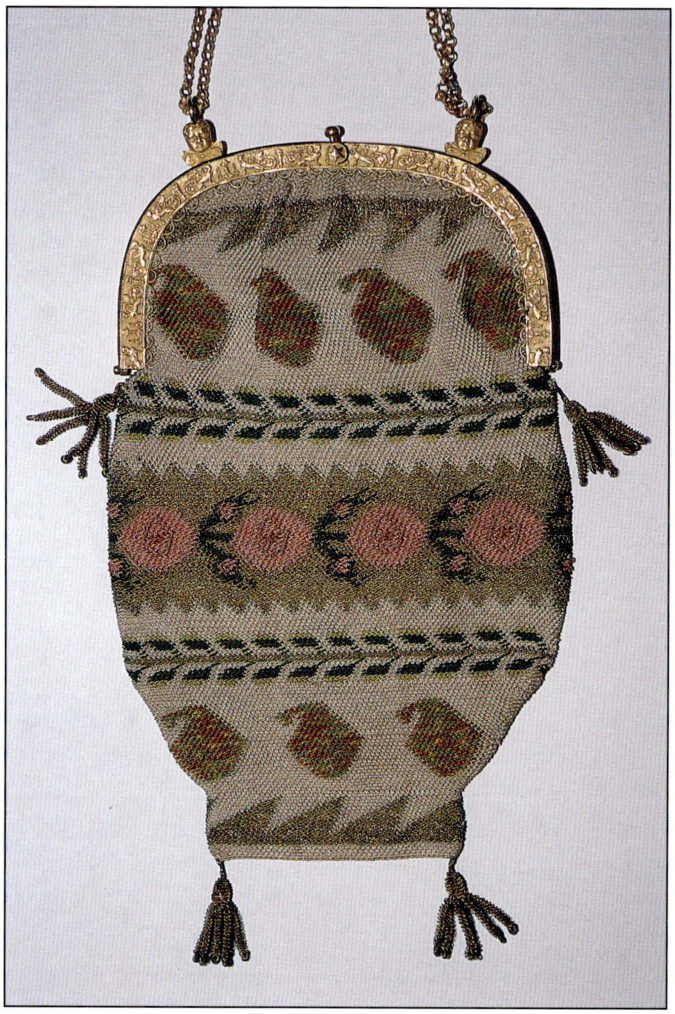

Early 19th century French knitted purse. Made from silk and gold threads in a floral and stylized buta design. This purse retains its original gold wire tassels and its pinchbeck frame. The frame has a design of torches, and figures with Griffin bodies and human heads. Napoleon's conquest of Egypt impacted all areas of design, including purse frames. Everything classical and Egyptian became the height of fashion. 8.5 x 5 in. *Collection of Paula Higgins.* $600-650.

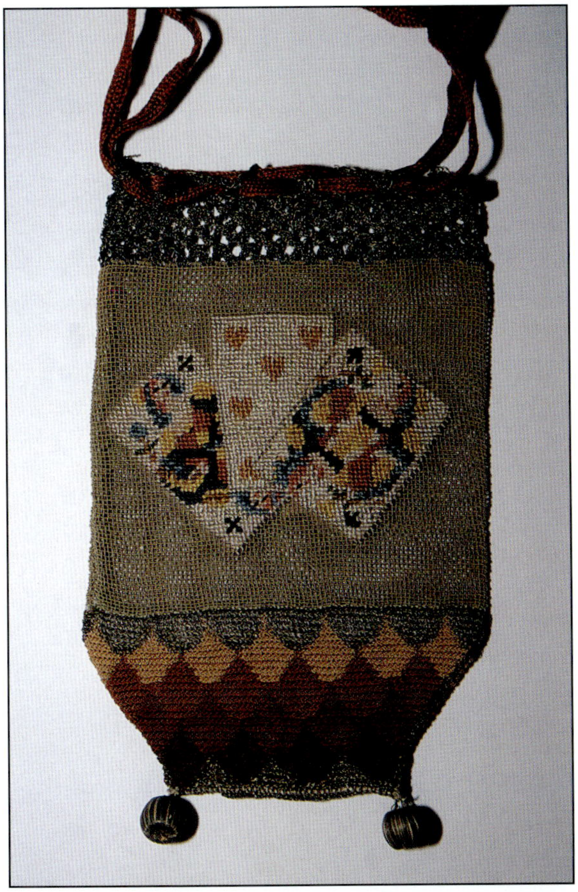

Early 19th century coin purse embroidered in a design of playing cards on fine net. The top is made from netted silver thread and the bottom is knitted in a fish scale design. Its shape, and the two small ball tassels, are typical of early 19th century purse design. 4 x 2.5 in. *Collection of Paula Higgins.* Rare.

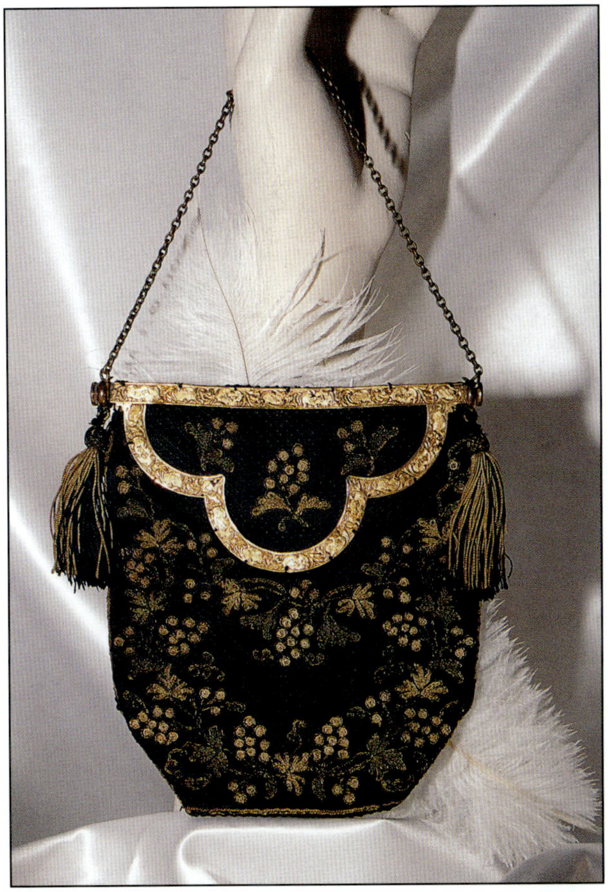

Early 19th century French embroidered purse. The grape and leaf design is worked on fine netting, which overlays black silk. The frame is made from pinchbeck. 6 x 5 in. *Collection of Paula Higgins.* $450-650.

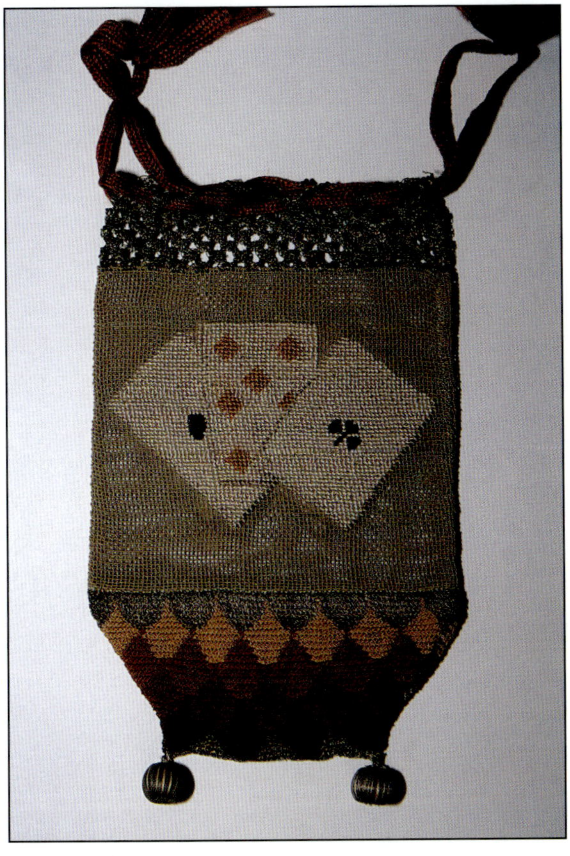

The reverse of the coin purse.

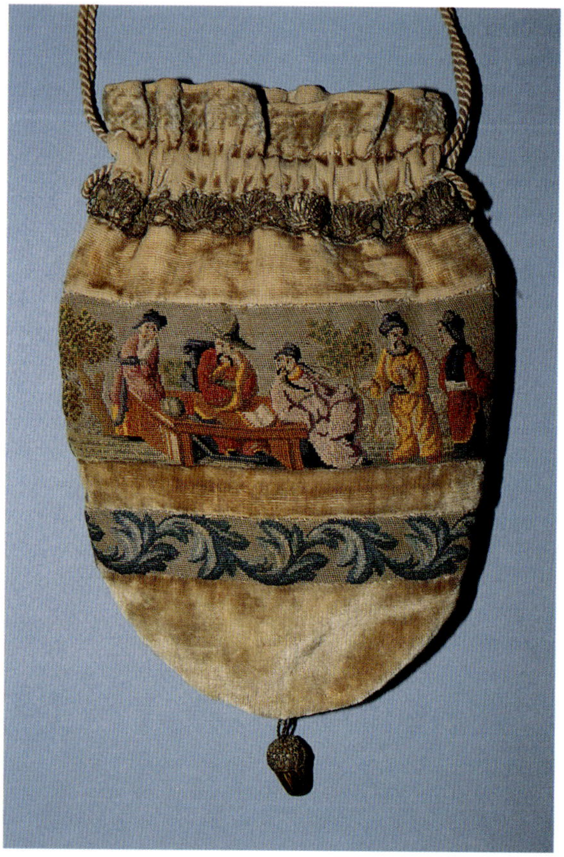

Early 19th century velvet and petit point purse with a design of Oriental figures transacting business at a table. The acanthus leaf design, gold lace, and acorn tassel are all early 19th century features. 8 x 6 in. *Collection of Paula Higgins.* $450-650.

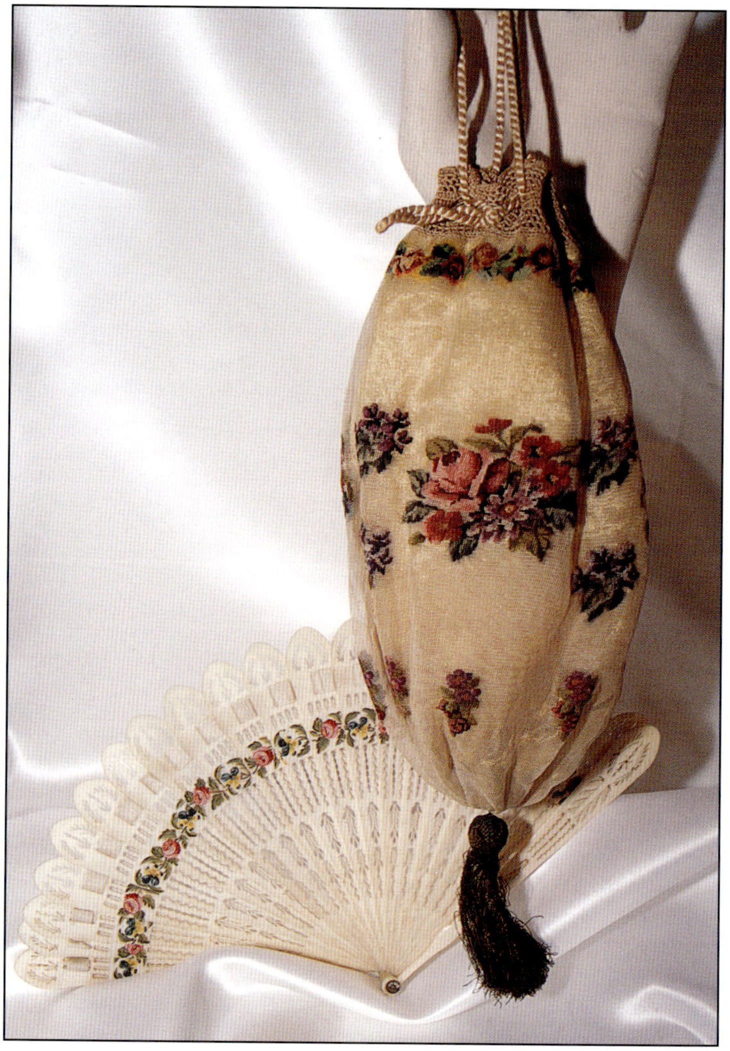

Beautiful, early 19th century petit point purse worked on fine gauze. The tassel is made from gold threads. 8 x 5 in. *Collection of Paula Higgins.* $450-650.

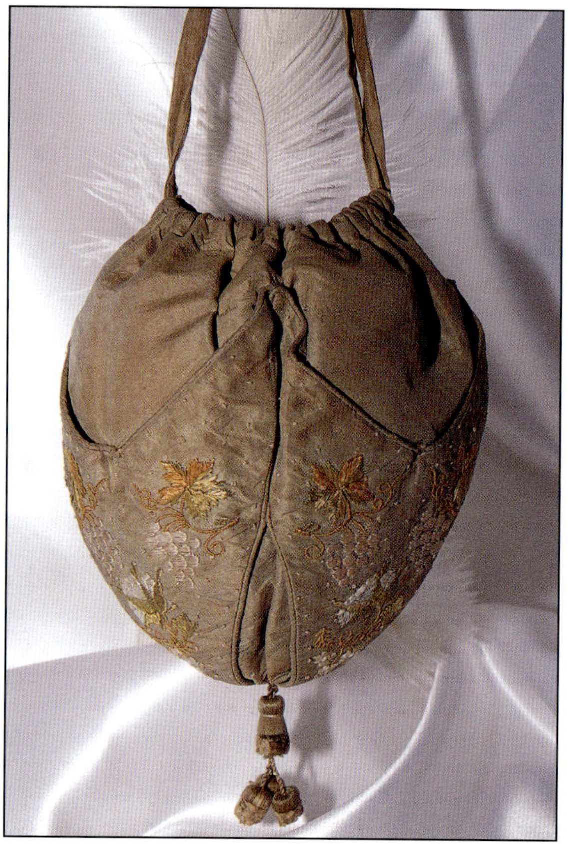

Early 19th century, American embroidered purse. Early purse features include: the grape and leaf design, the petal shaped overlay, the rolled edge on the petals, the color of the silk (green), and the tassels. 6 x 5 in. *Collection of Paula Higgins.* $450-650.

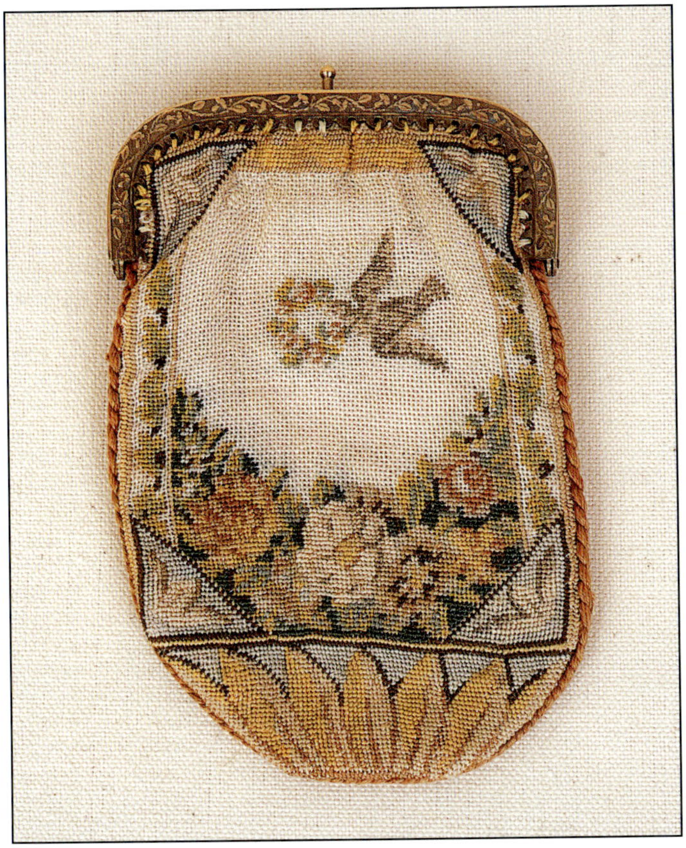

Lovely, early 19th century, petit point coin purse with a design of a bird and wreath, mounted on a gold frame. The bird and wreath design is a classic Biedermeier design. 4.75 x 2.75 in. *Collection of Lori Blaser.* $450-650.

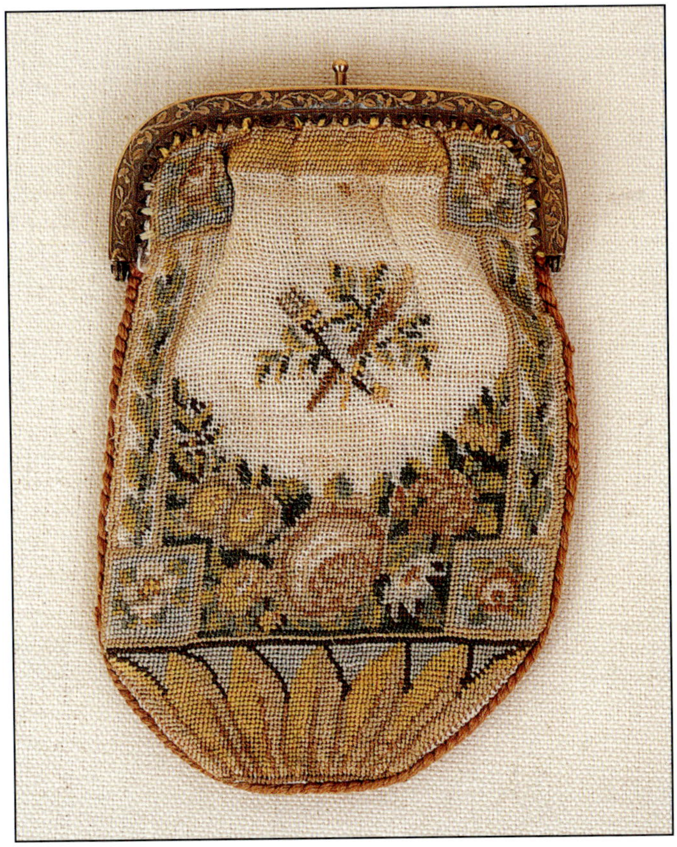

Classic designs of a quiver of arrows and a torch are embroidered on the reverse side of the petit point purse.

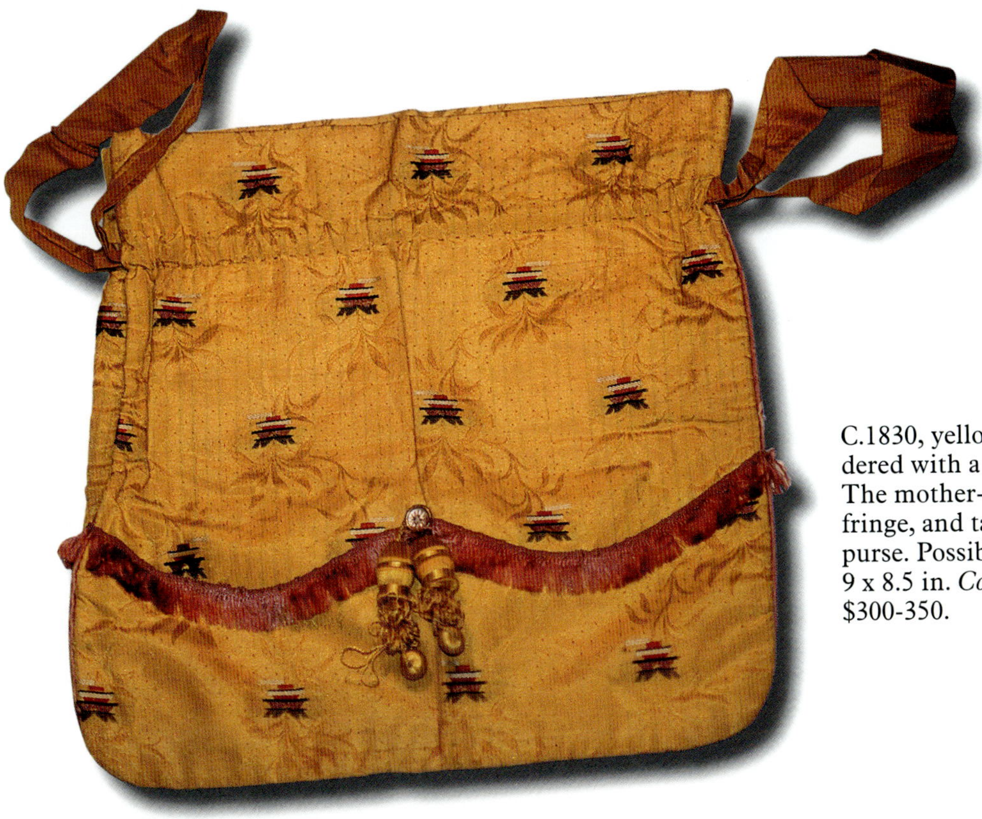

C.1830, yellow silk reticule embroidered with a Chinese pagoda pattern. The mother-of-pearl button, silk fringe, and tassels are original to the purse. Possibly made to match a dress. 9 x 8.5 in. *Collection of Paula Higgins.* $300-350.

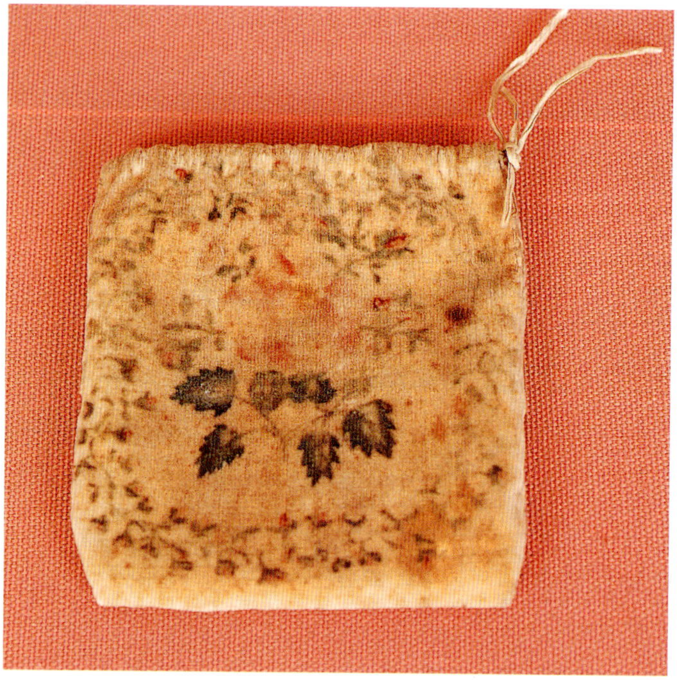

C.1820-1830 American Theorem purse stenciled in a rose and leaf design on velvet. Theorem purses were a schoolgirl art form, especially in America. Designs were stenciled and then set with a spirit gum type substance. This purse was used to store sewing items. 3.5 x 3 in. *Collection of Lori Blaser.* Rare.

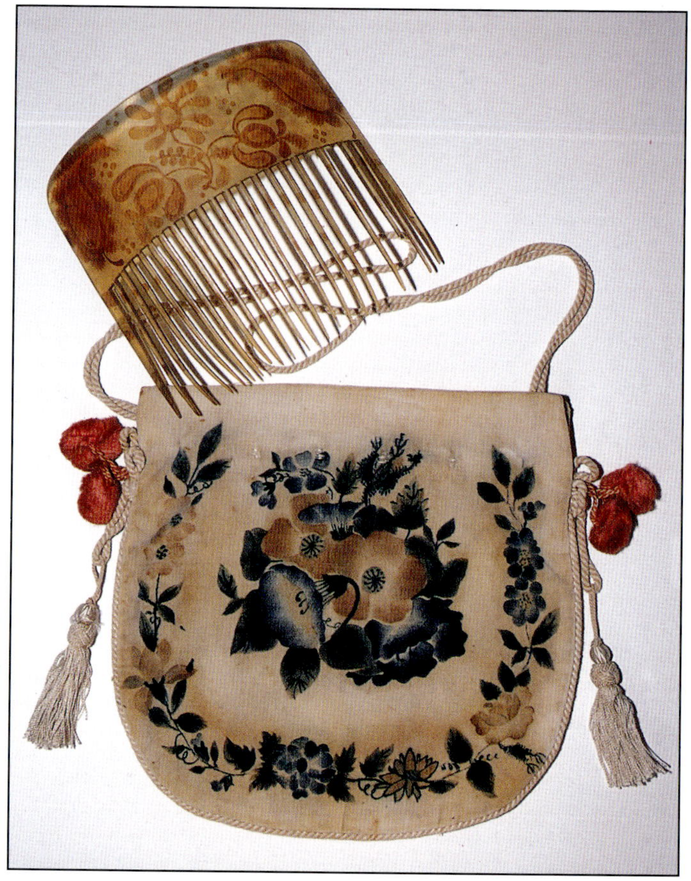

C.1830, velvet Theorem purse from New England. The stenciled half wreath and floral design are classic Theorem designs. Chenille tassels are another purse feature from this period. The American horn comb, also c.1830, is stenciled as well. 8.25 x 8.25 in. *Collection of Paula Higgins.* Rare.

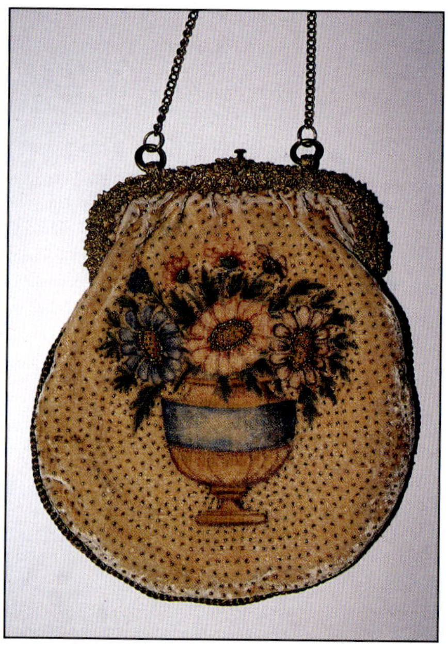

C.1830 Theorem purse mounted on a gilt frame. Parts of the design may have been free hand painted, as well as stenciled. The vase of flowers is decorated with gold beads and the surrounding velvet is studded with small gold beads. Gold metal roping borders the whole bag. 8 x 7 in. *Collection of Paula Higgins.* Rare.

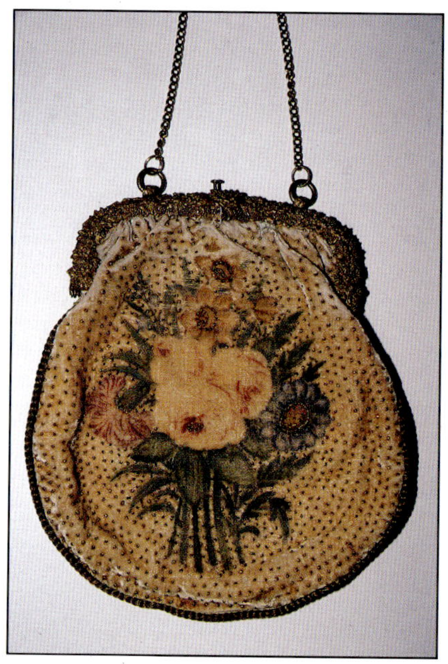

The reverse side of the Theorem purse.

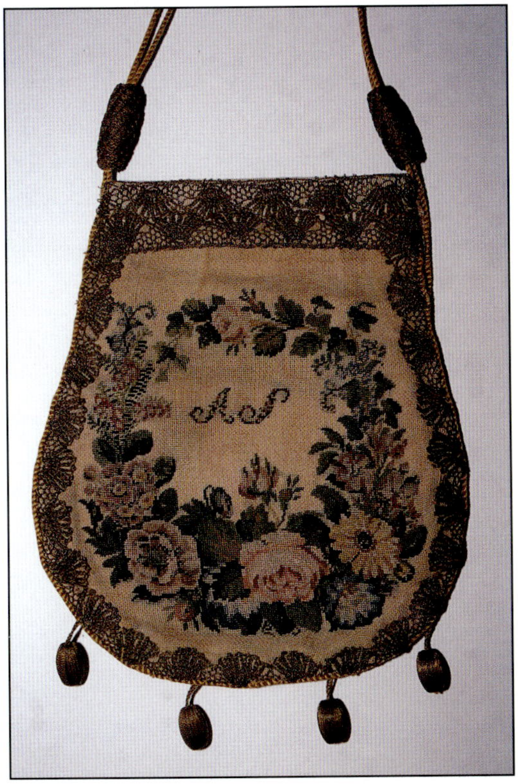

C.1830 petit point reticule decorated with gold lace and gold tassels. The initials *A* and *S* are in the center of a floral wreath. The petit point is beautifully worked on fine net. The silk drawstrings have wood sliders covered with gold net, which slide to open and close the purse. 8.5 x 7 in. *Collection of Paula Higgins.* $450-600.

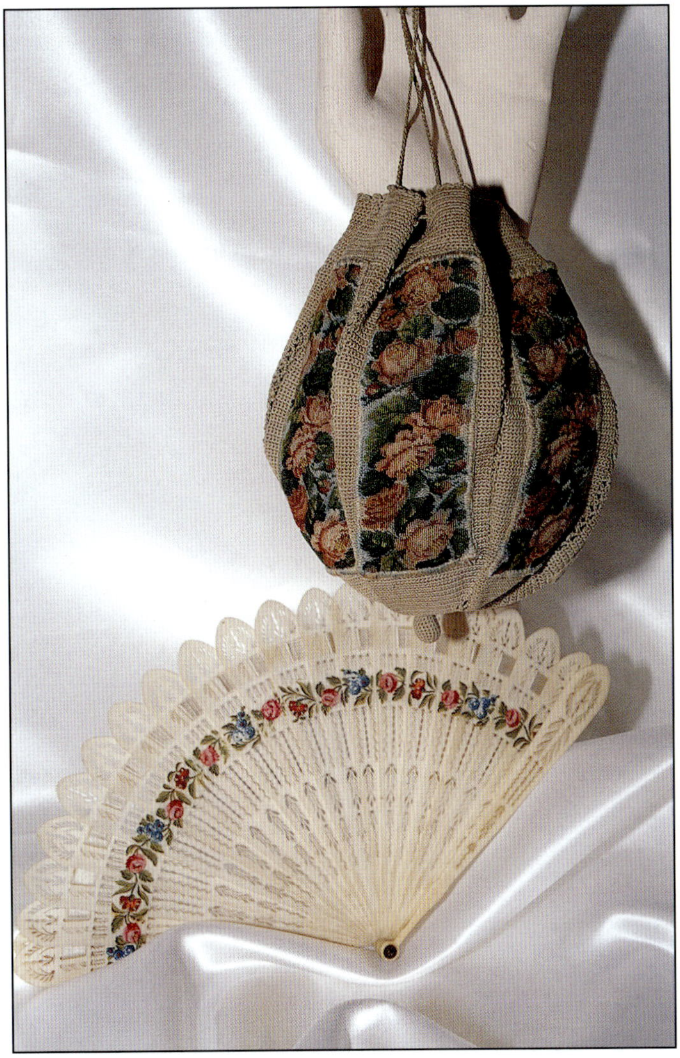

C.1830-1840 crocheted purse with petit point panels. 5.5 x 4.5 in. *Collection of Paula Higgins.* $250-300.

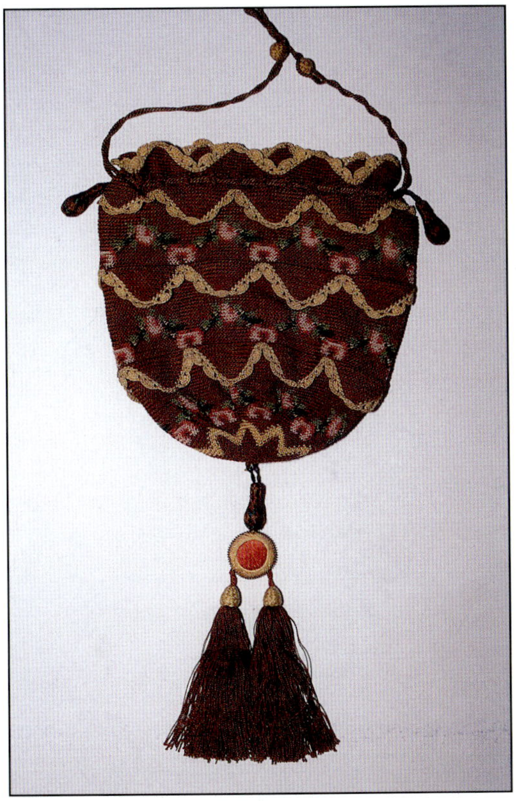

C.1830-1840 reticule with a design of roses, scalloped tiers, and a beautifully worked chandelier tassel. 8.5 x 5 in. *Collection of Paula Higgins.* $250-350.

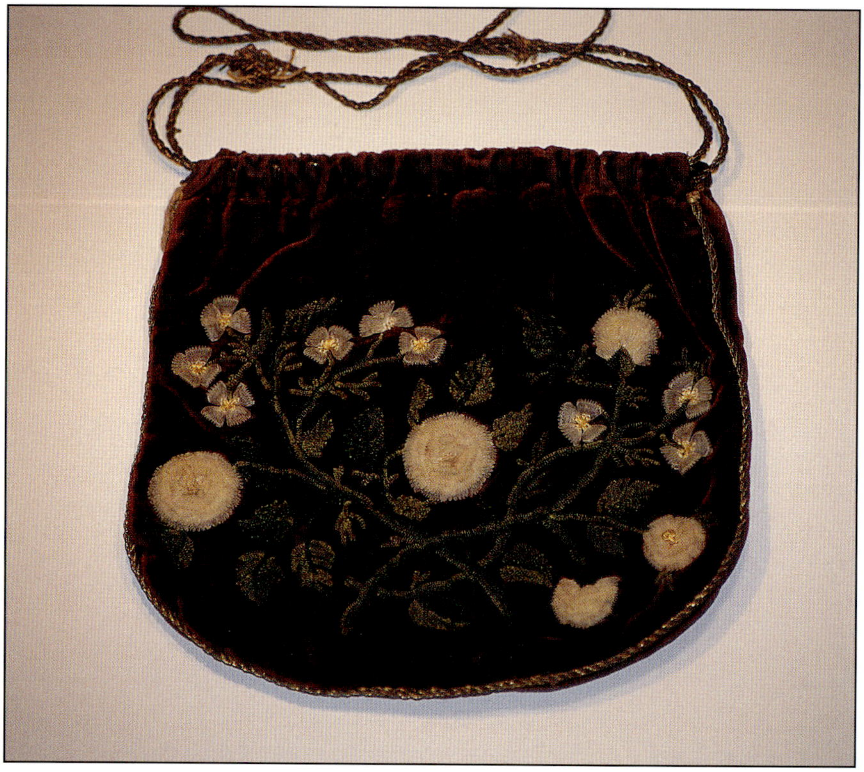

Cranberry velvet reticule embroidered with fish scales and chenille thread. A note that came inside the purse states: "Velvet bag worked by Mrs. Hill of Birmingham (England) 1838-flowers are fish scales." Each of the flowers was made from layered fish scales, which had been soaked, perforated, tinted, varnished, and then pierced with a needle. The preferred fish for this were carp, perch, or goldfish. Most fish scale embroideries were made in England. 7.25 x 7 in. *Collection of Paula Higgins.* Rare.

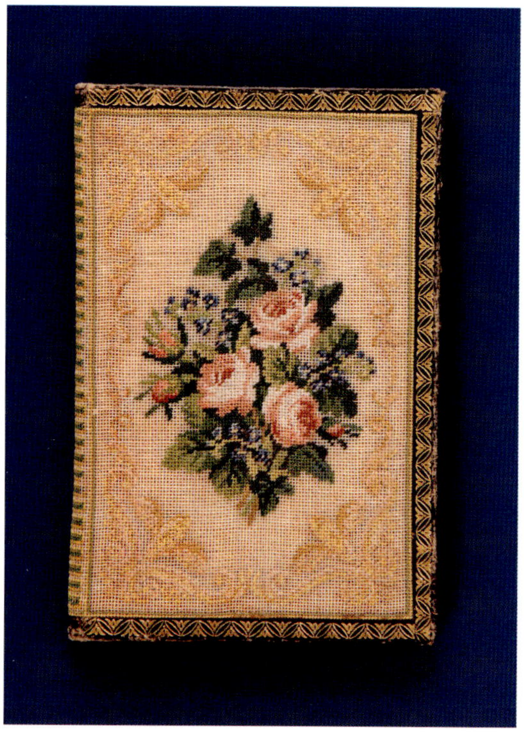

Beautifully designed and worked petit point and leather wallet, dating to c.1830-1840. The leather edge is embossed with gold. 6 x 4 in. *Collection of Sharon LuVisi.* $350-375.

The reverse of the petit point wallet depicting a lyre surrounded by roses. The lyre and rose design was very popular during the Biedermeier Period.

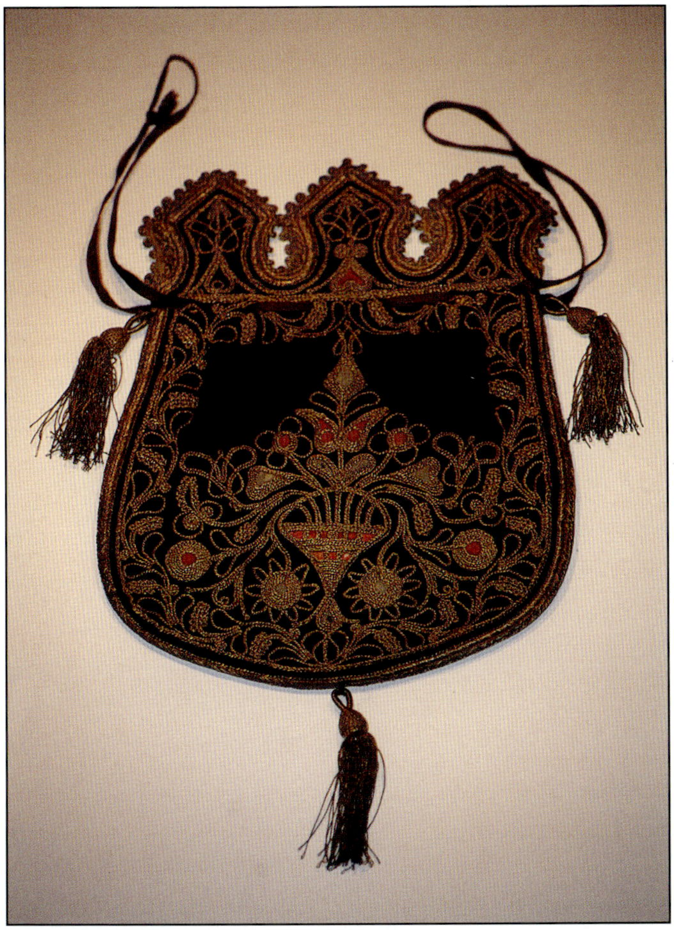

A note inside this purse states: "Uncle (Great) John Stockton brought this purse back from Mexico after the Blackhawk War." This dates the purse to c.1832. The overall design is very Spanish, with heavy, gold thread embroidery on a purple velvet background. The stylized vase of flowers has areas of padding for added dimension. At the top, the purse is crenellated, which is a Gothic Revival design element. Gold metal thread tassels hang from the sides and bottom. 11 x 6.5 in. *Collection of Paula Higgins.* $500-600.

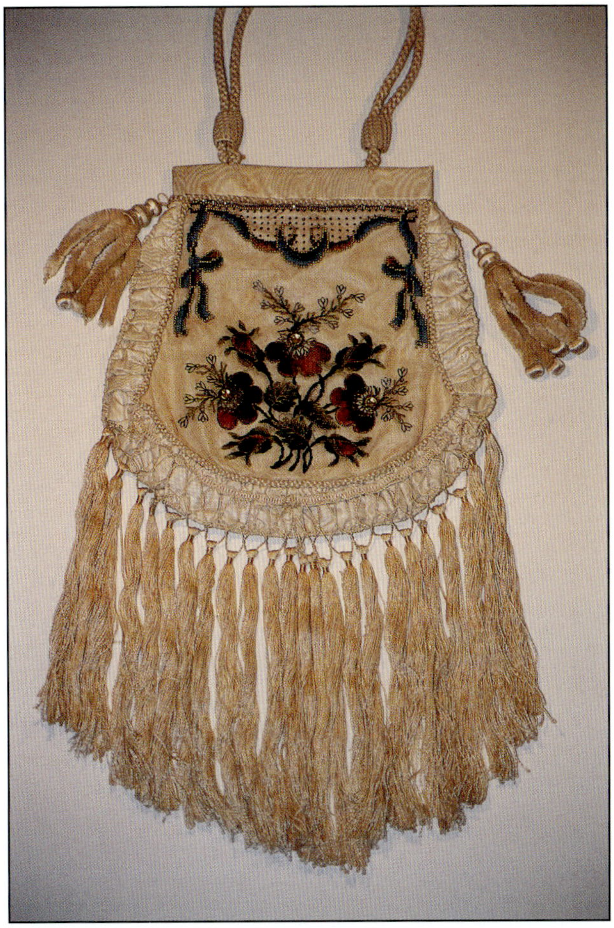

This purse is the epitome of Victorian design and craftsmanship. Although it incorporates numerous types of handwork, the overall effect isn't excessive. Made with appliqué, beads, cut steel buds, gold discs, embroidery, hand tied silk tassels, netted sliders, and chenille tassels, this purse has it all. It is American and dates to c.1840. 14 x 8 in. *Collection of Paula Higgins.* $500-600.

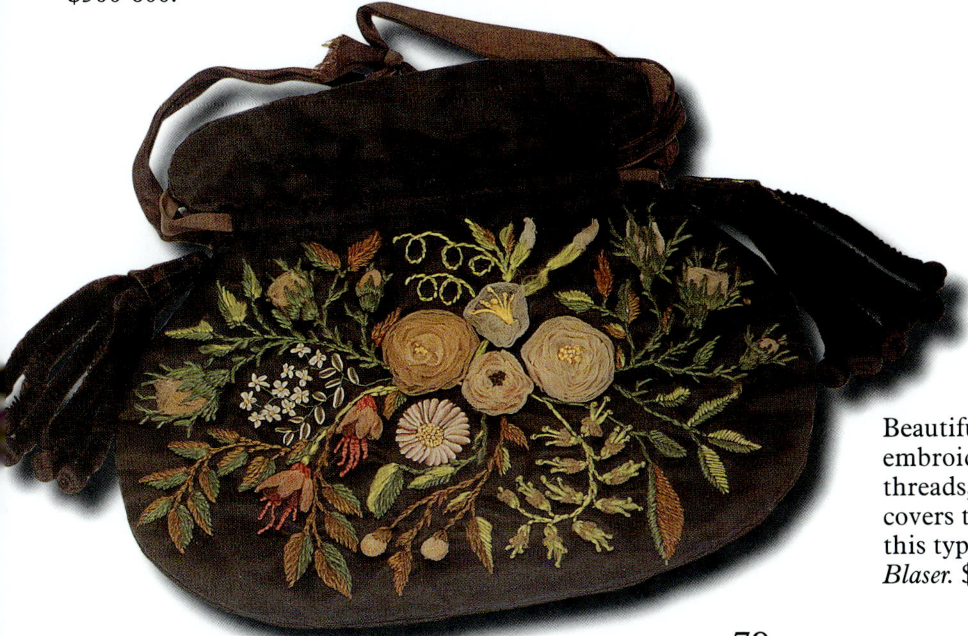

Beautiful, c.1830-1840 black silk reticule embroidered with aerophane gauze, chenille threads, and silk ribbons. The floral design covers the whole purse, which is unusual for this type of purse. 9 x 8 in. *Collection of Lori Blaser.* $350-450.

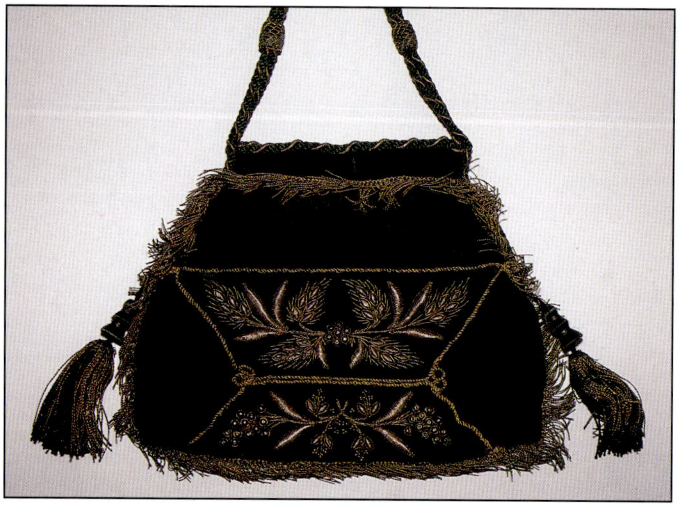

C.1830-1840 green velvet reticule with a wheat design embroidered in gold thread. The whole purse is bordered with gold fringe, and two silk and gold thread tassels hang from the sides. Netted sliders close the purse. 8.5 x 8 in. *Collection of Paula Higgins.* $350-450.

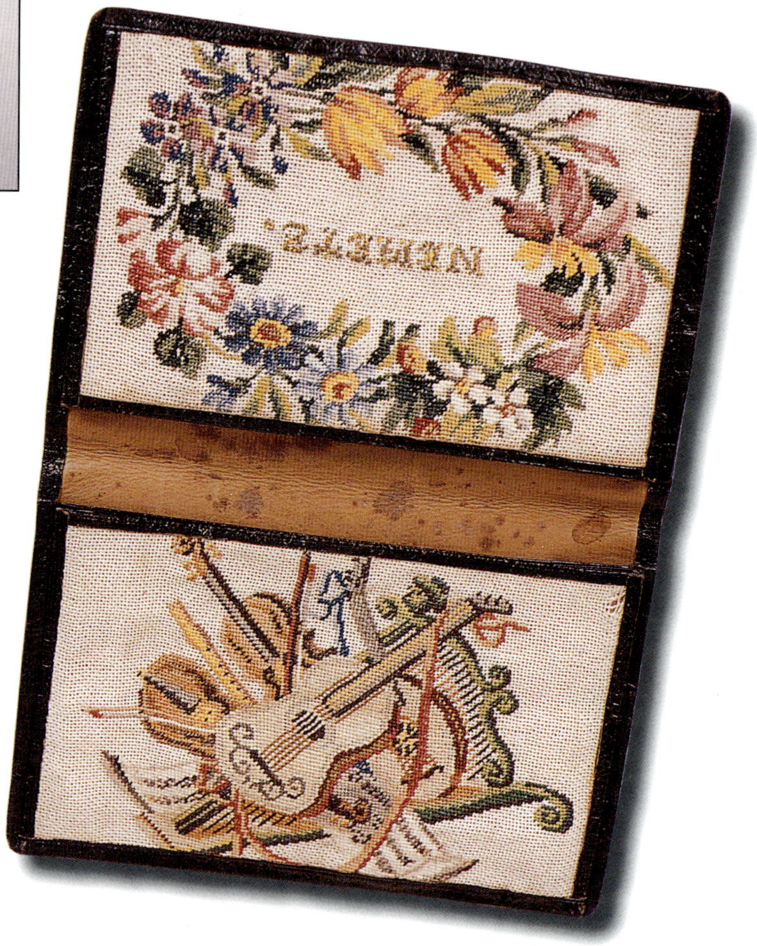

Wonderful c.1830-1840 petit point embroidered wallet with a colorful floral wreath on one side and a scene of musical instruments including a harp, mandolin, and violin on the other side. The exterior is made from leather. 5 x 3.5 in. *Collection of Lori Blaser.* $350-450.

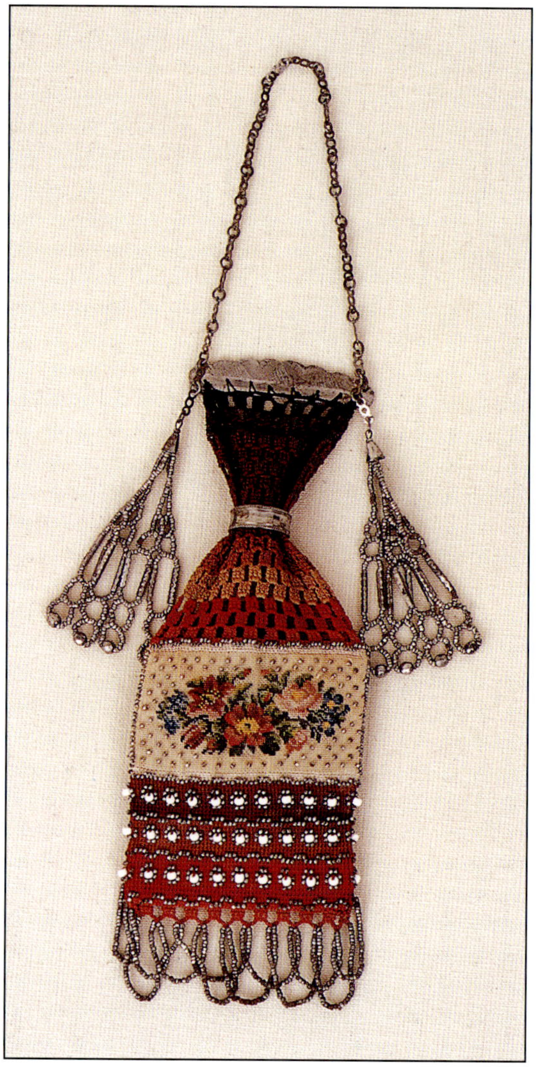

Unusual c.1840 coin purse. Although it has a metal top, it opens by accessing a slit below the ring like a miser purse. It is decorated with a petit point panel, and glass and cut steel beads. It is finished with side tassels and fringe made from cut steel beads. 8 x 2.75 in. *Collection of Lori Blaser.* $300-350.

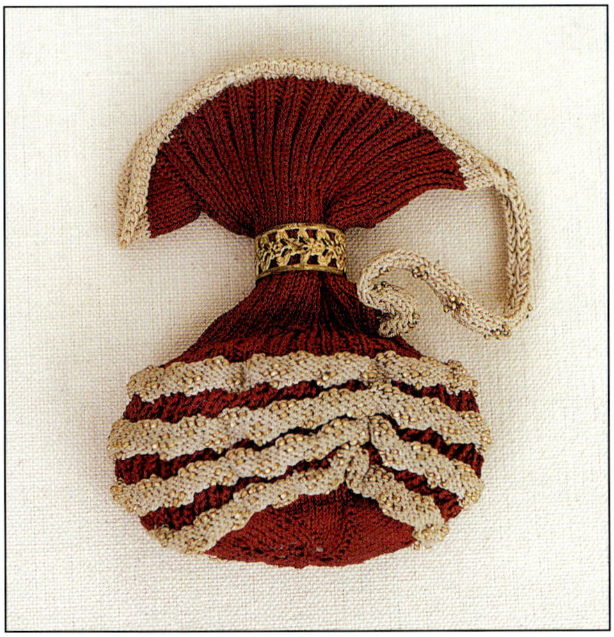

This charming coin purse is shaped like a jug. The gold ring slides up and over onto the handle so that coins can be deposited. It dates to c.1840. 4 x 3 in. *Collection of Lori Blaser.* $200-250.

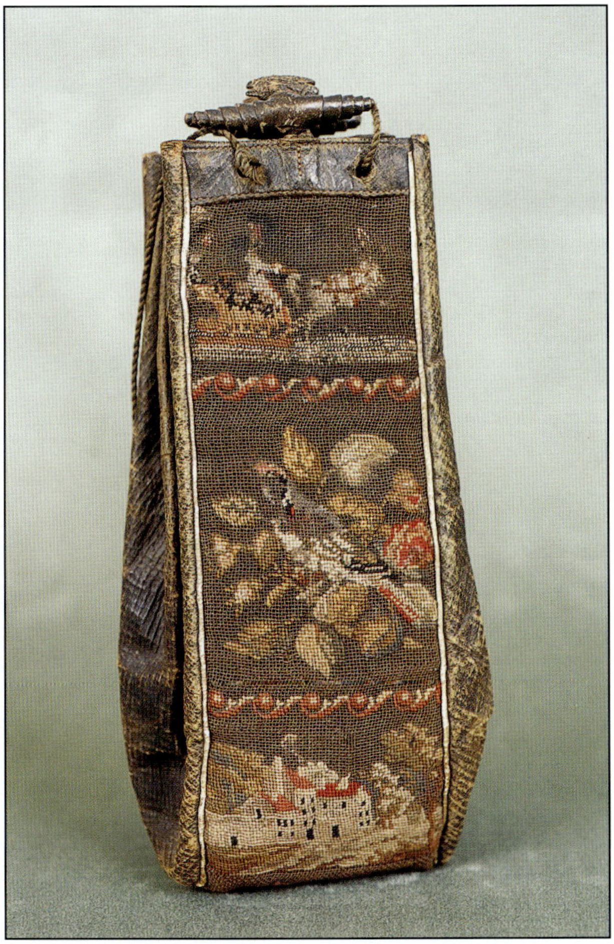

Wonderful Victorian leather and petit point purse made with six different panels. This purse is unusual because of its shape. The petit point is beautifully worked and the designs are very detailed. 8.5 x 3.5 in. *Collection of Lori Blaser.* Rare.

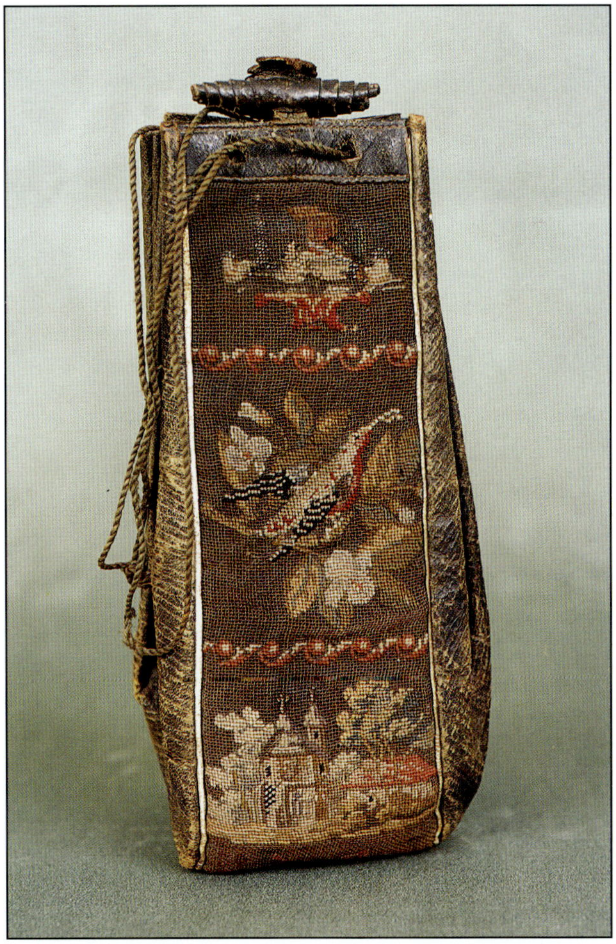

The reverse side of the petit point purse with three completely different scenes.

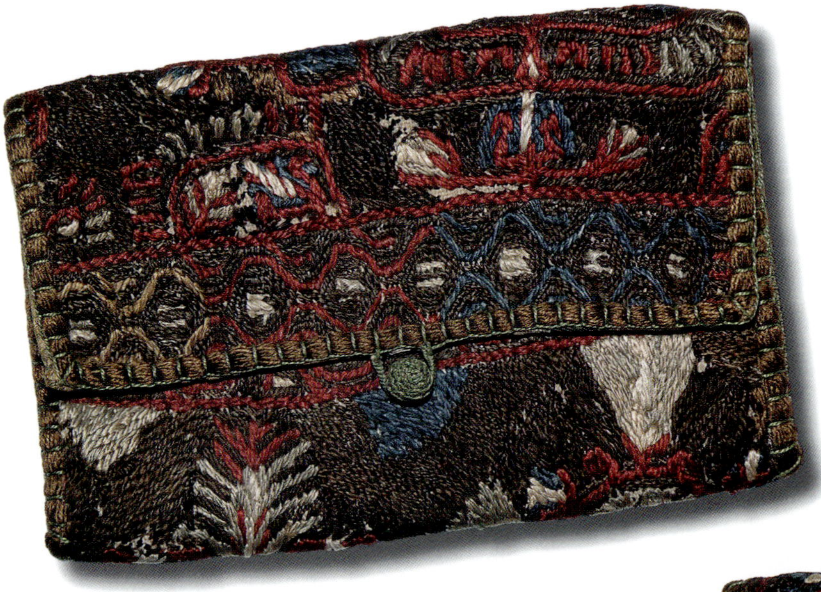

Nineteenth century, American folk art pocketbook, densely crewel worked with silk threads against an olive green background. The interior is lined with a green plaid silk lining. 6.5 x 5 in. *Collection of Paula Higgins.* Rare.

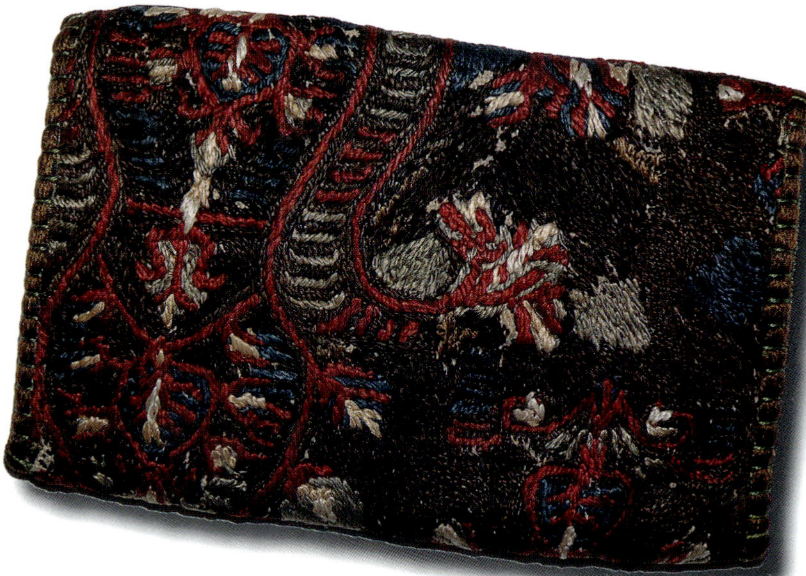

The backside of the purse with more of the compelling free-style embroidery.

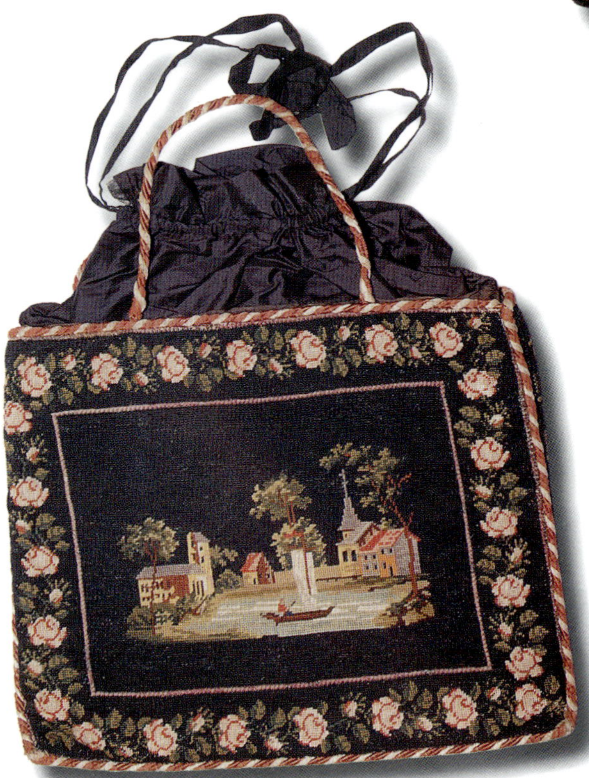

French, mid-nineteenth century purse worked in needlepoint with a petit point scenic design. Inside the bag is an attached black silk reticule, which is original to the purse. Twisted roping borders the whole purse. 10 x 10 in. *Collection of Paula Higgins.* $400-450.

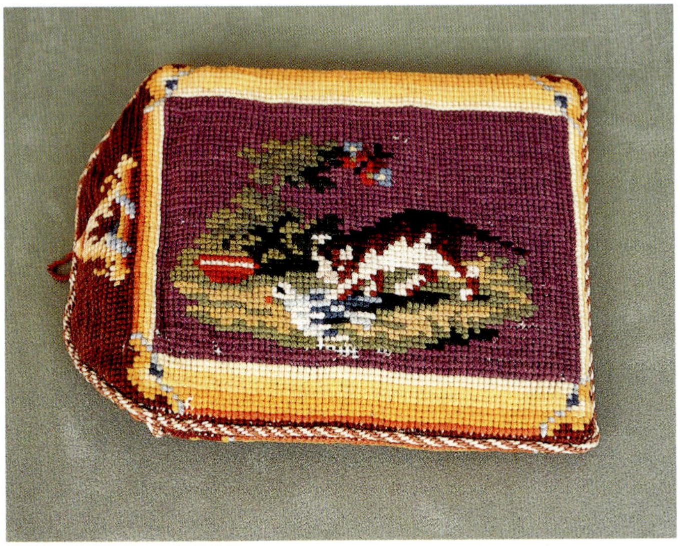

This envelope shaped case is needleworked in colorful wools. Designs featuring animals were popular during the Victorian years. This one shows a cat and a bird. A note was found inside the purse written to Captain Ash from Harriet Hollings, while on board the *Havering*, September 23, 1851. 5.5 x 5 in. *Collection of Lori Blaser.* $300-350.

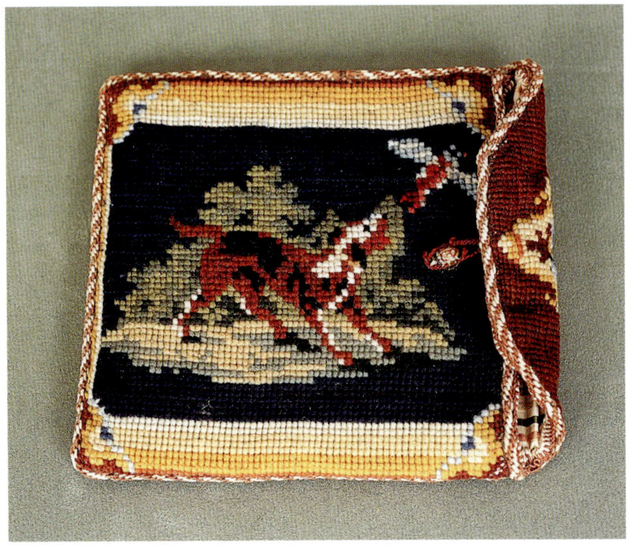

The reverse side of the case shows a dog and bird in flight.

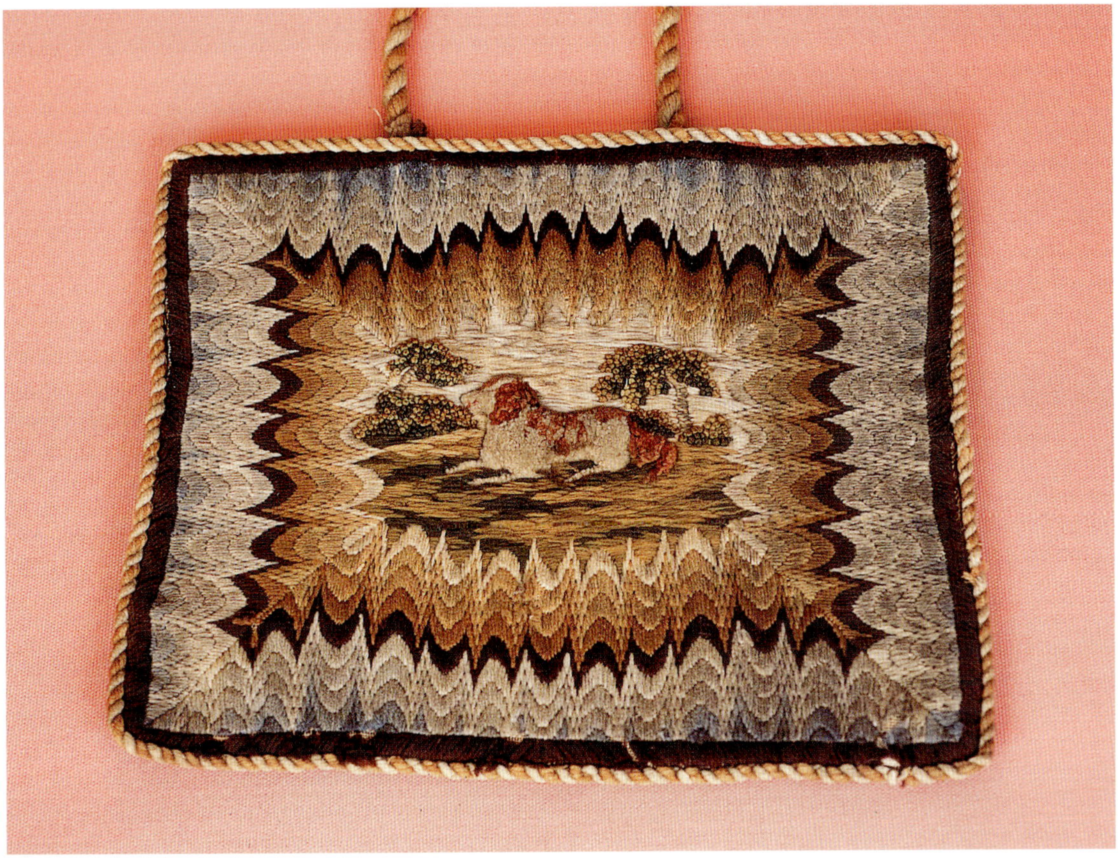

Mid-nineteenth century Berlin woolwork bag with a design of a spaniel set against a flamepoint background. The dog is padded for added dimension. This is a particularly appealing design. 10.25 x 8.5 in. *Collection of Lori Blaser.* $350-450.

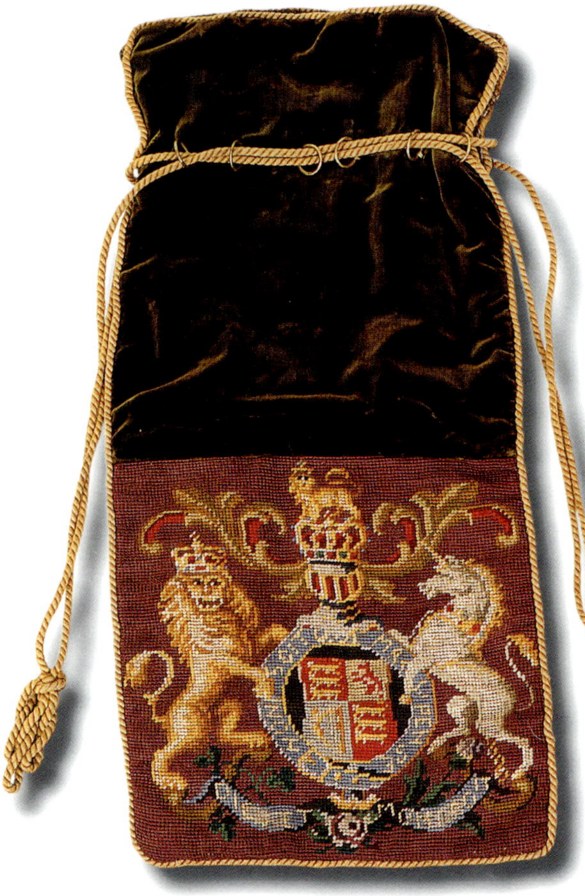

Mid-nineteenth century needlepoint and velvet bag designed with a coat of arms. The coat of arms may be authentic or imagined. The bag is quite long and may have been made for a specific purpose. 15.5 x 7.5 in. *Collection of Lori Blaser.* $350-450.

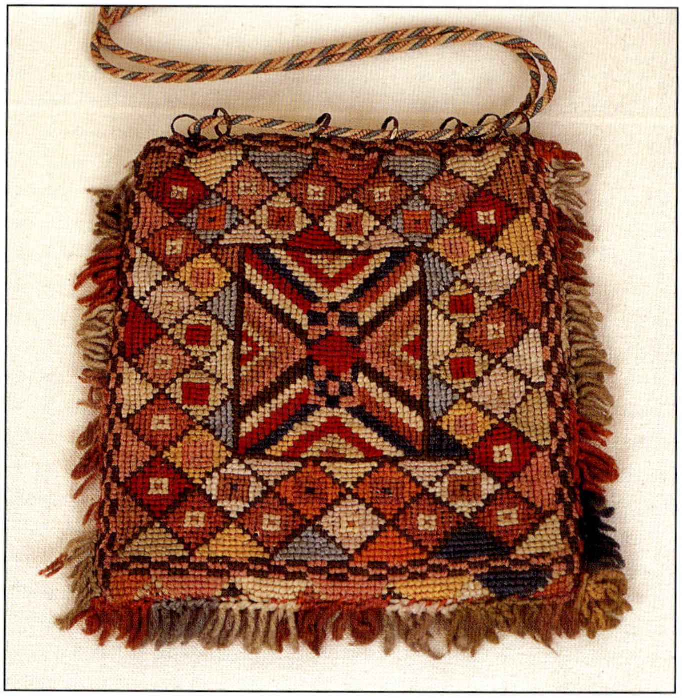

Mid-nineteenth century Berlin work purse. The design and color palette are less traditional and more creative than typical Berlin wool work. It has a folk art quality seldom found on these pieces, which adds to its value. 7 x 6.5 in. *Collection of Lori Blaser.* $400-500.

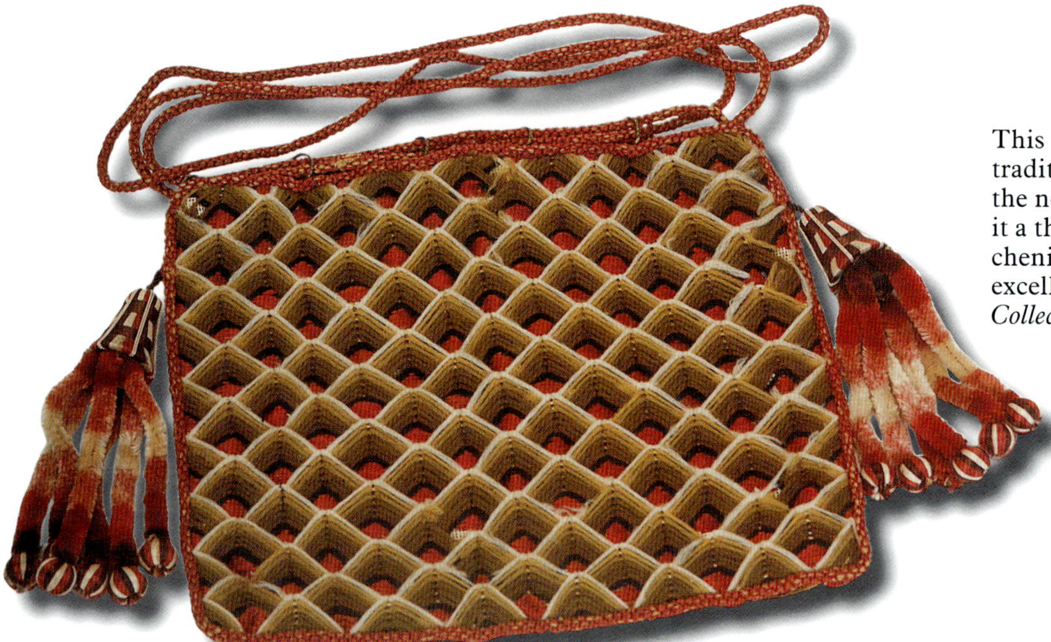

This Berlin work purse has a more traditional, geometric design but the needlework is raised, giving it a three dimensional look. The chenille tassels with silk balls are in excellent condition. 7.25 x 6.25 in. *Collection of Lori Blaser.* $300-350.

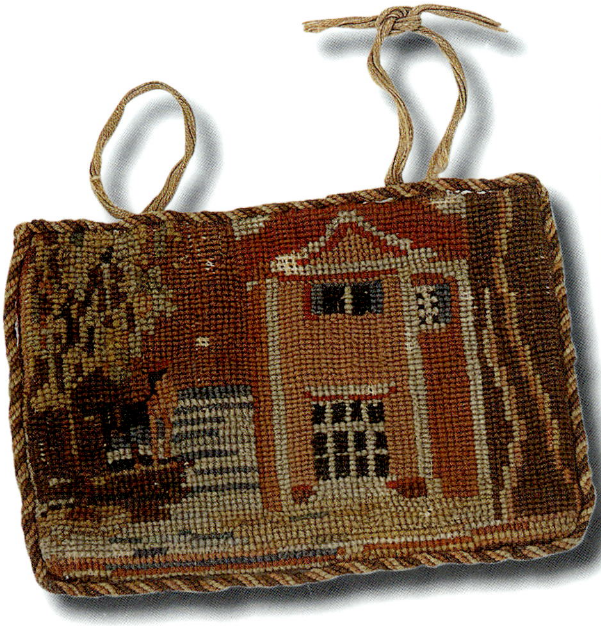

Mid-nineteenth century, needle worked reticule from Maine. This purse is very much in the folk art tradition with its free hand design. It may have been meant for a child since it is fairly small in size. 6 x 4.5 in. *Collection of Lori Blaser.* $300-350.

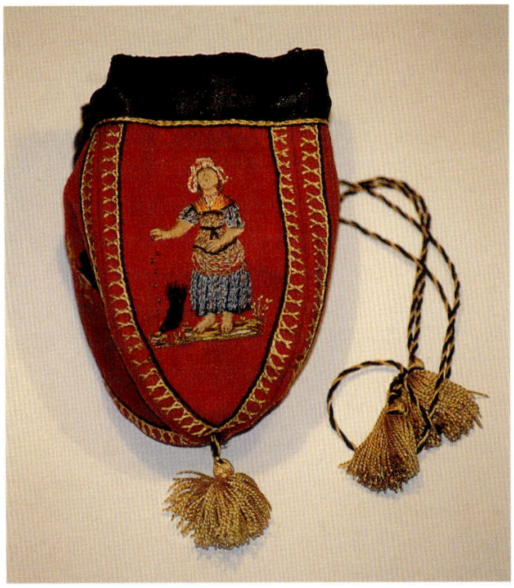

Nineteenth century red wool purse embroidered with a figure of a woman feeding a chicken. This purse has four different panels, each embroidered with a different design. The figures are dressed in the traditional clothing of Bretonne, France and resemble the figures seen on Quimper pottery. 5 x 3.5 in. *Collection of Paula Higgins.* $300-350.

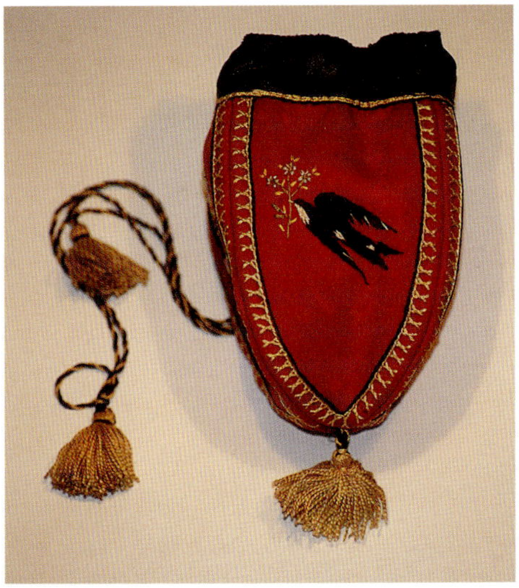

Another panel of the French embroidered purse showing a bird with a sprig of flowers.

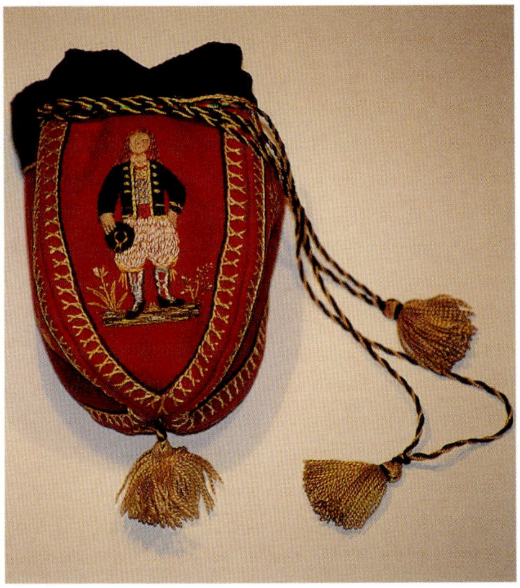

The second figural of a man holding his hat.

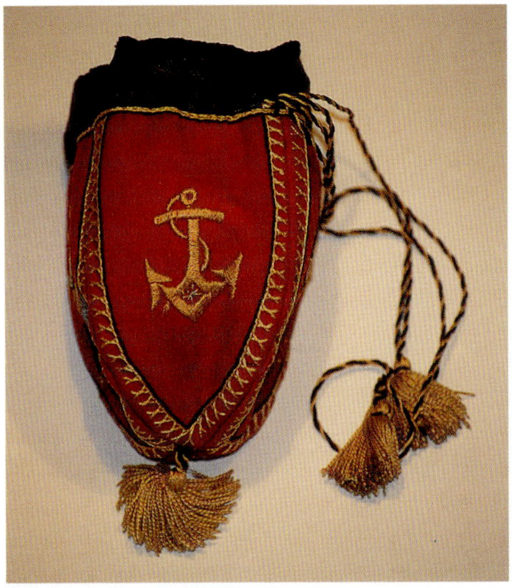

The last panel of the red wool purse embroidered with an anchor. All of these designs would have been popular in French towns along the seacoast. It's possible this was a type of souvenir purse.

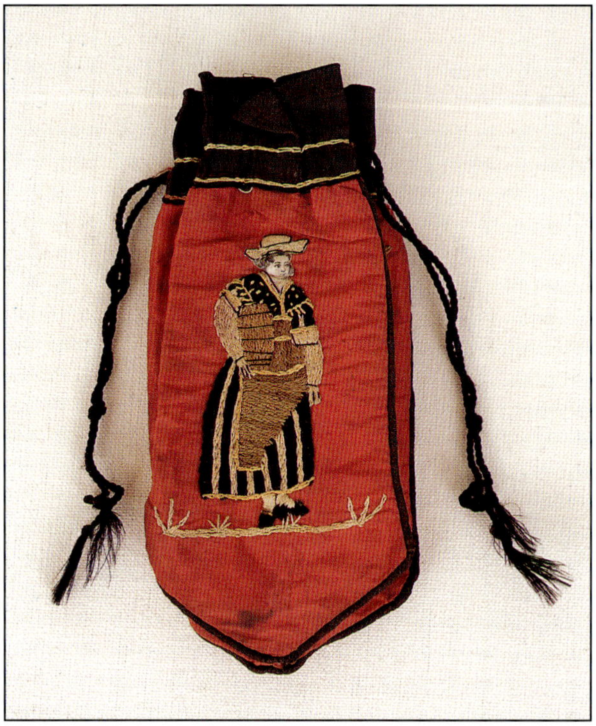

Nineteenth century figural, needleworked on silk with a hand painted face. This purse has four panels with different designs. Bretonne, France. 5.5 x 3 in. *Collection of Lori Blaser.* $350-400.

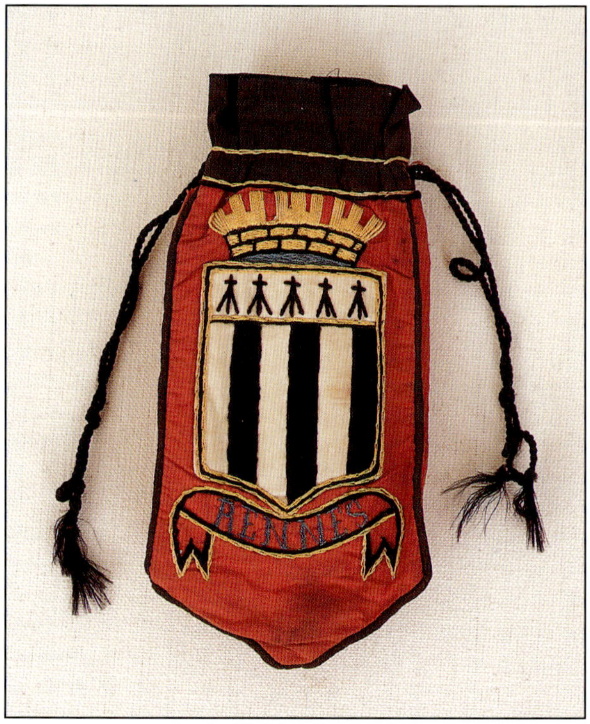

Another view of the silk purse with a coat of arms.

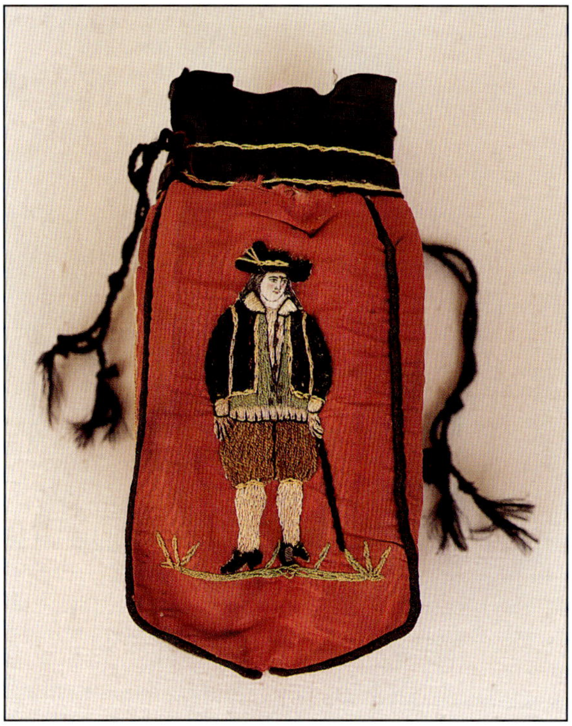

A third panel embroidered with a man dressed in traditional French clothing. His face is hand painted.

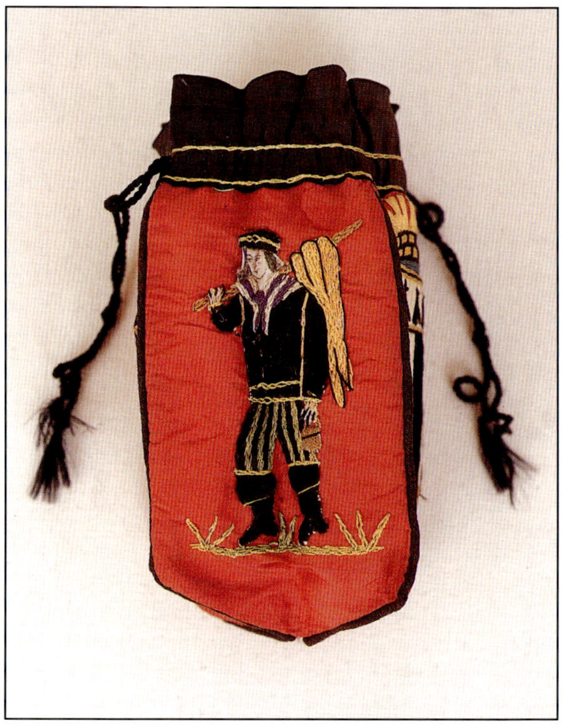

The last panel shows a man in uniform, possibly a sailor. The face is hand painted.

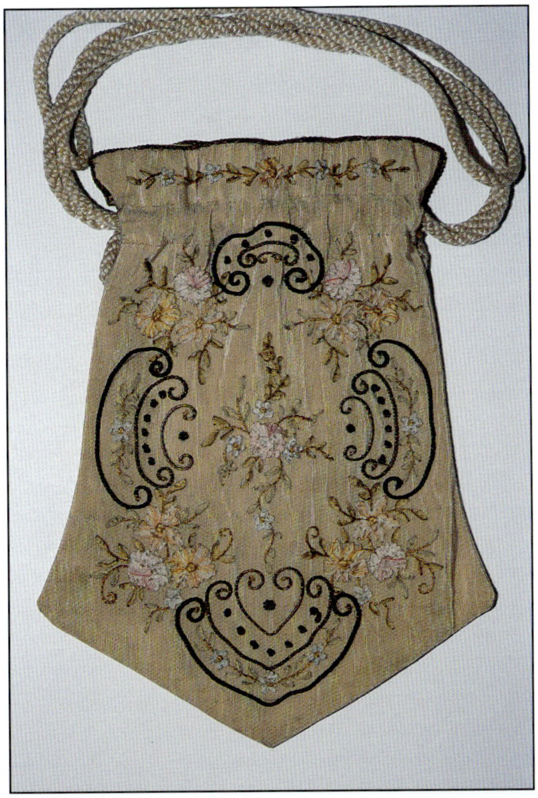

Nineteenth century ribbon worked purse with metal thread accents. Ribbon work was popular from the late 18th century into the early 20th century. Earlier purses were made from China silk ribbons, which were beautifully shaded. 7.5 x 6 in. *Collection of Paula Higgins.* $250-350.

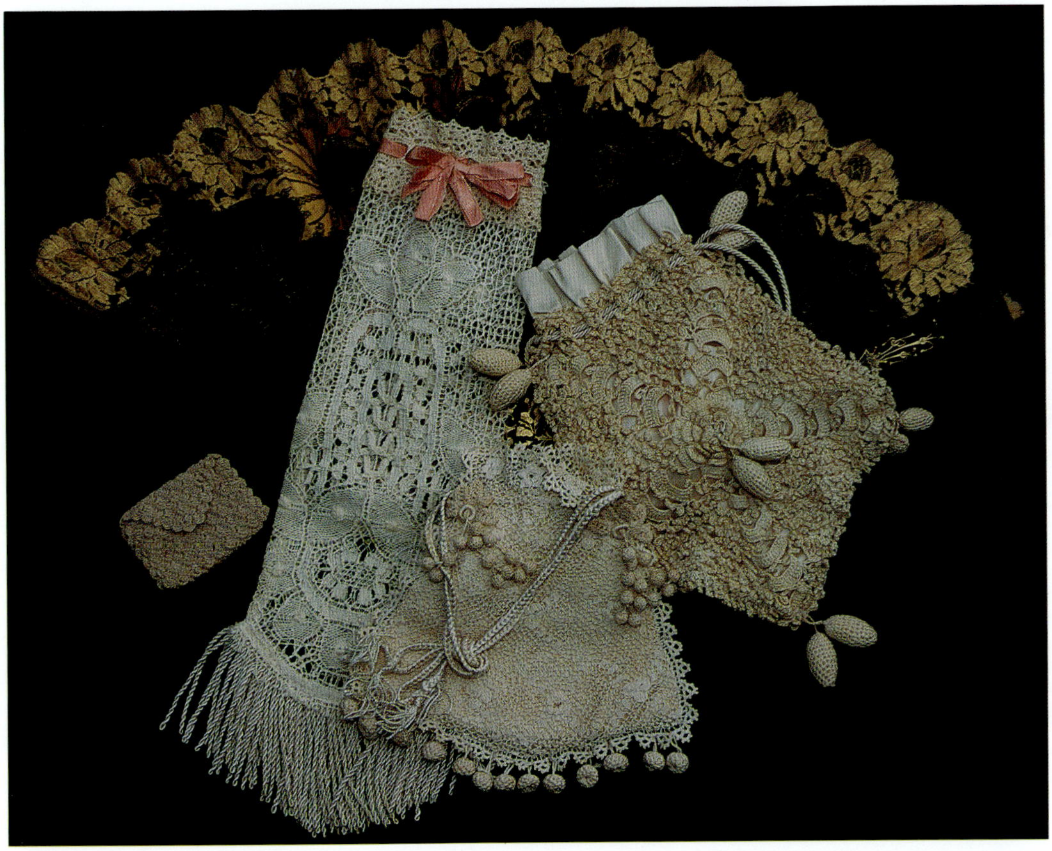

Three lovely, late Victorian crocheted purses. The long crocheted bag was used as a glove bag. The purse in the center is exceptional and made entirely from silk. The ball tassels at the bottom and the sides are beautifully worked. *Collection of Linda Marshall.* Left: $200-250. Center: $300-350. Right: $200-250.

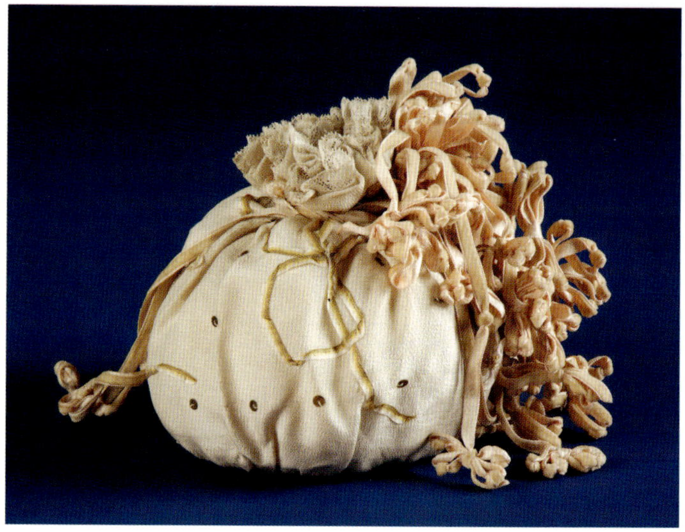

Early 20th century wedding purse. The bag is made from a profusion of beautiful velvet ribbons, which have been knotted to form flower-like tendrils. Lace edging trims the top and sequins dot the body. The overall effect is feminine and lovely. 7.5 x 7 in. *Collection of Sharon LuVisi.* $350-450.

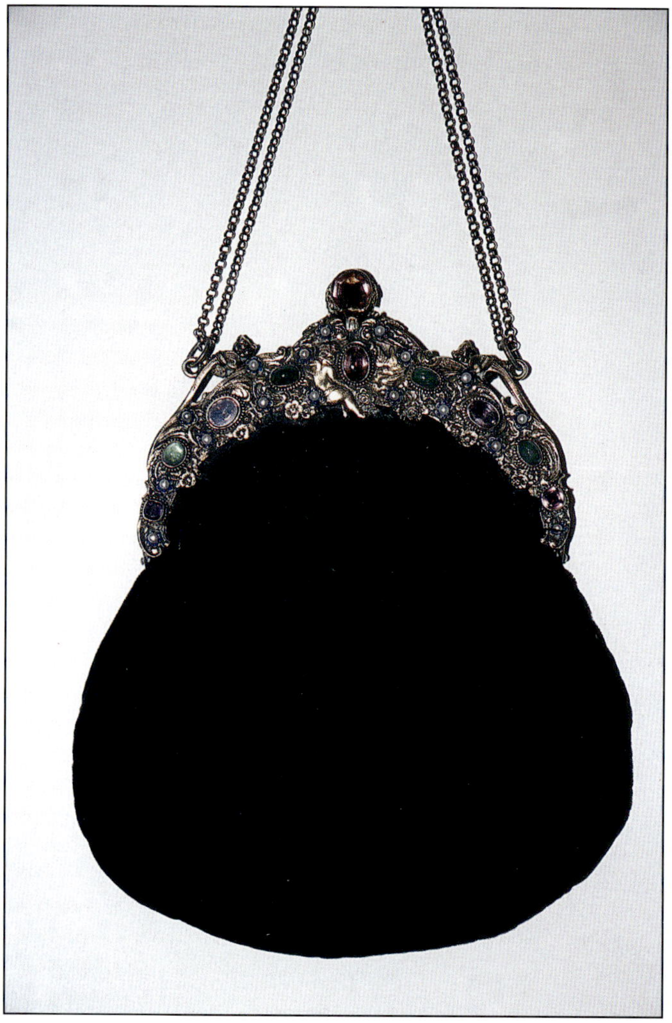

This c.1900 purse was owned by the wife of Gutzon Borglum, the designer and sculptor of Mt. Rushmore in South Dakota. It was sold by their niece in the late 1990s. The plain black velvet bag is attached to an 800 silver-gilt frame set with genuine pearls, emeralds, and amethysts. A cherub, bird, and small flowers decorate the rest of the frame. 8 x 7 in. *Collection of Paula Higgins.* $1,500-1,700.

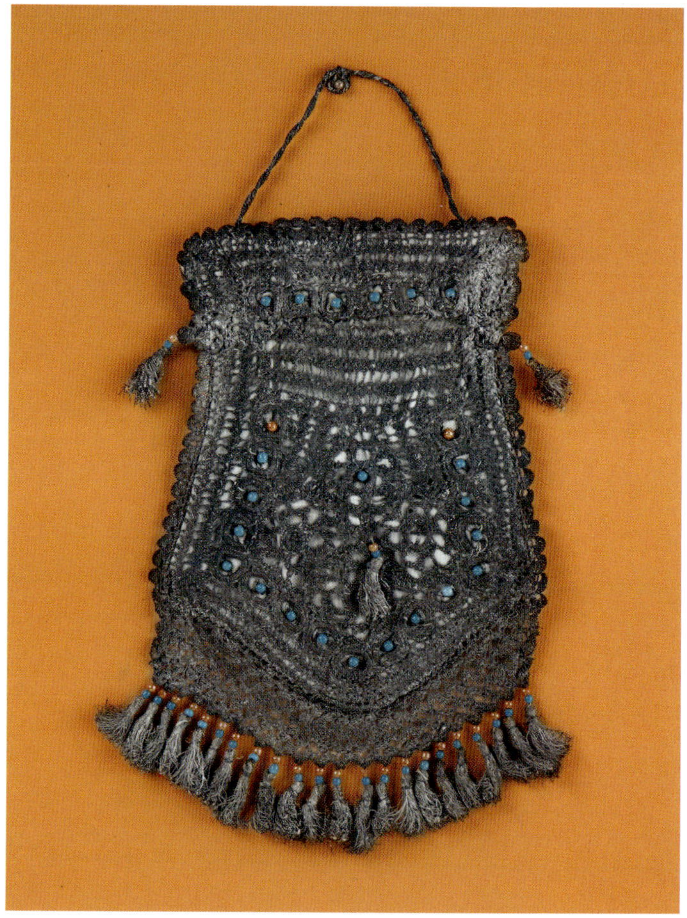

Beautiful metal thread purse, needleworked in an open work design, which is interspersed with coral and turquoise beads. The same beads are also worked into the tassels. Metal thread purses are seen from time to time, but few are as beautifully worked as this one. Late 19th century to early 20th century. Probably Turkish. 8.5 x 6 in. *Collection of Sharon LuVisi.* $450-550.

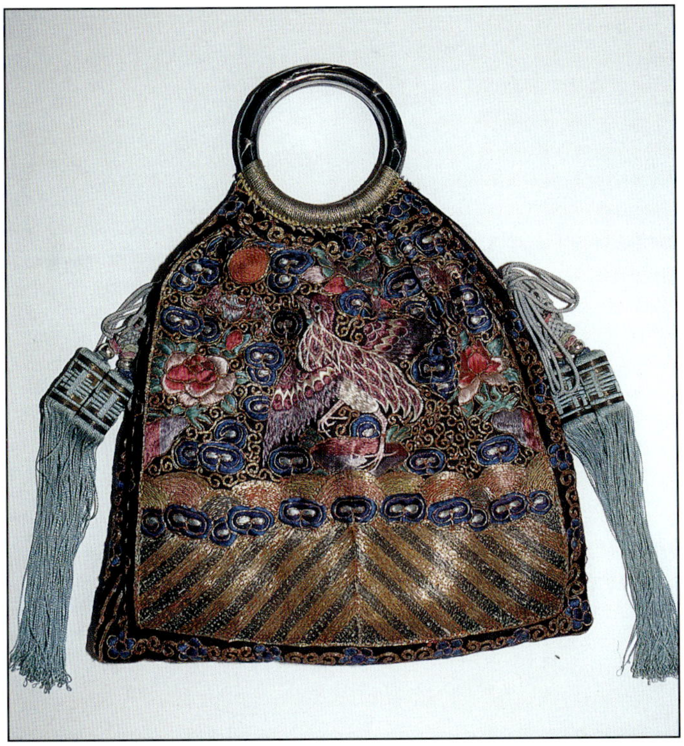

Chinese embroidered silk purse made for the western export market. This style of purse was often made from renk badges worn by Chinese civil servants. This example is quite colorful, which adds to its appeal. The handles are made from green glass covered with brass fittings. Early 20th century fashion design was heavily influenced by exoticism and the orient. Many of the purses designed during this period reflect this influence. 13 x 10 in. *Collection of Paula Higgins.* $250-300.

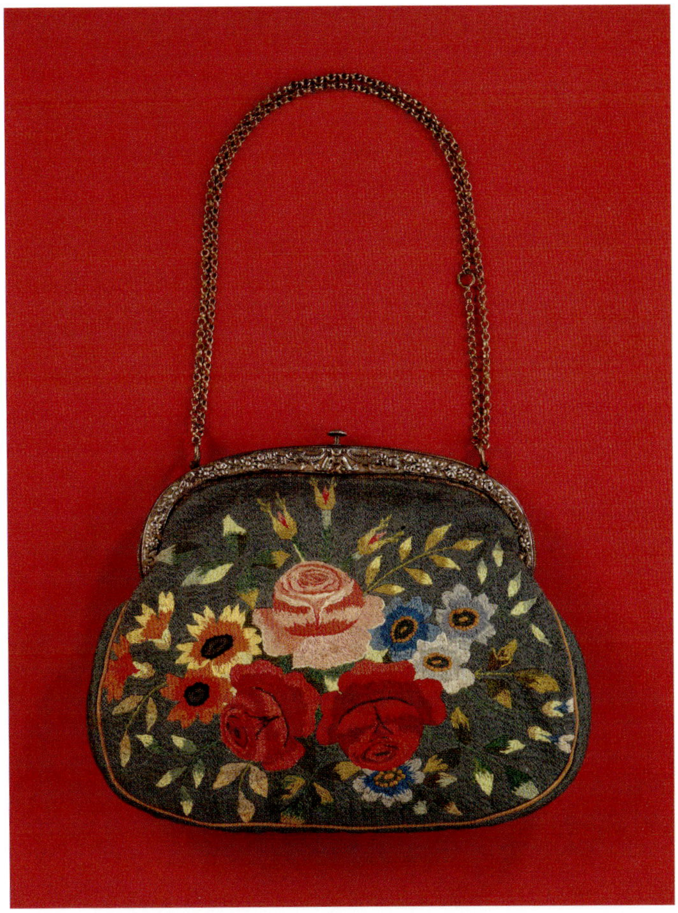

Early 20th century silk stitched purse, mounted on a silver frame. The design covers the whole purse, creating a lush scene. 8.5 x 7 in. *Collection of Sharon LuVisi.* $400-450.

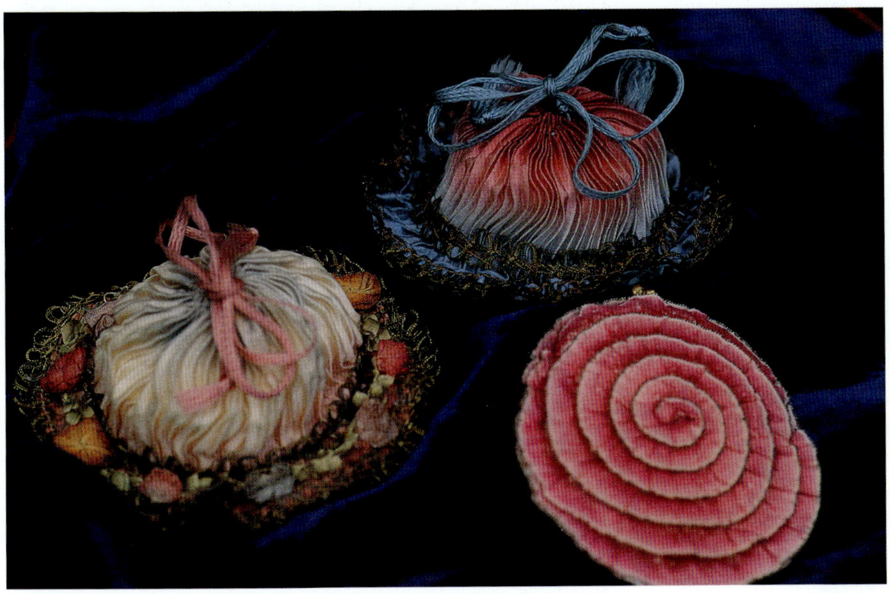

These early 20th century silk purses make for a beautiful picture. The purses at the left and top are made from pleated silks and metallic laces. Silk roses decorate the purse on the left for a particularly lovely example. The purse on the bottom right is made from shaded silk, worked in a circular design. *Collection of Linda Marshall.* Left: $300-350. Top: $250-300. Right: $200-250.

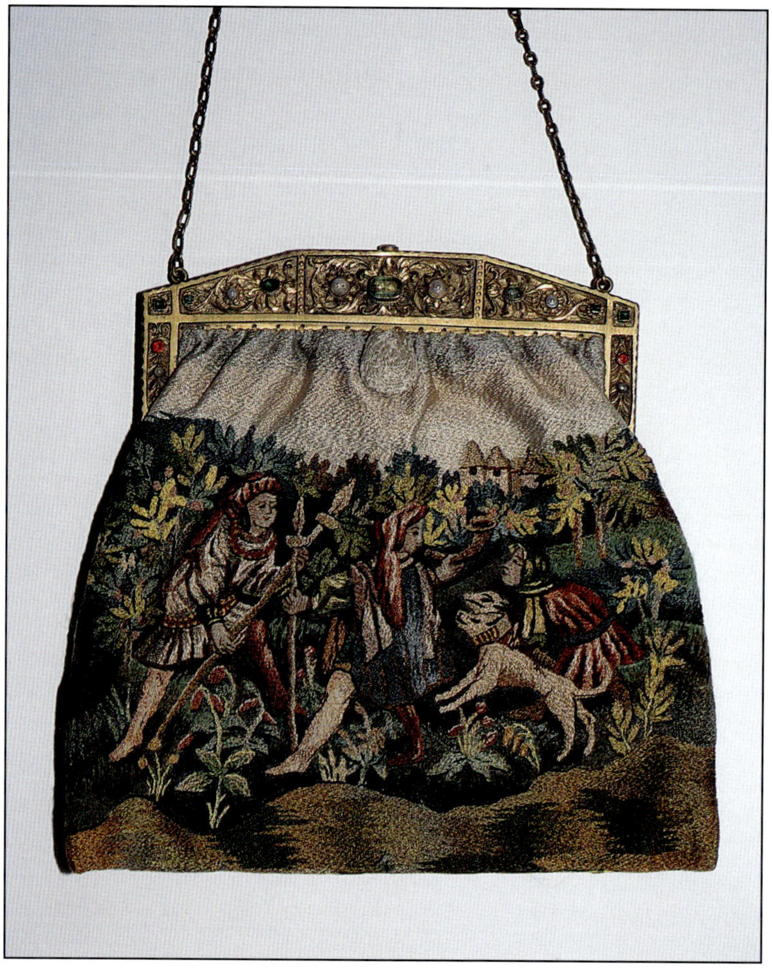

Early 20th century silk stitched purse mounted on a gilt frame set with genuine stones. The medieval hunting scene is unusual, detailed, and covers most of the purse. This purse was expensive when it was originally sold. 9 x 7.5 in. *Collection of Paula Higgins.* Rare.

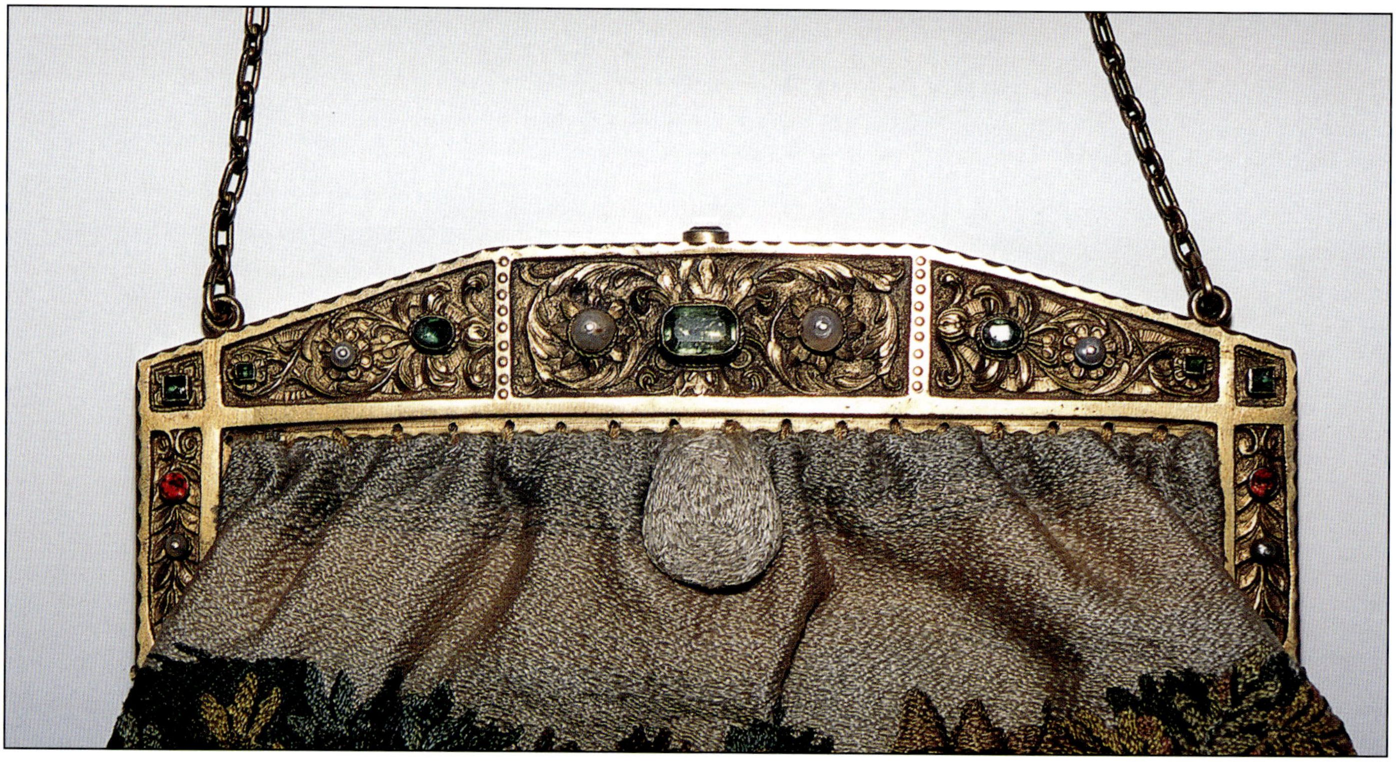

A close-up of the frame set with emeralds, pearls, and possibly rubies.

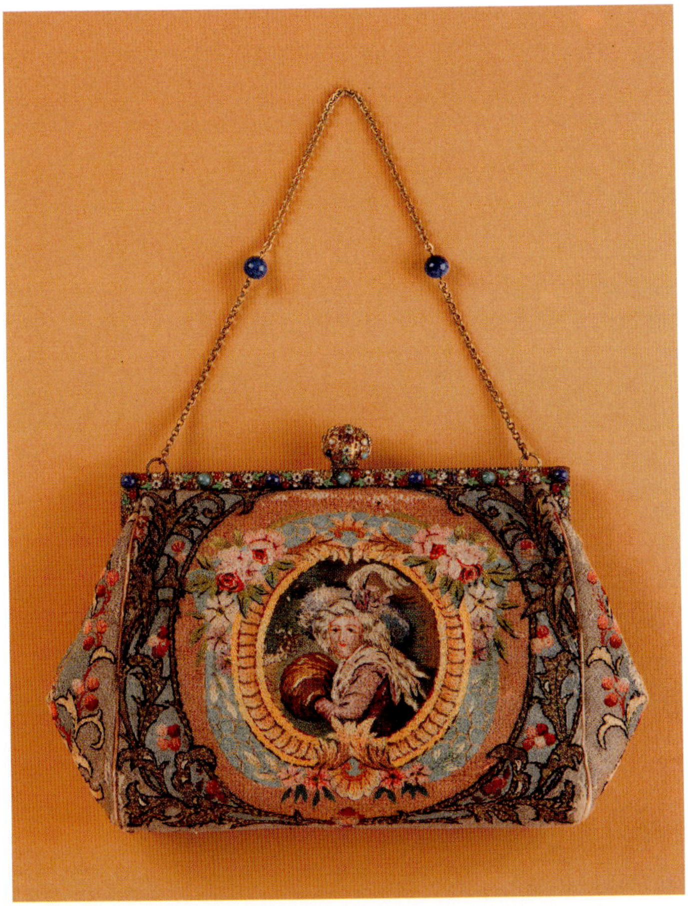

Early 20th century silk stitched purse. In the center is a portrait of an 18th century woman holding a fur muff. The portrait is surrounded by a wreath of flowers, and a border of vines. Even the gussets are silk stitched. The frame and clasp are jeweled and enameled, creating an even richer effect. 9 x 8 in. *Collection of Sharon LuVisi.* $450-600.

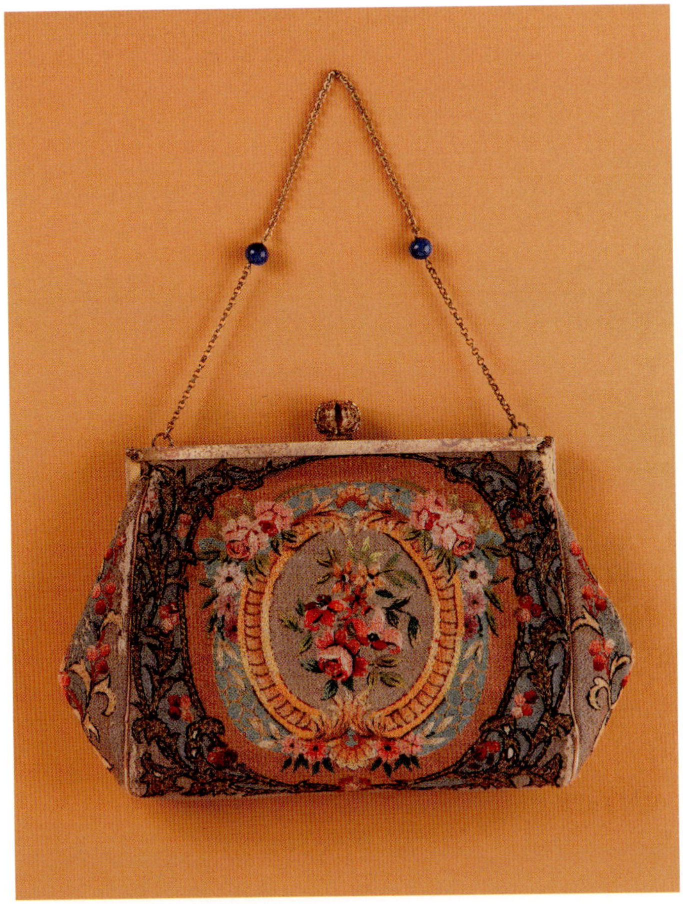

The reverse of the silk stitched purse. The color scheme and floral design are lovely.

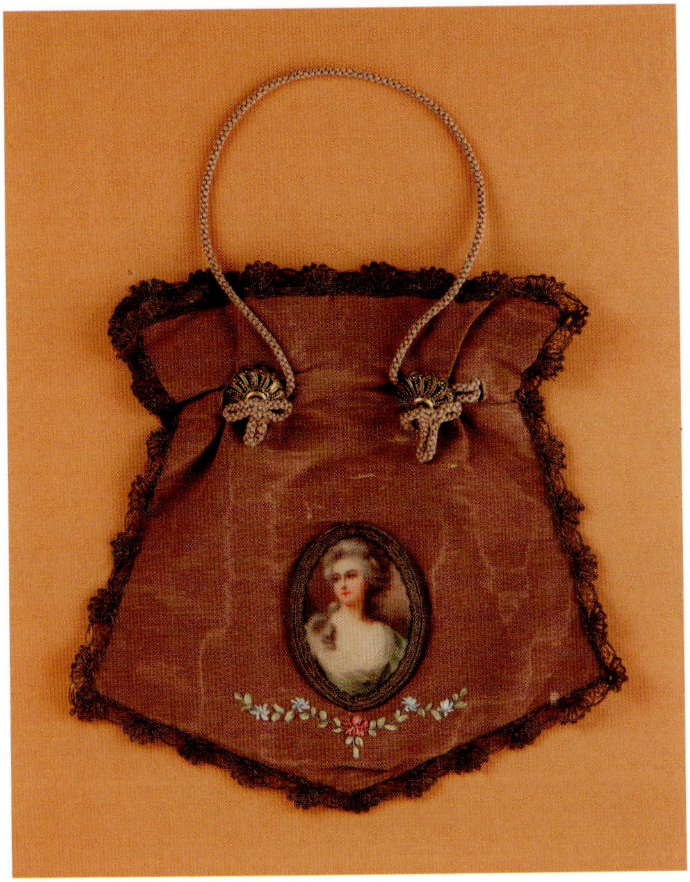

During the early 20th century, reticules were made with portraits of 18th century women. At this time there was a resurgence of interest in the colonial period and all areas of design were influenced by this trend. This is a fine example of the genre. 9 x 9 in. *Collection of Sharon LuVisi.* $300-350.

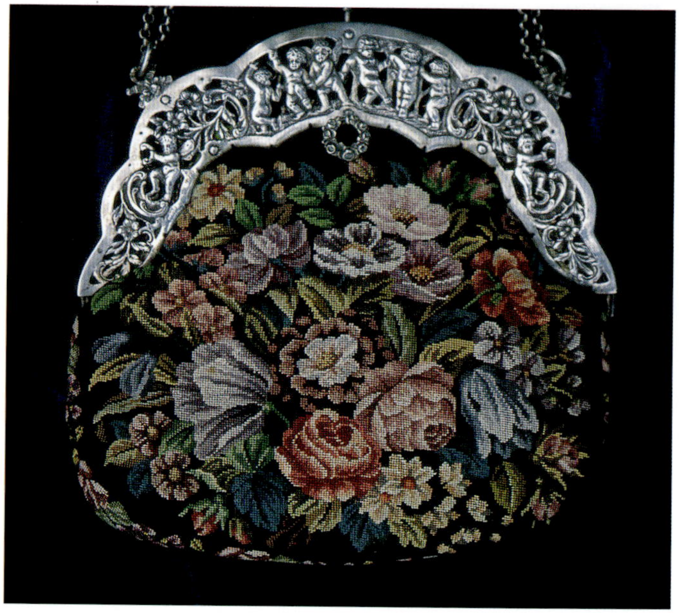

Floral petit point with ornate, pierced silver frame decorated with cherubs. 8.5 x 8.5 in. *Collection of Linda Marshall.* $350-450.

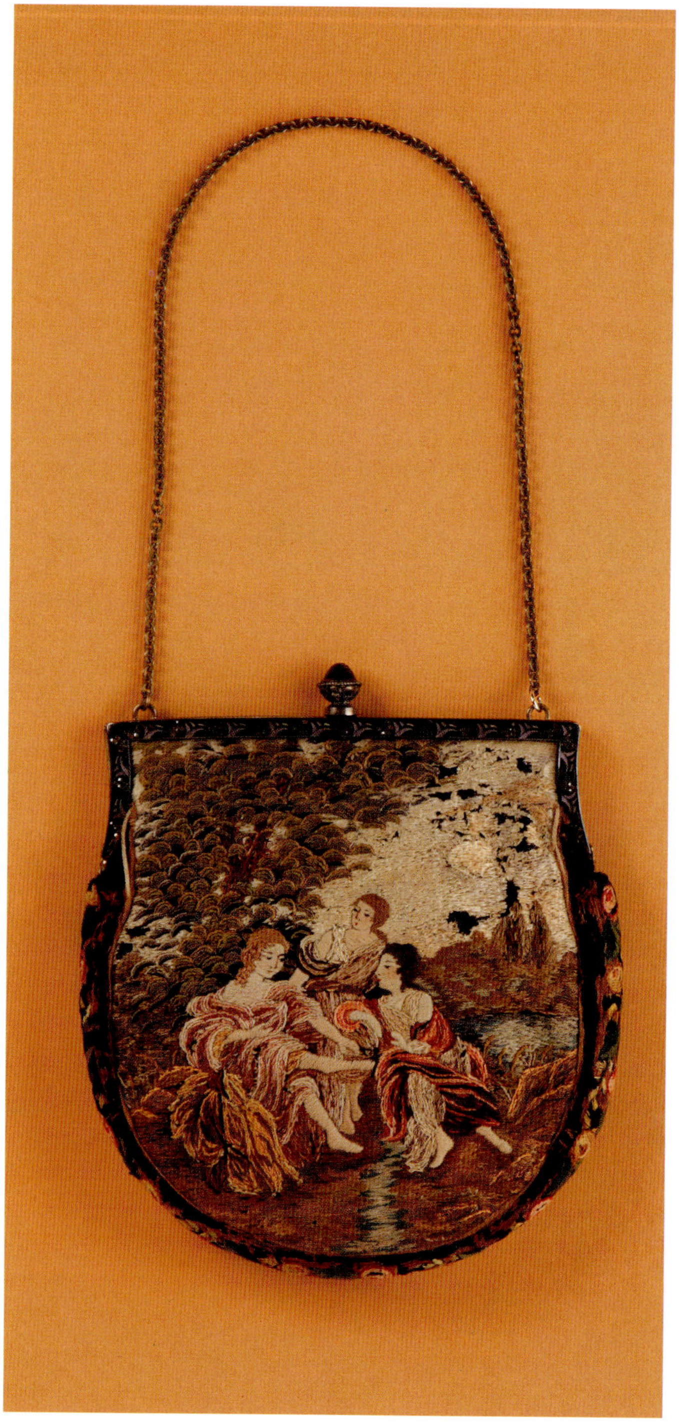

Beautiful silk stitched purse of three women reclining in front of a lake. The effect is like a painting in oils.7 x 7 in. *Collection of Sharon LuVisi.* $450-500.

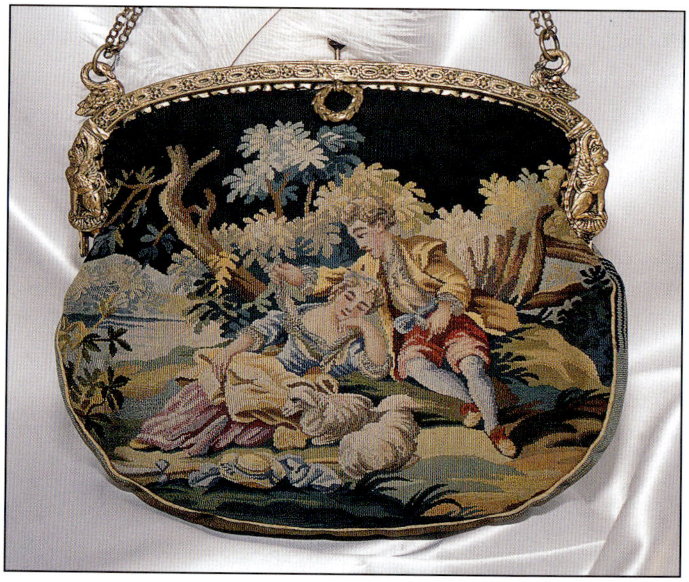

Early 20th century tapestry purse. Tapestry purses from this period often depict 18th century couples in bucolic settings. These purses are also called Aubusson tapestry purses because they resemble the Aubusson tapestry designs from an earlier period. Tapestry purses were usually nicely mounted on gold or silver frames, which were sometimes jeweled. 8.5 x 8.5 in. *Collection of Paula Higgins.* $450-600.

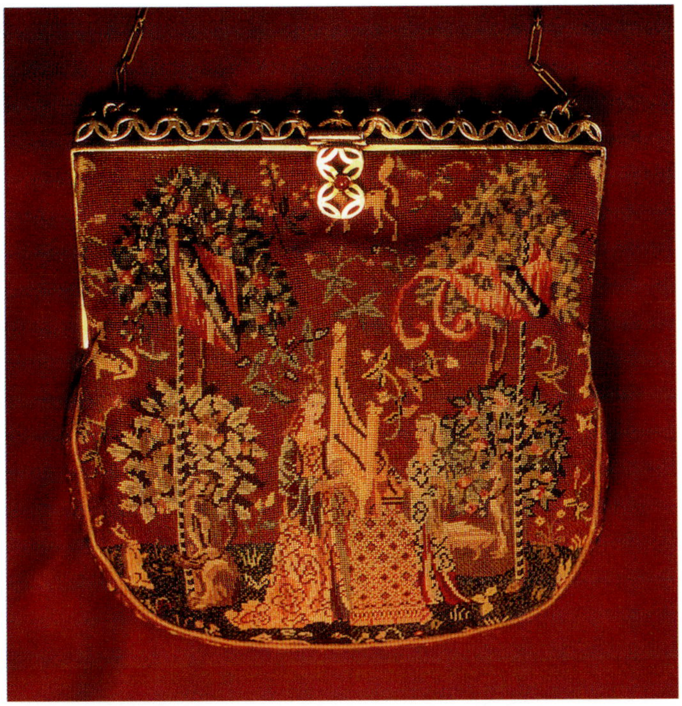

Early 20th century petit point purse. The design of The Lady, Lion and Unicorn is familiar to most purse collectors. Taken from the LeViste family tapestries, the designs vary from purse to purse, but they all have the same theme. The petit point is very finely worked and the red background is very effective. 6 x 6 in. *Collection of Linda Marshall.* $450-550

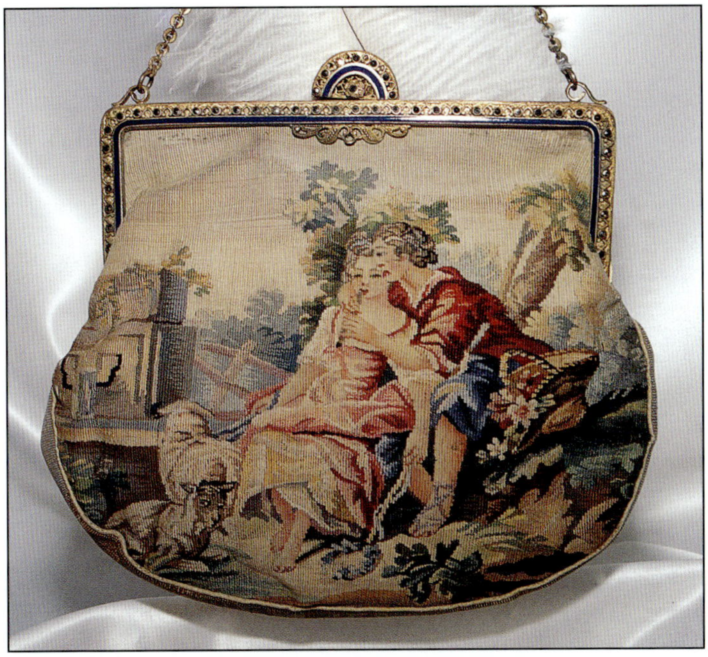

Early 20th century tapestry purse showing an 18th century couple, a basket of flowers, and a lamb. The background is light, which many collectors prefer. 7.5 x 7.5 in. *Collection of Paula Higgins.* $400-500.

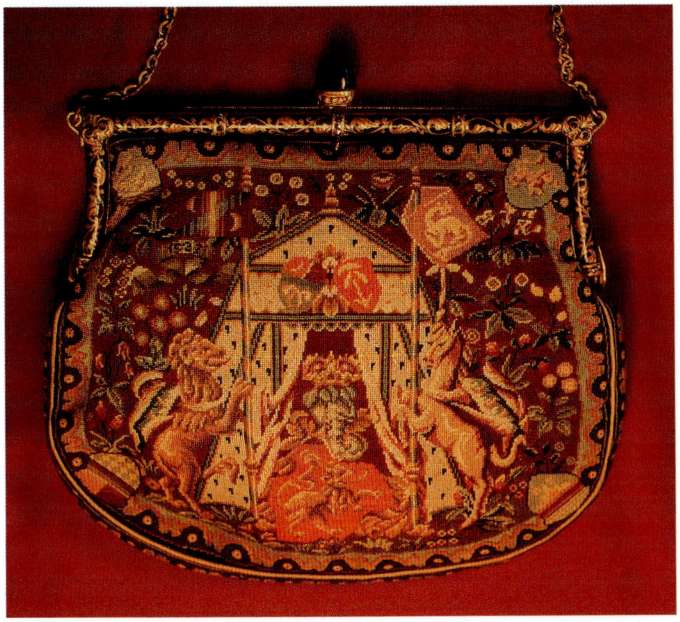

Early 20th century petit point purse showing another version of The Lady, Lion and Unicorn series of tapestries. The purse is mounted on a gold and black damascene frame for a rich effect. 7.5 x 7 in. *Collection of Linda Marshall.* $450-550.

An elegant and beautifully designed and executed purse. Gold thread embroidery surrounds a vase of flowers made from petit point. Small pearls are set into the embroidery at the top and bottom. 6 x 4.75 in. *Collection of Lori Blaser.* $350-450.

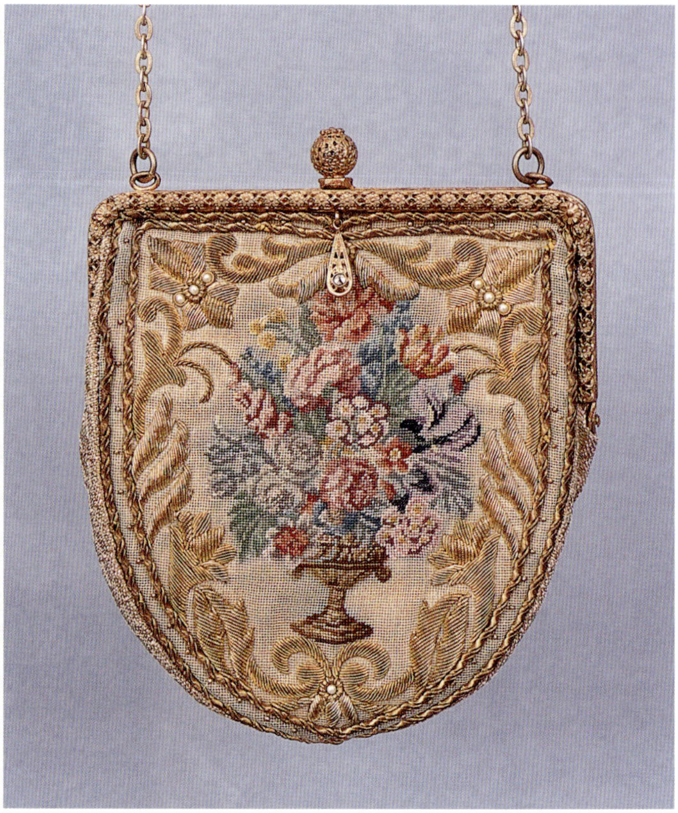

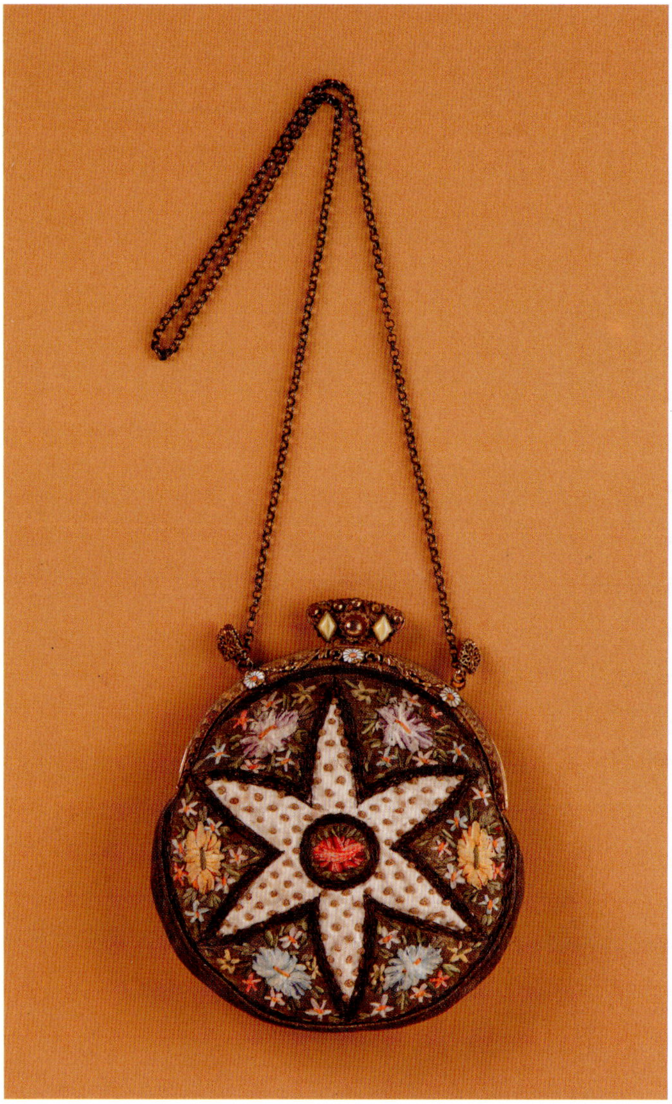

This needleworked purse is unusual. Silk stitched flowers circle a star design in the center. The brass frame is jeweled and compliments the purse design. 6.5 x 6.5 in. *Collection of Sharon LuVisi.* $350-450.

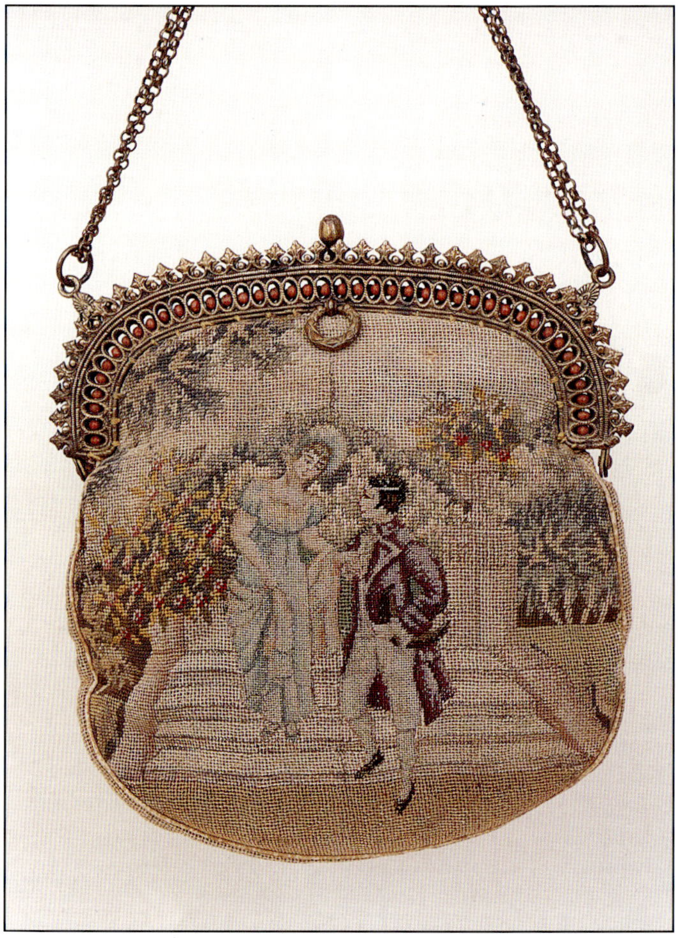

Early 20th century, petit point purse mounted on a frame set with genuine coral beads. 8 x 7 in. *Collection of Lori Blaser.* $450-550.

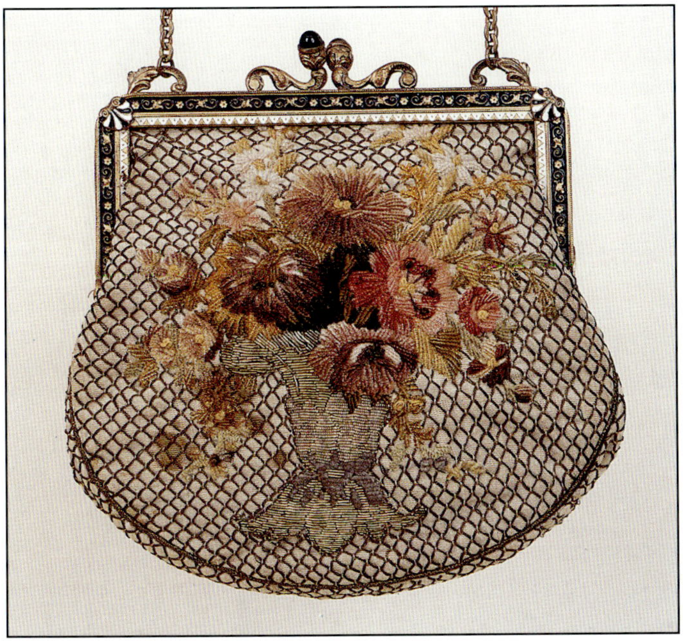

Early 20th century purse with a vase of flowers silk stitched against a background of gold threads. 5.5 x 5.5 in. *Collection of Lori Blaser.* $400-500.

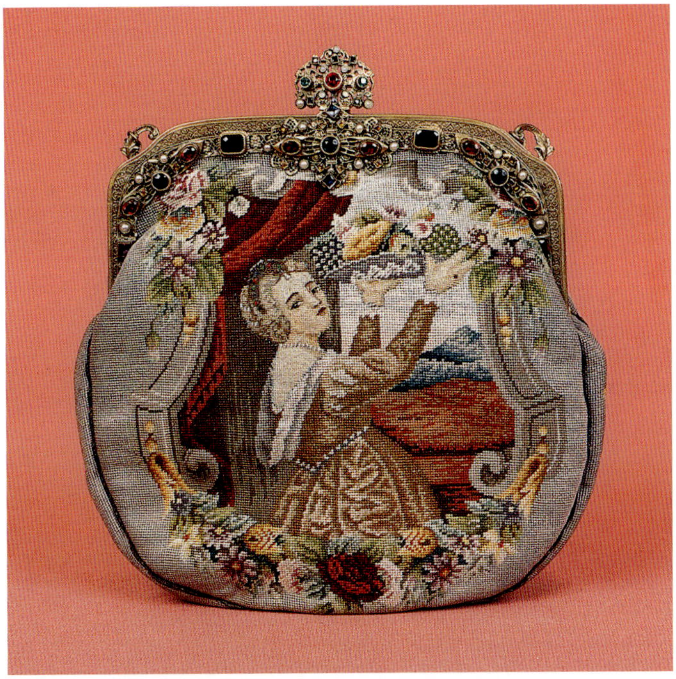

Early 20th century petit point purse. The design is atypical and charming, but the real treasure is the double-sided jeweled frame, which is extraordinary. Frames of this quality add significantly to the value of a purse. 8 x 7.75 in. *Collection of Lori Blaser.* $600-700.

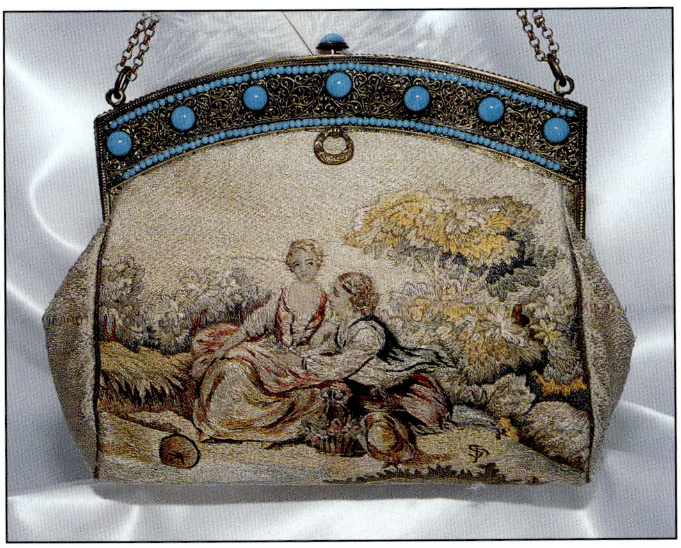

A silk stitched purse with a design of an 18th century couple in a pastoral setting. The figures are also padded for dimension. Again, the frame adds to the value of the purse. The frame is made of pierced brass, and set with faux turquoise stones and beads strung on wire. 8.5 x 6 in. *Collection of Paula Higgins.* $450-550.

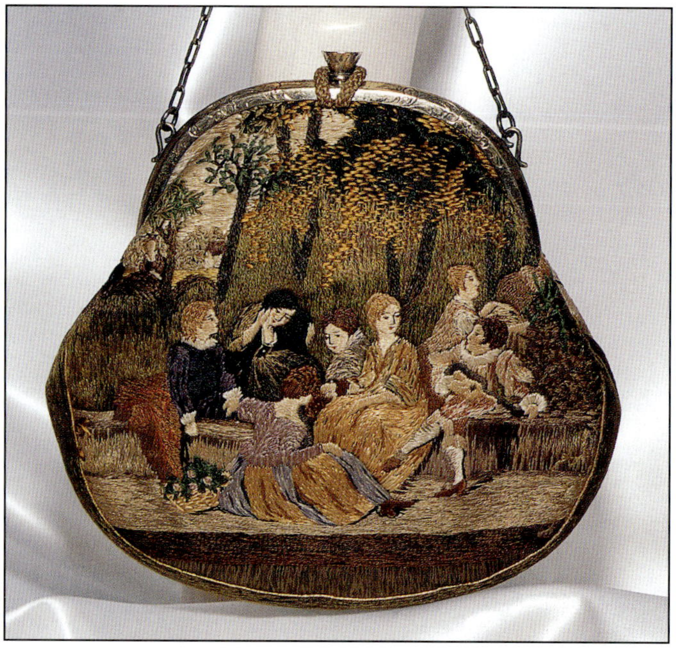

Exceptional silk stitched purse with a multi-figural design. The detail, number of figures, and atypical color scheme sets this purse apart from other silk stitched purses. The reverse side has a different scene. It is mounted on an engraved sterling silver frame. 7 x 6 in. *Collection of Paula Higgins.* $600-750.

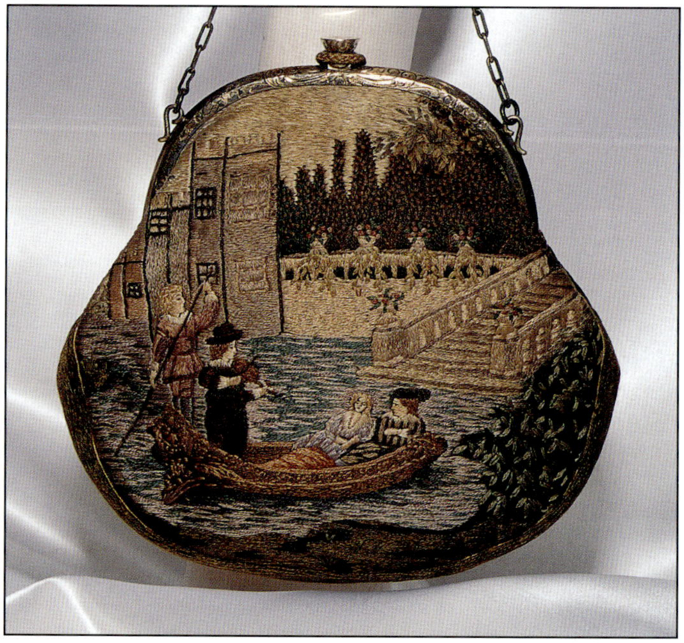

The reverse side of the silk stitched purse with a Venetian gondola scene.

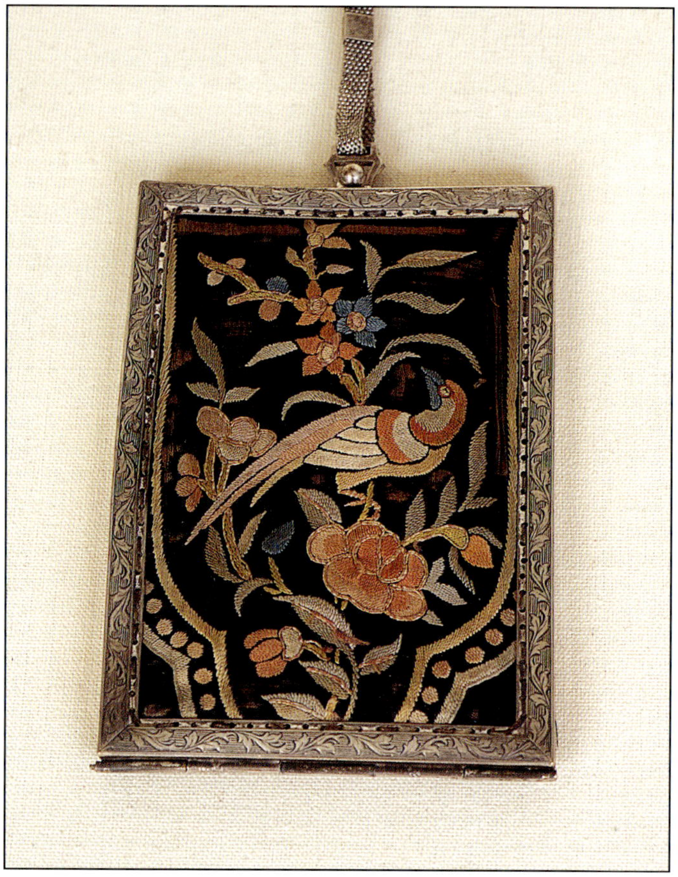

Early 20th century dance purse made from a Chinese embroidery, set in an engraved silver frame with a mesh strap. 5.5 x 3.5 in. *Collection of Lori Blaser.* $250-300.

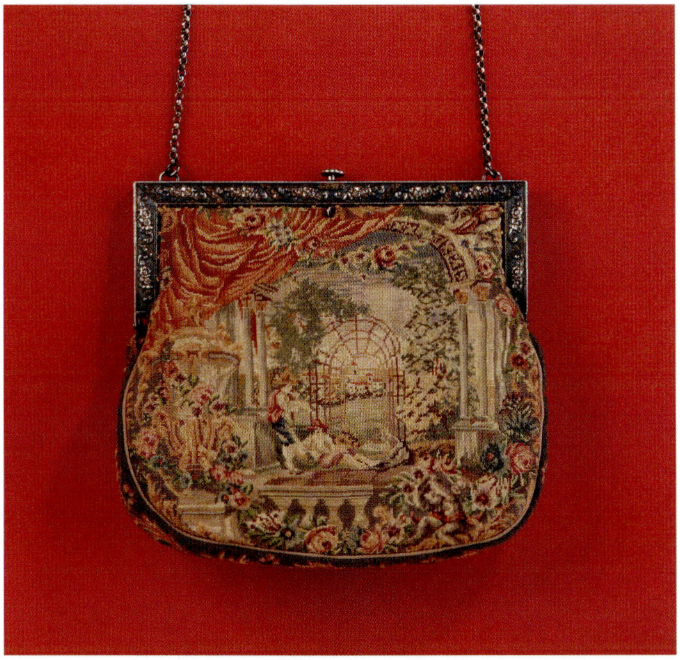

Petit point purse with a detailed scene and a lovely color scheme. 7.5 x 7.5 in. *Collection of Sharon LuVisi.* $400-450.

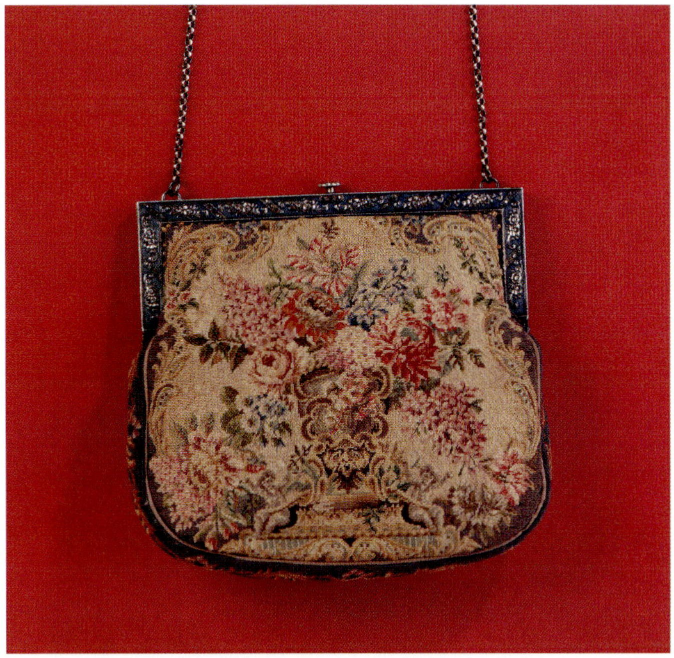

The reverse of the petit point purse has a design of a vase overflowing with flowers.

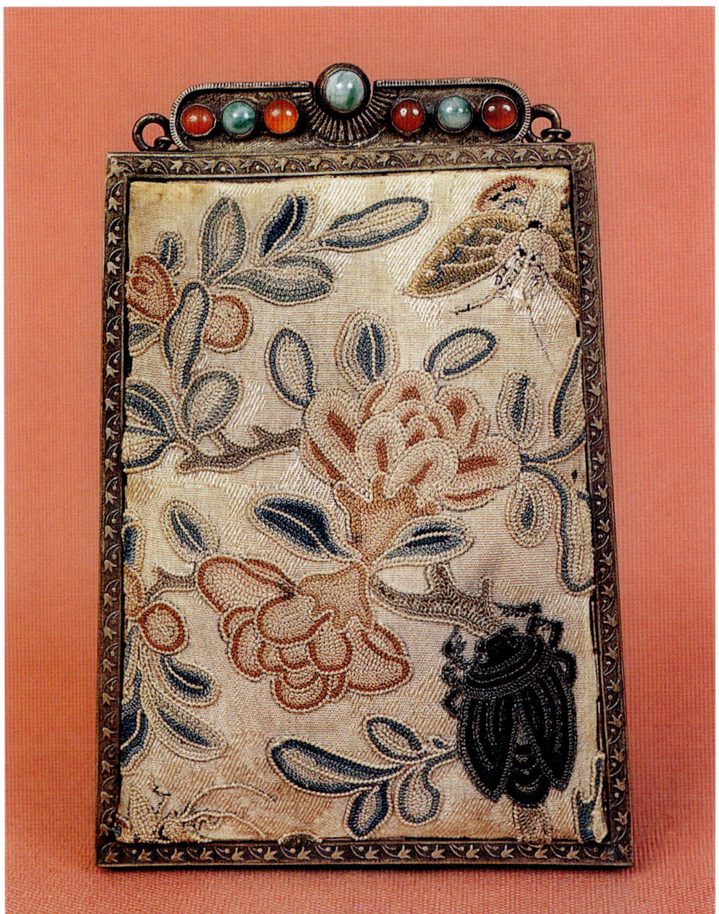

Dance purse made from tambour stitched Chinese embroidery, set into a jade jeweled frame. At the bottom, a black beetle can be seen climbing up one of the flowers. 5.75 x 4 in. *Collection of Lori Blaser.* $350-450.

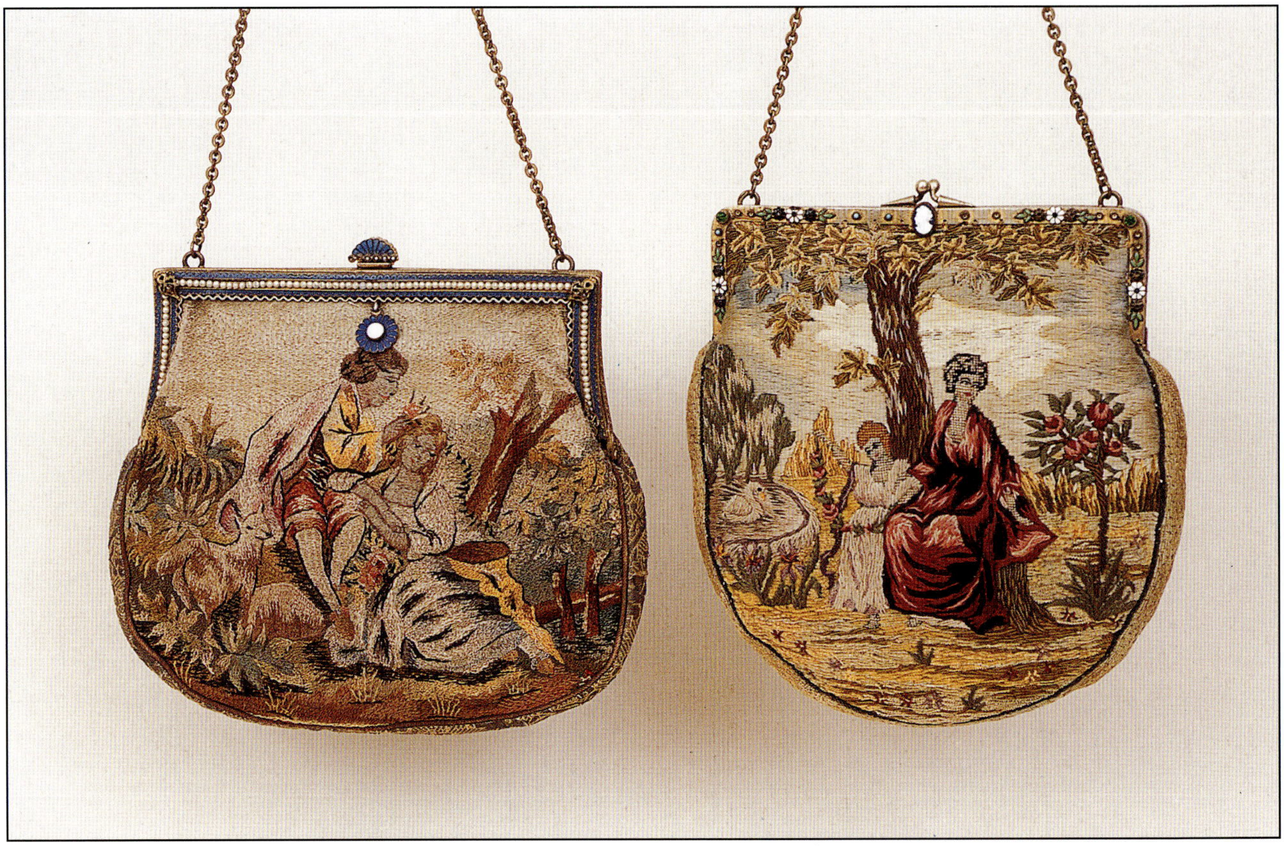

Two silk stitched purses. The design on the right is more unusual and the color scheme is very attractive. Left: 7 x 6.5 in. Right: 7.25 x 6.25 in. *Collection of Lori Blaser.* $450-550.

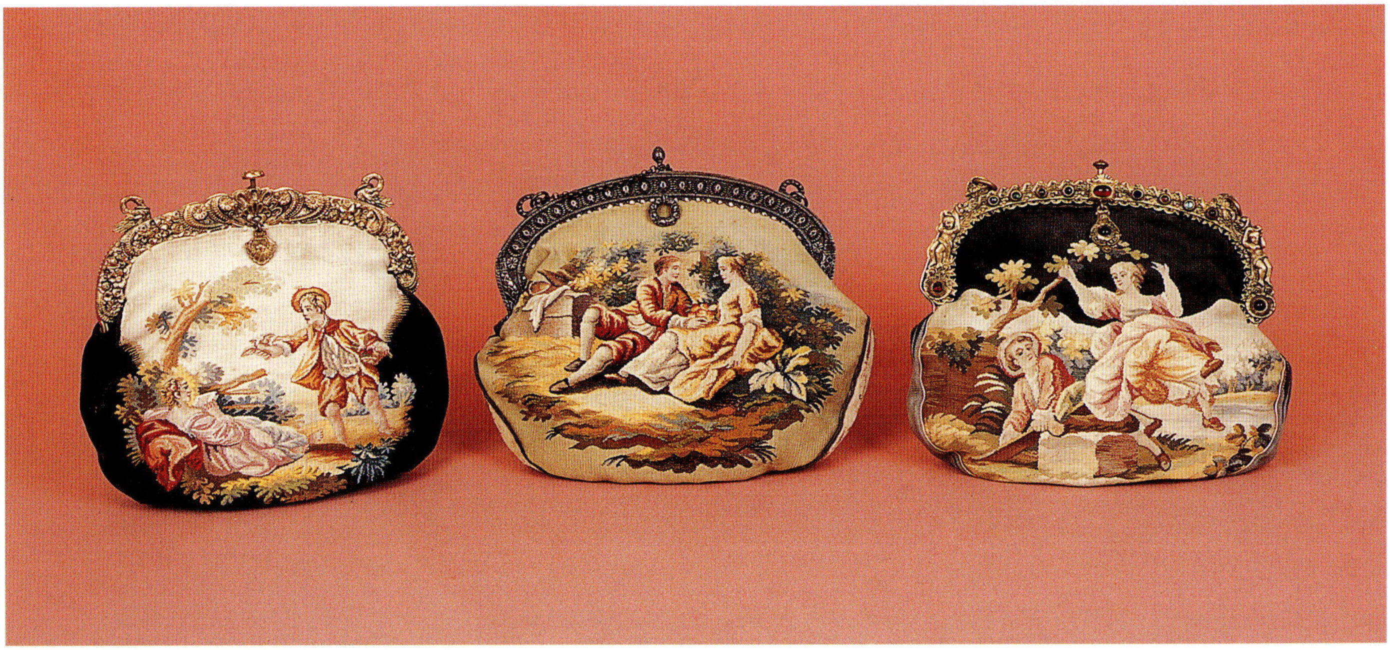

Three early 20th century tapestry purses. The popularity of the 18th century courting scene is obvious. Many of these scenes were actually taken from tapestry designs made in the 18th century by Boucher, Watteau, and Fragonard. Left: 8.5 x 8 in. Center: 7.75 x 7.75 in. Right: 8 x 8 in. *Collection of Lori Blaser.* $450-600.

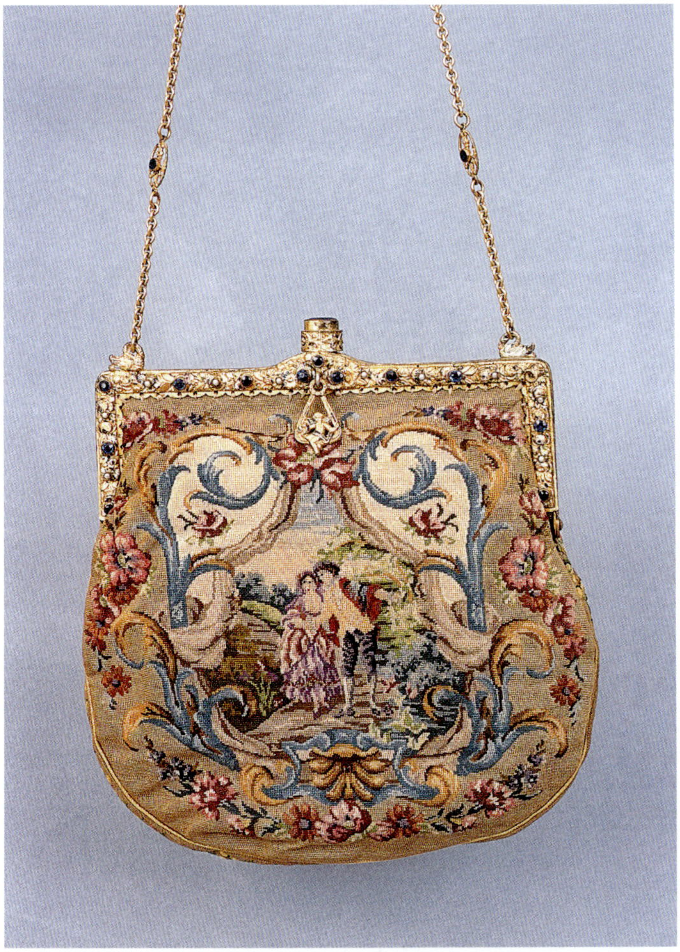

Traditional petit point with a double sided jeweled frame. 7.5 x 7 in. *Collection of Lori Blaser.* $400-550.

Tapestry purse with jeweled frame. 7.5 x 6 in. *Collection of Lori Blaser.* $600-650.

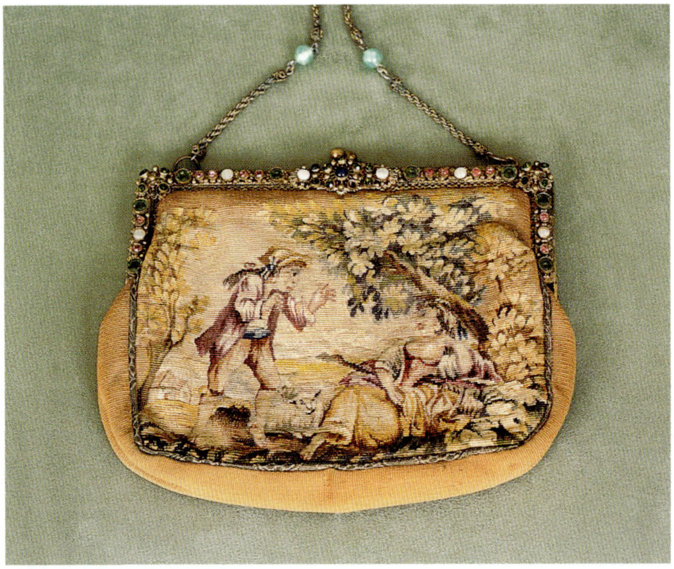

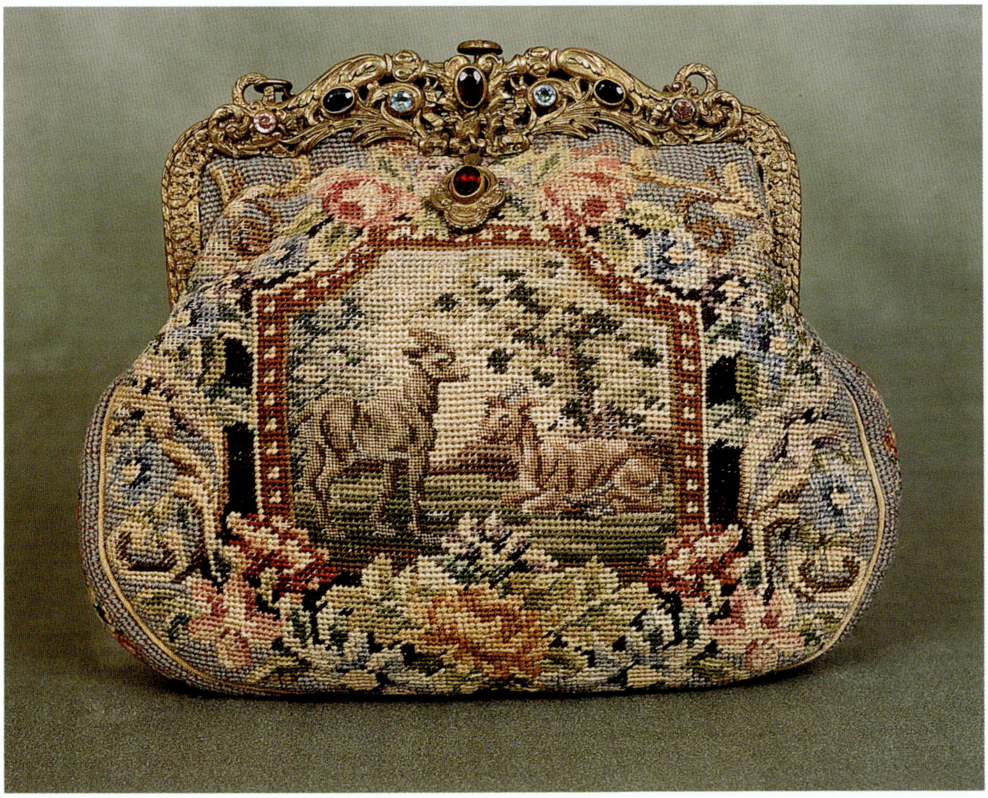

The beautiful needlepoint design, soft color palette, and exceptional double-sided jeweled frame, combine to make a truly beautiful purse. 8 x 7 in. *Collection of Lori Blaser.* $450-550.

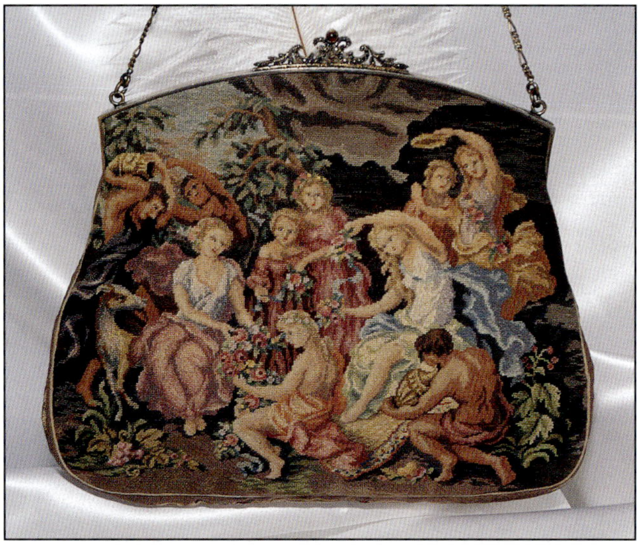

Austrian petit point designers seeking inspiration for new designs, would occasionally copy works from famous artists. The makers of this purse based their design on a Franz Anton Maulpertsch fresco painted in 1765. On the bottom of the purse is the name "Maulpertsch 1765." The sterling frame has a "tiara" clasp set with marcasite and carnelian stones. 7.5 x 6 in. *Collection of Paula Higgins.* $450-550.

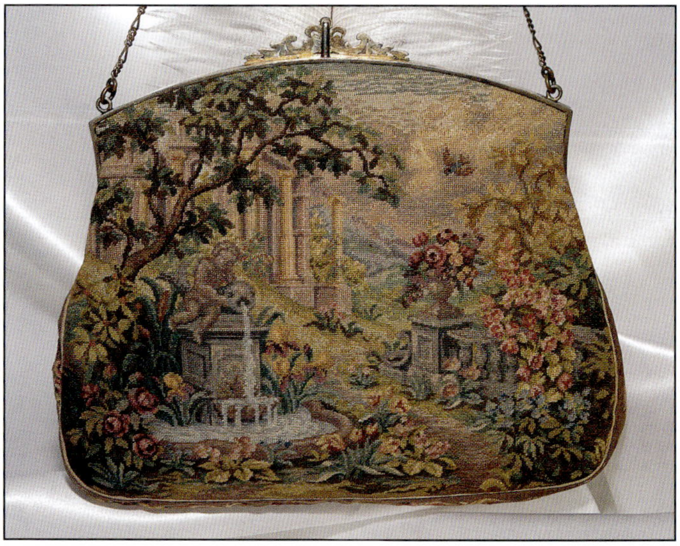

The reverse side of the petit point purse with a more traditional garden scene.

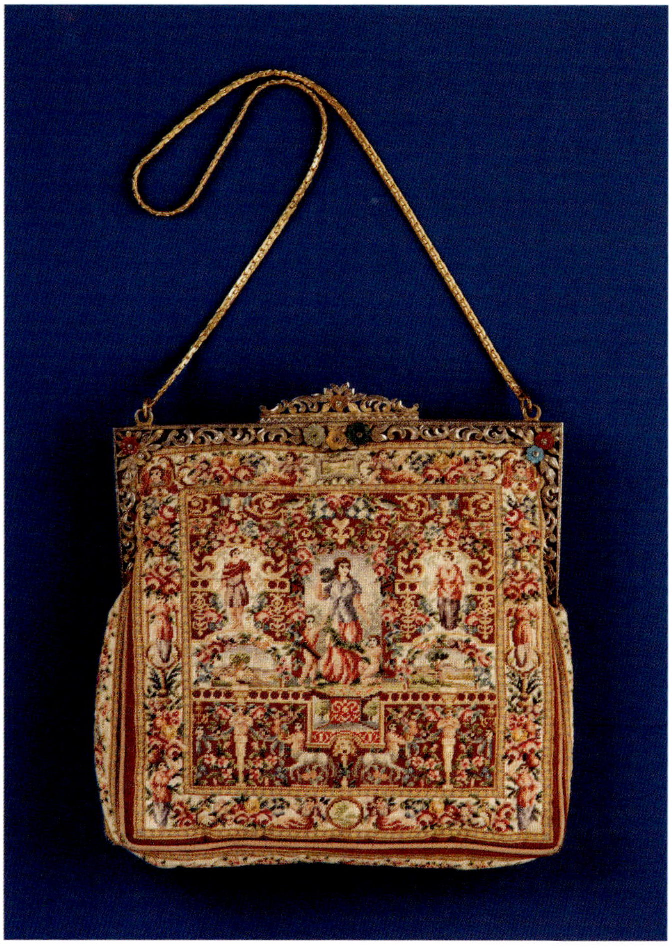

This petit point is exceptional because of its fine detail, numerous design elements, lovely color palette, and decorative frame. The design is also well balanced, which is noteworthy considering the amount of detail and numerous color changes. 7.5 x 7 in. *Collection of Sharon LuVisi.* $450-550.

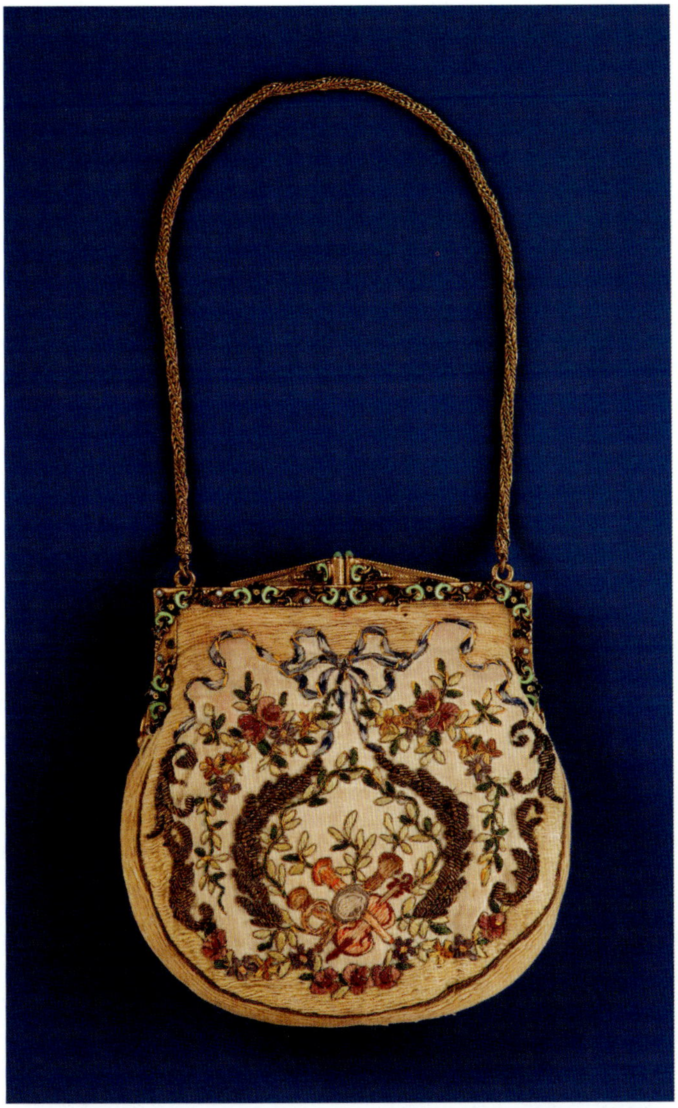

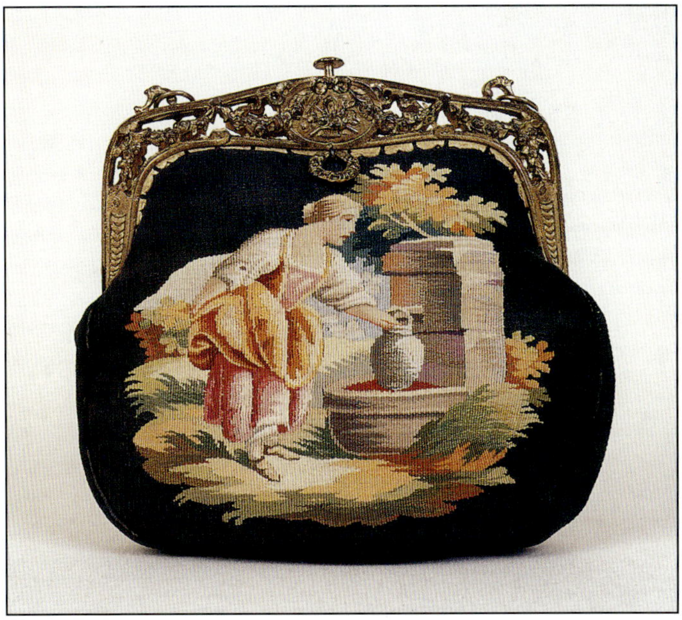

Early 20th century tapestry purse with an unusual design of a woman at a well. 7 x 7.5 in. *Collection of Lori Blaser.* $450-550.

Lovely silk stitched and metal thread embroidered purse. The design is reminiscent of 18th century embroideries. An enameled frame compliments the purse design. 6.5 x 6 in. *Collection of Sharon LuVisi.* $350-450.

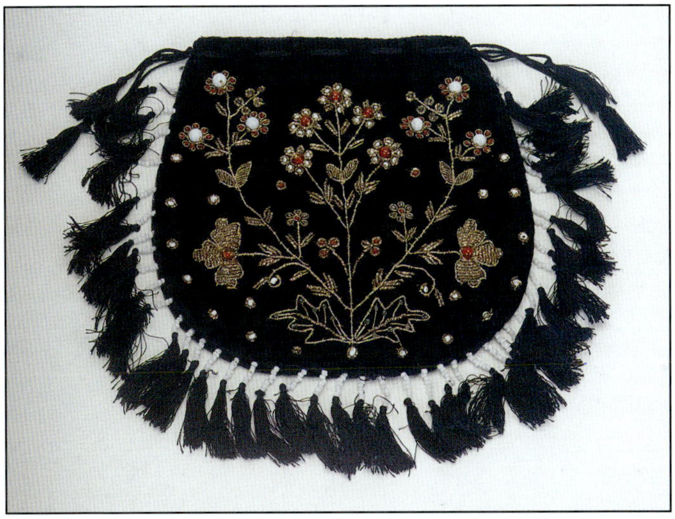

C.1930 velvet reticule made in India. Most Indian embroidered purses made for export were clutch shaped. This reticule is beautifully decorated with gold metal threads, silk, and glass beads. The hand tied tassels are a perfect finishing touch. 10 x 10 in. *Collection of Lori Blaser.* $250-300.

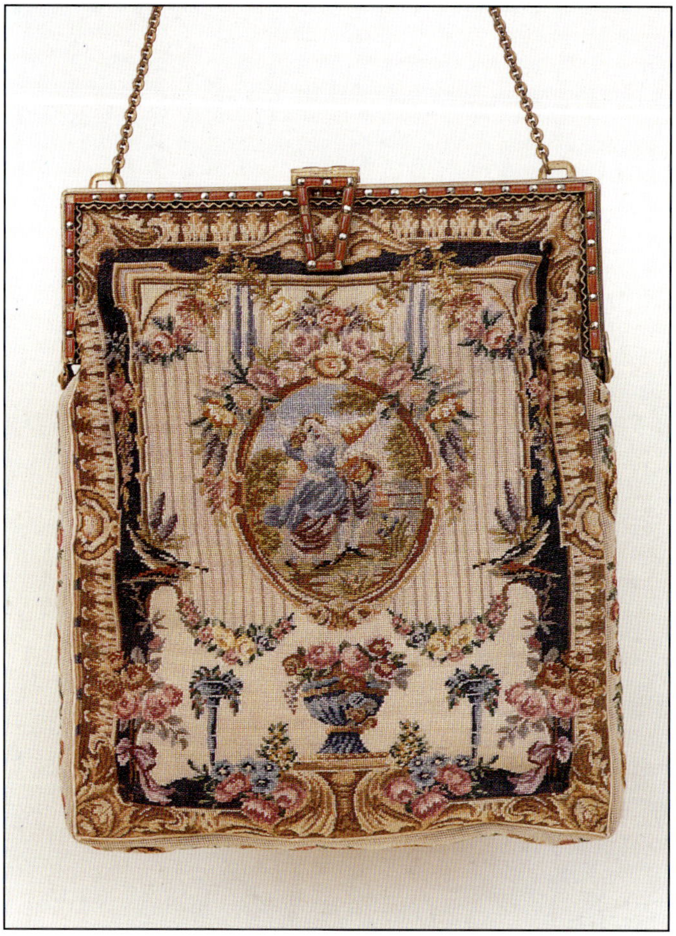

This rectangular shaped, Austrian petit point is mounted on a coral and marcasite frame. 8 x 6.5 in. *Collection of Lori Blaser.* $450-550.

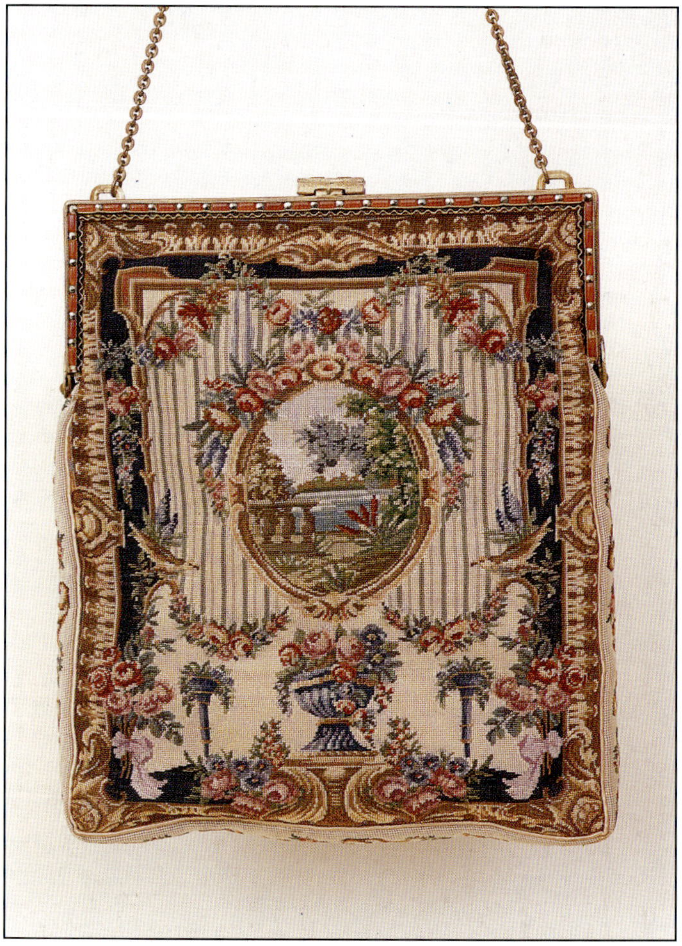

The reverse side of the petit point.

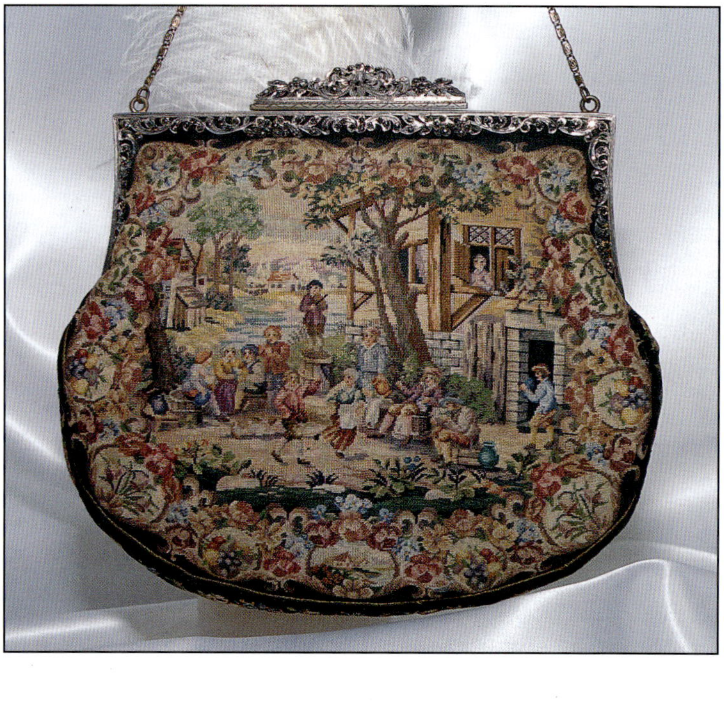

An Austrian petit point designed with a village scene, and people dancing and playing musical instruments. This design is filled with activity and there are numerous color changes. It is mounted on a sterling and marcasite frame. 7.5 x 7 in. *Collection of Paula Higgins.* $450-500.

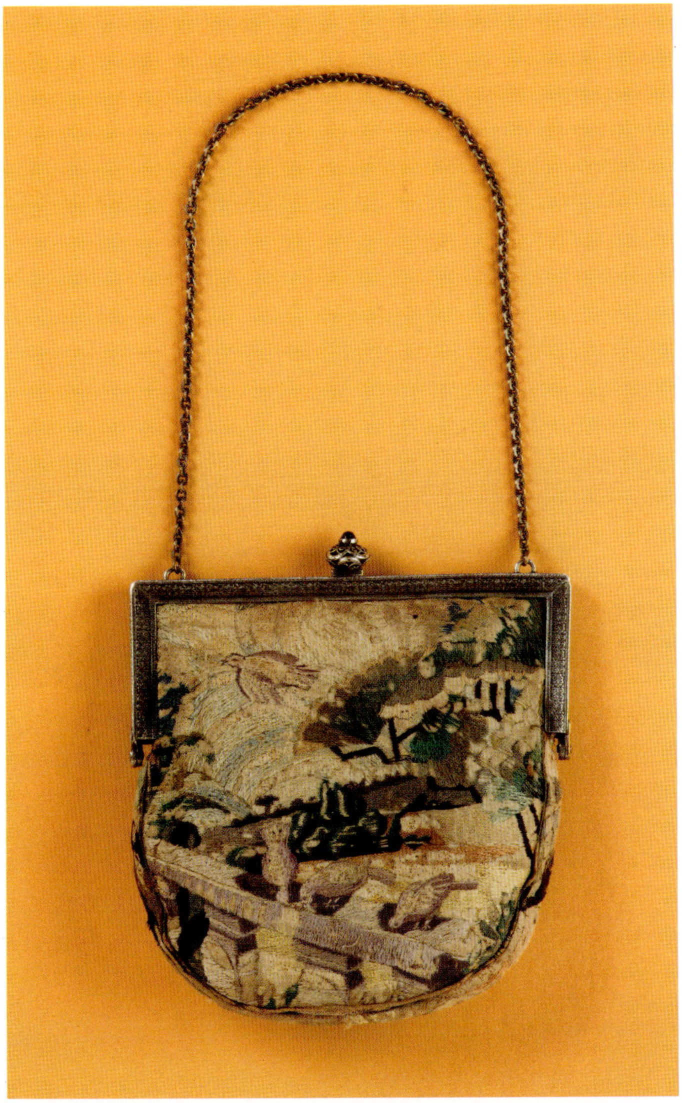 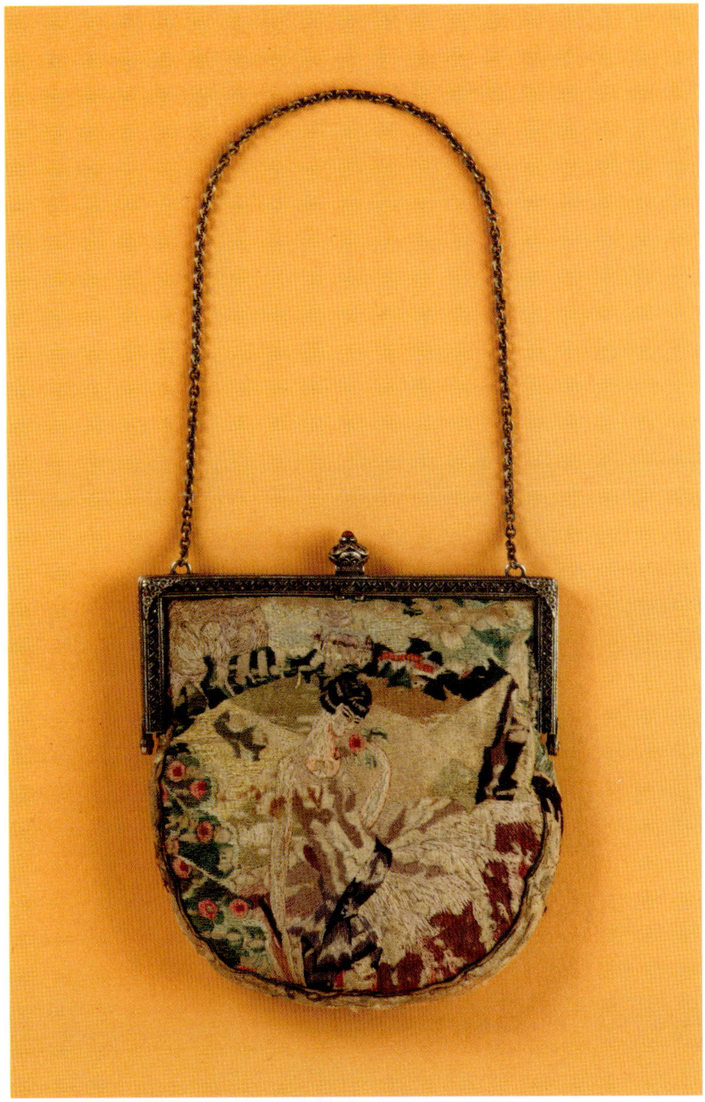

C.1920-1930 silk stitched purse with a stylized figural of a woman wearing a bobbed hairstyle. This is an unusual and refreshing design. 6.5 x 6.5 in. *Collection of Sharon LuVisi.* $450-550.

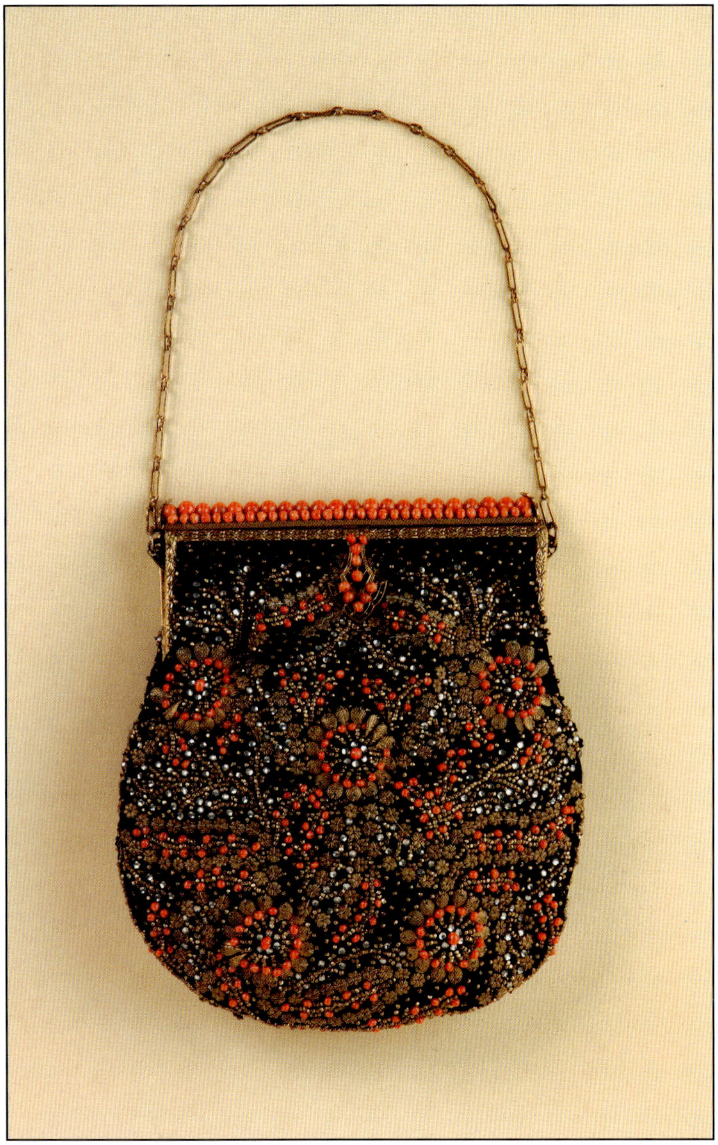

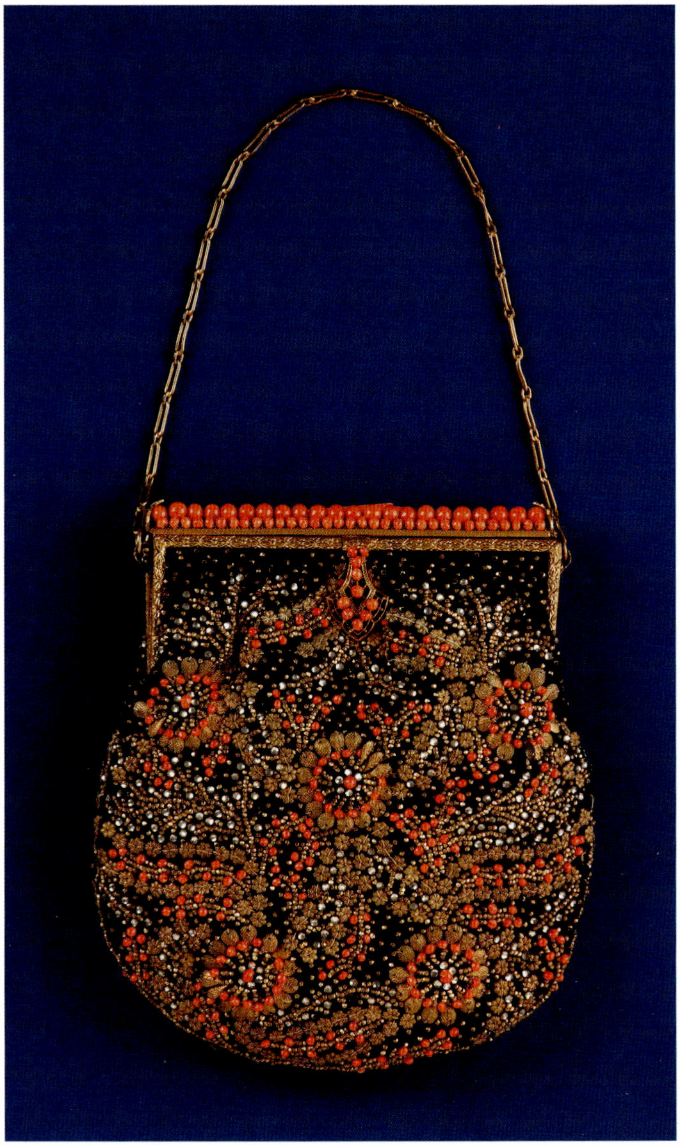

C.1930 embroidered and coral beaded purse. Genuine coral beads and gold thread flowers decorate this exceptionally lovely purse. More coral beads are wired onto the frame and clasp. This purse would appeal to any collector. 7.5 x 7 in. *Collection of Sharon LuVisi.* $500-600.

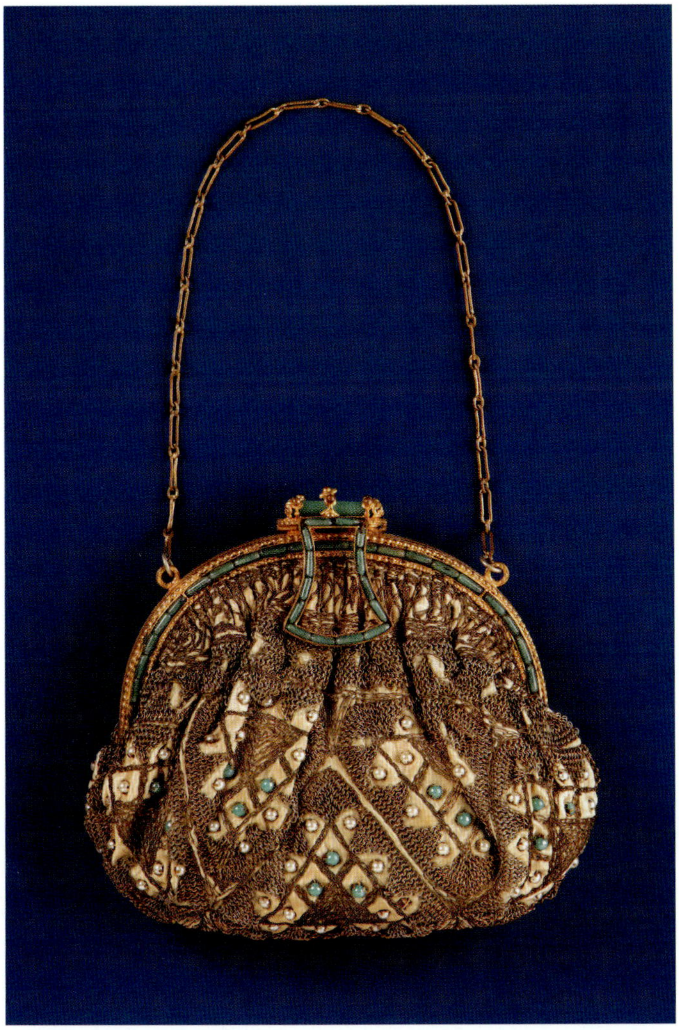

C.1930 embroidered and jeweled purse. Claw set pearls and jade decorate the body of the bag. Bars of jade are set into a lovely coordinating frame. 8 x 7 in. *Collection of Sharon LuVisi.* $350-450.

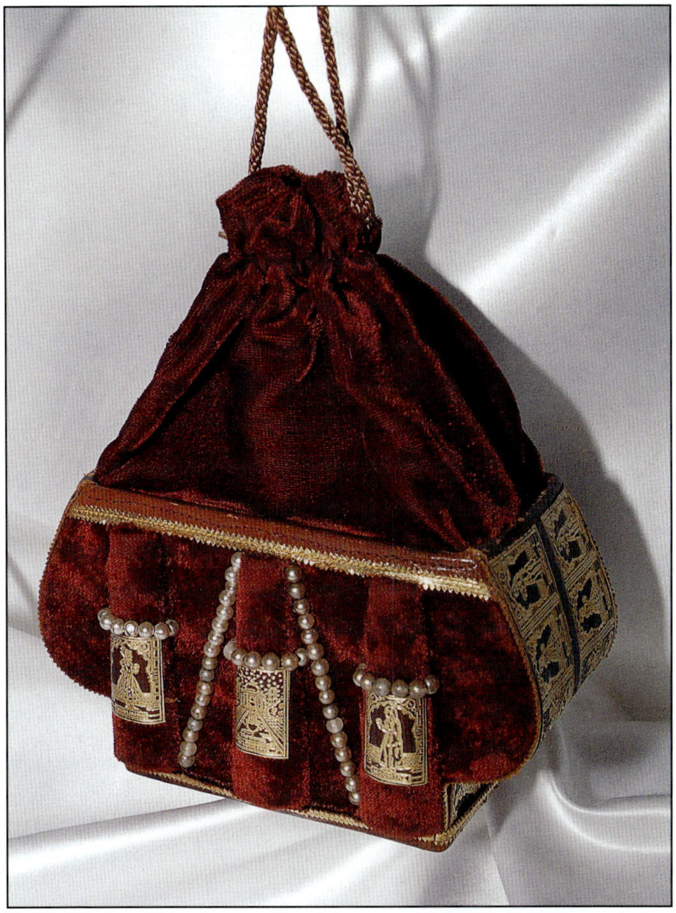

C.1930 crimson velvet reticule decorated with gold embossed leather and pearls. Indian designs of the Taj Mahal, Shah Jehan, and Mumtaz Mahal are embossed on the leather. Oriental, Indian, and Arabic designs were popular during the first thirty years of the 20th century. 7 x 6 in. *Collection of Paula Higgins.* $250-300.

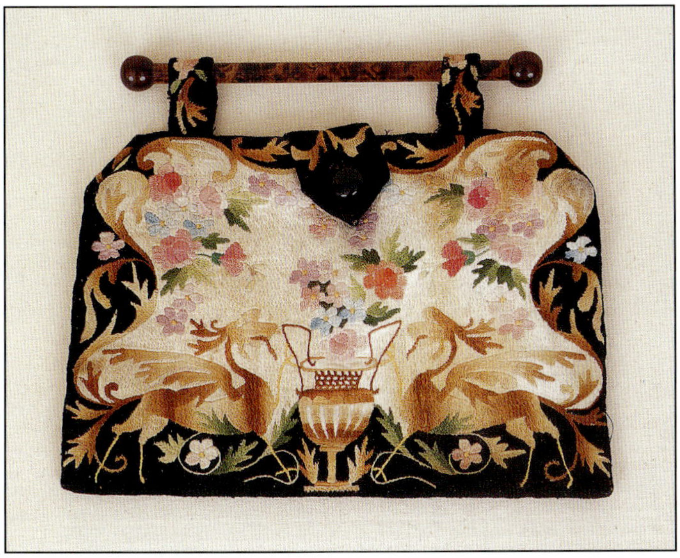

C.1930 silk stitched purse with an oriental design influence. The bar is made from plastic. This is an unusual and colorful purse, with considerable appeal. 8.5 x 7 in. *Collection of Lori Blaser.* $350-450.

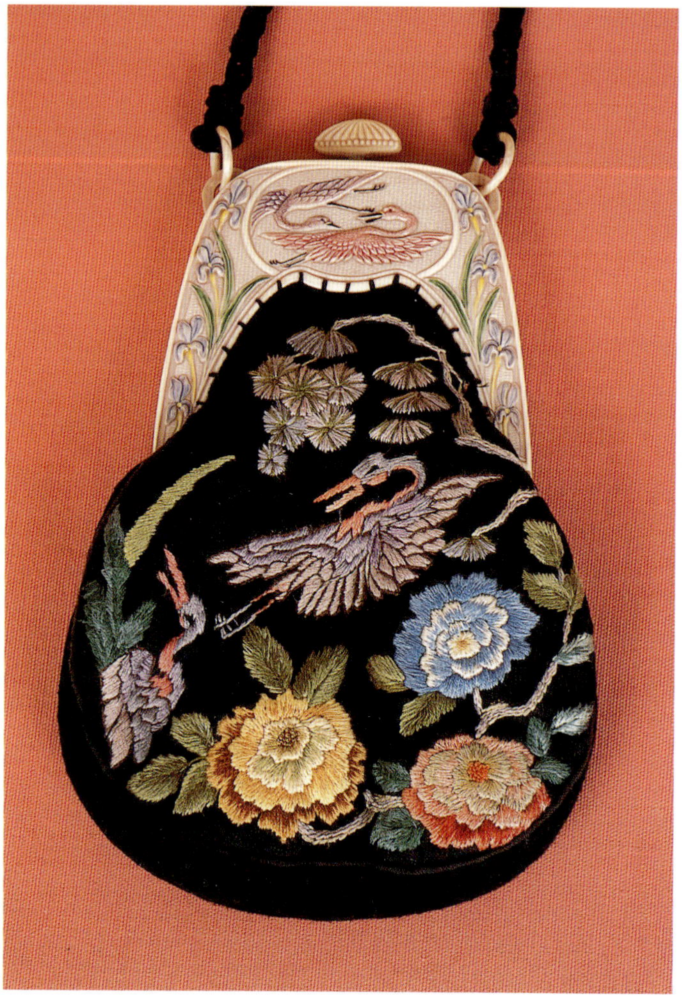

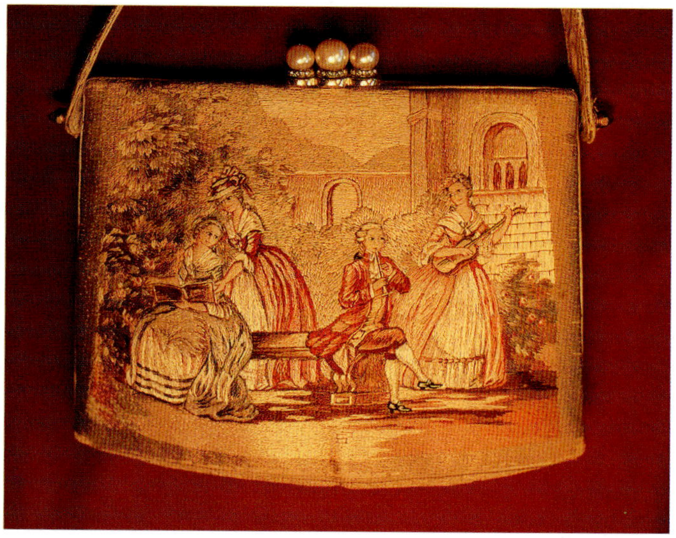

Silk stitched purse with a design of 18th century figures sitting in a garden scene. Two of the figures are playing musical instruments. The design is detailed and the clasp is jewel set with three large pearls and rhinestone rondels. 8 x 6 in. *Collection of Linda Marshall.* $450-550.

C.1930 Chinese style embroidered purse. The crane design is repeated on the coordinating celluloid purse frame. Many celluloid framed purses have plain fabric bodies attached to them. This is an imaginative exception. 9.25 x 6 in. *Collection of Lori Blaser.* $600-700.

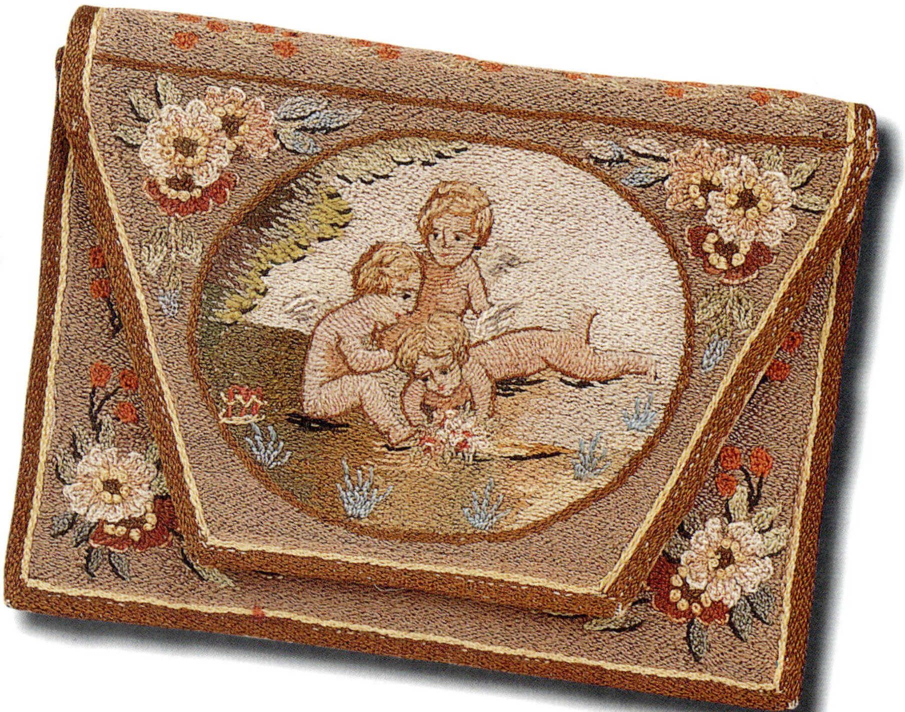

Silk stitched clutch embroidered with an unusual design of three cherubs or putti, flanked by flowers. 5.5 x 4.5 in. *Collection of Lori Blaser.* $350-450.

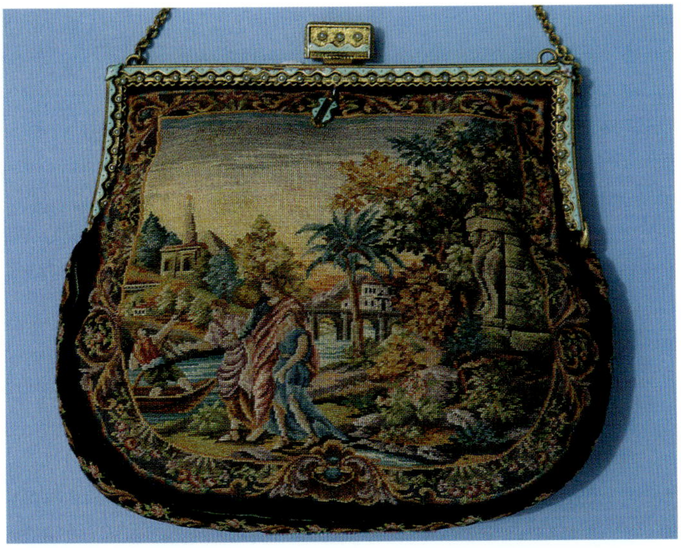

Mid-twentieth century petit point with robed figures greeting a man in a boat. This may be a religious themed petit point. Religious scenes were popular among petit point designers. The frame is enameled and set with small pearls. 8 x 7 in. *Collection of Linda Marshall.* $400-450.

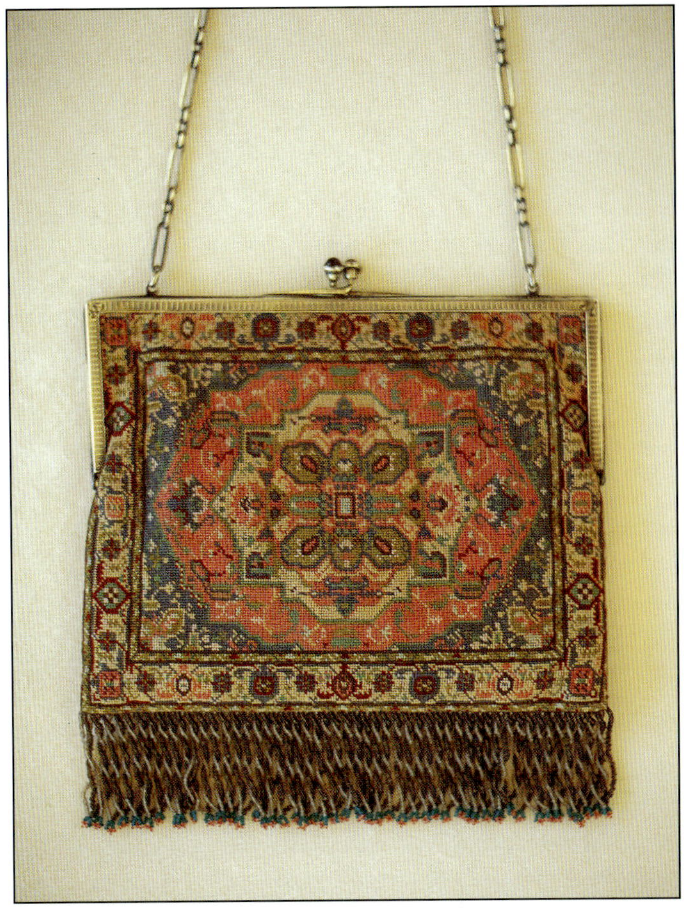

This lovely petit point purse bears the Tiffany & Co. stamp, which makes it rare and desirable. Made in an oriental rug design, it is less common than a floral. Tiffany & Co. petit points are also notable for their use of beaded fringe, attached to a textile body. The frame is sterling. Mid-twentieth century. 5.5 x 5 in. *Collection of Linda Marshall.* Rare.

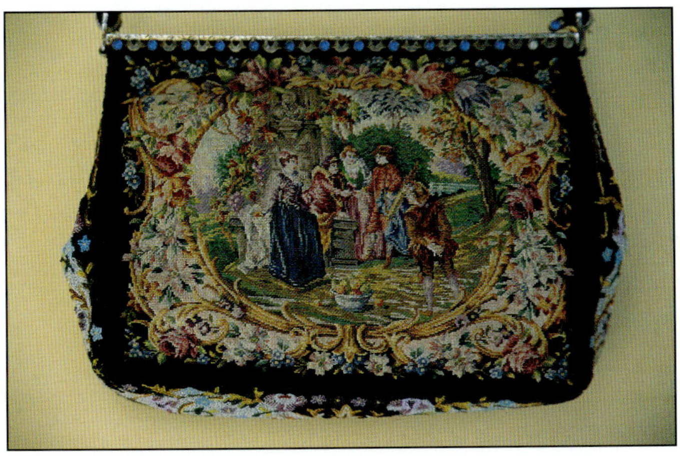

A petit point purse which is marked "Moralito-Paris" is unusual for its fine beaded gusset and strap. The beading matches the floral design on the petit point. It is mounted on a frame set with sapphire colored jewels. Mid-twentieth century. 8.5 x. 6.5 in. *Collection of Linda Marshall.* $450-550.

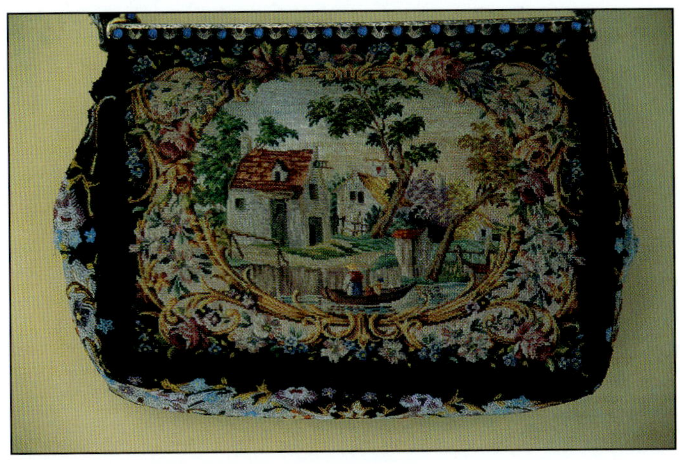

The reverse of the petit point purse.

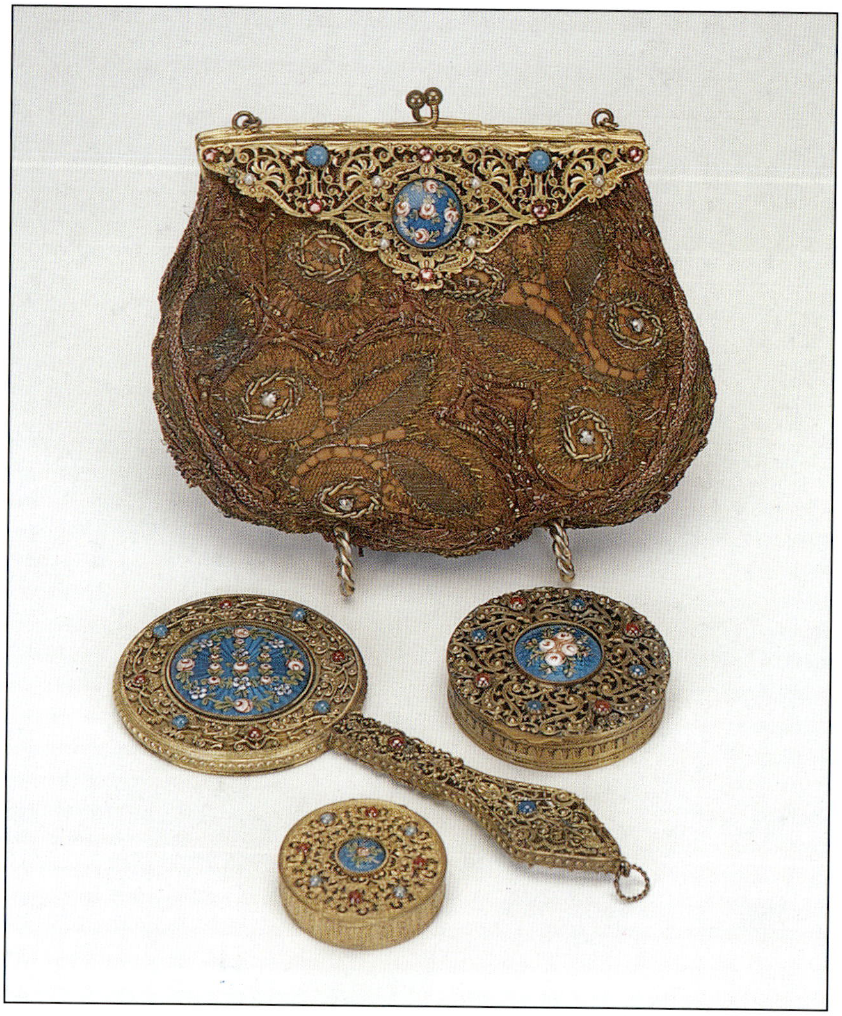

Beautifully made French silk purse, decorated with an overlay of metallic lace, metal strips, and pearls. The gilt frame is set with a guilloche enamel, hand painted floral plaque and jewels. In front of the purse is a dresser set made from the same filigree and enamel work. 6.5 x 5.5 in. *Collection of Lori Blaser.* $450-550.

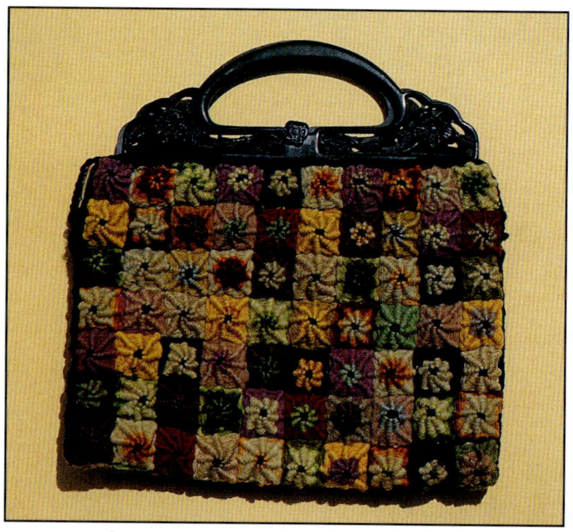

This needleworked purse is interesting because it was made in the first half of the 20th century, using a much older needlework technique. The "spider web" design is seen on small coin purses from the early 19th century. To see it resurrected approximately 100 years later is unusual. The handle is made from black plastic.9 x 9 in. *Collection of Linda Marshall.* $150-200.

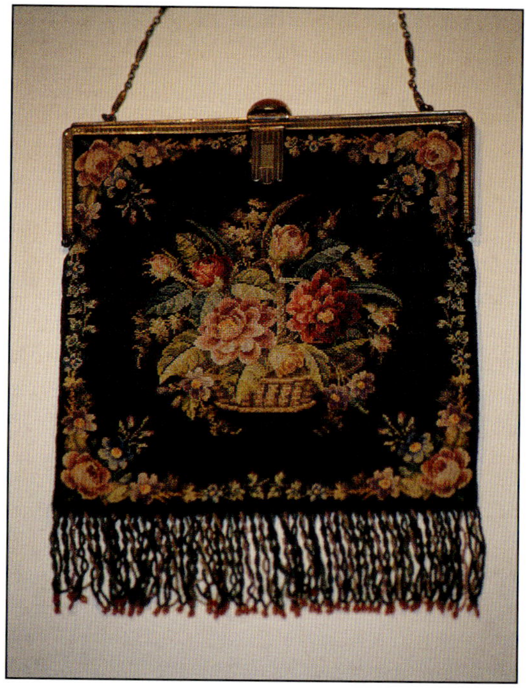

Tiffany & Co. marked petit point purse, with twisted, interlocking beaded fringe. The beaded fringe on the textile body was a Tiffany & Co. signature. The basket of flowers design is a classic Tiffany & Co. petit point design. Another version was made with a cream background. The frame is made from sterling and set with a carnelian clasp. 7.75 x 6 in. *Collection of Paula Higgins.* Rare.

C.1930 silk stitched clutch. This 18th century figural is a commonly seen design on the clutch model. 7 x 6.25 in. *Collection of Paula Higgins.* $300-350.

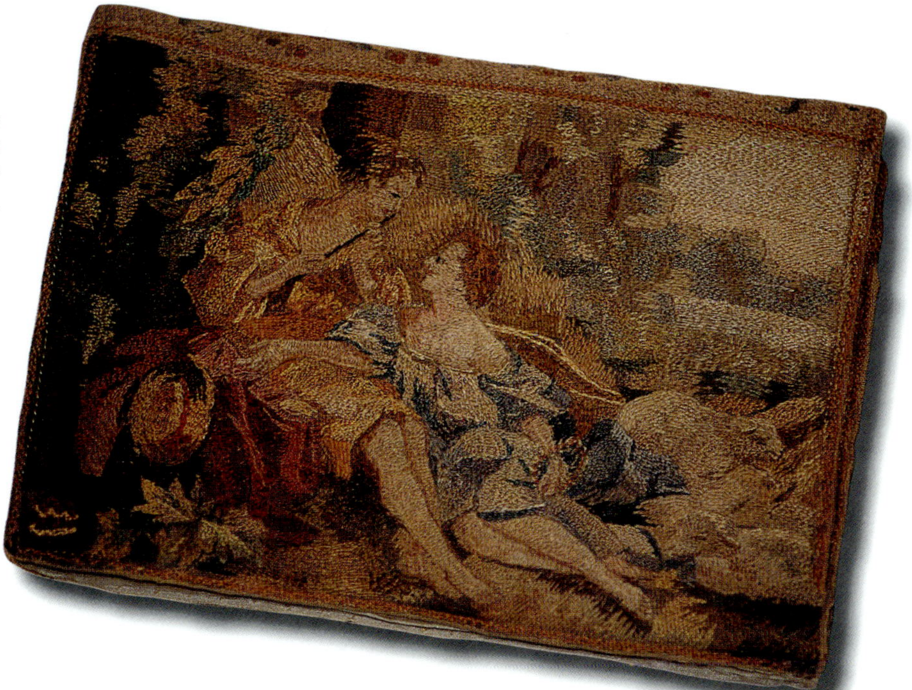

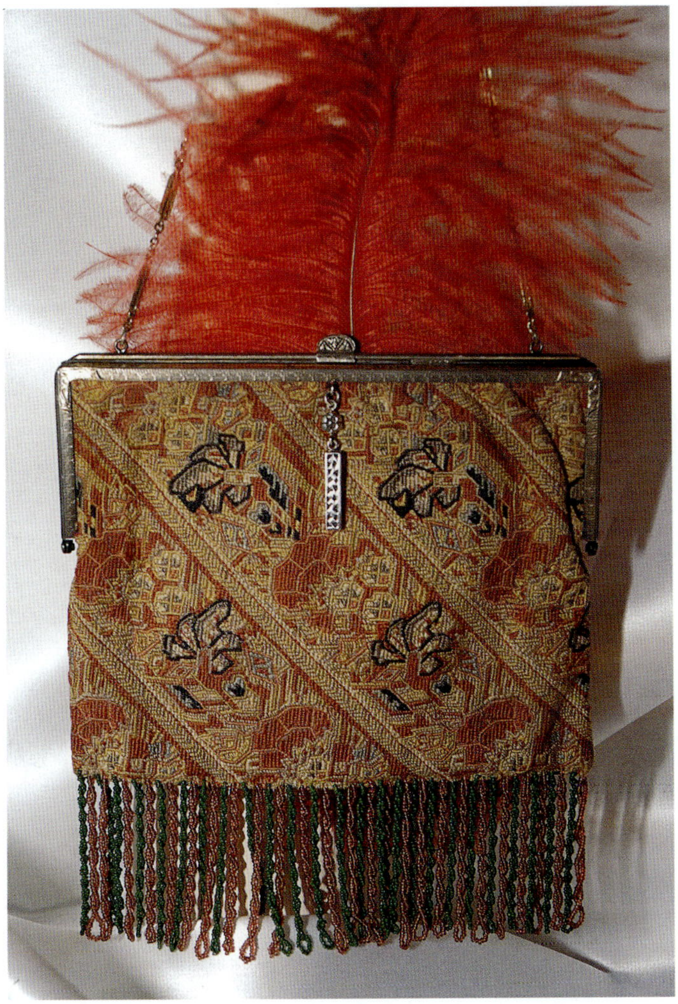

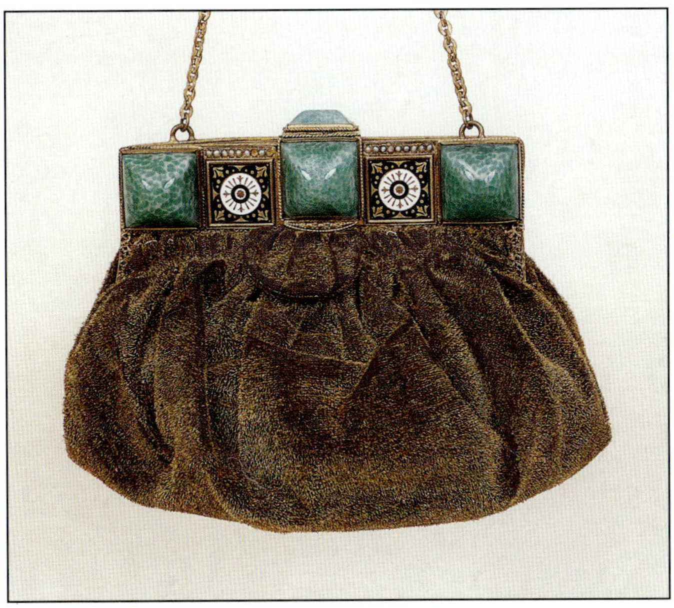

Velvet bag made from silk and metallic threads, mounted on a jade, enamel, and pearl frame. 6.5 x 5.5 in. *Collection of Lori Blaser.* $250-300.

A Tiffany & Co. needleworked purse with the Tiffany & Co. signature beaded fringe. Mounted on a sterling silver frame, the slide clasp is typical of Tiffany & Co. frames. 6.25 x 5 in. *Collection of Paula Higgins.* Rare.

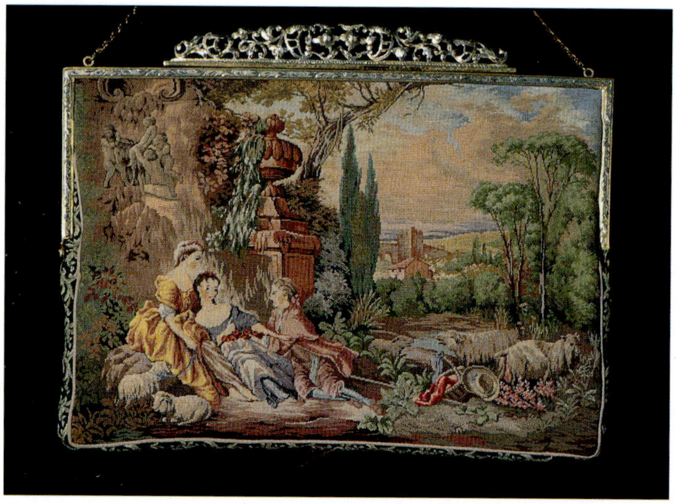

Austrian petit point with a classic 18th century pastoral scene, and a stand-up clasp. This purse dates to the mid-twentieth century. It is a superior quality petit point. 9 x 6.5 in. *Collection of Linda Marshall.* $400-450.

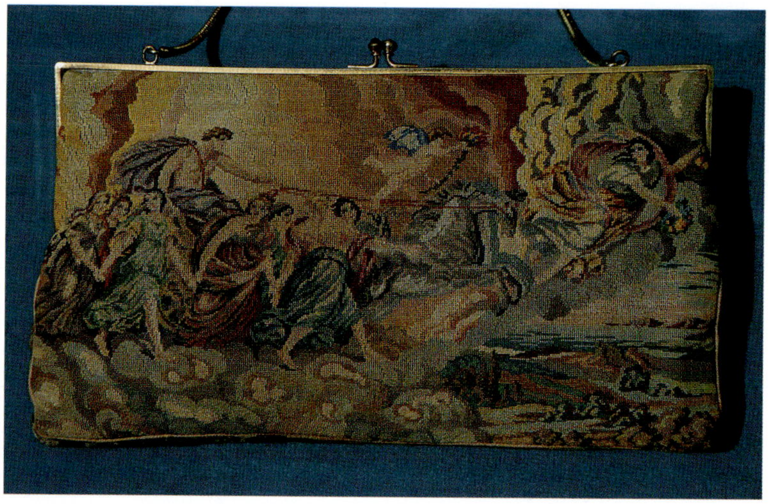

A petit point purse with a religious scene of a figure in a chariot, ascending into heaven, surrounded by angels. This is an unusual scene and it creates a strong visual impact. 9 x 5.5 in. *Collection of Linda Marshall.* $400-450.

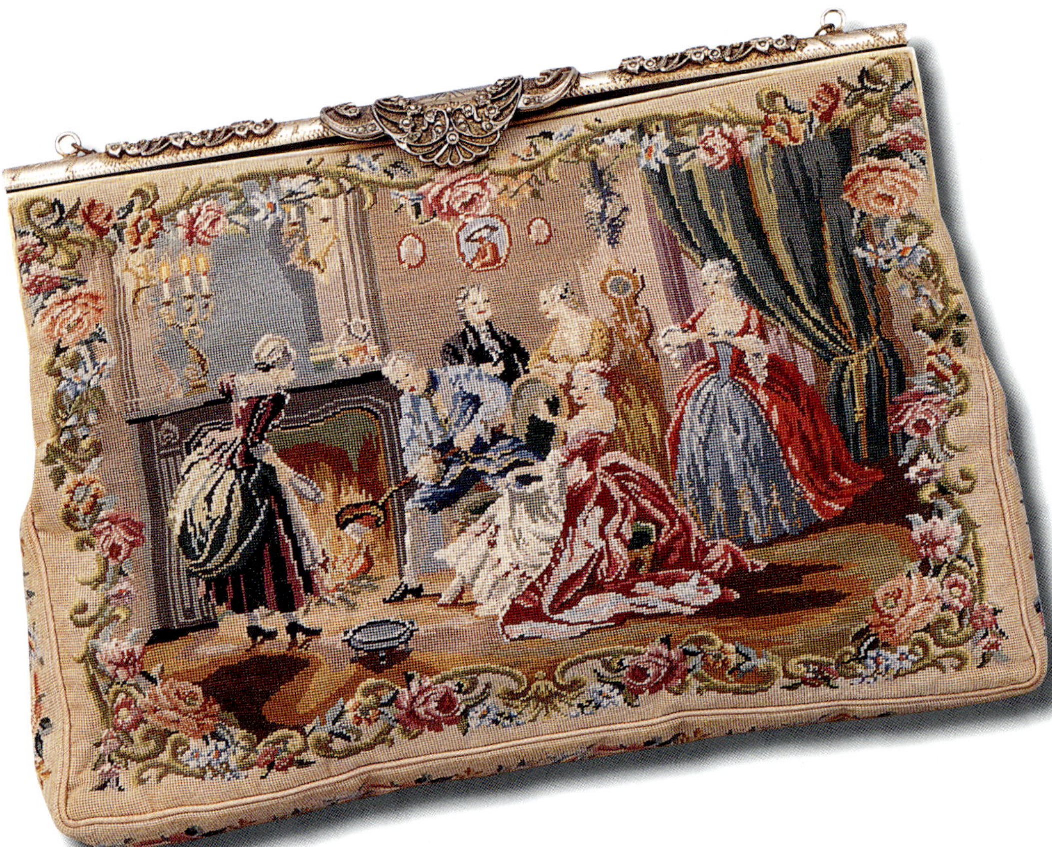

An Austrian petit point with a less common interior scene. The design, number of figures, and the high quality of the petit point make this a desirable purse. 9.25 x 7 in. *Collection of Lori Blaser.* $400-450.

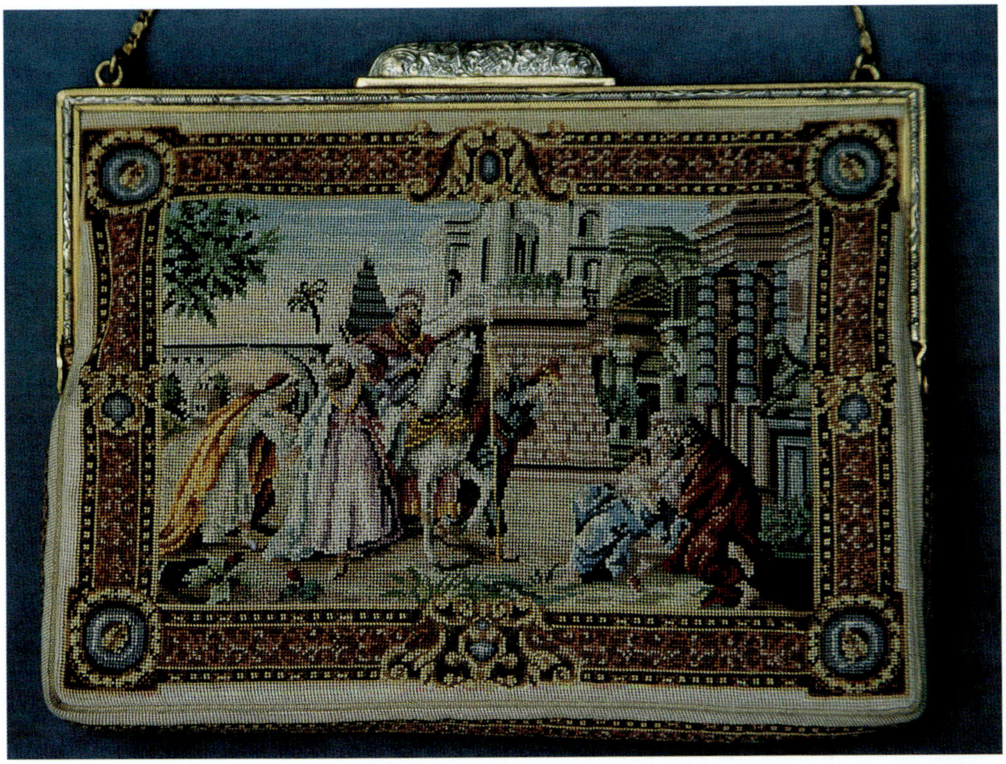

Another religious inspired petit point from the mid-twentieth century. Beautifully designed and executed. 7 x 5.5 in. *Collection of Linda Marshall.* $400-450.

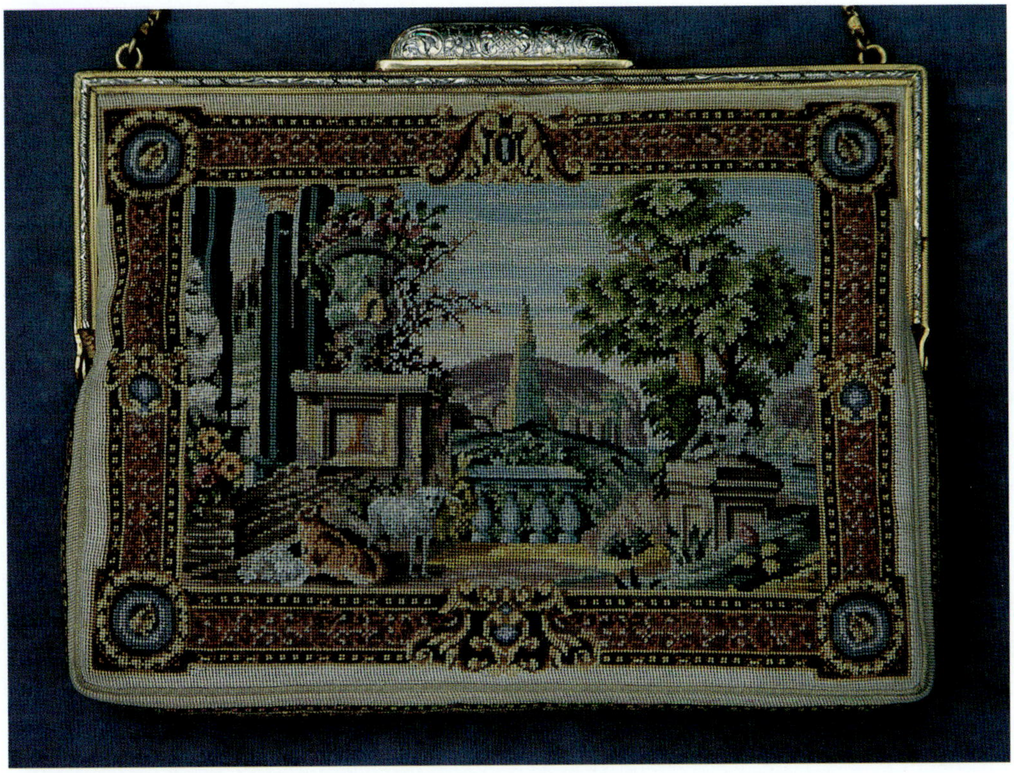

The reverse of the petit point purse.

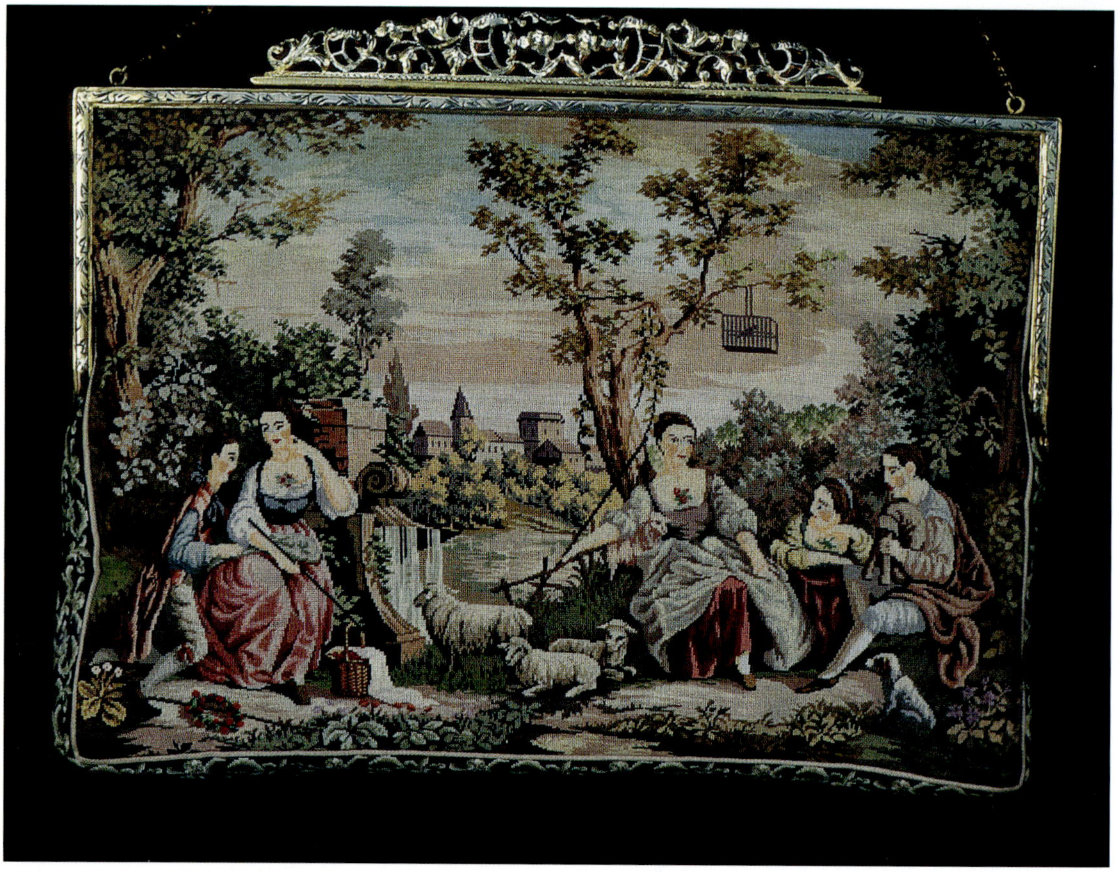

Mid-twentieth century, Austrian petit point with a multi-figural scene. The color scheme is atypical, giving the purse a painting-like quality. Mounted on a sterling silver frame with a standing, pierced clasp. 9 x 6.5 in. *Collection of Linda Marshall.* $400-450.

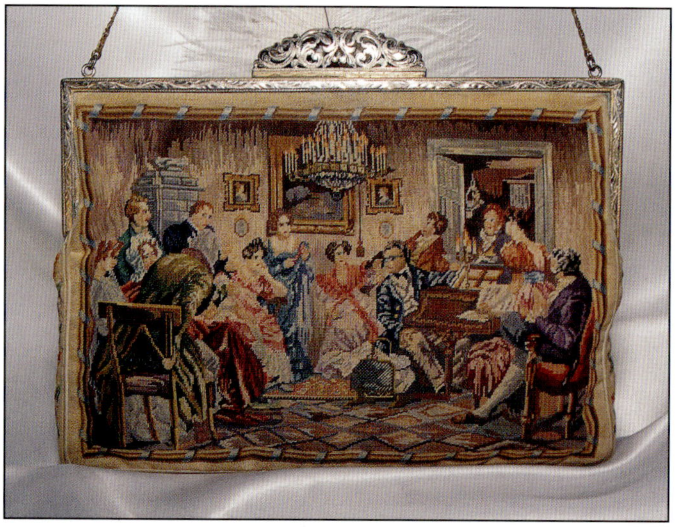

Mid-twentieth century petit point designed with an interior scene of famous 19th century musicians. The man sitting in the chair with the white hair may be Franz Liszt, the famous pianist. He was known for his long white hair, and his green coat with a brown collar. The man seated at the piano may be Schumann. 8. 5 x 7 in. *Collection of Paula Higgins.* $700-750.

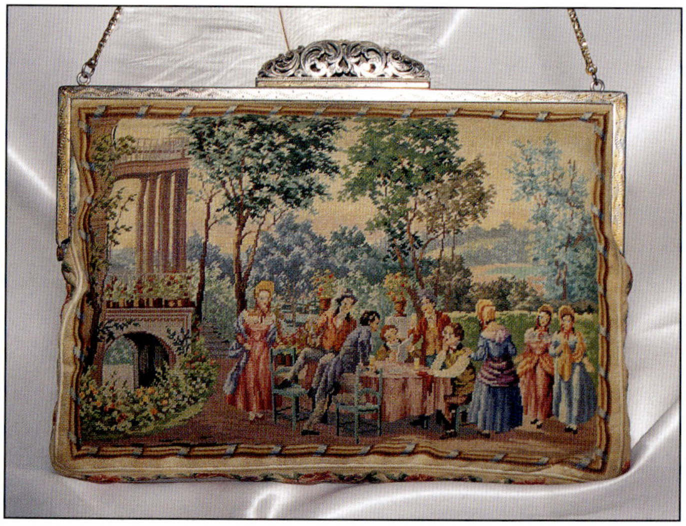

The reverse of the petit point purse featuring an exterior party scene.

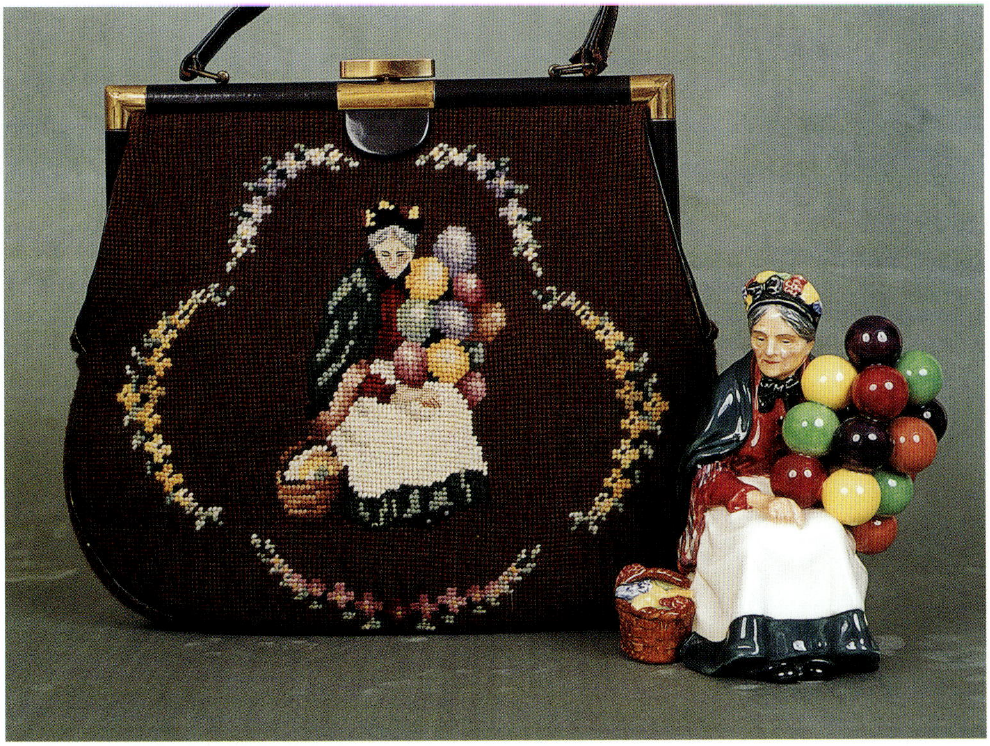

A mid-twentieth century, needleworked purse with a design of a balloon seller. This design was taken from the Royal Doulton figurine entitled "The Old Balloon Seller." This purse design is a beautiful recreation of the figurine, which belonged to the grandmother of the owner's husband. 14 x 13. *Collection of Lori Blaser.* $250-300.

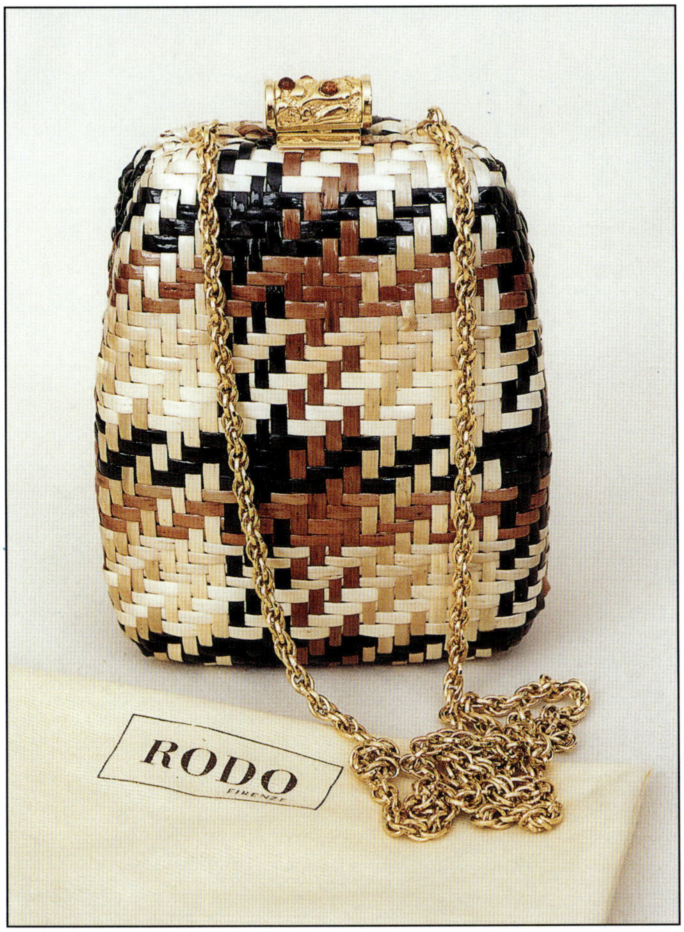

A Rodo Firenze lacquered and woven straw purse from the 1980s. The clasp is set with glass stones and the bag retains its original dust bag. 8 x 6 in. *Collection of Lori Blaser.* $150-200.

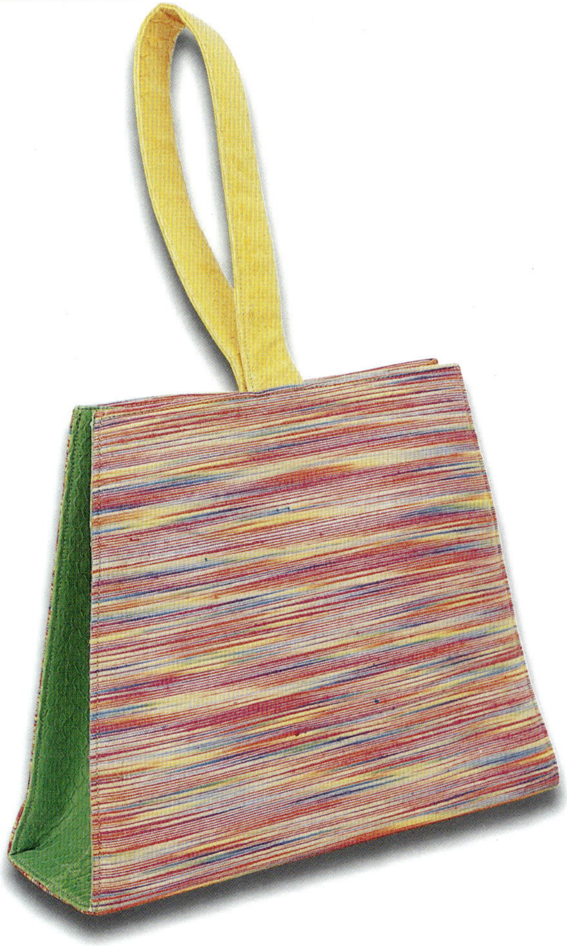

A c. 1990 Claudio Merazzi purse made from woven silk fabric and dyed lizard skin trim. 11 x 9 in. *Collection of Lori Blaser.* $300-400.

Chapter 6
Leather and Skin Purses

Leather bags pre-date the 1600s but most collectors will only encounter the very early examples in museums. The most common early leather purses available to the contemporary collector are the pocketbook and the gaming purse. Leather gaming purses were made in the pouch form, with short sides and flat bottoms. They were specifically made to hold coins for betting. The bottoms of these purses were often decorated with family crests in gold threads. They are very rarely offered for sale, especially in the United States. Early leather pocketbooks from Constantinople, Turkey, and Tetuan, Morocco were very much like a souvenir purse, with names embroidered on the purse in metal threads. Later 18th century leather pocketbooks were more ornately embroidered with metal threads on dyed leathers. Eighteenth century waist bags (chatelaines) were also made from leather, and attached to Rococo style hooks and frames. These waist bags are also rare and seldom seen.

Early 19th century leather bags are among the most charming of all leather purses. Leather bags were decorated with cut steel flowers, rivets, carry chains, and clasps. The clasps often took the shape of a lyre, which was a popular design during the early 19th century. These leather handbags are rare and European in origin. Early leather coin purses dating to c.1800 were made in a horseshoe shape with reverse painted scenes. Another version of this coin purse was made with a glass-covered scene of a small bird sitting on grass. The bird was made from real feathers.

The leather and fabric combination reticule dates to c.1830-1840. The bottom half of the purse was made from colored leather, in a bucket shape, which was then embossed with a gold design along the perimeter. The center of the leather was decorated with a gold colored button or other design, and the top half of the bag had a velvet or silk drawstring top. These purses are also rare and can be confusing to date because they are so infrequently seen by collectors. One offered on Ebay five years ago was identified by the seller as an Arts and Crafts purse. Leather bags with reticule tops also date to the mid-twentieth century, but typically the leather bag was barrel shaped and they lacked decoration. However, to prove that here are always exceptions to the rule, one example dating to the 1920s was decorated with Egyptian designs.

Mid- to late-nineteenth century leather purses were typically of the chatelaine or handbag variety. The handbags looked like small satchels or pieces of luggage. A less common style is the small box purse from the mid-nineteenth century. They were rectangular in shape and embossed with scrolling designs. Some were made with fitted interiors for sewing items. Leather handbags from c.1870-1890 were not very large and had metal fittings with round leather handles. Some examples were embossed with medieval scenes and figures. Leather chatelaine bags from the late 19th century to the early 20th century are also highly collectible. Decorated with pierced metal work and embossing, they were hung from wrist rings, belts, and hooks. The finer examples are quite rare.

Leather opera bags, from the turn of the 20th century, were fitted with opera glasses and small fans. Small in size, and elegant in design, they were made for women of means. Larger leather bags were made for everyday use during the early 20th century and they can be seen in many of the photographs from the period. Bags were made from goatskin, ostrich, sealskin, antelope, alligator, crocodile, suede, cowhide, and kidskin. Prices ranged from a dollar and a half to five dollars. Closed with twist clasps, sliding closures, or locks, they were stylish and accessible for the average woman. Jemco provided the majority of the frames for these purses, which included copper and Bakelite frames, to the more ordinary nickel fames. The leather purses most collectors are familiar with are those made by Meeker, Bosca, Reed, Roycroft, and Amity. Roycroft deserves special mention because they were handmade in the Arts and Crafts Style. They have been seen with hand hammered copper plaques as part of their decoration, making them rare and desirable.

Art Deco leather and skin bags with marcasite, enameled, and jewel set frames are among the most collectible of vintage purses. Usually structured and linear, they are sophisticated and elegant, reflecting the streamlined look of the Art Deco Period. Other Art Deco leather bags were made with bold geometric designs, in the Wiener Werkstatte tradition, with fold over flaps. By the 1930s, alligator bags were made with the head and feet attached as part of the design. Not particularly attractive to us now, they were considered very stylish at the time. Later alligator and crocodile bags were made without the head and feet, which was a considerable improvement.

Leather and skin shoulder bags were the height of fashion during World War II. Hanging from the shoulder with flair, they signaled the emergence of the modern, working woman. The leather shoulder bag was to remain a popular handbag choice for the next 60 years and beyond. Designers from the later half of the 20th century competed to produce sophisticated and unique leather purses to appeal to the wealthy, as well as the less affluent. Because women were now a major part of the work force, they had more disposable income, which they could spend on designer purses. There were still exceptional leather purses, such as the Kelly bag, made by Hermes, which only the wealthy could afford. Made by hand, they came in alligator skins, patterned fabrics, and colored leathers. Their distinctive belt closure and lock was unique, and a symbol of status.

Novelty leather bags are very hard to find, and the ones from the 1920s and 1930s are very desirable. Made in the shape of ships, cars, and airplanes in the 1920s and 1930s, they required an owner with self-confidence since they were sure to be noticed. Anne Marie of France made gold decorated, black suede bags in clock, champagne bucket, and piano shapes in the 1940s and 1950s. Again, they weren't carried by the timid. By the late 20th century, purses were disguised as footballs, flowerpots, books, and telephones. Besides having investment value, novelty bags put a smile on our face.

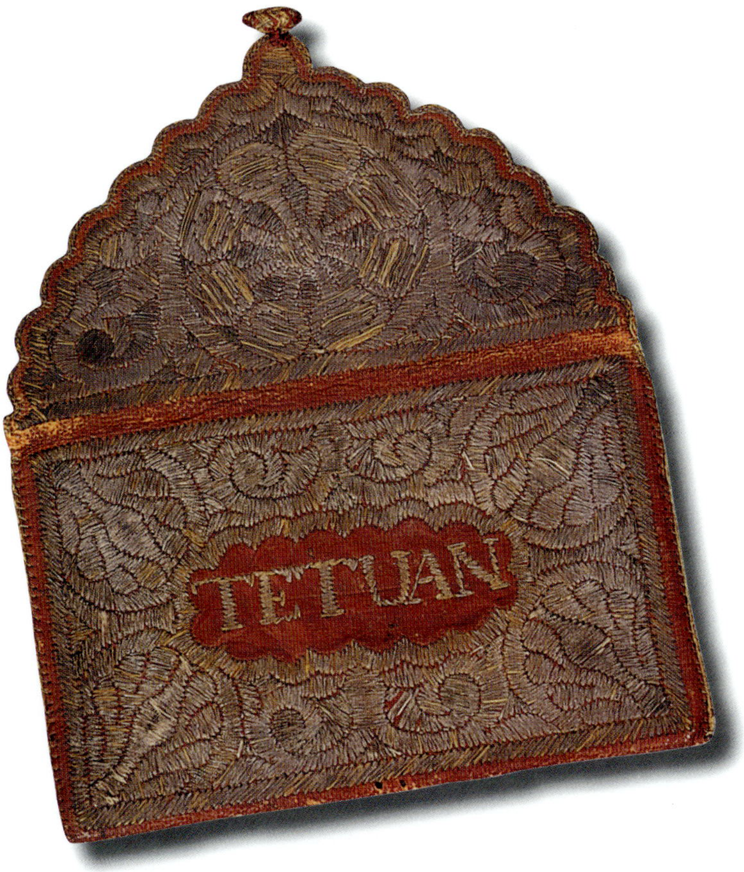

Dated 1734, this leather pocketbook was made in Tetuan, Morocco. Worked in gold threads on burgundy leather, the name of the owner, *Joana Scot*, is embroidered with the date on the reverse side. Turkey and Morocco made many purses for export during the 18th century. The names of their capitols were often embroidered on the purse as a form of advertising, for example *Constantinople* (Turkey) and *Tetuan* (Morocco). 6.5 x 4.25 in. *Collection of Lori Blaser.* Rare.

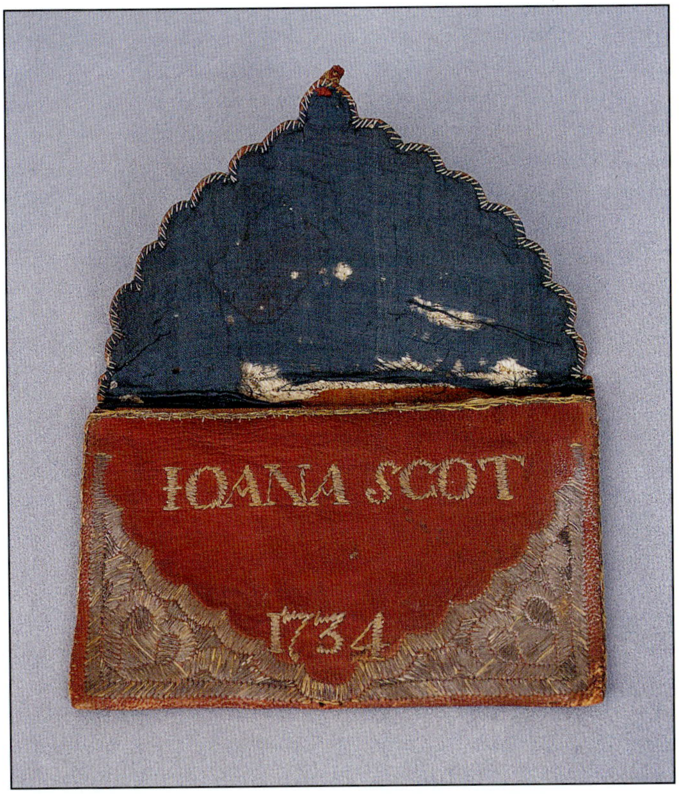

The reverse side of the leather embroidered purse.

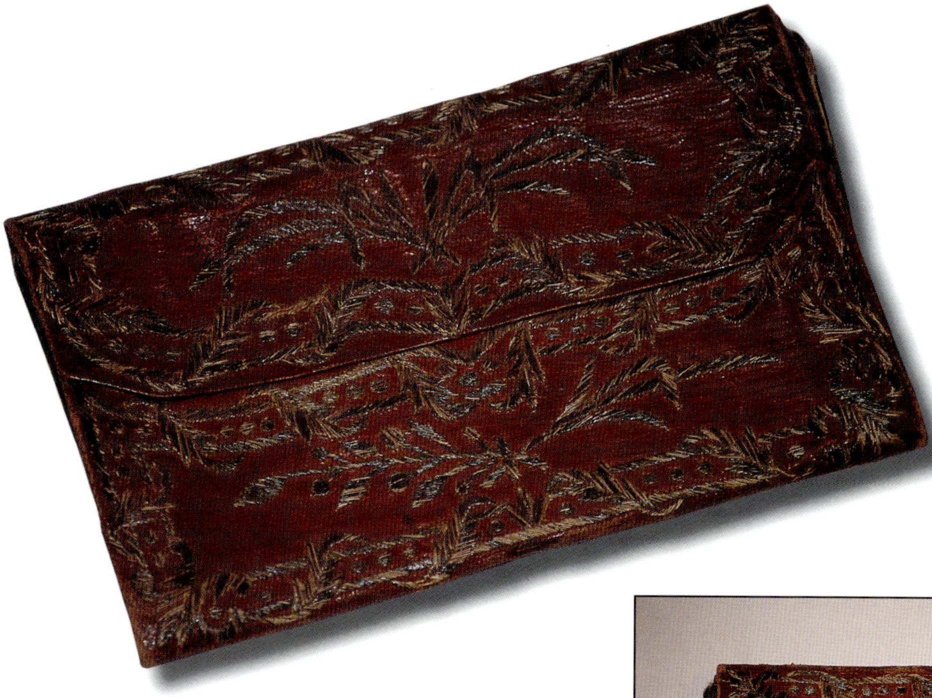

Eighteenth century American leather pocketbook, embroidered with metal threads. This purse was formerly owned by Martha Genung Stearns, author of the book *Homespun and Blue*. On the front of the purse is a wheat design and on the back are two initials and a cornucopia. The leather is irregularly cut and the embroidery does not appear to be professionally worked. 6 x 4 in. *Collection of Paula Higgins.* $650-750.

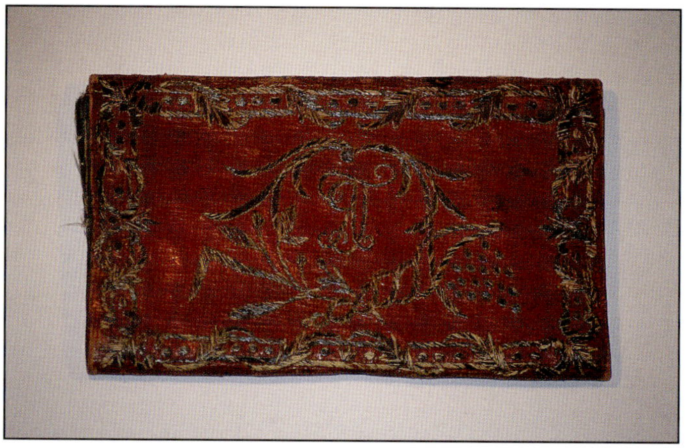

The reverse of the leather pocketbook showing two initials, possibly *A* and *T*, and a cornucopia.

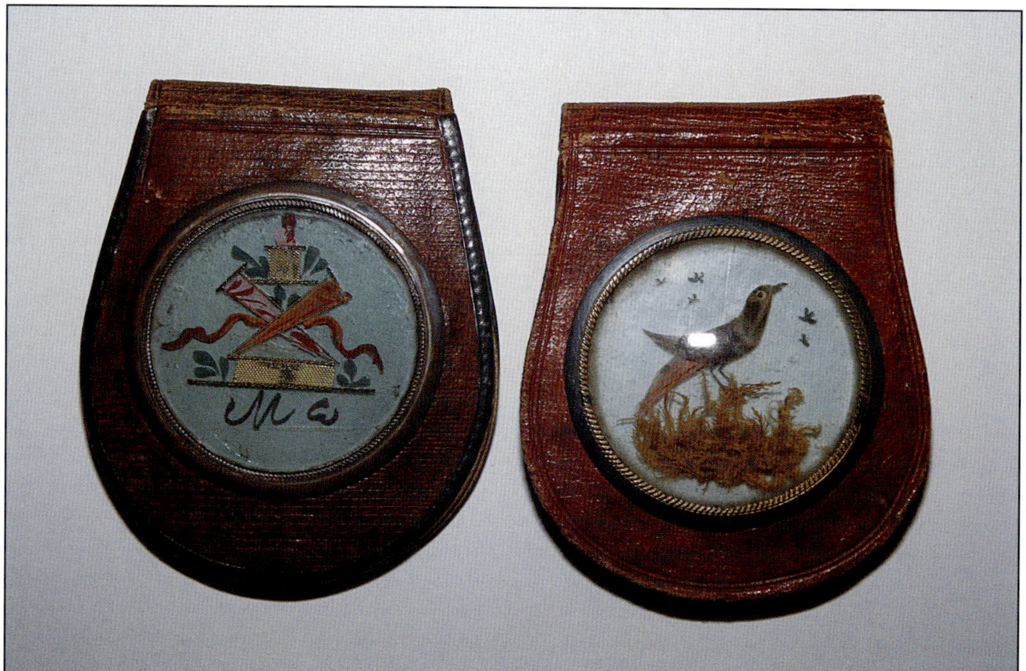

Two, c.1800 leather and glass coin purses. The purse on the left is reverse glass painted with an altar and torch scene, commemorating a victory in battle. The purse on the right is decorated with an applied scene of a bird made from actual feathers and grass. The background has been painted. To access the purses, you lift a flap in the back. The purse on the right is marked on the inside "given to me by Mrs. Riley 1802." Left and right: 3.75 x 2.5 in. *Collection of Paula Higgins.* $350-400.

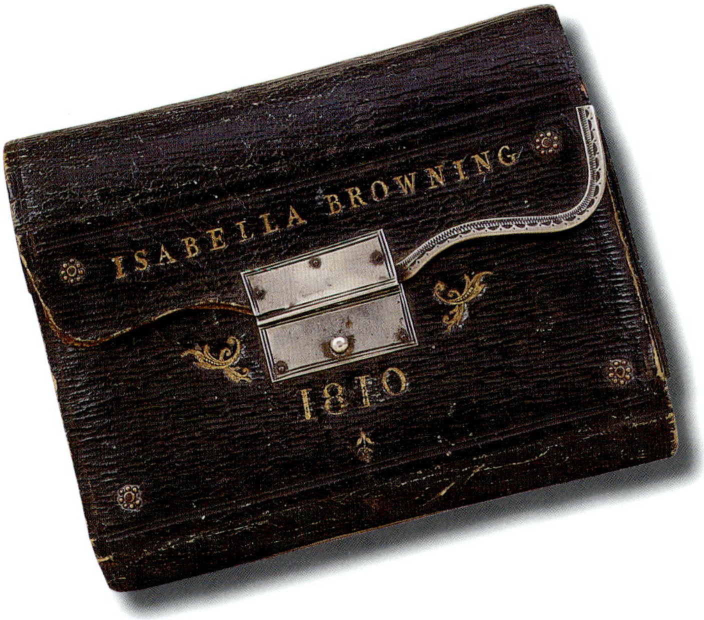

Leather sewing purse embossed with the owner's name, *Isabella Browning*, and the date 1810. Early purses with dates and names on them are prized by collectors. 4 x 3 in. *Collection of Melissa Overdorf.* Rare.

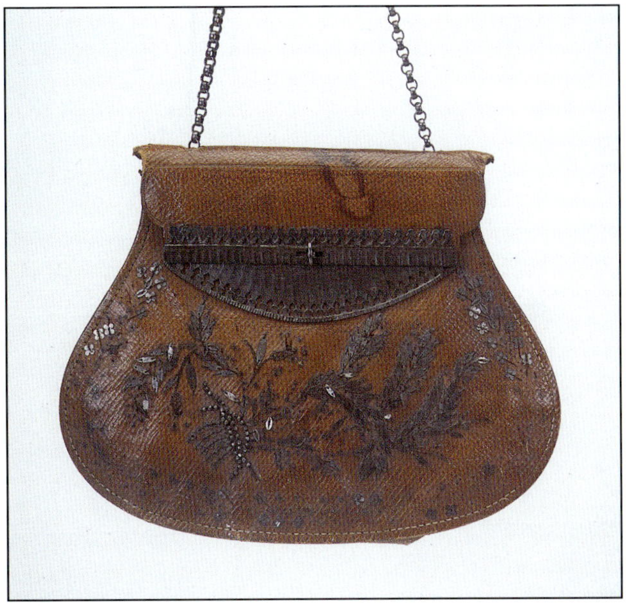

Early 19th century leather purse decorated with cut steel paillettes in a whcat design. The clasp and chain are also made from cut steel. These early cut steel and leather purses are unique to the early 19th century and very desirable. European made, possibly French. 8 x 6 in. *Collection of Lori Blaser.* Rare.

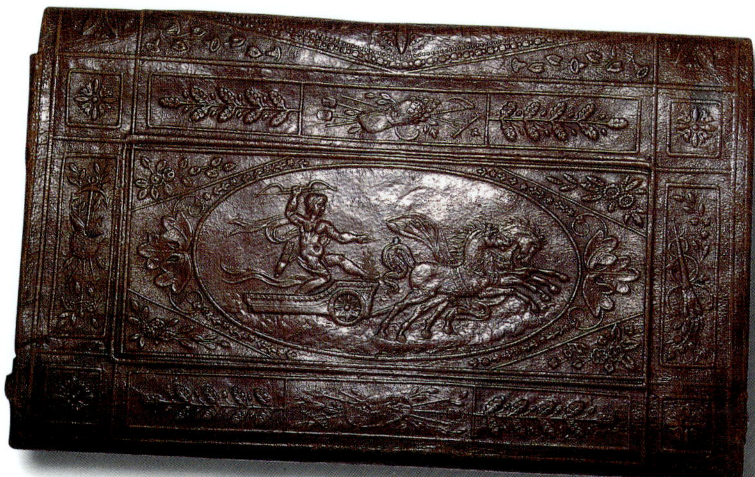

C.1830 leather pocketbook featuring embossed mythological scenes. The inside of the purse is lined with paper engravings. 7 x 4 in. *Collection of Paula Higgins.* $400-450.

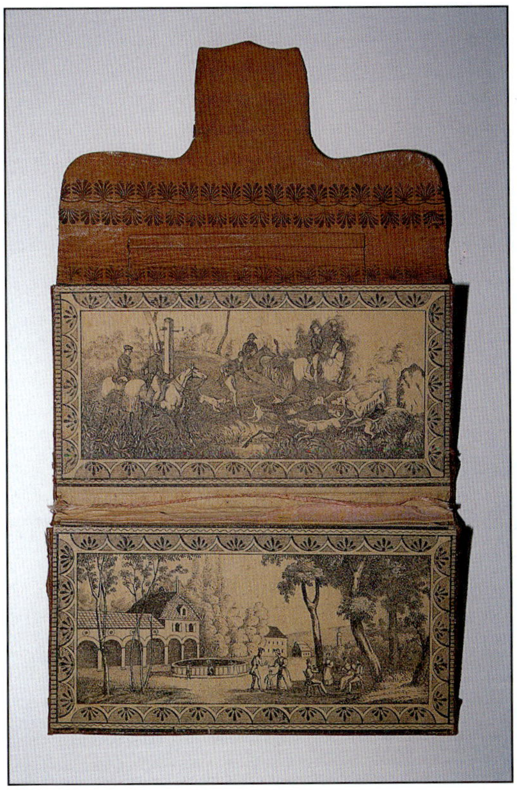

The interior paper engravings of a hunt scene and an outdoor party, possibly a wine party. Other subjects for these purses included engravings of European towns.

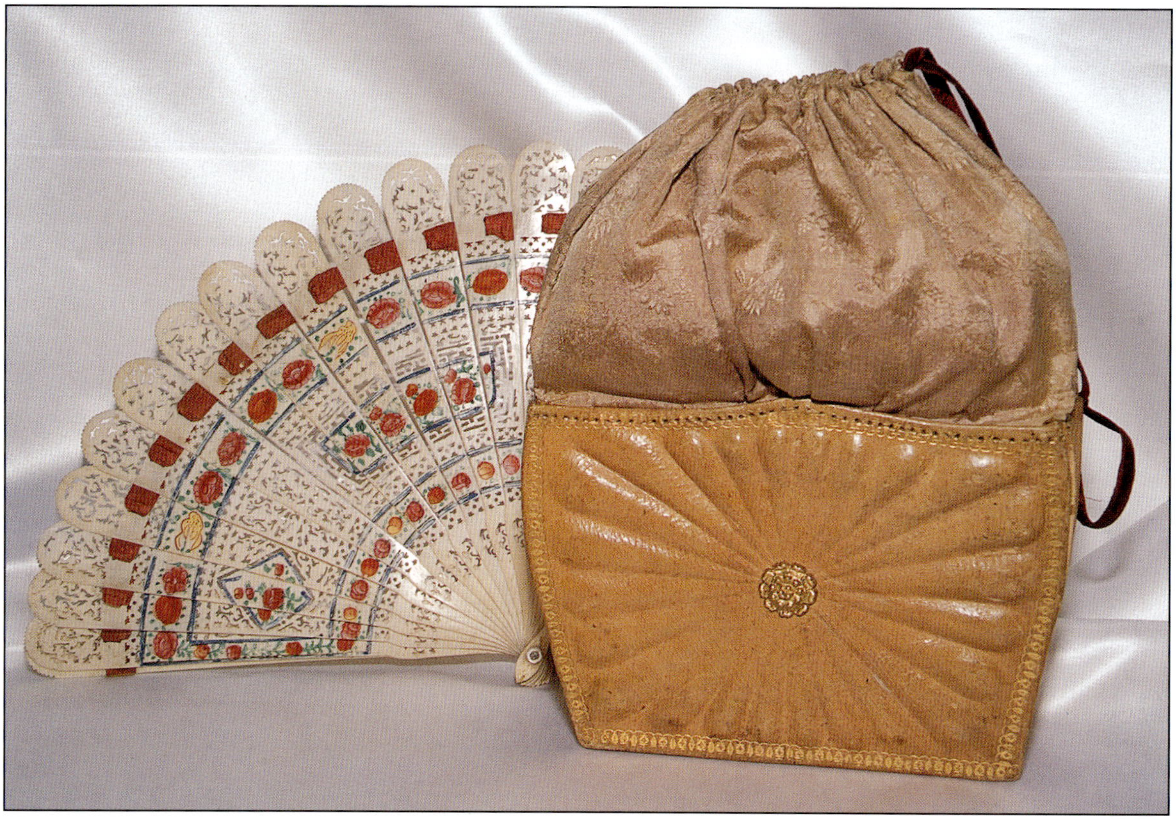

C.1830 leather bucket bag with a silk reticule top. The perimeter of the purse is embossed in gold. The leather body is molded in a sunray design and decorated with a gilt button. Another version of this purse was molded in a pillar design and made from cranberry leather. 8 x 6.25 in. *Collection of Paula Higgins.* Rare.

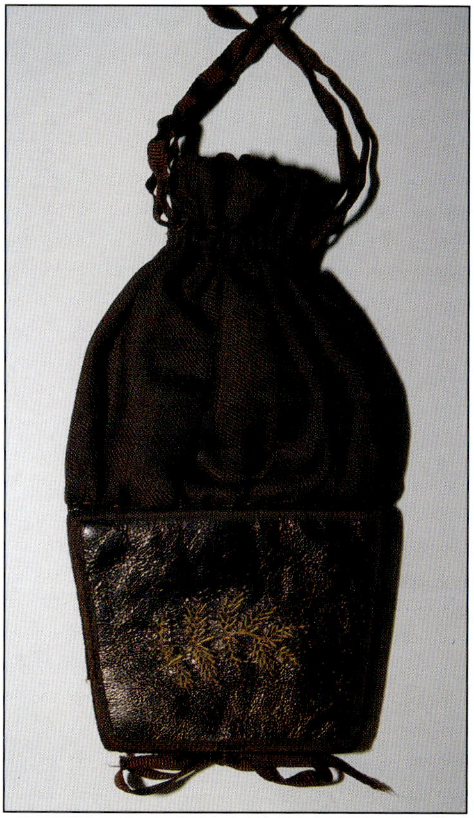

Early 19th century American sewing purse from Maine. This purse is actually a smaller version of the preceding bucket purse, but the bottom opens and closes with silk ties. It is believed that this purse was made by the Shakers. 6 x 3 in. *Collection of Paula Higgins.* $300-350.

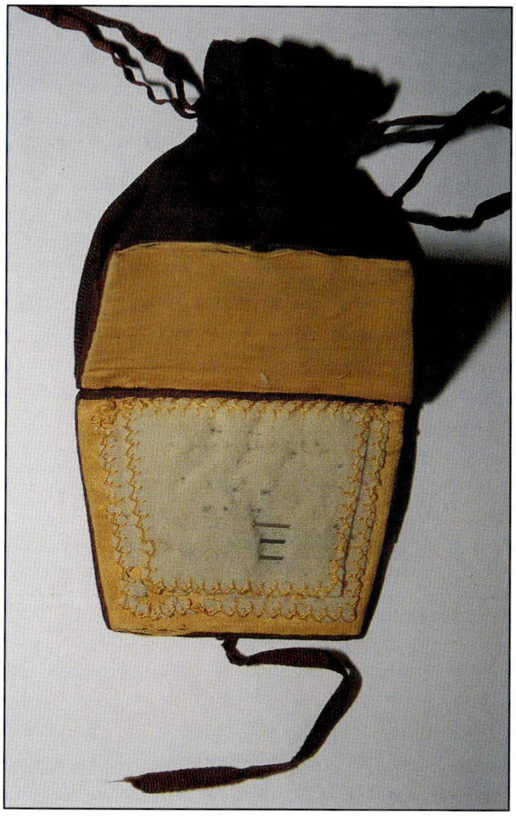

The interior of the sewing purse.

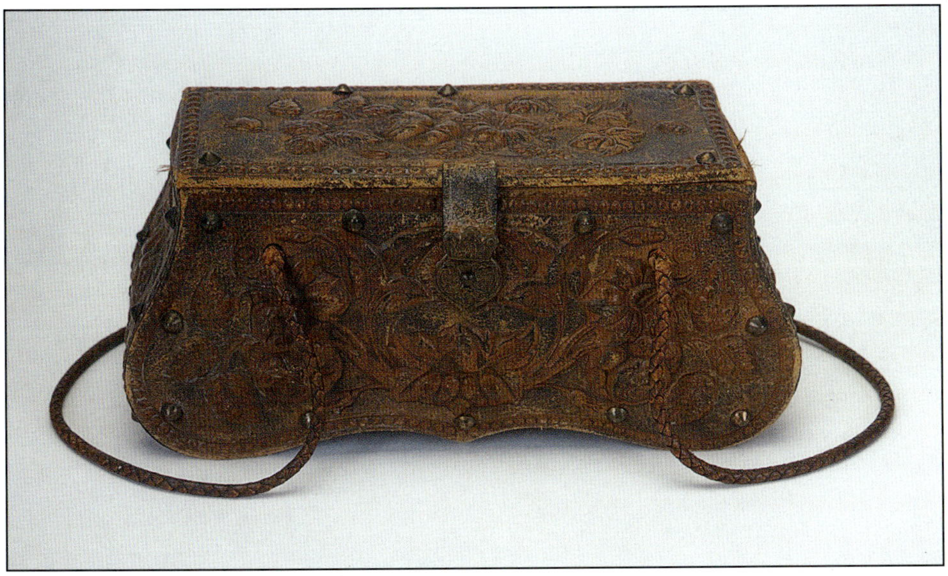

Mid-nineteenth century, hand tooled leather box purse. This is a relatively rare type of purse because they seldom survive in good condition. 8.5 x 4 in. *Collection of Lori Blaser.* $350-450.

Exquisite, mid-nineteenth century sewing purse. The leather is embossed with gold and the sides are decorated with petit point. Found inside the purse are a thimble, strawberry emery, needle holder, and a calling card with the name *Mrs. Whitman L. Mead* written on it. It is believed that this sewing purse was made by the Shakers. 3.5 x 2.25 in. *Collection of Lori Blaser.* $450-500.

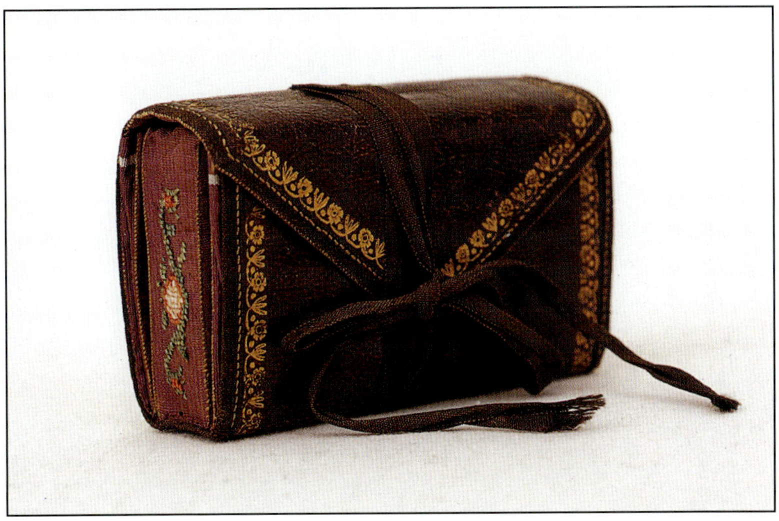

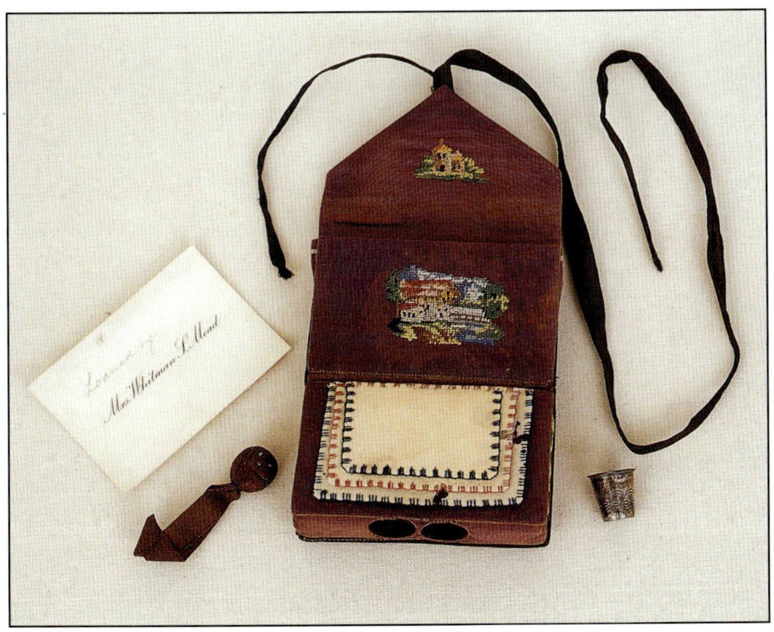

The interior of the sewing purse.

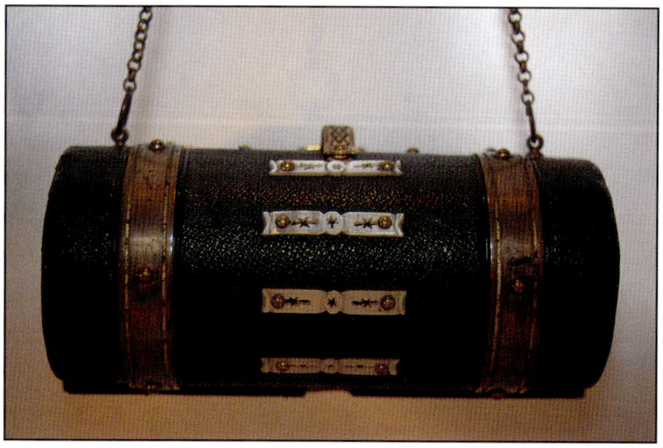

Mid-nineteenth century sewing purse decorated with mother-of-pearl bars. Made in the shape of a traveling trunk from the same period, the outer surface is covered with leather made to look like shagreen (sharkskin). 6.5 x 4 in. *Collection of Paula Higgins.* $250-300.

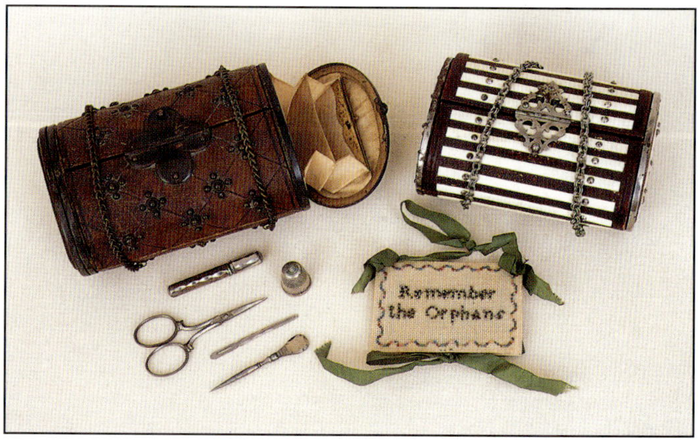

Two nineteenth century sewing purses with their sewing tools, and a beaded and punched, paper needle holder, which says "Remember the Orphans." The purse on the left has a side purse for coins. The sewing purse on the right is made from ivory and leather. Left: 5.5 x 3.5 in. Right: 4.5 x 3.25 in. *Collection of Lori Blaser.* $350-450.

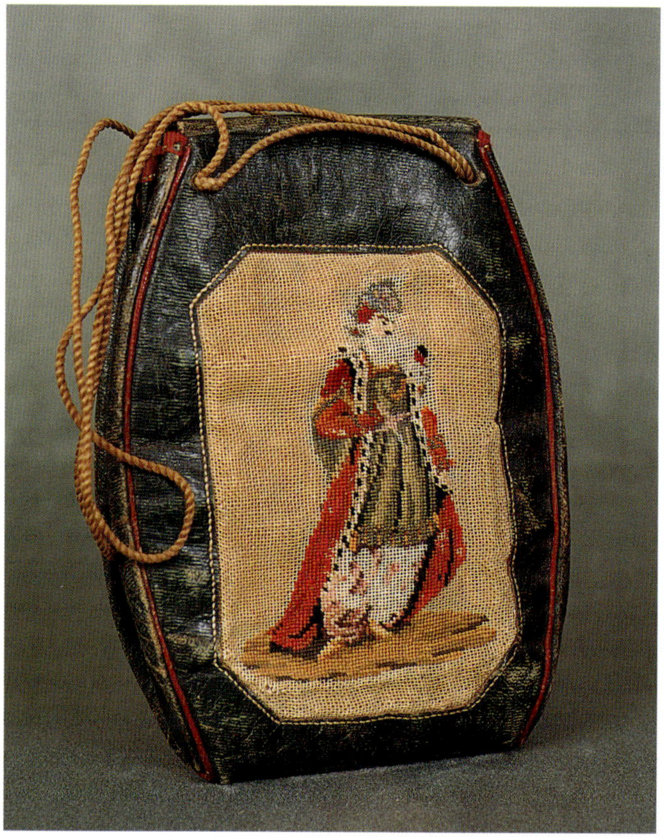

Nineteenth century green leather bag made with a petit point insert of an Ottoman figure. Mid-eastern designs were popular throughout the 19th century. 6 x 4.5 in. *Collection of Lori Blaser.* $300-350.

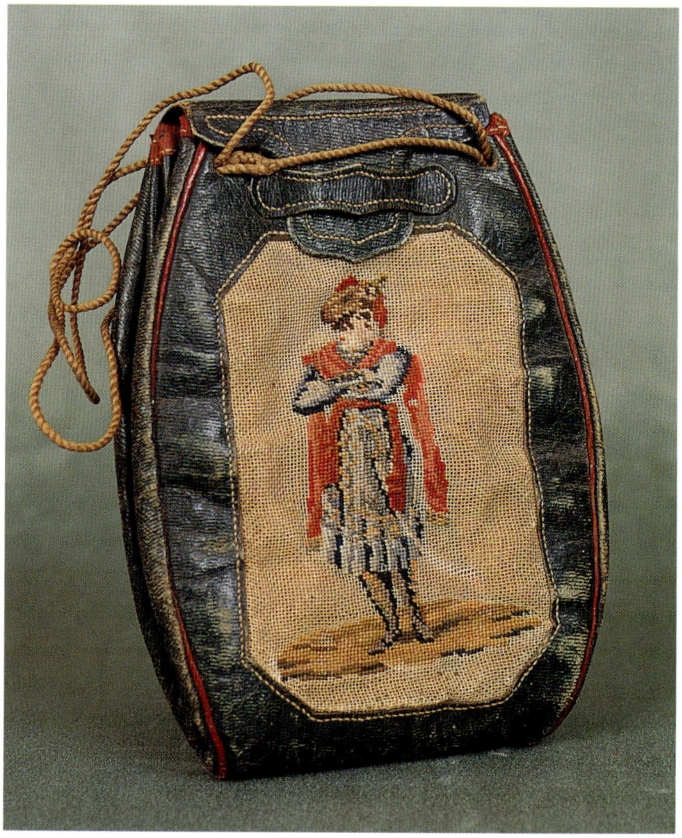

The reverse of the green leather bag.

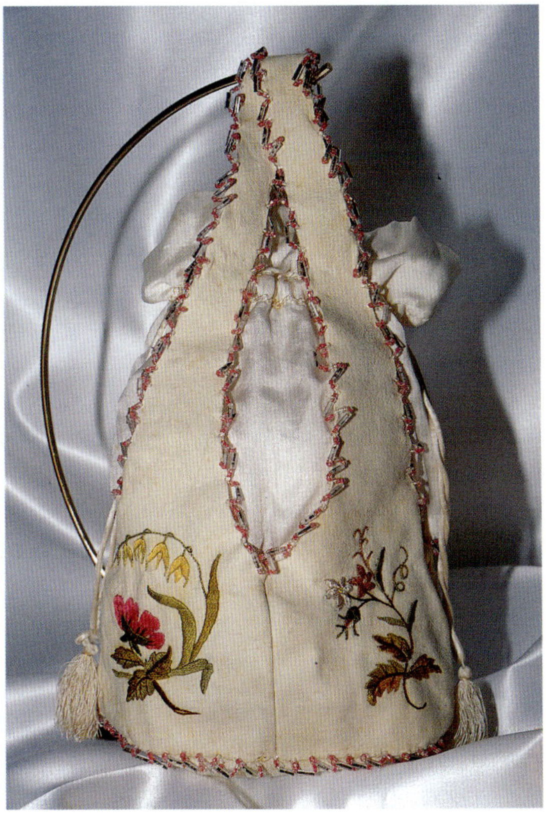

Victorian white leather purse, which has been embroidered with four different floral designs. Inside is an attached silk reticule, which is original to the purse. The beading along the edge is typical of Indian beadwork. This purse may have been made by American or Canadian Indians for the tourist market. 12 x 5 in. *Collection of Paula Higgins.* Rare.

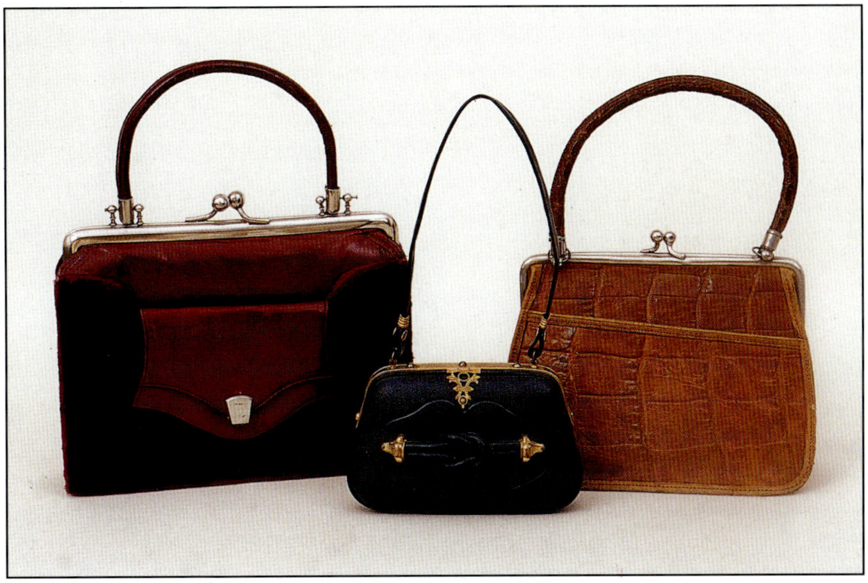

Three late 19th century purses. On the left is a burgundy leather and velvet purse with an exterior pocket. The handle is also made from leather and it closes with a twist clasp. In the middle is a green leather purse, trimmed with gold gilt. On the right is a caramel colored leather purse with an exterior pocket and a rolled leather handle. Left: 7.5 x 6 in. Center: 4.75 x 3 in. Right: 6.5 x 5.5 in. *Collection of Lori Blaser.* $250-300.

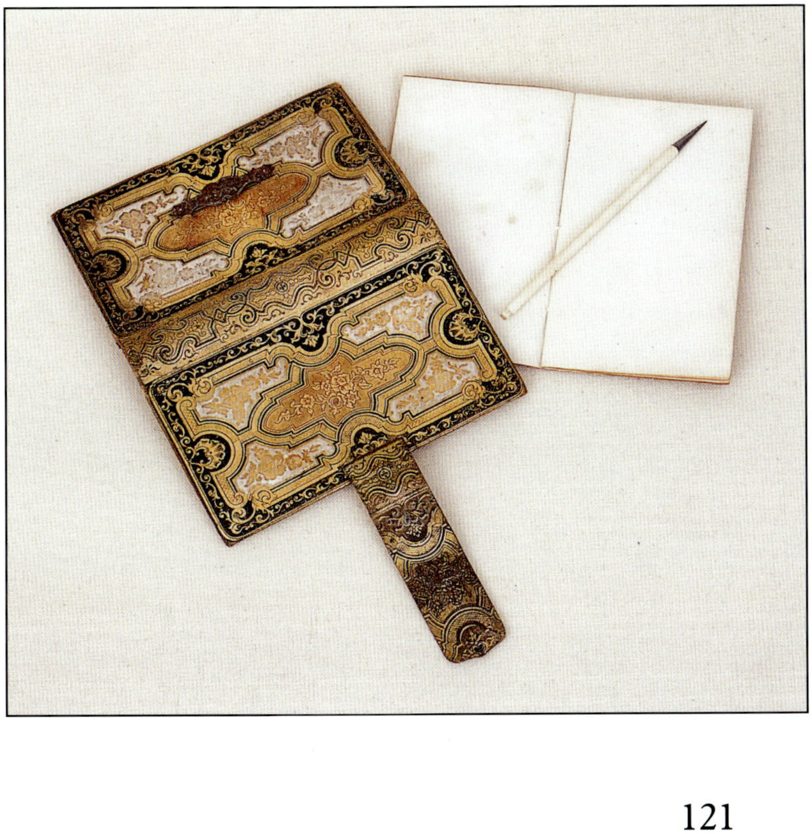

Beautiful Florentine worked, gold embossed leather wallet. Although similar pieces are still being made in Florence today, this wallet dates to the late 19th century. 5.25 x 3.25 in. *Collection of Lori Blaser.* $250-300.

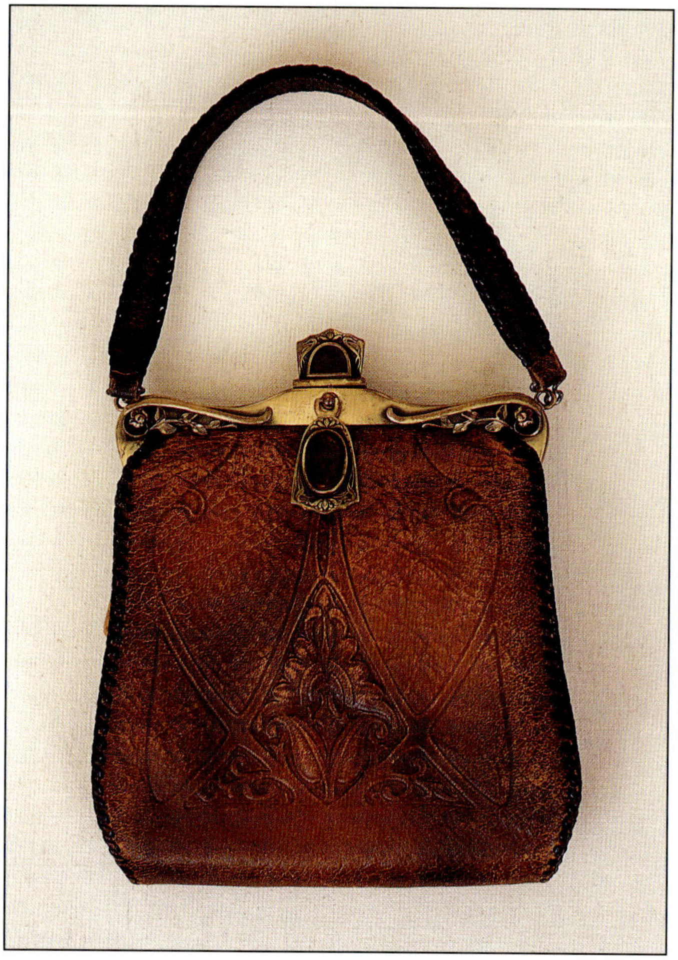

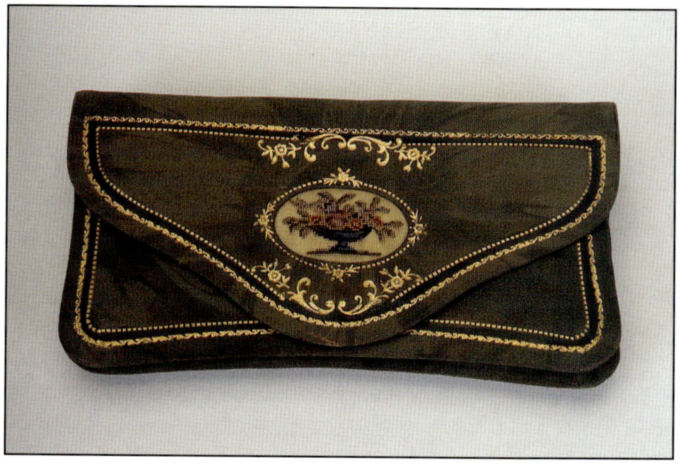

C. 1930 green suede pocketbook decorated with gold, and inset with a petit point urn. This beautifully made piece could be carried today. 6 x 3 in. *Collection of Lori Blaser.* $350-400.

Art Nouveau, tooled leather purse mounted on a lovely frame, which is dated 1917 and marked Jemco. 8 x 7 in. *Collection of Melissa Overdorf.* $300-350.

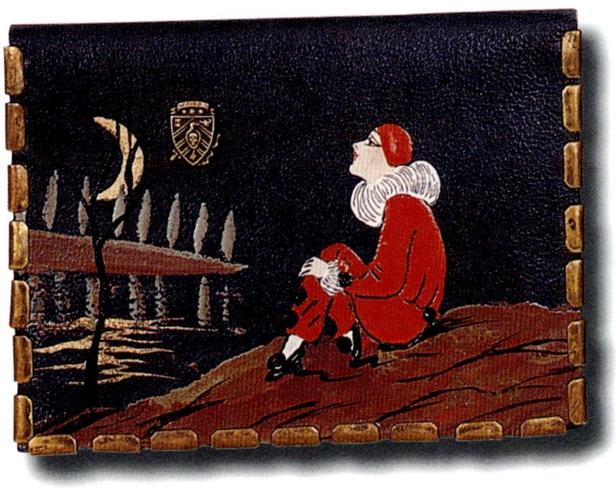

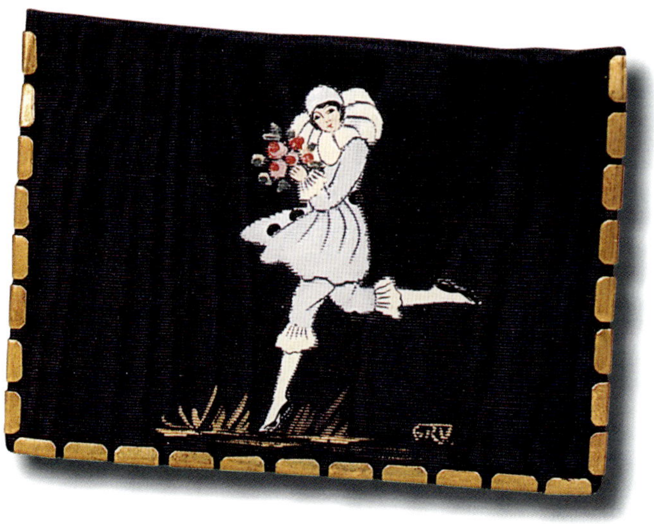

On the left is a leather wallet hand painted with a design of a Pierrot and on the right is a silk moiré wallet hand painted with a Pierrette. Left: 3.5 x 2.5 in. Right: 3.75 x 2.75 in. *Collection of Lori Blaser.* $350-450.

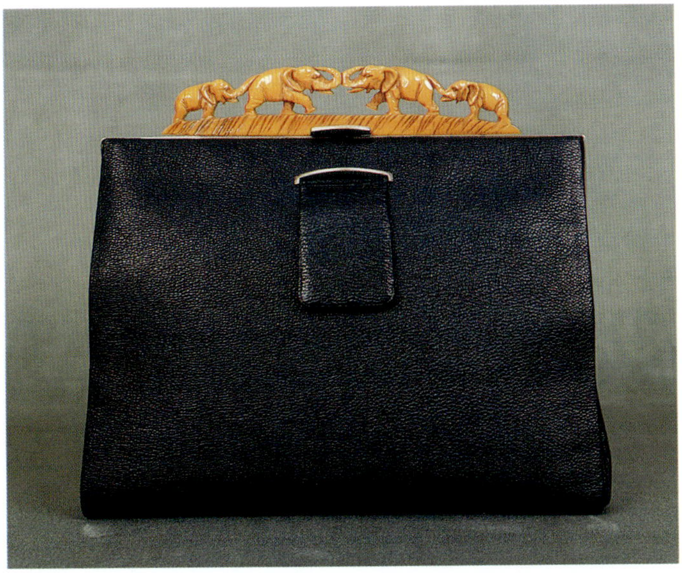

Elegant and sophisticated black leather bag mounted on an elephant carved bakelite frame. Made c.1920, this is another bag, which could still be carried today. 8 x 7.5 in. *Collection of Ruth Penson.* $500-600.

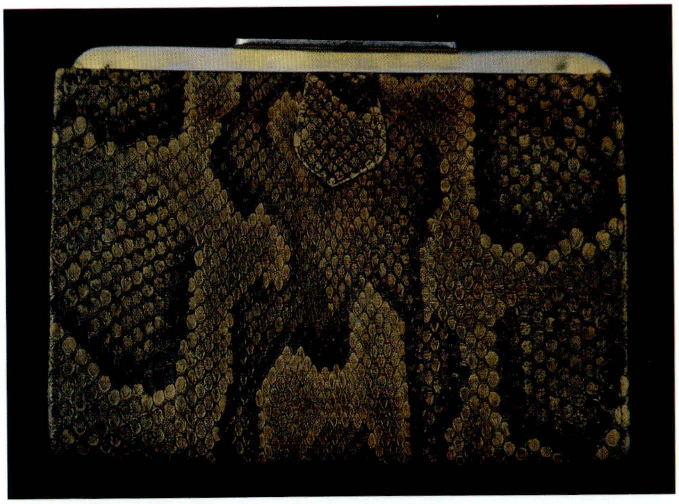

C.1930 snakeskin (python) clutch with a leather interior. 8 x 6.5 in. *Collection of Linda Marshall.* $250-350.

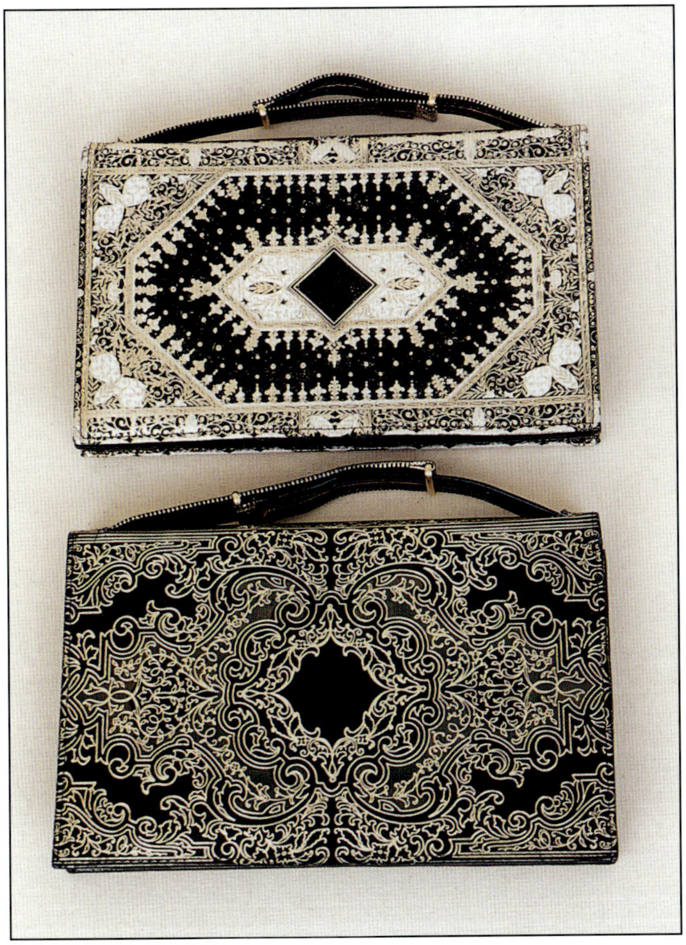

A pair of gold embossed, Florentine worked leather bags. Both 8.5 x 5.75 in. *Collection of Lori Blaser.* $200-300.

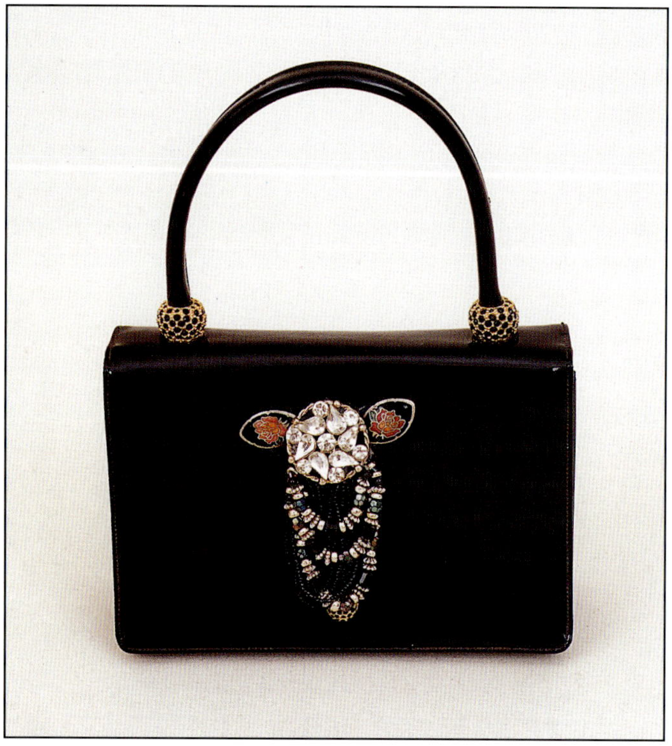

Patent leather bag decorated with paste stones, beads, and enamel. 7.5 x 6 in. *Collection of Lori Blaser.* $150-200.

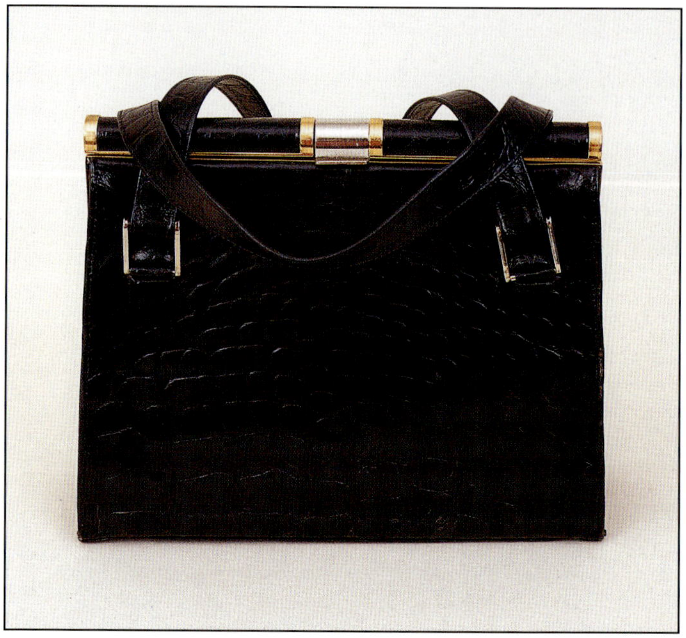

C.1950 Mark Cross alligator leather bag. 10 x 8.5 in. *Collection of Melissa Overdorf.* $400-450.

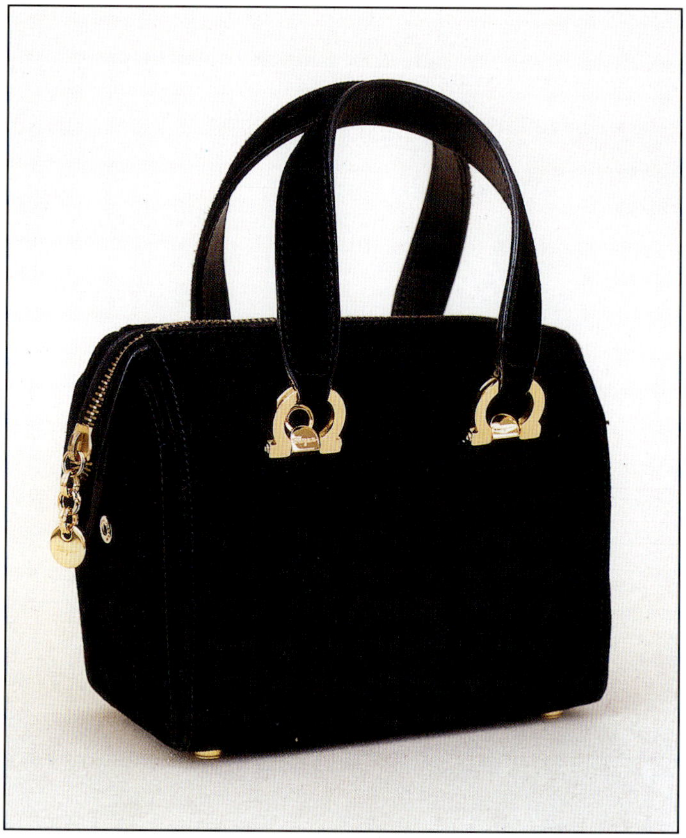

C.1990 black suede bag made by Salvatore Ferragamo. 7 x 6 in. *Collection of Lori Blaser.* $250-300.

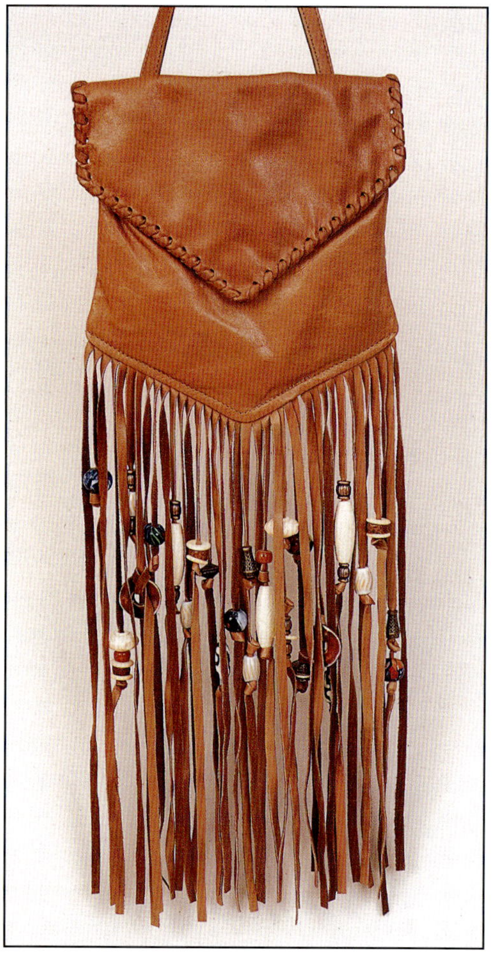

Leather pouch with long fringe hung with large beads. Made in 1992 by Nina Arjani Designs, San Diego USA. 21.5 x 8 in. *Collection of Lori Blaser.* $250-350.

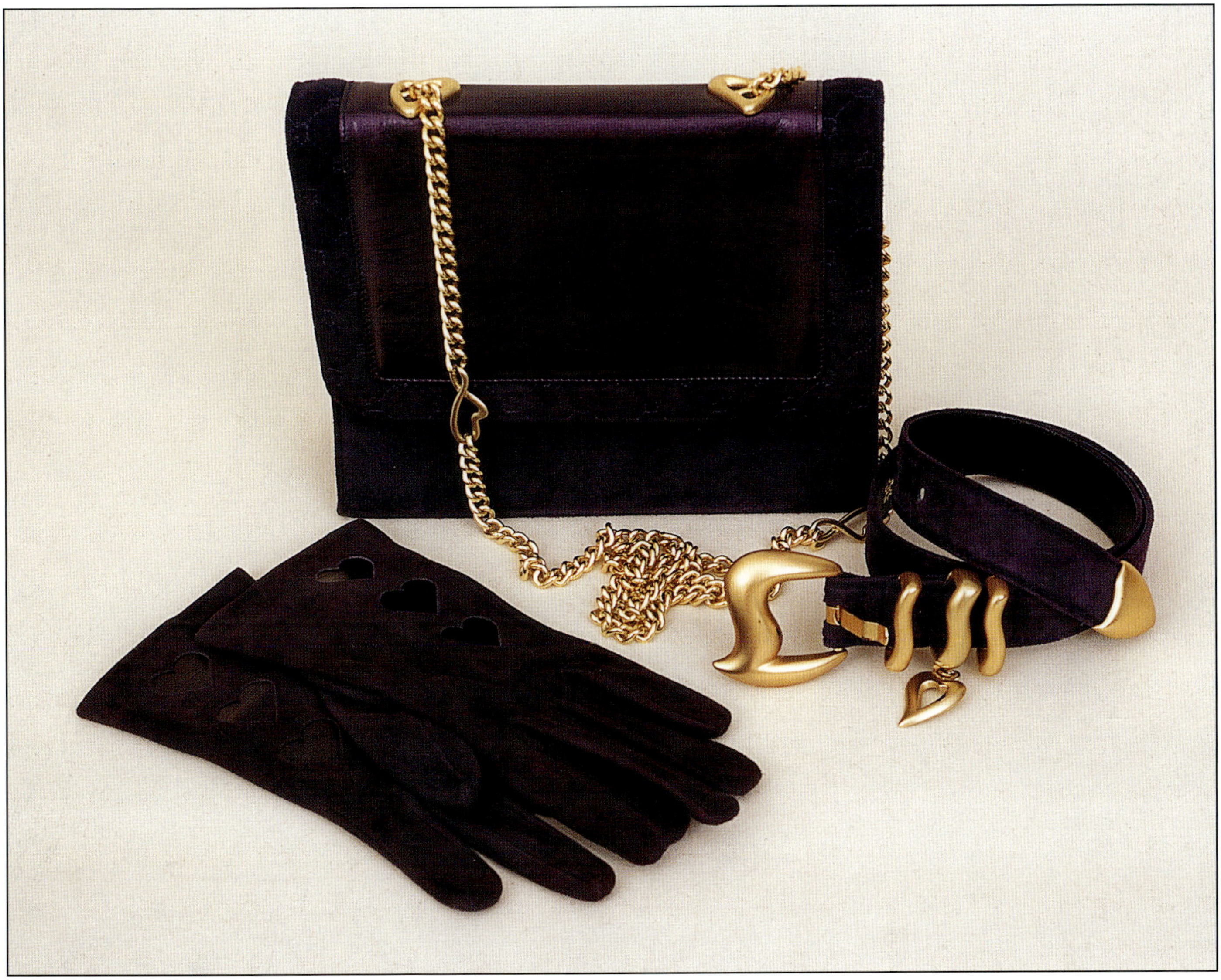

C.1990 plum suede and metallic leather purse by Escada, with a matching belt and gloves. 8.75 x 8 in. *Collection of Lori Blaser.* $350-450.

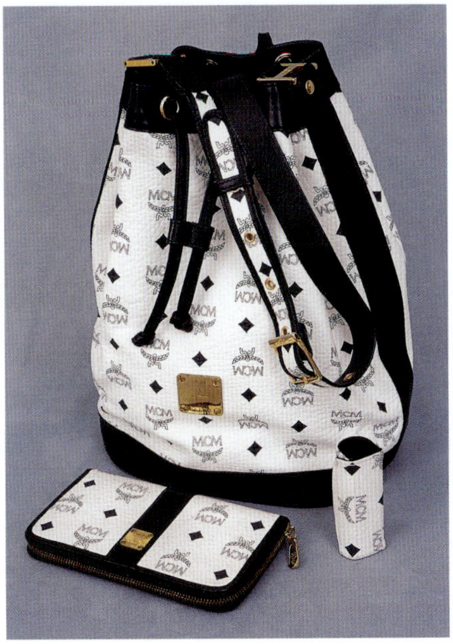

C.1990 MCM bucket bag with navy leather trim, matching wallet and lipstick case. 14 x 11 in. *Collection of Lori Blaser.* $350-450.

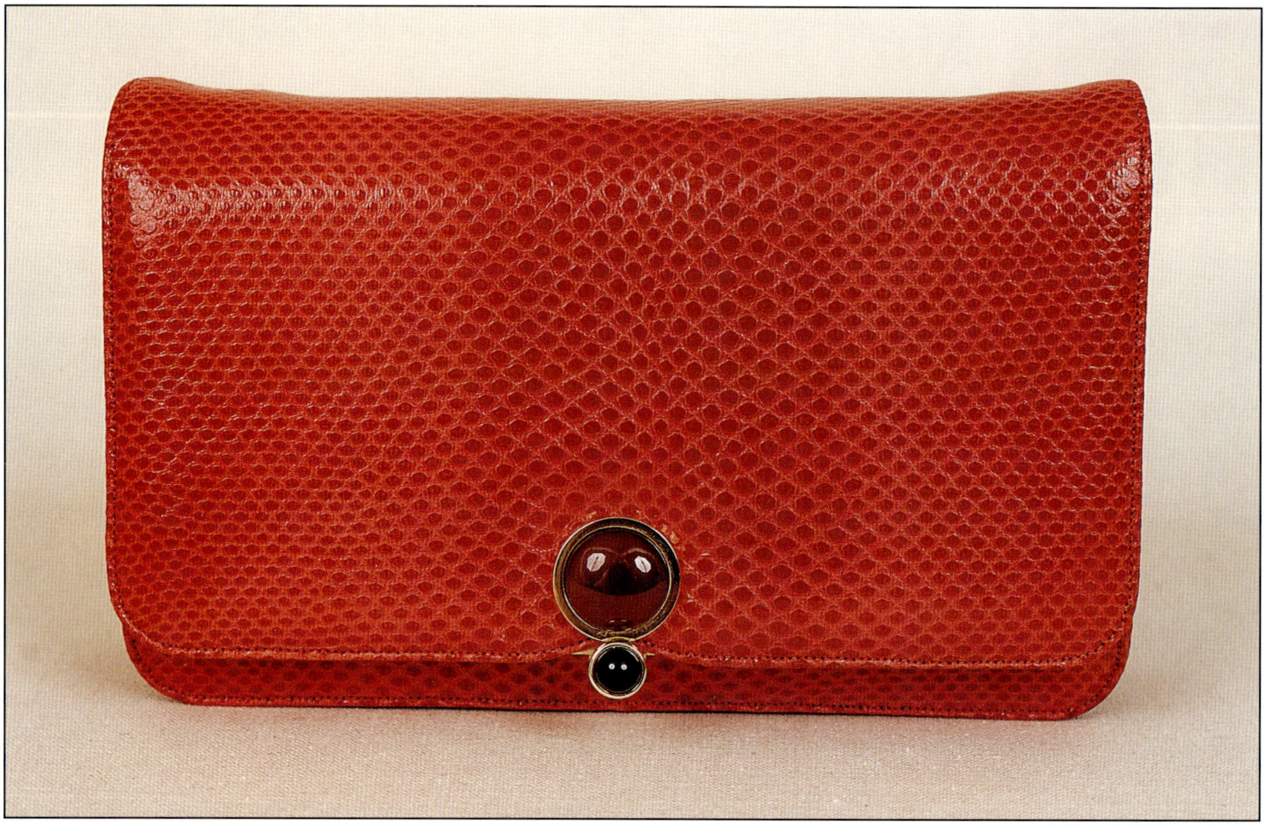

Streamlined elegance by Judith Leiber. Made from red Karung snakeskin, this clutch has a carnelian and onyx clasp. Judith Leiber started her own company in 1963. Her purses have become the gold standard for evening-wear because of their workmanship and creative artistry. 7 x 4.5 in. *Collection of Ruth Penson.* $450-500.

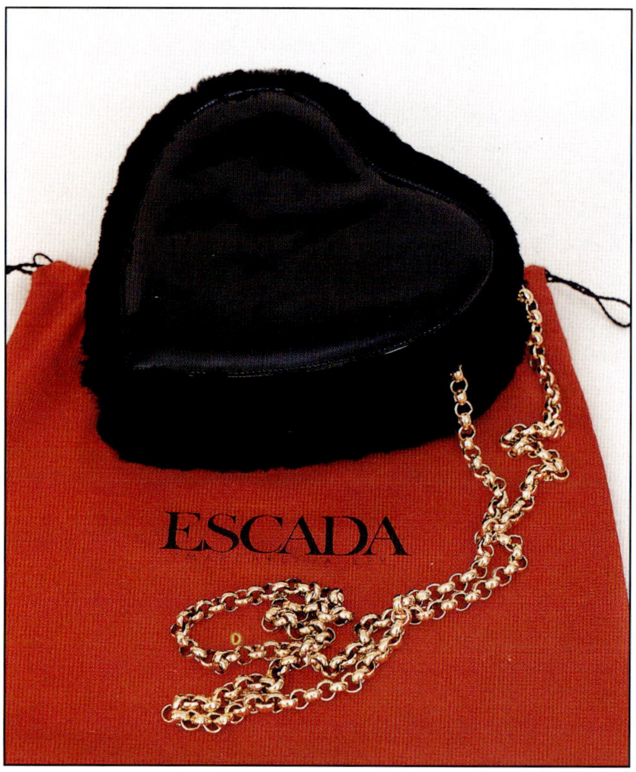

C.1990 Escada heart shaped purse. Made from black patent leather with faux fur trim on the sides. 8.75 x 8.5 in. *Collection of Lori Blaser.* $350-450.

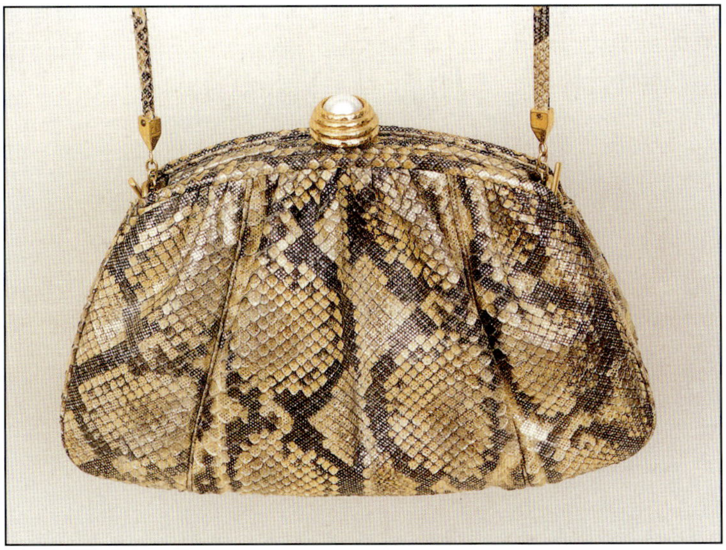

C.1990 Judith Leiber evening bag made from snakeskin. 8.5 x 6 in. *Collection of Lori Blaser.* $450-500.

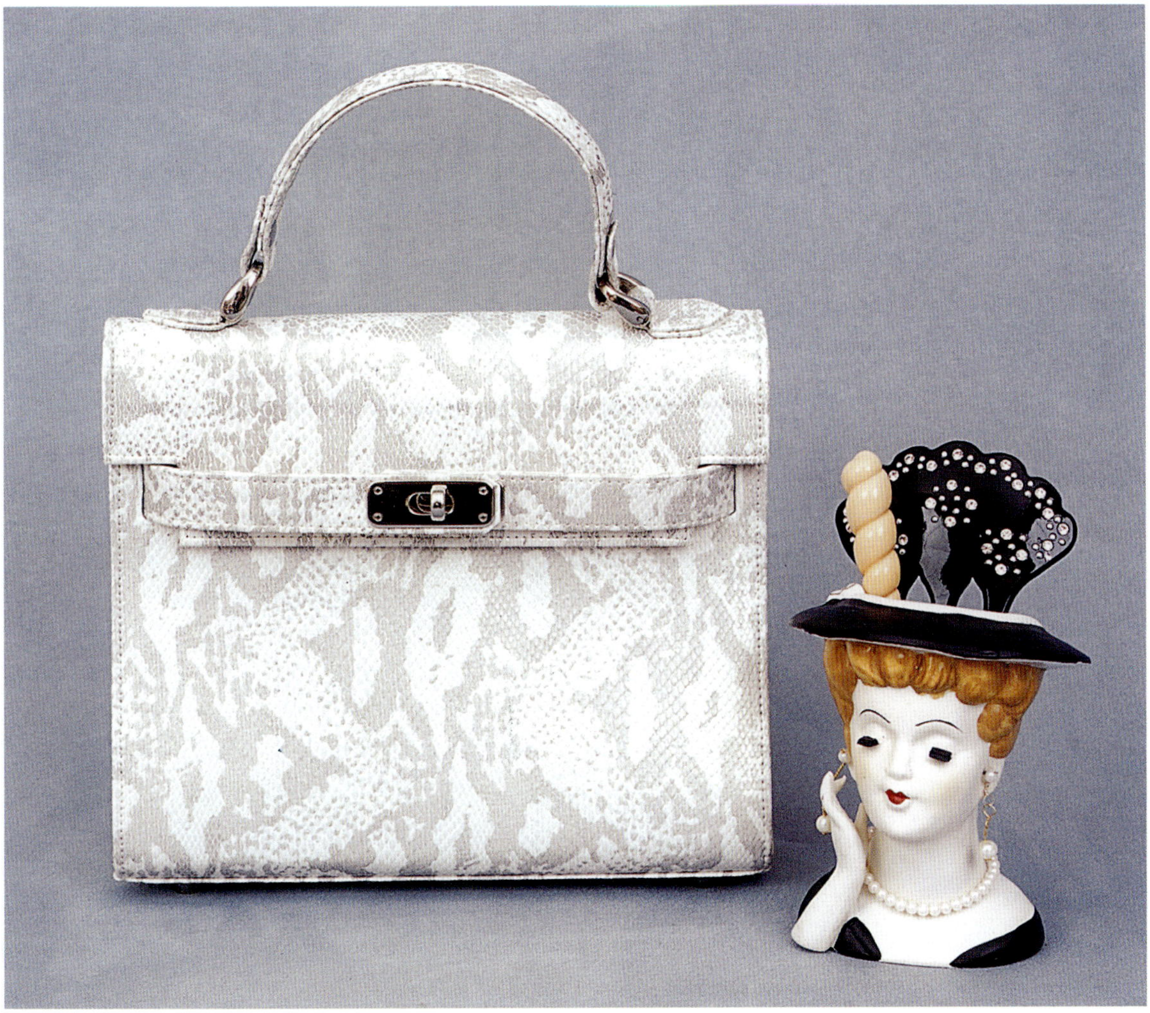

C.1990 B.C.B.G. bag made from a white lizard print on leather. 8.5 x 7.5 in. *Collection of Lori Blaser.* $150-250.

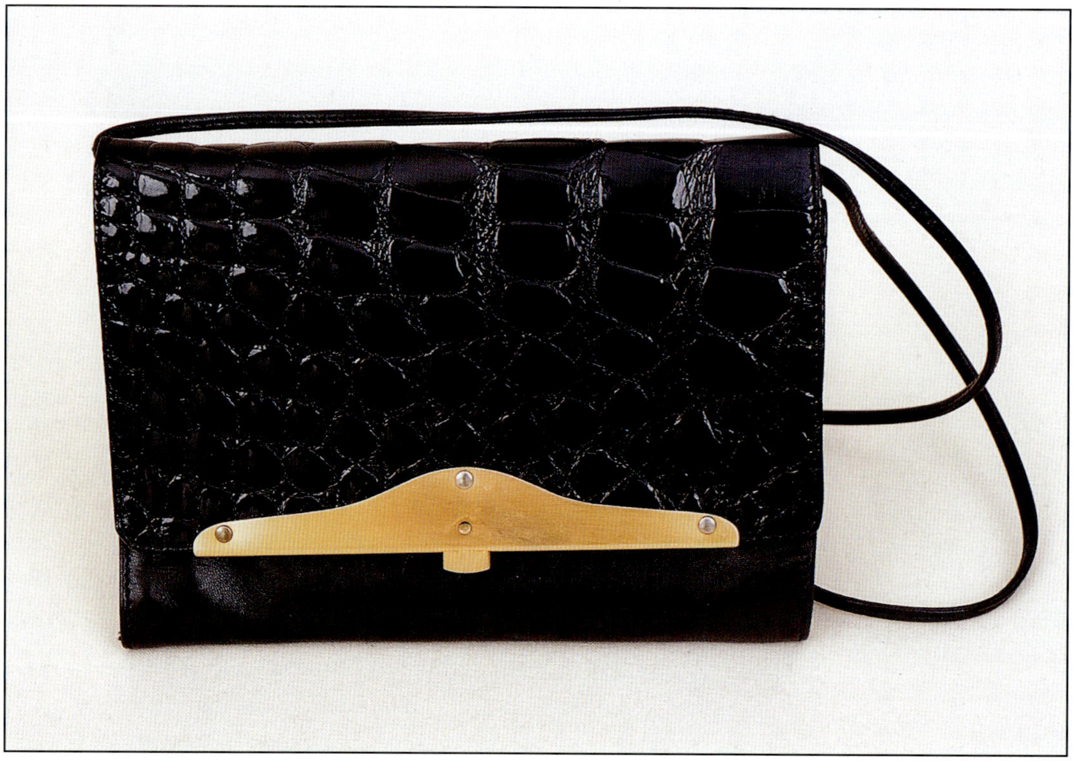

C.1990 black alligator bag made by Donna Karan. 8.5 x 6.5 in. *Collection of Lori Blaser.* $350-450.

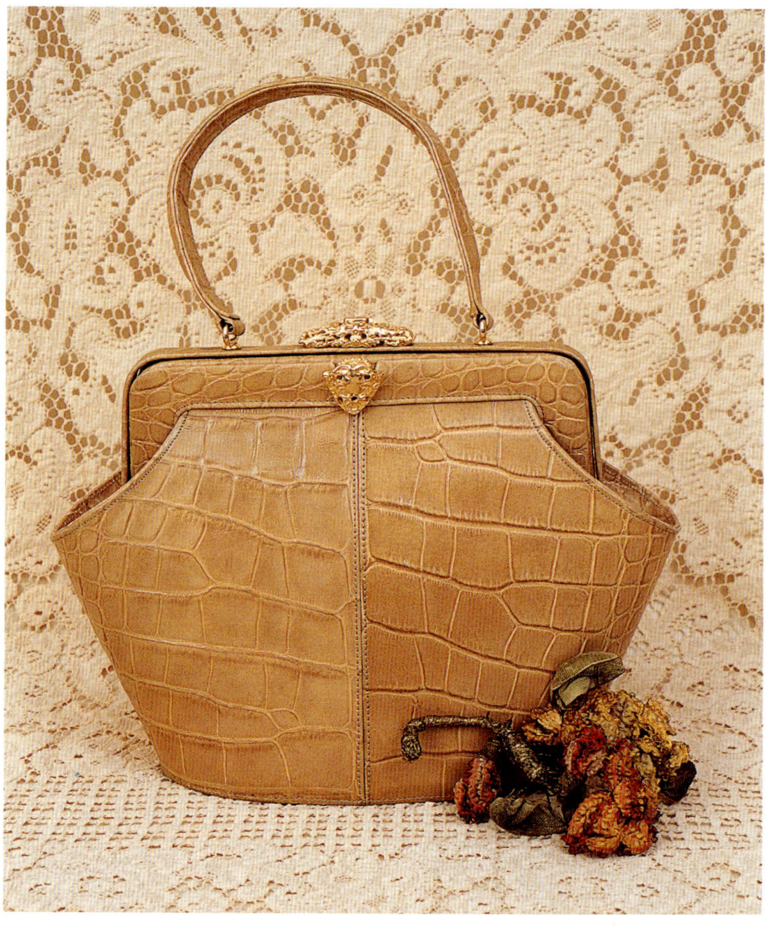

C.1990 structured bag made from alligator printed leather by Glen Miller for Ann Turk. 14 x 12 in. *Collection of Lori Blaser.* $200-250.

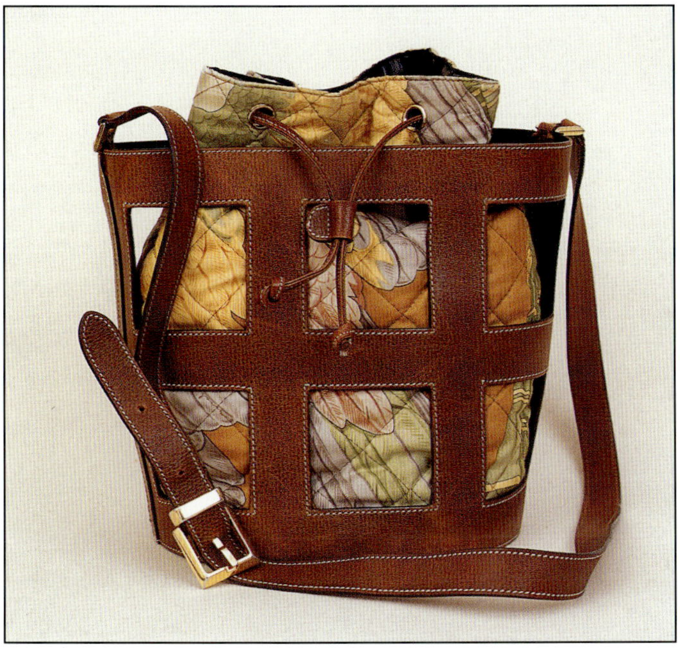

C.1990 Salvatore Ferragamo bag made from cutout leather. A separate bag made from quilted silk sits inside the leather bag. 11 x 10.5 in. *Collection of Lori Blaser.* $300-400.

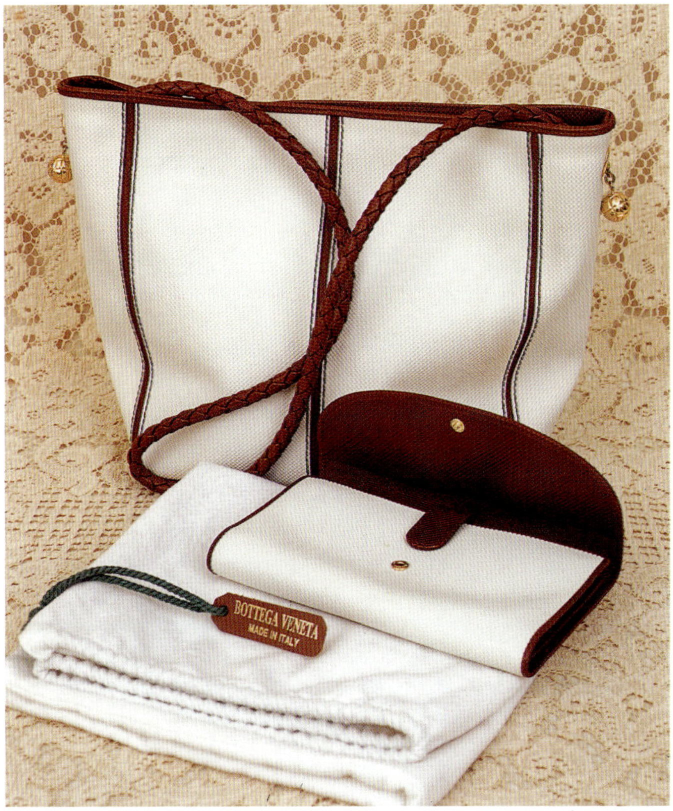

A timeless bag made by Bottega Veneta, trimmed in leather, with a braided leather strap. The original dust bag and wallet are in the foreground. 13 x 9.5 in. *Collection of Lori Blaser.* $350-450.

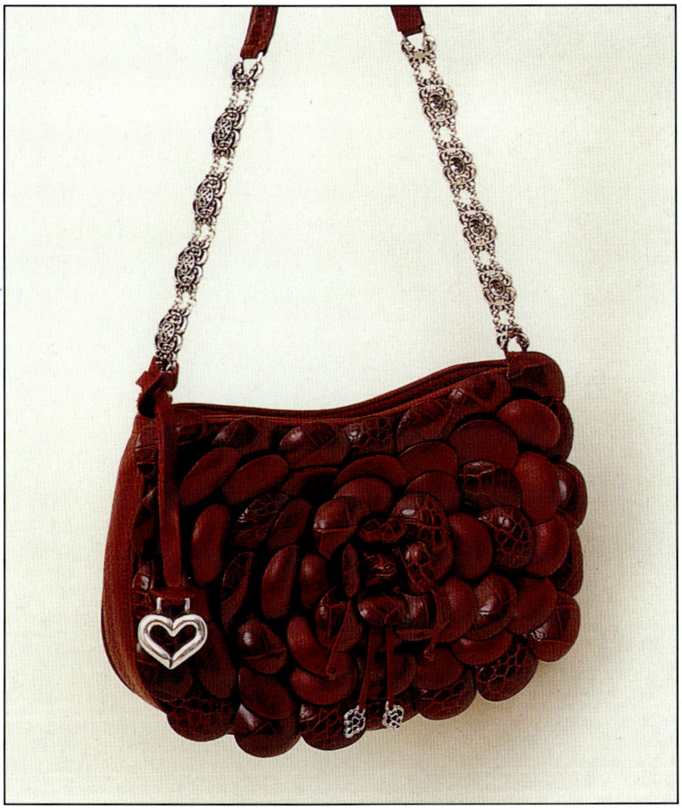

This Brighton cranberry leather purse was a gift to the author (Lori Blaser) from her son Jeffrey in 2005. Floral petals made from smooth leather and alligator stamped leather decorate the entire front of the purse. 9 x 6.5 in. *Collection of Lori Blaser.* Priceless.

Chapter 7
Dance, Compact, and Evening Purses

The idea of a purse designed specifically for evening wear, to use at restaurants, dances, and special events, wasn't fully realized until the early 20th century. There were ornate, beautifully decorated purses made prior to that time, but they weren't sold in volume to women until the early 20th century. An example of a 19th century evening purse is included in this chapter, but most of the purses in this category are from the 20th century.

Early 20th century evening reticules were heavily decorated with ribbons, laces, gold bullion, and embroidery. Beaded bags and mesh bags were also a favorite dress bag for evening wear. But it is the small, jeweled dance and compact purses from the 1920s that capture the imagination of so many purse collectors. The narrow and shortened silhouette of the 1920s required a smaller, more delicate purse to accompany the jewel-like beaded dresses. Women were now routinely wearing cosmetics, which created a need for special containers. So the dance and compact purse was created. It dangled from the wrist, functioning as a coin carrier, mirror holder, and in the case of the compact purse, a cosmetic container. Some models came with inset watches, lighters, fans, and compartments for cigarettes. The dance and compact purse came in a multitude of shapes including: egg, round, square, rectangular, figural, and triangular. Purses were made from many materials including: mesh, plastics, bone, mother-of-pearl, enamel, fabric, petit point, metals, jewels, feathers, and nuts. Hung from black carry cords or chains, they were lightweight and easily carried while dancing. Silk tassels, which hid cylindrical lipstick containers, were the perfect finishing touch for the compact purse and allowed easy access to the lipstick. Occasionally scent bottles were substituted for lipstick containers. A compact purse with all its original pieces (powder puff, lipstick holder) is desirable. While all dance and compact purses have undeniable charm, figural dance/compact purses are among the most rare and collectible.

By the 1930s evening purses were made in the clutch and envelope shapes. Beaded, embroidered, and made from luxury fabrics they were sophisticated and functional. Clasps and frames were decorated with real and faux coral, jade, and pearls, reflecting the oriental design influence prior to World War II. All collectors are familiar with the tambour embroidered and beaded purses of the 1930s. Not all of them were mediocre. Some were made with enameled and jeweled frames, and beautiful color schemes, making them more collectible.

Minaudieres, slender boxes containing compartments for cigarettes, combs, lighters, coins, and cosmetics make their appearance in the 1930s. Exceptional examples were made by jewelry houses such as Van Cleef and Arpels, and Cartier. Early minaudieres are highly collectible. Minaudieres were to gain even more prominence in the second half of the 20th century thanks to the artistry of purse designer Judith Leiber.

After the Second World War, beaded evening purses were made in Belgium, France, and Japan. Although expensive French purses also incorporated embroidery, many were beaded in one color, or in simple geometric patterns. Even the mesh bag, which was now made in either silver or gold, reflected a sameness and lack of creativity. Rhinestone purses also lacked their former Art Deco stylishness.

The name Judith Leiber is synonymous with evening bags. Since 1963, she has been making handbags for evening wear. Her first bags were made from leathers and silks and decorated with jeweled handles and clasps. By the late 60s, she was making beautiful minaudieres, hand decorated with Swarovski crystals. Made in the shapes of cats, fruits, dogs, pigs, Chinese boxes, shells, and flowers, they are individual works of art, carried by famous women world-wide. She also continues to make silk evening bags decorated with rhinestone clasps. First Ladies Barbara Bush, Hillary Clinton, and Laura Bush carried Judith Leiber silk purses to their husband's inaugurations. Leiber bags are in The Smithsonian Institution in Washington, D.C., The Metropolitan Museum of Art in New York, and The Victoria and Albert Museum in London. Her bags are sold today for $2,000 and up, as true investment pieces.

Anna Johnson shows evening purses made by current designers such as Anthony Luciano, Christian Dior, Valentino Garavani, Katherine Baumann, and Violette Nozieres in her book, *Handbags*. Handles decorated with lily of the valley flowers, made from green silk leaves, gold wire stems, and pearl and rhinestone buds decorate contemporary evening bags. These are the antique purses of the future. Another purse company, Revivals, uses vintage jeweled frames and attaches them to contemporary bags to create a whole new look. The idea is not new. During the early 20th century, 18th century embroidered fabrics were made into bags, and then attached to enameled, early 20th century frames, creating a very rich look.

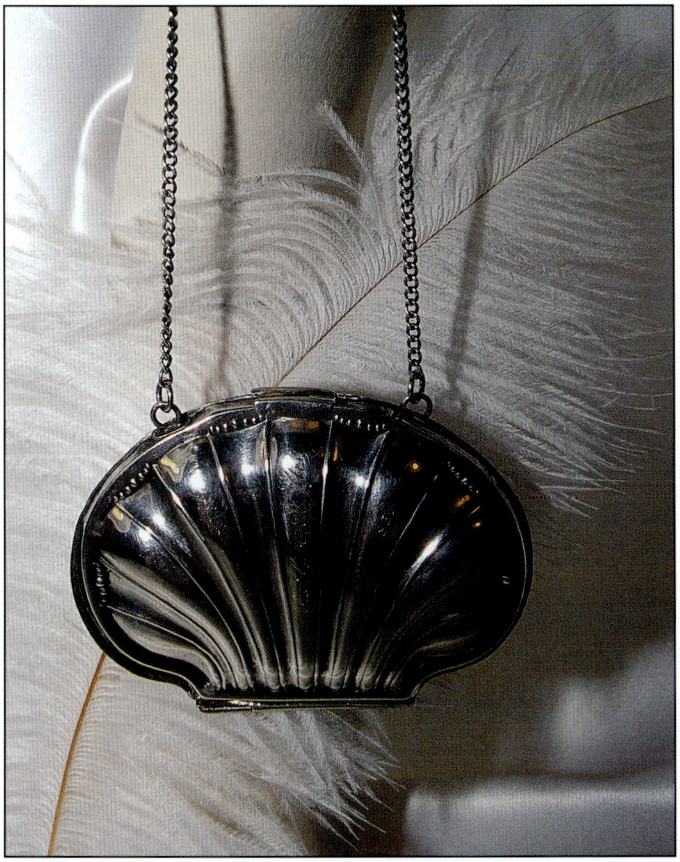

Shell shaped purses have been popular from the early 19th century to the twentieth century. This sterling silver evening purse is dated on one side 1851 and inscribed with the name *C. A. Bolles*. On the reverse side it is dated 1864 and inscribed with the name *Gracie Foster.* It was not unusual for mothers to pass fine purses on to their daughters and inscribe them with their names. This purse came from a New Haven, Connecticut estate. The interior has two compartments and it is lined with pink silk. 3 x 2.5 in. *Collection of Paula Higgins.* $350-400.

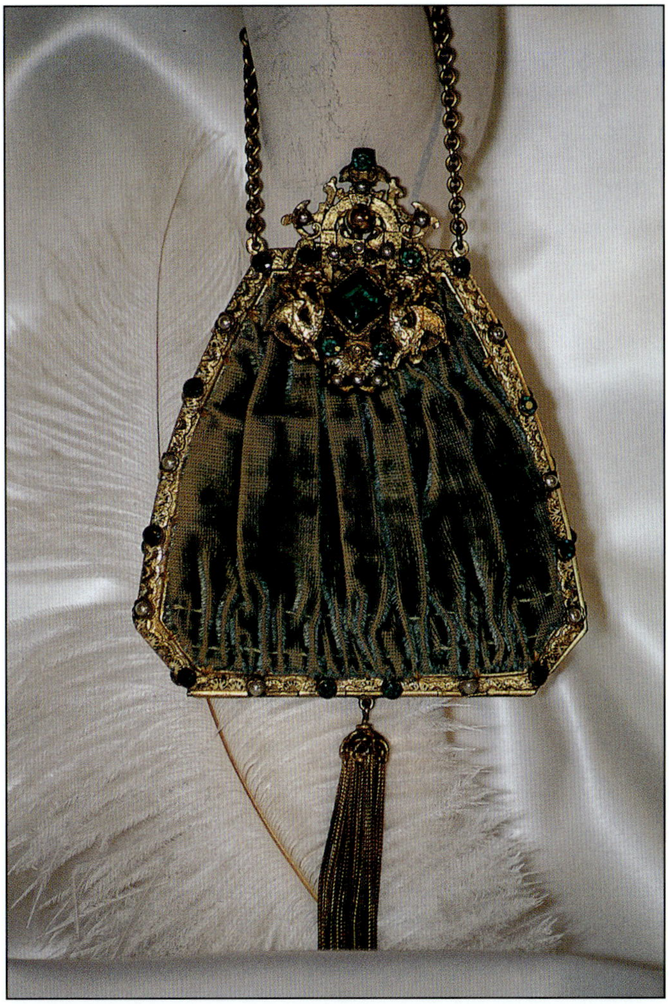

This 19th century green velvet evening purse is rare. The frame is hand made and set with pearls and foil-backed stones, to add depth and color. Traces of the original enamel work remain on parts of the frame. Two griffin-like creatures flank the large emerald stone. The interior is lined with an early silk fabric, which is finished with a fine silk braid. 5 x 4 in. *Collection of Paula Higgins.* Rare.

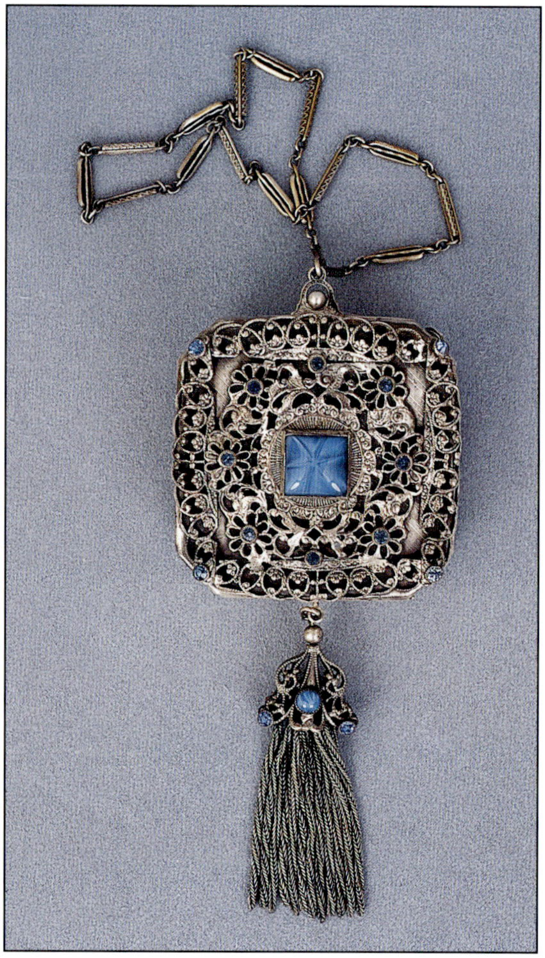

Early 20th century vanity/dance purse, beautifully made with filigree work and blue stones. 2.5 x 2.5 in. *Collection of Melissa Overdorf.* $450-500.

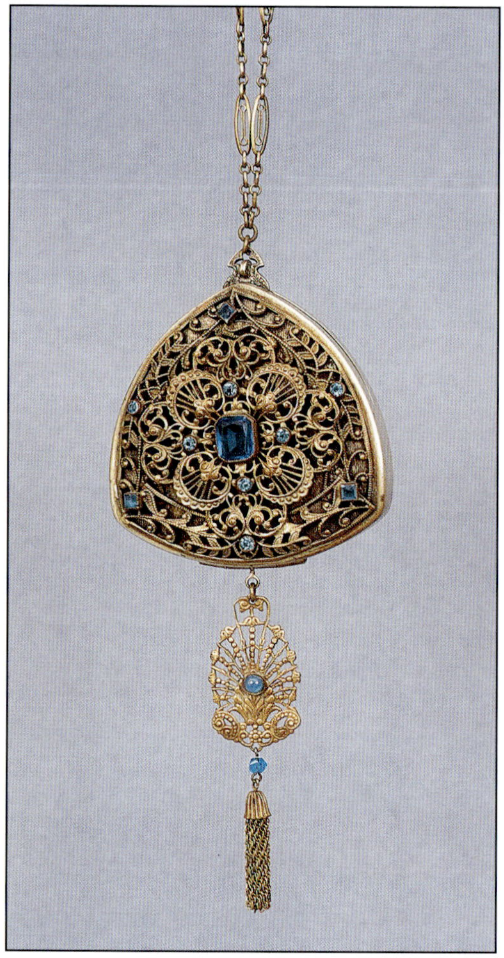

Early 20th century gold filigree vanity/dance purse set with blue stones. The delicate tassel is made in two sections, which is especially lovely. *Collection of Melissa Overdorf.* $450-500.

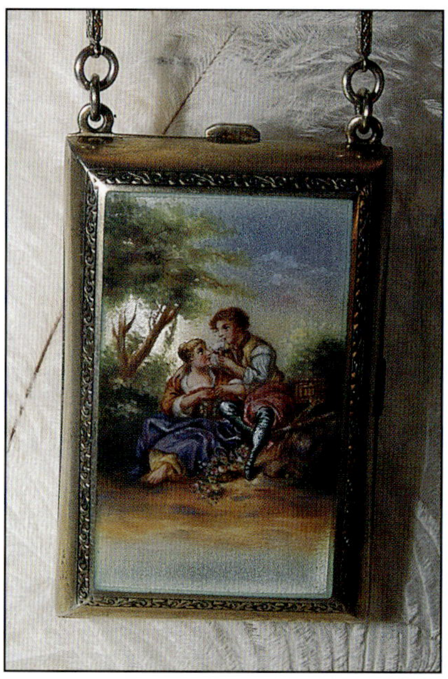

Early 20th century sterling and enameled vanity purse. Hand painted and enameled courting scenes are typically seen on compacts and not vanity purses. Inside the purse are a perfume container, lipstick holder, mirror, and a small area for coins. 2 x 1.75 in. *Collection of Paula Higgins.* $500-600.

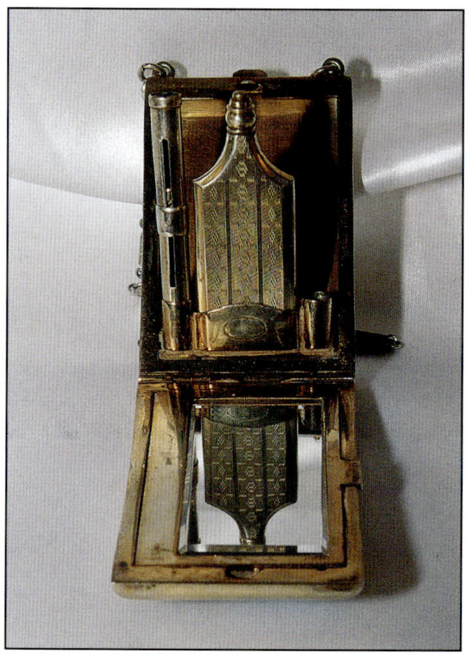

Interior of vanity purse showing a perfume flask, mirror, and lipstick holder.

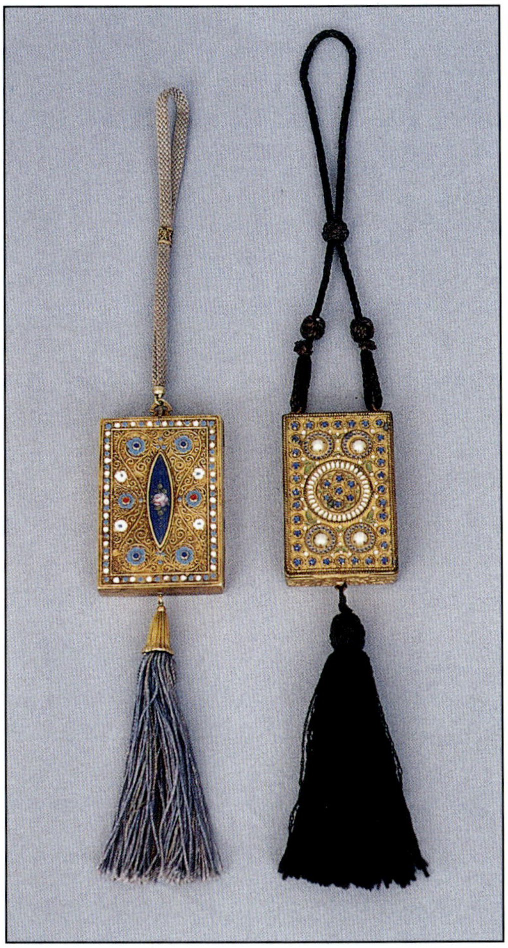

Two vanity/dance purses made with enamel and paste stones. Inside the purses are areas for lipstick, rouge, powder, and a mirror. Left: 14 x 2 in. Right: 15 x 3 in. *Collection of Lori Blaser.* $400-500.

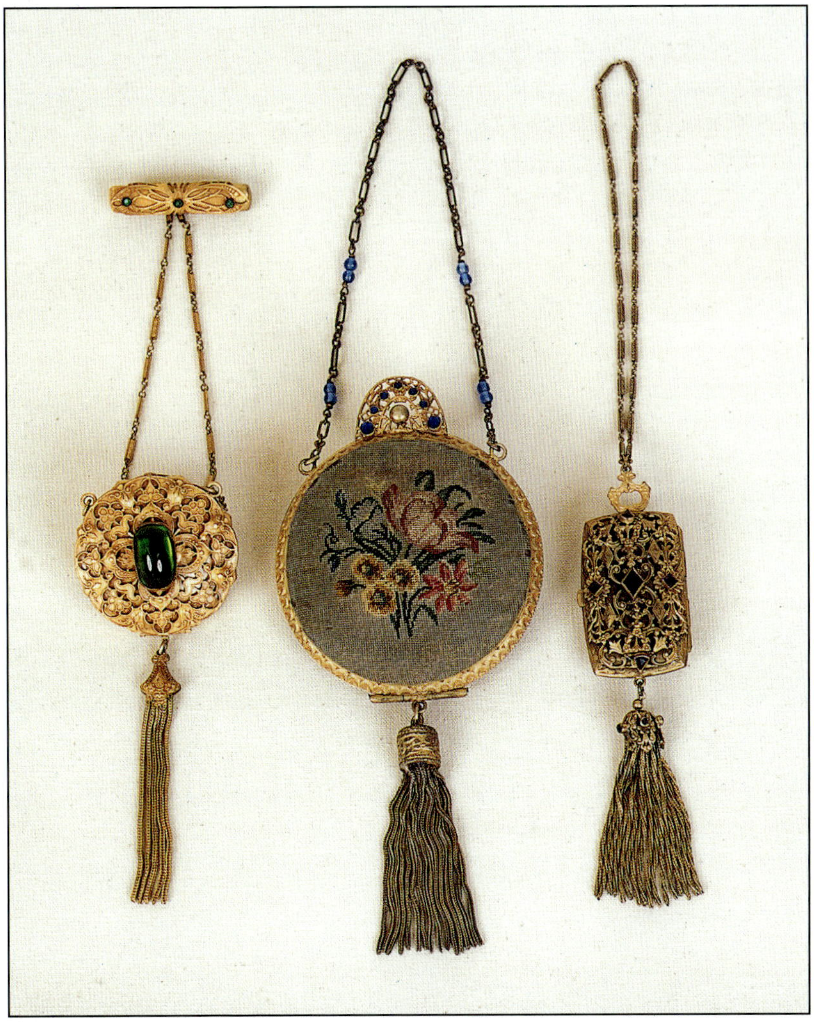

Three compact/dance purses from the early 20th century. On the left is a purse set with a large green stone. The attached lipstick case could be suspended between two fingers. Inside is a place for powder, rouge, and a mirror. The center dance purse has a trinity plate frame with a petit point insert. On the right, is a metal dance purse set with a glass jewel. Inside are two coin holders and an extra space for other necessities. Left: 6 x 2.25 in. Center: 8 x 3.75 in. Right: 6 x 1.5 in. *Collection of Lori Blaser.* $400-450.

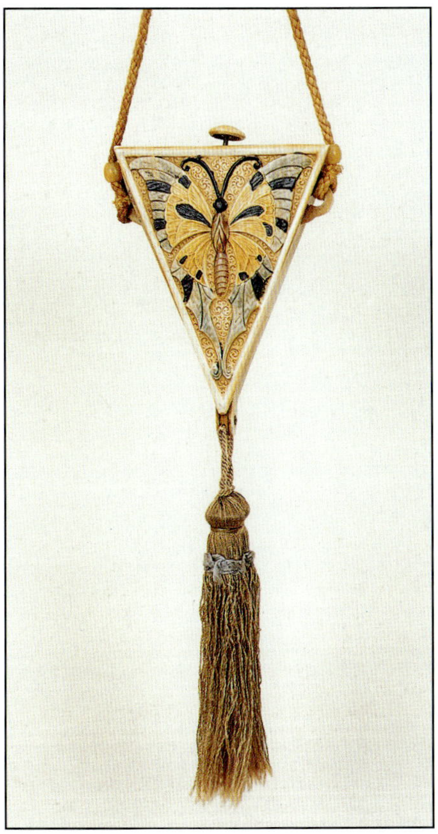

This is a very beautiful celluloid dance purse. Triangular shaped and painted with a design of a butterfly, it makes quite a statement. 13 x 4 in. *Collection of Lori Blaser.* Rare.

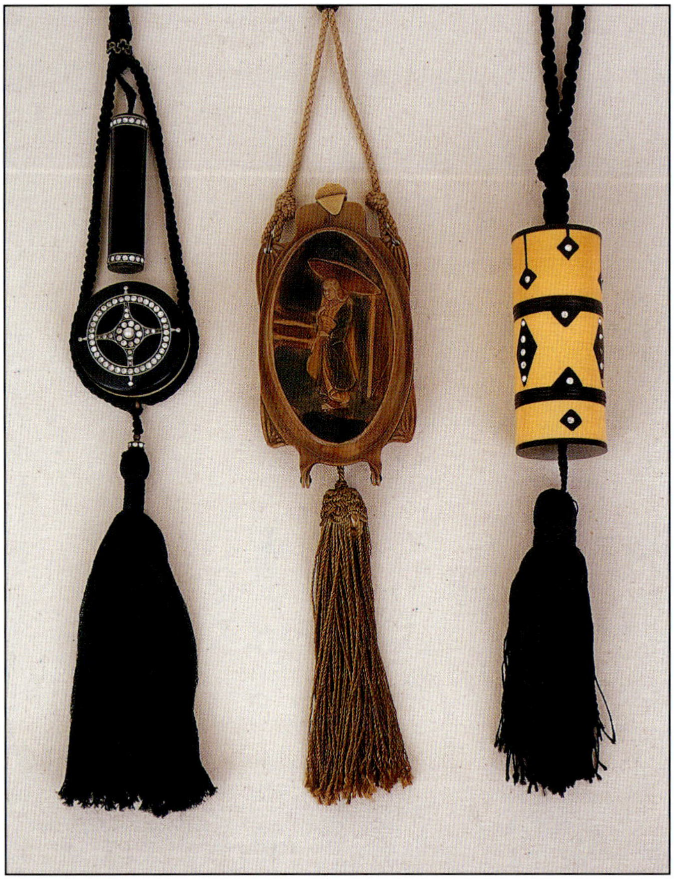

Three vanity or dance purses from the Art Deco Period. The purse on the left is made from plastic and set with paste stones. A lipstick holder hangs in the center. The celluloid purse in the center has an Asian figural design. On the right is a yellow plastic, cylindrical case, which is set with paste stones. All three purses have silk tassels. Left: 11.5 x 2.25 in. Center: 10.5 x 3 in. Right: 9.5 x 1.5 in. *Collection of Lori Blaser.* $400-600.

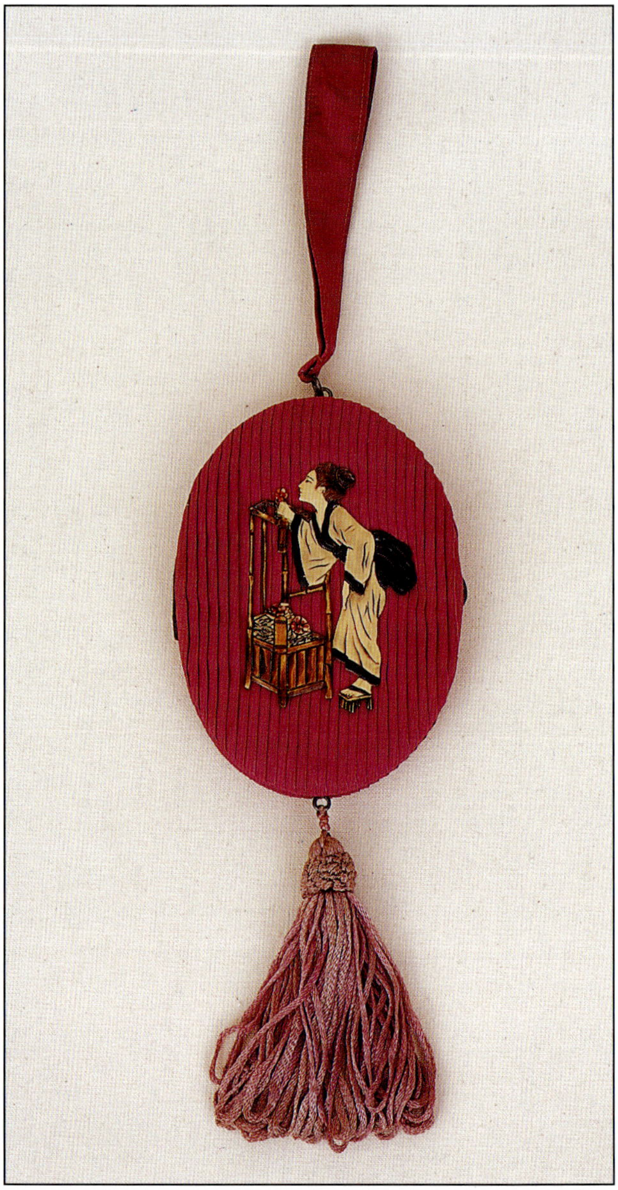

C.1920 dance purse made from pleated pink silk. The Japanese figural on the front of the purse is made from celluloid. The color, design, and materials make this a rare purse. 16.5 x 4 in. *Collection of Ellen Foster.* Rare.

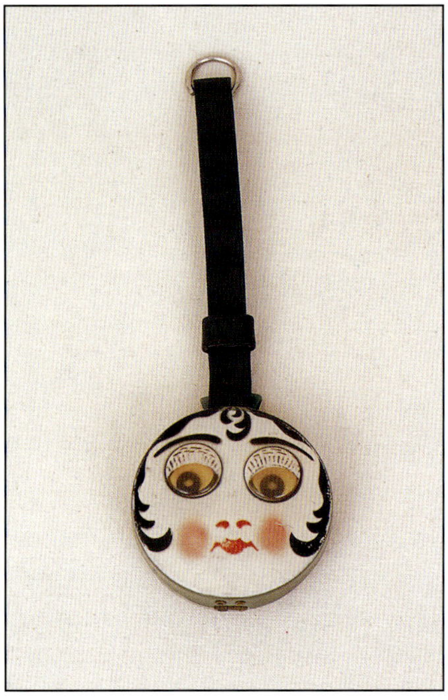

This dance purse wins the prize for the most amusing design. Made in the image of a flapper or Betty Boop (1930), with eyes that actually move. The case and strap are made from plastic. 9.5 x 3 in. *Collection of Ellen Foster.* Rare.

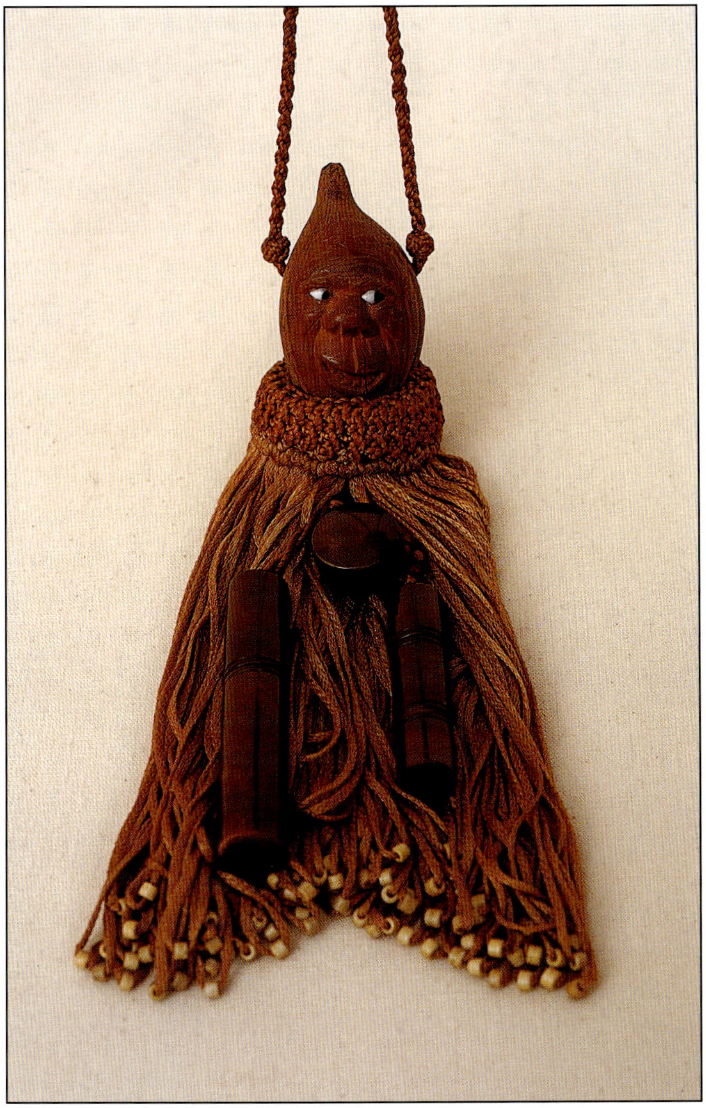

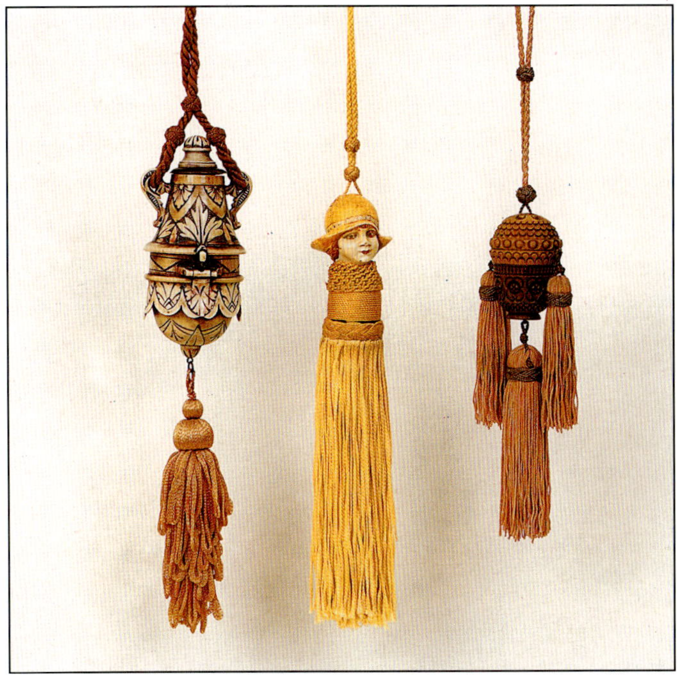

A trio of vanity/dance purses from the 1920s. On the left is a celluloid urn shaped purse, with decorative carving. In the center is a purse made in the shape of a woman's head, dressed in a cloche hat. The head unscrews to reveal a powder puff, and in the middle of the tassel is a lipstick holder. To the right is a carved nut vanity purse, which houses a powder puff with a dog's head. In the middle of the tassel is a celluloid container for a lipstick. Left:17 x 2.5 in. Center: 9.5 x 2.25 in. Right: 14 x 2.75 in. *Collection of Ellen Foster.* Rare.

In 1925, Josephine Baker, a black American dancer, captured the hearts of Parisians with her erotic and exotic song and dance shows. Dressed in little more than feathers, or as in one case bananas, she was the darling of café society. One theory is that this vanity purse was made in homage to her. The head is made from a nut, which has been carved. Hidden beneath the skirt are a cigarette holder inside a case, a lipstick case, and a powder container. This has to qualify as one of the most unique and unusual vanity purses ever known. 11 x 2.5 in. *Collection of Ellen Foster.* Very rare.

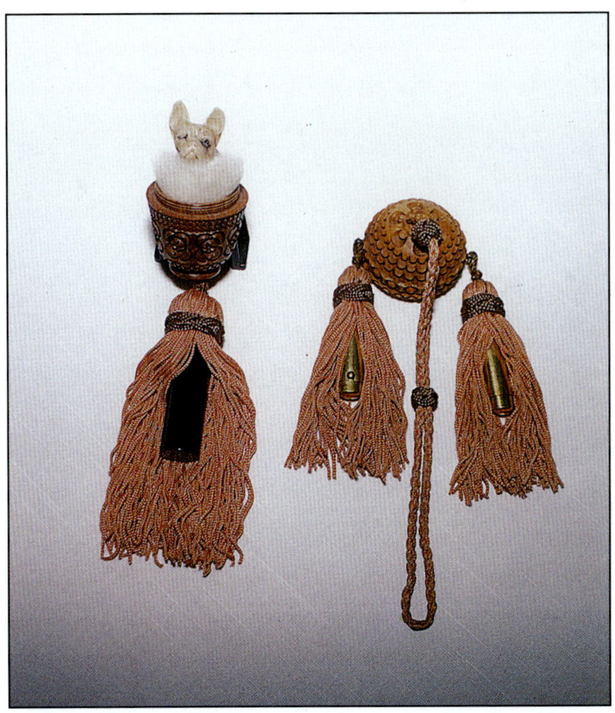

The vanity purse made from a nut shown open, revealing the powder puff decorated with a dog's head.

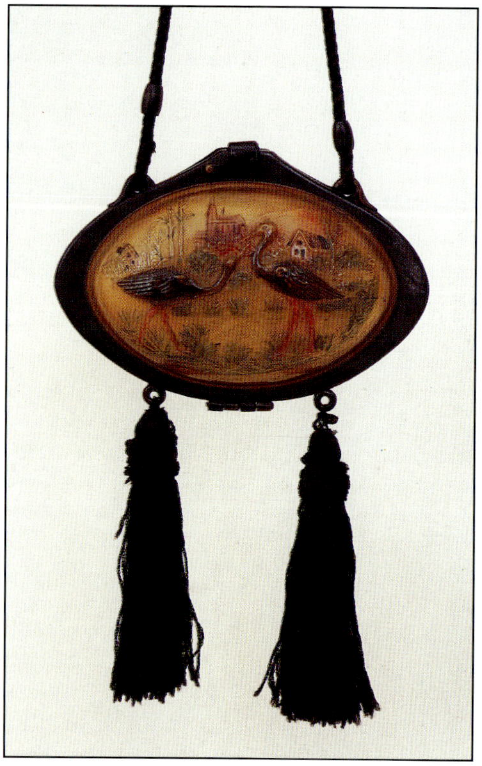

Elliptical shaped, vanity/dance purse made from plastic. Decorated with a scene of two cranes, it also has two decorative tassels instead of the usual one. 8.5 x 6 in. *Collection of Lori Blaser.* $400-500.

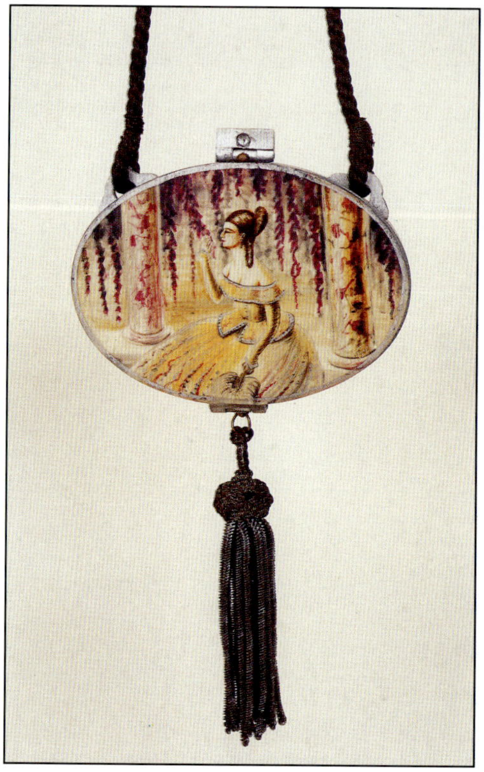

An oval shaped dance purse featuring a hand painted figural of a mid-nineteenth century southern belle. Feminine and charming, this purse would appeal to most collectors. 8.5 x 4.25 in. *Collection of Lori Blaser.* $400-500.

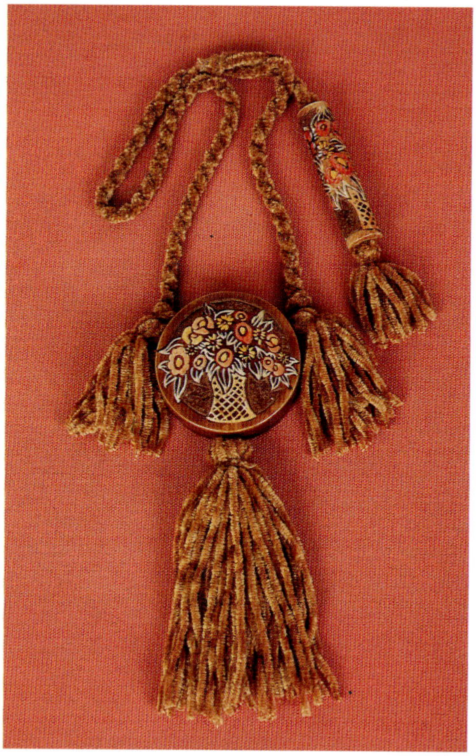

A plastic painted powder container with coordinating lipstick holder. The heavy chenille tassels and cord add texture and substance to the purse. 11 x 4 in. *Collection of Lori Blaser.* $400-500.

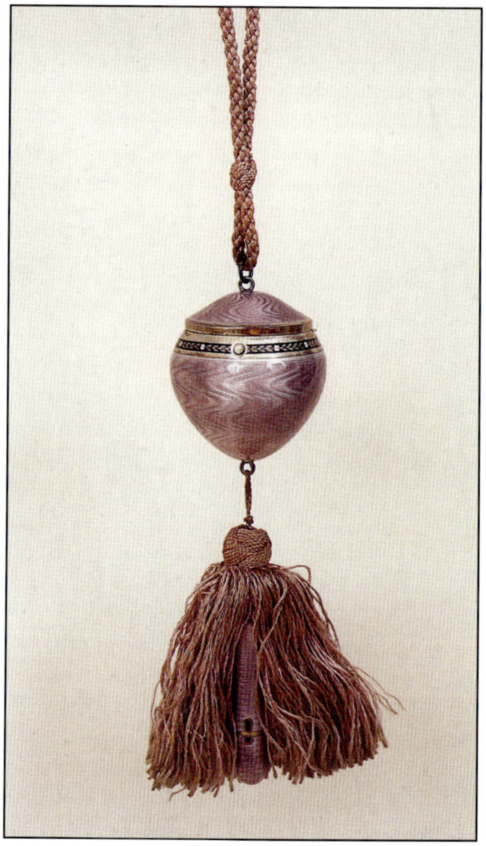

This is a beautiful vanity/dance purse, made from lavender guilloche enamel, with silver and enamel banding. The pushbutton clasp is made from a pearl. A matching enamel lipstick hangs from the middle of the tassel. Inside the purse is a swansdown powder puff. 13 x 3.75 in. *Collection of Ellen Foster.* Rare.

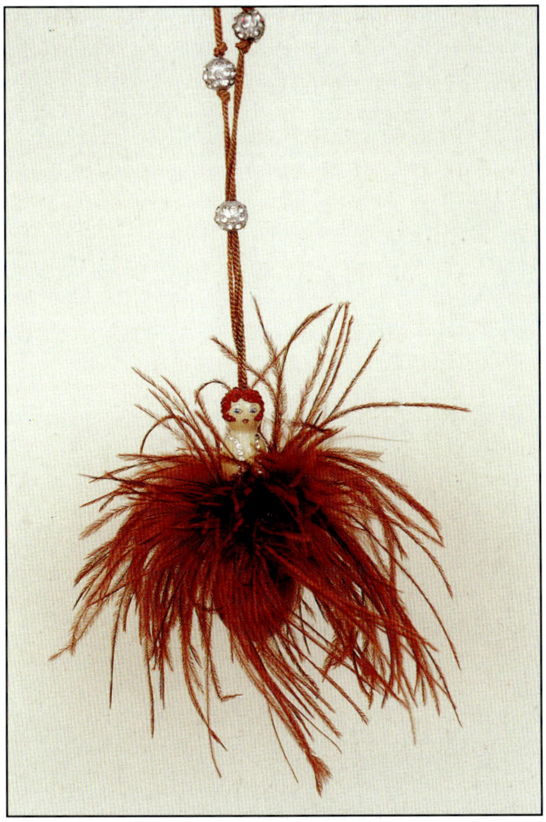

An extraordinary, figural vanity/dance purse decorated with marabou feathers. The egg shaped bottom unscrews to reveal a powder container and mirror. The carry cord is decorated with rhinestone balls. 12.5 x 5.5 in. *Collection of Ellen Foster.* Very rare.

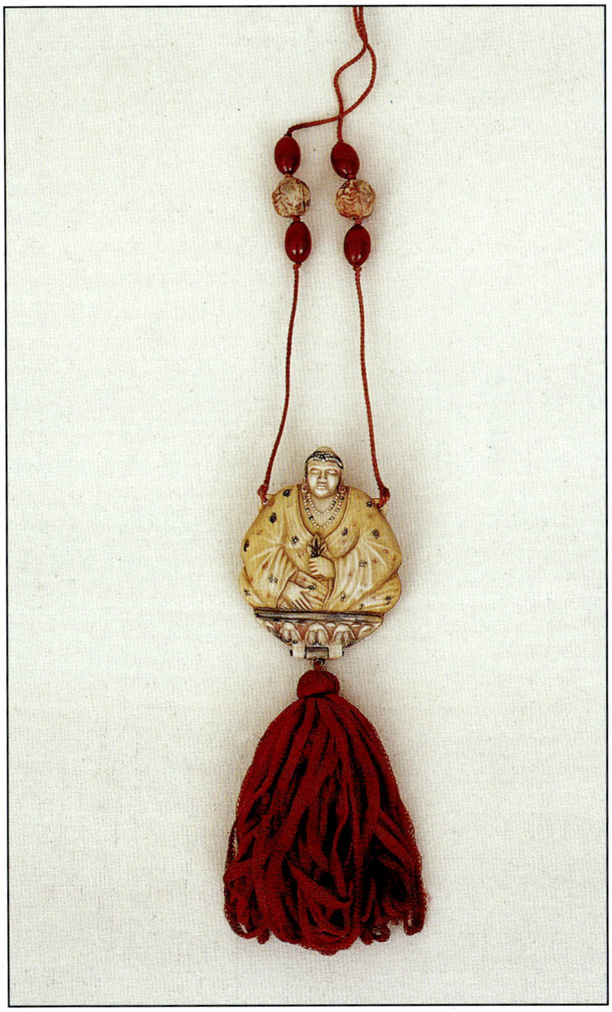

Celluloid vanity/dance purse in the shape of a sitting Buddha. It opens from behind to reveal a powder puff and mirror. A lipstick container is hidden in the thick red tassel. Celluloid beads decorate the carry cord. 7.5 x 2.5 in. *Collection of Ellen Foster.* Rare.

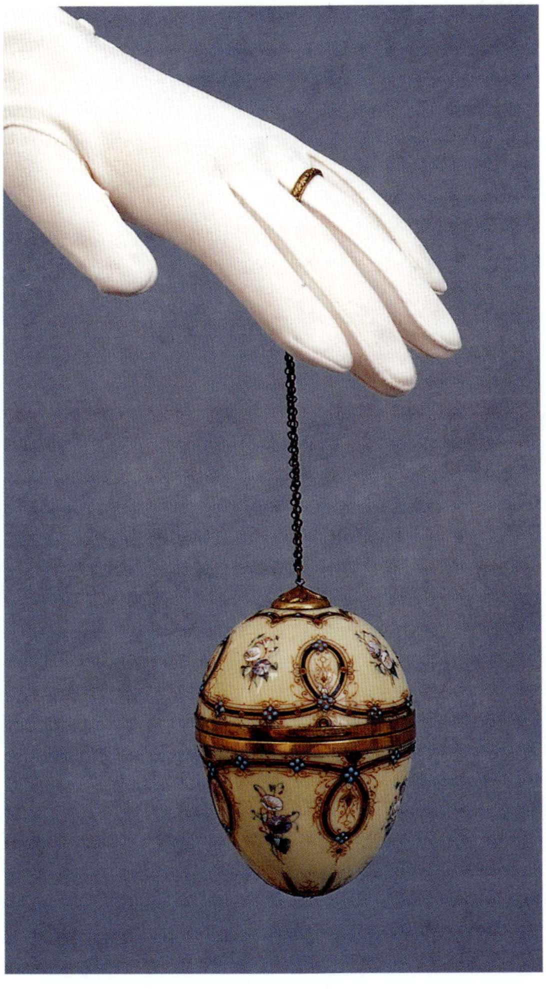

Exquisitely worked, enameled dance purse made in the shape of an egg. On top of the enameling, it has hand painted details, which are studded with turquoise stones. The beautiful workmanship reminds one of the Fabergé eggs made for the Romanov Dynasty. The inside is lined with accordion silk. 9 x 3 in. *Collection of Ellen Foster.* Very rare.

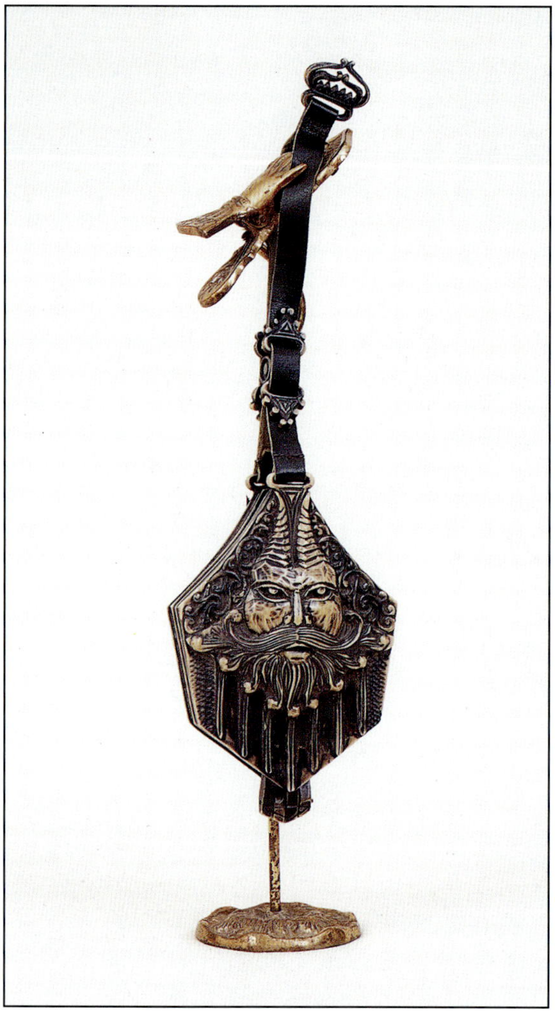

Celluloid, figural dance purse with a leather strap. This is an unusual subject for a dance purse. 13 x 3.75 in. *Collection of Ellen Foster.* Rare.

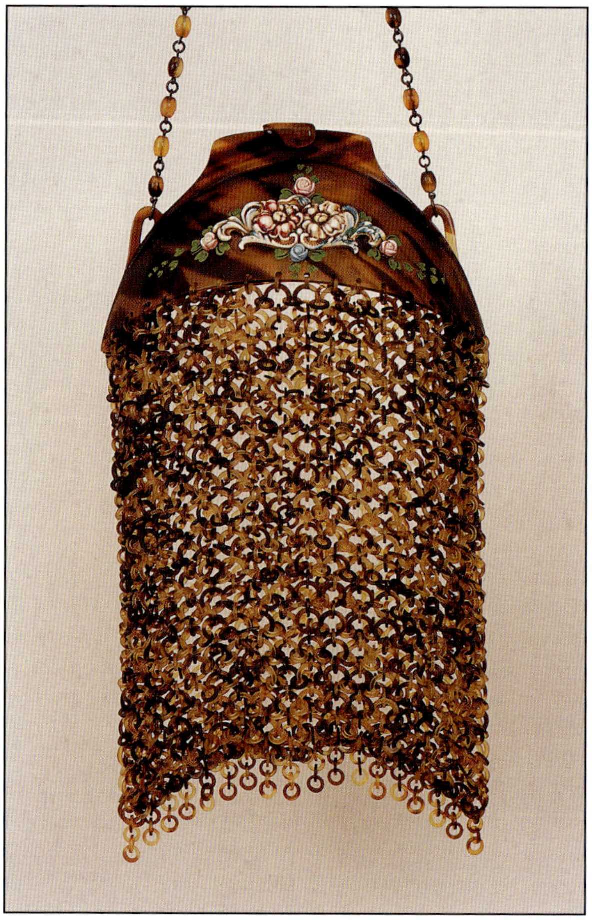

This dance purse is made entirely from celluloid. A raised floral design decorates the frame. Purses made from celluloid links are fragile, which is why they are seldom seen. 10 x 5.5 in. *Collection of Lori Blaser.* $450-550.

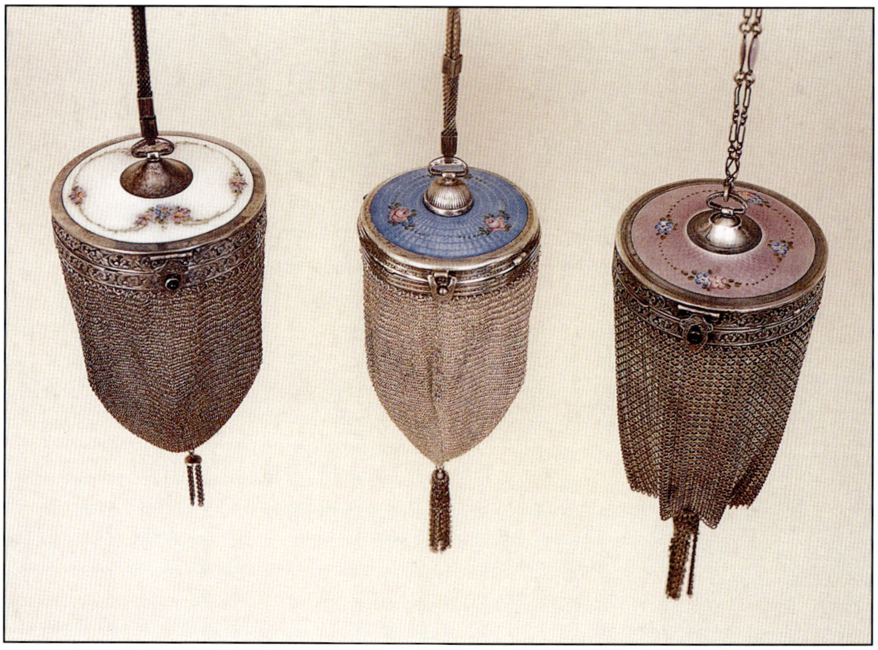

Three R & G Company sterling silver and guilloche enamel compact purses. On the left the purse is made from ring mesh. In the center the purse is made from ring mesh and on the right the purse is made from baby armor mesh. Left: 6 x 2.75 in. Center: 6 x 2.25 in. Right: 7 x 2.75 in. *Collection of Lori Blaser.* $650-750.

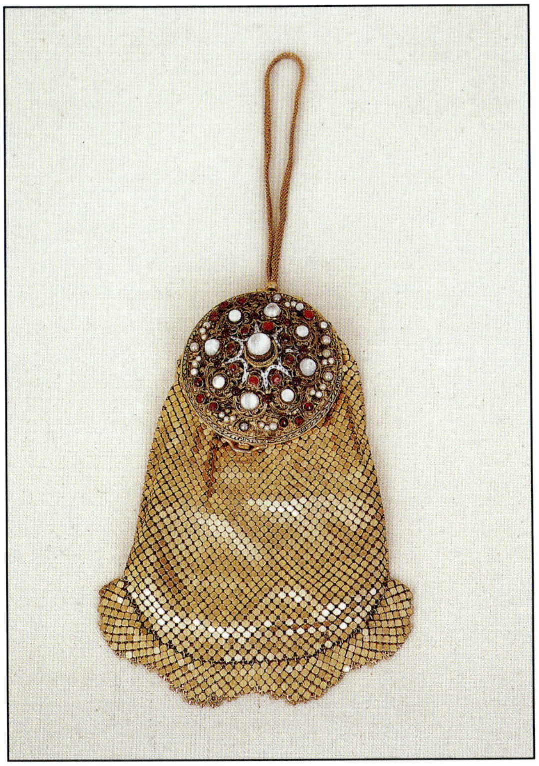

The Evans Company also produced some lovely vanity purses. Made with gold armor mesh, the lid is decorated with faux pearls and rubies. 10 x 5.75 in. *Collection of Lori Blaser.* $350-450.

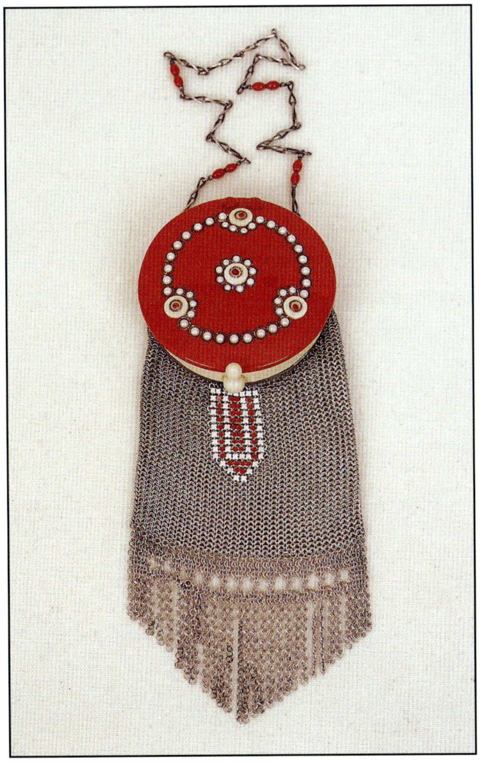

This compact top purse was made by Whiting & Davis. The body is made from ring mesh and the top from red celluloid decorated with jewels. 8 x 3.5 in. *Collection of Lori Blaser.* $500-600.

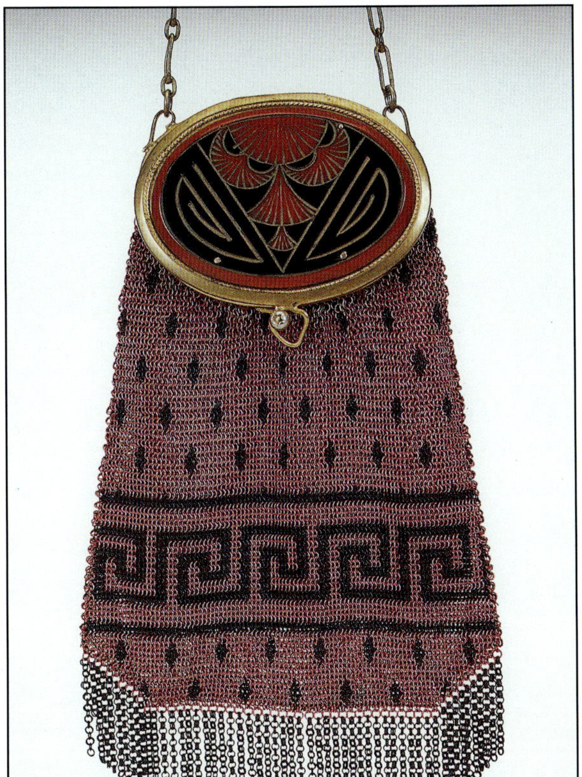

Rare, French made vanity purse. The top of the purse is enameled in an Egyptian design and the Dresden mesh body has a Greek key design. This particular purse was made in several color combinations, but the pink color is the most rare. 8 x 4.5 in. *Collection of Lori Blaser.* $700-750.

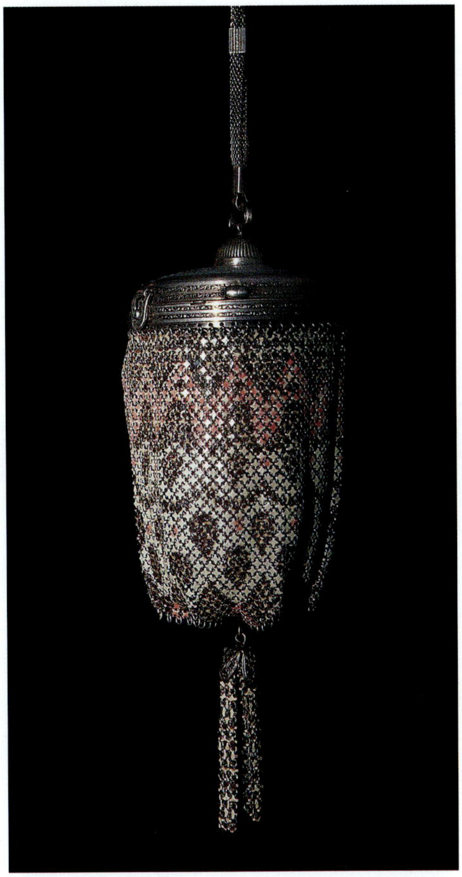

R & G Company sterling silver lidded vanity purse. The body is made from pink, tan, and brown enameled armor mesh. 3.5 x 2.25 in. *Collection of Linda Marshall.* $650-750.

Exceptional, 14kg ring mesh vanity purse. The tassels are finished with genuine pearls and two sapphires decorate the compact lid. These jewelry quality purses are very desirable, expensive, and difficult to find. 6.5 x 2.5 in. *Collection of Melissa Overdorf.* Rare.

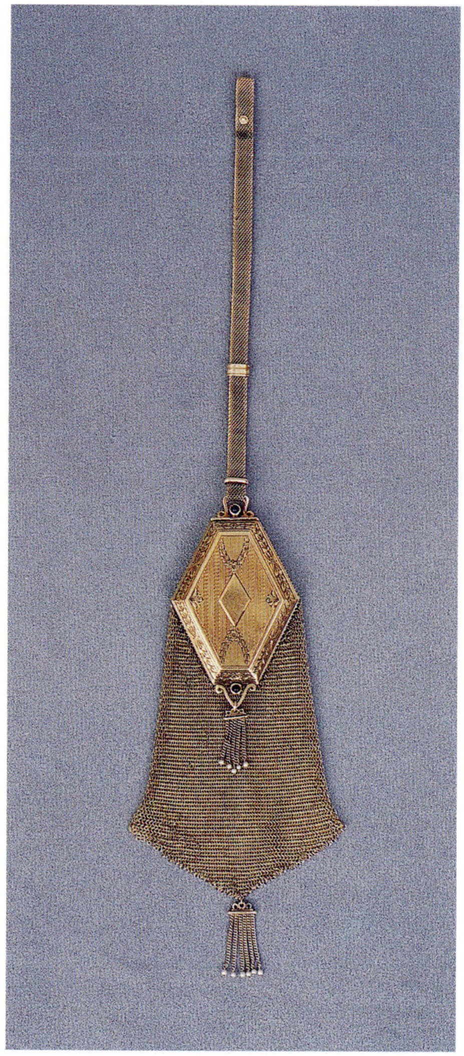

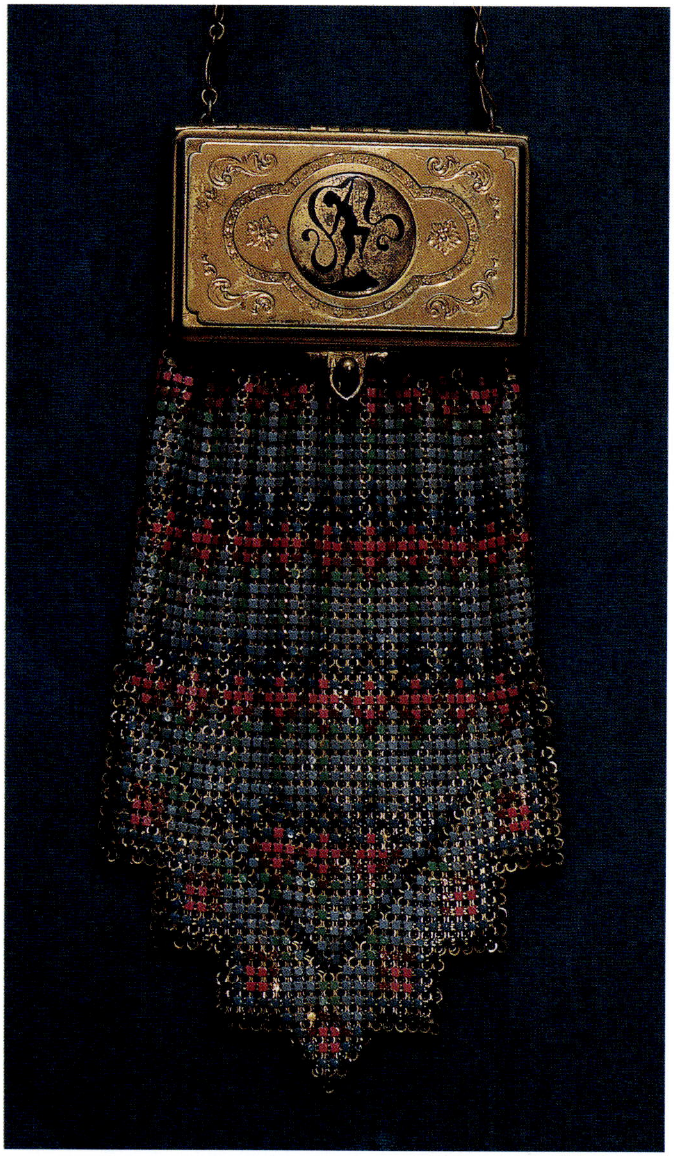

The hard, gold compact top creates a rich look when paired with the colorful armor mesh body. The bottom is finished in a stepped pattern. 7.5 x 3 in. *Collection of Linda Marshall.* $650-750.

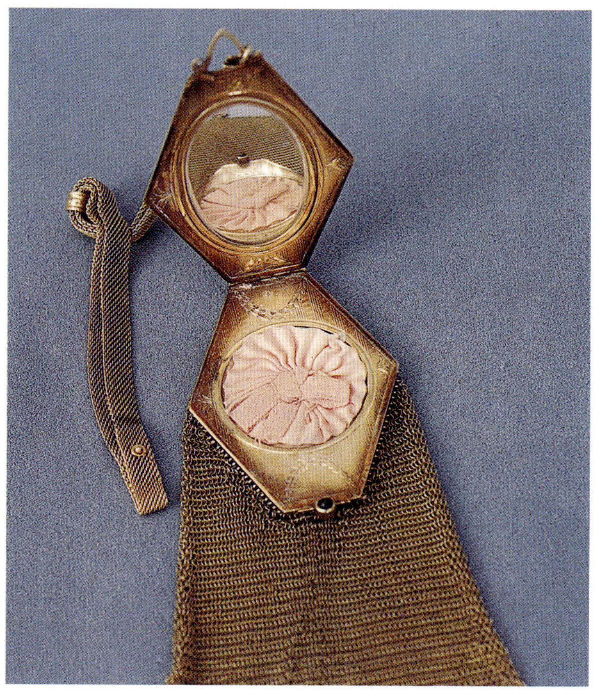

The interior of the 14kg compact top.

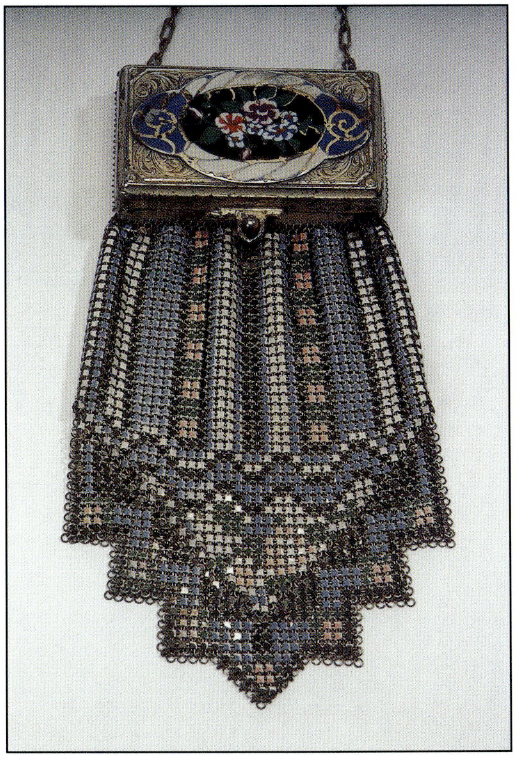

A Whiting & Davis compact purse made from armor mesh. The enameled compact top contains a comb, mirror, rouge pot, powder container, and puff. 8 x 4 in. *Collection of Lori Blaser.* $650-750.

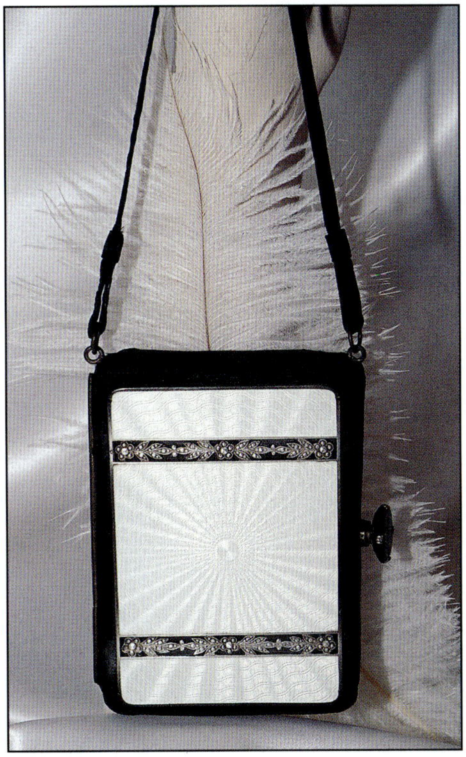

This guilloche enamel evening purse is decorated with a marcasite floral design and an onyx clasp. Inside the purse are three compartments, two pockets, and a mirror. Made by Lancel, Paris. C.1930. 4.5 x 3.25 in. *Collection of Paula Higgins.* $600-650.

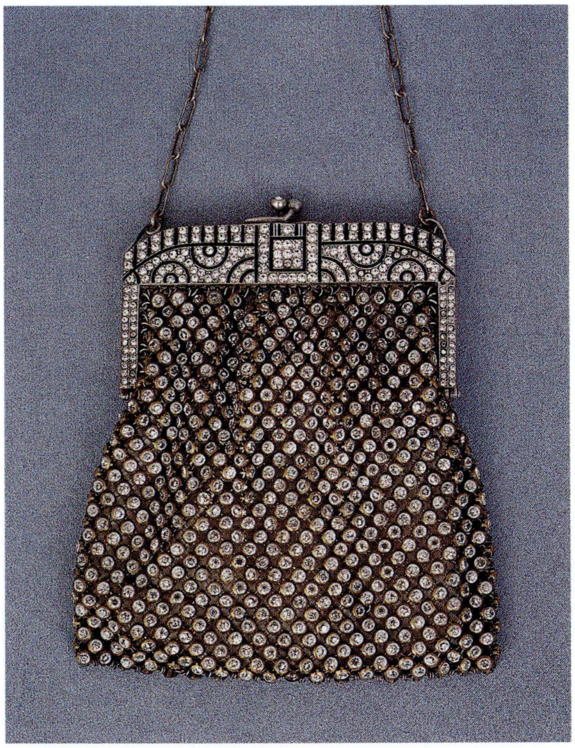

French purse made with bezel set rhinestones. The frame design is classic Art Deco, which adds to its value. 5.5 x 4.75 in. *Collection of Melissa Overdorf.* $700-750.

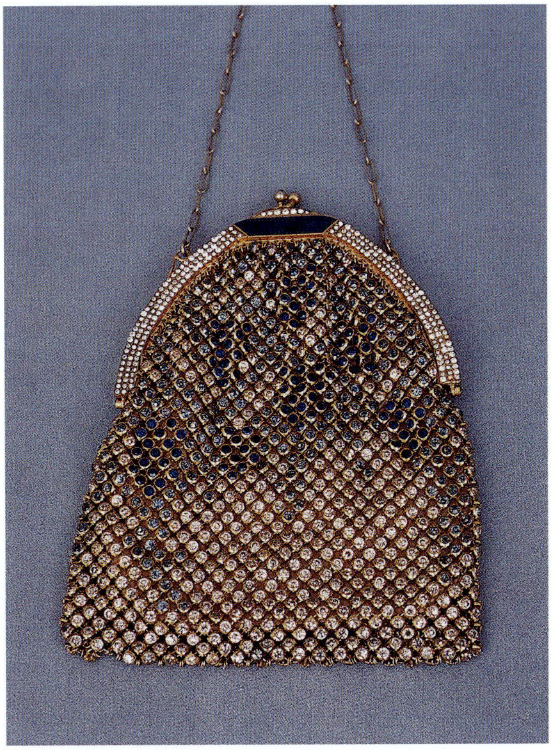

Another glorious bezel set rhinestone purse from the Art Deco period. French. 7.5 x 5 in. *Collection of Lori Blaser.* $700-750.

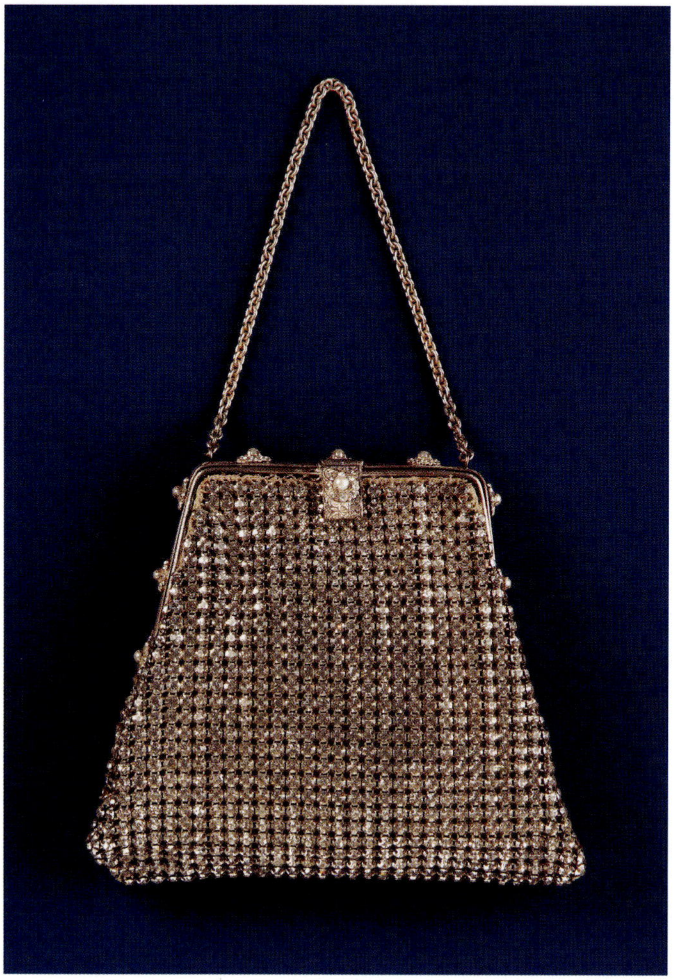

A beautiful rhinestone purse from c.1930 mounted on a pearl decorated frame. 5.5 x 4.75 in. *Collection of Sharon LuVisi.* $600-700.

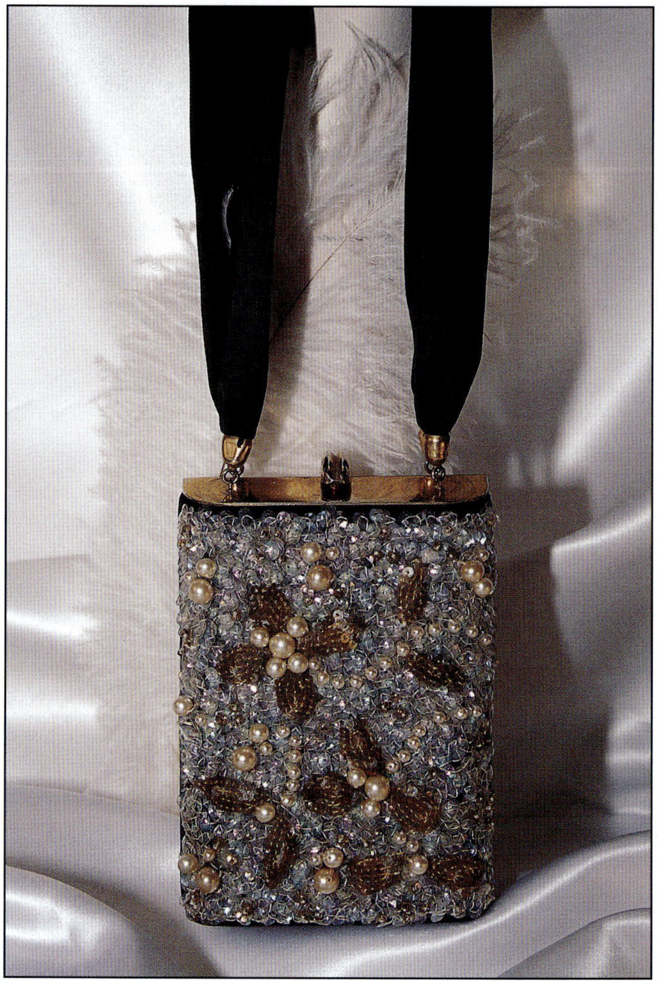

Mid-twentieth century vanity purse made from aurora borealis sequins, gold sequins, and pearls. Inside the bag are compartments for powder and lipstick. There is also a large mirror. The strap is made from black satin. 5 x 3.5 in. *Collection of Paula Higgins.* $250-350.

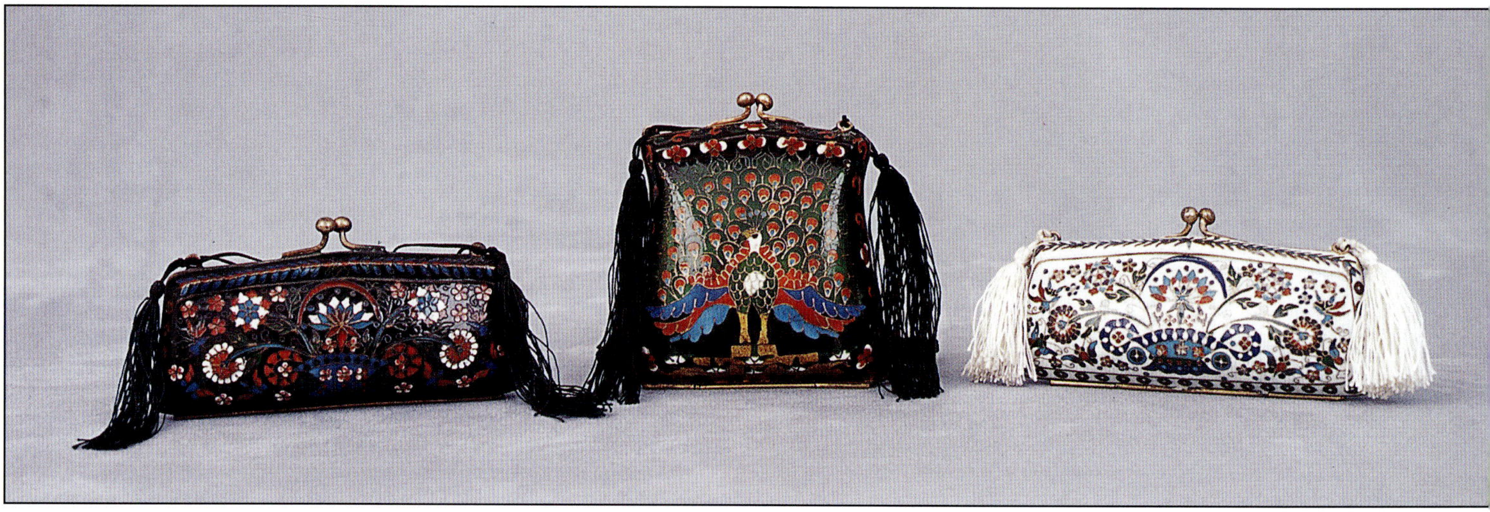

A trio of small enamel decorated purses. The center purse is enameled with a peacock design. Left and Right: 4.5 x 2.25 in. Center: 4.5 x 3.5 in. *Collection of Lori Blaser.* $200-250.

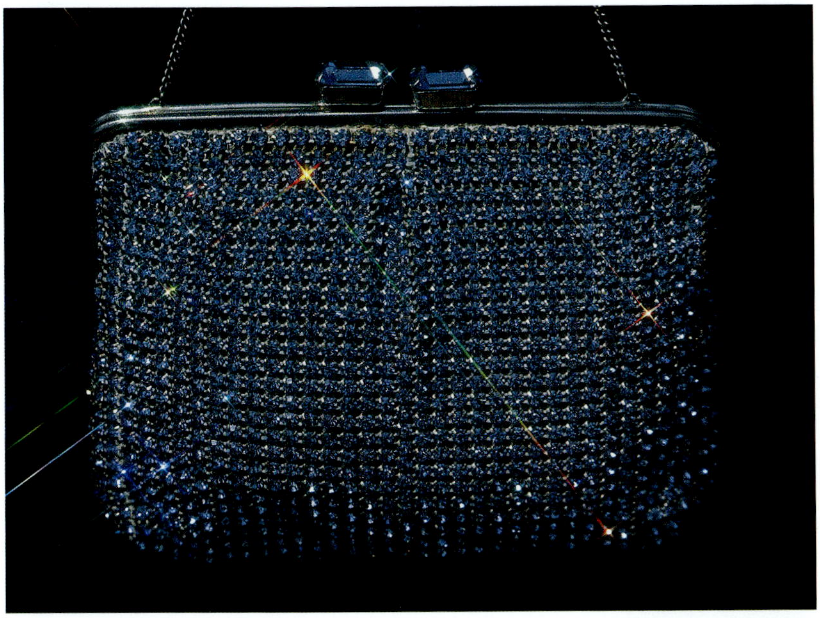

This is a stunning blue rhinestone purse from the mid-twentieth century. Two large blue rhinestones are set into the clasp. Blue rhinestone purses are rare. 7 x 5.5 in. *Collection of Linda Marshall.* $650-700.

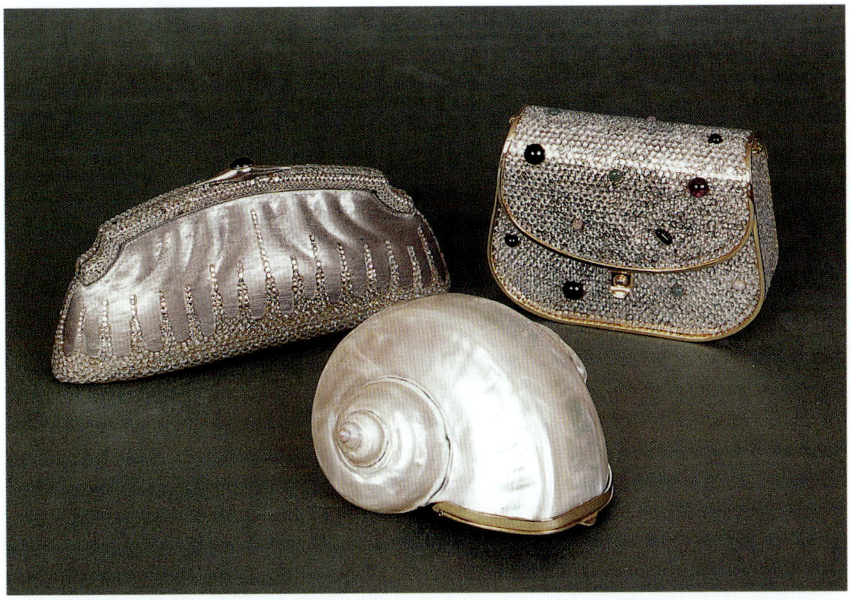

Three beautiful Judith Leiber evening bags. On the left is a c.1970 silver metal clutch inset with rhinestone decoration. The clasp is made from black onyx. In the center is a Judith Leiber conch shell purse c.1960. On the right is a c.1970 rhinestone bag inset with semi-precious cabochon stones. Left: 8 x 3.5 in. Center: 6 x 5 in. Right: 5.5 x 4 in. *Collection of Ruth Penson.* $500-1,000.

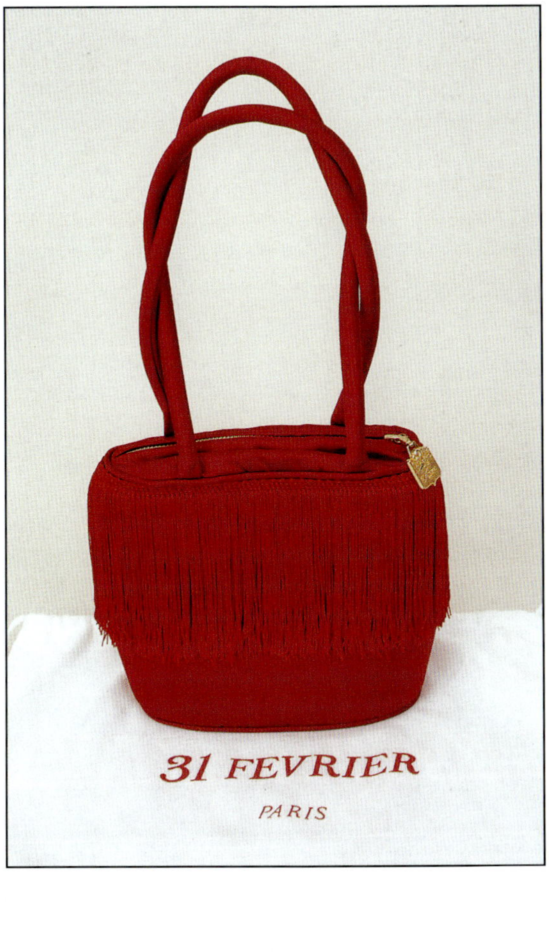

A made to be noticed, red satin evening bag with silk fringe by 31 Fevrier, Paris. 16 x 8.25 in. *Collection of Lori Blaser.* $200-300.

Chapter 8
Wirework and Mesh Purses

Early 19th century iron wirework, also known as Silesian wirework, Berlin iron work, and Fer de Berlin, is among the earliest type of metal mesh work associated with purses. Iron foundries in Silesia were moved to Berlin in the late 18th century, where they produced mesh wirework. When Napoleon conquered Prussia in 1806, he took the iron wirework patterns with him to France. It is most likely that the rare and delicate early 19th century wirework purses shown in the following chapter were made in France. Although other countries copied and produced wirework patterns, the most innovative purse designs during this period originated in France. The two examples pictured in the following chapter were made from fine iron wires, which were spun and meshed, and then decorated with steel button flowers, locks, and *paillettes*. Although a rare type of purse, at least four different versions dating to the same period have been seen.

By the mid-19th century, smaller, coin sized wirework purses were being made in France and they survive in volume. They were palm sized, and made from wire mesh inserts, which were set into steel frames. Lined with colored silks, they typically had tiny cut steel decorations in the center and short carry chains. In this chapter there is a wirework coin purse, with its original box, in excellent unused condition. Since rusting was a common problem for these purses, its pristine condition and original box make for a rare survival.

The majority of mesh purses pictured in this book were made by the firms of Mandalian and Whiting & Davis. Although mesh purses were also made in Europe, particularly in France, Germany, and England, the two American firms of Whiting & Davis, and Mandalian produced the highest volume. Some rare French examples are very desirable because of their unique and compelling designs.

Evelyn Haertig shows a flat mesh purse with a twist clasp dating to 1875 in her book, *More Beautiful Purses*. These early mesh purses are very rare and collectible. The first ring mesh purse made in the United States was made in 1892 by Wade-Davis Company. Very small in size, it could hold little more than a coin. Made in gold, silver, brass, and plated metals, these early ring mesh purses were made by hand. In 1909, A. Pratt invented a machine that produced sheets of mesh, which could be cut and then sewn together with wire. Mesh was made in two styles, ring and armor. Ring mesh was made from small circles of wire that were interlinked and soldered. Armor mesh, also called spider mesh, was made from cruciform links, which were linked together with round links. Once armor mesh was completed and cut, it was enameled with painted designs ranging from traditional florals to Art Deco abstracts.

In 1918, Whiting & Davis produced a fine ring mesh known as Dresden mesh, which was decorated with enamel paints using a stenciling method. This mesh had first been produced in Germany and England using Pratt designed machinery, which created legal problems because Whiting & Davis owned the patent rights. It was ultimately settled by the acquisition of all the Dresden machinery by Whiting & Davis, which they subsequently improved upon. By the 1920s, beautiful impressionistic designs were being made and sold in stores. The German Dresden mesh purses are less desirable because the mesh is much coarser than the Whiting & Davis mesh. The Evans Case Company also made Dresden mesh, which while rare, is also of a lesser quality.

Baby mesh, a fine armor mesh, is sought after by purse collectors. Baby mesh was made by both Whiting & Davis and Mandalian. The pearlized baby mesh purse by Mandalian sold for as much as $75.00. "Lustro-pearl" baby mesh was finished with the essence of pearls, giving the mesh a high luster. Made with elegant designs and beautiful color schemes, Lustro-pearl baby mesh purses by Mandalian are among the most prized by purse collectors. Mesh finishes made by Whiting & Davis included the fish scale or pearlized, beadlite, and ivory tone. Whiting & Davis also made an aluminum armor mesh purse for a short period of time. They have a much lighter feel than the standard armor mesh purses.

Mandalian purses are acknowledged as the most beautifully designed and manufactured of all mesh purses. Inspired by oriental carpets, peacocks, and naturalistic floral designs, they were mounted on gorgeous gold, silver, jeweled, and enameled frames. Mandalian's Gloria frame formed a box shape when opened for a completely unique look. The Martha Washington purse was attached to a fabric reticule top, and drawstrings with rings. The bottoms of Mandalian purses were finished with teardrop fringe in a V-shape or stepped shape, looped fringe, straight fringe with teardrops, V-fringe, and vandyke skirts. A Mandalian baby mesh purse with a lustro-pearl finish, looped fringe, and in its original box with a tag, is high on the list of most coveted mesh purses. Mandalian purses were all made with their individual armor links set diagonally. By 1944, the Mandalian Company was in financial difficulty, so the company was purchased by Whiting & Davis.

Whiting & Davis was the most prolific maker of mesh bags during the 1920s and 1930s. Purses featuring florals, figurals, landscapes, animals, buildings, abstracts, geometrics, cartoon characters, and dragons were all possible design options. Just when you think you have seen them all, a new Whiting & Davis design surfaces. The armor links on Whiting & Davis purses were usually set in a straight line, and not diagonally like the Mandalian purses. However, there were some exceptions to this rule, most notably those purses ending in a V-shape. Whiting & Davis was also known for decorating their purses with unusual and exotic touches. Purse bodies were jewel embedded, and frames were enameled, jeweled, pierced, open-worked, blown-out, and inset with Bakelite. Carry chains were decorated with stones, and rigid handles were made from Bakelite and metal. Fringe was scalloped, straight, vandyked, double-tiered, and V-shaped. It was made from beadlite, ring mesh, teardrops, and in an unusual combination of beads, tiny armor mesh, and ring mesh. The "Baby Peggy" mesh purse was made in both ring and armor mesh, with a reticule top. This should not be confused with the Mandalian Martha Washington purse, which was also made with a reticule top. A very rare Whiting & Davis *El Sah* purse style was made with an enamel body, which was inset with topaz-colored stones and a topaz carry chain.

The Princess Mary, with its fold over flap, came in a variety of styles. For example, the sunset mesh Princess Mary was made with red gold, green gold, and platinum colored ring mesh. The Princess Mary was made in a number of styles including armor mesh, Dresden mesh, and with a delicate Venetian fringe. The one common denominator for all the Princess Mary labeled purses was their fold over flap.

The Dresden mesh purse, with its lovely soft, watercolor effect, was a popular alternative to the more structured armor mesh. Made by stenciling and layering different colors on the mesh, it could take weeks to make. The most desirable Dresden mesh purses were mounted on beautiful enameled and stippled frames (also called eggshell frames) or enameled frames set with faux pearls. The soft impressionistic effects created by the Dresden mesh are very appealing to many collectors.

Compact bags like the Delysia and the Piccadilly were expensive then and remain even more so now. The Whiting & Davis enameled bag with the jeweled compact top is especially beautiful and is among the most sought after. A very rare version is the Dresden mesh purse with the small, flat gold compact inserted into the frame, or alternatively, an enameled, hanging compact. Another equally rare type is the double mesh vanity bag. Two separate, mesh bags were separated by a compact containing a mirror, rouge, and powder compartments. A rigid, box shaped purse, with a fold over flap and Dresden paint finish, also came in a compact form.

Whiting & Davis made the holy grail of mesh purses in 1976, known as the "Star Series." To commemorate their 100th anniversary, they produced four bags with enameled likenesses of Marion Davies, Clark Gable, Charlie Chaplin, and Renee Adoree. With the exception of the Charlie Chaplin purse, which was enameled in black and white, they were made with colored mesh. Their long, twisted mesh chains indicate their later date of manufacture. It is somewhat ironic that a firm that is most notable for their 1920s and 1930s purses issued today's most rare and valuable purses, in 1976, for a very short time.

Whiting & Davis made a mesh purse in a small handbag shape in 1929, which was designed by French designer Paul Poiret. It was made in beadlite, enamel, and the Dresden mesh form. Today, this is an undervalued purse that deserves consideration by mesh purse collectors. By the late 1930s, mesh purses were made in solid gold or silver-colored mesh, and while they had considerable "flash," they lacked the artistry of their predecessors. Plain mesh purses are still sold by Whiting & Davis today.

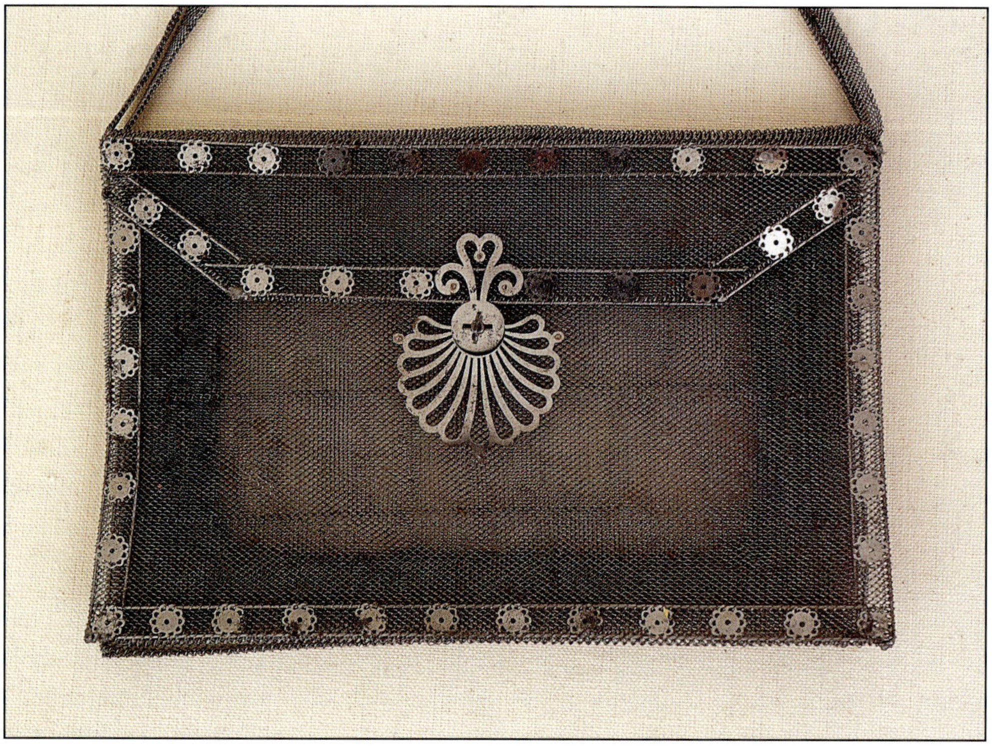

C.1810-1820 Fer de Berlin wirework purse. The fine wire mesh is decorated with cut steel paillettes and a steel, shell shaped clasp. Berlin wirework designs were taken to France by Napoleon, where this purse was made. Early 19th century wirework purses came in several shapes; all of them rare. 7.5 x 5 in. *Collection of Lori Blaser.* Rare.

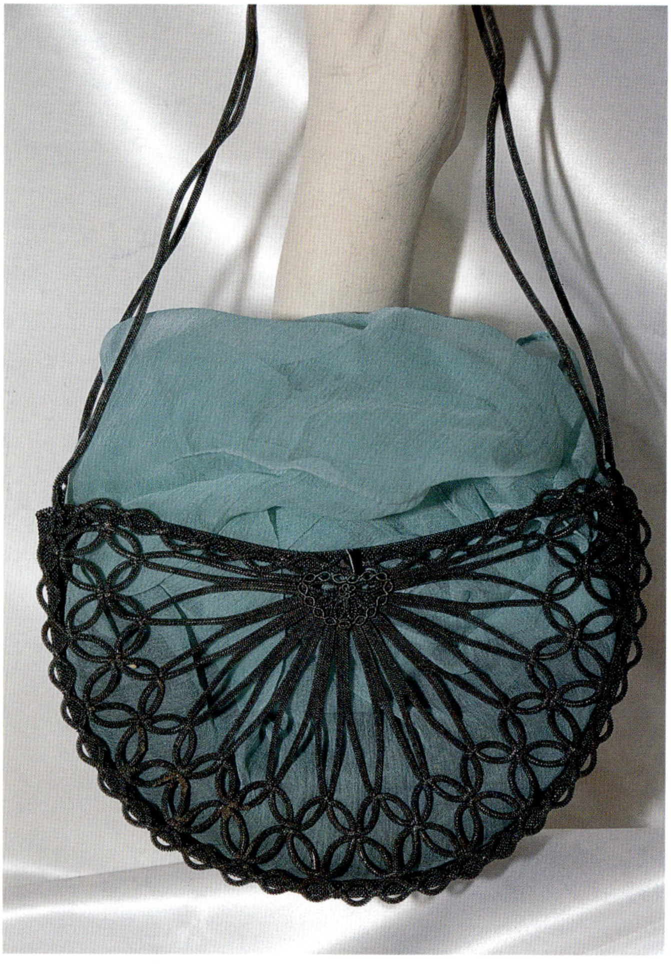

Another early 19th century (c. 1800-1810), Fer de Berlin wirework purse made from mesh strands. Openwork designs were popular during the early years of the 19th century. A key clasp closes the purse; a common feature of wirework purses. 6 x 4 in. *Collection of Paula Higgins.* Rare.

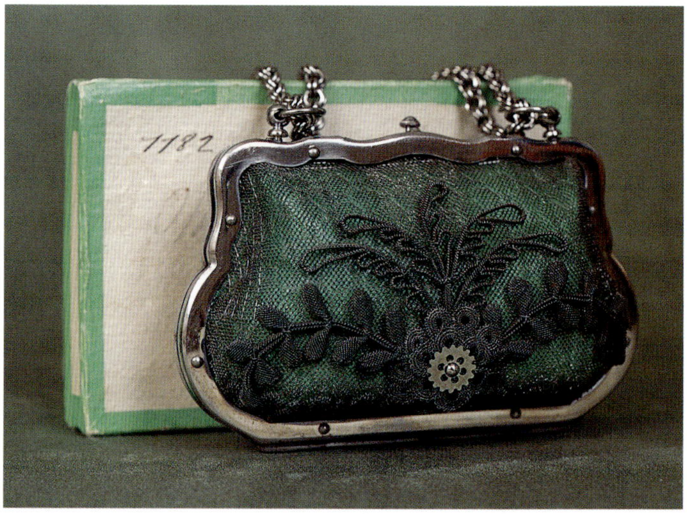

C.1840 wirework purse, decorated with cut steel. Although this type of wirework purse is not rare, this one came in its original French box, which is very rare. It is in amazing condition and a lovely example of the type. 4.25 x 3 in. *Collection of Lori Blaser.* Rare.

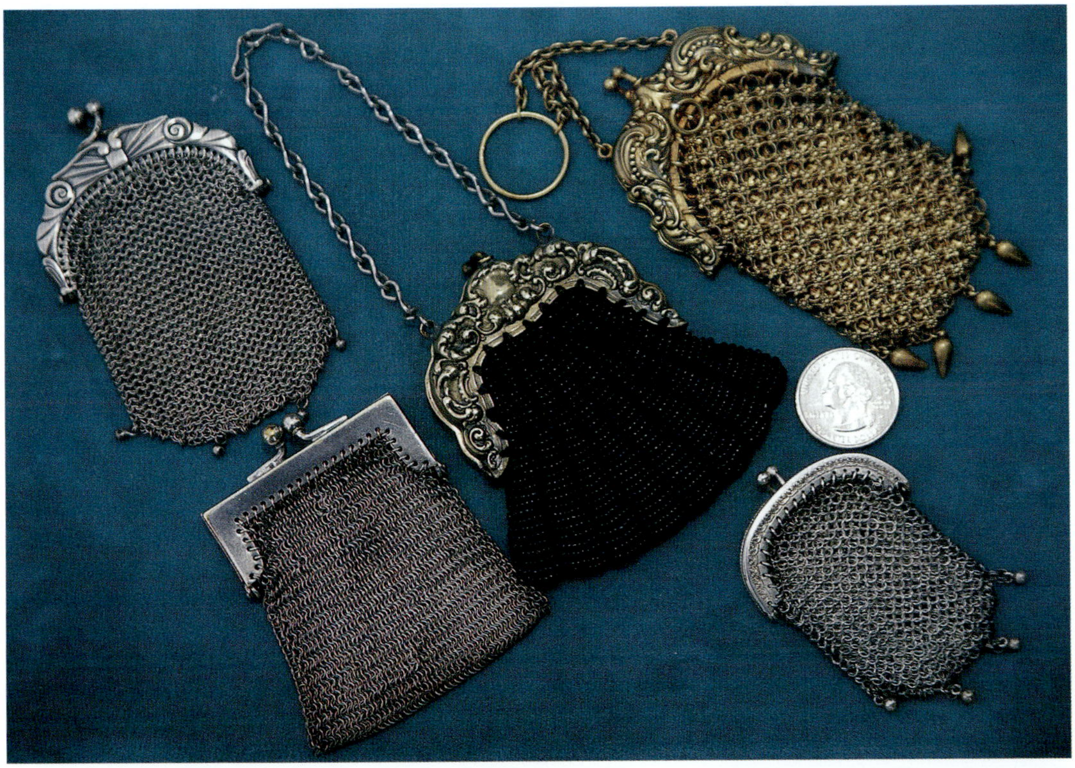

A selection of very small mesh purses dating to c.1900. The gold mesh, finger chatelaine purse on the right is made from sterling with a gold wash and it is marked Blackinton, North Attleboro, Mass. The purse on the top left divides into two sections. Left: 2.5 x 2 in. Top left: 3 x 2 in. Right: 3.5 x 2.5 in. Bottom: 2.5 x 1.75 in. *Collection of Linda Marshall.* $50-200.

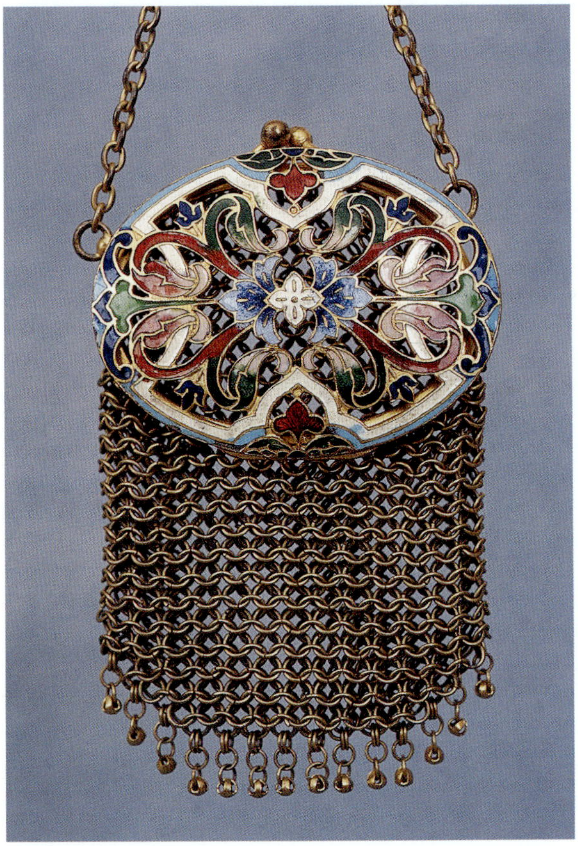

Pretty enameled coin purse, made from ring mesh and decorated with tiny ball tassels. 4 x 2.5 in. *Collection of Lori Blaser.* $275-300.

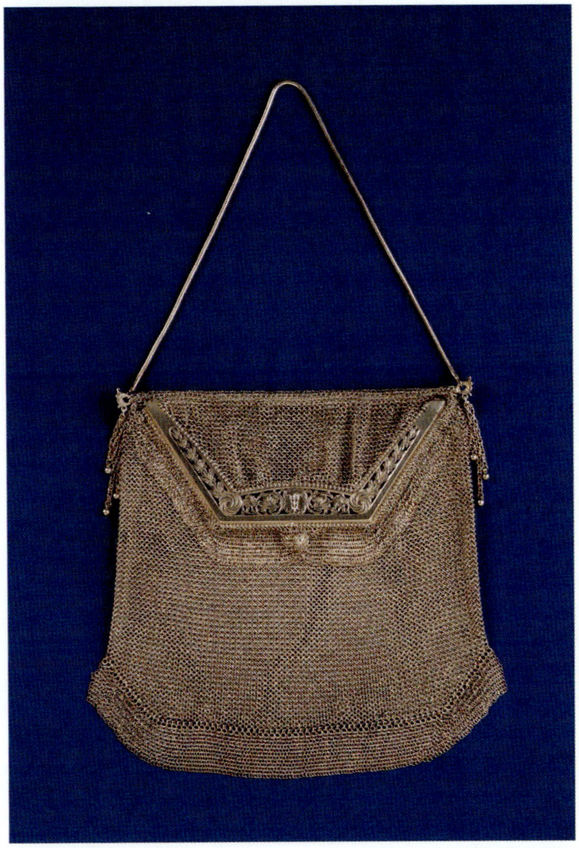

Early 20th century, silver mesh purse made in a flap over style. This mesh purse is exceptionally nice, with its side tassels and pierced, floral decoration. 7 x 6 in. *Collection of Sharon LuVisi.* $300-350.

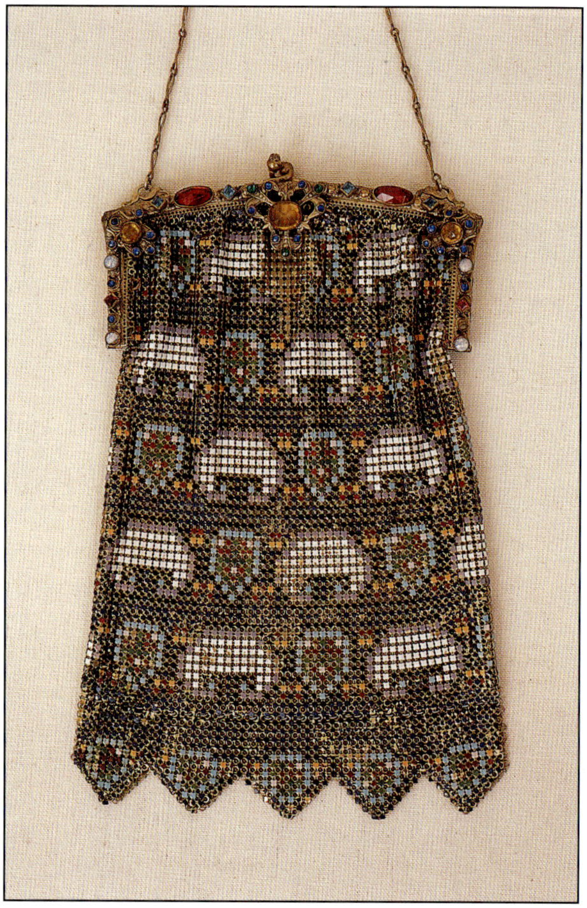

Enameled, armor mesh purse, with a vandyke skirt, made by Whiting & Davis. The jeweled frame is exceptional and adds considerably to its value. 9 x 5.5 in. *Collection of Melissa Overdorf.* $375-450.

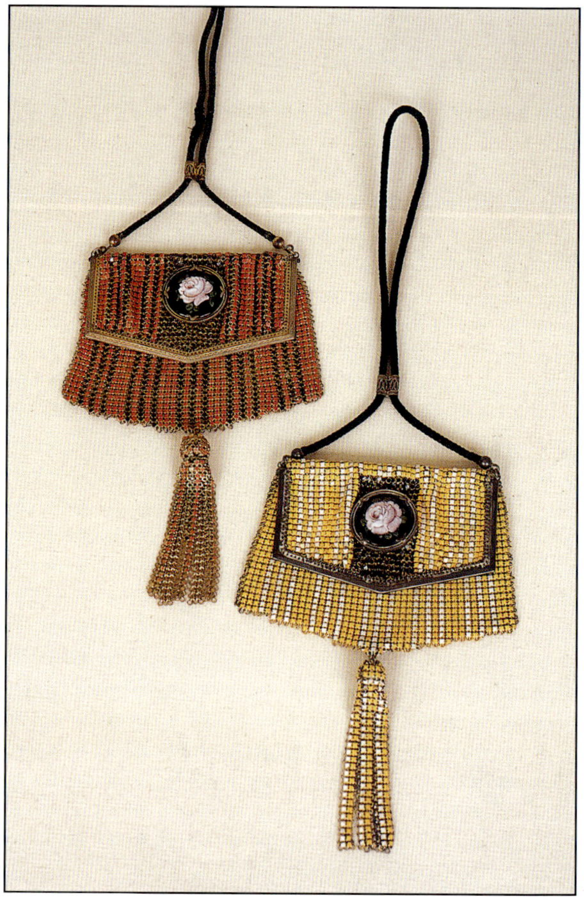

Two Princess Mary purses in different color combinations. Made from armor mesh with fold over frames, each one is decorated with hand painted roses on porcelain. 4 x 4 in. Left: *Collection of Ruth Penson.* Right: *Collection of Lori Blaser.* $400-450.

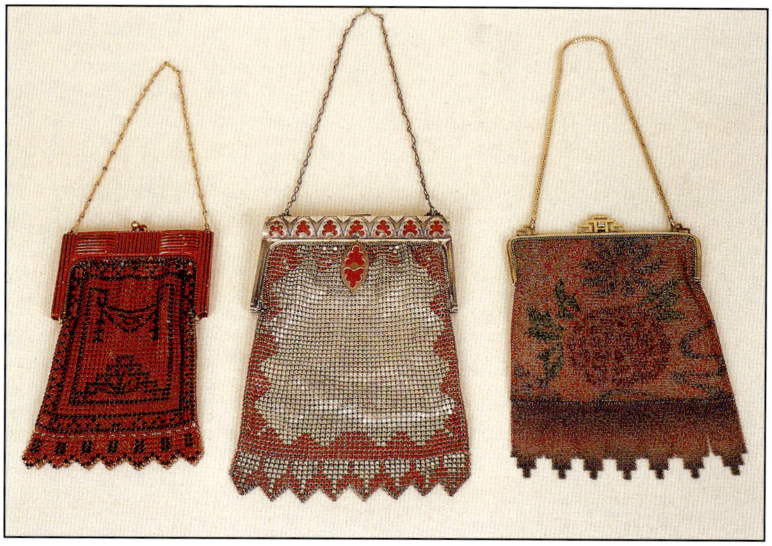

Three Whiting & Davis Art Deco mesh purses. The purse on the left is made from red enameled, armor mesh and mounted on a wide, red enameled frame. The center purse is made from armor mesh and the silver frame is enameled in an arched, gothic window design. The purse on the right is an uncommon red Dresden mesh with a distinctive floral design. Left: 6 x 4 in. Center: 7.5 x 5 in. Right: 6.5 x 5 in. *Collection of Ruth Penson.* Left: $325-350. Center: $450-475. Right: $450-475.

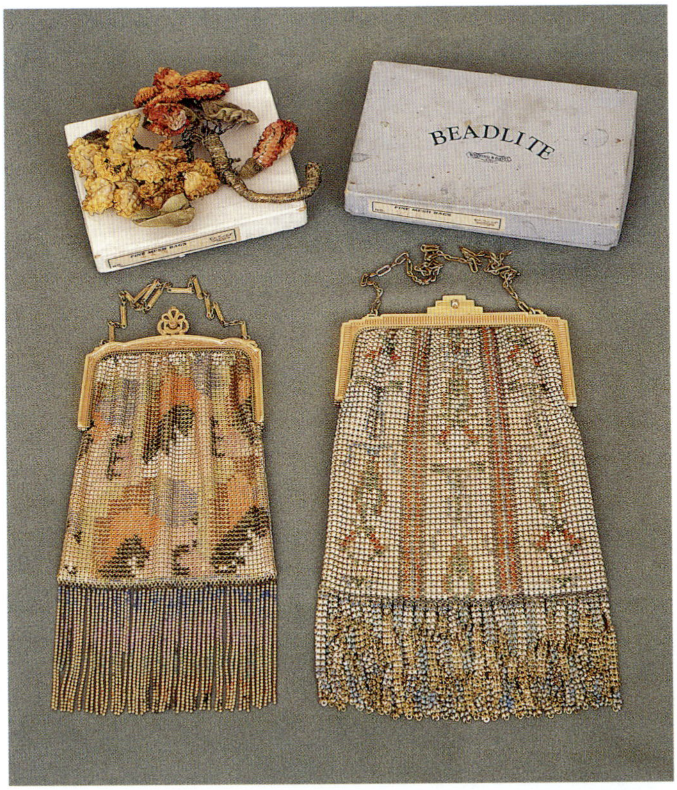

Two mesh purses with their original boxes. The purse on the left has key chain fringe and the larger purse on the right has back to back, beadlite strip fringe. Beadlite mesh was created by placing a dot in the center of each link, creating a raised design. The intent was to imitate beaded purses. Left: 9 x 4.5 in. Right: 9.5 x 6 in. *Collection of Lori Blaser.* Left: $400-450. Right: $495-550.

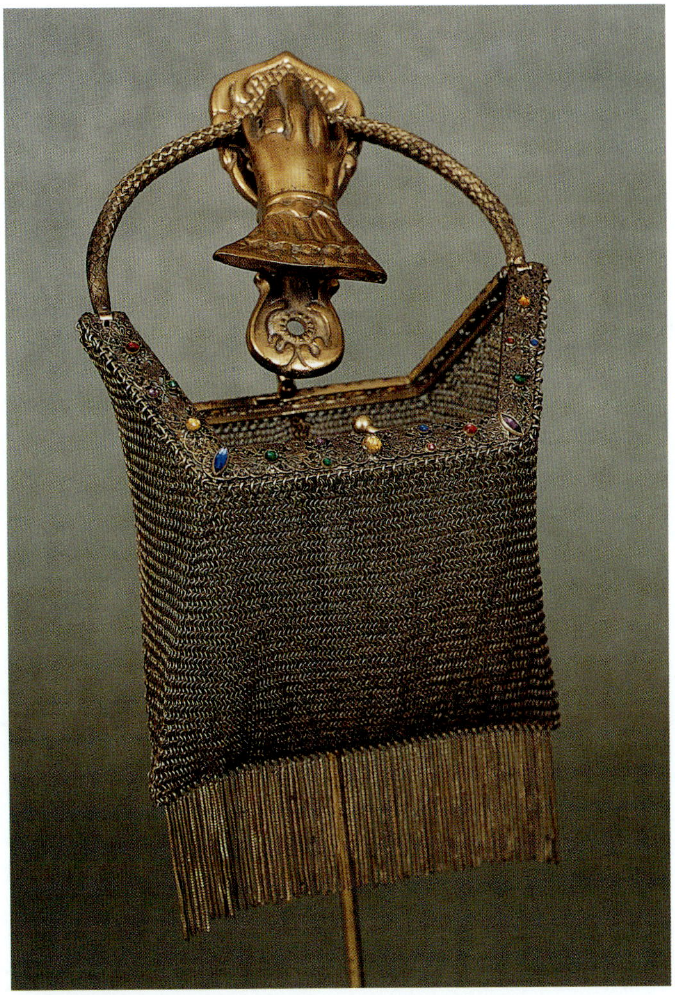

This very unusual ring mesh purse was made with a hard braided handle and a jeweled frame that springs open into a square. The fringe is also braided. 9.5 x 5.5 in. *Collection of Lori Blaser.* $350-450.

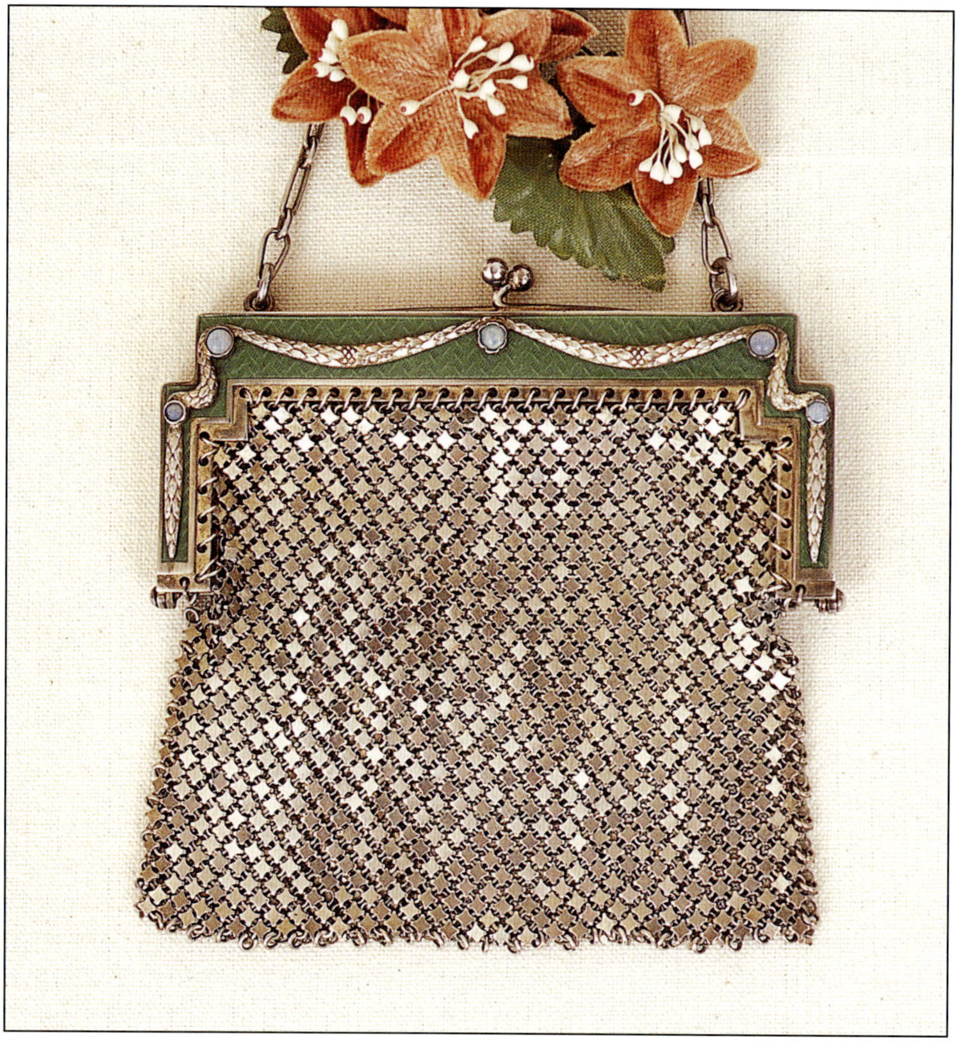

900 silver purse made by Georg Adam Scheid. Scheid was a Viennese silversmith who worked until 1921 producing high quality silver items. This exceptional guilloche enamel frame is decorated with a swag design and genuine opals. Scheid favored this swag design on his frames. Another very interesting example, made by Scheid, can be seen in the book *Bags*, by Hendrikje Ivo of The Tassenmuseum. 4.25 x 4.25 in. *Collection of Lori Blaser.* Rare.

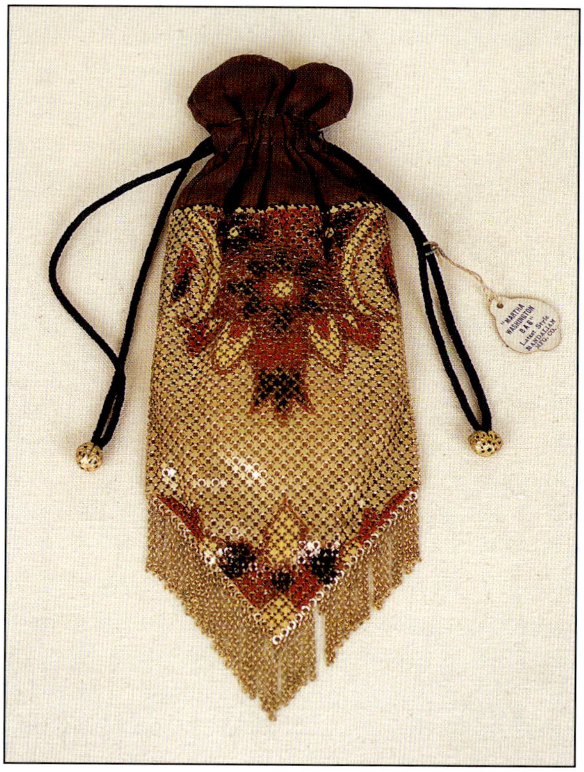

Commonly known as the "Martha Washington" purse, it was made by Mandalian. The original Mandalian tag is still attached. Made from armor mesh in a stylized floral design, it ends in a V fringe. 9 x 3.5 in. *Collection of Ruth Penson.* $350-400.

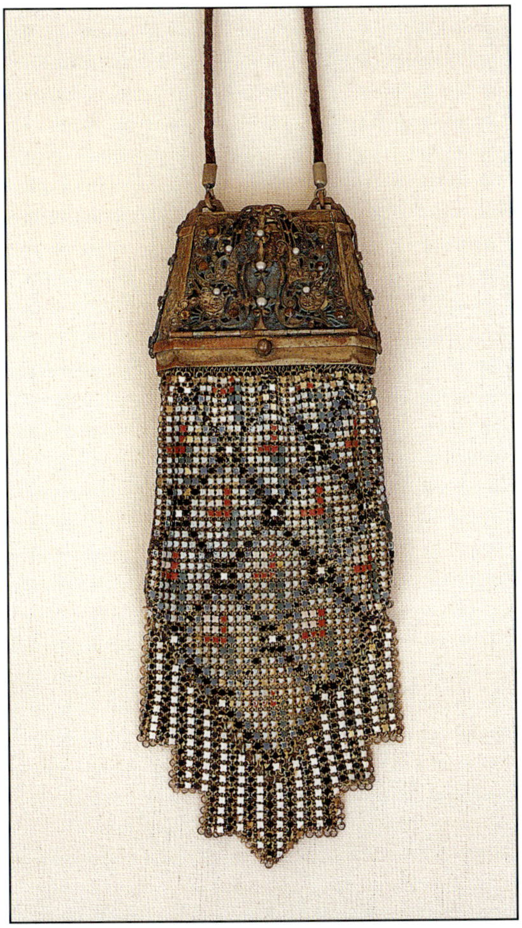

A Whiting & Davis compact top purse made from enameled armor mesh. The hard compact top is jeweled. The frame opens into a square. 8 x 3 in. *Collection of Melissa Overdorf.* $650-750.

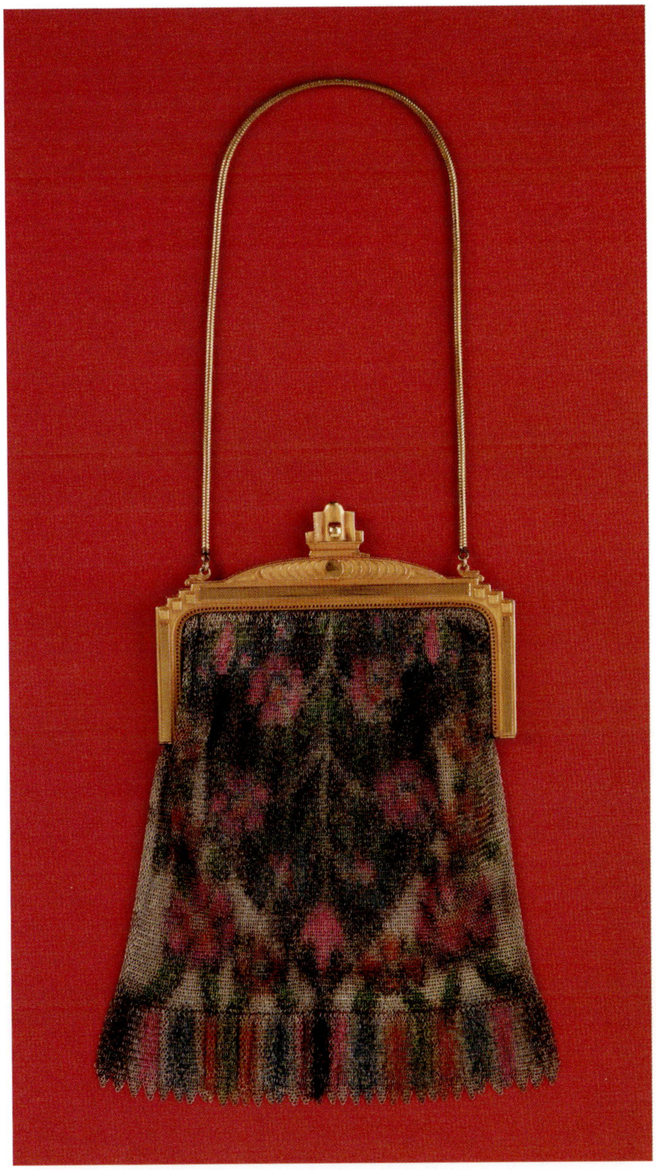

Colorful, Whiting & Davis Dresden mesh purse with a 24kg plated frame. The impressionistic designs appeal to many collectors. Ideally, the colors should be strong and the fine ring mesh without holes. 5.5 x 4.5 in. *Collection of Sharon LuVisi.* $275-325.

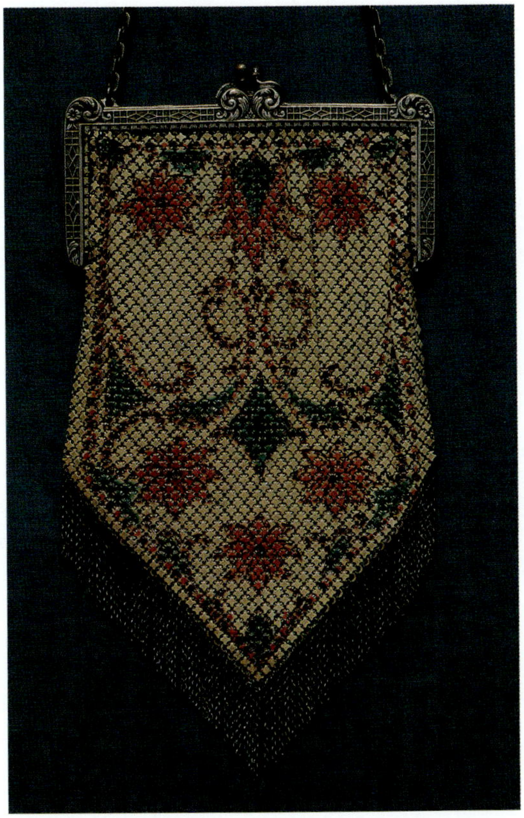

Floral designed armor mesh purse on a silver frame by Mandalian. 7.5 x 4.5 in. *Collection of Linda Marshall.* $325-350.

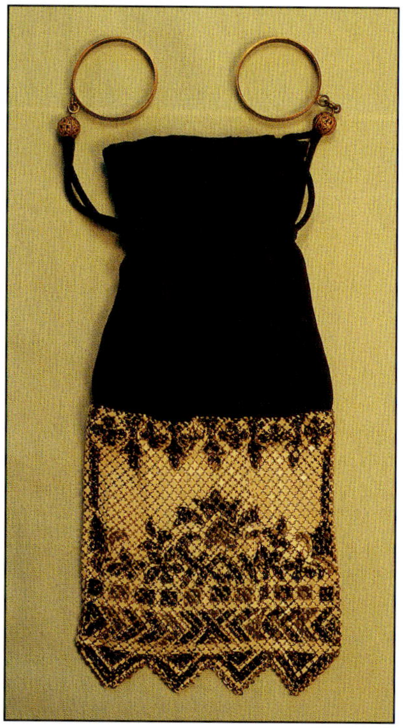

Another "Martha Washington" purse made by Mandalian with its original rings attached to the drawstring. Made in black and white armor mesh with a Vandyke skirt. 7.5 x 4.5 in. *Collection of Linda Marshall.* $350-400.

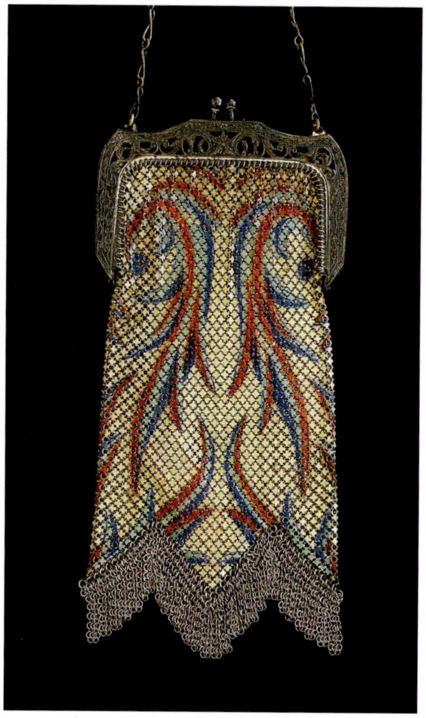

Visually striking, Whiting & Davis mesh purse made with a tri-point fringe and a silver, open worked frame. 7 x 3 in. *Collection of Linda Marshall.* $275-300.

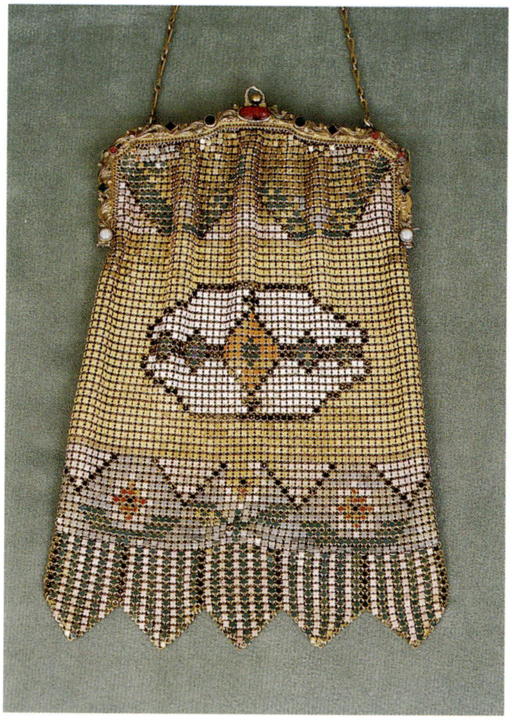

Whiting & Davis armor mesh purse with a lovely jeweled frame. Jewel framed mesh purses are very desirable. 9 x 5.5 in. *Collection of Lori Blaser.* $375-450.

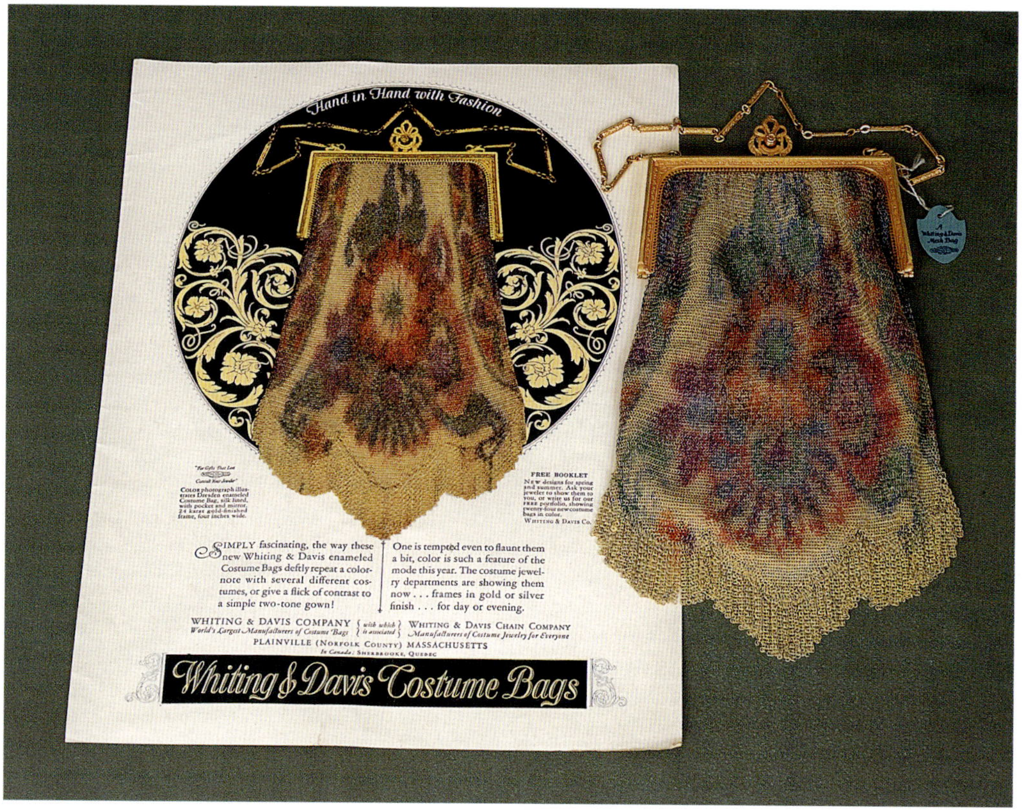

A Whiting & Davis Dresden mesh purse with its original tag and an original ad showing the same purse. The frame is 24kg plated. This purse is in excellent condition and it even retains its original lining. The combination of the purse, ad, and tag are rare. 9 x 5 in. *Collection of Lori Blaser.* Rare.

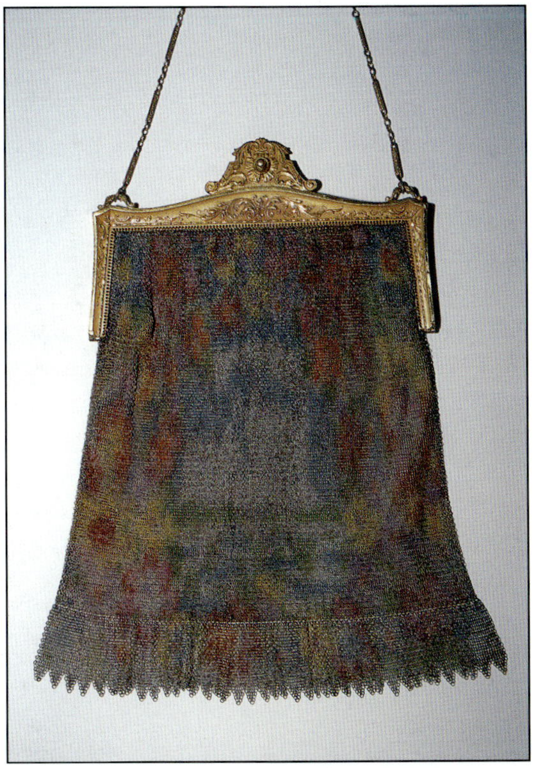

Large Dresden mesh purse with a 24kg plated frame by Whiting & Davis. 9 x 6 in. *Collection of Paula Higgins.* $300-350.

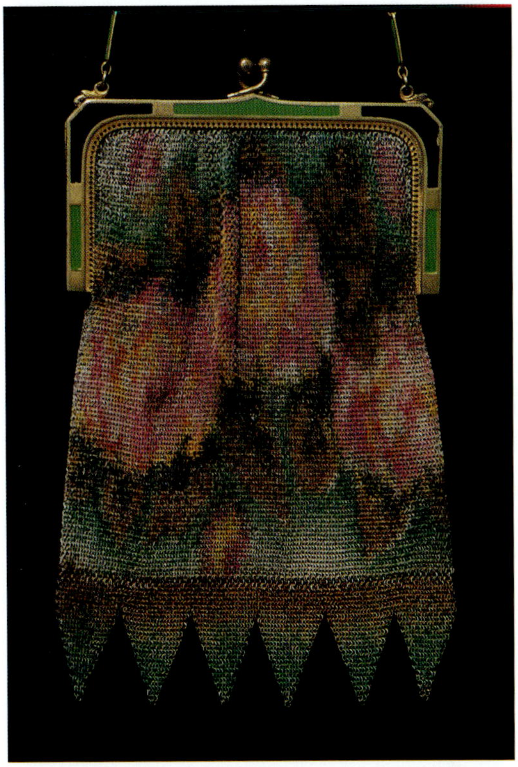

Beautiful Dresden mesh purse with an enameled frame by Whiting & Davis. The colors on this purse are quite vibrant. 6 x 4 in. *Collection of Linda Marshall.* $300-350.

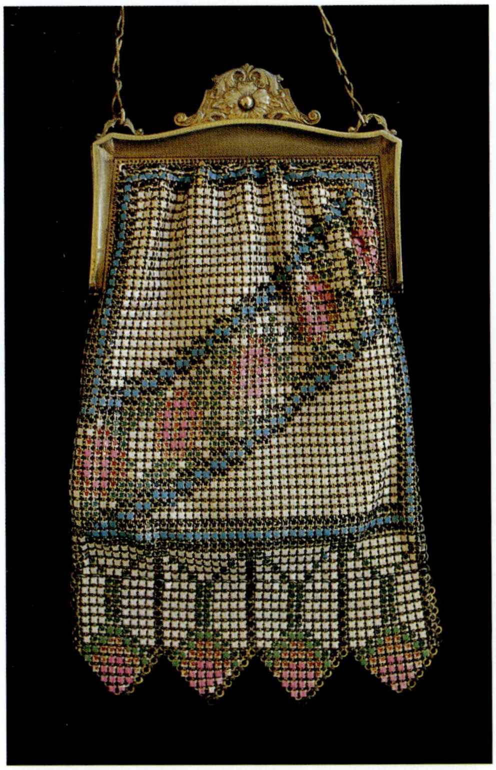

Pink and turquoise Whiting & Davis armor mesh purse with a vandyke skirt. 7 x 5 in. *Collection of Linda Marshall.* $250-275.

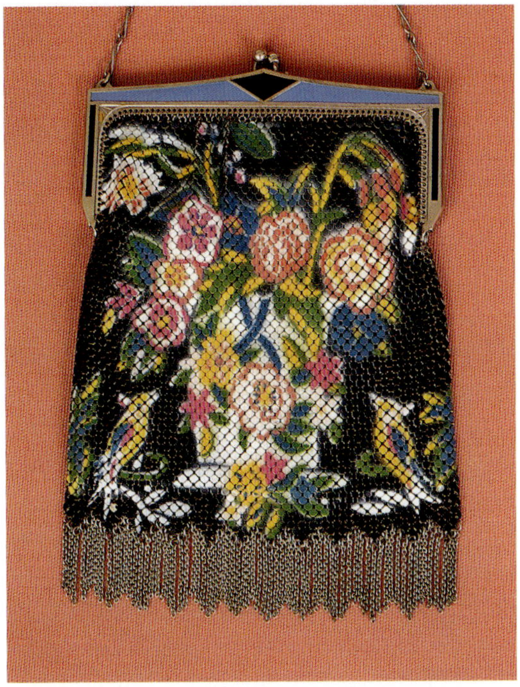

Mesh bags don't come more colorful than this. This Whiting & Davis purse is decorated with a floral arrangement flanked by two birds. Made from armor mesh, it also has an enameled frame and ring mesh fringe in a saw tooth design. 8 x 5 in. *Collection of Lori Blaser.* $450-500.

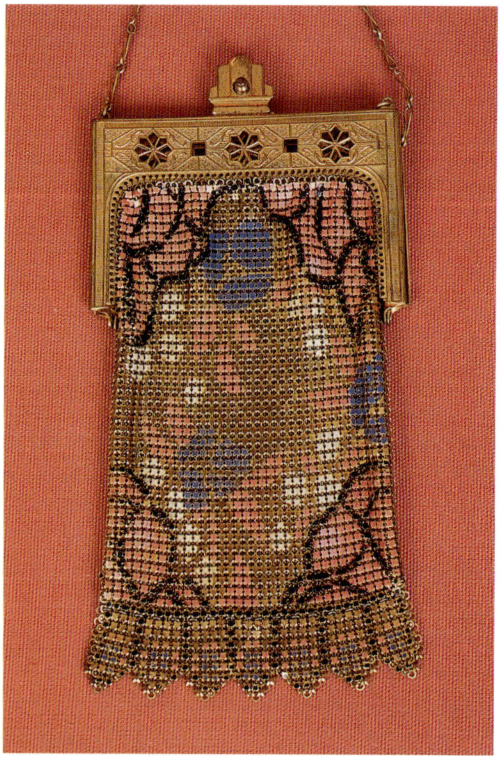

A Whiting & Davis armor mesh purse made with an open worked 24kg plated frame. 8 x 4 in. *Collection of Lori Blaser.* $250-275.

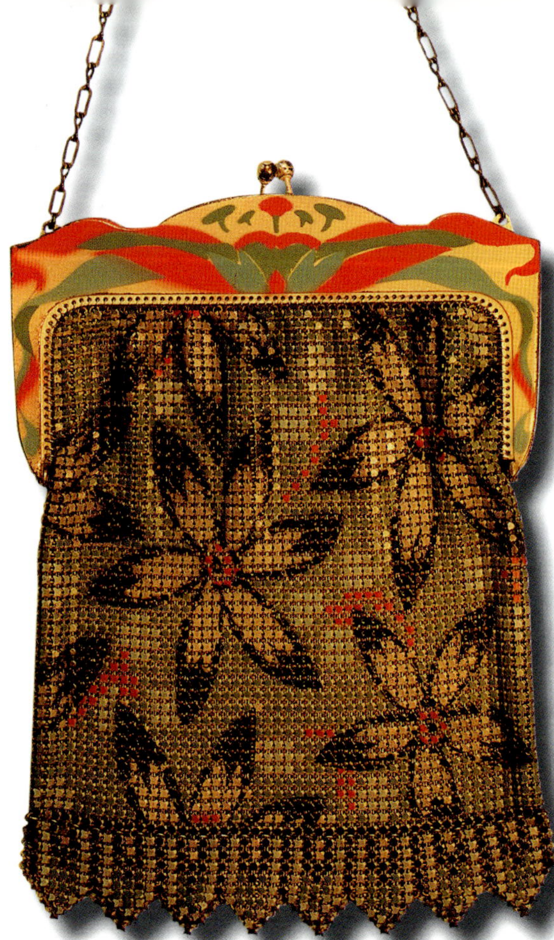

This Art Deco inspired daisy design is complimented by a beautifully enameled frame. The frame adds considerable value to the purse. Made by Whiting & Davis in armor mesh. 7 x 5 in. *Collection of Linda Marshall.* $350-400.

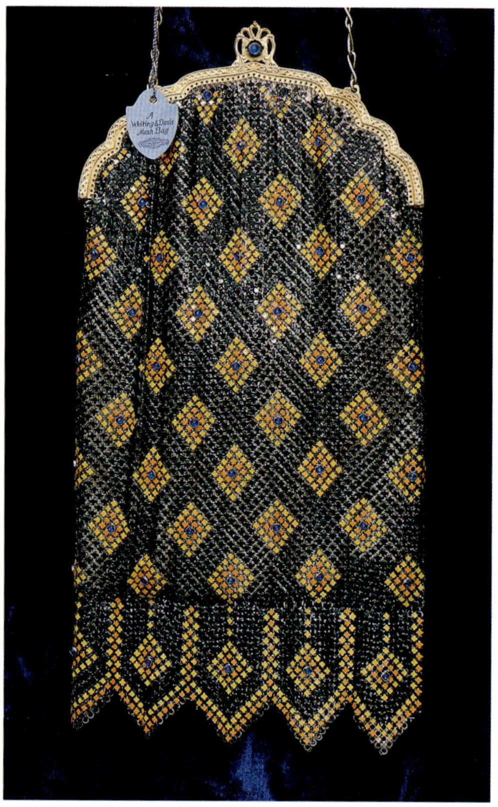

Mesh purses, with jeweled bodies, are very desirable. This purse has tiny blue stones set into each enameled diamond. Whiting & Davis made this purse and it still retains its original tag. 8 x 4 in. *Collection of Linda Marshall.* $450-600.

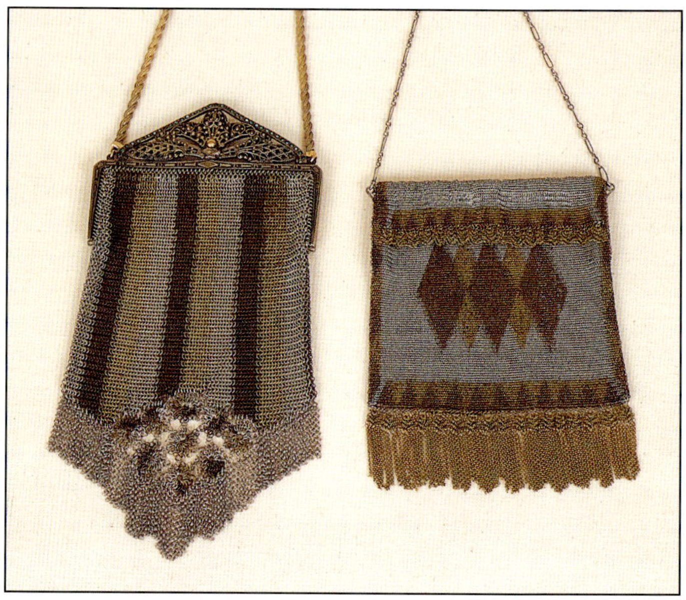

Two sunset mesh purses. The purse on the left has a Venetian fringe and a twisted rope chain. The purse on the right is made in the Princess Mary style in Dresden mesh. Left: 8.5 x 4 in. Right: 6 x 4 in. Left: *Collection of Lori Blaser.* Right: *Collection of Ruth Penson.* Left: $350-400. Right: $350-400.

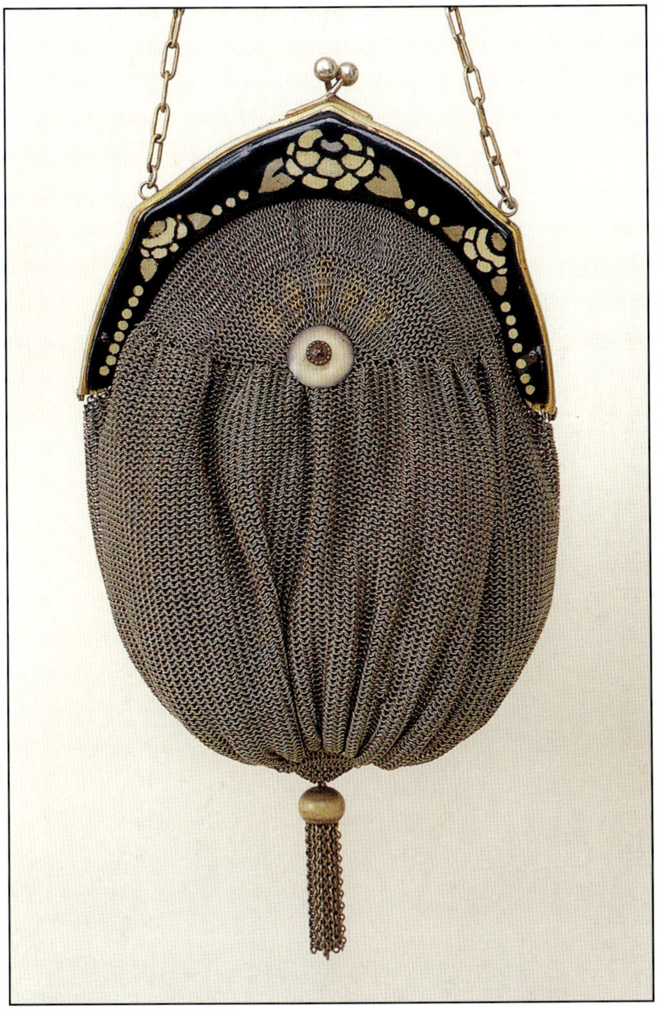

Two tone, ring mesh bag attached to an enameled frame. Possibly French made. 7 x 4.5 in. *Collection of Lori Blaser.* $300-375.

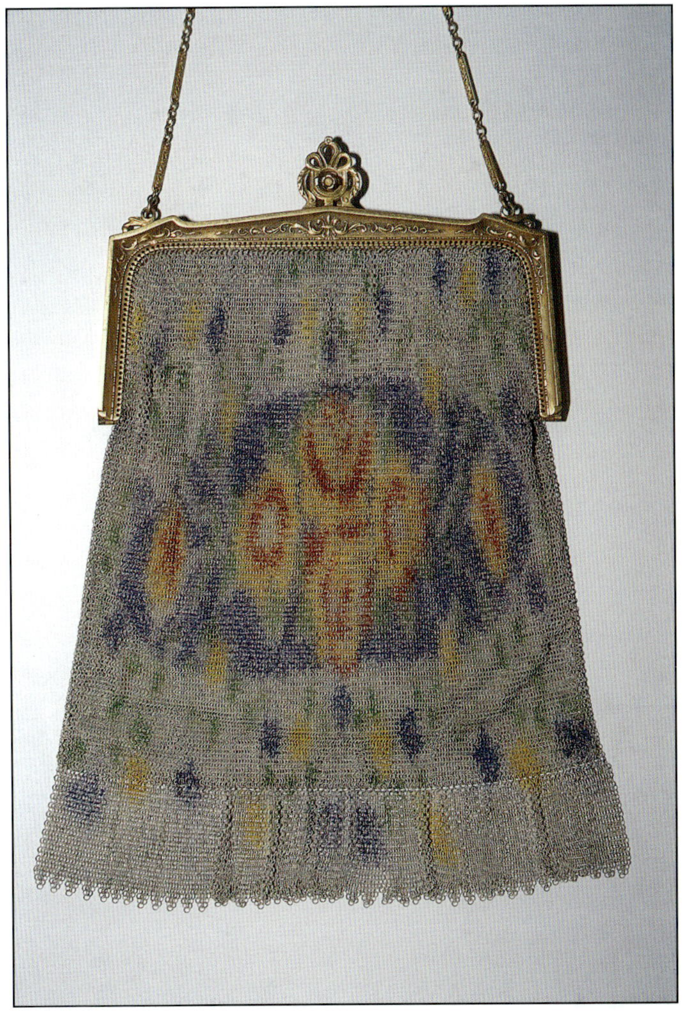

Whiting & Davis Dresden mesh purse with its original lining and 24kg plated frame. 7 x 5 in. *Collection of Paula Higgins.* $250-300.

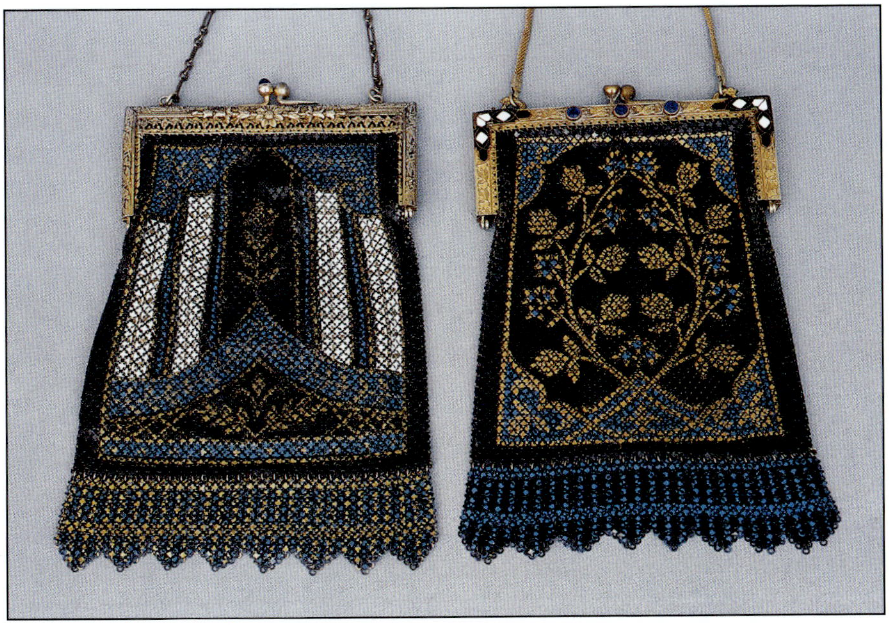

A pair of Mandalian armor mesh purses. Jeweled frames add to the value of any mesh purse. Mandalian produced balanced and elegant designs, with a touch of the exotic. Left: 8.5 x 5.5 in. Right: 8 x 5.25 in. *Collection of Lori Blaser.* $375-450.

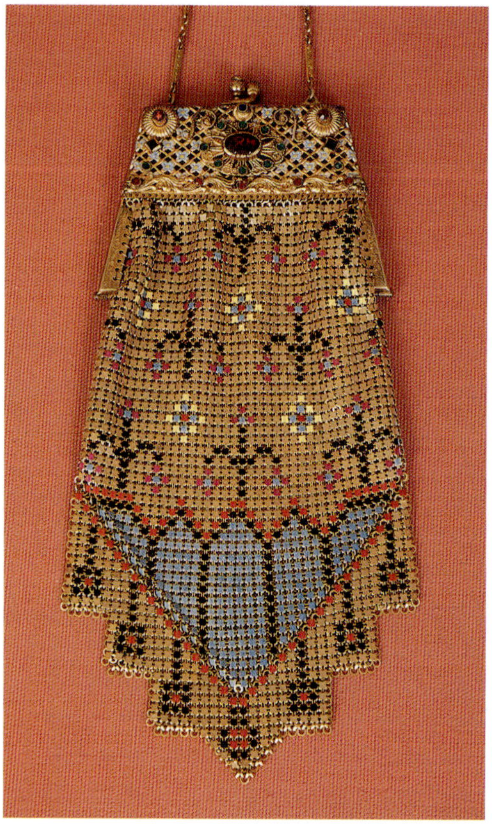

Whiting & Davis also made exquisite bags. Purses like this one, bring high prices. The armor mesh body is beautifully enameled and in excellent condition. It also has a stunning jeweled and enameled frame, which compliments the design on the purse. 8.5 x 4 in. *Collection of Lori Blaser.* $650-750.

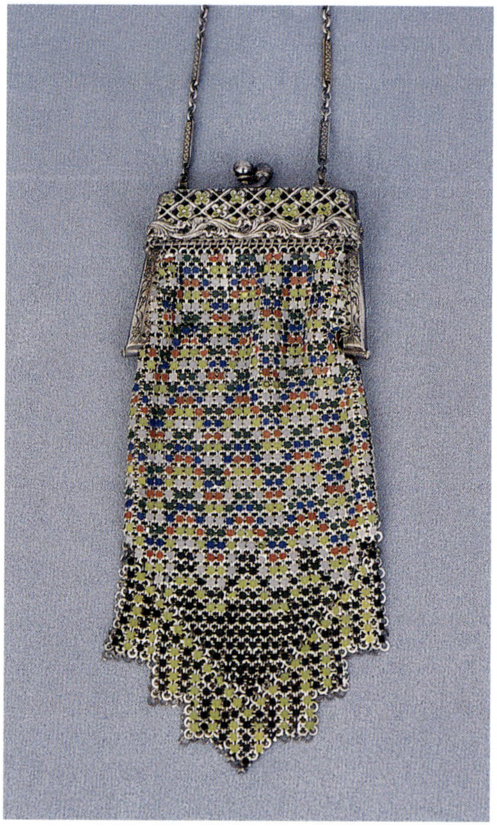

Mesh firms also made children's purses. This small, armor mesh purse by Whiting & Davis has a reticulated frame and a step style bottom. 6 x 2.5 in. *Collection of Lori Blaser.* $350-375.

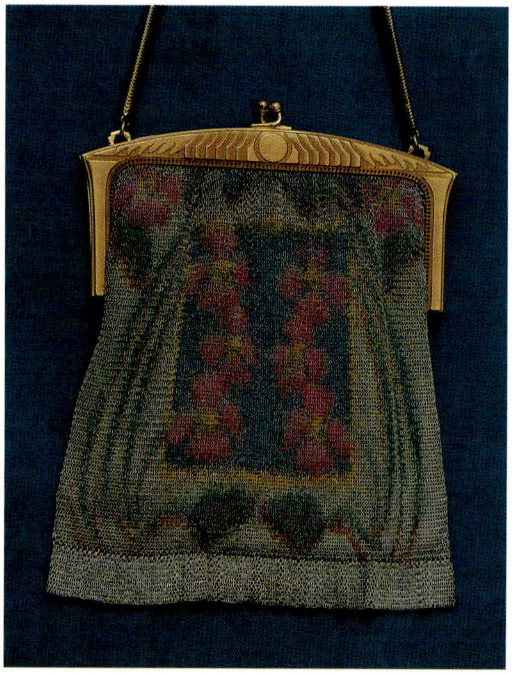

Pretty floral Dresden mesh by Whiting & Davis with a 24kg plated frame. 6 x 5 in. *Collection of Linda Marshall.* $300-350.

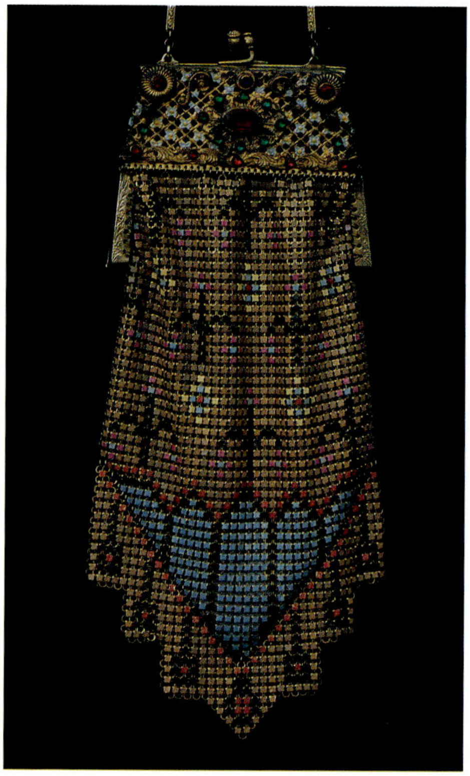

Another high quality Whiting & Davis, enameled armor mesh purse with a jeweled and enameled frame. If a collector could only own one mesh purse, this might be it. 8 x 4 in. *Collection of Linda Marshall.* $650-750.

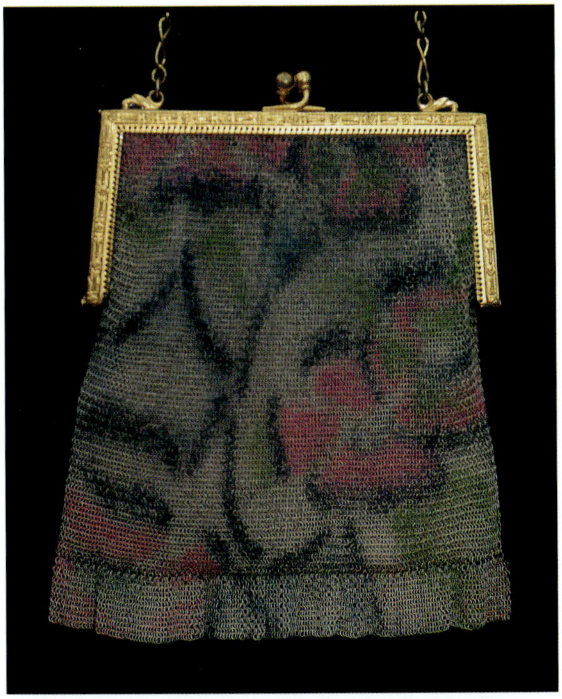

Whiting & Davis Dresden mesh purse with 24kg plated frame. 8 x 5 in. *Collection of Linda Marshall.* $275-300.

An armor mesh purse made by Whiting & Davis with a dome shaped, blown out, and cut out frame. 7.25 x 3.25 in. *Collection of Linda Marshall.* $300-350.

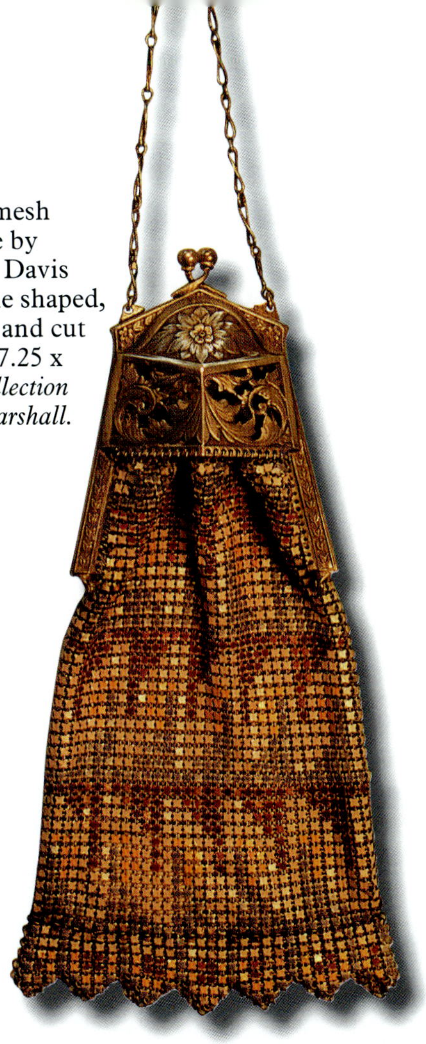

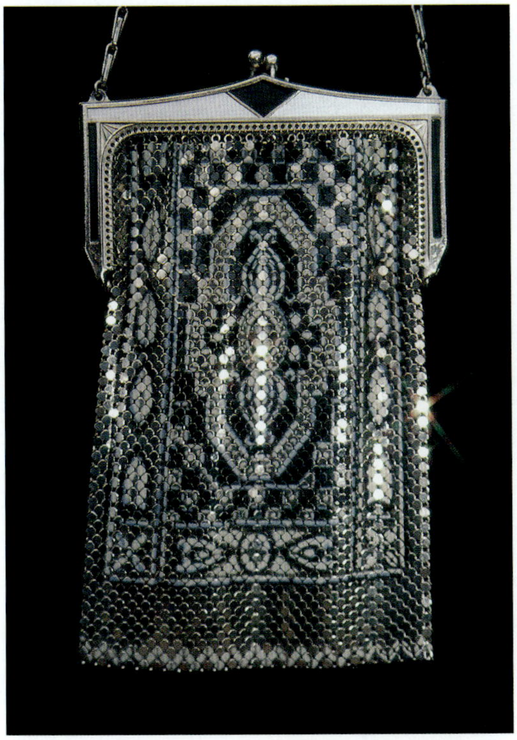

This black and silver Whiting & Davis purse was made with round armor mesh links. The coordinating enameled frame and the exotic rug design make for a sophisticated purse. 7 x 4 in. *Collection of Linda Marshall.* $250-275.

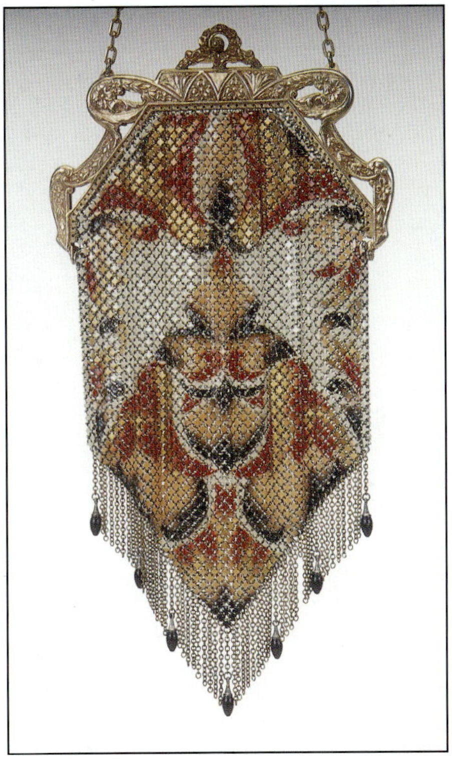

Mandalian made some truly beautiful and rich looking purses. This is a prime example. Earth tones and sumptuous lines decorate this armor mesh purse. The sinuous lines of the frame add to the overall effect. At the bottom is a V fringe made from ring mesh and drops. 9.5 x 4.75 in. *Collection of Lori Blaser.* $600-700.

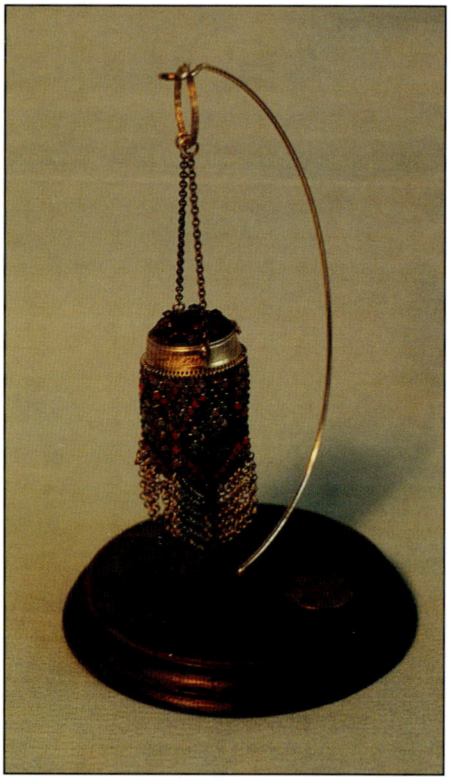

Rare, miniature, enameled armor mesh purse with a jeweled top and finger ring. Whiting & Davis made these small purses to hold rosaries. An ad for one of these purses is seen in Evelyn Haertig's book, *More Beautiful Purses.* 2.5 x 1 in. *Collection of Linda Marshall.* Rare.

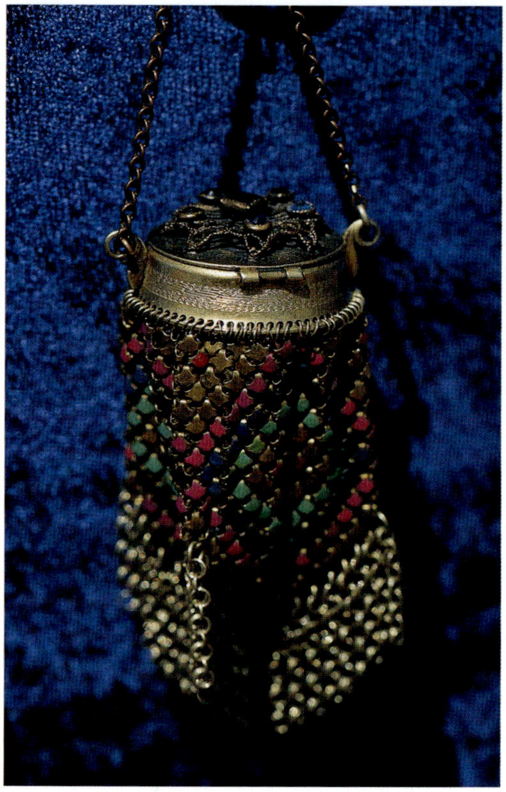

A close-up of the miniature purse.

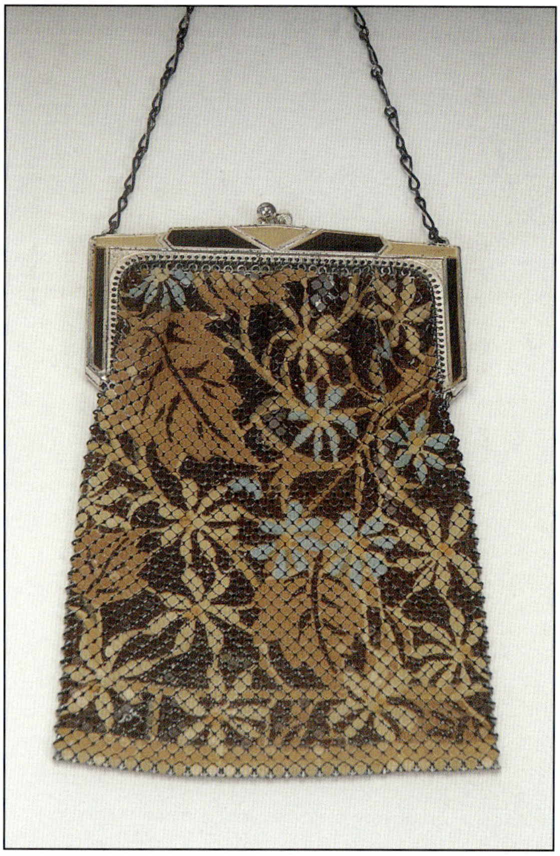

A Whiting & Davis purse made from aluminum armor mesh. Aluminum armor mesh was made for a brief period of time. Much lighter weight than other metals, it has a distinctive feel. The frame is enameled. 7 x 4.4 in. *Collection of Lori Blaser.* $350-375.

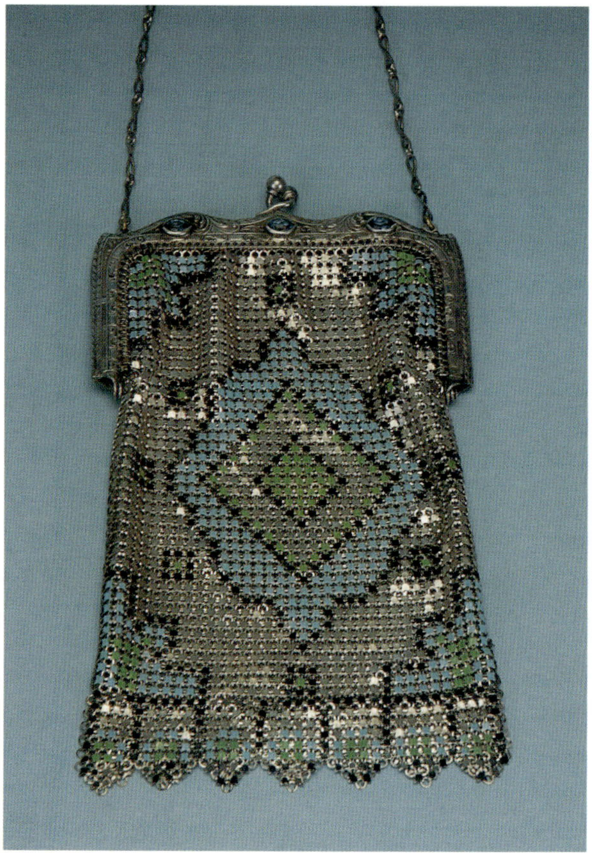

The frame on this Whiting & Davis armor mesh purse is decorated with bezel set, faceted stones. 7 x 3.75 in. *Collection of Lori Blaser.* $350-375.

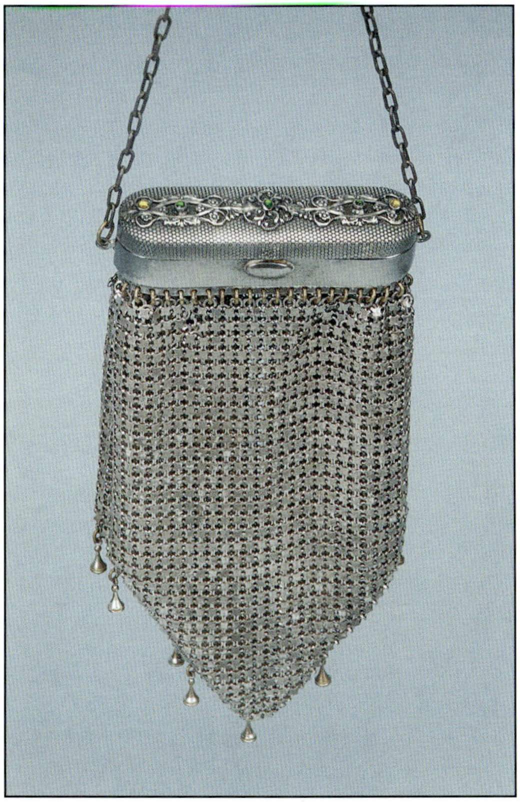

This silver mesh purse is unmarked. The unusual frame is set with rhinestones and opens like a box. Drops hang from a V shaped bottom. 7.5 x 3.5 in. *Collection of Lori Blaser.* $325-375.

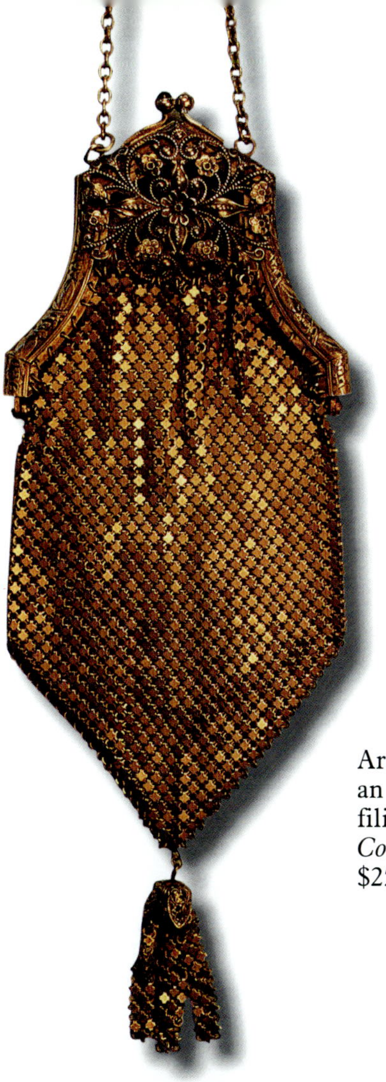

Armor mesh purse with an embossed and floral filigreed frame. 7 x 3 in. *Collection of Linda Marshall.* $250-275.

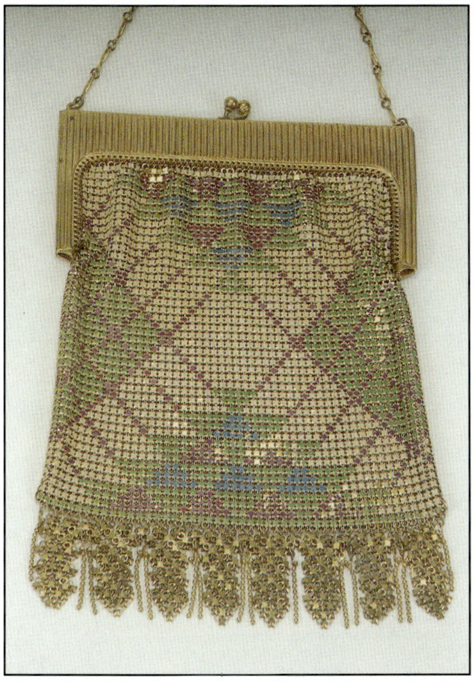

This Whiting & Davis armor mesh purse has an unusual fringe design. Vandyke mesh segments alternate with key chain fringe, creating a glittering effect. 8.25 x 5 in. *Collection of Lori Blaser.* $300-375.

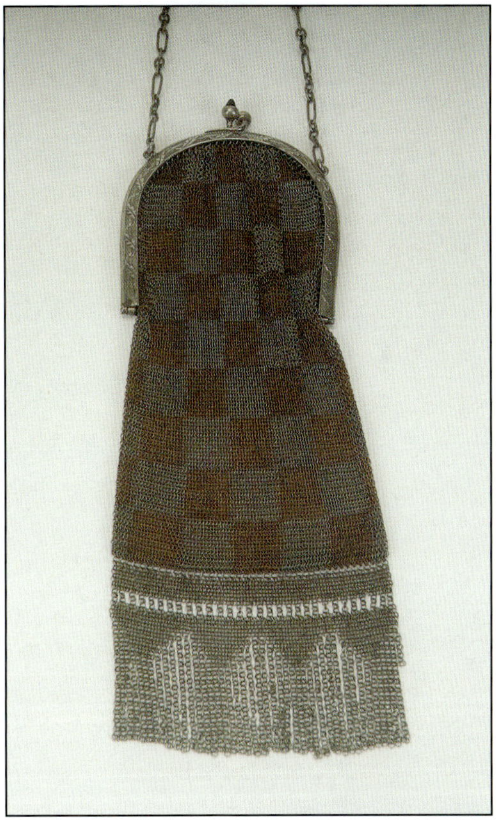

Fine ring mesh, designed like a checkerboard, is finished with tiers, vandyke points, and long fringe. This purse is unmarked. 8.5 x 2.5 in. *Collection of Lori Blaser.* $300-325.

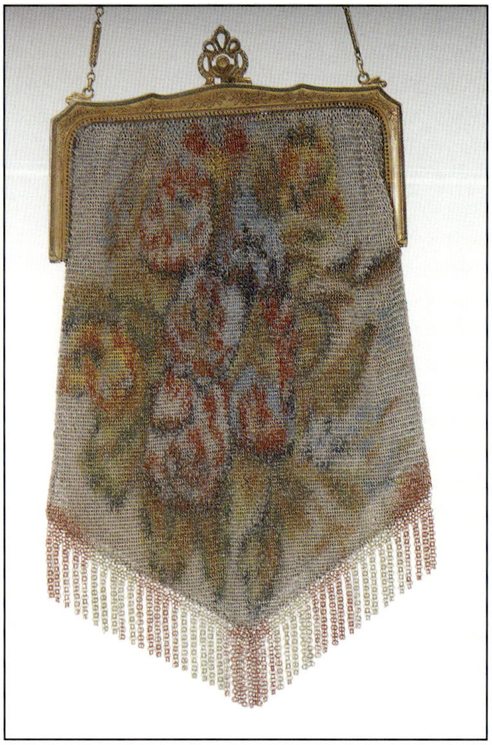

A large Dresden mesh purse with a 24kg plated frame. This design was made in several color combinations. 9.25 x 5.5 in. *Collection of Lori Blaser.* $300-350.

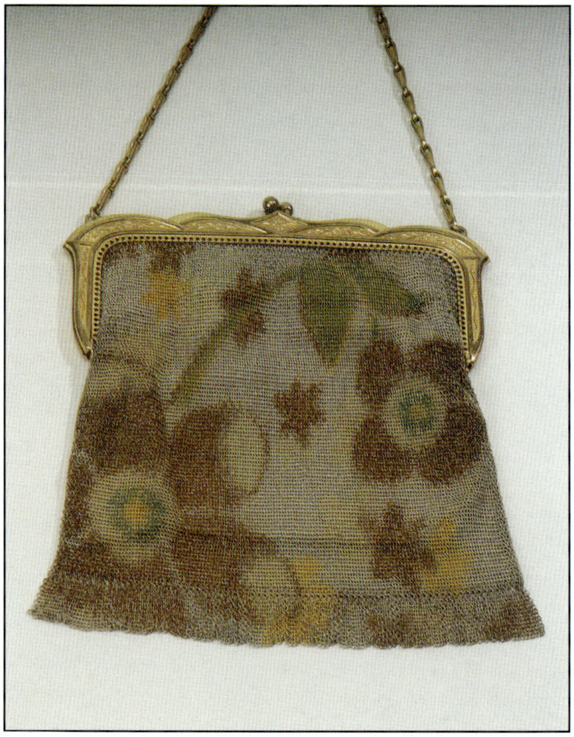

A smaller, Dresden mesh with an earth tone color scheme and skirted bottom. 6 x 5.25 in. *Collection of Lori Blaser.* $225-250.

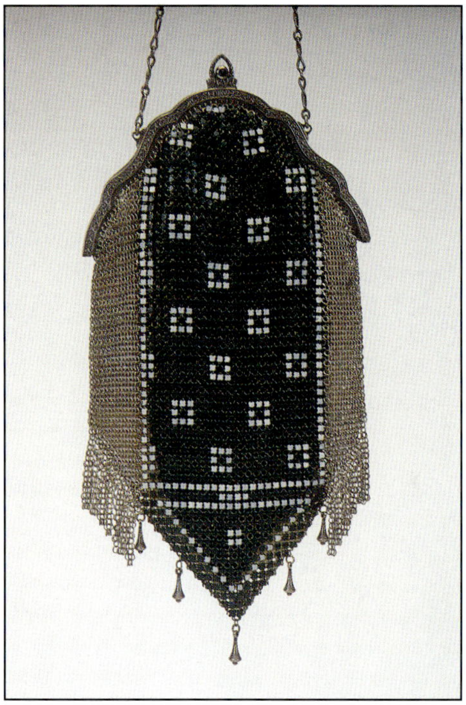

Another Whiting & Davis purse with an unusual design. The body of the purse is made from ring mesh sides, flanking an armor mesh center. On the bottom, ring mesh and drop fringe continue the theme. This is known as the "batwing" design. 8.5 x 4 in. *Collection of Lori Blaser.* $350-450.

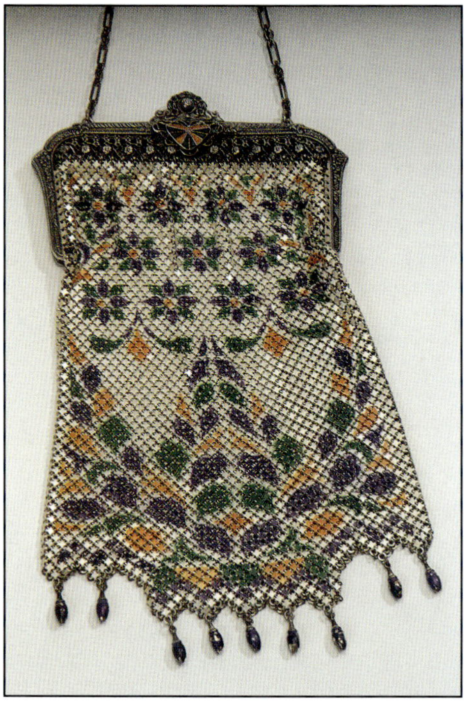

A Mandalian beauty made from armor mesh with a lustro-pearl finish. Whiting & Davis also produced a similar finish, which they called "fish scale." The Byzantine, drop decorated bottom adds to its value. 9 x 4.5 in. *Collection of Lori Blaser.* $375-425.

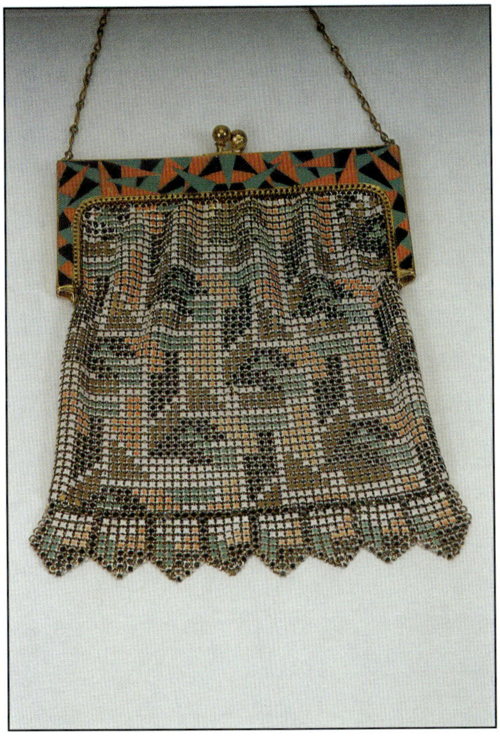

Whiting & Davis specialized in Art Deco geometric designs. This purse is an excellent example of the style. Their enameled frames often took their inspiration from the purse body design. 8 x 5 in. *Collection of Lori Blaser.* $250-275.

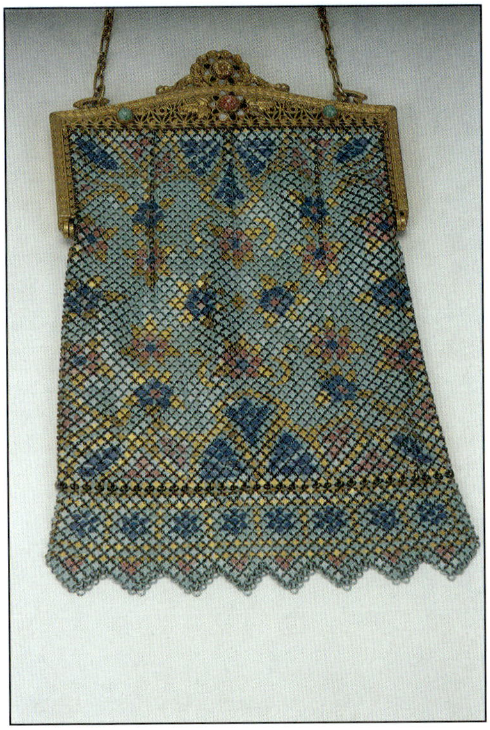

This color combination is beautiful and among Mandalian's most popular. The Persian influenced design is made from armor mesh. It is finished with a vandyke skirt, and the frame is set with cabochon stones. 9 x 5 in. *Collection of Lori Blaser.* $350-425.

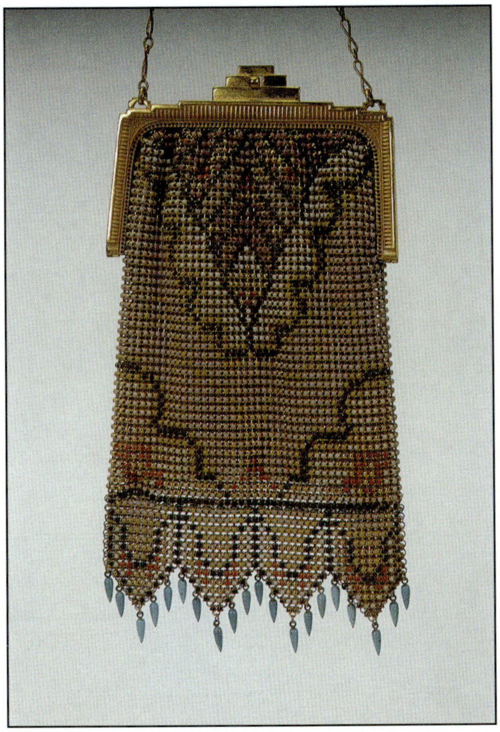

Whiting & Davis also made drop finished purses, and with twenty drops, this is an excellent example. The mesh is made from beadlite and the frame is 24kg plated. 8 x 4 in. *Collection of Lori Blaser.* $300-375.

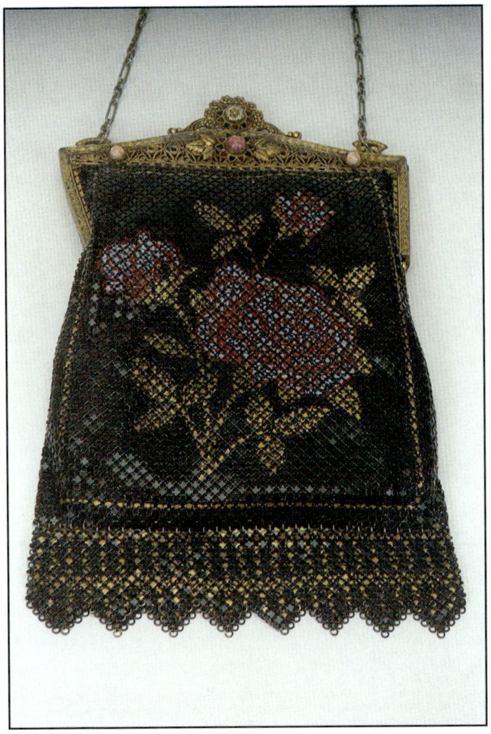

This is a well known Mandalian purse made from armor mesh in a bold floral design. The frame is set with marbleized cabochon stones and enamel work. 9 x 5.5 in. *Collection of Lori Blaser.* $325-350.

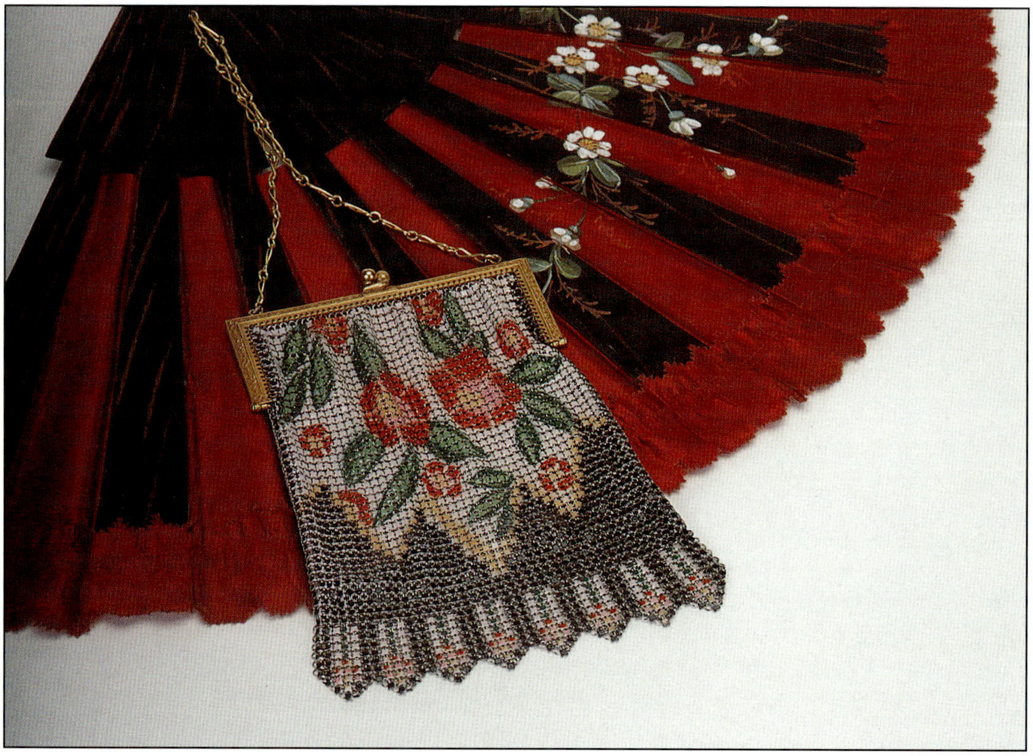

The visual appeal of black and red is captured beautifully in this picture. Whiting & Davis made many beautiful floral designs like this one. Their floral designs were more contemporary looking than those produced by Mandalian. 6.5 x 4.5 in. *Collection of Lori Blaser.* $300-325.

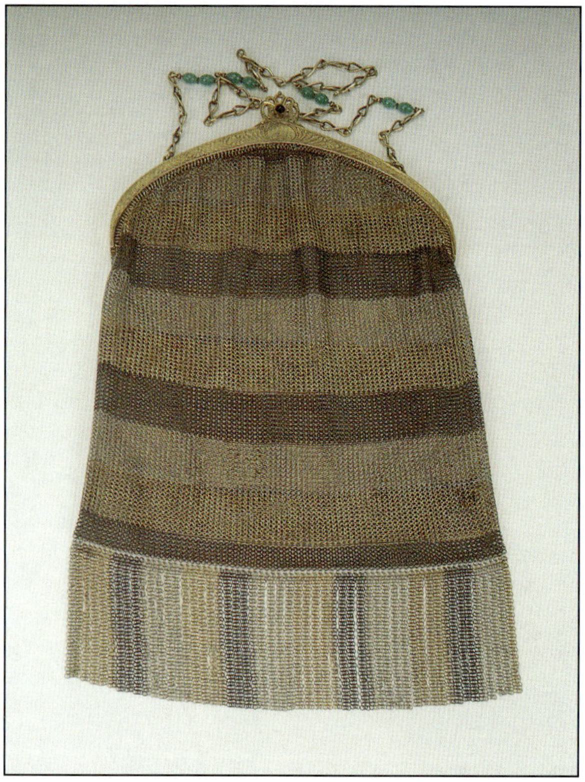

Sunset mesh by Whiting & Davis came in a variety of designs. The name sunset describes purses made in alternating segments, using plated metals of gold, bronze, silver, or brass. This purse has both horizontal and vertical stripes, which extend into the fringe. 10.5 x 5.5 in. *Collection of Lori Blaser.* $300-350.

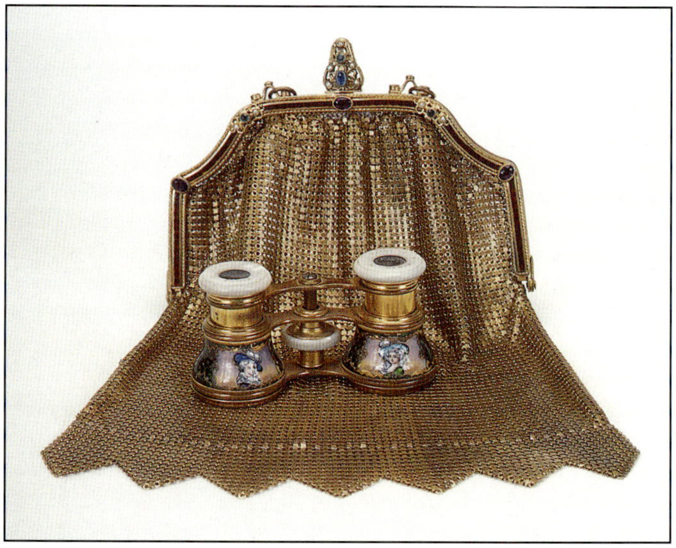

Frames can add substantially to the appeal and value of a mesh purse. The frame on this large armor mesh bag is enameled and decorated with bezel set stones in an elegant and sophisticated design. 11 x 7 in. *Collection of Lori Blaser.* $300-350.

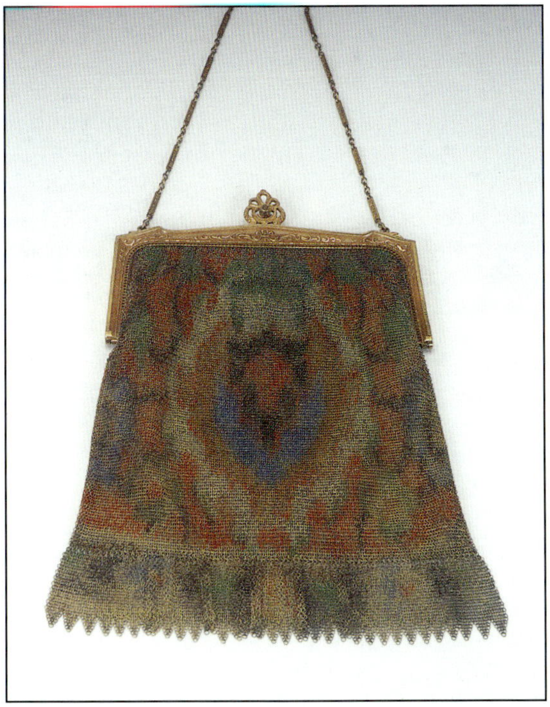

Coral, green, tan, and blue make for a colorful Dresden mesh design. The frame is 24kg plated. 8.25 x 5.5 in. *Collection of Lori Blaser.* $225-250.

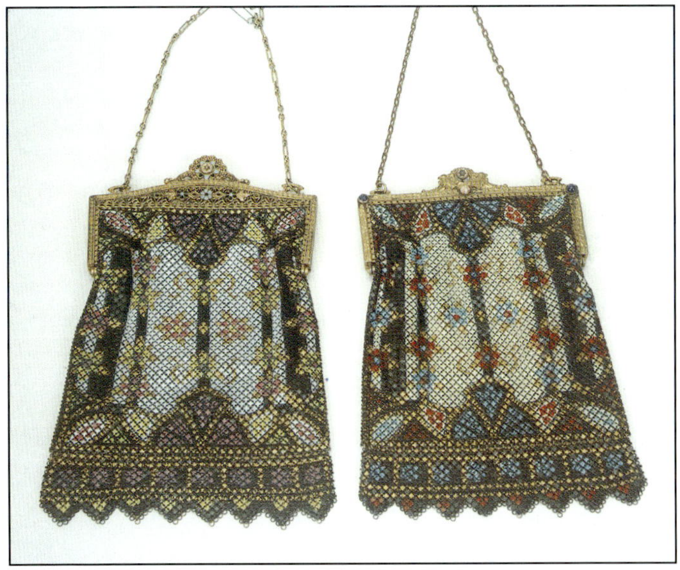

A pair of Mandalian armor mesh purses made in the "stained glass window" design. The jeweled and enameled frame on the left is among the finest Mandalian produced. Left: 8 x 5.5 in. Right: 8 x 5 in. *Collection of Lori Blaser.* Left: $400-450. Right: $400-425.

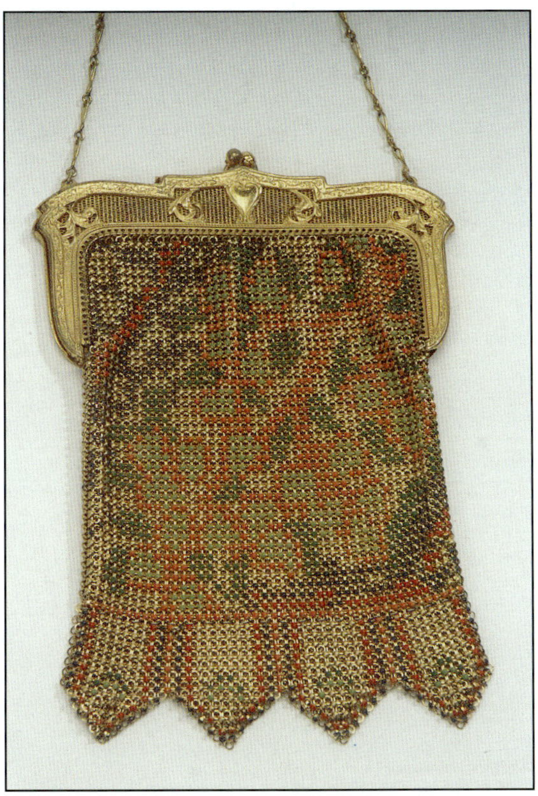

Coral, green, and gold beadlite mesh purse with a 24kg plated frame and a vandyke skirt. Made by Whiting & Davis. 7.75 x 5 in. *Collection of Lori Blaser.* $200-225.

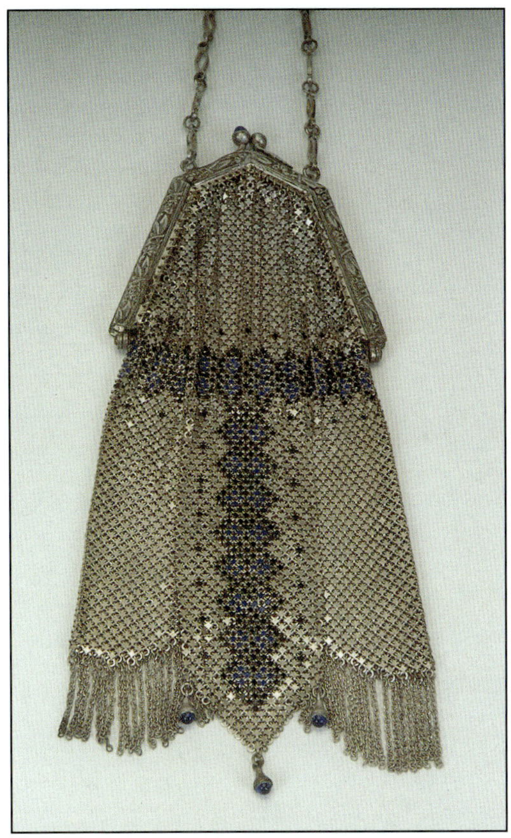

This batwing style purse is made completely of armor mesh. Other examples were made from both ring and armor mesh. The drops are made from blue cabochons, which have been bezel set. 8.5 x 3 in. *Collection of Lori Blaser.* $400-450.

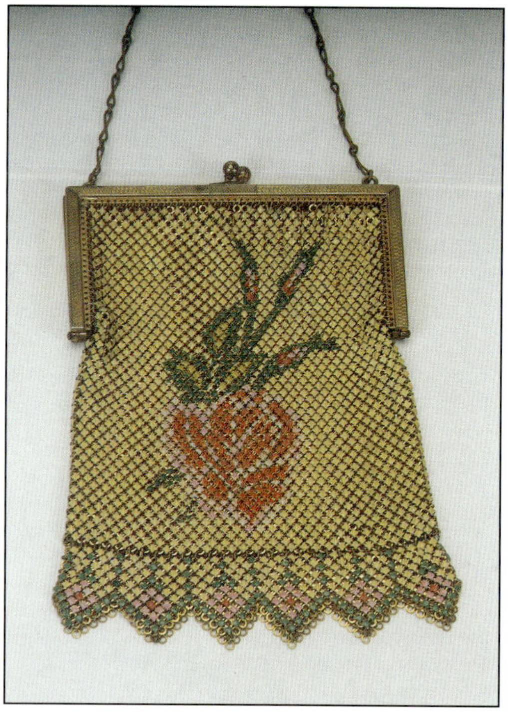

A Whiting & Davis floral designed armor mesh purse. Compare this purse with the Mandalian floral (with a black background), also in this chapter, to see the difference in production values. 6.5 x 4 in. *Collection of Lori Blaser.* $200-225.

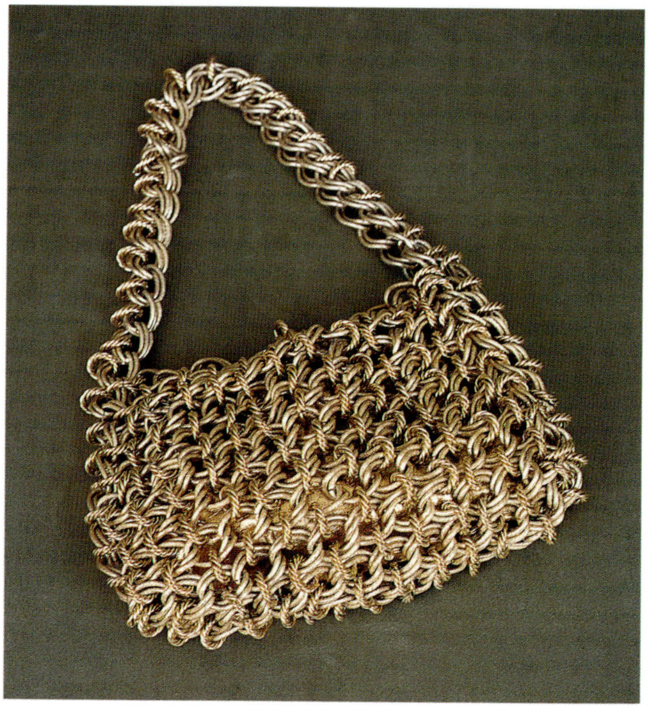

Mesh purses were also made later in the century as this 1960s example proves. Large intersecting links replace the armor and ring mesh of the 20s and 30s. The maker is unknown. 8.5 x 6 in. *Collection of Ruth Penson.* $75-100.

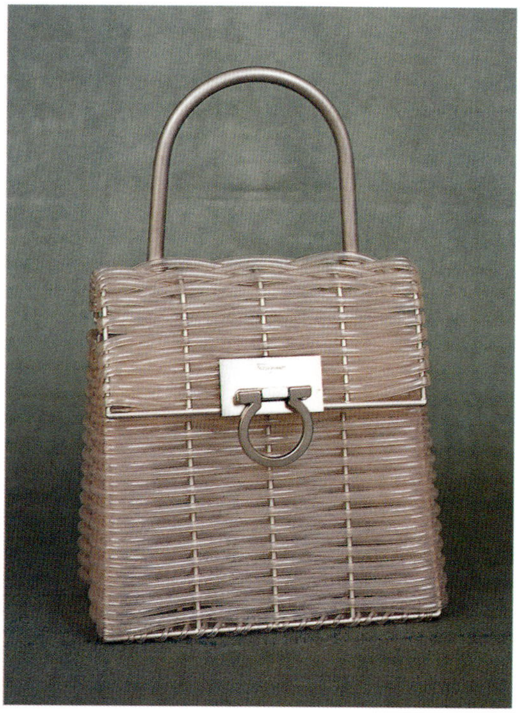

Although this Salvatore Ferragamo purse is not made from metal mesh, the plastic weaving has the appearance of woven mesh. 8 x 7.5 in. *Collection of Ruth Penson.* $200-250.

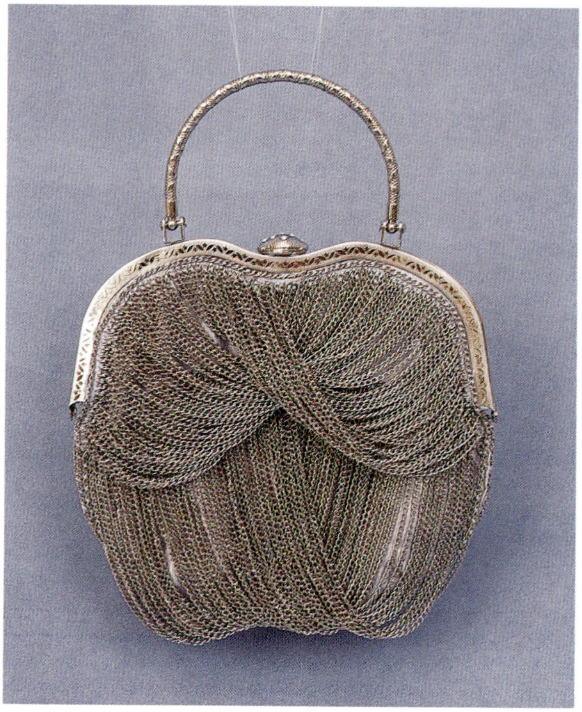

The latest in mesh bags made by Chico's. This apple shaped, swag mesh handbag has a rigid handle and an optional carrying chain. Made in 2005. 8 x 8 in. *Collection of Lori Blaser.* $200-250.

Chapter 9
Beaded Purses

Early 17th century beaded purses were made with a network technique, which resulted in a mesh of beadwork. Square or slightly rectangular in size, they were often finished with three short tassels across the bottom. Vanda Foster dates these beaded purses to a very narrow time period, from 1620 to 1640. Beaded in all-over diaper patterns (repetitive geometric designs) or acorn designs, many had mottos beaded at the top, such as "Remember the Pore." It is believed these purses were made in England. France also produced early beaded purses. No 17th century American examples are known to exist. Any 17th century beaded purse is very rare.

Other beadwork methods used during this early period included stitching beads onto fabric, couching, and sewing beads onto fine net. Caroline Crabtree and Pam Stallebrass note in their book, *Beadwork—A World Guide,* that steel needles were made as early as the 16th century in Germany and Spain, and that by the end of the 16th century they were also being produced in England.

Sablé beaded purses from the 18th century are another rare type of beaded purse. Sablé means "grain of sand" in French, but the term also refers to the technique used to make them. Made with a horizontal and vertical looping method, the finished result resembled a buttonhole or basket stitch surrounding the bead. These beads were so fine, at size 22 or greater (possibly up to size 30), needles could not pass through their center holes. Charles Germain de Saint-Aubin is believed to have set up the first sablé beadwork shops in Paris. Saint-Aubin was also the chief designer to Louis XV. He discusses in his book, *Art of the Embroiderer,* published in 1770, how the tiny beads were threaded by folding a hair over a thread, then the hair (human or horse) was inserted through the bead, and then onto the thread. Another method involved pointing the silk thread with shellac. Whatever method was used, the process was time consuming and labor-intensive, which meant that only wealthy people could afford to buy them. Sablé purses were decorated with scrolling, Rococo designs, nymphs, shepherds, cherubs, florals, and phoenix. They were made as wallets, square bags, and in a pouch shape. While sablé beadwork of any kind is quite rare, sablé pouches and bags are very rare. An extraordinary sablé wallet, formerly in the collection of the late textile authority and collector, Cora Ginsburg, had three different panels beaded with mythological scenes and figures, cherubs, peacocks, a ship, and hearts aflame. The Museum of Fine Arts in Boston, Massachusetts has an excellent collection of sablé beadwork, especially purses.

By the early 19th century, most beaded purses were knitted. Early 19th century reticules were very finely knitted, with areas of beading interspersed throughout the knitting. By 1830, most glass beaded purses were totally covered with beadwork. Beads were strung onto the thread according to the pattern, before the knitting was started. A few misplaced beads could result in disaster, ruining the design. By c.1830 beaded purses were also crocheted. Crocheted beadwork has a tighter feel and often the beads sit at a slight angle. Early 19th century beaded purses were also embroidered on canvas, beaded on a mold, and sewn onto fabric.

Early purse designs ranged from the three-sectional, "primitive" florals, to the detailed European town scenes. Other designs included: Carib Indians, funereal designs, shepherds and sheep, wreaths, angels, and hunt scenes. Although less sophisticated than later figurals and scenes from the late 19th and early 20th centuries, they have a charm that is undeniable. The women who made them used their life experiences for inspiration. Although many early beaded purses were made with a header in the reticule style, some were mounted on frames of pinchbeck, iron (rare), silver, cut steel, and brass. Frame clasps were made in the push-button style or the more rare ball-push-through style (a ball which pushed through a hole in a standing clasp). During the mid-nineteenth century, velvet purses decorated with beadwork were also popular.

By the late 19th century, beaded purses were loomed, embroidered, knitted, crocheted, and woven with a needle. The bead knitted purse is still the favorite of most purse collectors, but fine examples were made using other methods. In the following chapter there are purses made from a variety of techniques. They were included because they have merit by virtue of their designs, historic merit, color schemes, framing, rarity, or beauty. A colored, cut steel loomed purse in good condition might be more attractive and valuable than a bead knitted purse of no particular merit. Beadwork purses from the late 19th and early 20th centuries were frequently mounted on a frame.

Turkish and Eastern Mediterranean beadwork is

distinctive; once you become familiar with its characteristics, it is easy to spot. Exported to Europe in the 19th and early 20th centuries, many pieces have made their way to the United States. Turkish and Eastern Mediterranean purses were typically crocheted or netted. Designs include sharp angular bird or floral designs, diamond shapes, and triangular amulets. Turkish beaded misers were often finished with short, bushy silk tassels ending in beads. Turkish and Eastern Mediterranean purse makers were also partial to gold colored glass beads and bright color schemes. Because the designs are so angular, some people confuse this with American Indian beadwork. Turkish and Eastern Mediterranean beadwork can be seen on the following pages and in Chapter Three. Turkish prisoner-of-war beadwork from World War I is also distinctive. Usually made of netted beadwork, these purses were decorated with dates and crosses.

French cut steel purses have inherent structural problems because they were loomed and not knitted. Once the threads start to give away, they require relooming to repair them, which is very time consuming. However, there are purse restorers who can do this work if the purse is worth salvaging. Colored cut steel purses also fade over time when exposed to light. Since they are loomed, the design is the same on both sides and some bags can be turned inside out, which allows the brighter side to be shown. This work is best left to a knowledgeable purse restorer, as there are some loomed purses that cannot be turned inside out.

Dating beaded purses can be difficult and confusing. For example, beaded bags were made in the 20th century with early 19th century beads. Early 19th century purse designs were also being used as late as the early 20th century (especially in Germany), and early 19th century bags were mounted on late 19th century or early 20th century frames. Learning the difference between an early 19th century silk lining and a 20th century silk lining is helpful. Determining if a frame is original to the purse is another useful clue, since twist clasp purse frames date to the 1870s. It is important to know that some early 19th century frame designs were being manufactured in the early 20th century with twist clasps. But if you should have a Pinchbeck frame attached to a beaded purse with an early 19th century design, you can be pretty sure it is all original and early. Figurals and scenes mounted on original jeweled and enameled frames usually date to the early 20th century.

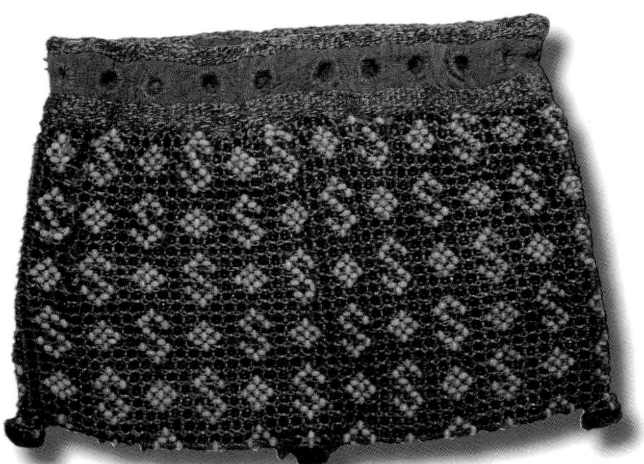

Early 17th century beaded purses are very rare. Made from a network of beads, many of them were designed in allover diaper patterns like this purse. Other purses were made with acorn patterns or geometric flower designs. This purse originally had three tassels at the bottom, where the stubs remain. It retains its original silk and silver thread header. This purse was originally advertised by its E-Bay seller as a beaded purse with $ signs. It was won for $9.00. It dates to c.1600 and is either British or French in origin. 5.25 x 4 in. *Collection of Paula Higgins.* Very rare.

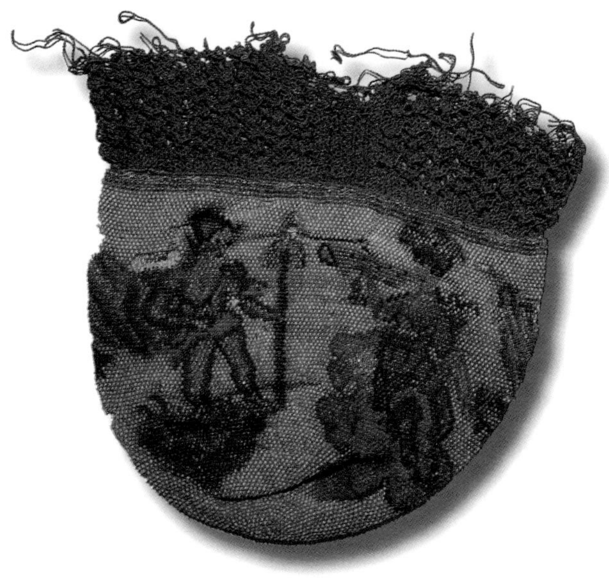

Eighteenth century sablé beaded purses with figural designs are very rare. Sablé means "grain of sand" which refers to the size of the beads. This type of beadwork was made in a few specialty shops in Paris, France during the 18th century for the wealthy. The purse pictured here, was made with a horizontal and vertical looping method, with extremely fine beads. It is in very fragile condition. The female figure on the right appears to be blowing a horn, and the figure on the left has a spear in his hand. During this period it was popular to use symbolic figures to represent the new and the old world (America and Europe). They also might represent mythological figures like Diana, the goddess of the hunt, and a hunter. 4 x 3 in. *Collection of Paula Higgins.* Very rare.

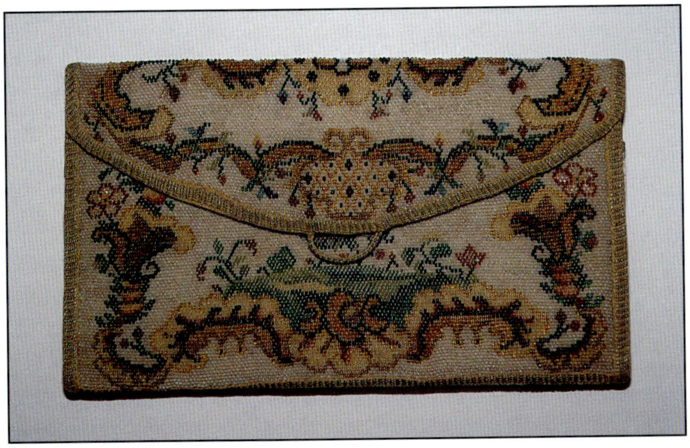

An 18th century sablé beaded pocketbook originally owned by Charles Germain de Saint-Aubin, chief designer to Louis XV of France. Saint-Aubin also set up the first sablé beadwork shops in Paris. The scrolling Rococo and floral design is typical of beadwork from this period. It is in excellent condition. 6.25 x 3.75 in. *Collection of Paula Higgins.* Very rare.

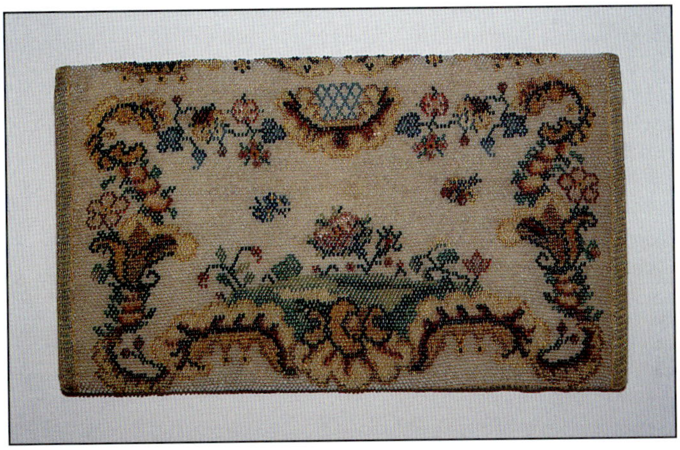

The reverse of the sablé beaded pocketbook.

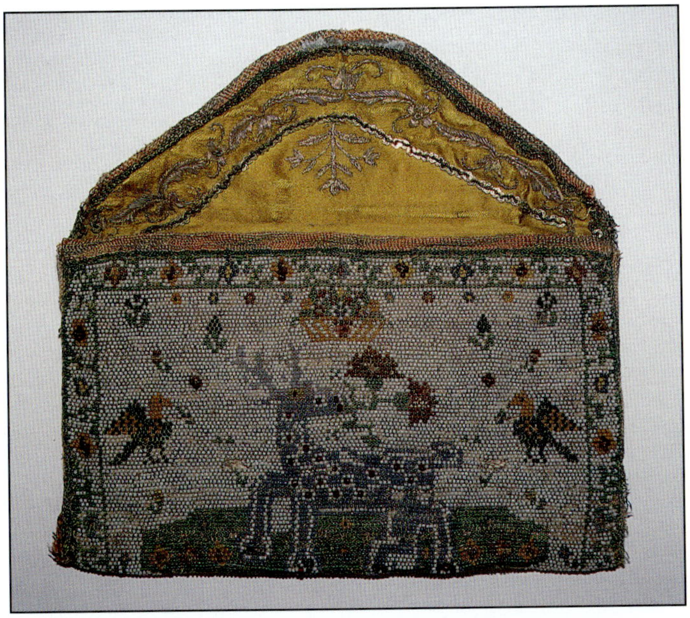

This early 18th century beaded pocketbook was made with a stag, bird, and floral design. The angularity of the design is typical of early beadwork. Inside the purse is a lining of gold silk, which is embroidered with gold metal thread and gold paillettes. 7 x 4.5 in. *Collection of Paula Higgins.* Rare.

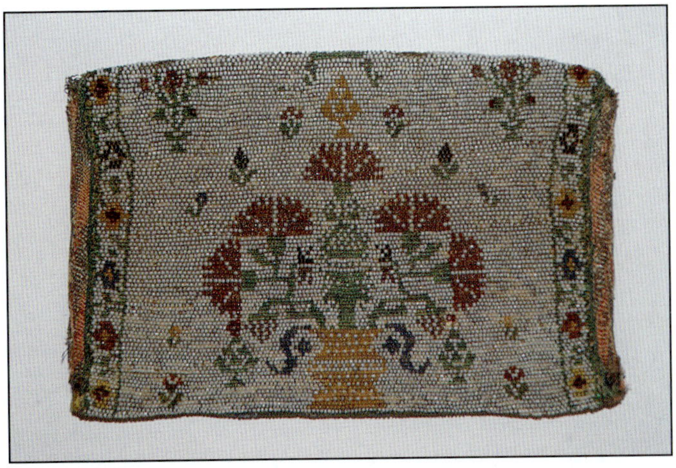

The reverse side of the beaded pocketbook showing a vase filled with carnations. The splayed carnation is typical of 17th and early 18th century design.

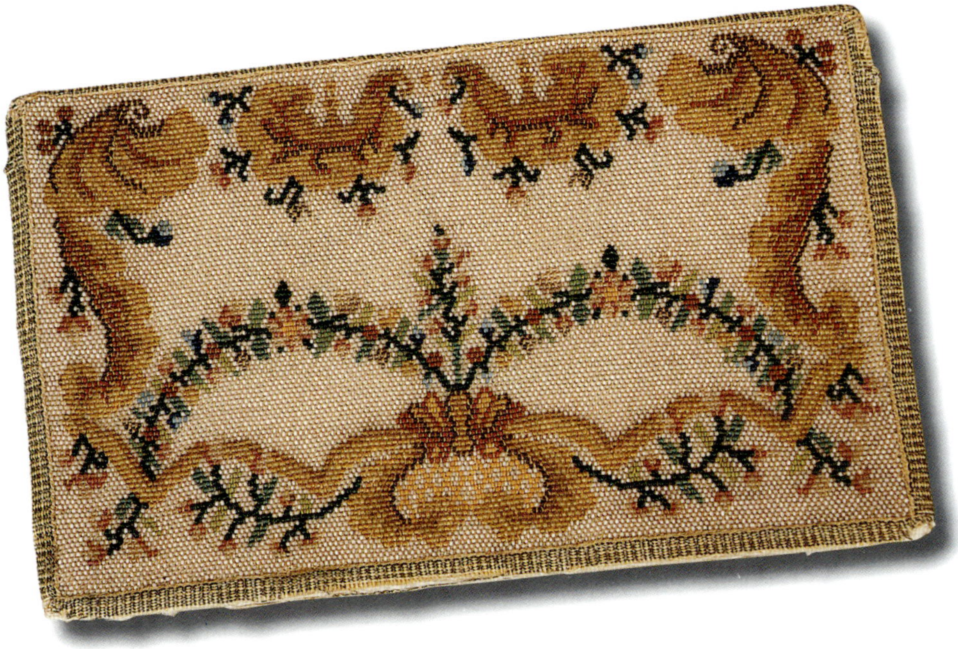

A beautiful 18th century sablé beaded pocketbook in excellent condition. The Rococo design is elegant and balanced. 6 x 3.75 in. *Collection of Lori Blaser.* Rare.

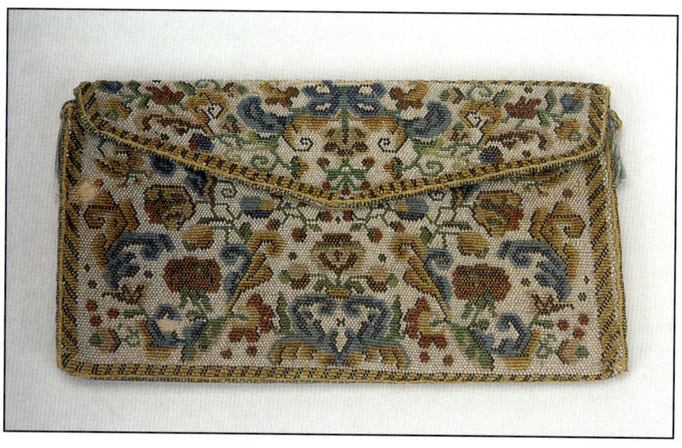

This 18th century sablé beaded purse has a densely worked floral design on the front and a phoenix design on the reverse with a motto. Phoenix designs were popular sablé purse subjects, and the French often used mottos on their pocketbooks. 6.5 x 4 in. *Collection of Lori Blaser.* Very rare.

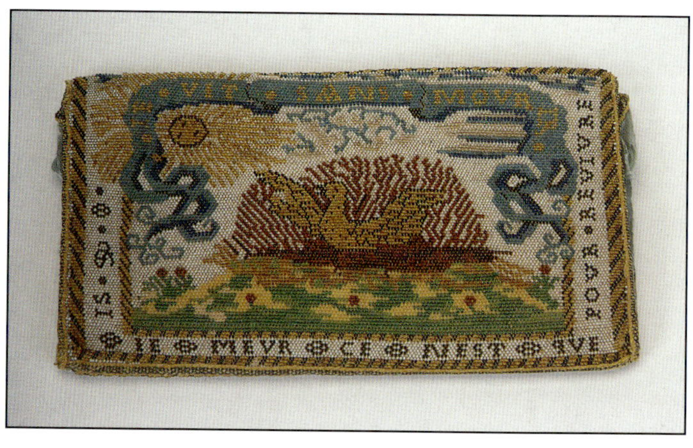

The reverse of the pocketbook showing a phoenix in flames, signifying rebirth. The French motto roughly says "Live without dying, death is only for being reborn." The phoenix was a popular design motif.

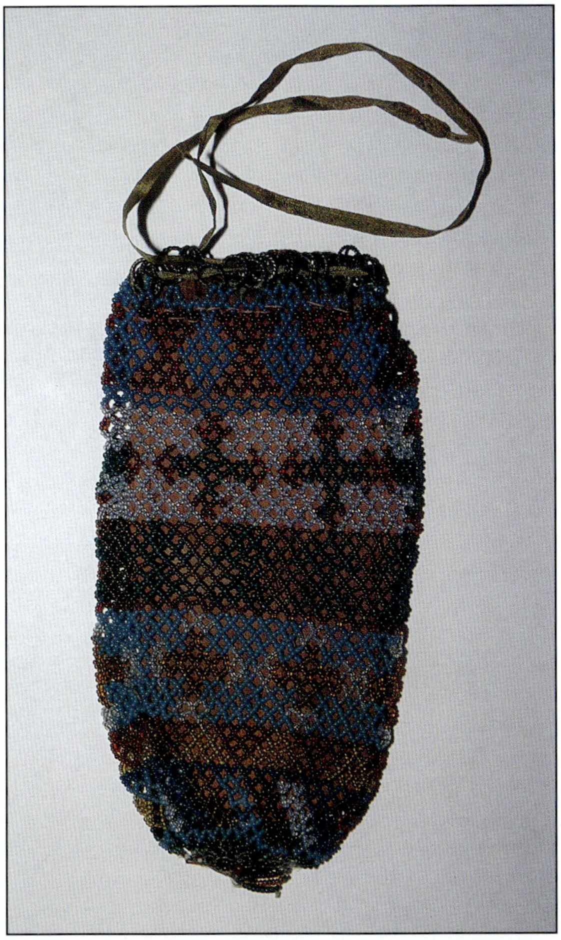

C.1800 American beaded reticule made from a network of beads. The unusual geometric pattern suggests an Indian design influence. It retains its original, early silk lining and green silk drawstring. The color combination of blue and brown was popular during this period. 5 x 2.5 in. *Collection of Paula Higgins.* $200-300.

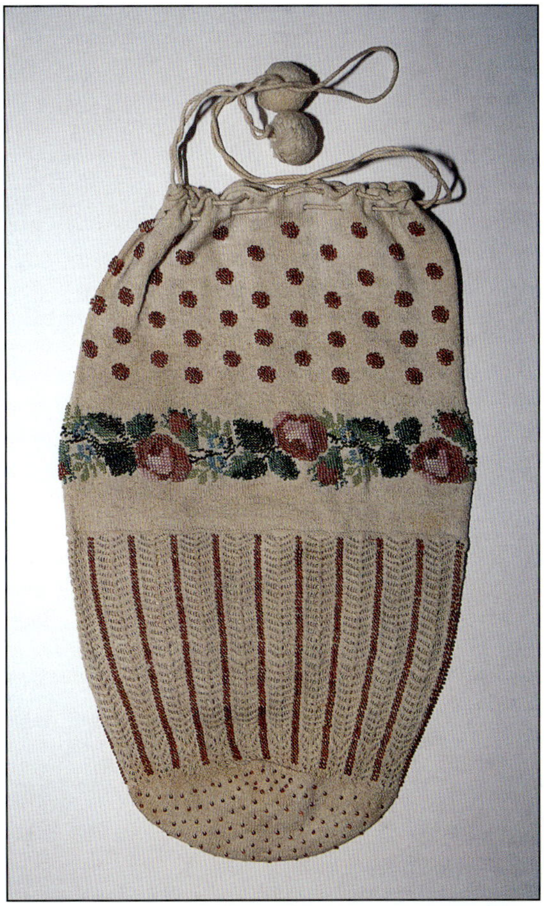

Early 19th century beaded purses were made with large areas of plain knitting, interspersed with beadwork. The bucket bottom is also typical of early purse design. 10 x 6 in. *Collection of Paula Higgins.* $300-350.

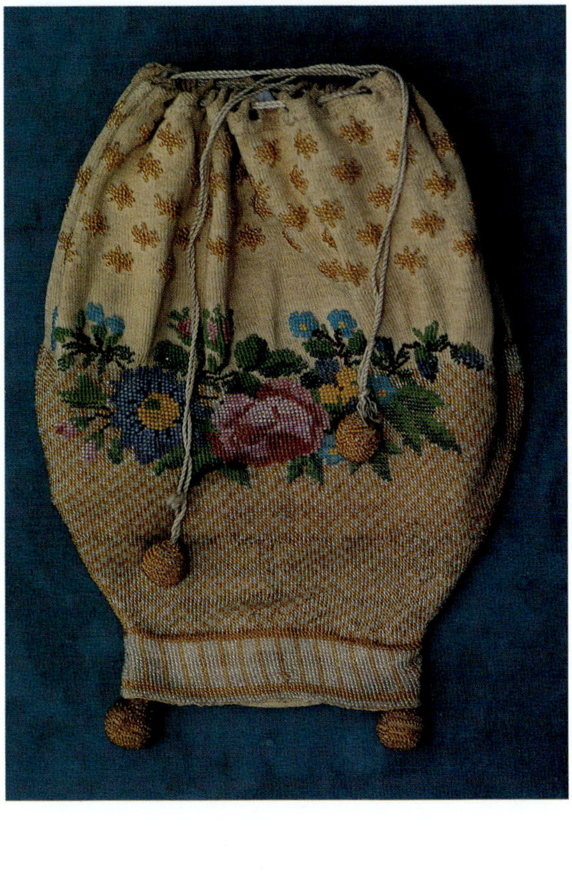

An early 19th century knitted purse, decorated with beadwork. The knitting at the top feels like cotton jersey. The two ball tassels, hanging from the squared off bottom, are typical of early 19th century design. 8 x 7.5 in *Collection of Linda Marshall.* $300-350.

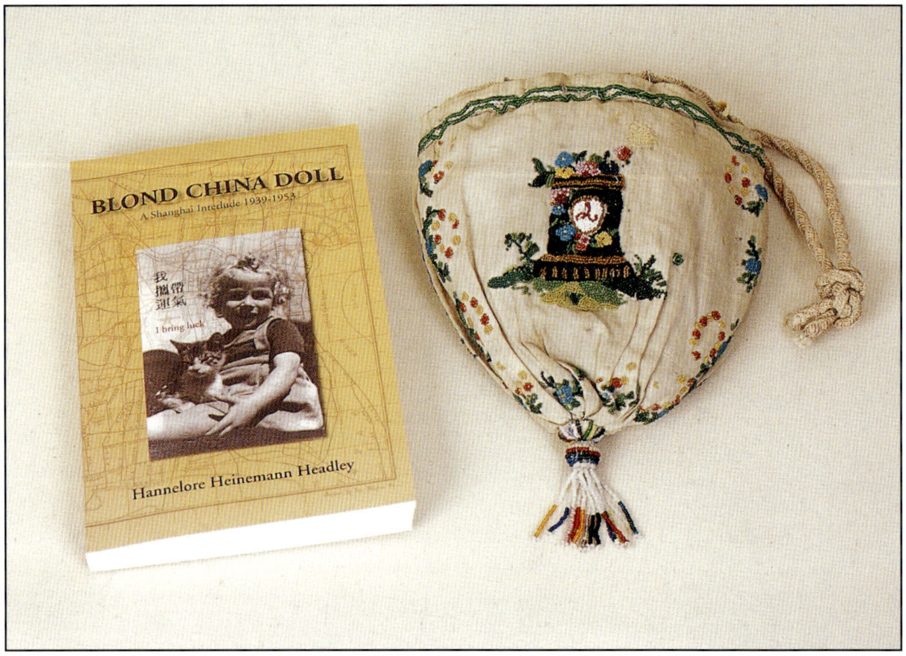

This early, 19th century silk reticule is decorated with a beadwork memorial and floral design. It was originally owned by the grandmother of the author of the accompanying book, Hannelore Heineman Headley. She brought it to Shanghai when she fled the Nazis, and then to Canada when she fled the Communists. So this purse has quite a history. The beadwork is unusually colorful for an early memorial purse. 9 x 7 in. *Collection of Lori Blaser.* $450-650.

This early, dated scenic of a European town and waterway is rare. Most scenics from this period are of the "primitive" or folk art style and not nearly as detailed as this one. They are among the rarest of the early beaded purses. The owner completed major restoration on this purse and attached the frame. 10.5 x 6.5 in. *Collection of Terri Lykins.* $2,000-2,500.

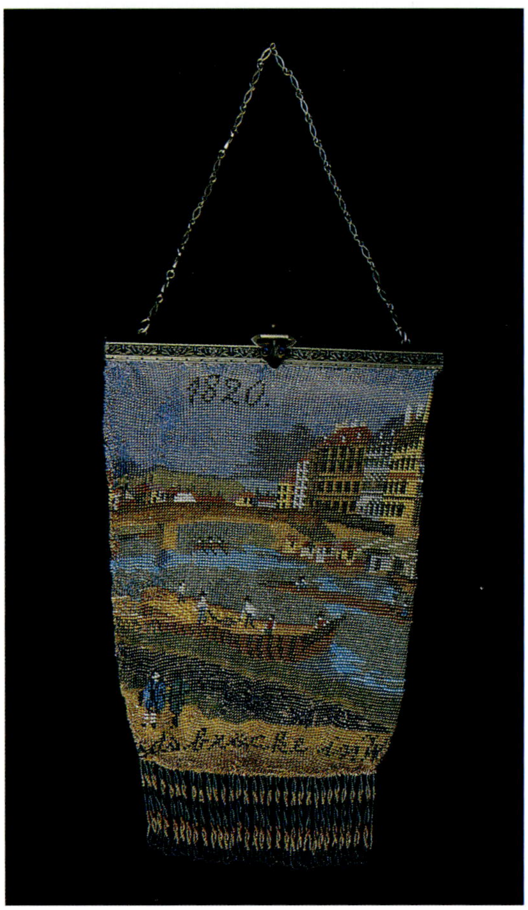

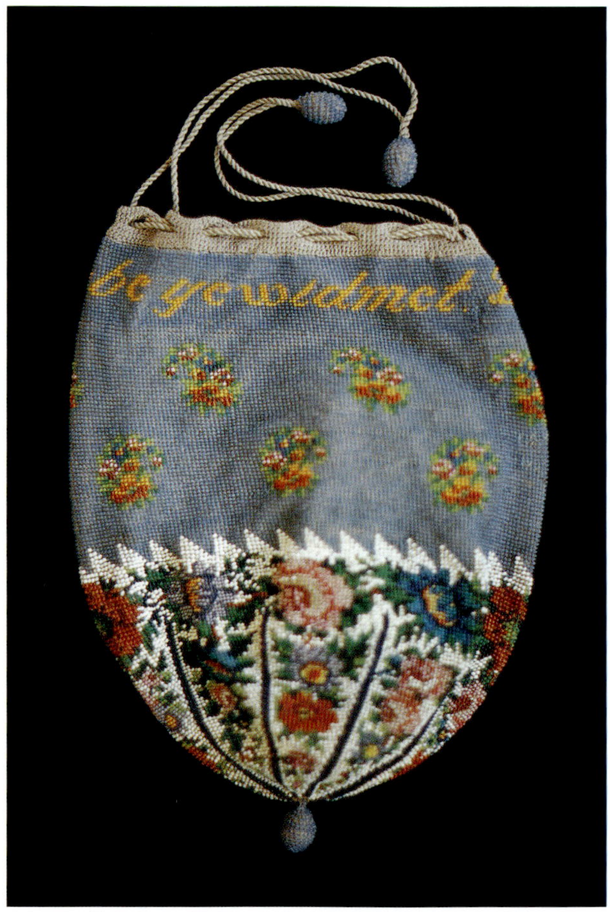

German beaders often incorporated mottos into their beadwork at the top of the purse. The design and the colors used to make this purse are especially lovely, and the knitting is of a very high quality. 7 x 6 in. *Collection of Linda Marshall.* $300-375.

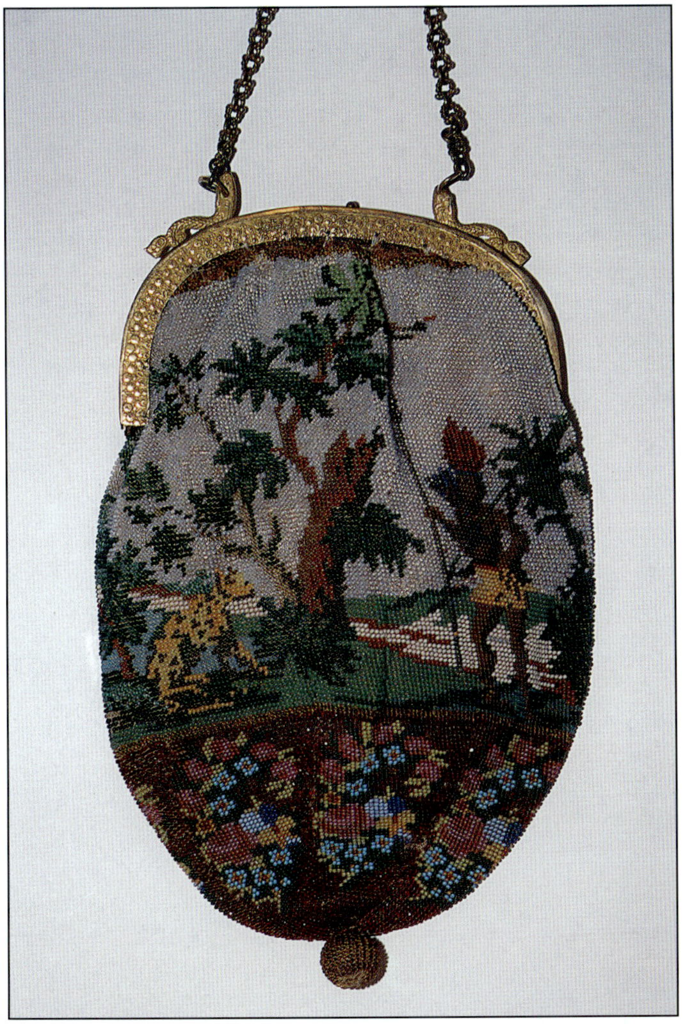

Early 19th century beaded scene of a Carib Indian and a jaguar facing off in a tropical setting. It is a continuous scenic and the reverse shows the Indian shooting an arrow at two jaguars. This design is reminiscent of the famous Dufours wallpapers from the same period. It is mounted on a pinchbeck frame with a stirrup link chain. The original silk lining is trimmed with silver lace. 9 x 5.5 in. *Collection of Paula Higgins.* Rare.

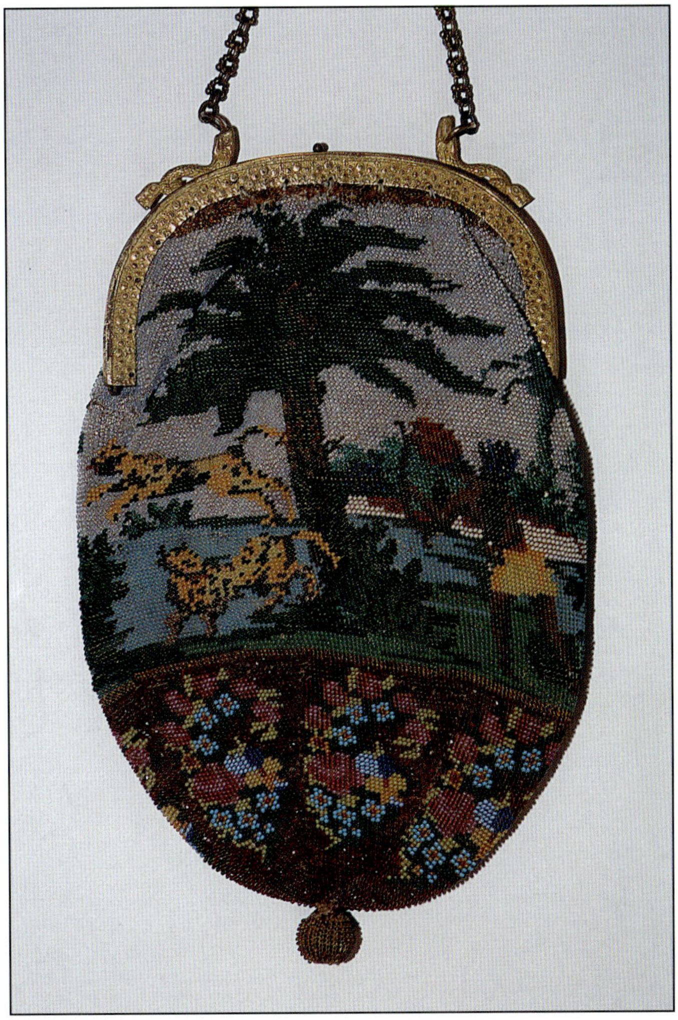

The reverse side of the continuous scenic.

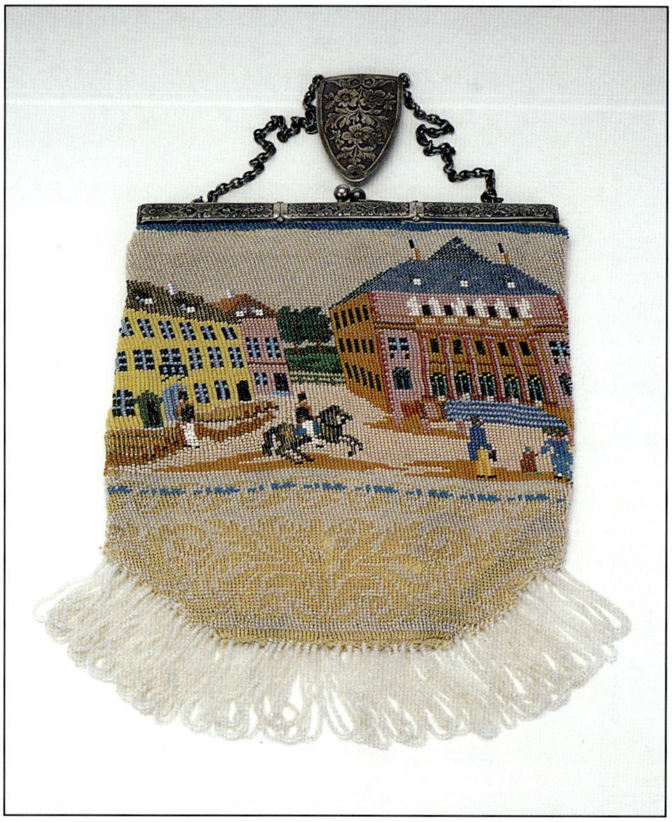

C.1820 continuous scenic of a European town and a man on a horse. The reverse side shows another view of the town square. The Museum of Fine Arts in Boston has the same purse in their collection. The chatelaine frame was added later in the 19th century. 9 x 6.25 in. *Collection of Lori Blaser.* $2,000-2,500.

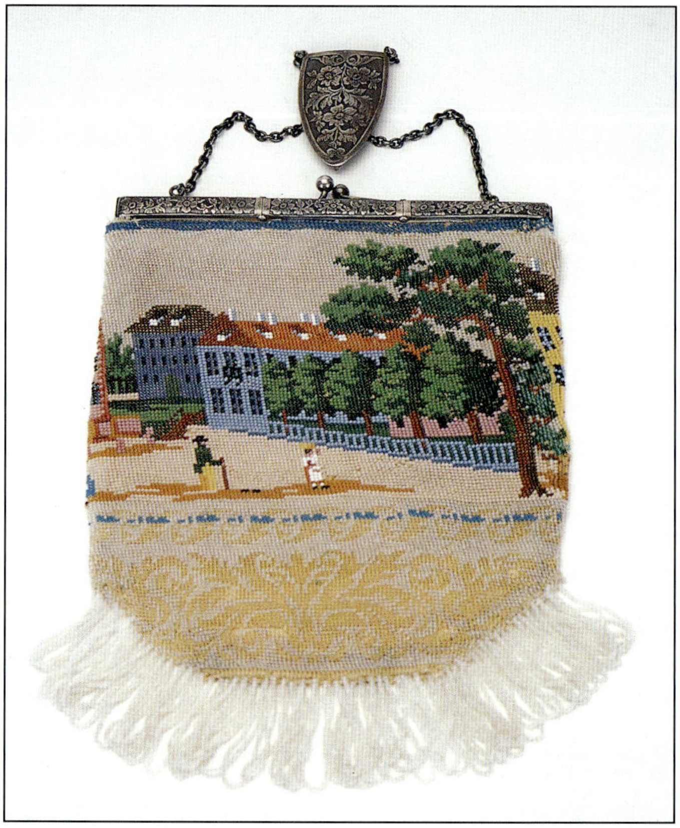

The reverse side of the continuous scenic.

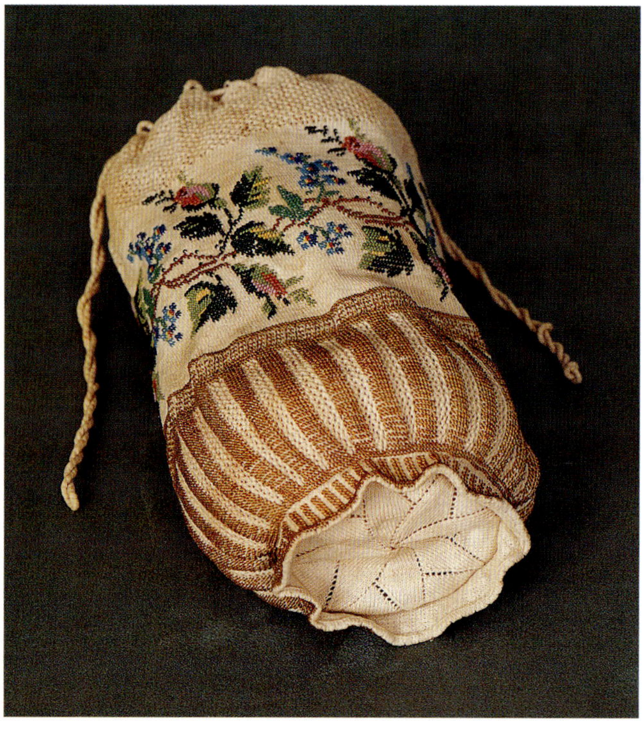

An unusual reticule from the Biedermeier Era. This reticule is knitted, with areas of beadwork interspersed throughout. The bottom of the purse has an added band of bead knitting, which looks like a base. When the purse is carried, it resembles a vase of flowers. 9 x 5 in. *Collection of Lori Blaser.* $450-600.

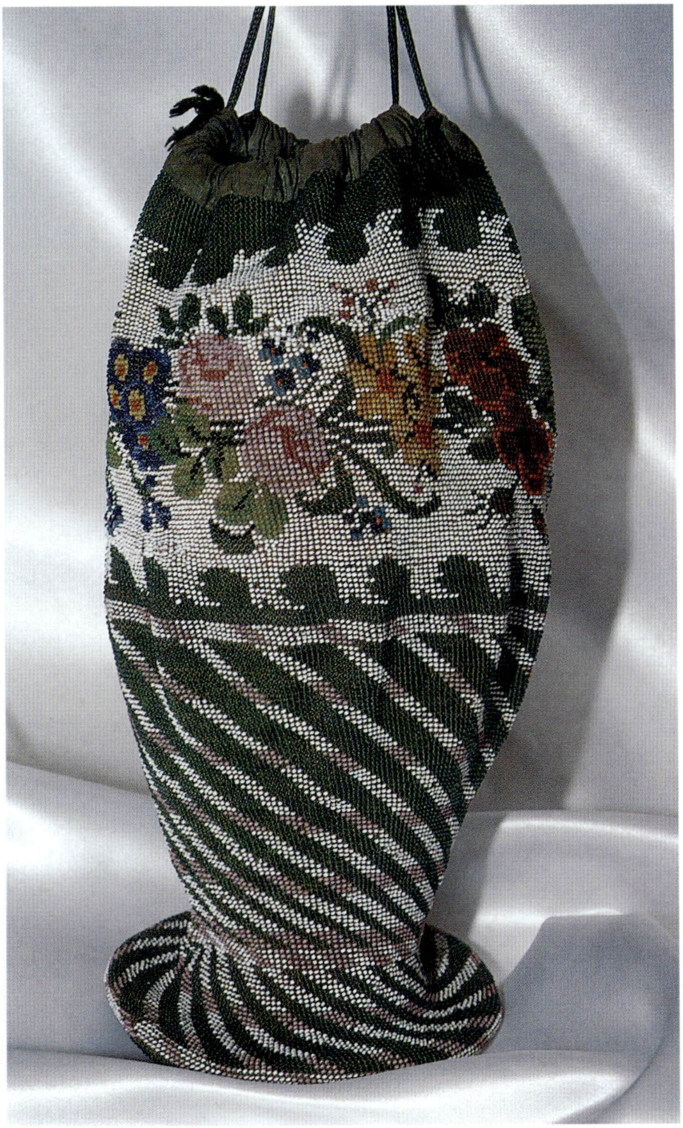

This completely beaded reticule from c.1830 is a slimmer version of a Biedermeier basket purse. These purses were made for a fairly short period of time, making them desirable and rare. 8.5 x 5 in. *Collection of Paula Higgins.* Rare.

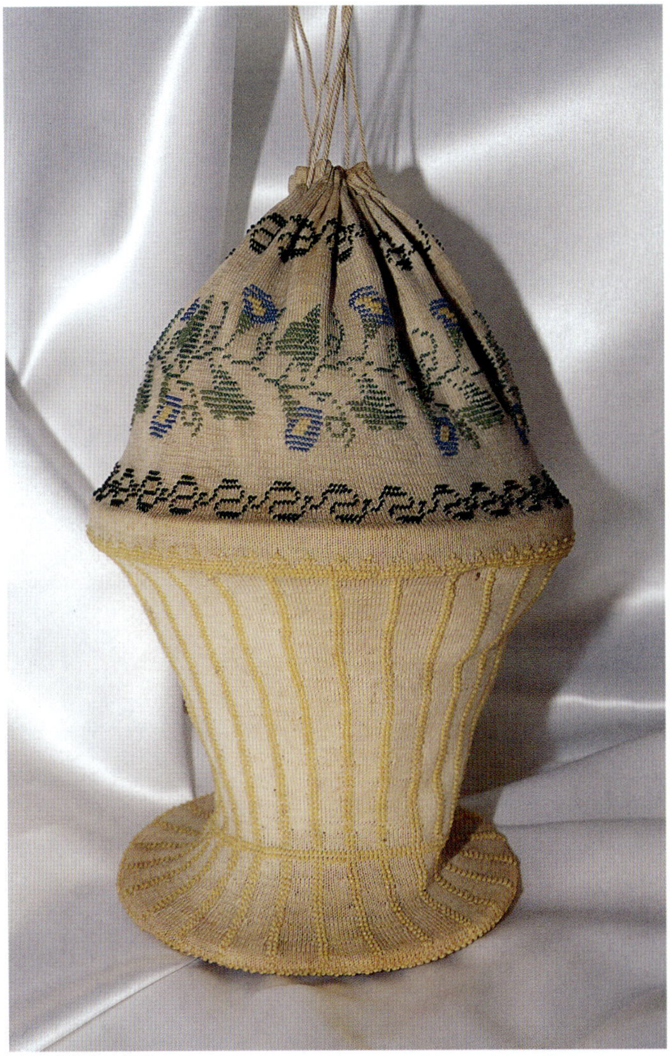

C.1820-1830 knitted and beaded basket purse. Basket purses were popular during the Biedermeier Period in Germany. The majority of these purses were made from knitted material, interspersed with beading, although there are examples which were completely beaded. Floral decorations were the favored designs. Baleen or wooden hoops were inserted into the middle of the purse to provide support and shape. The footed bottoms were made from round pieces of card inserted into the purse. 10 x 7 in. *Collection of Paula Higgins.* Rare.

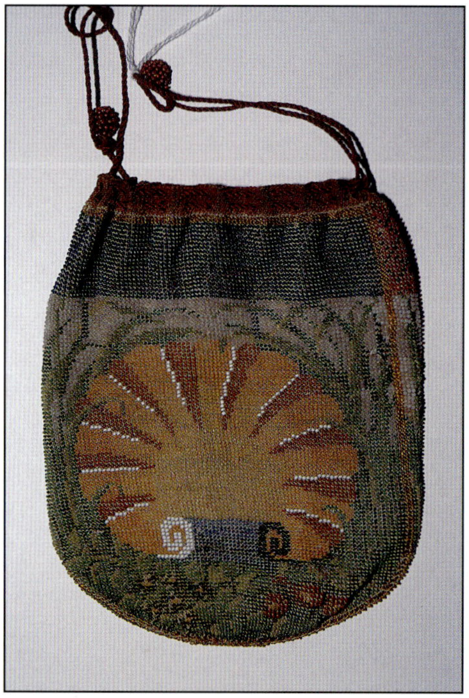

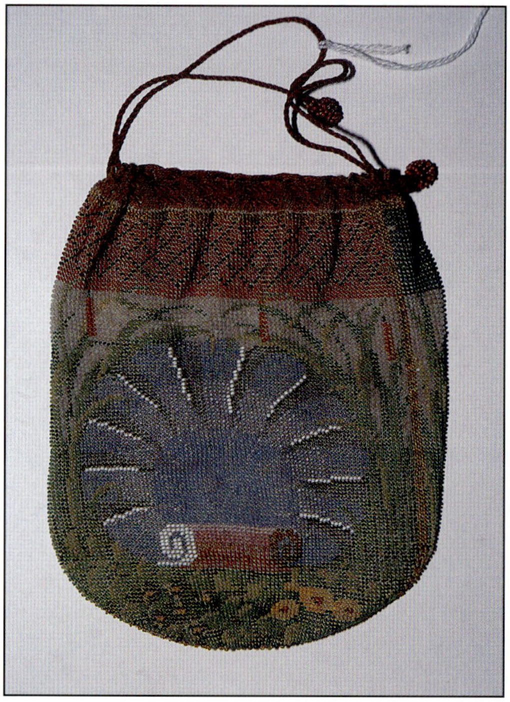

An early 19th century beaded reticule with a shell design. Shell designs were popular in all areas of design during the early years of the 19th century. 5 x 5 in. *Collection of Paula Higgins.* $275-325.

The reverse of the purse with the shell design.

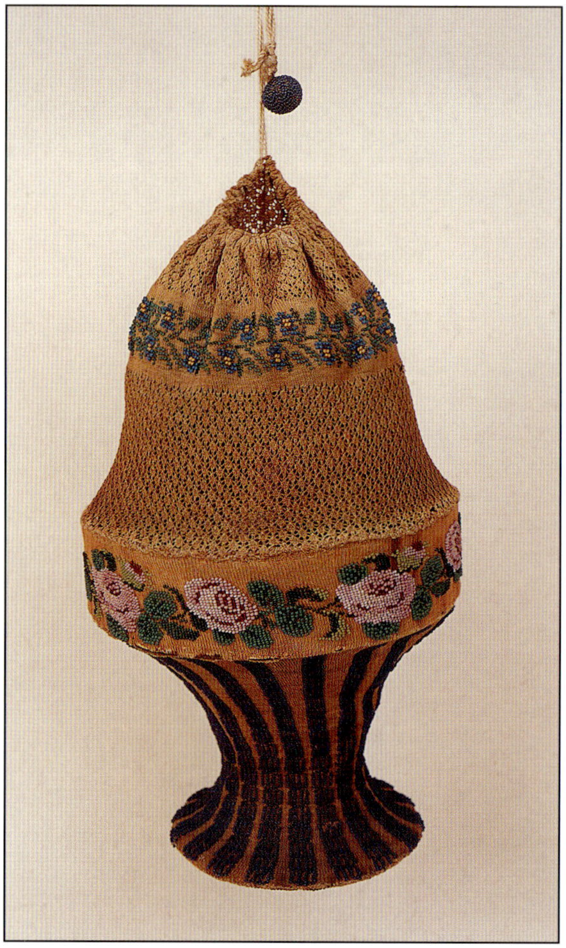

This is another version of a Biedermeier basket purse with a wider midsection and a more colorful design. On the bottom of the footed base is a beaded eight point star design. 10 x 6 in. *Collection of Lori Blaser.* Rare.

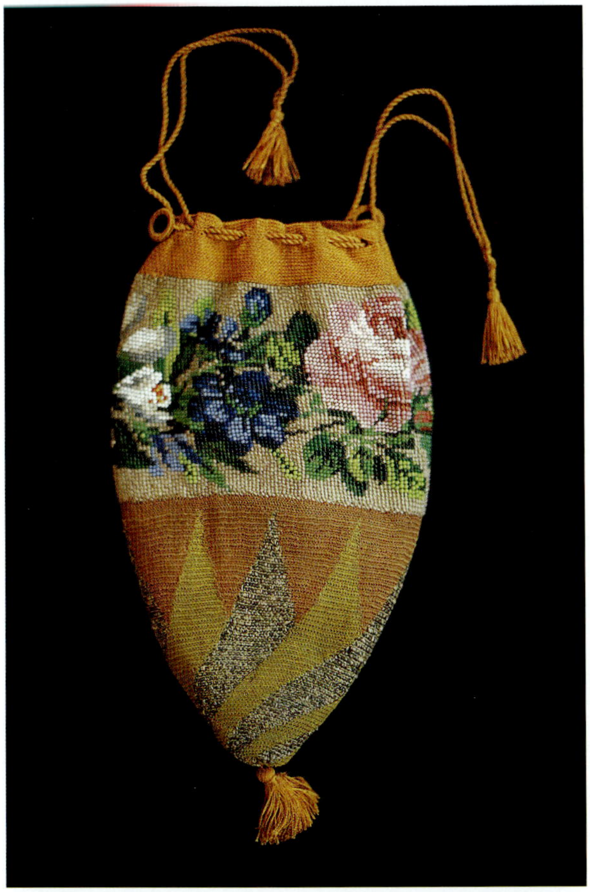

Early 19th century reticule with a classic floral design, knitted with areas of beading interspersed throughout. Earlier beaded purses were often finished with silk tassels, rather than beaded tassels. 6.5 x 4 in. *Collection of Linda Marshall.* $300-375.

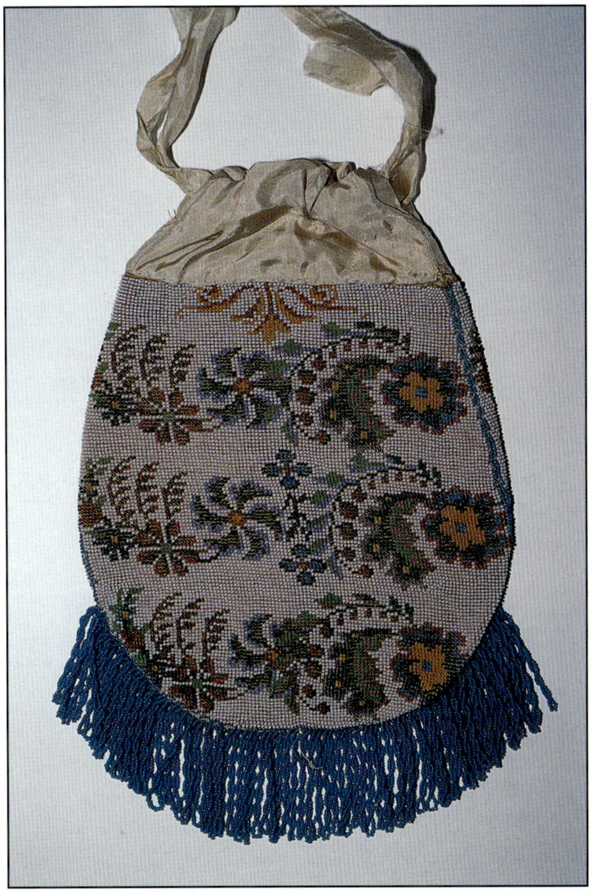

The floral design on this purse is somewhat atypical, and the beader even added holly leaves and berries. The maker of this purse penned her name, city, and state inside the purse. Written on the original leather lining in script lettering is: "Catherine Thorndike, Charlestown, Mafs." "Mafs" was how they wrote Mass. in early 19th century New England. 9.5 x 6.5 in. *Collection of Paula Higgins.* $350-375.

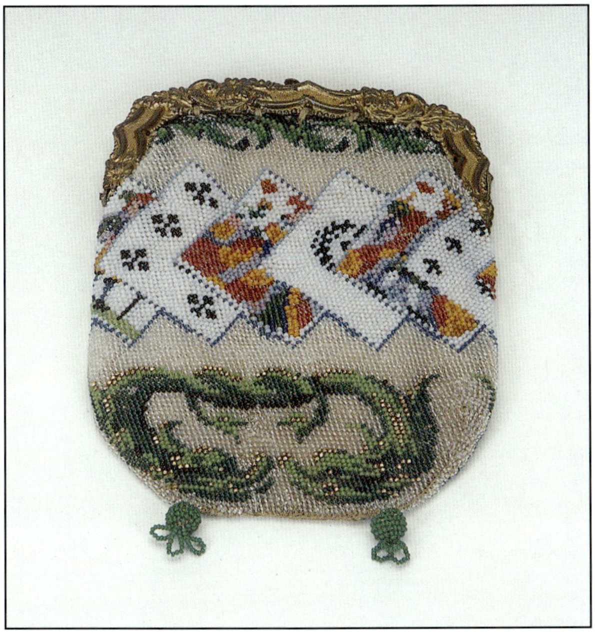

Early 19th century purses with beaded card designs are rare and desirable. This purse is mounted on its original gilt metal frame. The design continues around the whole purse, each side depicting different cards. Card playing was a very popular pastime in the late 18th and early 19th centuries. 4.5 x 3.75 in. *Collection of Lori Blaser.* Rare.

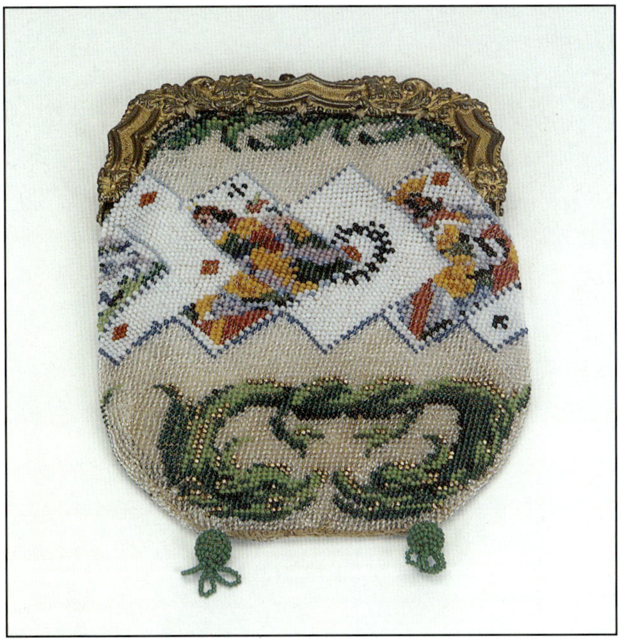

The reverse side of the card purse.

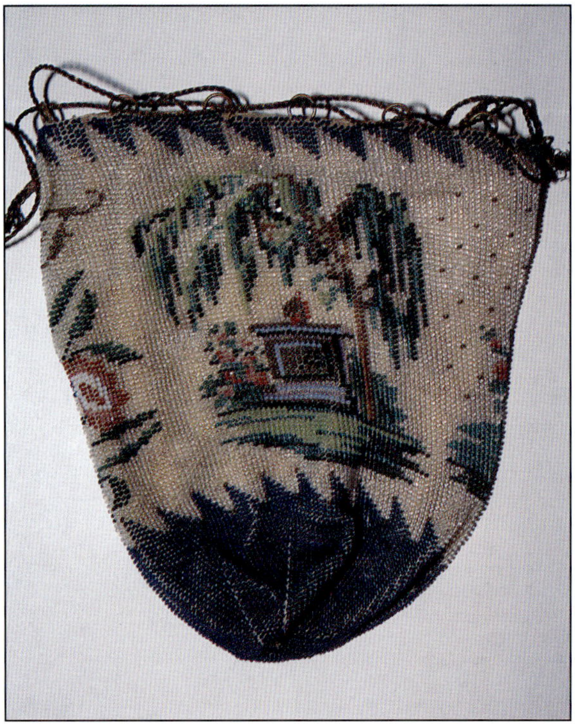

This c.1830 beaded reticule has several designs circling the purse, giving it a sampler-like quality. One side has a memorial or funeral design with a weeping willow tree. The monument has the letter A on it. Purses with memorial designs typically have the letter A or the letter S as part of their design. Different theories have been offered as to their significance. One writer thought the letter A stood for angel and the letter S for salvation. Script letters also circle the purse. The twisted metal drawstring and linen lining are original to the purse. 6 x 5.5 in. *Collection of Paula Higgins.* $400-450.

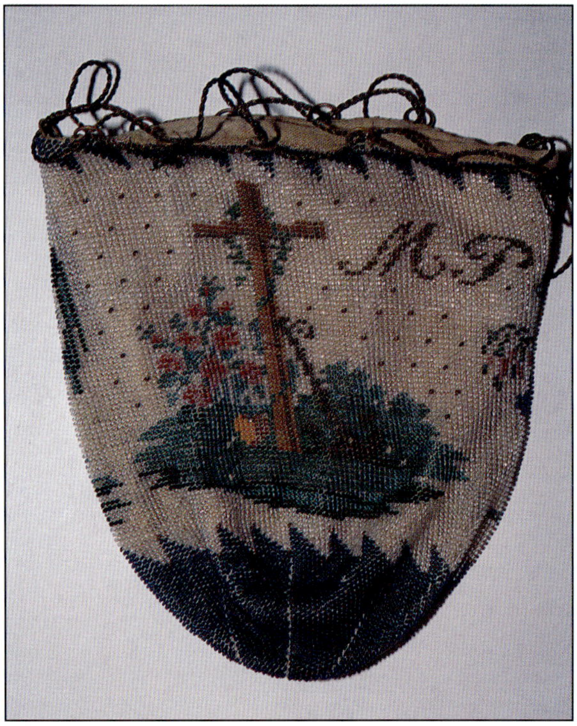

The reverse side of the purse shows a cross, anchor, and heart. The heart represents love, the anchor represents hope, and the cross represents faith. The sawtooth bottom is solid, which is an early design element.

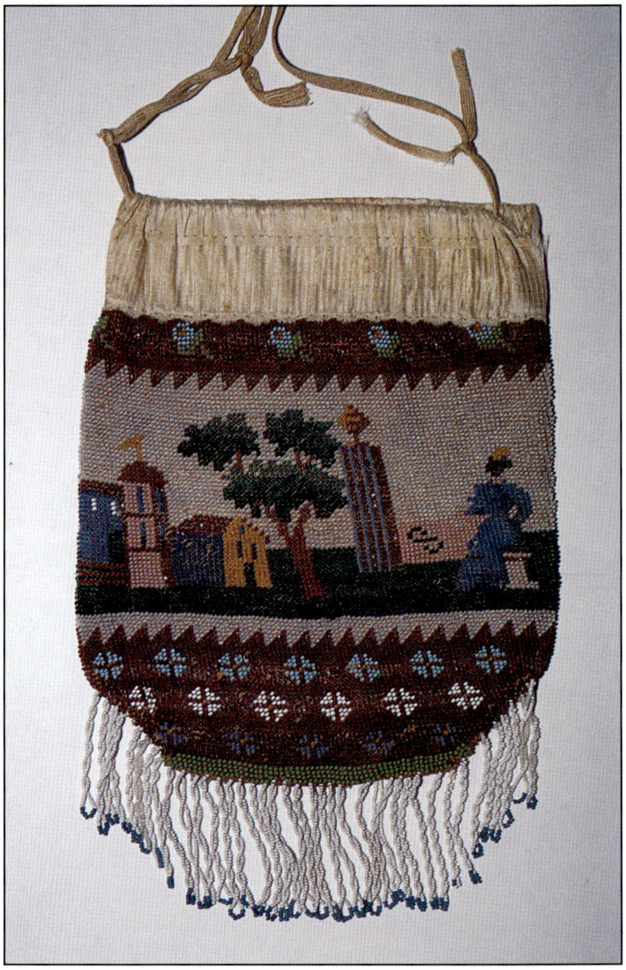

A memorial purse with the letter S on the tombstone. The woman sitting on a bench beside the tomb has a comb in her hair and is dressed in c.1830 clothing. 8.5 x 6 in. *Collection of Paula Higgins.* $350-400.

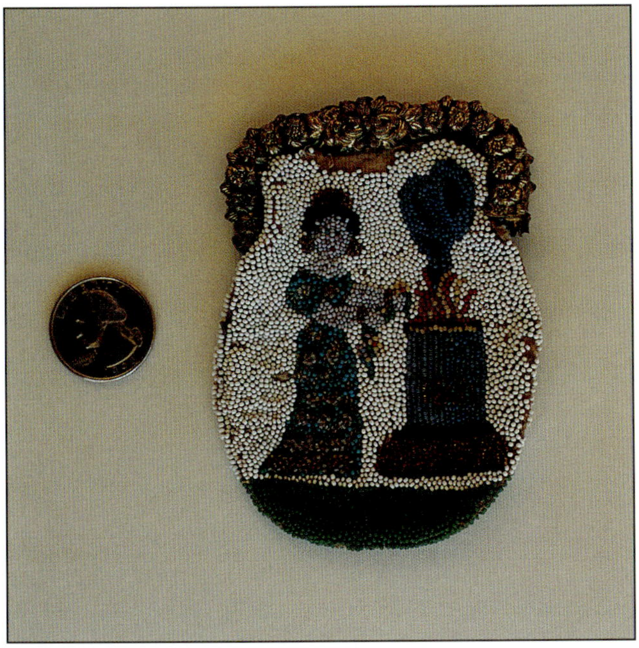

This 1831 dated figural coin purse depicts a woman burning laurel leaves on a pyre, possibly symbolizing victory in battle. The reverse side shows her writing at a table. Many of these designs were symbolic and commemorated significant events. It is possible the woman represents Clio the Greek Muse of History. 4 x 2.75 in. *Collection of Linda Marshall.* $325-375.

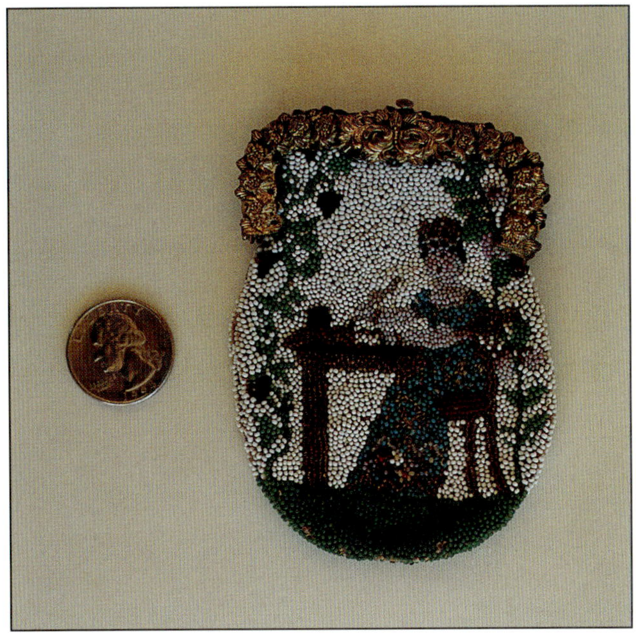

The reverse side of the 1831 coin purse.

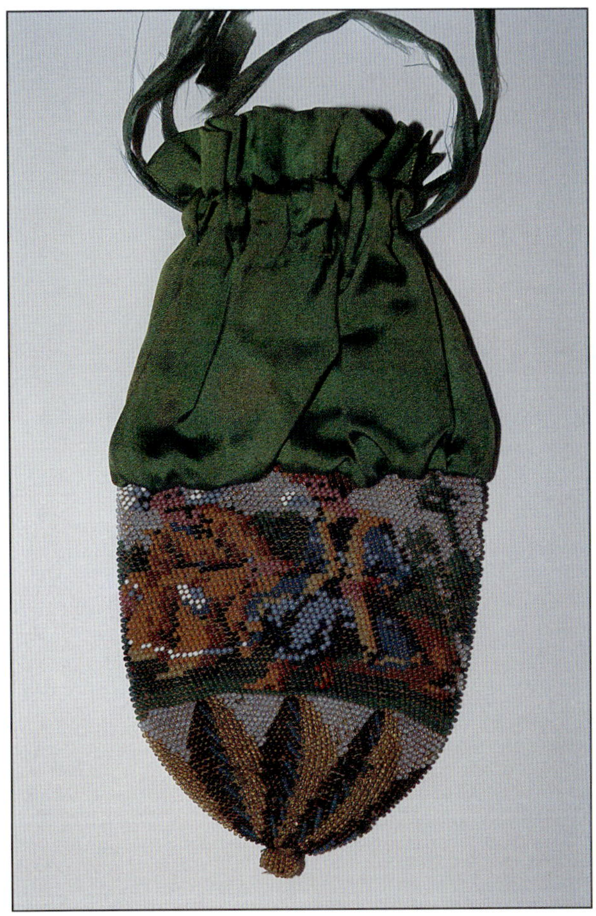

Small, early 19th century coin purse decorated with the two Turkish figures. Everything exotic was popular during the early years of the 19th century after Napoleon conquered Egypt and when the Greeks fought for their independence from Turkey. 5 x 3 in. *Collection of Paula Higgins.* $300-325.

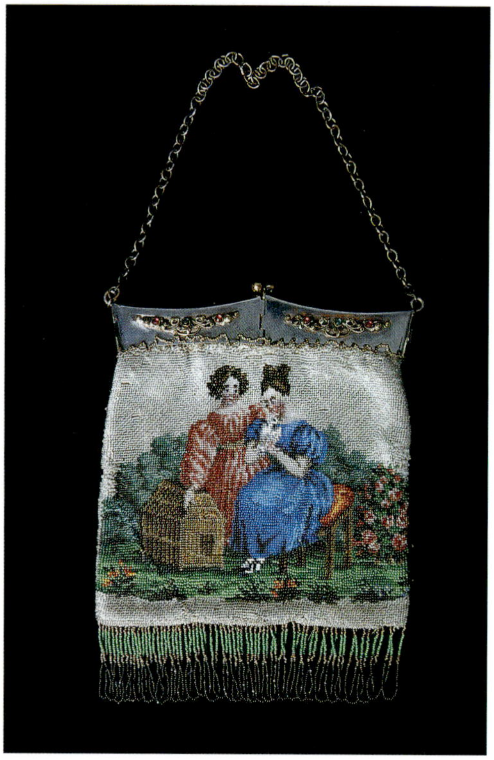

A mother and daughter dressed in c.1830 clothing make a delightful subject for a purse design. The mother is holding a dove, and the daughter stands next to an early birdcage. All the details are nicely beaded including the clothing and the mother's hair comb. A later 19th century frame was added during restoration. This purse was bead embroidered on canvas. 8.5 x 6.5 in. *Collection of Terri Lykins.* $750-800.

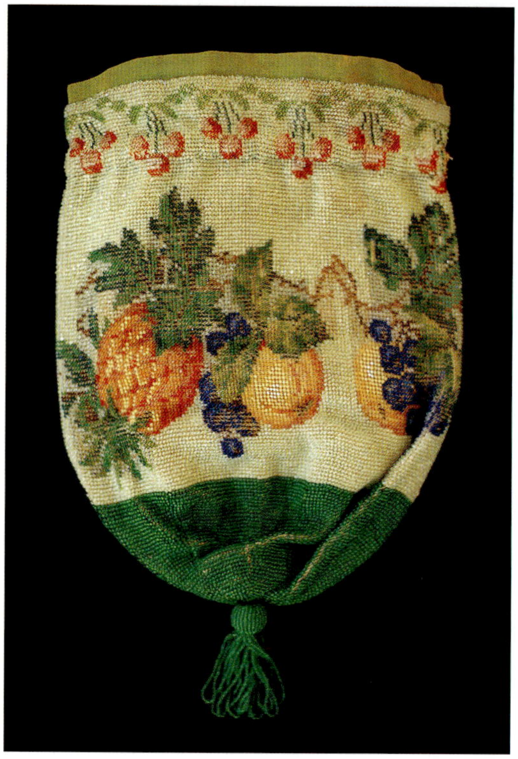

Early beaded purses with realistic designs of fruit are uncommon. This is a lovely example, which even has a border of cherries at the top. 11 x 8 in. *Collection of Linda Marshall.* $375-450.

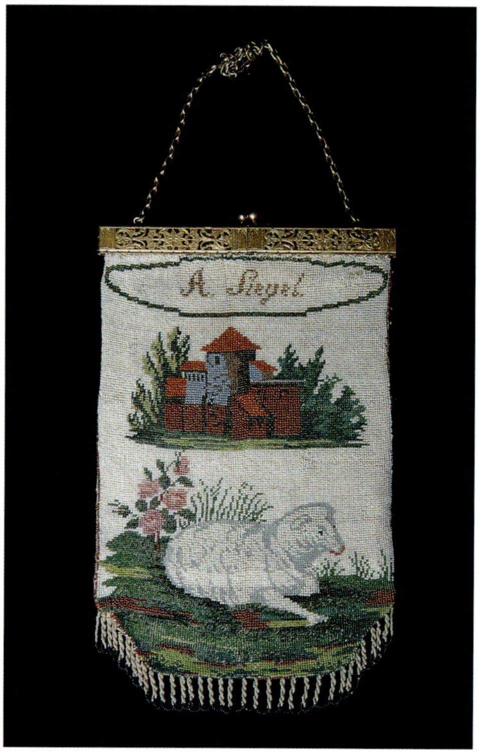

Lambs were a popular early 19th century purse design subject. This purse has several designs, including a lush basket of fruit and flowers on the back. The front has the name A. Siegel worked in gold beads above a European town. The box frame was added at a later date. 11.5 x 6.75 in. *Collection of Terri Lykins.* $750-850.

The reverse side is beautifully beaded with a basket of fruit.

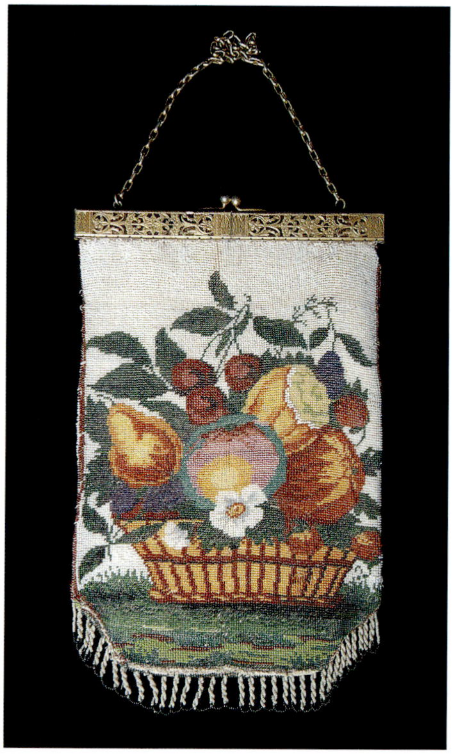

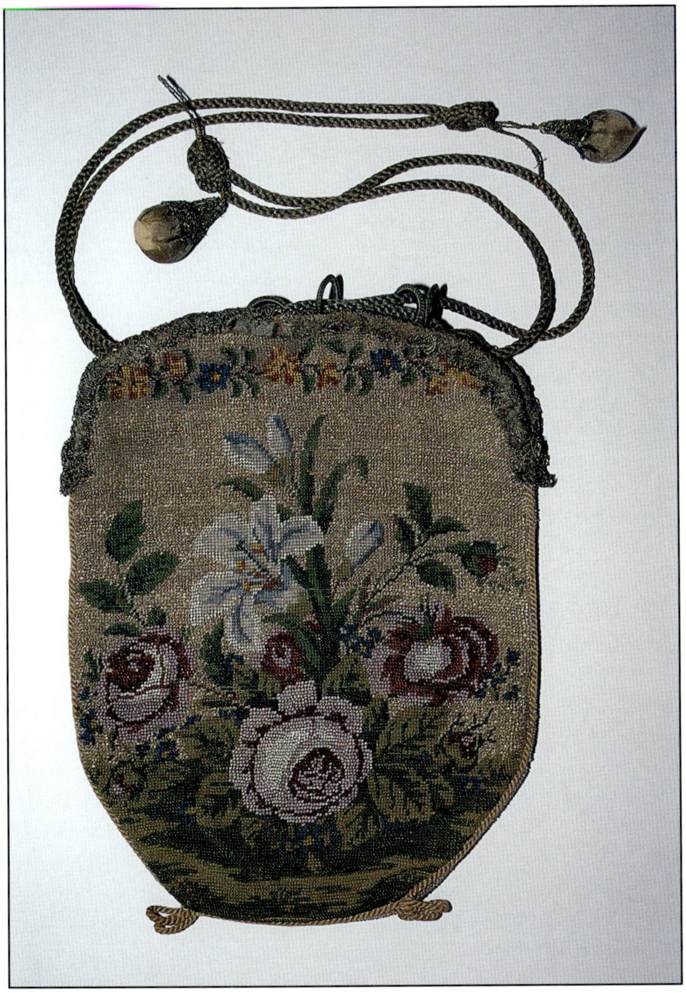

An unusual, early floral design, beaded on canvas. This purse has several early purse features including: a pea green silk lining, loops on the bottom, silver lace at the top, hand whipped rings, and padded tassels at the end of the drawstrings. American. 9 x 6 in. *Collection of Paula Higgins.* $350-375.

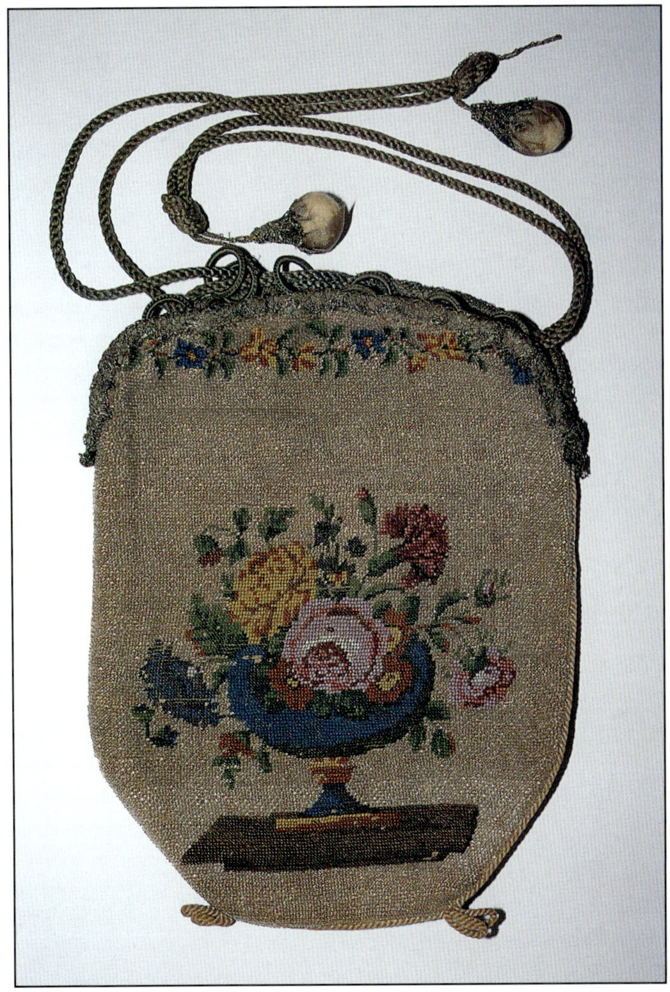

The reverse side of the floral beaded purse depicts a pedestal bowl, sitting on a table, overflowing with flowers.

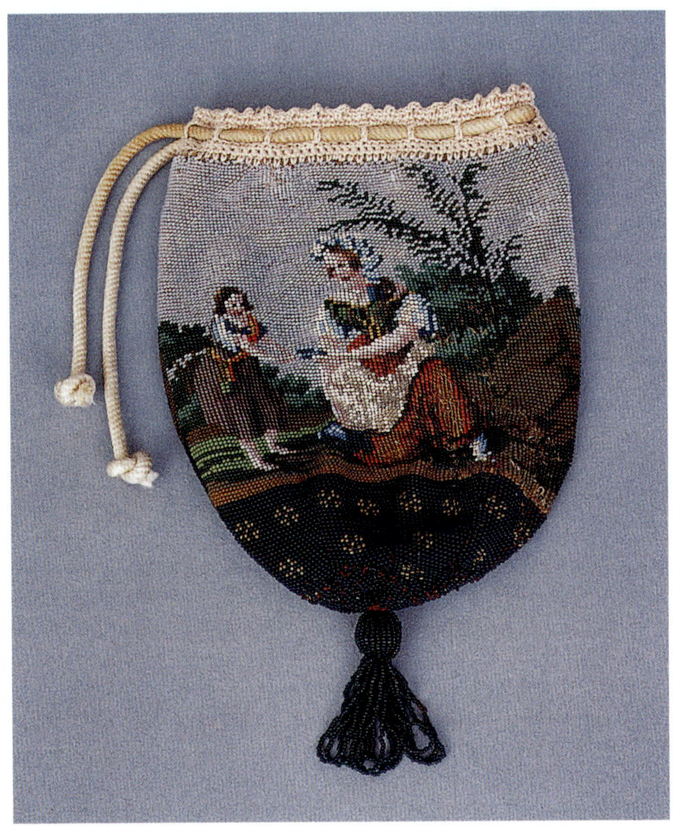

This bead knitted purse from c.1830 features a wonderful design of a woman and child in period clothing. The clothing is nicely detailed, including the turban on the woman's head. Purses like this one, are among the most desirable of early beaded purses. 9 x 5.5 in. *Collection of Lori Blaser.* $850-1,000.

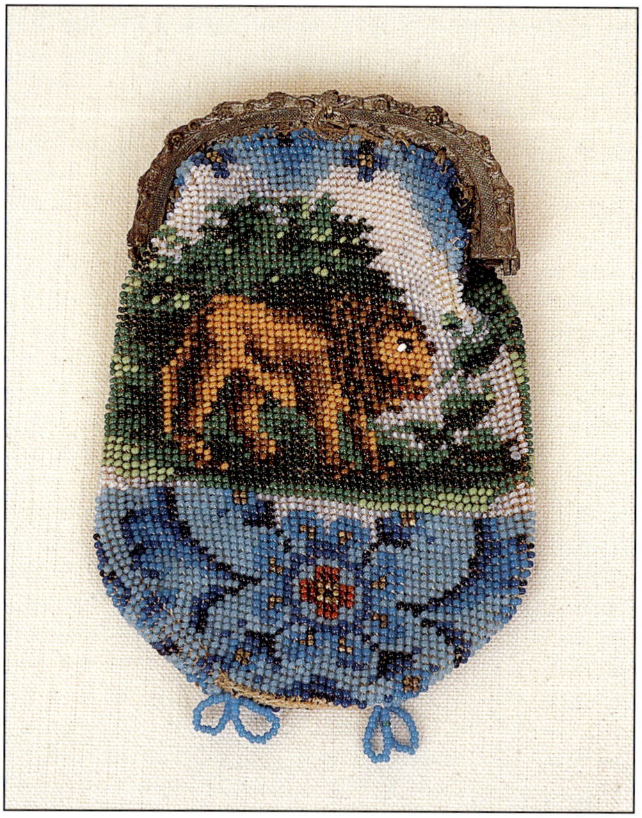

A little lion with personality, mounted on its original frame. Early coin purses don't come any more charming than this. Made in Germany. 5 x 3.25 in. *Collection of Lori Blaser.* $350-400.

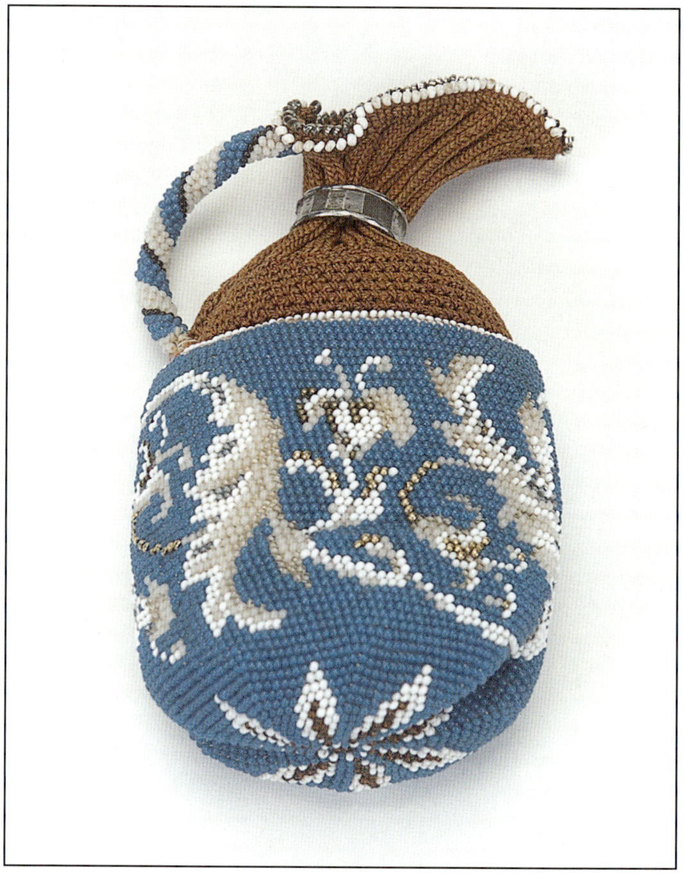

An exceptional, Russian beaded jug purse formerly in the collection of Mrs. Dewitt Cohen. The silver ring slides back over the jug handle so that coins can be deposited inside. Few examples are as beautifully made as this one. 4.5 x 2.5 in. *Collection of Lori Blaser.* $600-650.

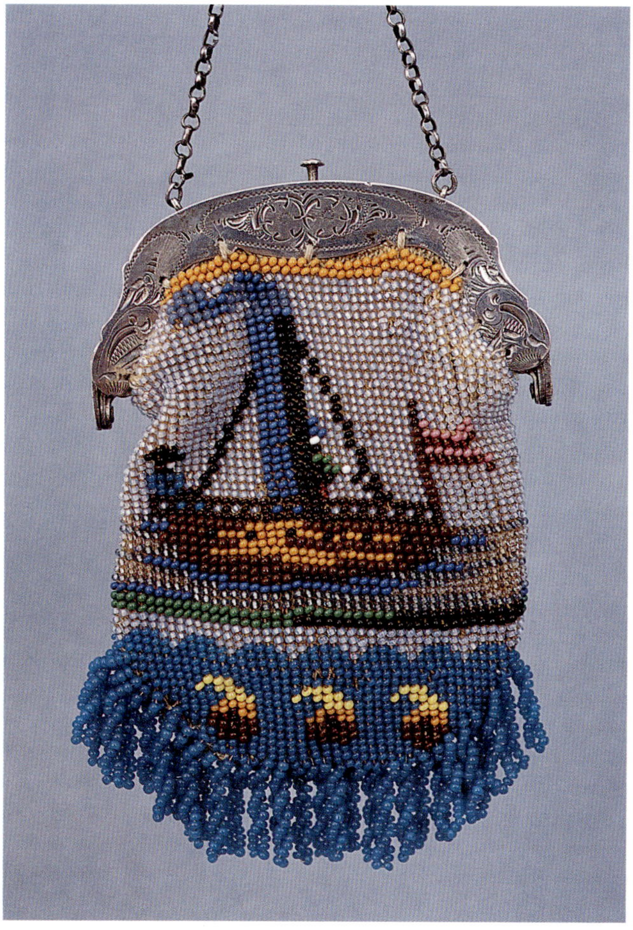

Small c.1840 coin purse with a design of a man in a steam and sail ship, attached to its original engraved frame. The transition from sail, to steam and sail, was a popular purse subject prior to 1860. 4.75 x 3 in. *Collection of Lori Blaser.* $300-350.

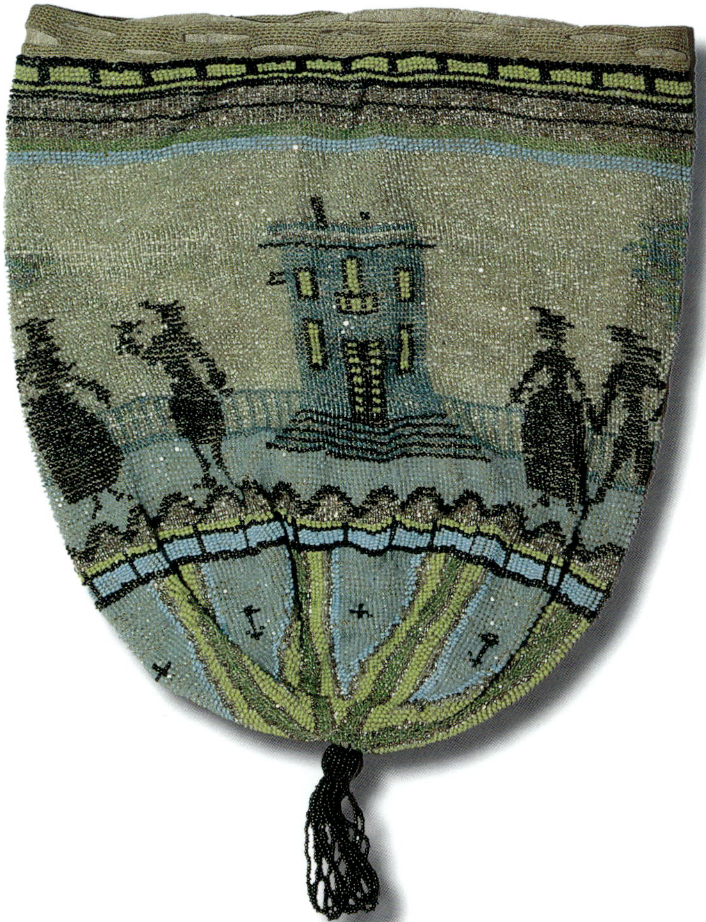

This fine bead knitted reticule is a continuous scenic. The front shows an 18th century house, flanked by silhouetted figures dressed in period clothing. This particular house design is more commonly seen on embroidered samplers from the early 19th century. The bottom design is decorated with anchors and crosses; both early design elements. 9.5 x 8 in. *Collection of Paula Higgins*. $750-850.

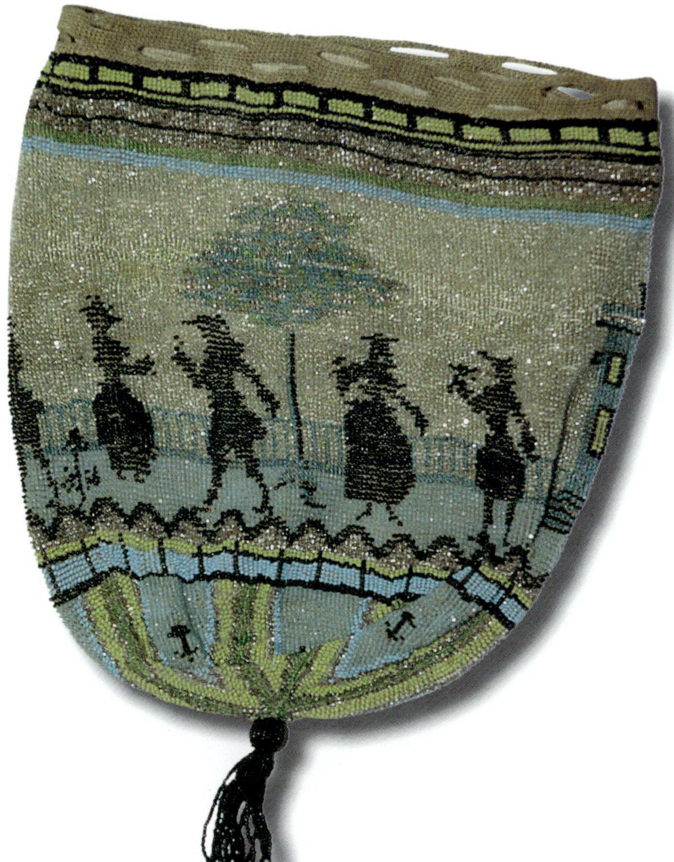

Another view of the continuous scenic.

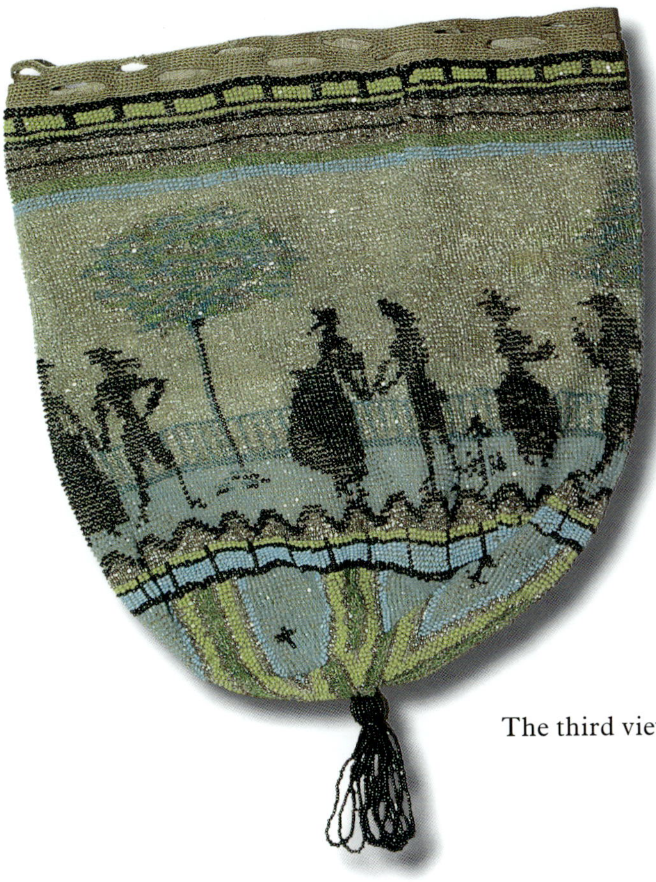

The third view of the continuous scenic.

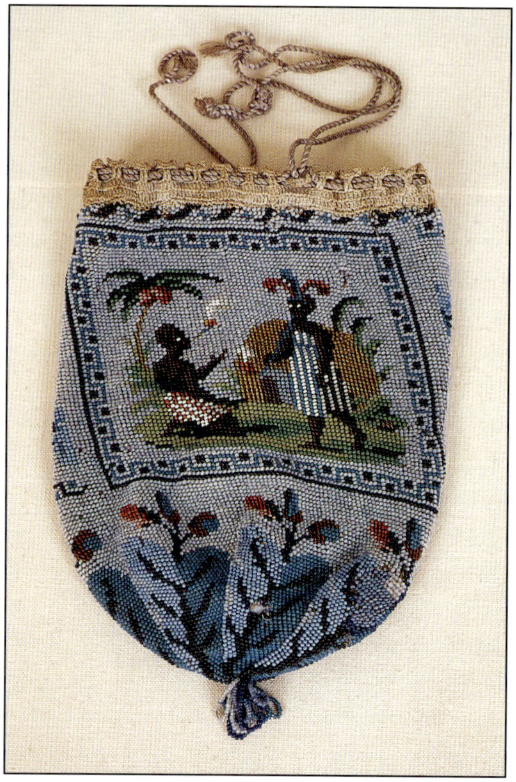

A wonderful and rare figural of a black man and woman in a tropical setting. The man is smoking a pipe and the woman has plumes in her hair. 8.5 x 5.5 in. *Collection of Lori Blaser.* $750-950.

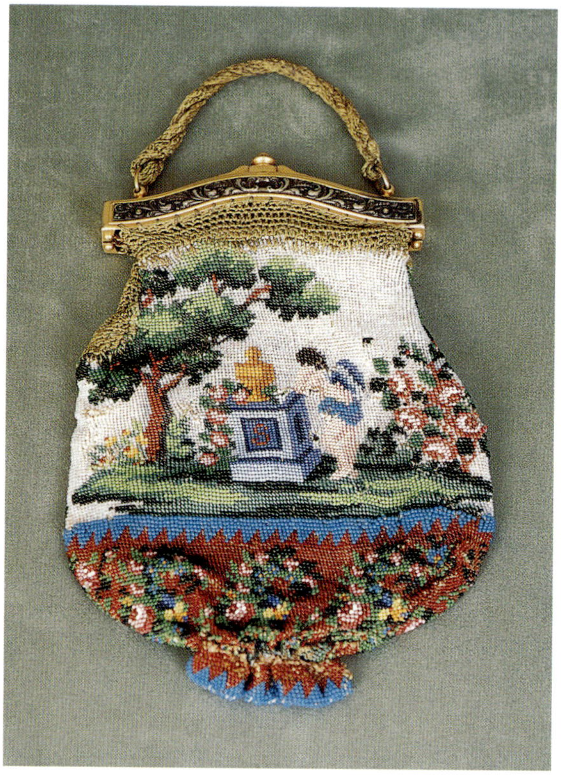

A memorial scene with an angel/cherub standing beside a monument. Repairs of varying degrees of success have obviously been attempted, so this purse awaits more skillful restoration. But the design is colorful, beautifully knitted, and unique to the period it was made in. 8.5 x 5.75 in. *Collection of Lori Blaser.* $450-500.

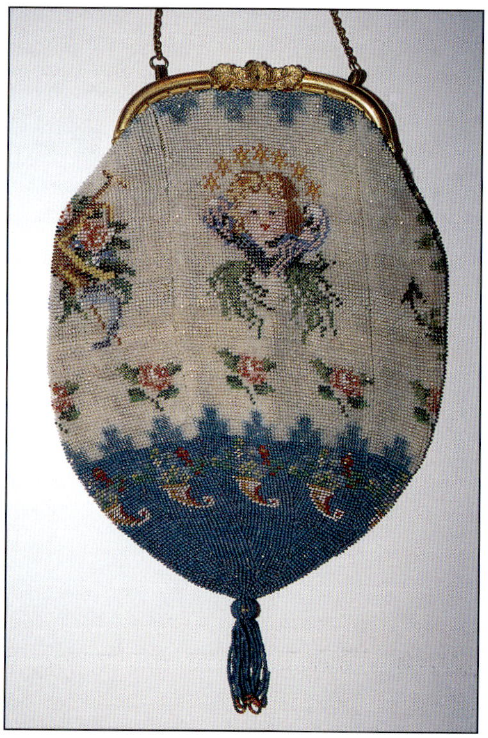

A c.1830-1840 purse made with several designs circling the purse, in a sampler-like style. The front shows an angel's head. The left side has an anchor and the right side, a wheel barrow. The frame is original to the purse. Another interesting feature of this purse is that it was made in vertical sections, which have been sewn together. 11 x 7 in. *Collection of Paula Higgins.* $650-750.

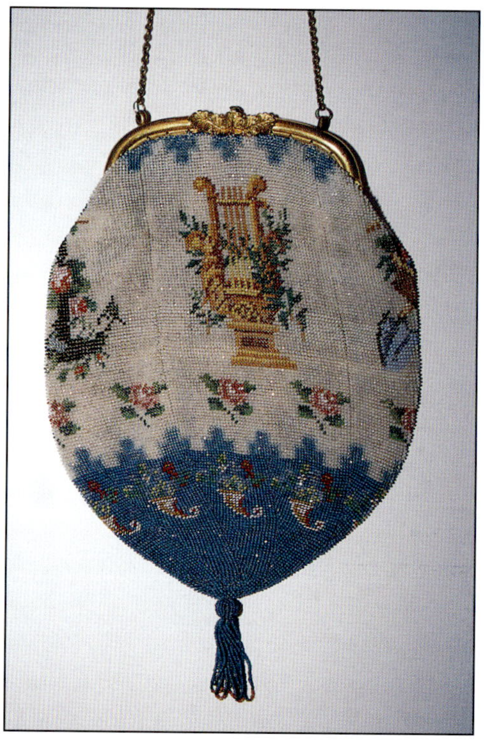

The reverse side showing a lyre and rose vine design.

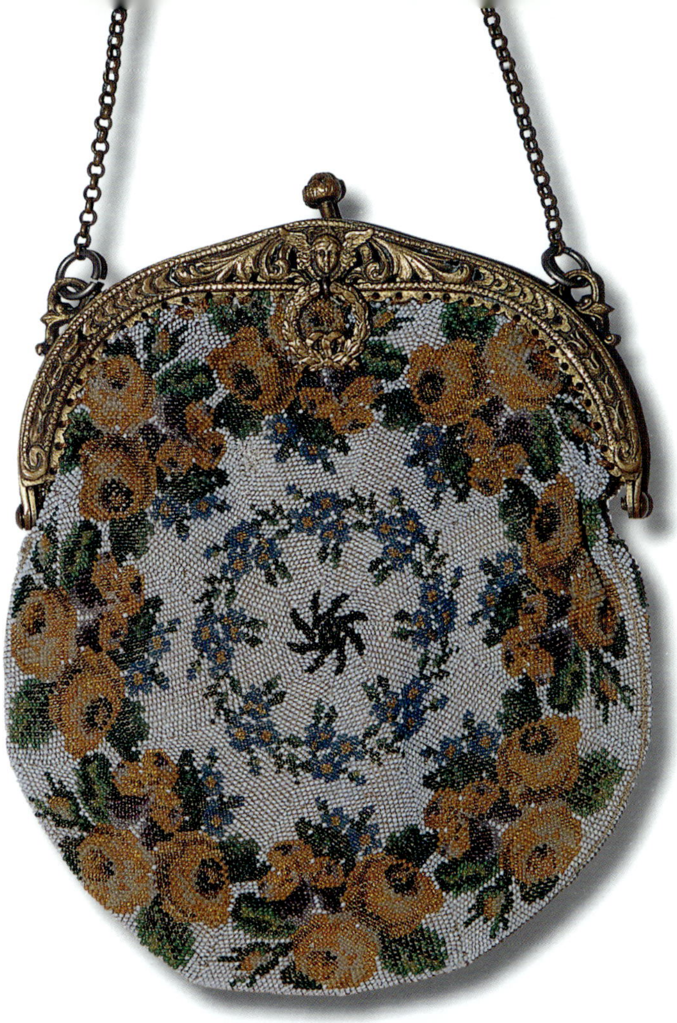

Fine bead knitted piecrust purse in colors of gold, green, and blue. Piecrust purses were made in pie shaped wedges, which were then sewn together to form a round purse. The frame is original to the purse, and it is decorated with acanthus leaves, a winged Mercury head, and a wreath tab. This purse was made c.1830. 6.5 x 5 in. *Collection of Paula Higgins.* $450-650.

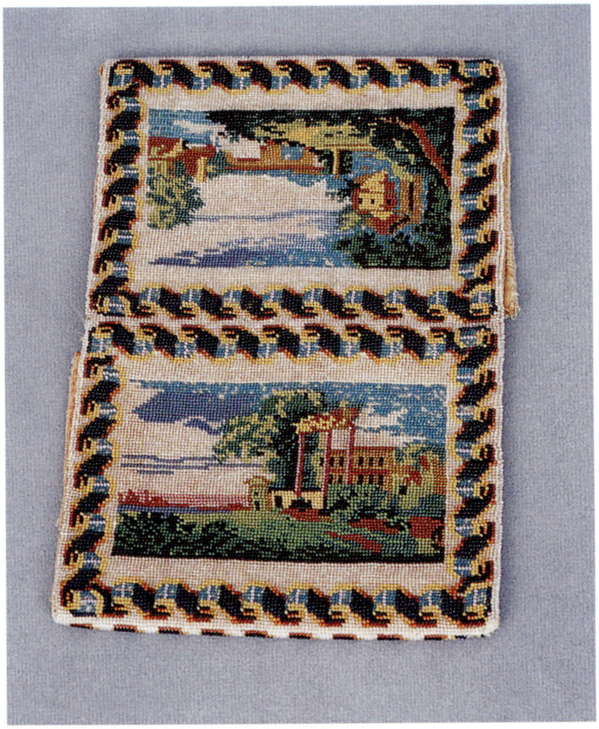

C.1840 beaded pocketbook featuring a villa scene. The interior is also beaded with two more different designs. 8 x 5.5 in. *Collection of Lori Blaser.* $375-425.

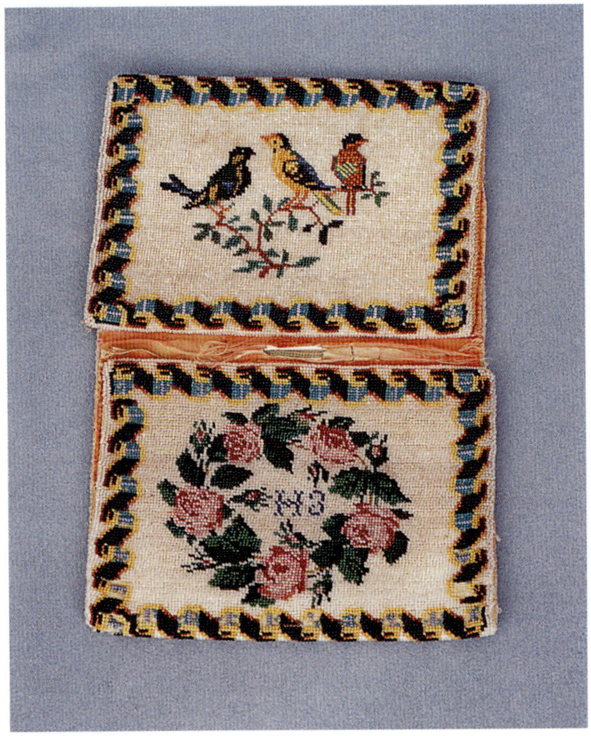

The inside of the beaded pocketbook shows a delightful bird scene and a wreath of roses.

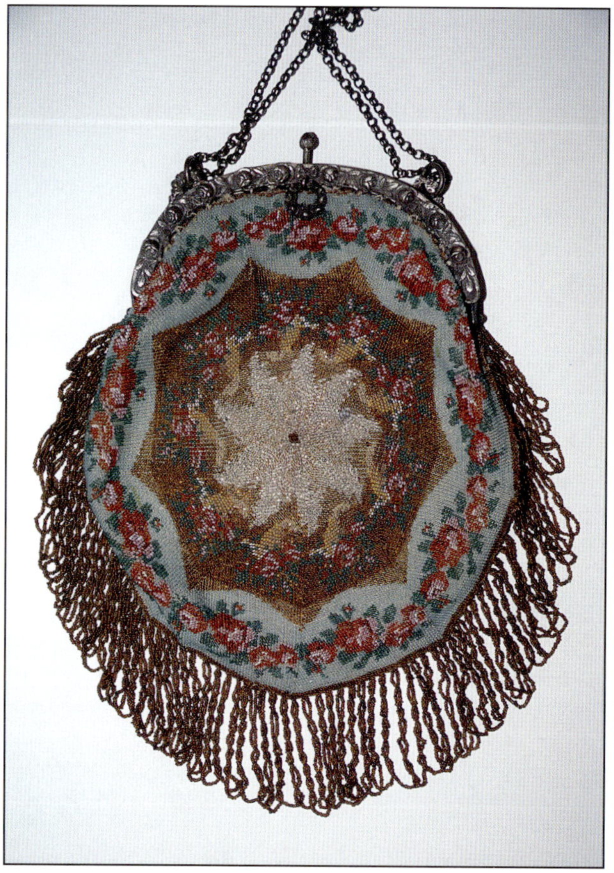

A large c.1830-1840 beaded piecrust purse with its original silver frame, lining, and fringe. This purse is beautifully knitted and constructed. The seams connecting the pie shaped wedges are barely visible. 9.25 x 7 in. *Collection of Paula Higgins.* $600-650.

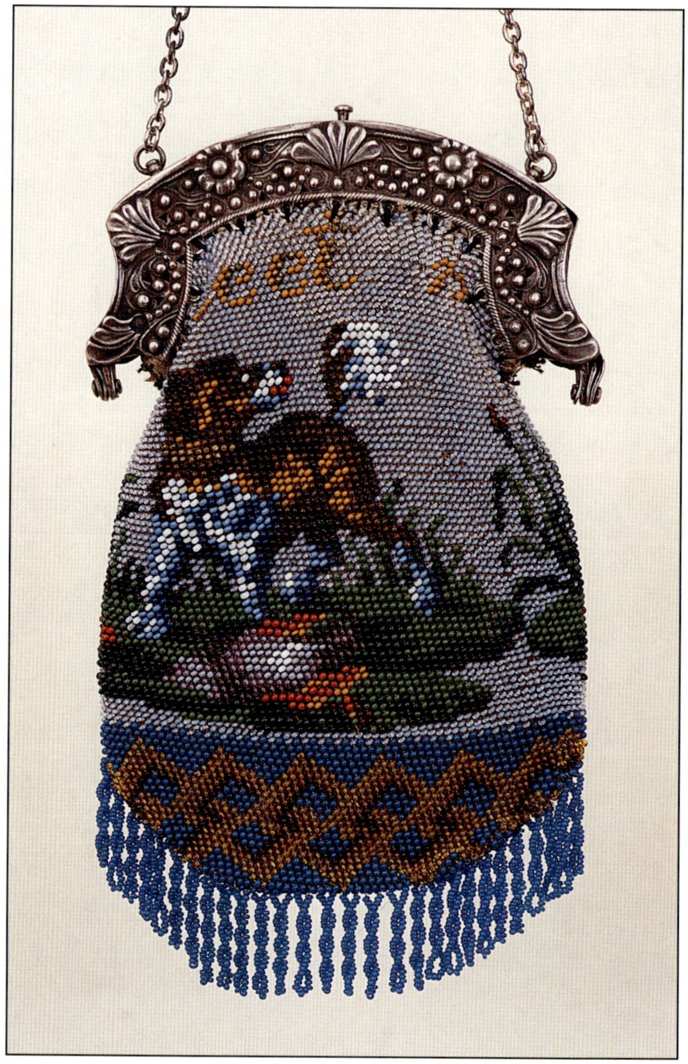

Dogs were another popular design for early beaded purses. This German made purse is in excellent condition for its 160 years. The silver frame is original to the purse and a nice example of early frame design. 7 x 4 in. *Collection of Lori Blaser.* $450-600.

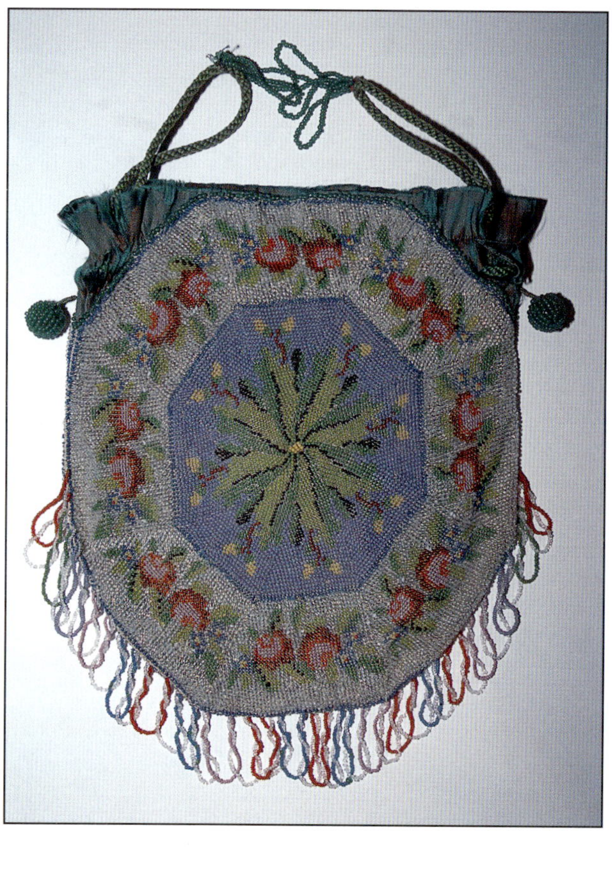

Piecrust purses were also made in the reticule style, without a frame. The lining, header, and drawstrings are original to the purse. Inside is a very faded tag that says Duveleroy Paris. 9 x 6 in. *Collection of Paula Higgins.* $400-500.

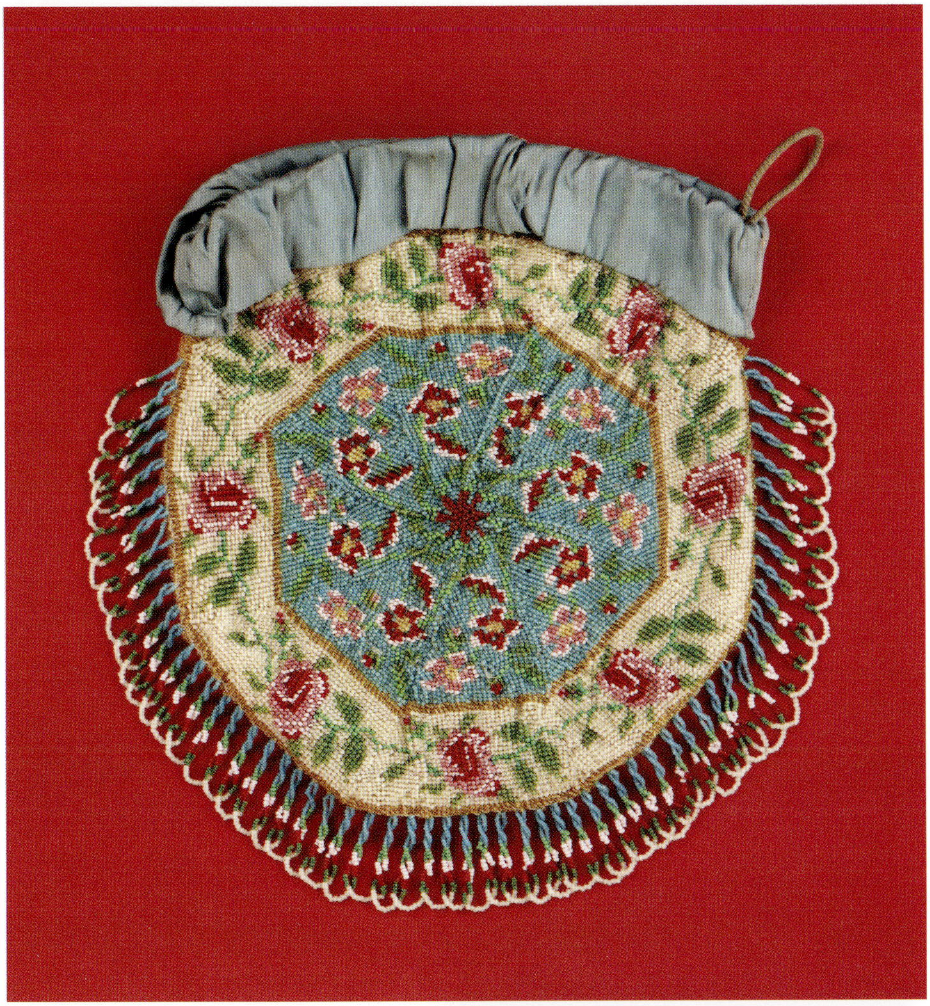

This is another example of a piecrust made in the reticule style. The color scheme is very attractive and feminine. Although many piecrusts date to c.1830, it is important to know that they were being made into the late 19th and early 20th centuries. 9 x 9 in. *Collection of Sharon LuVisi.* $425-500.

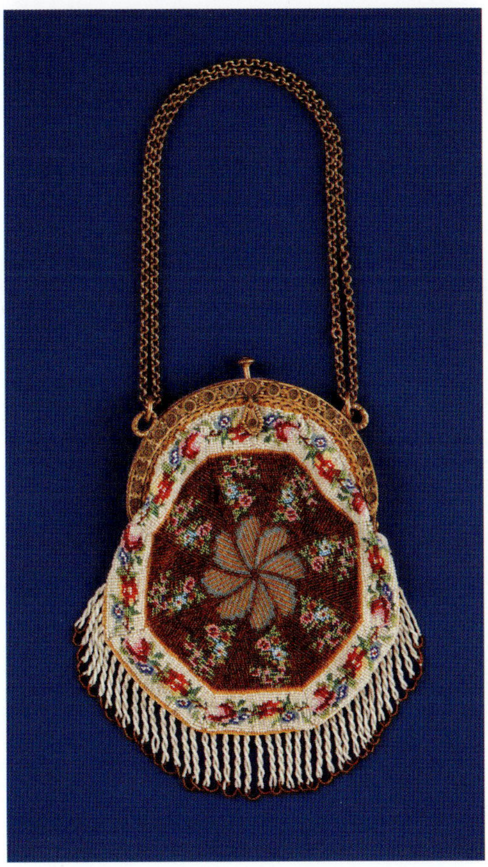

A beautifully preserved, piecrust beaded purse with its original frame. The long double chain is typical of early frame design. 9 x 7 in. *Collection of Sharon LuVisi.* $600-650.

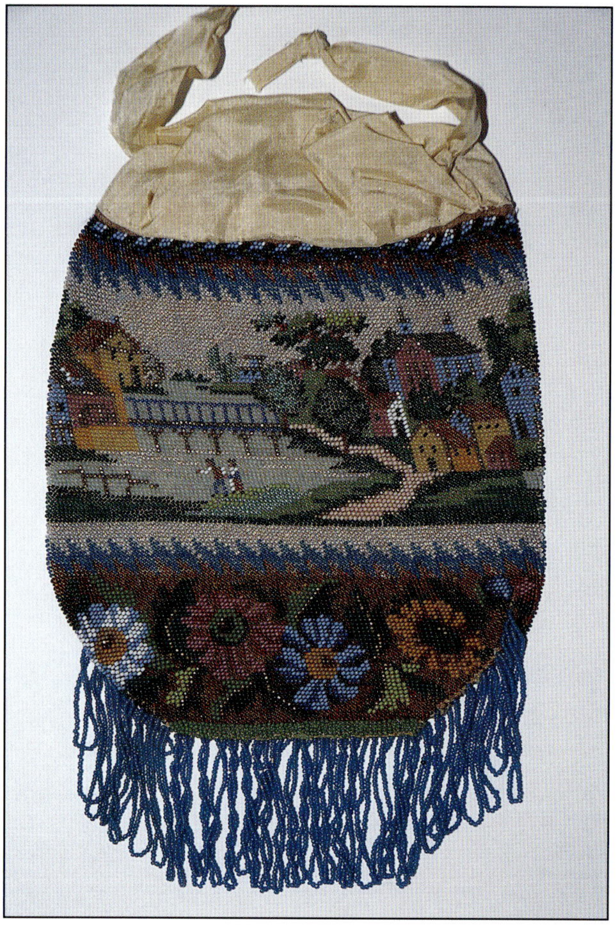

Most purse collectors are familiar with the early beaded "primitive" or "sampler" style purses. Typically divided into three sections, the more interesting versions have a scenic or figural design in the center. This example has a fairly detailed scenic design. It is bead knitted with fine beads. 8.5 x 6 in. *Collection of Paula Higgins.* $325-375.

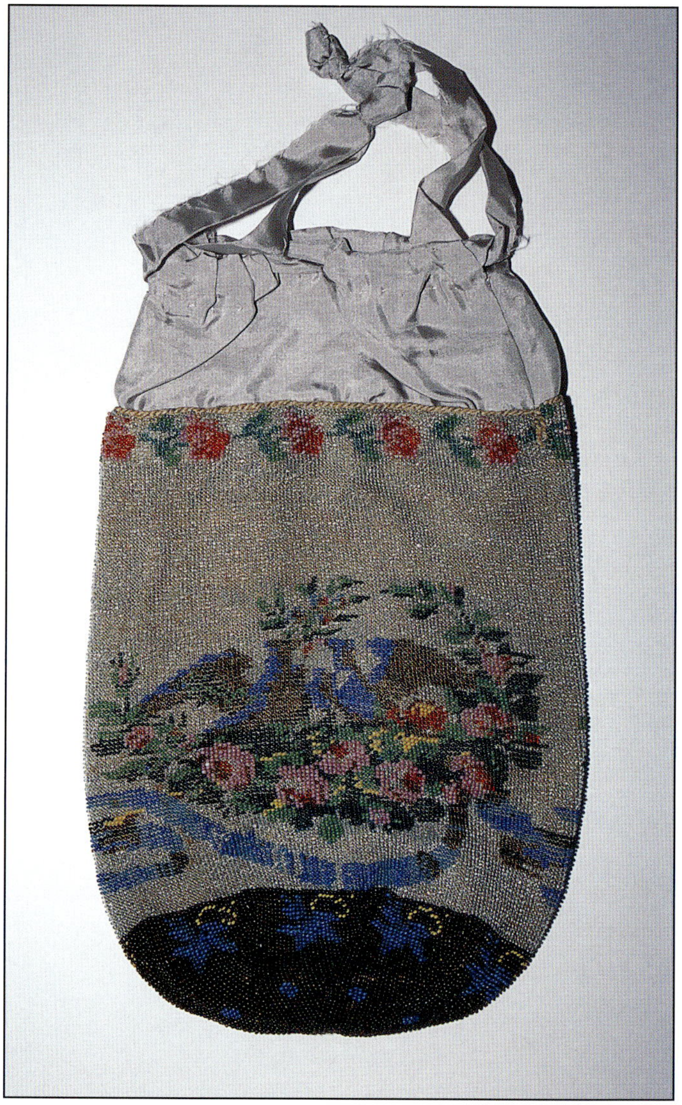

This c.1840, bead knitted purse has a classic Biedermeier design. A naturalistic design of birds sitting among roses and holding a branch is characteristic of the period. Many beaded purse designs originated from the needlework designs of the same period. 9 x 6.5 in. *Collection of Paula Higgins.* $300-325.

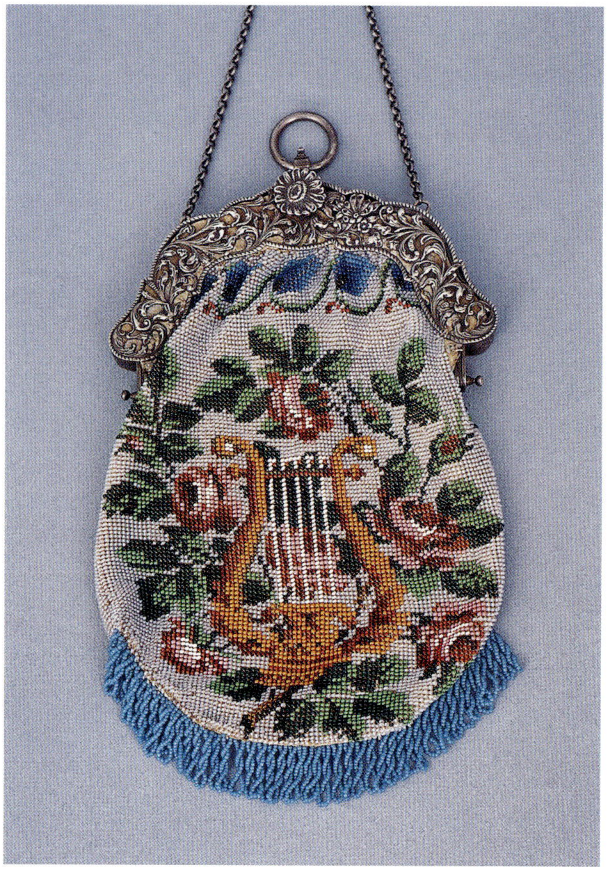

The lyre and rose design is another notable Biedermeier design. Variations of this theme, such as the lyre and vine, are also seen on beadwork from this period. This particular frame style was in use for over 100 years. 11 x 6 in. *Collection of Lori Blaser.* $450-550.

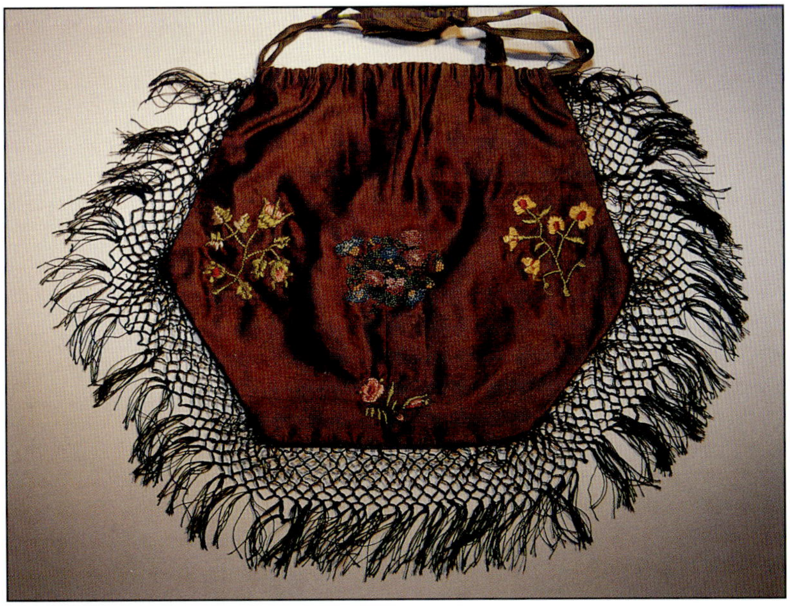

A very unusual c.1830-1840 silk purse decorated with beaded flowers and a wide border of netting and tassels. Decorative netting was also used on table cloths and bedspreads during the first half of the 19th century. American. 13 x 9.5 in. *Collection of Paula Higgins.* $350-400.

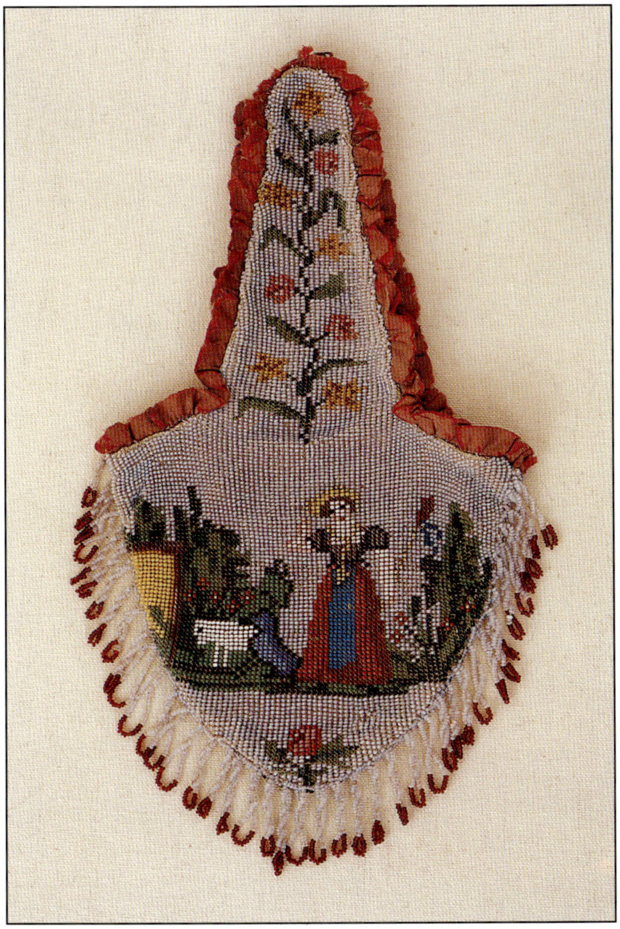

Another wonderful variation of the reticule style, designed to be worn over the arm. A woman and lamb decorate one side, and the reverse shows a man leaning against a tree. Pleated silk edges the top of the purse. 10 x 5 in. *Collection of Lori Blaser.* $650-750.

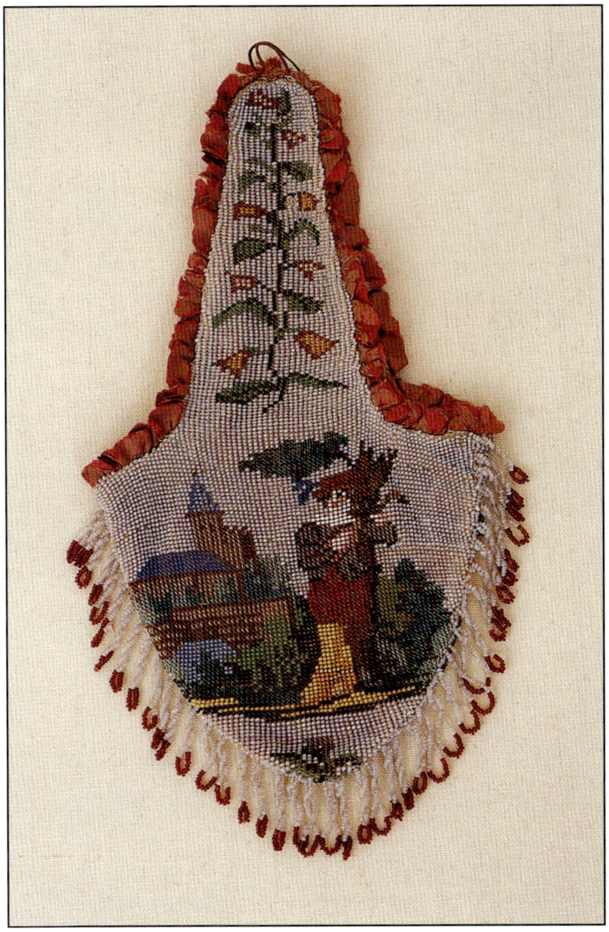

The reverse side of the arm reticule.

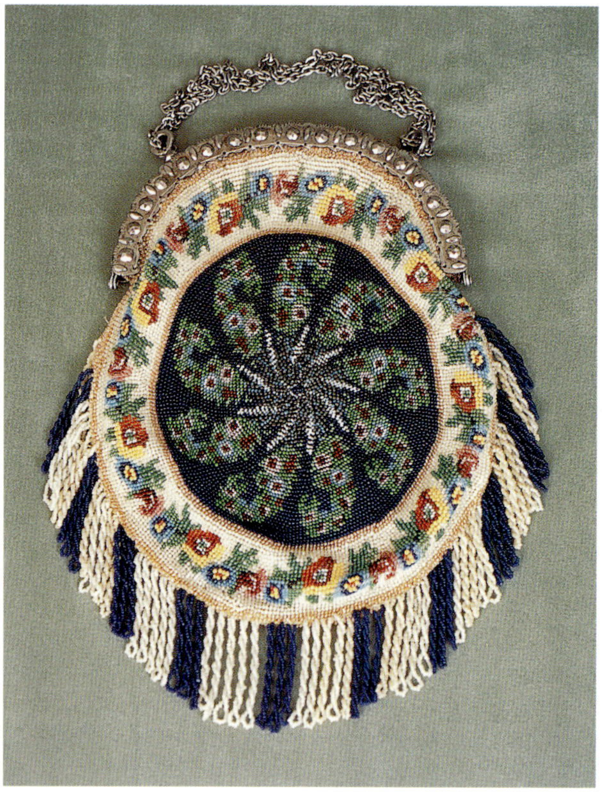

This bead knitted, piecrust purse is mounted on an early cut steel frame. The alternating fringe is striking and unusual. 9 x 6.5 in. *Collection of Lori Blaser.* $650-750.

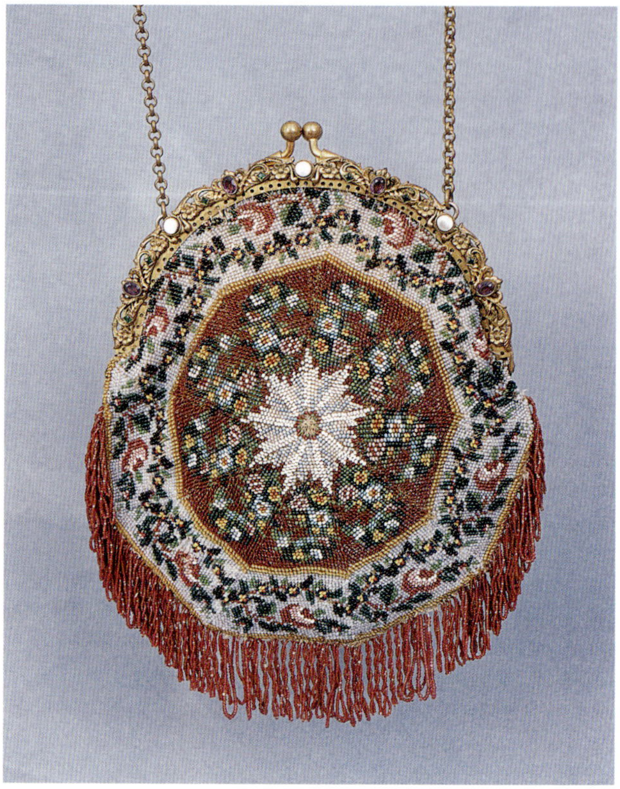

A rich, ruby red fringe makes this piecrust a standout. Multi-faceted red beads in this color are rare. The beautiful frame was added later to replace a shattered header. 8.5 x 6.25 in. *Collection of Lori Blaser.* $700-800.

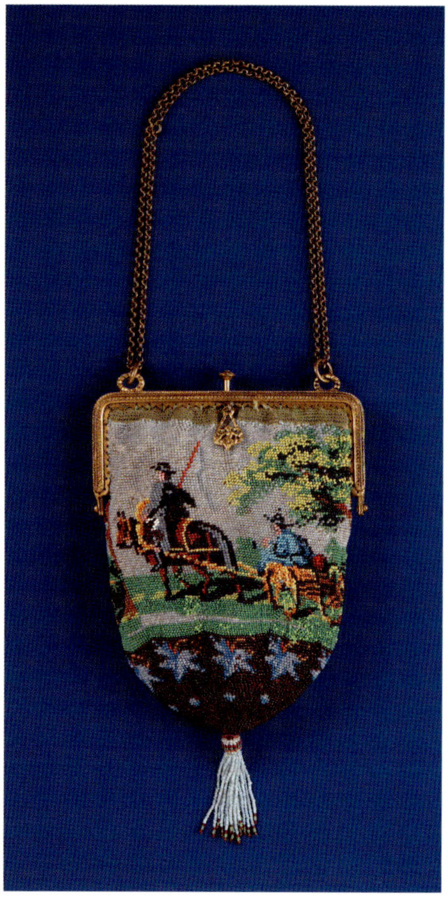

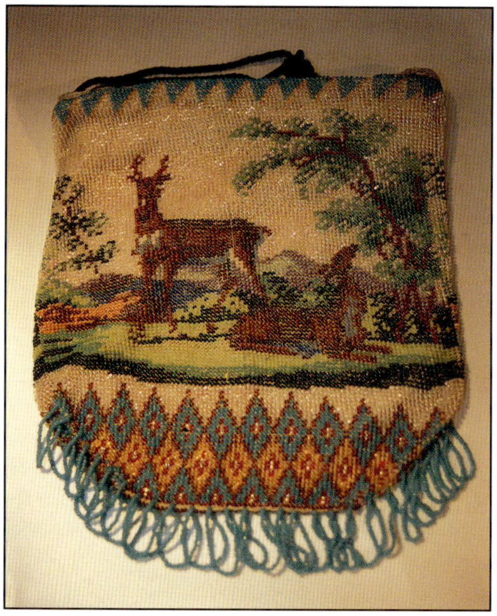

Deer and stags were another common design theme in the first half of the 19th century. This purse dates to c.1840. 7 x 5 in. *Collection of Paula Higgins.* $350-375.

Transportation scenics are always desirable. This early horse, rider, and cart scenic is charming, and it shows a nice sense of perspective. 9.5 x 7 in. *Collection of Sharon LuVisi.* $750-850.

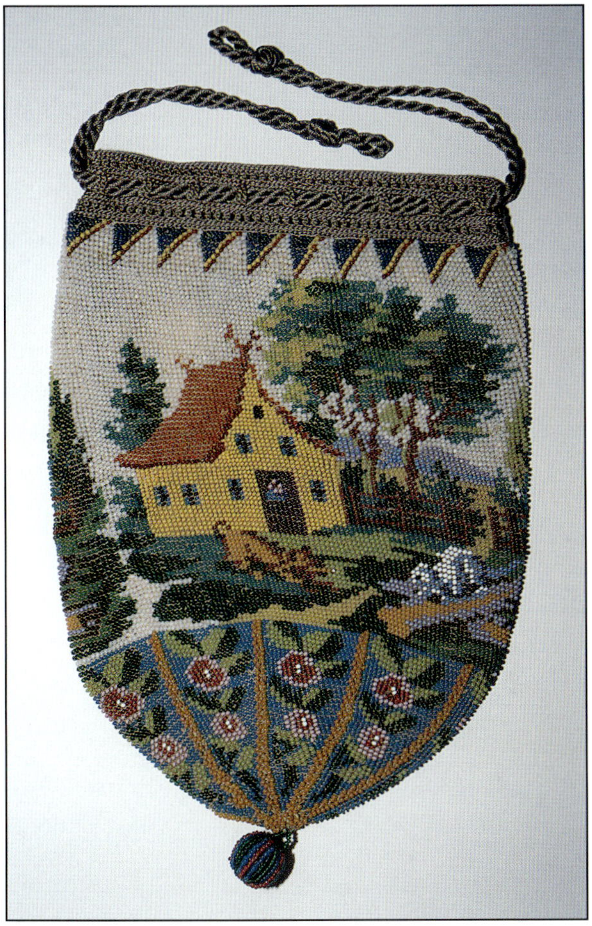

A European style farmhouse forms a backdrop for the antics of a dog and cat in the foreground. The design on the bottom, the sawtooth border at the top, and the early silk lining date this purse to c.1840. 8.5 x 5.5 in. *Collection of Paula Higgins.* $400-450.

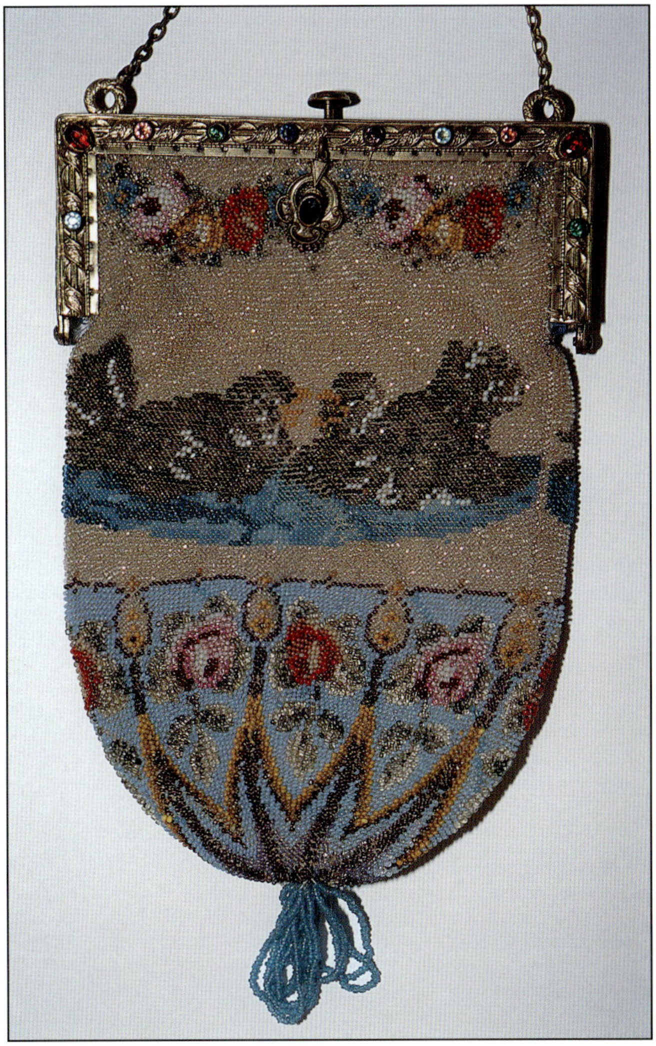

Two birds sitting in water are flanked by colorful floral designs. The purse is attached to its original frame. C.1840. 8 x 5.5 in. *Collection of Paula Higgins.* $500-650.

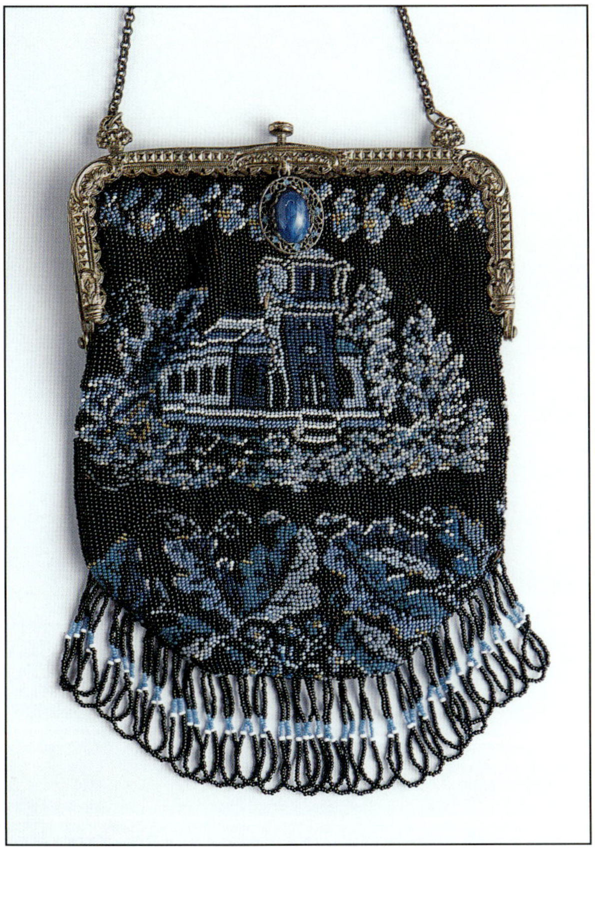

Religion played a prominent role in everyday life in the 19th century, so it is only natural that churches were used in beadwork designs. This blue, black, and white beaded purse is nicely detailed. 8 x 6 in. *Collection of Kim Stonecipher.* $375-500.

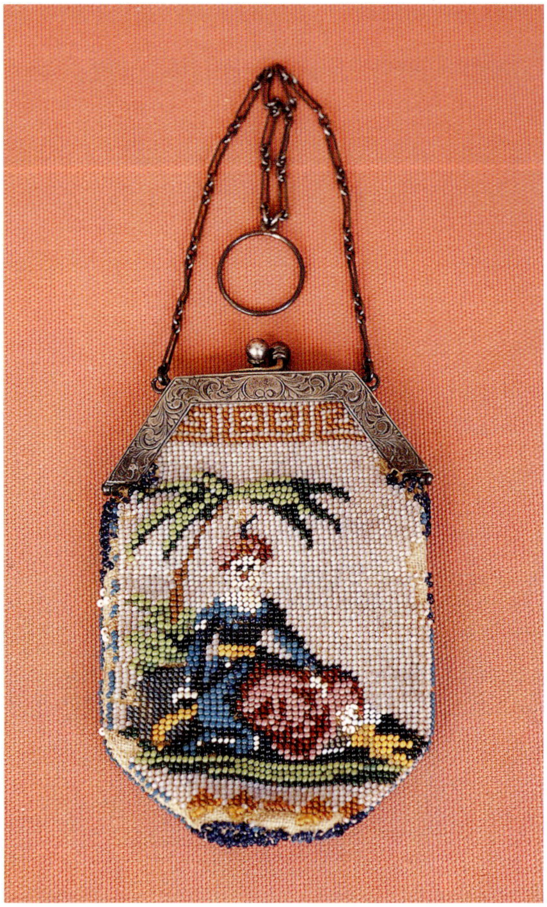

This small, early coin purse was probably reframed later in the 19th century. The beaded figural design is early, but the twist clasp frame is believed to date to the 1870s. 4.5 x 3 in. *Collection of Lori Blaser.* $350-375.

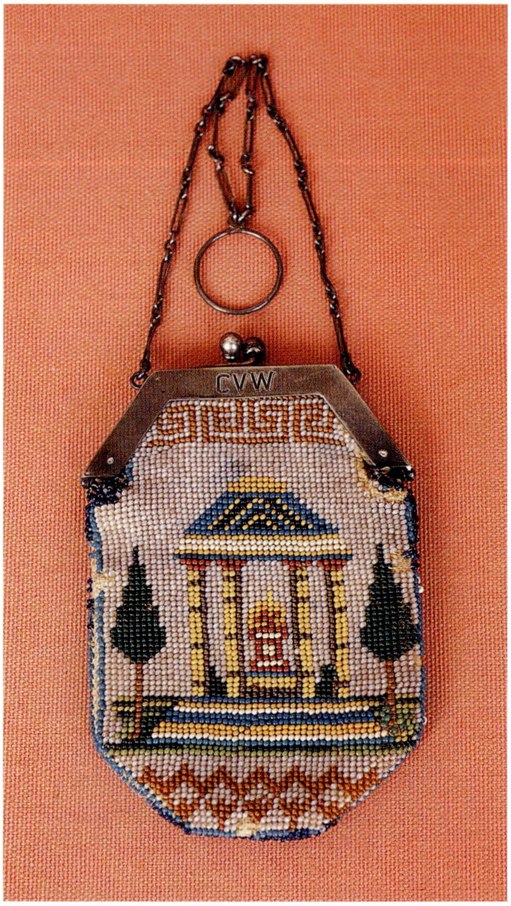

The reverse side of the coin purse.

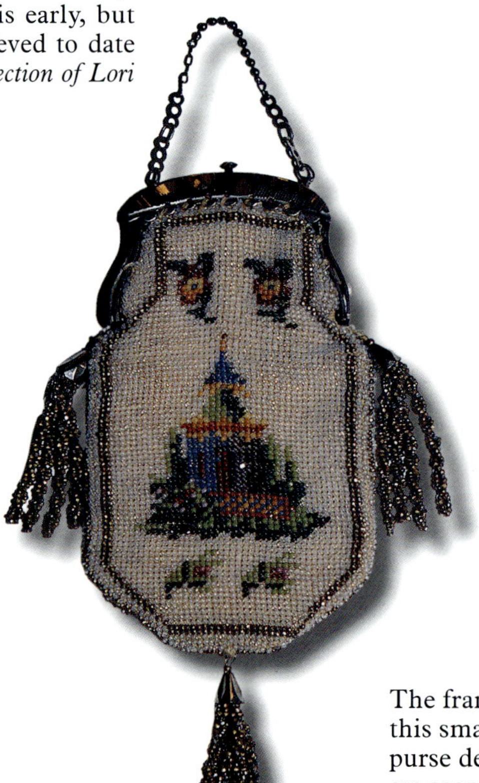

The frame and cut steel side tassels seen on this small coin purse are typical of c.1840 purse design. Larger versions of this frame are seen on other purses from the same period. 4.5 x 3 in. *Collection of Paula Higgins.* $325-350.

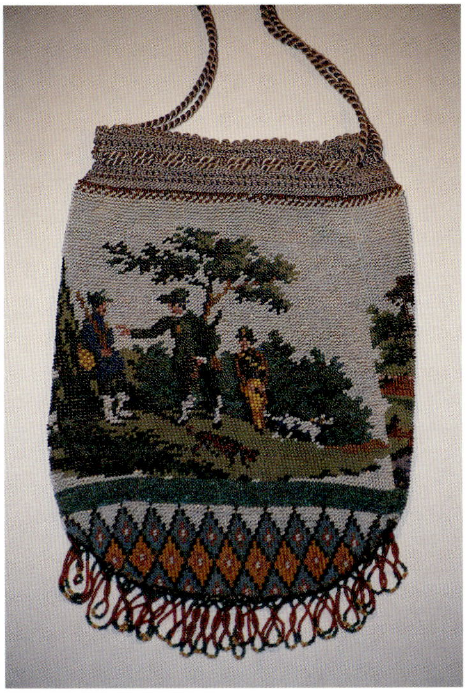

C.1840 hunting scene with three hunters and their dogs. The reverse side shows an alpine scene with a woman in the foreground. This purse came from Holland. 8 x 6 in. *Collection of Paula Higgins.* $750-850.

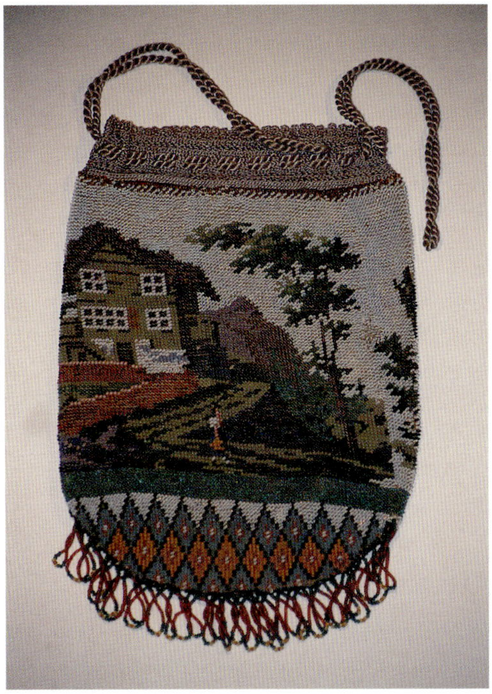

The reverse side of the hunting scenic showing the alpine scene.

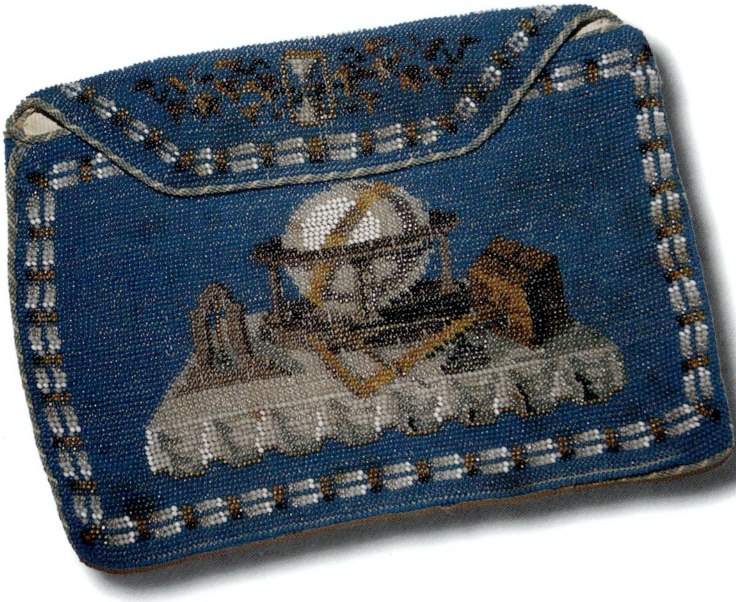

Beaded Masonic pocketbook worked with Masonic symbols such as the astrolabe, plumb, sextant, and hourglass. The colors used to bead the purse represent chastity and fidelity. The Masonic Order found its origins in the stonemason guilds of the 17th century. Their philosophic beliefs were based on the principles of enlightenment and self-improvement. Famous Masonic members included George Washington and Paul Revere. The purse is lined in white kid. 8 x 6 in. C.1840. *Collection of Paula Higgins.* $500-600.

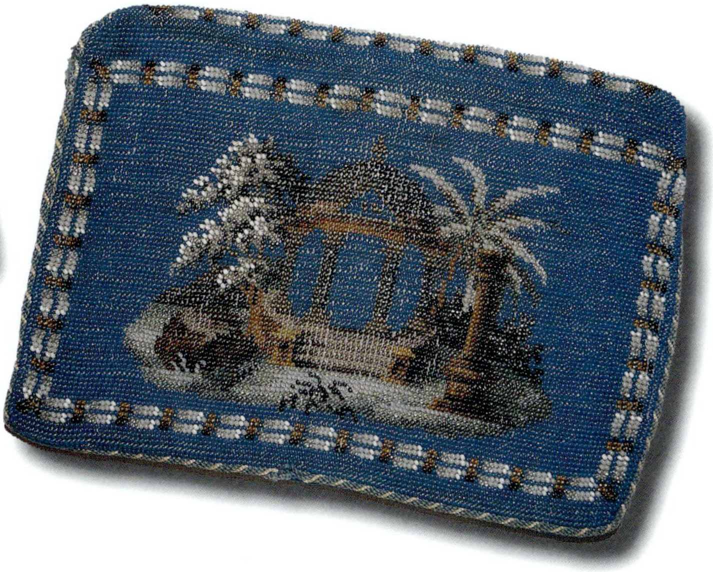

The reverse side of the Masonic beaded purse.

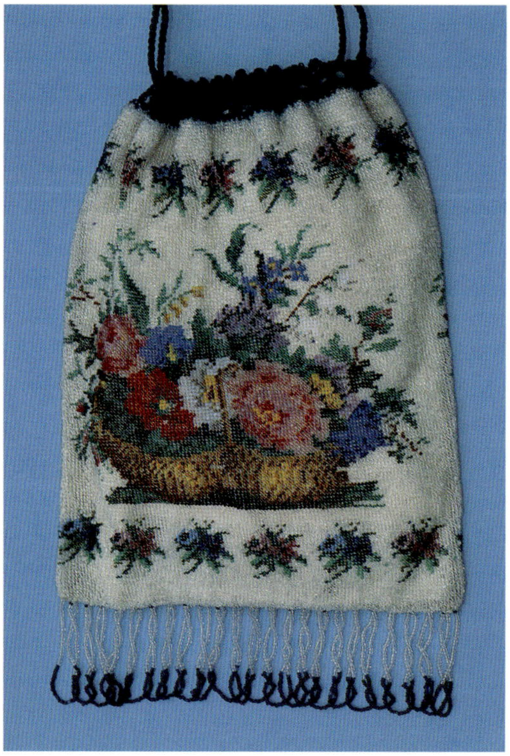

Designs featuring a flat basket of flowers typically date to the first half of the 19th century. Later, the baskets became taller or the flowers were placed in tall vases. But it is still important to look at the purse in its entirety to determine age, because old designs were reproduced many years later. 9.5 x 7 in. *Collection of Linda Marshall.* $350-425.

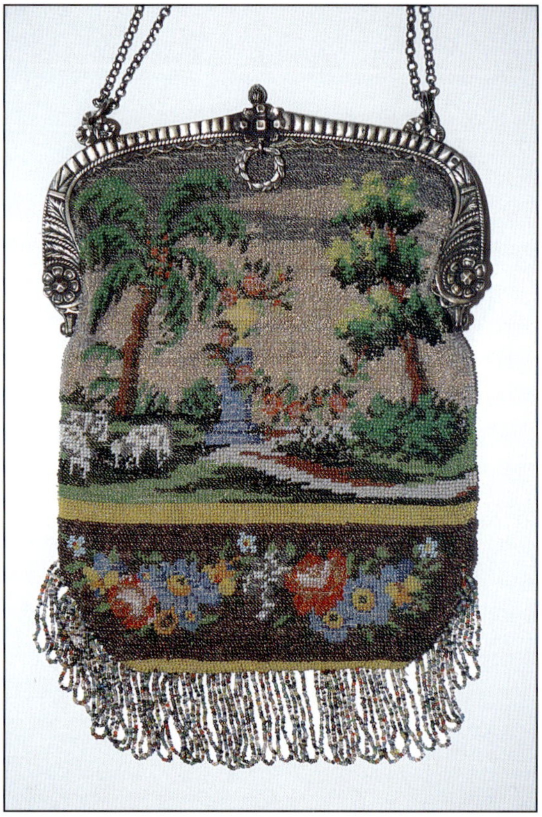

A c.1840 beaded purse with its original frame and lining. On the front is a memorial scene with a pedestal and urn, entwined with roses. Sheep graze on the left. It is continued on the reverse side with a pastoral scene of a young man playing a flute, a shepherdess, and sheep. 10 x 6.5 in. *Collection of Paula Higgins.* $900-1,200.

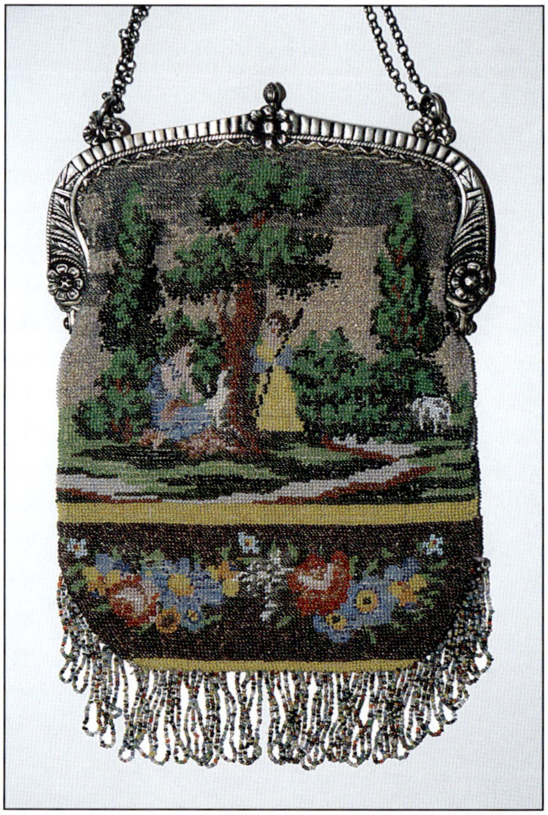

The reverse side of the continuous scenic.

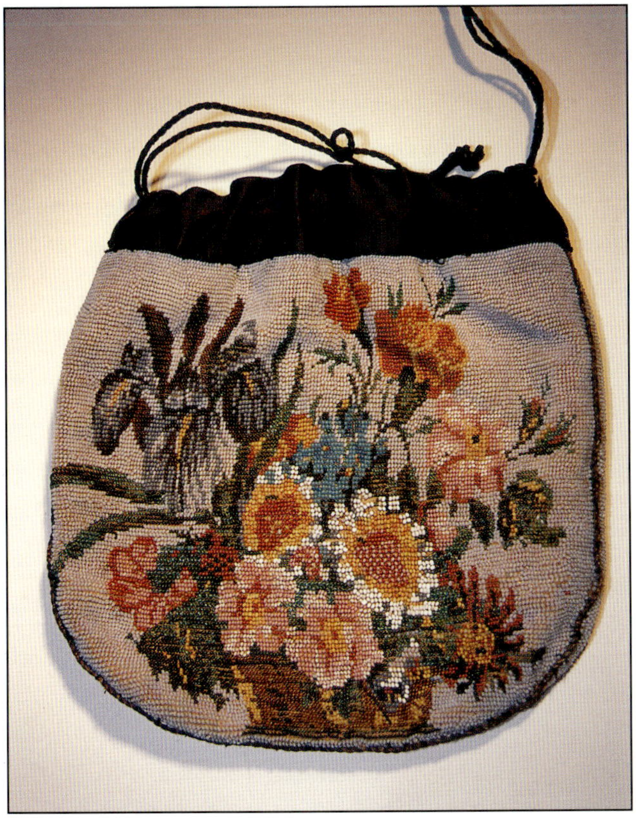

Another flat basket of flowers dating to c.1840. The overflowing basket covers the entire front of the purse. On the reverse side is a scene of two hares. This purse is made with fine beads embroidered on canvas. 7 x 7 in. *Collection of Paula Higgins.* $400-500.

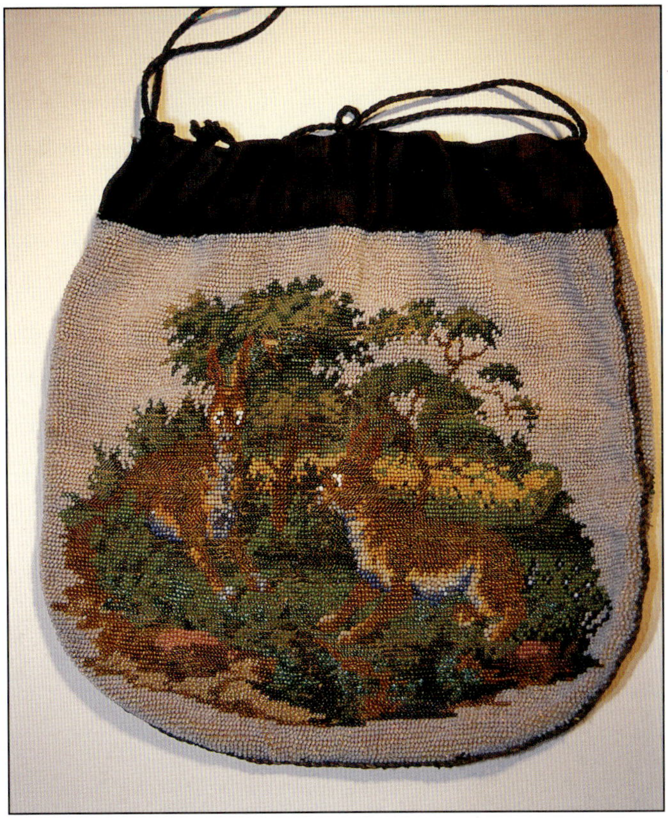

The reverse side of the basket of flowers purse.

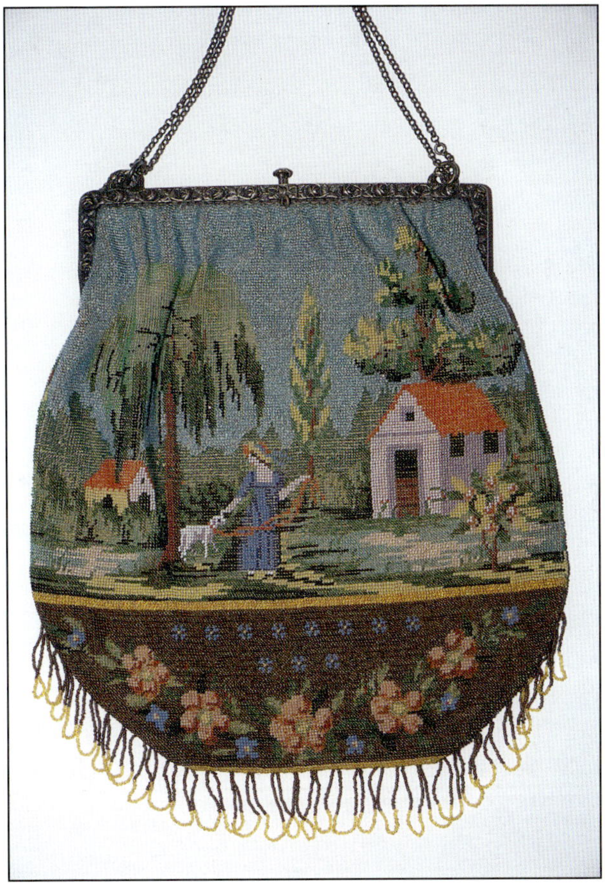

This c.1830-1840 scene is sometimes called the "Mary Had a Little Lamb" design. It has another completely different scene on the reverse side. The lining and frame are original to the purse. This purse is made with very fine beads embroidered on canvas. 12 x 10 in. *Collection of Paula Higgins.* $900-1,200.

The reverse side of the purse on page 193 bottom depicts a tropical scene with a man, a woman, and a dog at a gate. The trees, brick wall, and gazebo to the right are nicely designed and beaded.

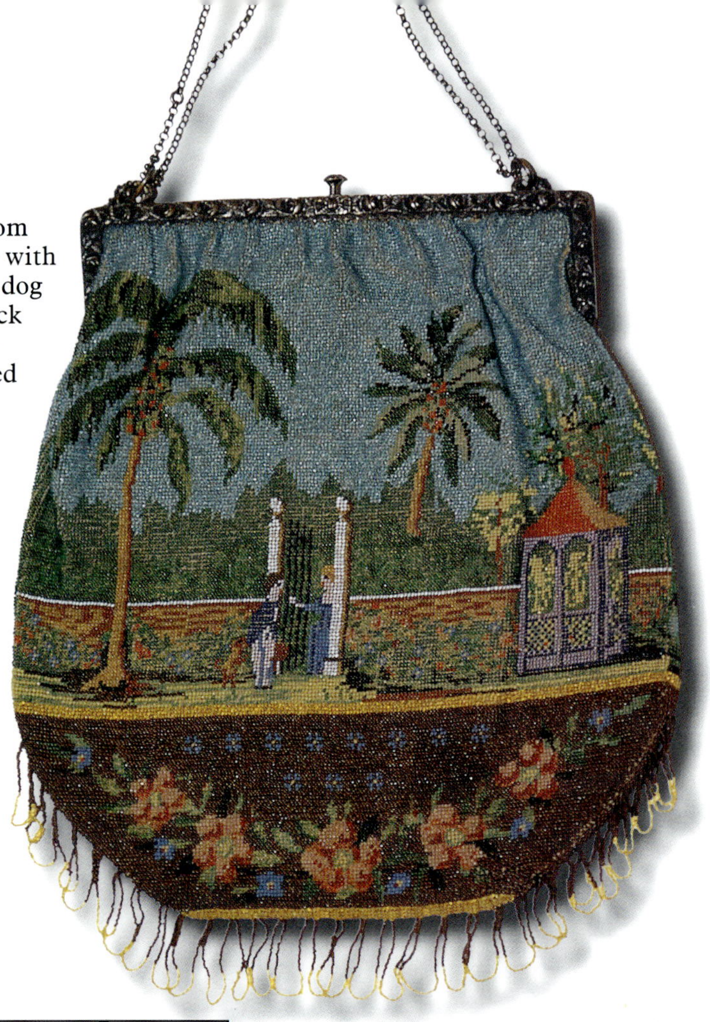

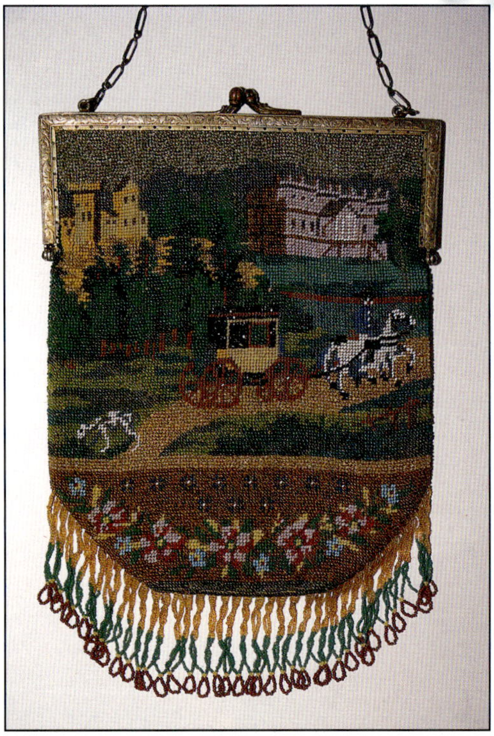

Originally made with a reticule top, a later 19th century frame was added because the top wasn't salvageable. The purse itself, dates to c.1840. The carriage design on the front is part of a continuous scenic. 8.5 x 6.5 in. *Collection of Paula Higgins.* $1,000-1,200.

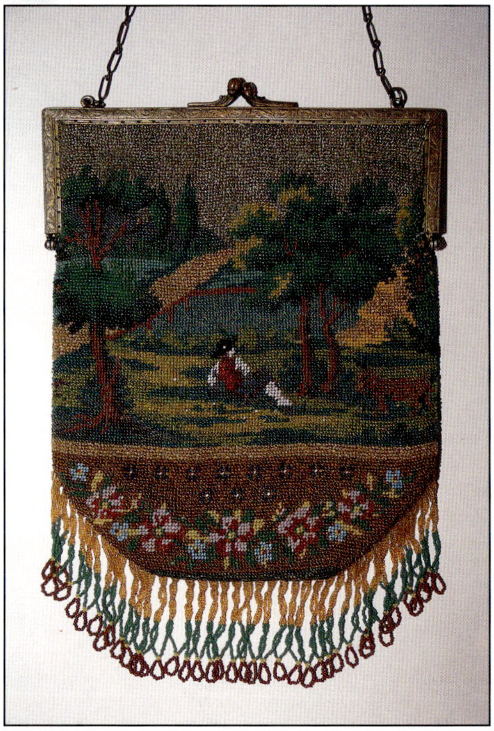

The reverse side of the purse.

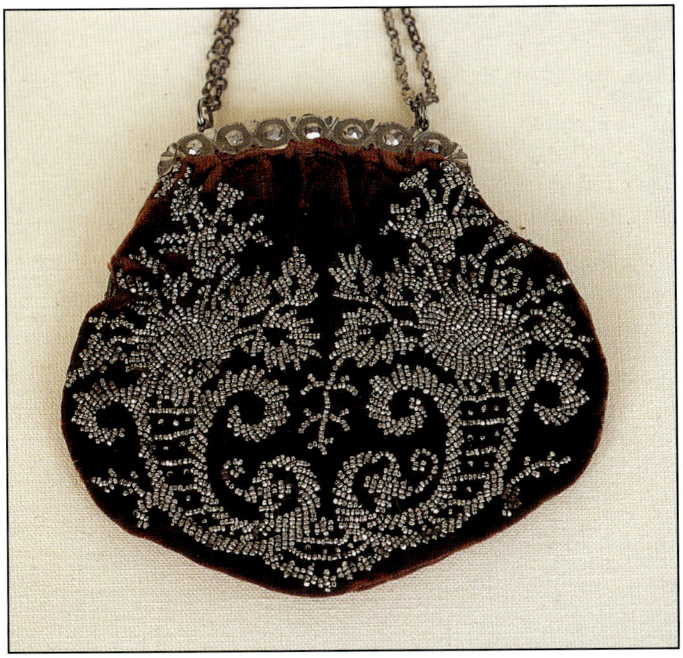

Cut steel decorated velvet purses were made c.1840, and also later in the 19th century. This is an early example and an extraordinarily beautiful one as well. The two cornucopias facing each other create a very rich effect. The cut steel frame is from the same period and it is original to the purse. 5.5 x 5.5 in. *Collection of Lori Blaser.* $450-500.

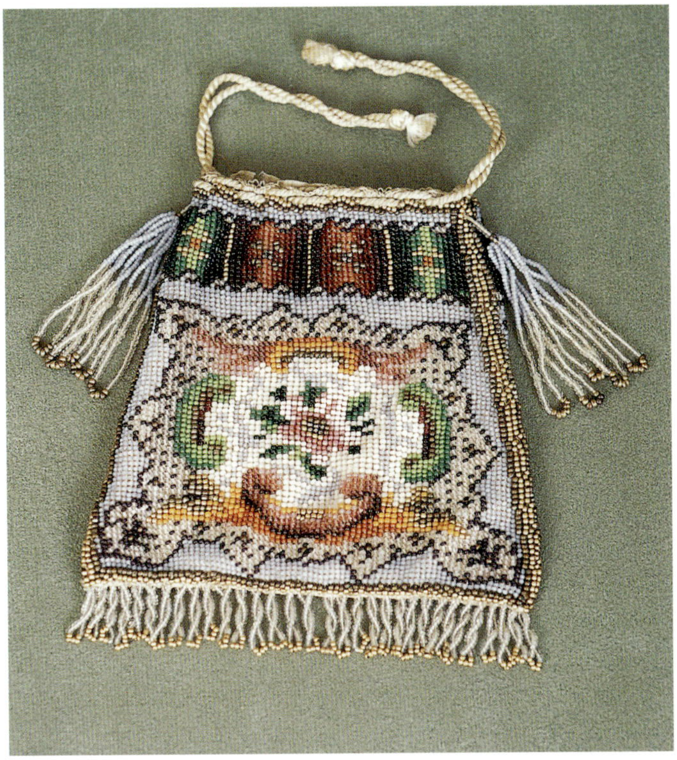

Made in Europe, this is an unusual and attractive purse design. The side tassels are typical of the early Victorian period. 3.75 x 3.5 in. *Collection of Lori Blaser.* $275-350.

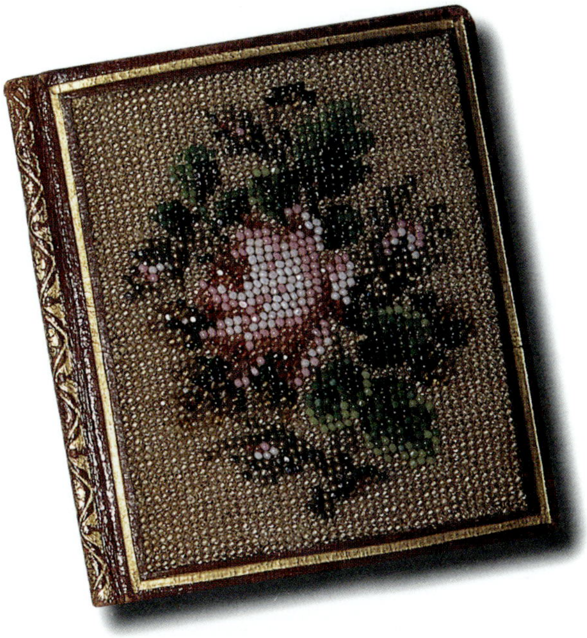

Tiny coin purses came in some clever forms. This one is shaped like a book. 3 x 3 in. *Collection of Paula Higgins.* $150-200.

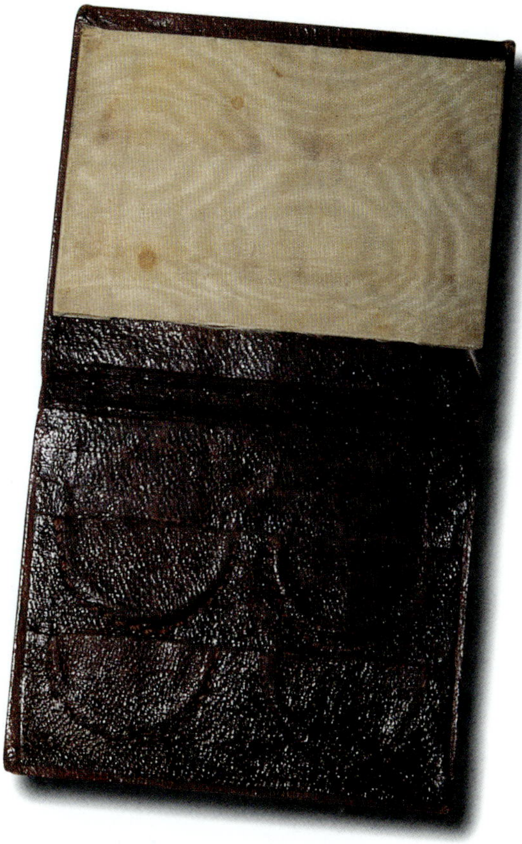

The inside of the coin purse.

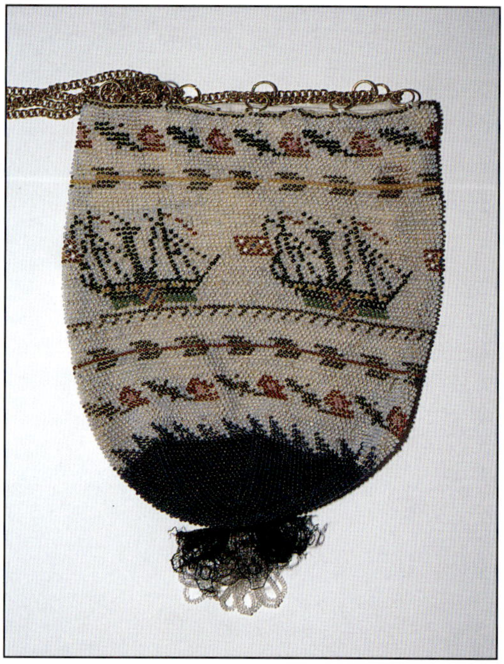

This purse was made in England at a time when Britain ruled the seas. It was also at this time that ships were making the transition from sail, to steam and sail. It is believed that this design commemorates the sailing of the *Sirius.* Four steam and sail ships circle the purse, along with an arrow or dart design. The bottom is finished with a beaded ball and tassel, surrounded by lace. Mid-nineteenth century. 9 x 5 in. *Collection of Paula Higgins.* $350-425.

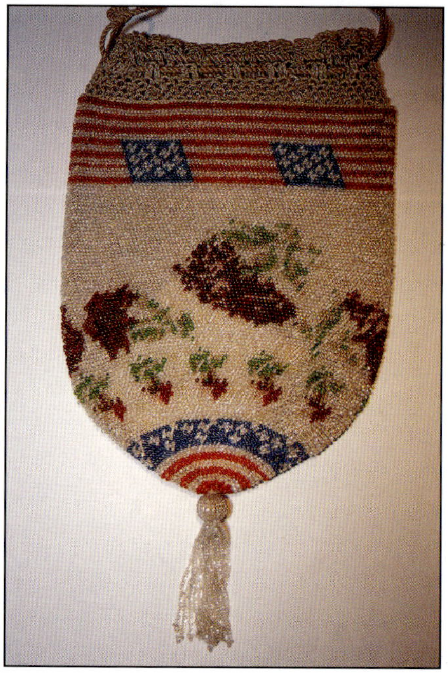

Nineteenth century purses designed with representations of the American flag are a rare type of purse. The beader used elements of the flag at the top and bottom, rather than trying to bead the whole flag on the purse. The carnation design in the center is an early 19th century design, but this purse probably dates to the mid or late 19th century. 9 x 6.5 in. *Collection of Paula Higgins.* $450-600.

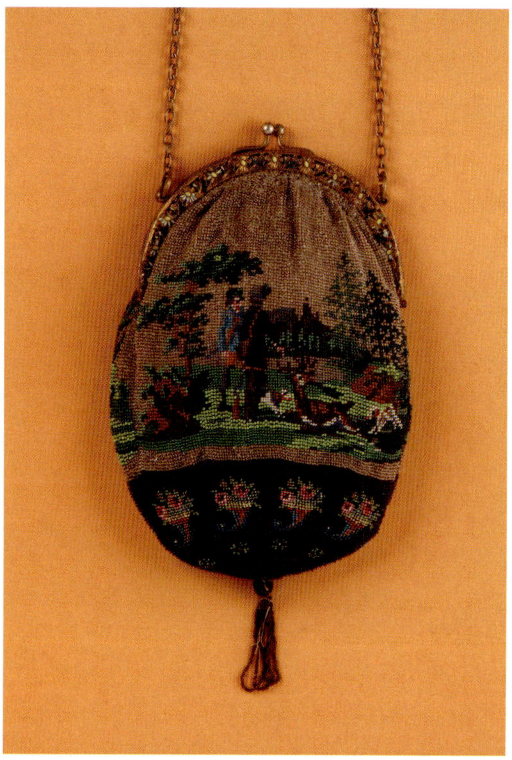

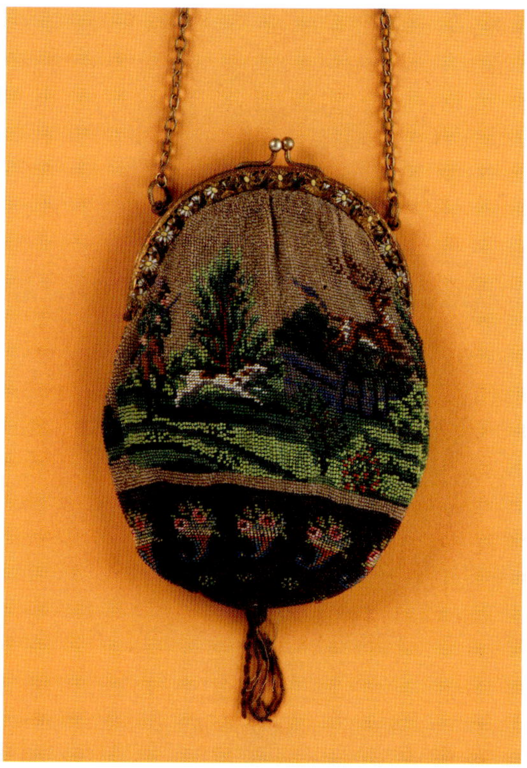

Two hunters, a dead stag, and a dog are the focal point of this scene. Hunting scenes were extremely popular subjects for beaded purses. It is attached to an enameled 19th century frame. 9.5 x 6 in. *Collection of Sharon LuVisi.* $650-750.

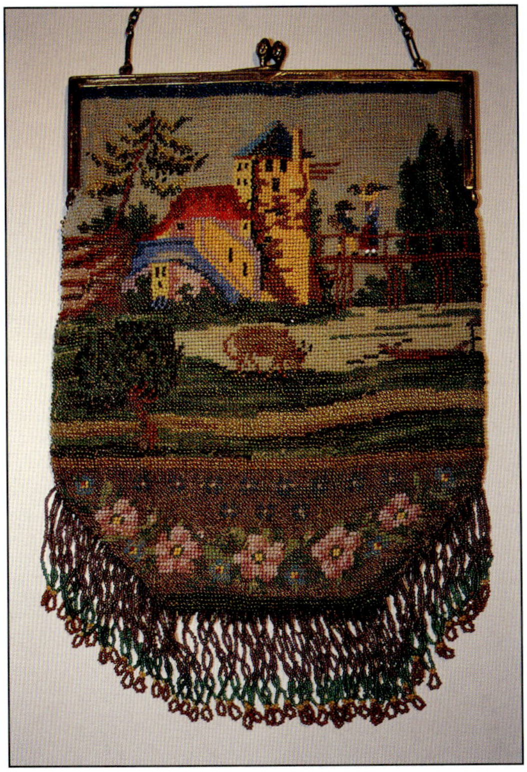

Another continuous town and castle scenic on its original frame. The frame has a twist clasp, which dates it to the 1870s. Although no patent date has been established for the twist clasp in the current literature, the curators of the Tassenmuseum (Museum of Bags and Purses) in Holland believe that this date is correct. 9 x 6.5 in. *Collection of Paula Higgins.* $900-1,200.

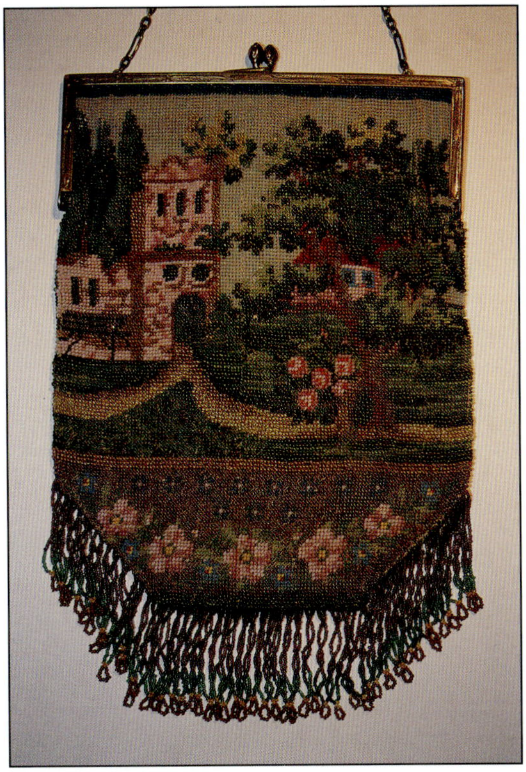

The reverse side of the continuous scenic.

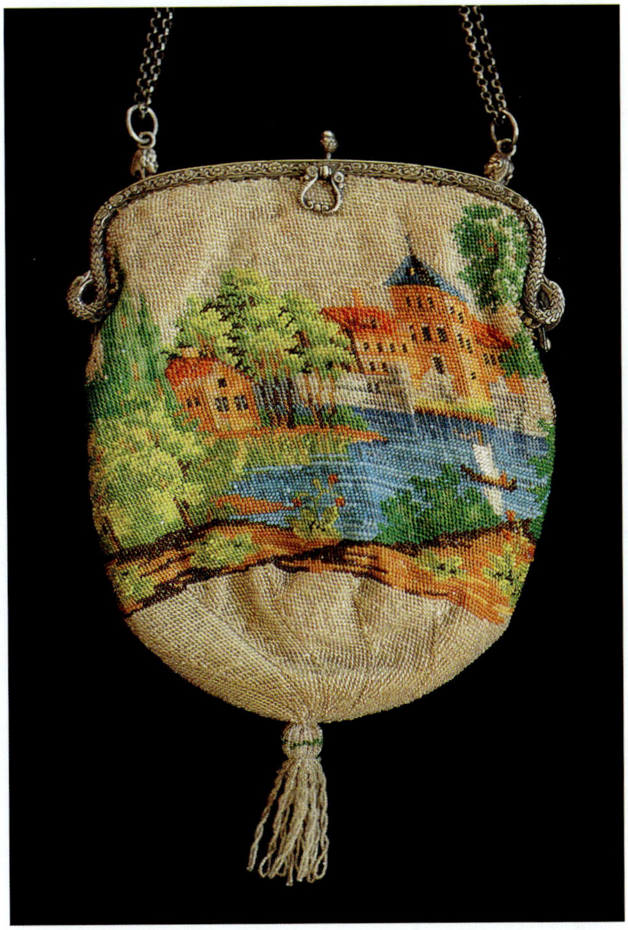

This colorful and uncommon European village and lake scene would appeal to almost all collectors. It is still attached to its original sterling frame, which is made in a long serpent design. 8 x 6.5 in. *Collection of Linda Marshall.* $700-850.

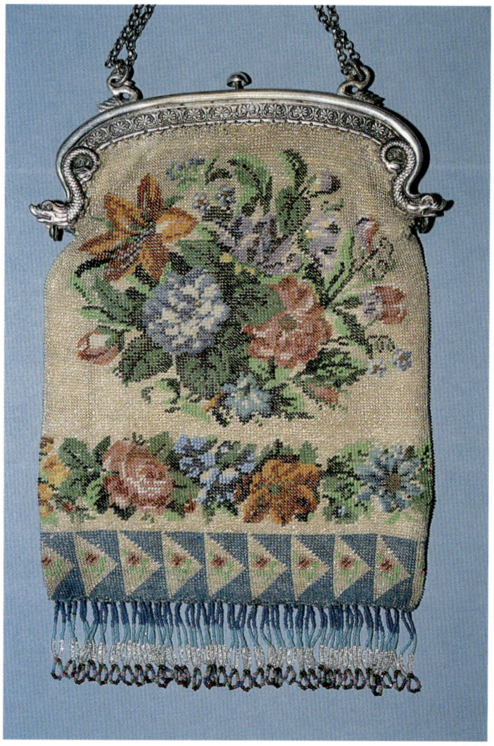

Late 19th century beaded florals retained earlier design elements, but they were modified as tastes changed. This purse has three sections, like the earlier designs, but the floral design is large, like a bouquet. The sterling silver frame has sea serpent heads. 9.25 x 6 in. *Collection of Paula Higgins.* $550-650.

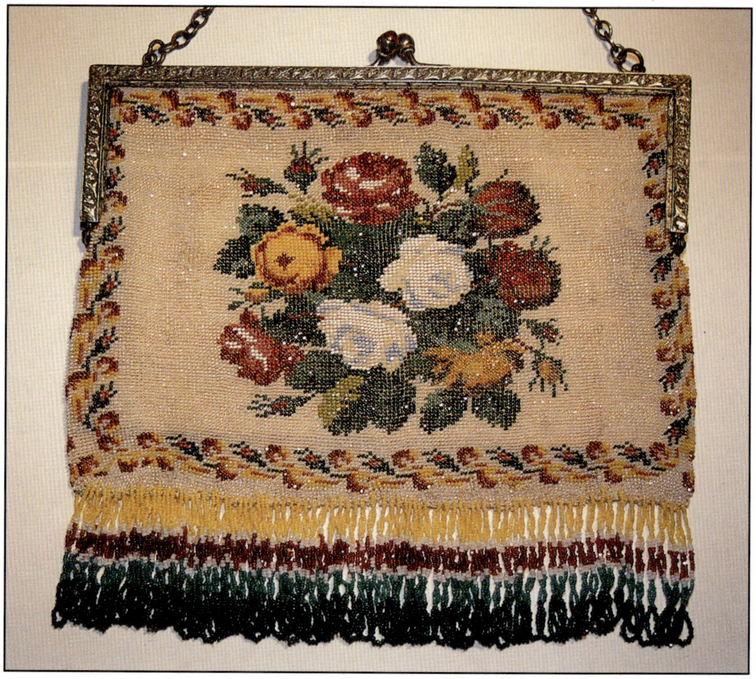

This purse was originally found unframed and without fringe. It was sewn together, attached to a frame, and then an attractive fringe was added. 8.5 x 7.5 in. *Collection of Paula Higgins.* $350-375.

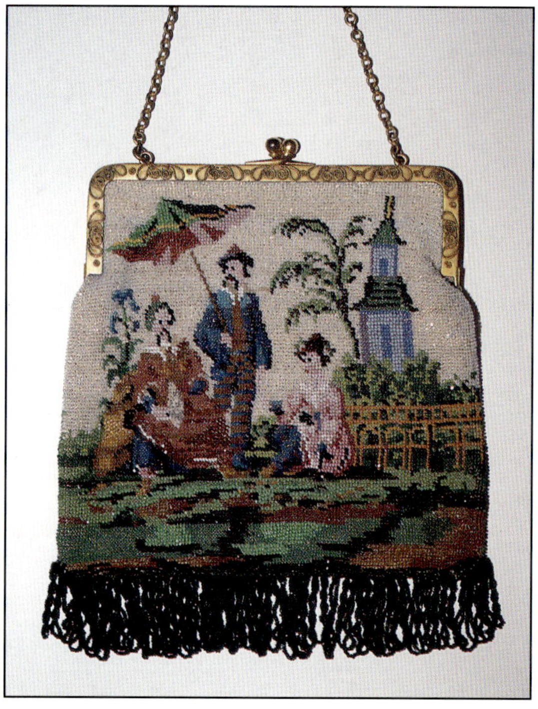

The earlier trend for Turkish and Asian figurals continued into the late 19th century. This purse dates to the last 30 years of the 19th century. It is bead embroidered on canvas. The frame is original to the purse. 8 x 7 in. *Collection of Paula Higgins.* $850-950.

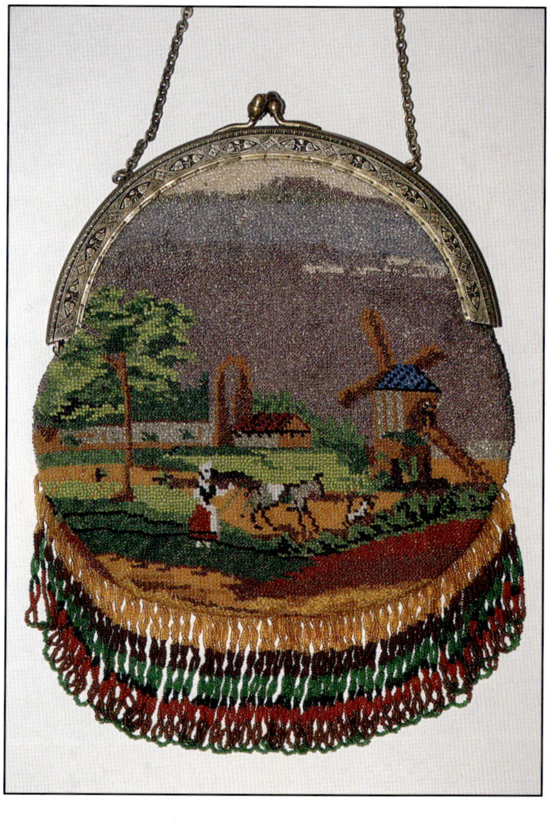

A Dutch windmill scenic, bead embroidered on canvas. 10 x 7 in. *Collection of Paula Higgins.* $650-700.

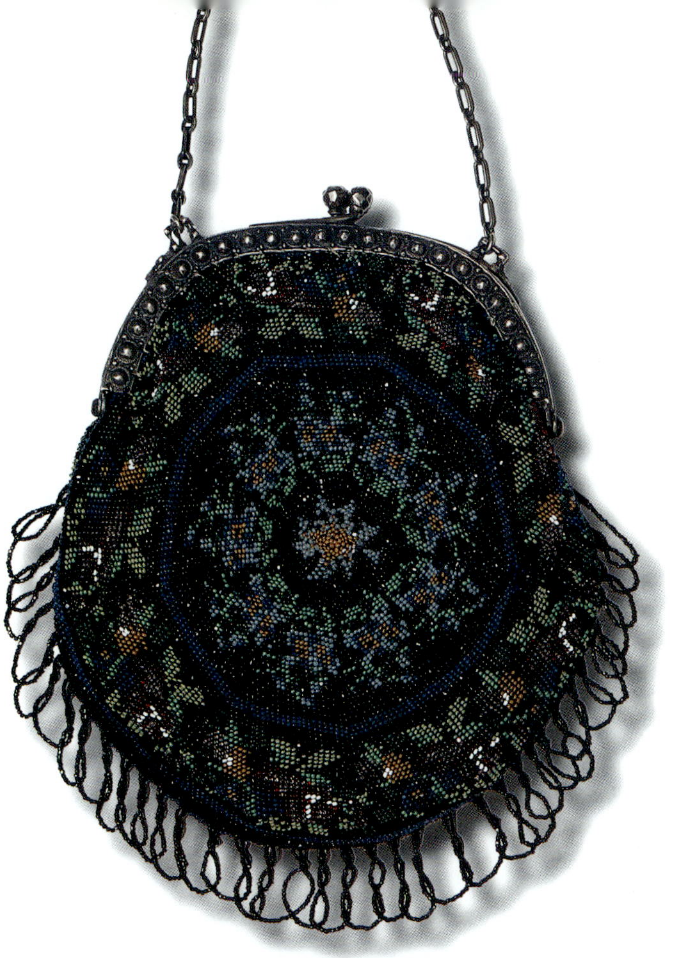

Piecrusts were made into the late 19th century and early 20th century. This piecrust is mounted on its original steel frame, with a twist clasp (c.1870s). 7.5 x 7 in. *Collection of Paula Higgins.* $450-600.

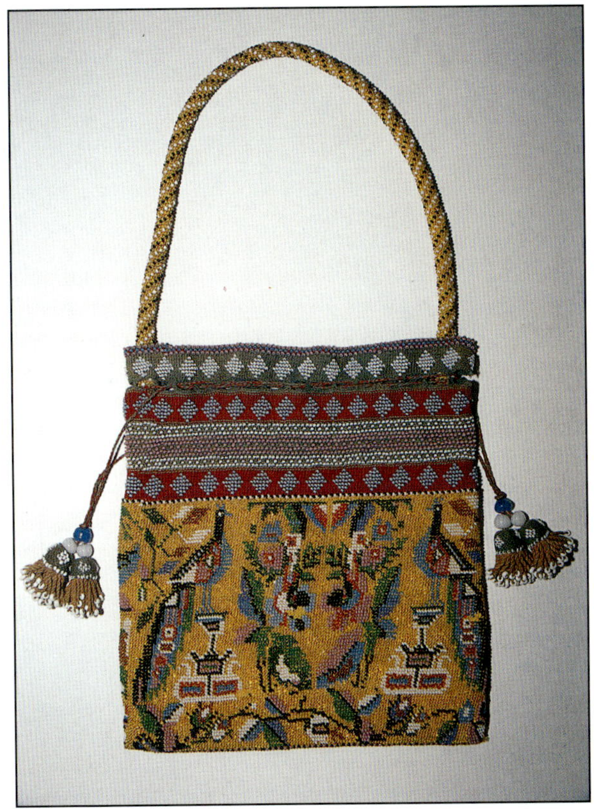

Turkey and other Eastern Mediterranean countries exported purses throughout the 19th century. The angular design, diamond pattern at the top, beaded rope handle, and the uniquely constructed beaded tassels, all identify this purse as Turkish/Eastern Mediterranean. Occasionally, Greek and Turkish beadwork is misidentified as American Indian beadwork because of the angularity of their designs. 7.5 x 7.5 in. *Collection of Paula Higgins.* $450-550.

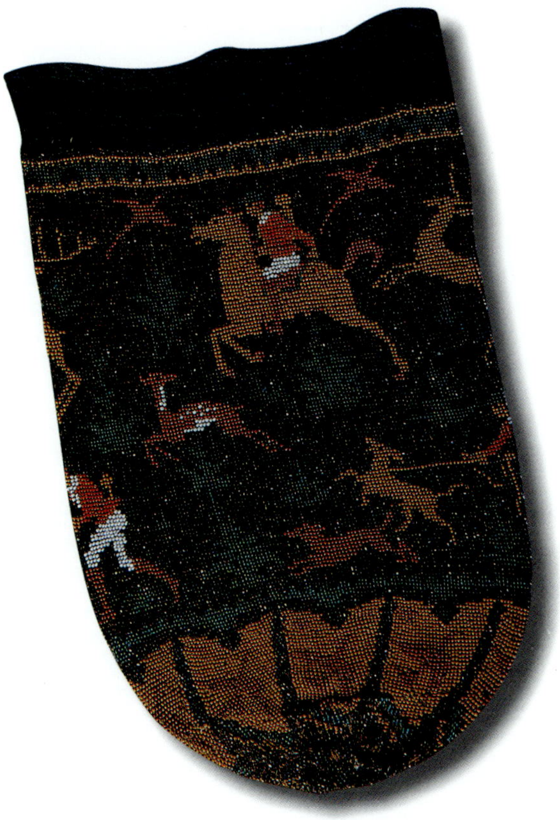

In this hunt scene, red jackets and riding boots present a more sophisticated impression than the early 19th century hunt scenes. Bead knitted in size 16/0-18/0 beads, this is an uncommon design. Black faceted beads create a glistening background. 12.5 x 6.5 in. *Collection of Terri Lykins.* $600-700.

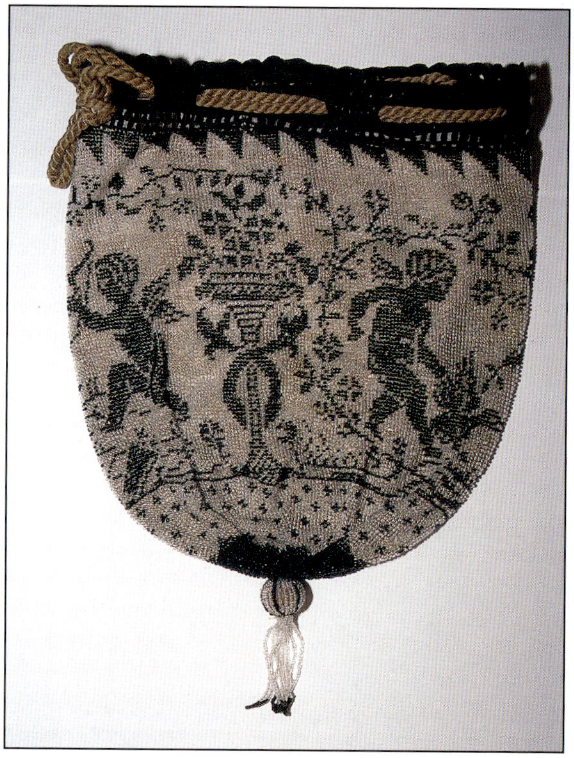

A late 19th century, bead knitted purse featuring cherubs gamboling about in various forms of play. This design circles the purse. 9 x 6 in. *Collection of Paula Higgins.* $600-700.

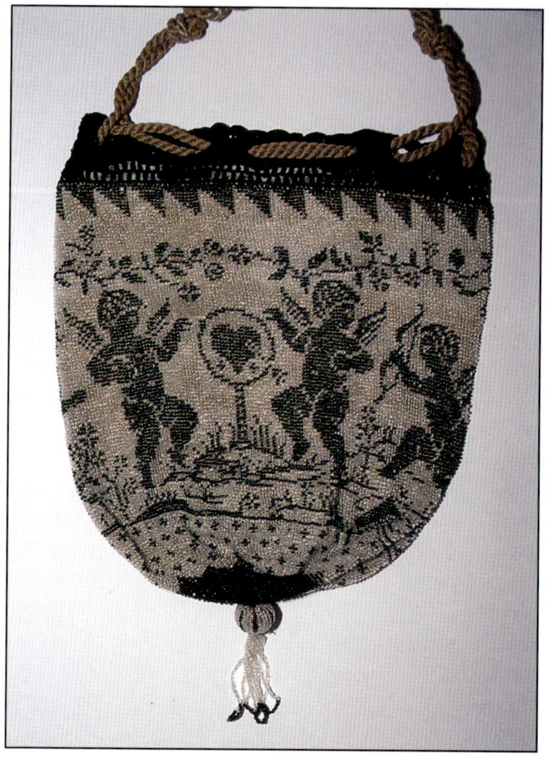

Another view of the cherub purse.

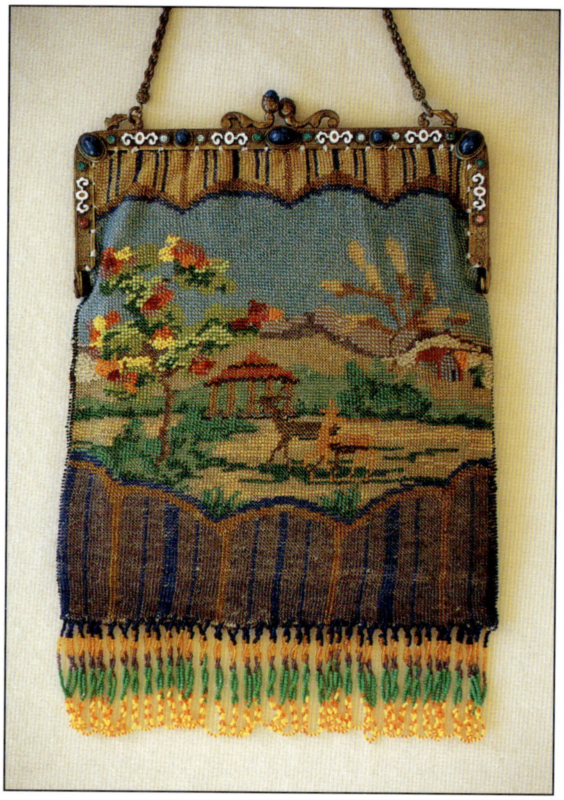

This colorful scenic purse has a picture frame quality because it is outlined in blue and brown beads. Bead knitted with fine beads, it has a jeweled and enameled frame. 9 x 6.5 in. *Collection of Linda Marshall.* $650-750.

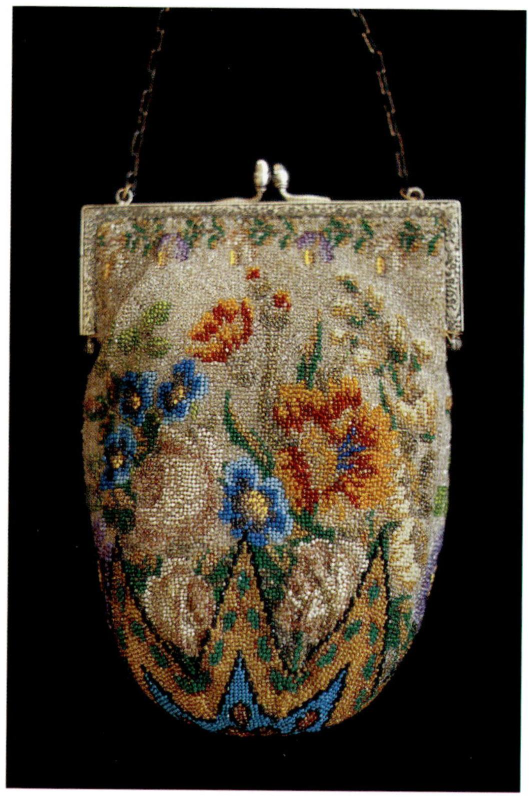

The colors of blue and orange are used effectively on this beaded floral. It is bead knitted with fine beads. 8 x 6 in. *Collection of Linda Marshall.* $325-350.

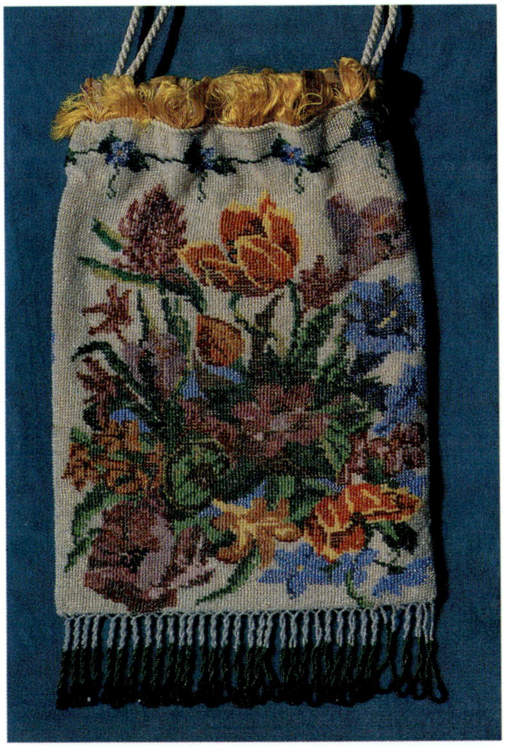

Another colorful bead knitted purse with a realistic floral design. 8.5 x 6 in. *Collection of Linda Marshall.* $350-375.

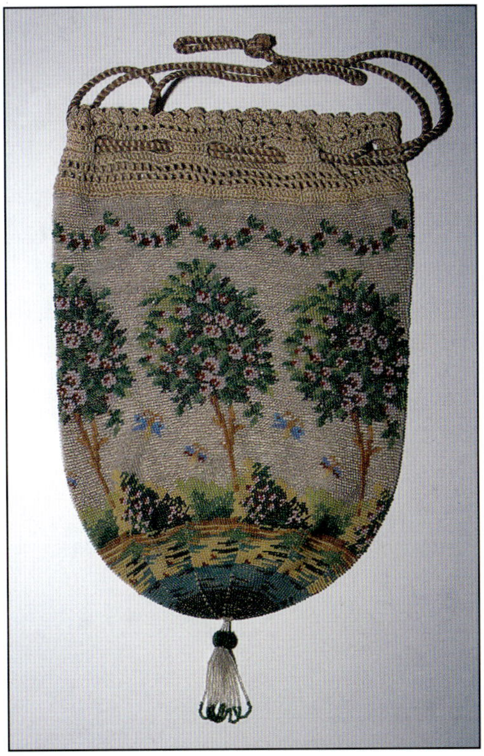

This is an unusual scenic purse, bead knitted with very fine beads. The elegant design of flowering trees is repeated around the purse. 10.5 x 6.5 in. *Collection of Paula Higgins.* $600-650.

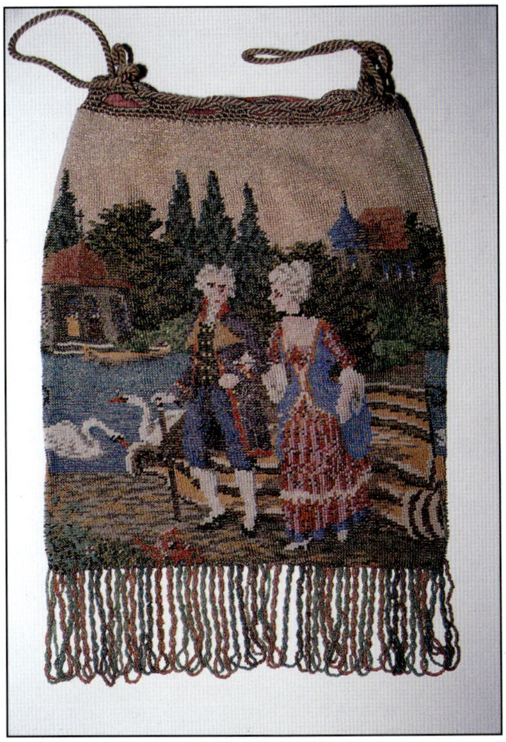

Purses featuring 18th century courting scenes are among the most costly of beaded purses. This purse has considerable detail from the watering can in the foreground, to the 18th century clothing. The whole design is balanced and in proper perspective. 11 x 8 in. *Collection of Paula Higgins.* $2,000-2,500.

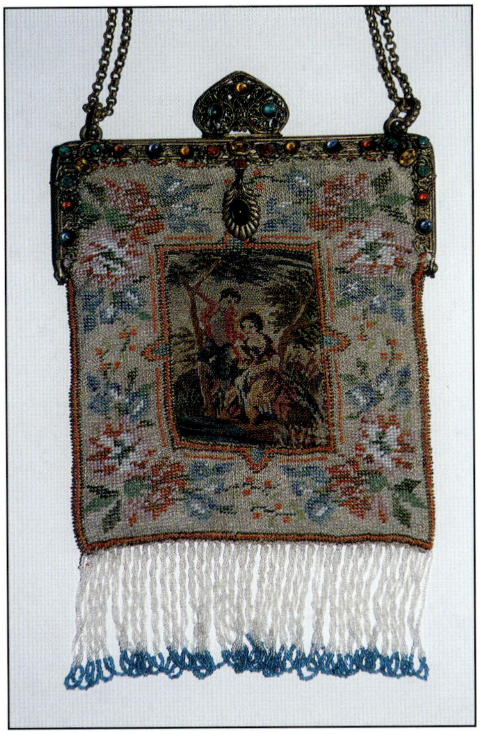

Bead knitted purses, with petit point inserts, are another favorite among collectors. The beaded floral border acts as a picture frame for the petit point courting scene. The heavily jeweled frame with the standing clasp adds color and value to the purse. Purses with petit point inserts on both sides are especially desirable. 9 x 5.5 in. *Collection of Paula Higgins.* $1,000-1,250.

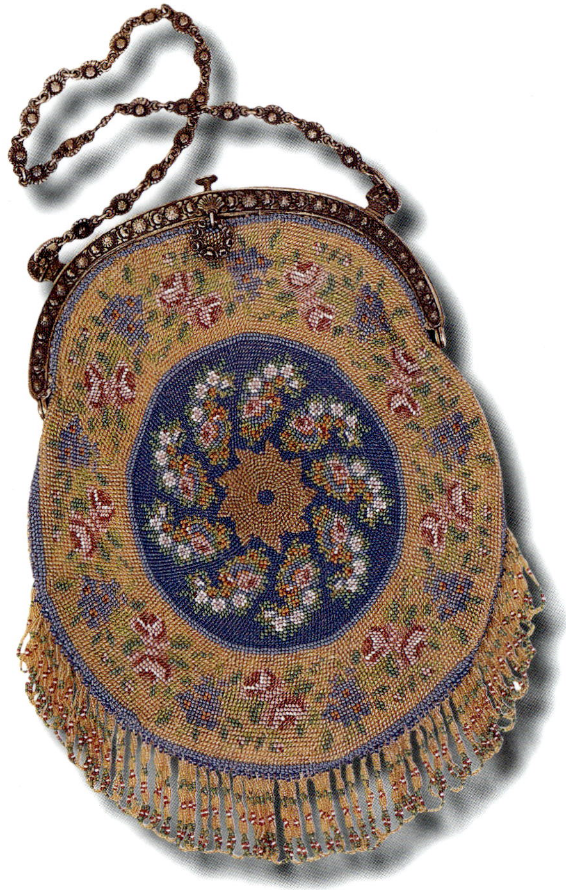

This very beautiful piecrust purse dates to the late 19th or early 20th century. The color combination of gold and blue beads is very rich, elegant, and unusual. 10.5 x 7.25 in. *Collection of Melissa Overdorf.* $750-800.

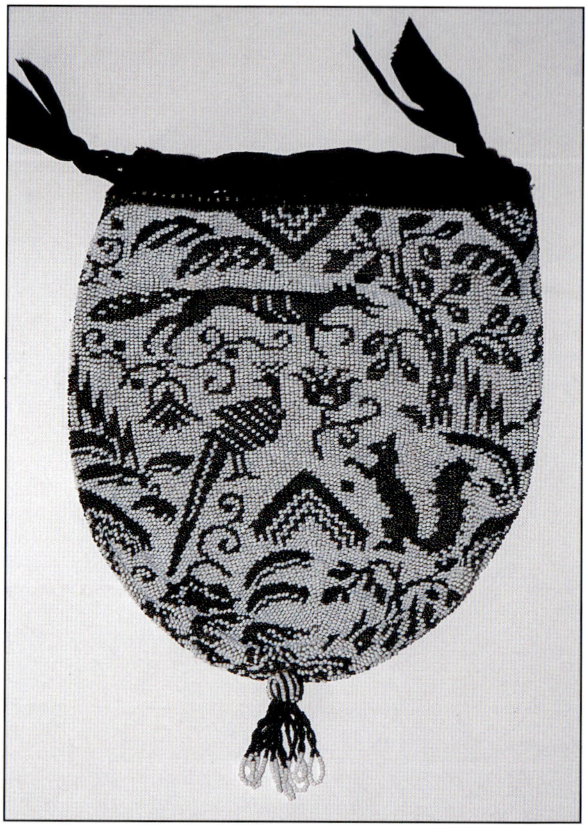

A fox, squirrel, and pheasant design decorate this black and white beaded reticule. Leaves and random geometric designs create an eclectic impression. 9 x 7.5 in. *Collection of Paula Higgins.* $325-350.

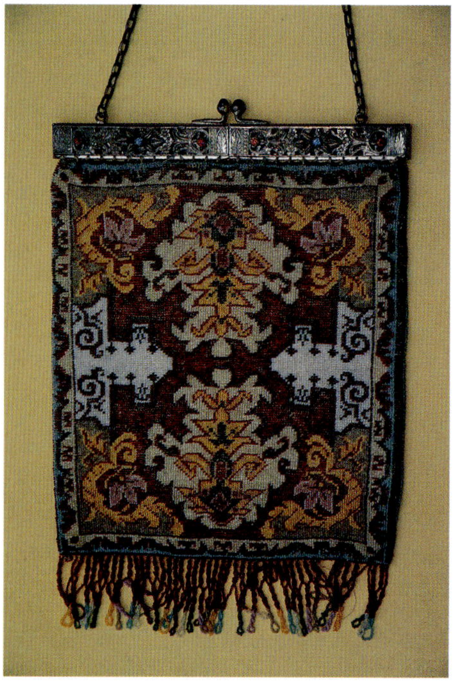

Geometric beaded purses are seldom as striking as this one, with its deep red background. It is mounted on a jeweled, silver box frame. 10 x 7 in. *Collection of Linda Marshall.* $600-700.

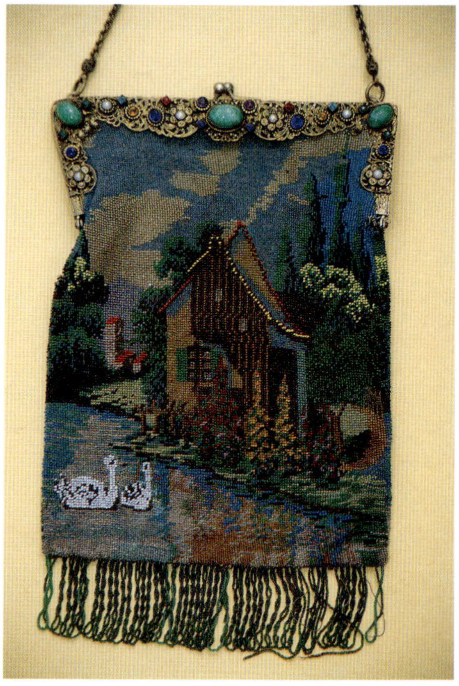

A small house on a pond, with swans in the foreground, makes for a tranquil purse design. It is bead knitted with very fine beads and mounted on a beautiful jeweled frame. 9.5 x 7 in. *Collection of Linda Marshall.* $1,500-1,800.

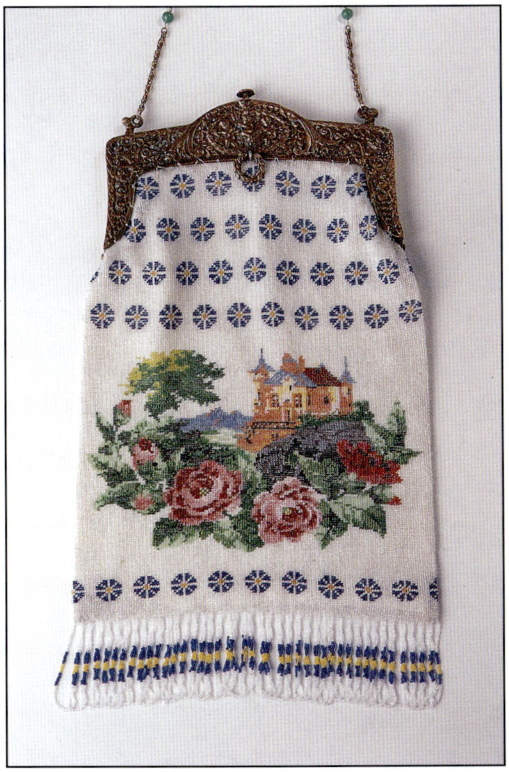

The pure white background on this purse is lovely and it shows off the castle and rose design very effectively. Bead knitted with very fine beads, this purse would appeal to most collectors. 13 x 8 in. *Collection of Kim Stonecipher.* $1,000-1,200.

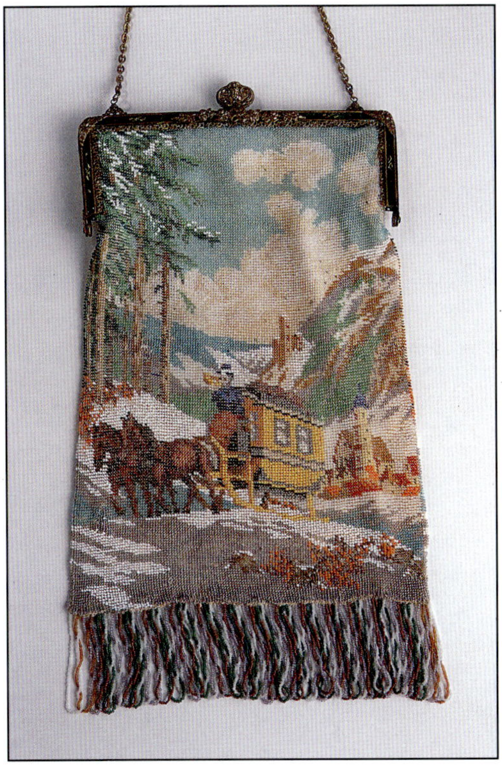

This exceptional transportation scenic has snow covered mountains, trees, a town in the distance, and a 19th century carriage with horses. The driver even has a blanket covering his legs. There is also a nice use of perspective in this finely beaded scenic. Transportation purse designs are among the most desirable of all scenic beaded purses. 12 x 7 in. *Collection of Kim Stonecipher.* $2,000-2,500.

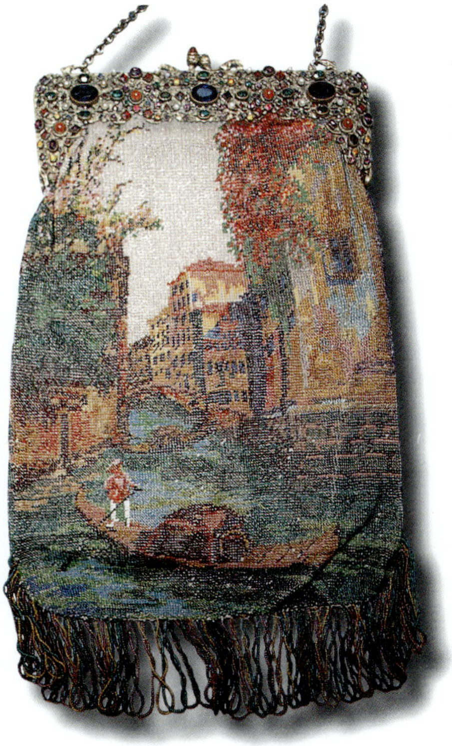

Venetian scenics, like this one, bring some of the highest prices in the purse world and for obvious reasons. Beautifully bead knitted, with the extremely fine beads, the scene portrays historic buildings and a Venetian canal in detail. The covered gondola on this purse dates to the 19th century. It wasn't until the 20th century that gondolas were made open to the air. An extraordinary jeweled frame also adds to the value of the purse. 11 x 7.5 in. *Collection of Shara Stewart.* Rare.

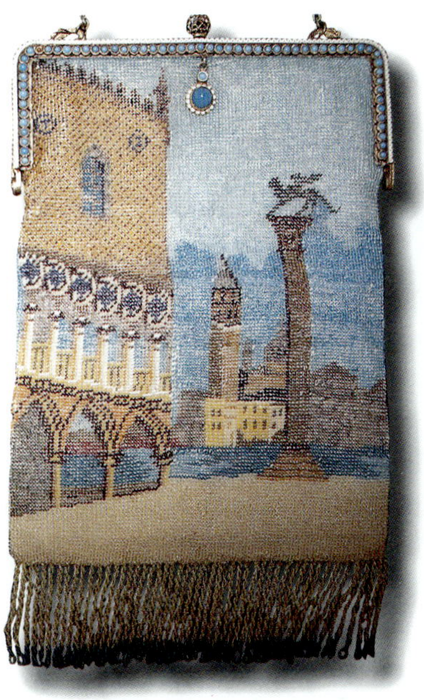

Another view of Venice, looking out to Saint Mark's basin. The Lion of Venice sits atop a pillar on the right and the Dogés Palace is on the left. Beautifully bead knitted, it is mounted on a frame set with turquoise stones. It is believed that Venetian scenic purses were made in Venice from glass beads produced by the glass factories in nearby Murano. 11 x 6 in. *Collection of Shara Stewart.* Rare.

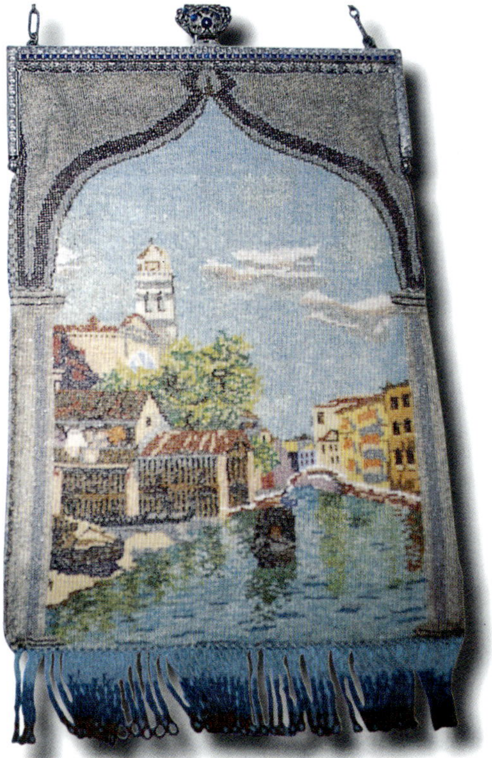

A beautifully conceived design featuring a view of the Grand Canal in Venice. The design is framed by a Gothic arch. 12 x 8 in. *Collection of Shara Stewart.* Rare.

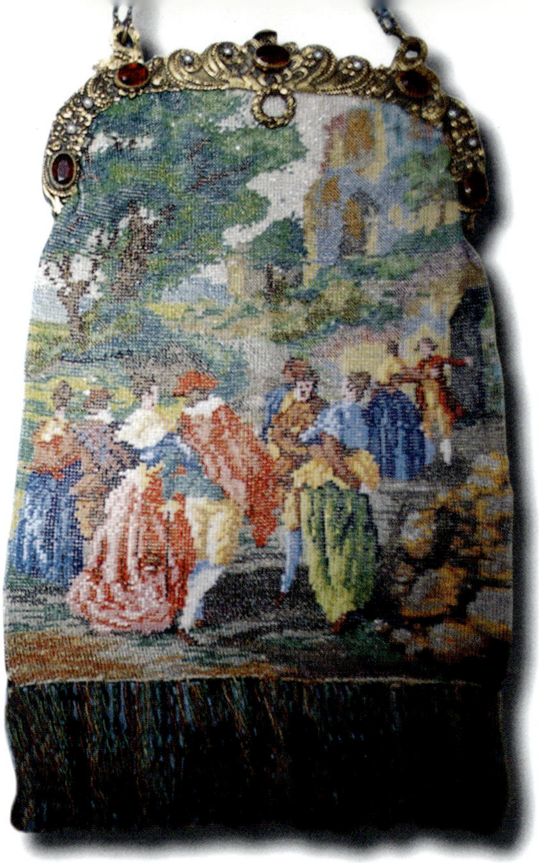

Eighteenth century figural purses of this quality, are highly valued by purse collectors. This scene has a painting like quality, which is difficult to convey in beadwork. The color scheme is especially lovely and the jeweled frame adds to the overall effect. Framing purses with this much color and detail can be challenging because the goal is to enhance the design and not to detract from it. 12 x 7 in. *Collection of Shara Stewart.* Very rare.

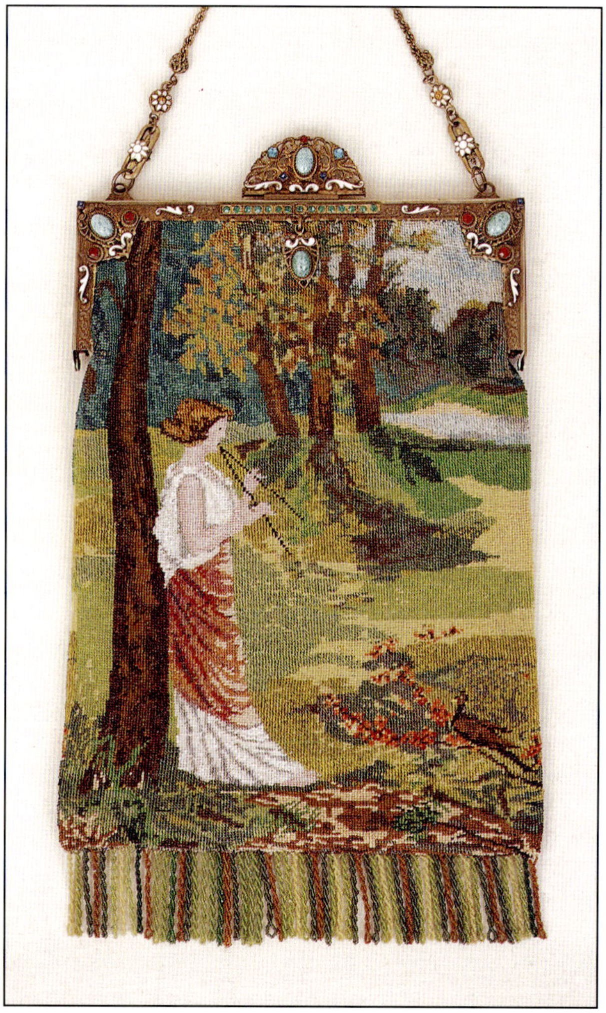

This extraordinary purse also has a painting like quality. A woman, draped in Grecian style clothing, is seen playing an Aulos (a type of ancient flute) in a forest setting. The graceful human form, colors, use of perspective, shadowing, and the realistic rendering of a natural setting create an exceptional piece of beadwork. The jeweled frame is a perfect match for this spectacular purse. 13.25 x 8 in. *Collection of Lori Blaser.* Very rare.

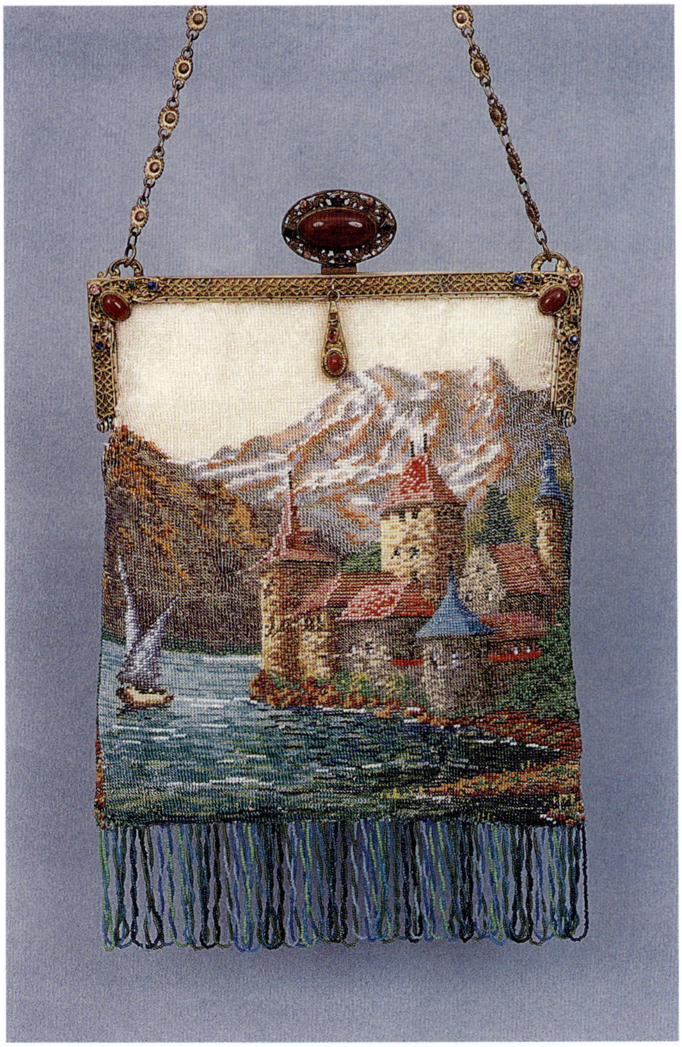

A castle scene, bead knitted with fine beads, has a beautiful color scheme, considerable detail, and a lovely jeweled frame set with cabochon stones. 12.5 x 8 in. *Collection of Lori Blaser.* $1,500-1,800.

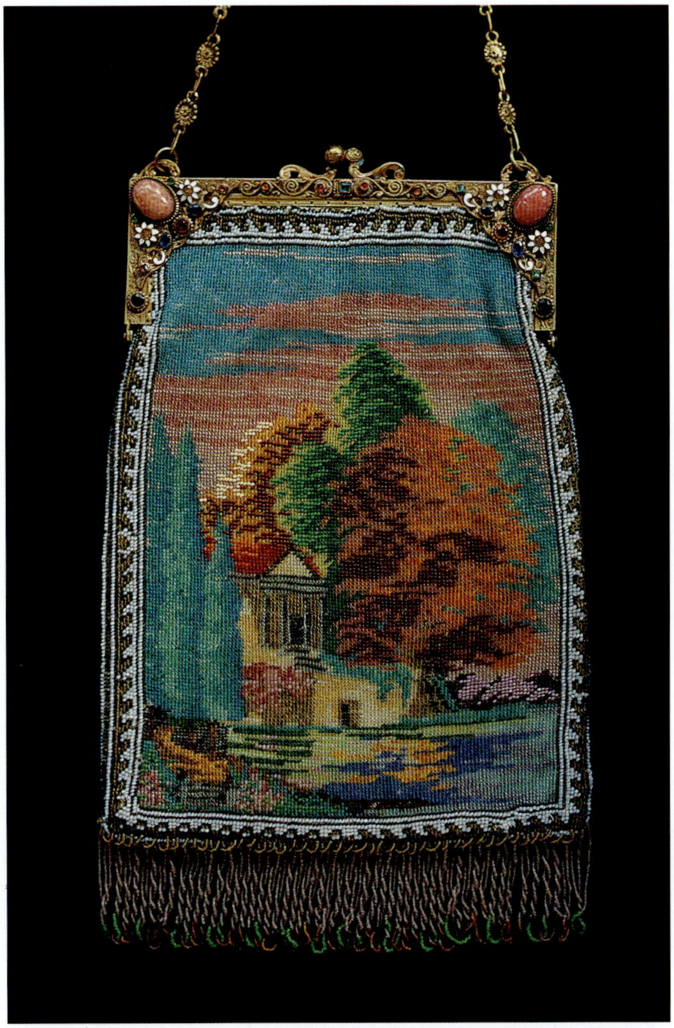

Rich colors set this scenic purse apart. A building on the left, surrounded by trees, sits on a lake. Bead knitted with fine beads, this purse is in excellent condition. The jeweled and enameled frame works perfectly with this purse design. 8 x 6.5 in.*Collection of Linda Marshall.* $1,500-1,800.

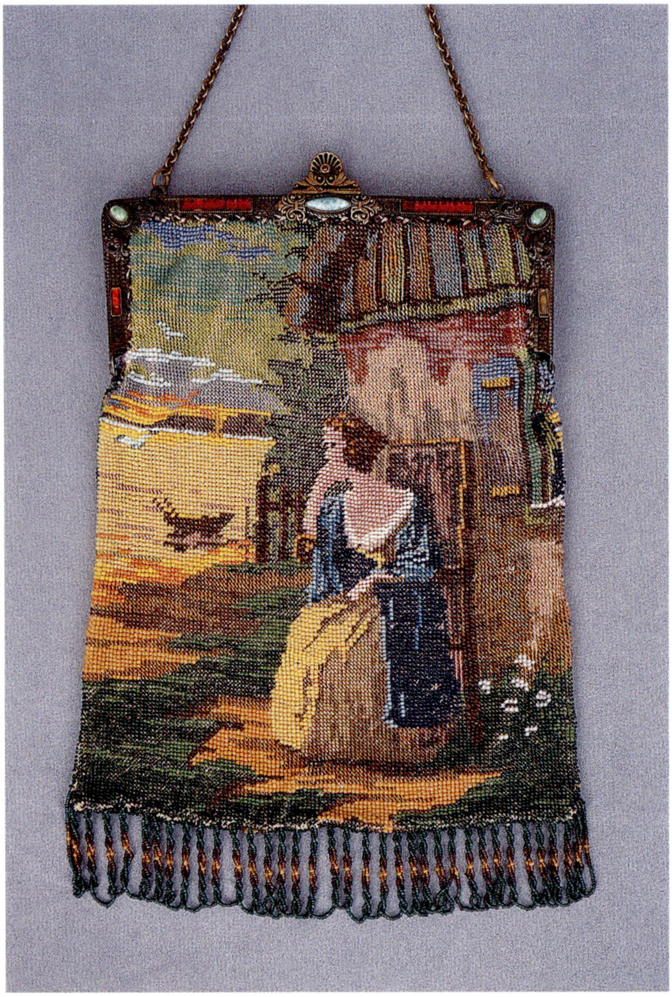

This figural is lovely. Again, perspective, figural proportion, and shading techniques elevate this beadwork to painting quality. This purse design is unusual and rare. 10.5 x 7.5 in. *Collection of Melissa Overdorf.* Rare.

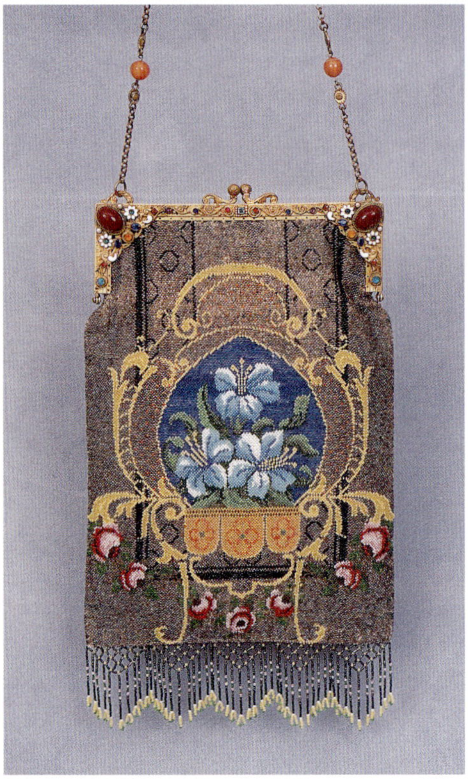

Bead embroidered purses can be ordinary, but not this one. The gold beaded scroll work enhances the colorful and balanced floral design. The fringe is in excellent condition. Red stones in the jeweled and enameled frame match the red flowers on the purse. 14 x 8 in. *Collection of Lori Blaser.* $650-750.

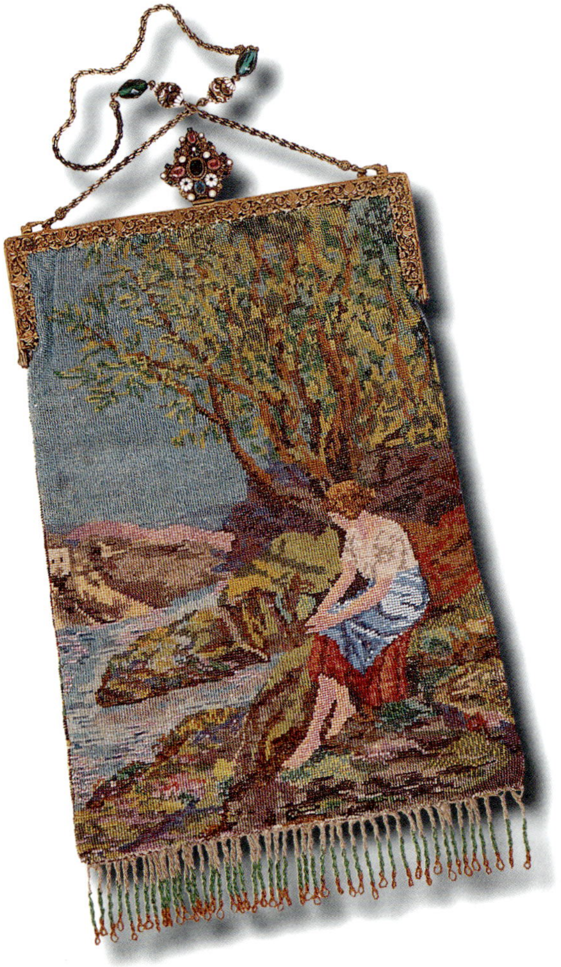

This scenic of a lady by a brook is exceptional. In this case, beadwork has been elevated to an art form. The human form is difficult to bead in any case, but especially in this languid pose. A stream, rocks, and trees are executed to perfection, creating a beautiful backdrop. Bead knitted with very fine beads, this purse would be a prize in any collection. 15 x 8.5 in. *Collection of Melissa Overdorf.* Rare.

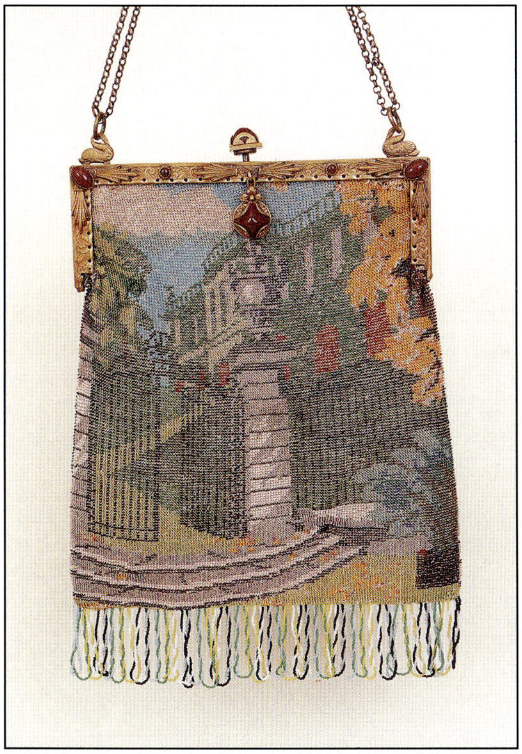

Behind the black iron gates, sits a mansion on top of a hill. Bead knitted with fine beads, the jeweled frame compliments the colors in the purse.10 x 7.25 in. *Collection of Lori Blaser.* $1,800-2,000.

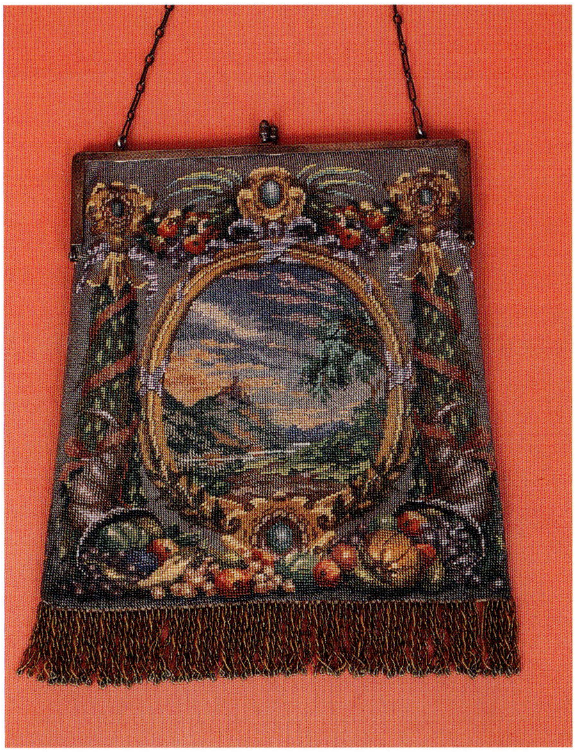

This cartouche scenic is wonderful because of the vegetable and fruit filled cornucopias on the bottom. Cornucopias have been beaded on purses for 200 years, but these are the finest representations anyone is ever likely to see. The colors are rich and the effect is lush. 10.25 x 8 in. *Collection of Lori Blaser.* $1,500-2,000.

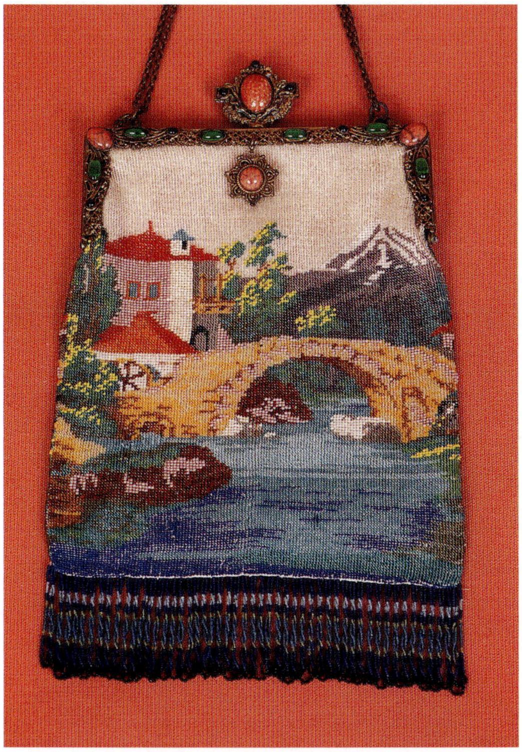

The European countryside provided inspiration for many beaded purse designs. This European scenic has a vibrant color scheme and a jeweled frame with a stand-up clasp. The stone bridge and blue river are prominent features in this design. 11.5 x 7 in. *Collection of Lori Blaser.* $1,500-2,000.

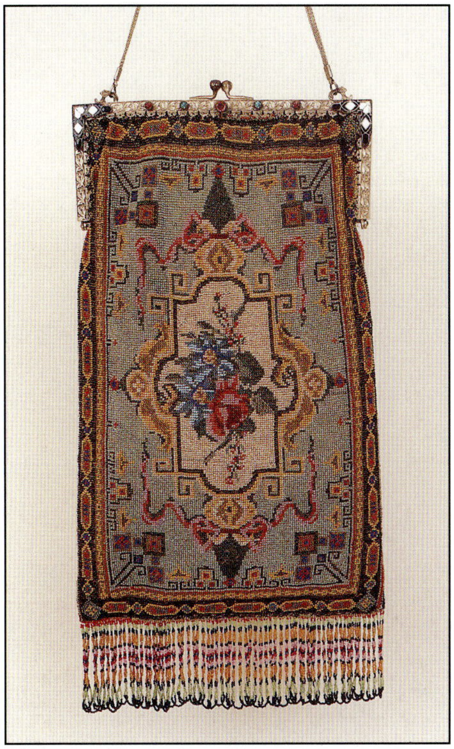

A combination of geometric and floral designs creates a visually striking purse. A rarely seen shade of green was used to bead the background. The colorful twisted, interlocking fringe is the perfect finishing touch. 14 x 7.75 in. *Collection of Lori Blaser.* $750-850.

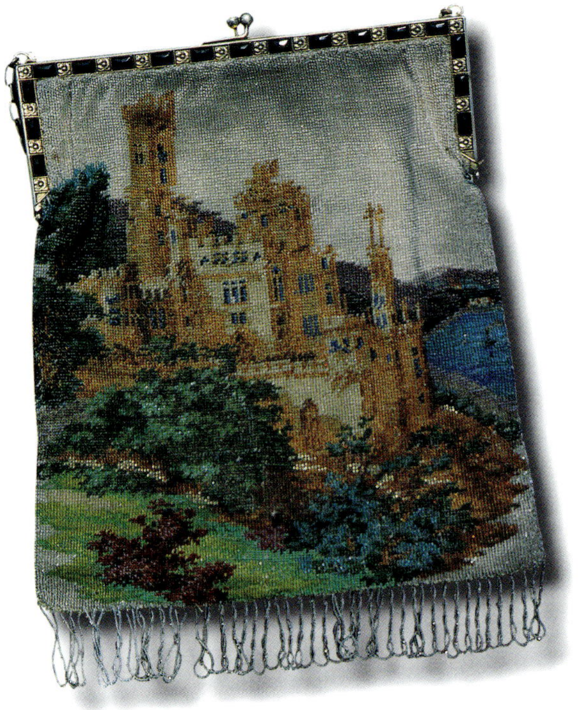

A castle with crenellated battlements sits on the side of a hill, next to a lake. This purse is bead knitted with fine beads and mounted on an jeweled frame. 11 x 9 in. *Collection of Linda Marshall.* $1,500-1,800.

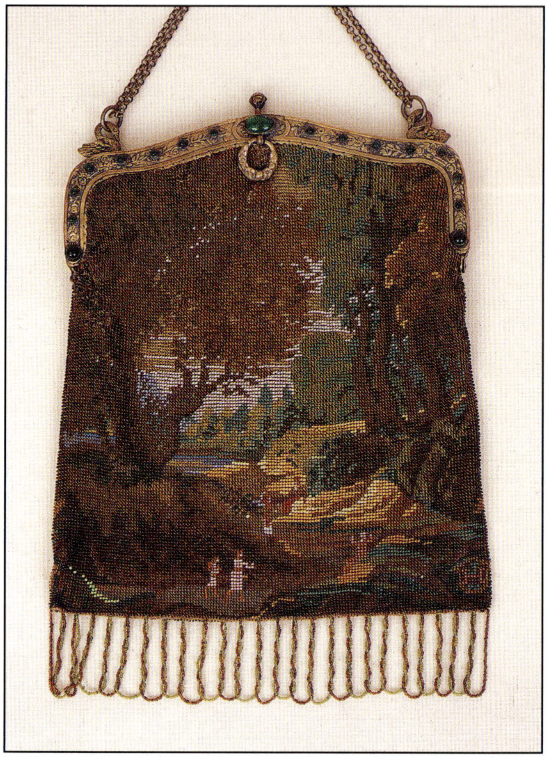

Brown and green beads have never been used to such beautiful effect as on this purse. A woodlands scene, with sinuous trees and a winding road, is an unusual purse subject. The scene is reminiscent of the Hudson River school of painting, which celebrated man's relationship with America's pastoral surroundings. The initials JNH are beaded in the lower right hand corner. 12.25 x 8.75 in. *Collection of Melissa Overdorf.* Rare.

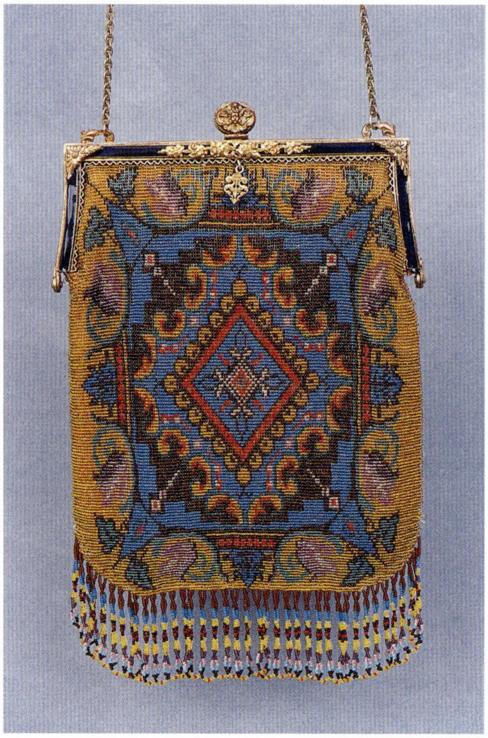

Many purse collectors prefer not to buy loomed purses because of possible inherent structural problems. But this is a glass beaded loomed purse which should appeal to everyone. The gold and blue geometric design is made even more beautiful by the gorgeous gold and blue enameled frame. 11 x 7 in. *Collection of Lori Blaser.* $700-750.

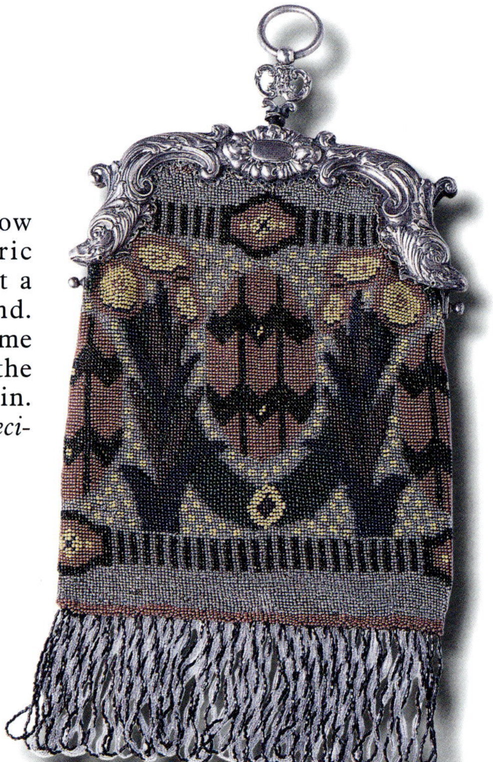

Stylized pots of yellow flowers and geometric shapes are set against a silver-gray background. The scrolling silver frame works perfectly with the color scheme. 11 x 8 in. *Collection of Kim Stonecipher.* $450-600.

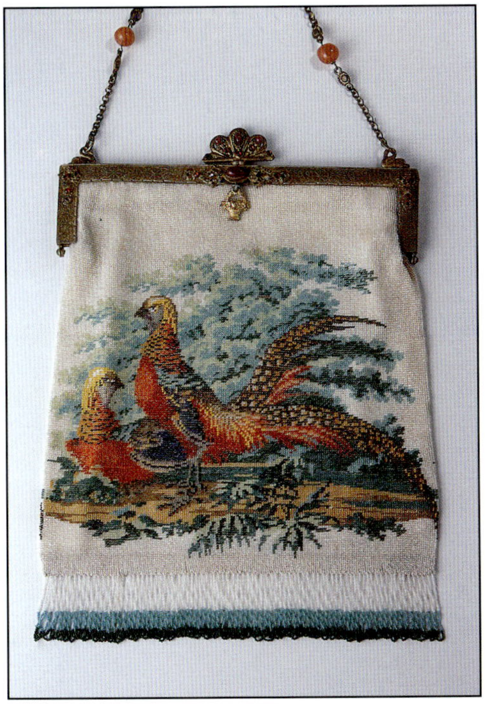

This purse has one of the most beautiful bird designs ever beaded. Two pheasants, in all their colorful glory, are set against a predominantly white background. The realism of the bird design is also impressive. 11 x 9 in. *Collection of Kim Stonecipher.* $1,400-1,600.

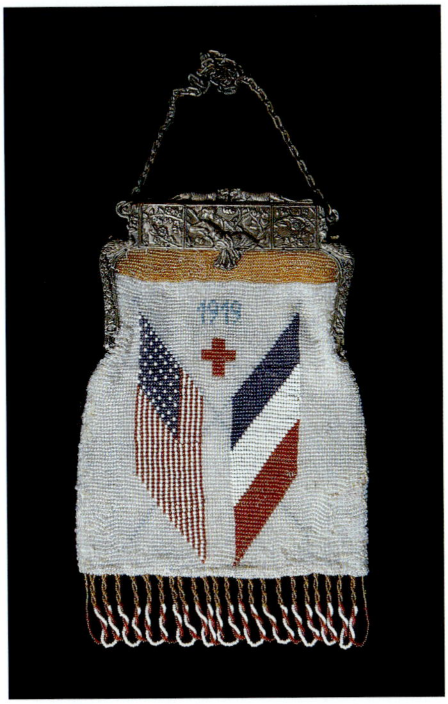

Purses with historical significance are always worth investing in. This beaded bag features the date "1919" and the American and French flags. In 1919, the League of Nations was established as a result of the Paris Peace Conference. France and America were two of the founding members. It is likely that this purse design commemorates that event. On the reverse side is a house with two eagles on the roof. The ornate Art Nouveau frame is original to the purse. 10.5 x 6.5 in. *Collection of Terri Lykins.* Rare.

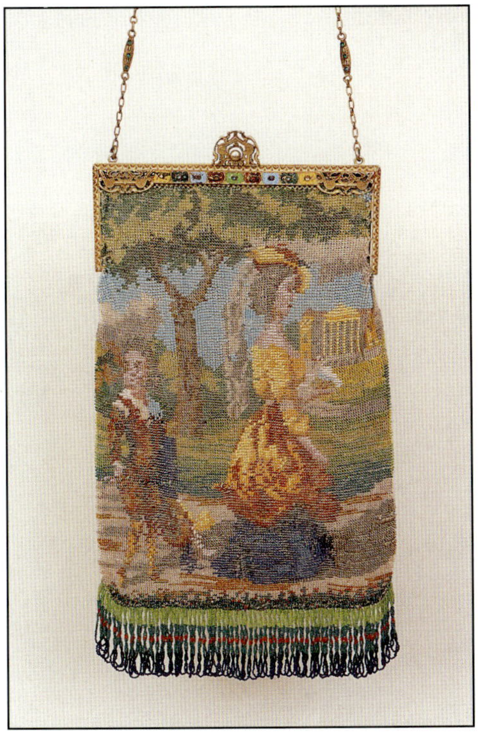

This whimsical figural has an Alice in Wonderland quality because the figures are not in proportion. But that is part of its undeniable charm. This design may represent a mother and her son. 13.5 x 7.5 in. *Collection of Melissa Overdorf.* $2,000-2,500.

Most purse collectors have at least one swag beaded purse in their collection. Typically beaded in only one color, they were a perfect accessory for beaded evening dresses. This silver beaded example, mounted on a silver filigreed frame, is a fine example. 9 x 4 in. *Collection of Kim Stonecipher.* $275-450.

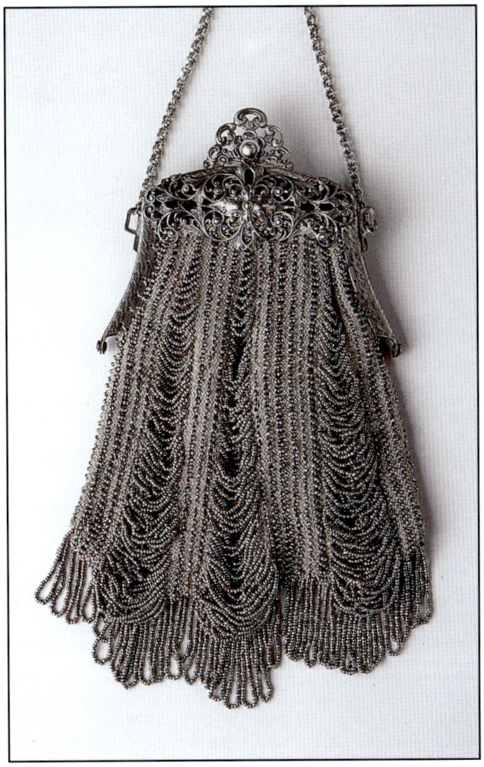

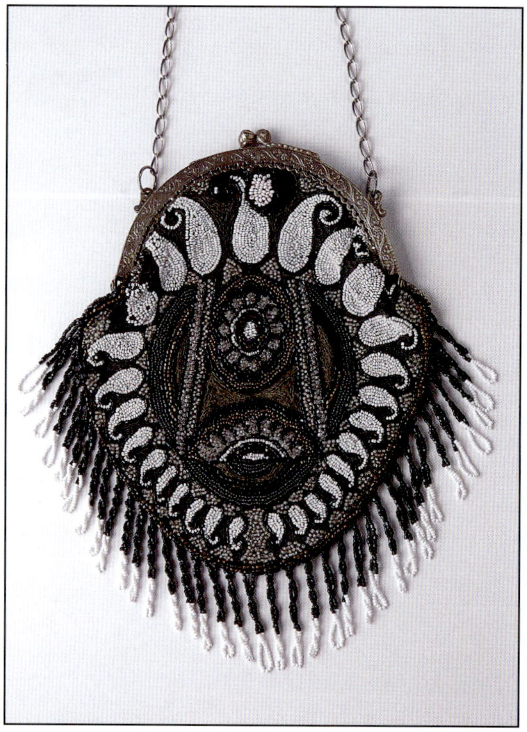

A bold design in black and white is meant to be noticed. This purse is bead embroidered and finished with a matching fringe. 9 x 8 in. *Collection of Kim Stonecipher.* $375-400.

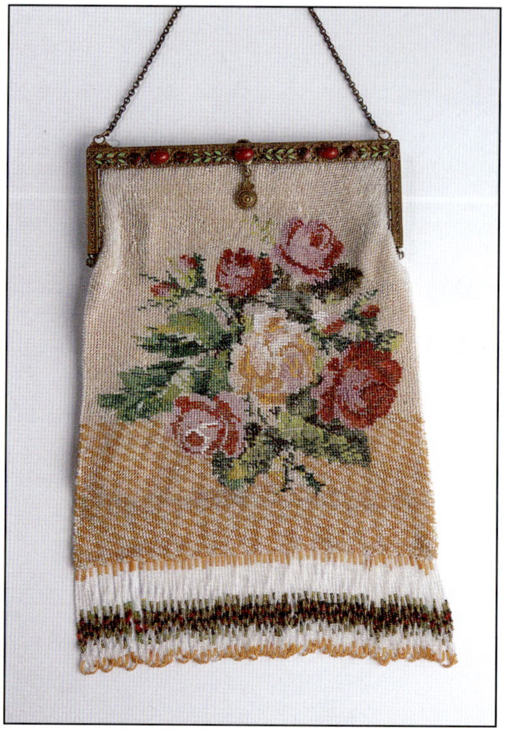

Gold and red roses are set against a checkerboard and cream background to great effect. A thick fringe, and an enameled and jeweled frame add value to the purse. 12 x 8 in. *Collection of Kim Stonecipher.* $600-700.

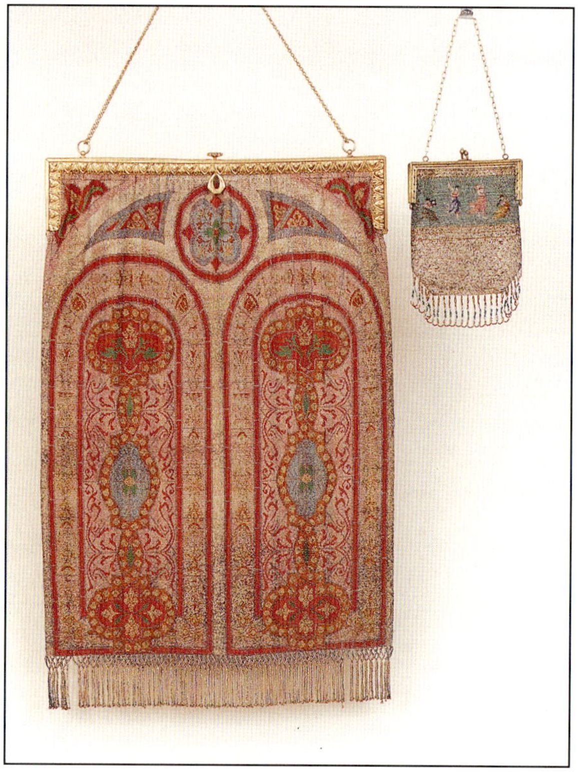

This beautiful, colored cut steel purse has the fine detail of a stained glass window. Loomed with fine beads, it is in remarkable condition considering its extremely large size. Because it is so large, it may have been made for advertising purposes. The smaller cut steel purse to the right is decorated with Greek mythological dancing figures. Left: 22 x 14 in. Right: 7 x 4.5 in. *Collection of Melissa Overdorf.* Left: Rare. Right: $400-450.

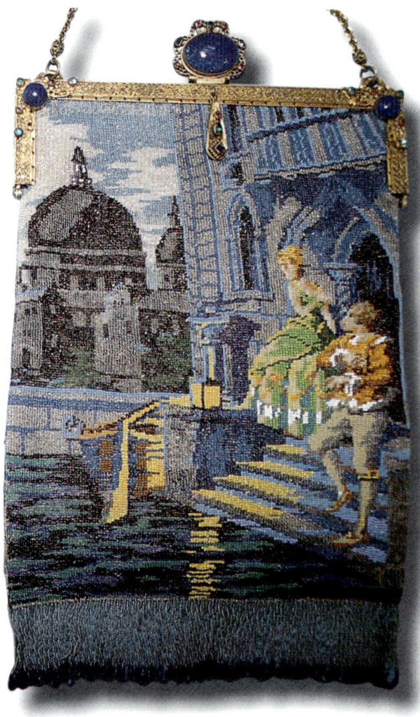

An 18th century couple are standing on the steps of a Venetian building, which end at the water's edge. This is certainly a rare and unusual Venetian scenic, beaded mostly in blues, grays, and black. A frame set with blue cabochon stones matches the colors of the purse. 12 x 8 in. *Collection of Shara Stewart.* Rare.

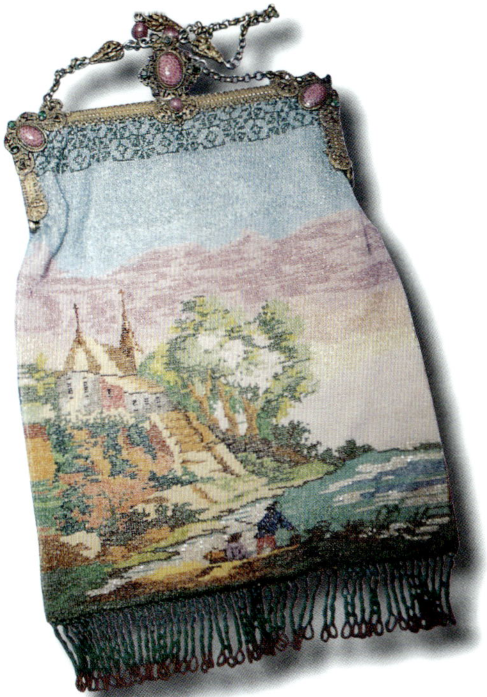

This imaginative European scenic shows steps leading up to a church from the water's edge. The purse is bead knitted with very fine beads. 7 x 12 in. *Collection of Shara Stewart.* $2,500-3,000.

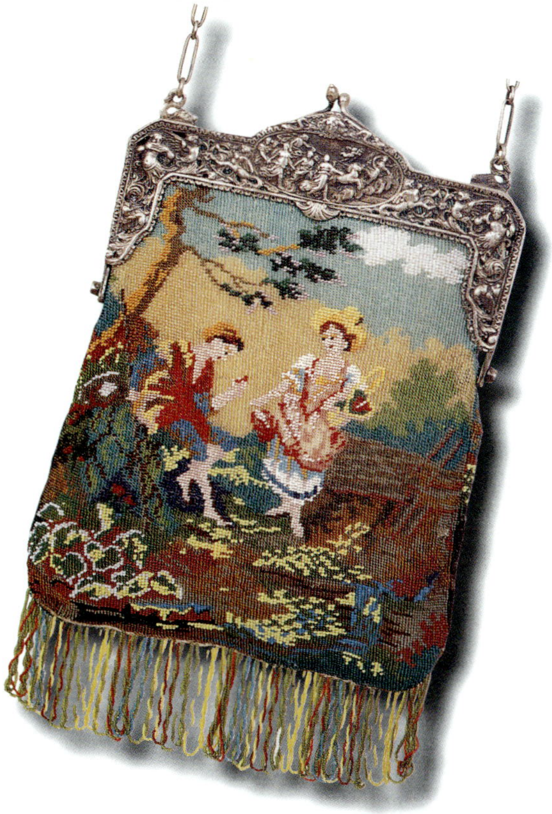

A classic, 18th century, pastoral courting scene is bead knitted in vibrant colors. Many 18th century pastoral courting scenes took their inspiration from the paintings of Boucher, Watteau, and Fragonard. The figural frame is made from 800 silver. 11.5 x 7 in. *Collection of Lori Blaser.* $2,000-2,500.

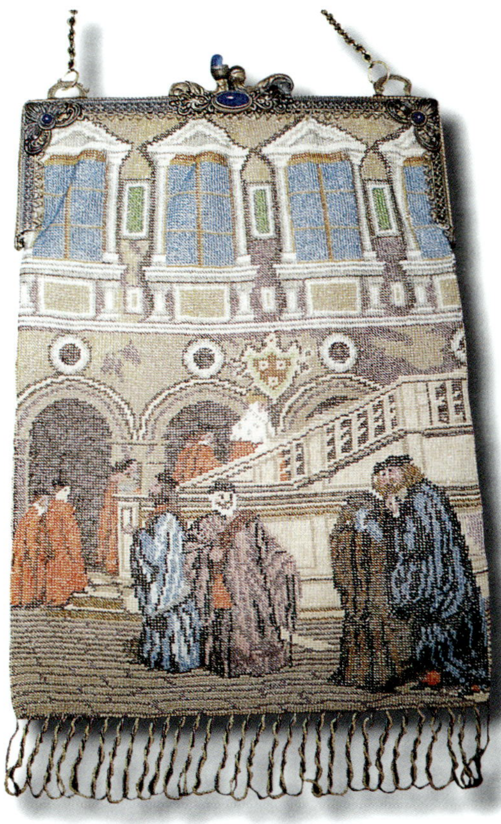

Purse designs don't come much rarer than this. Venetian men congregate at the steps of what may be the Dogés Palace or the Biblioteca. Two of the men even appear to be masked. Masks were used during the regattas and the carnival. But they were also used when people wished to be anonymous, for example while gambling at the Ridotto. It is even said that members of the church occasionally wore masks when they did not want to be recognized. 12 x 7 in. *Collection of Shara Stewart.* Very rare.

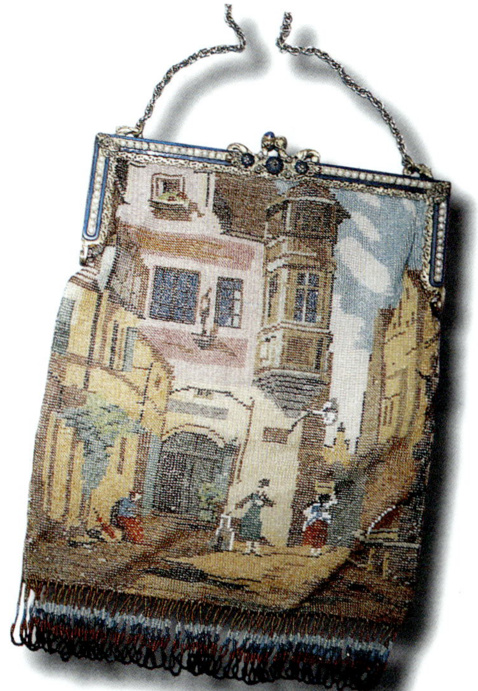

This very detailed European town scenic has a fountain at the far right, a woman with a basket on her head, and a turreted building. It is bead knitted with very fine beads. The frame is decorated with pearls and enamel work. 11 x 6.5 in. *Collection of Shara Stewart.* $3,000-3,500.

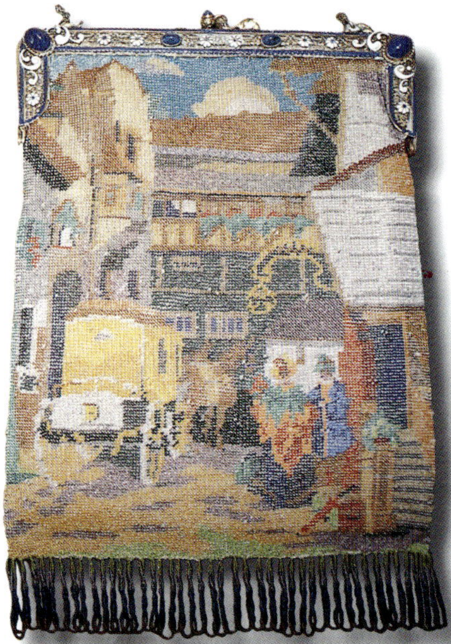

This purse also has a highly detailed design with buildings, people, and a horse and carriage. The carriage even has a trunk on the back. It is bead knitted with very fine beads. A jeweled and enameled frame is attached to the purse. 12 x 7 in. *Collection of Shara Stewart.* $3,000-3,500.

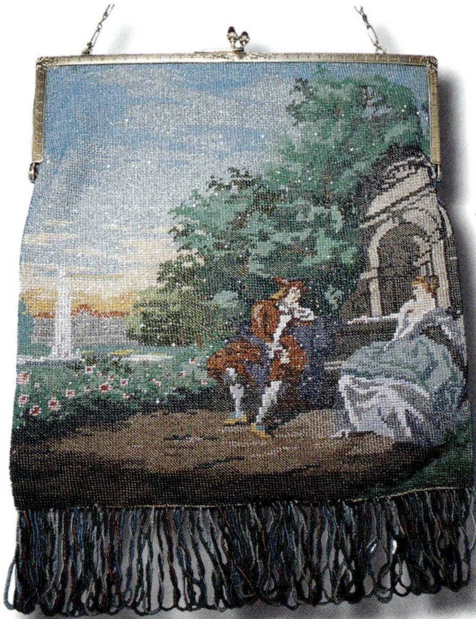

An uncommon 18th century courting scene with a fountain to the left, and a palace behind the fountain. It is bead knitted with very fine beads and mounted on a 14 karat gold frame. 9.5 x 7 in. *Collection of Shara Stewart.* $2,500-3,000.

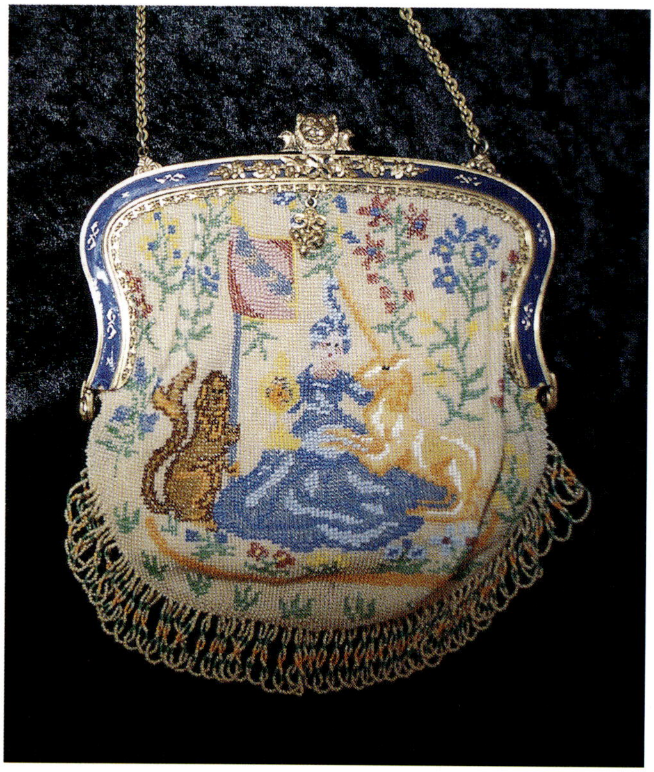

The Lady, Lion, and Unicorn design from the LeViste Family tapestries is most commonly seen on needleworked purses. The very beautiful purse pictured here, is beaded with this famous design. The stunning blue and gold enameled frame is a perfect match for the purse. 6.5 x 6 in. *Collection of Shara Stewart.* $1,800-2,000.

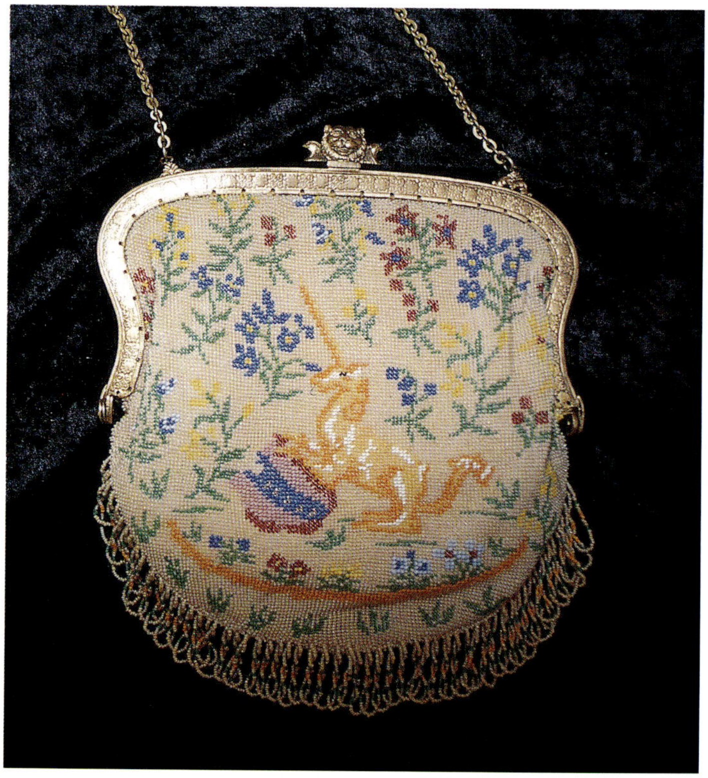

The reverse side of the purse.

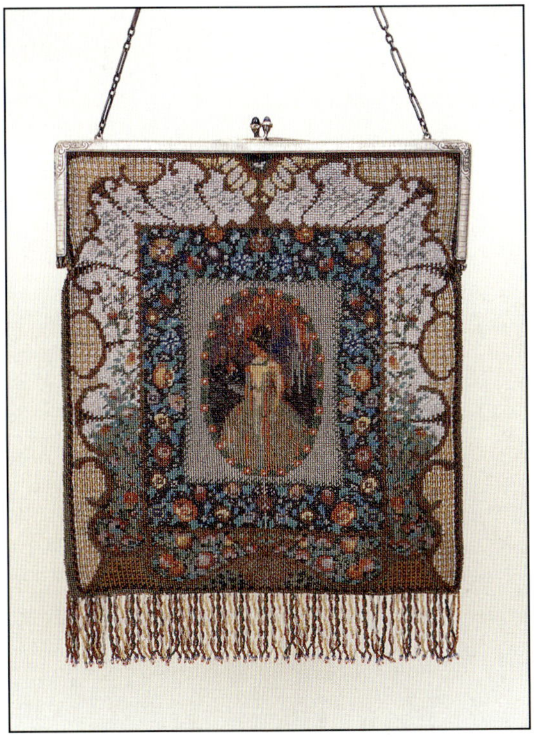

This remarkable beaded purse has a unique design, a rich color scheme, tiny beading, and beautiful floral borders framing the figure in the center. It is attached to a sterling silver frame. 9.5 x 7 in. *Collection of Lori Blaser.* $2,000-2,500.

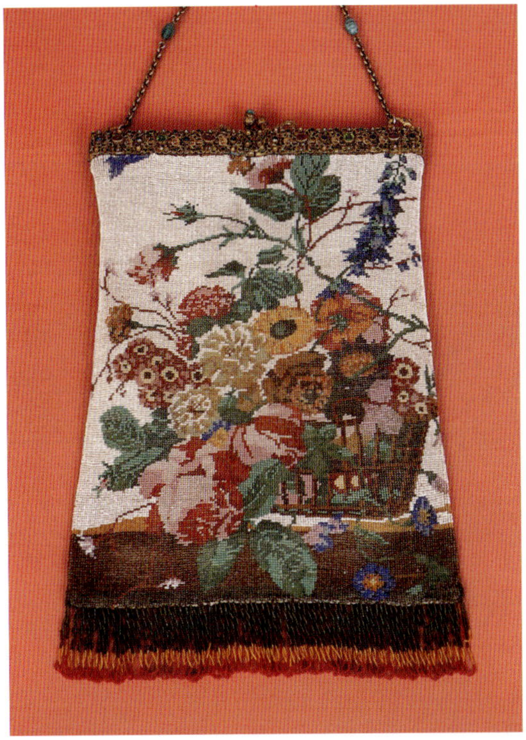

A beautiful design of a basket overflowing with flowers makes for a desirable purse. The color scheme adds to the beauty of this purse with its rich reds, oranges, browns and greens. The frame opens into a box shape. 13.5 x 8 in. *Collection of Lori Blaser.* $750-850.

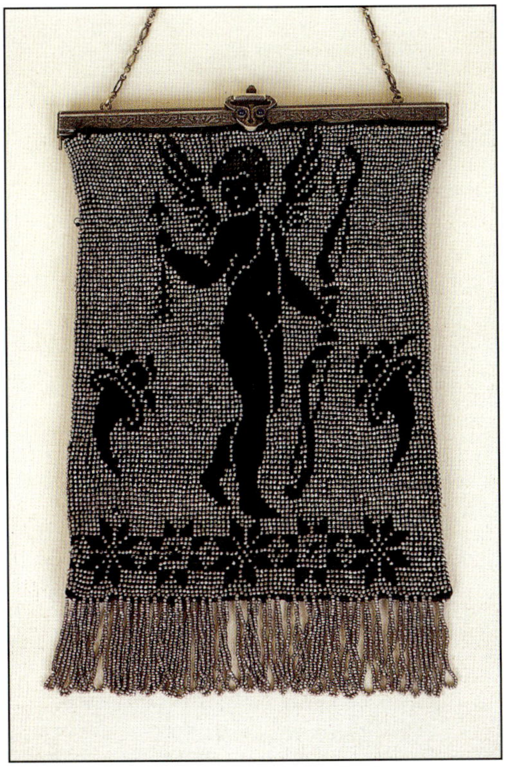

The silhouetted designs of an angel, cornucopias, and flowers were made by voiding the areas of beadwork. The remainder is beaded with cut steel beads. The frame opens into a square. 10.5 x 7 in. *Collection of Lori Blaser.* $450-600.

This knitted beaded purse is made with beads that are so tiny that it looks like petit point. The horizontal geometric designs are also very unusual, giving it the look of an ethnic or tribal weaving. The original gilt frame is made with a design of cherubs. 9.5 x 8 in. *Collection of Lori Blaser.* $750-800.

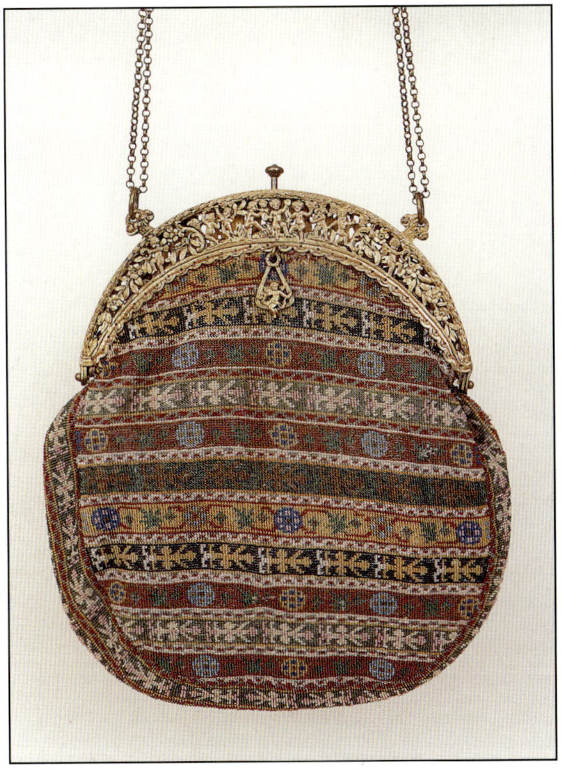

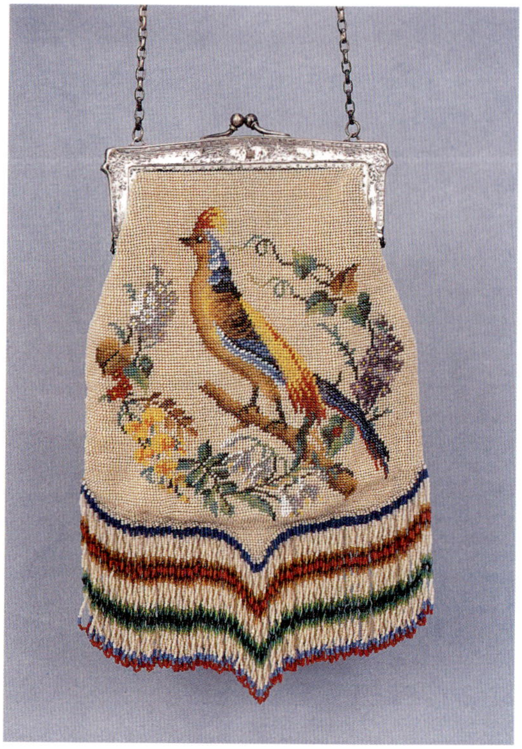

Purses this stunning would be a welcome addition to any collection. The bird is beaded in rich and vibrant colors, which are repeated on the thick curving fringe. Inside is a suede lining and the frame is silver plated. 12 x 8 in. *Collection of Lori Blaser.* $750-850.

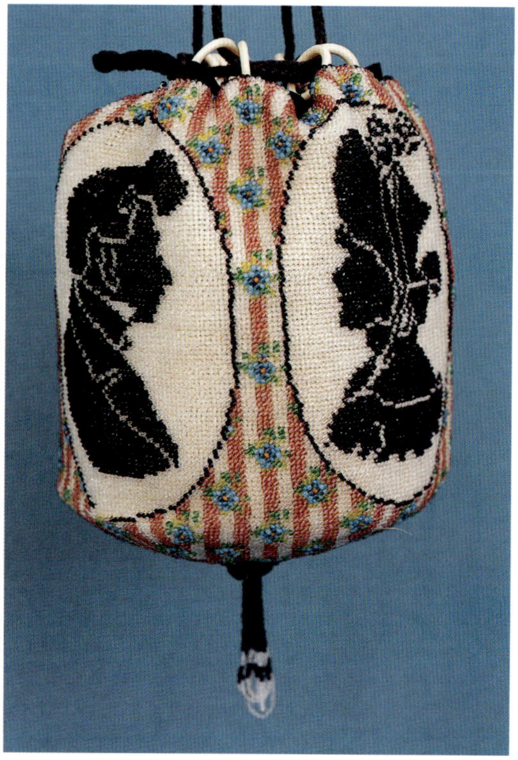

Silhouettes of a 19th century man and woman are set cartouche style against a floral and striped background. Another unusual feature of this purse is that cardboard has been placed between the lining and beadwork to create a rigid form. 9 x 5 in. *Collection of Lori Blaser.* $650-750.

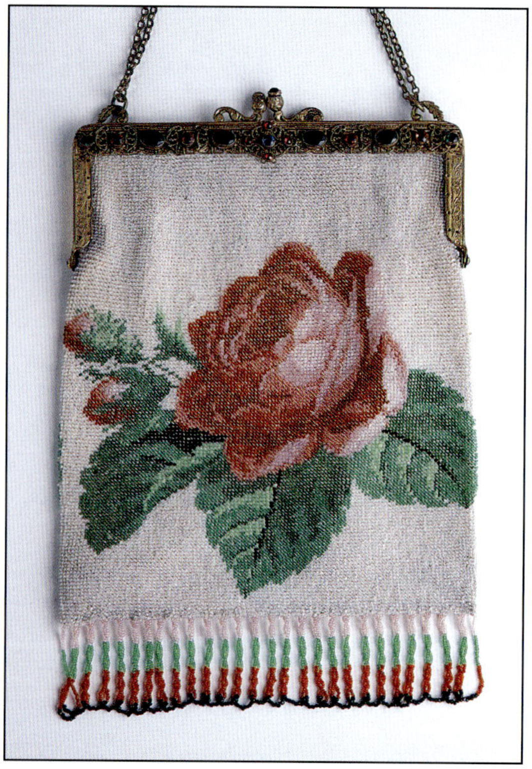

One large rose creates a beautiful impression on this purse. The coordinating jeweled frame and fringe complete this bead knitted purse. 10 x 7 in. *Collection of Kim Stonecipher.* $650-750.

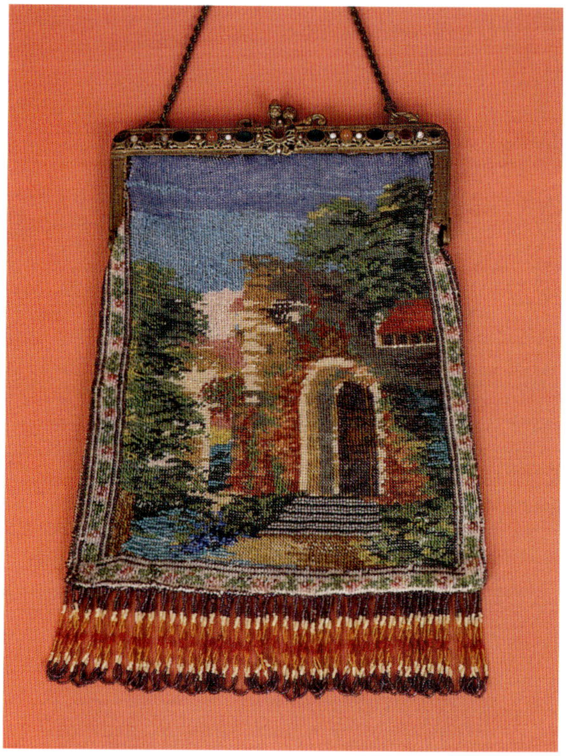

Beaded purse designs included subjects as simple as stairs and a doorway, beautifully bead knitted in jewel tones. The thick fringe and lovely jeweled frame add value to an already desirable purse. 11.5 x 7.5 in. *Collection of Lori Blaser.* $1,800-2,200.

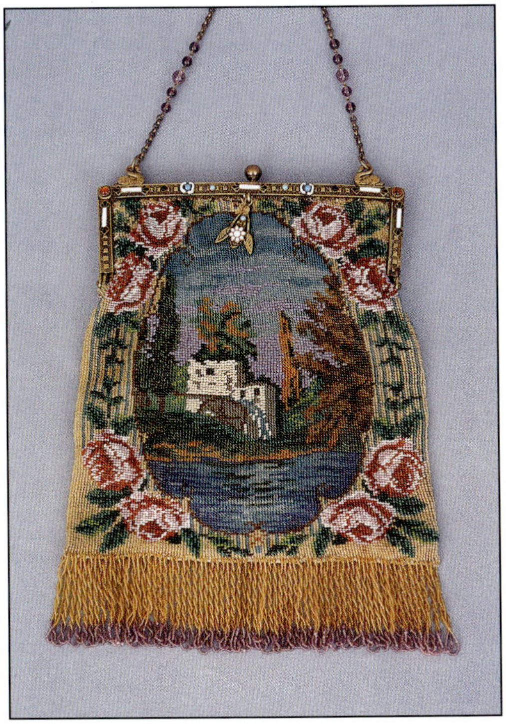

This villa scene was beaded inside a cartouche design, and then surrounded by roses. The thick fringe and jeweled frame are prized by purse collectors. 10.5 x 7.5 in. *Collection of Lori Blaser.* $1,200-1,500.

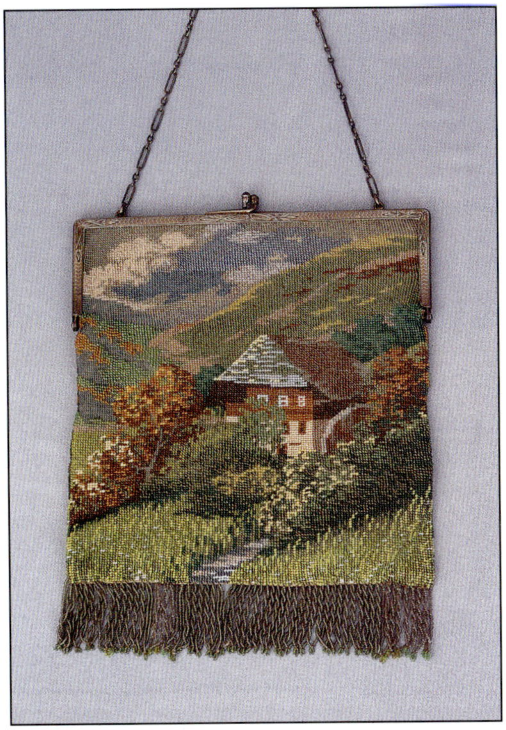

Some purse designs benefit from simpler sterling silver frames, like this one. The mountain chalet scene is beautifully designed and beaded, giving the impression of an oil painting. 9 x 7 in. *Collection of Lori Blaser.* $1,800-2,200.

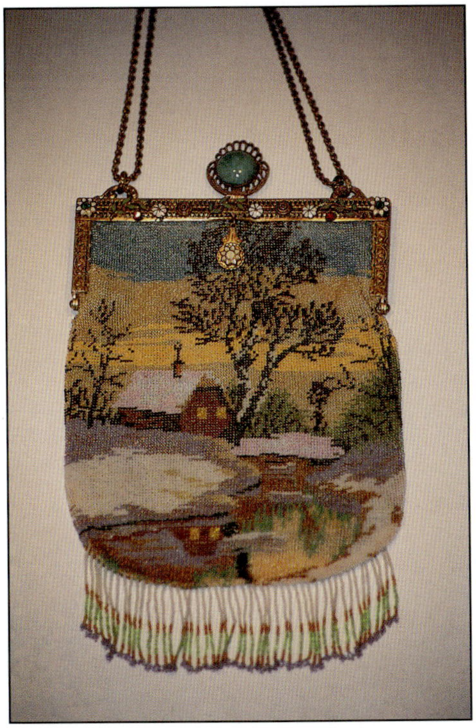

Beaded purses with winter scenes are uncommon. This purse is bead knitted with fine beads and mounted on a jeweled and enameled frame. The simple stick and loop fringe is original to the purse. 9 x 6 in. *Collection of Paula Higgins*. $1,500-1,800.

The beauty of cut steel purses is very difficult to capture on film. Such is the case with this fine beaded and woven cut steel purse, which is even more colorful in person. The design of the Lion, Lady, and Unicorn, taken from the LeViste Family tapestries, is most typically seen on needleworked purses, making this a rare, cut steel beaded purse design. The floral decorated gilt frame is original to the purse. 10 x 7 in. *Collection of Paula Higgins.* $1,200-1,500.

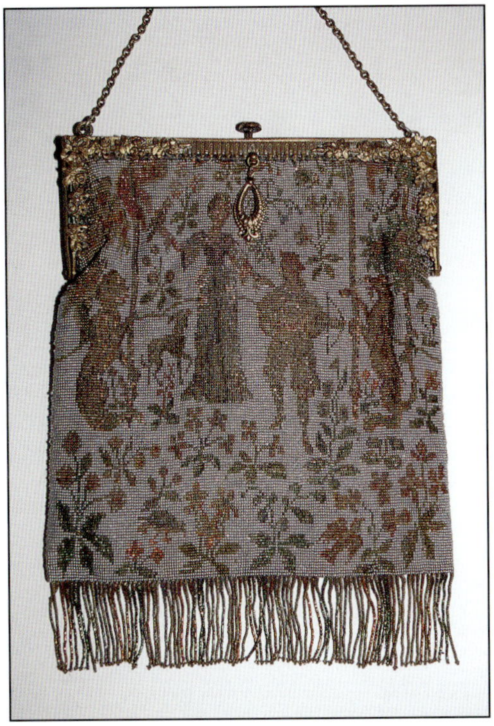

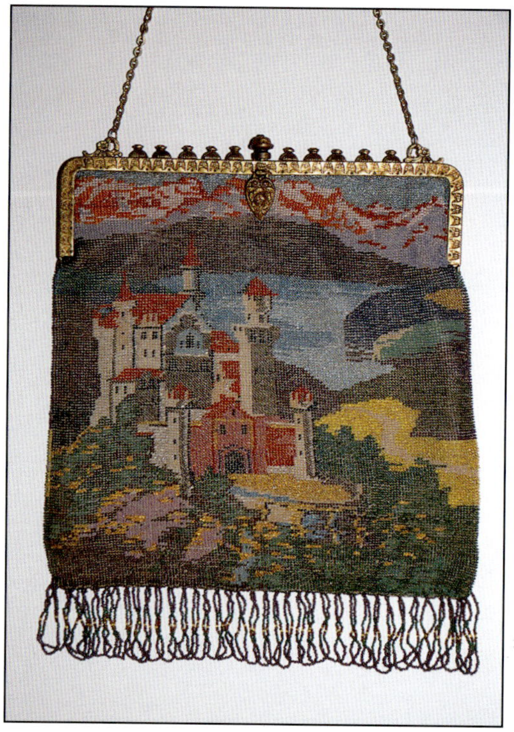

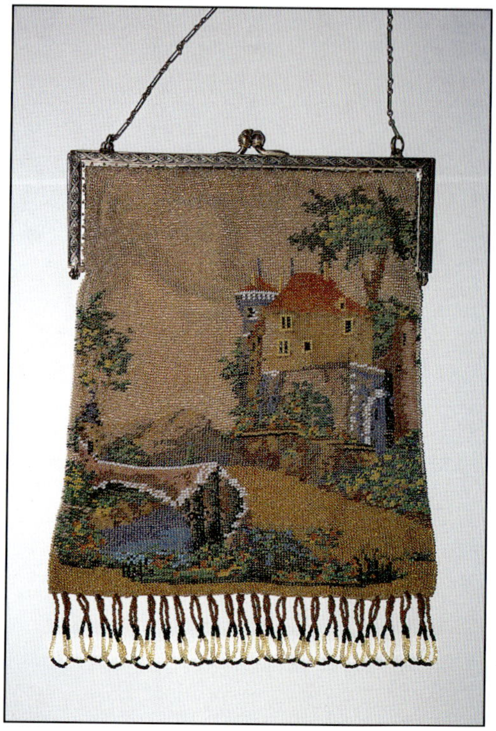

A European villa, bridge, and stream make up this scenic. Bead knitted with fine beads, it is attached to a simple engraved frame. 8.25 x 7 in. *Collection of Paula Higgins.* $1,500-1,800.

The castle of Neuschwanstein, also known as the "Sleeping Beauty Castle," was built by King Ludwig of Austria. This bead knitted version of the castle captures the beauty of the exterior design. The inside of the castle was an overly decorated mess, epitomizing the worst of 19th century romantic design. King Ludwig ultimately went mad, but he will always be known for his fairy tale castle. The frame is made with faux topaz stones, set in carbuncle style settings. 10 x 8.25 in. *Collection of Paula Higgins.* $2,000-2,500.

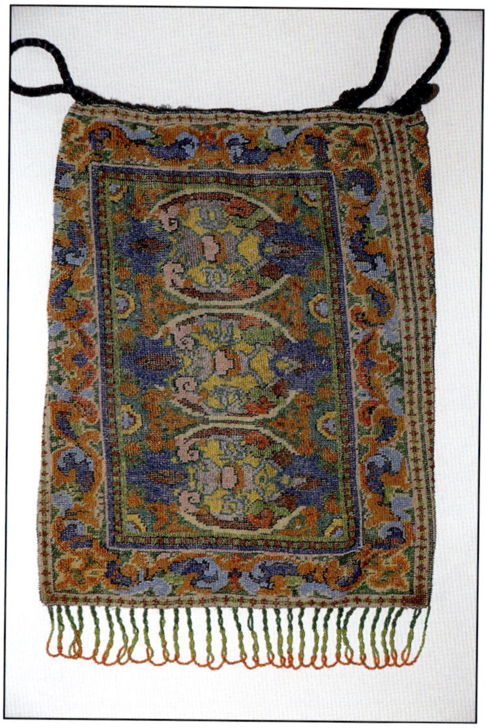

Geometric designs from the 1920s can create a strong visual impact with their color schemes. This purse has a vibrant color palette, and a striking geometric design. However, the fringe is sparse, not in its original state, and it should be redone. Terri Lykins refers to this as "McFringe." 10 x 7.25 in. *Collection of Paula Higgins.* $375-425.

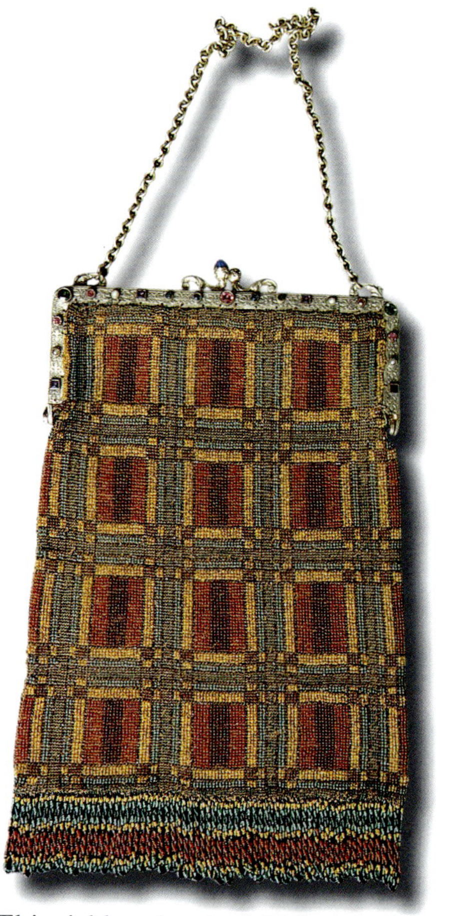

This richly colored, plaid designed purse is woven with size 18/0-20/0 beads. The fringe and jeweled frame are original to the purse. Plaid beaded purses are uncommon. 10.25 x 6.5 in. *Collection of Terri Lykins.* $700-750.

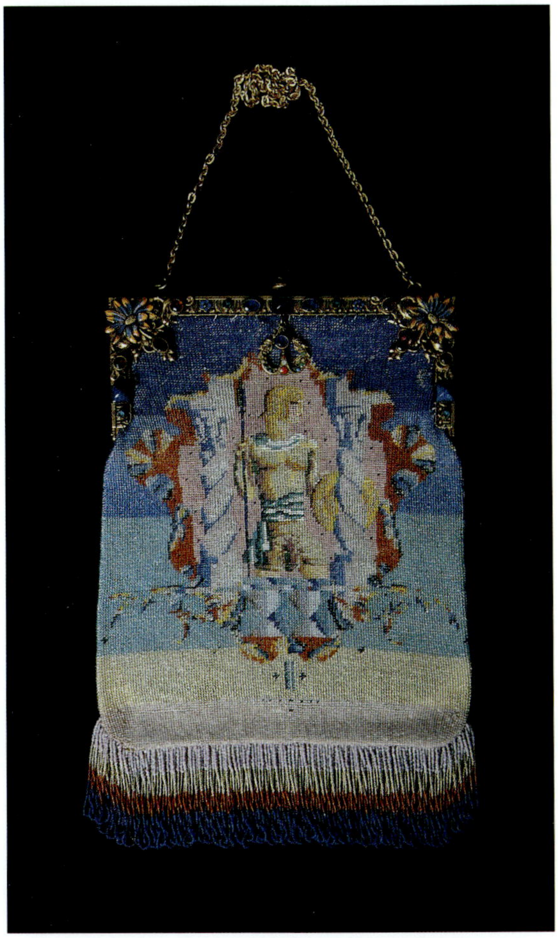

After Egyptian King Tutankhamen's tomb was discovered in 1922 by Howard Carter, Egyptian purse designs became popular. This fine beaded purse shows an Egyptian man in profile, holding a spear, and flanked by two columns. Beaded with size 18/0 beads, it retains its original fringe and frame. 10 x 6.5 in. *Collection of Terri Lykins.* $2,000-2,500.

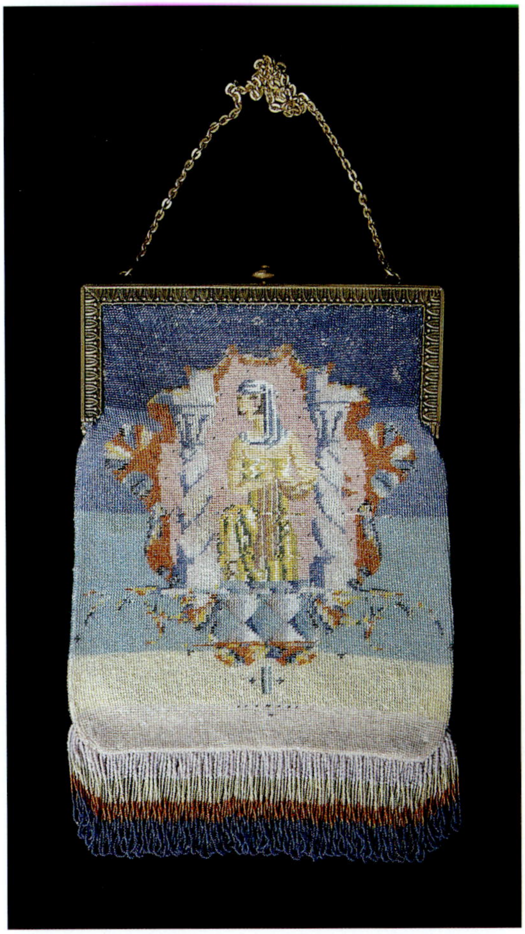

The reverse side of the figural shows an Egyptian woman.

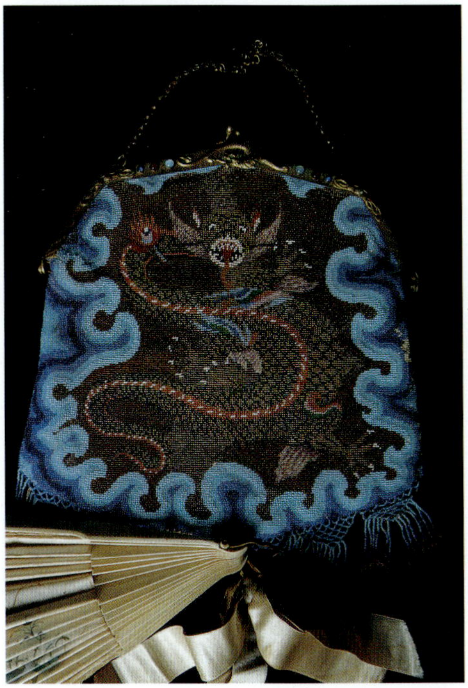

This wonderful bead embroidered purse is made with glass and steel beads, which have oxidized to a rich, even brown. The ferocious looking Chinese dragon is surrounded by Chinese style clouds. In the Chinese culture, the dragon is a positive symbol of power, weather, rivers, peace, and prosperity. The imperial dragon has five claws, and the remaining dragons have four, like this one, or three. The original jeweled frame is decorated with a dragon scale design. 12.5 x 9.5 in. *Collection of Terri Lykins.* $1,200-1,500.

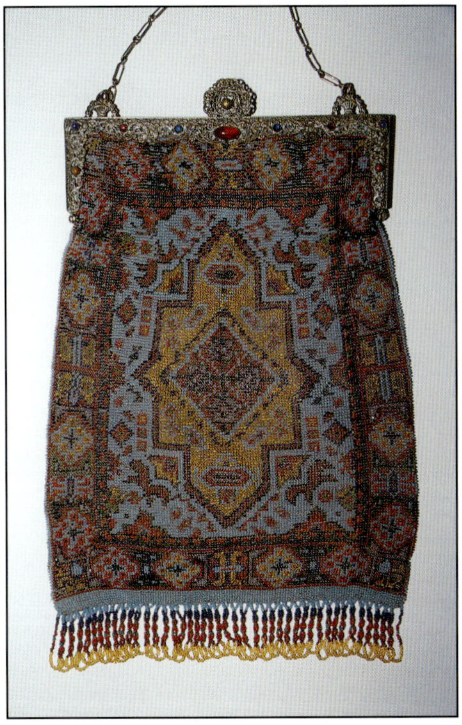

Shown is a rug designed purse made with numerous borders, very fine beading, and a jeweled frame. It is not known if this purse was made from an actual oriental rug design, but many were. 12 x 7 in. *Collection of Paula Higgins.* $750-850.

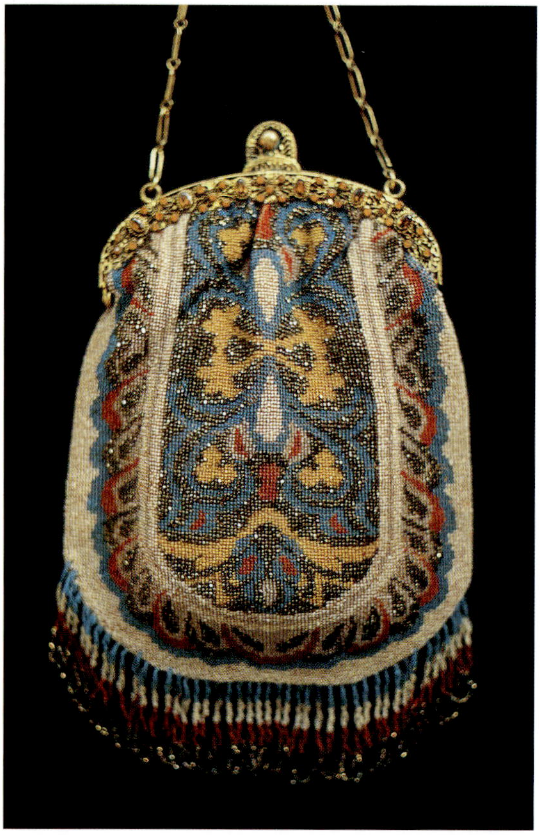

A glass and cut steel beaded purse, made in a geometric design, has its original frame and coordinating fringe. The heavily jeweled frame compliments the color scheme of the purse. 11.5 x 9 in. *Collection of Linda Marshall.* $650-750.

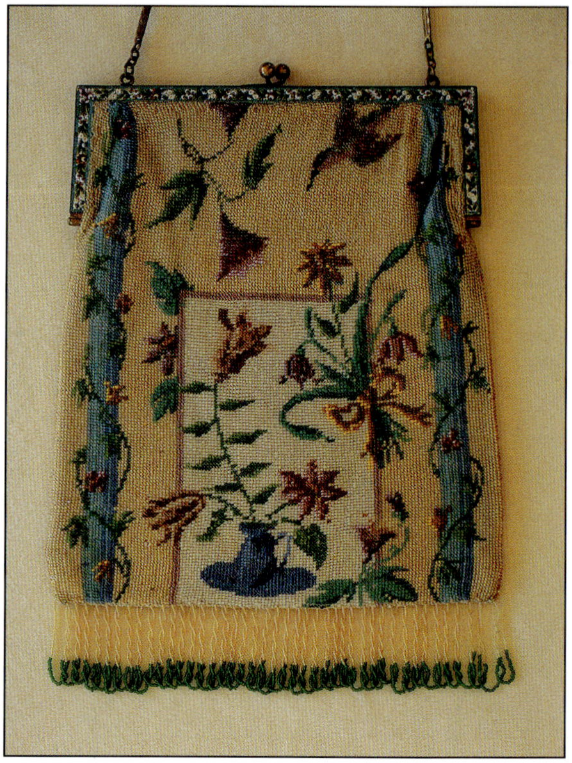

This lovely purse has a floral and hummingbird design, flanked by vine wrapped pillars. The owner describes them as 'Maypoles" and it is easy to see why. The micromosaic frame is beautiful and works very well with the floral design. Micromosaic frames were made in Italy and they add value to any purse. The finer the micromosaic work, the more valuable the frame. 9.5 x 7 in. *Collection of Linda Marshall.* $750-800.

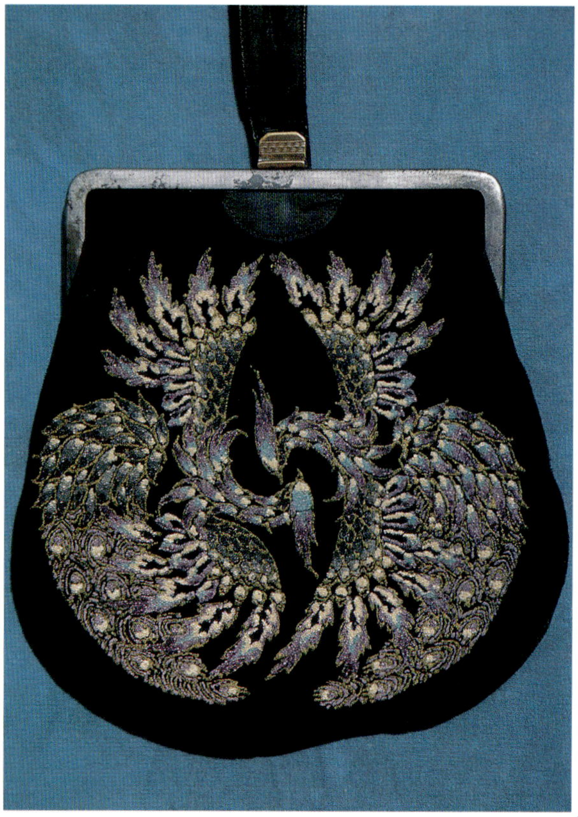

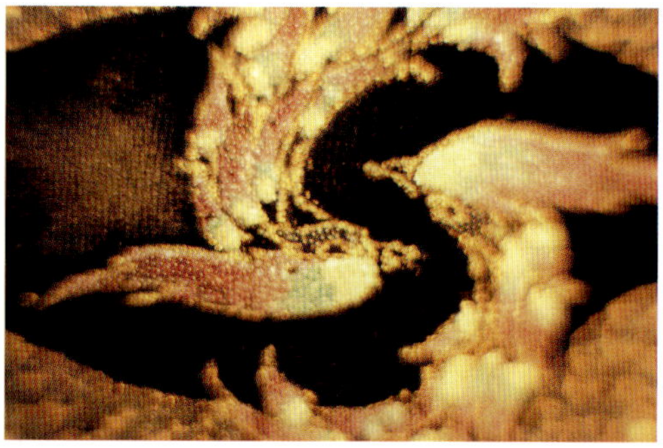

A close-up of the sugar glass beadwork on the purse.

Purses made from "sugar" glass are rare. These beads were named "sugar" glass because they were not much larger than sugar crystals. The mythical bird (possibly a Phoenix) design on this purse was beaded with the finest glass beads made since the 18th century. In the Victorian Period, lampshades were covered with sugar glass, in an effort to imitate stained glass designs. The beads were most likely applied with adhesive onto the velvet background. 7 x 7 in. *Collection of Linda Marshall.* Rare.

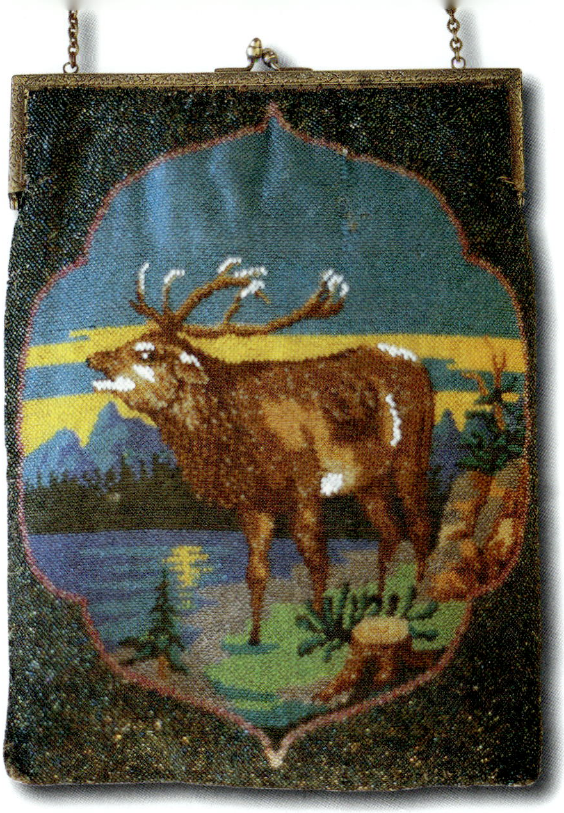

Bead embroidered with a design of a caribou, this purse will appeal to all animal lovers. The finely beaded design is presented in a cartouche, against a steel black background. 11 x 8 in. *Collection of Linda Marshall.* $600-650.

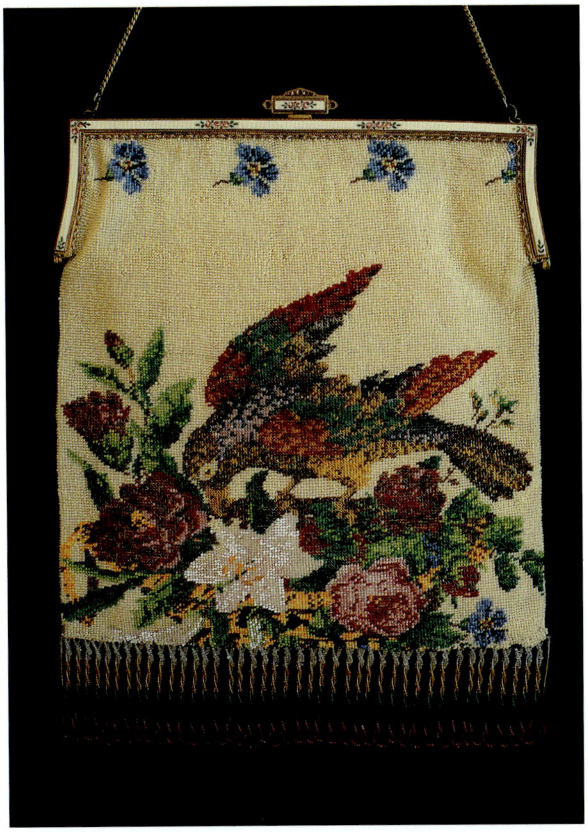

Gorgeous is the only way to describe this purse. The rich colors "pop" against the white background. Knitted with fine beads, it is attached to an elegant enameled frame. This is a purse that should appeal to any and all collectors. 11 x 8 in. *Collection of Linda Marshall.* $1,500-1,800.

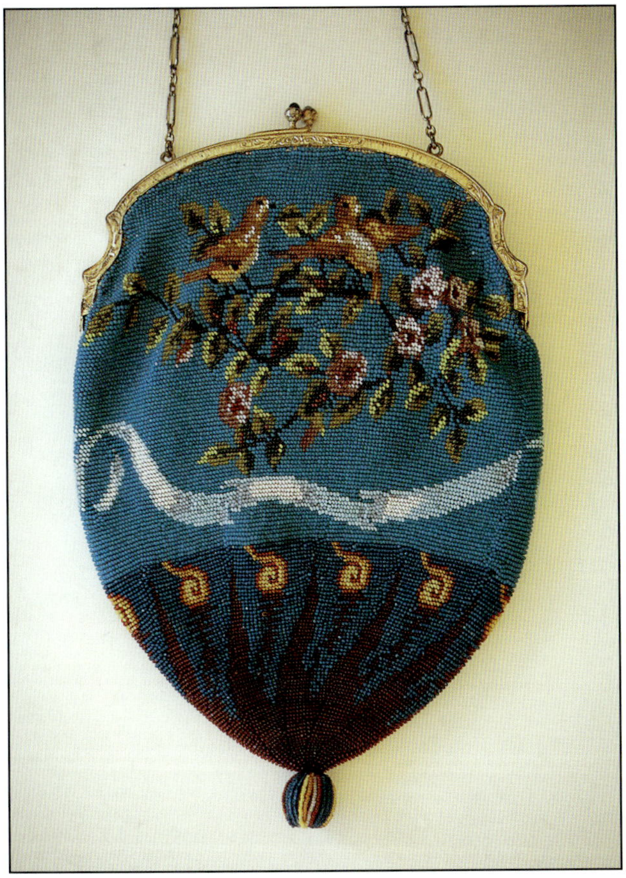

Tiffany & Co. beaded purses are a rare type of purse. Elusive and costly, they disappear into private collections, never to be seen again. The engraved sterling and gold washed frame is marked Tiffany & Co.. The beadwork and frame design are refined and elegant, which are hallmarks of Tiffany & Co. craftsmanship. 8.5 x 6 in. *Collection of Linda Marshall.* Rare.

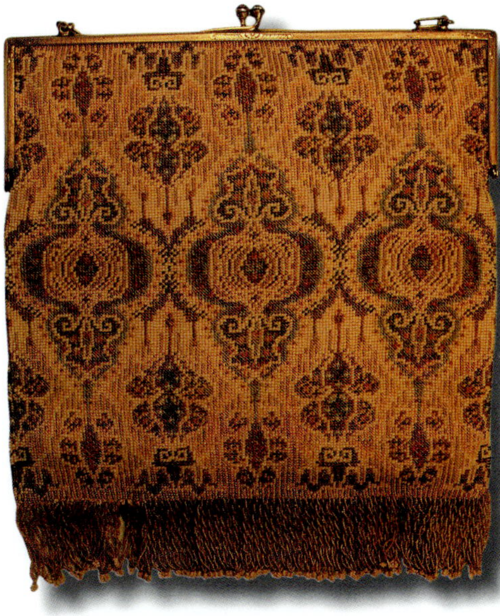

Purses of this quality were typically sold from jewelry stores. The very fine beaded arabesque design is beautiful and represents beadwork at its finest. The simple sterling frame was the favored mounting for this type of purse, which didn't distract or detract from the lovely beadwork. 7 x 7 in. *Collection of Linda Marshall.* $1,000-1,200.

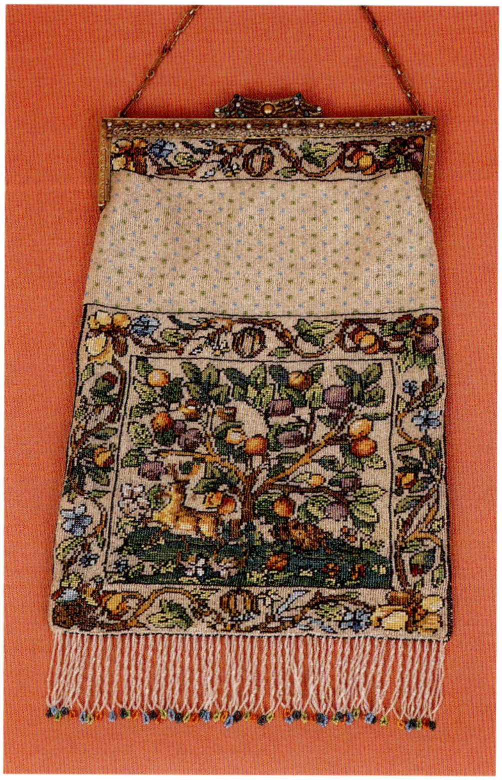

This is a rare purse design, which took its inspiration from seventeenth century needlework designs. A unicorn and stylized fruit tree are the focal points, bordered by a meandering vine. The color scheme also reflects an early needlework design influence. It is an extraordinary purse from any viewpoint. 14.5 x 8 in. *Collection of Lori Blaser.* Rare.

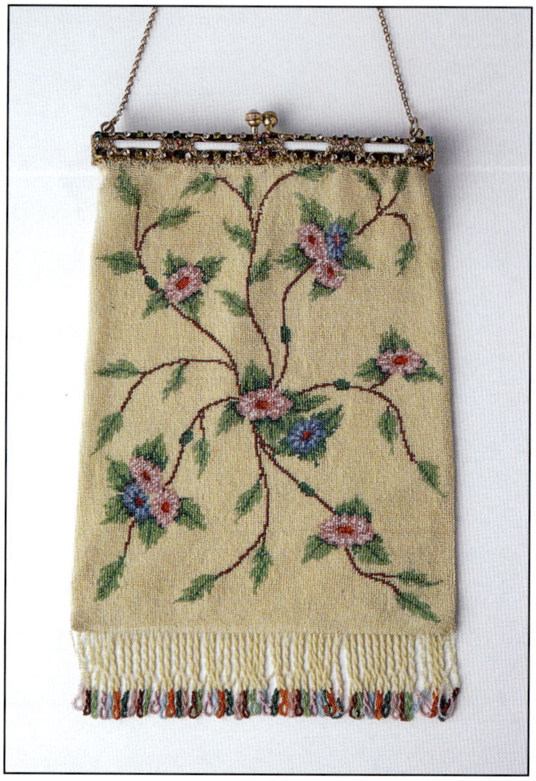

Pink dogwoods flourish against a yellow beaded background. This lovely floral is attached to a beautiful enameled and gold frame. Unusual floral designs like this one, have considerable appeal. 11 x 7 in. *Collection of Kim Stonecipher.* $700-750.

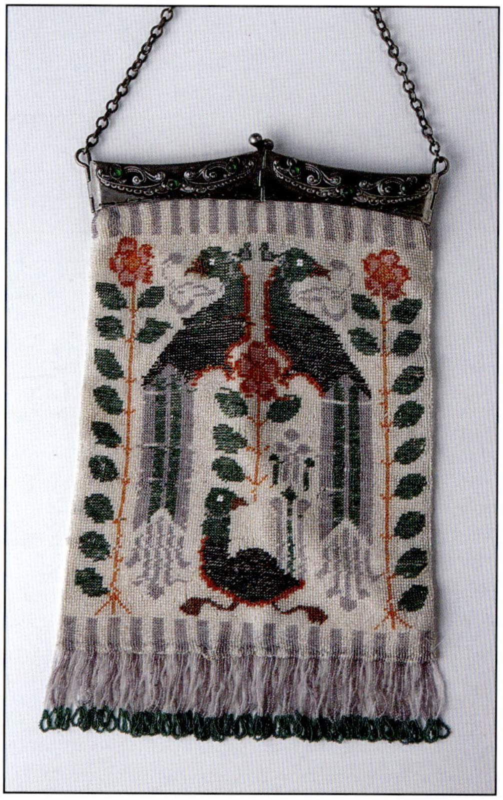

This purse dates to 1920-1930 with its stylized bird and geometric design. The silver box frame is set with green stones, complimenting the colors in the purse. 10 x 7 in. *Collection of Kim Stonecipher.* $475-525.

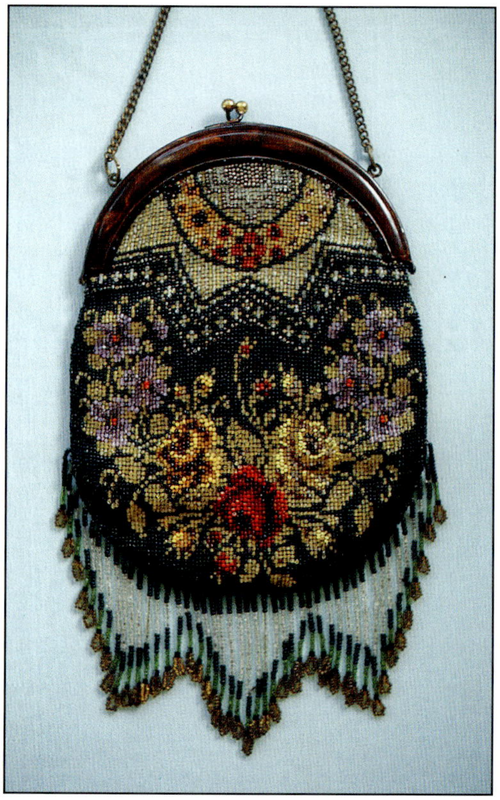

The beads used to make this purse are somewhat larger than average, but the overall look of the purse is very attractive thanks to a wonderful vandyke fringe. The faux tortoiseshell frame is original to the purse, which is in perfect condition. 9 x 7 in. *Collection of Linda Marshall.* $350-450.

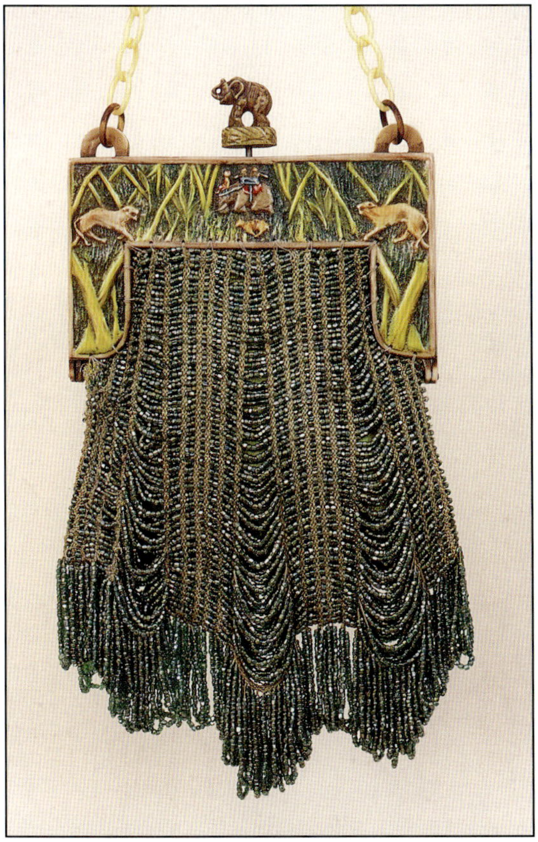

A swag beaded purse taken to its highest incarnation. The amazing, jungle animal decorated, celluloid frame is a perfect match for the green beaded bag. Celluloid frames of this caliber are highly sought after. 10.5 x 6 in. *Collection of Lori Blaser.* $850-950.

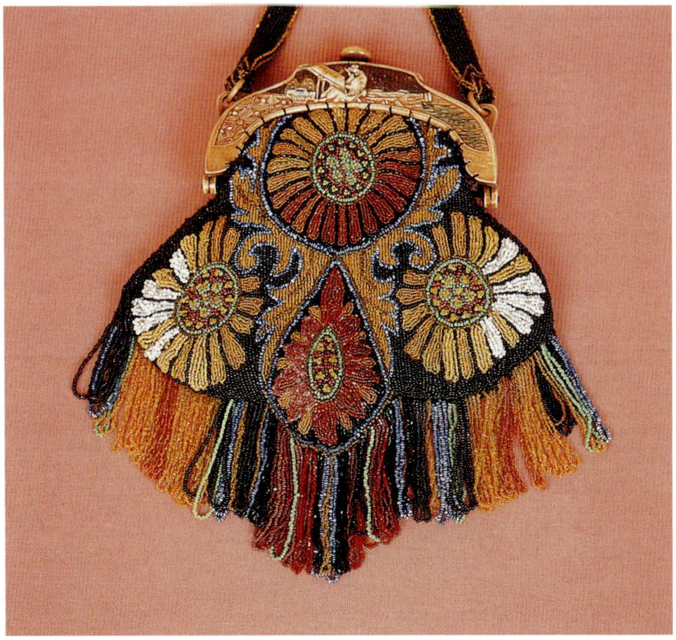

Another exceptional celluloid-framed purse. The frame features a design of a woman weaving at a loom, and there is a sea scene to her right. It has been suggested that the woman is the Greek heroine Penelope, who wove during the day and then took her weaving apart at night, while waiting for Odysseus, who was fighting in the Trojan War. 11 x 8 in. *Collection of Lori Blaser.* $850-950.

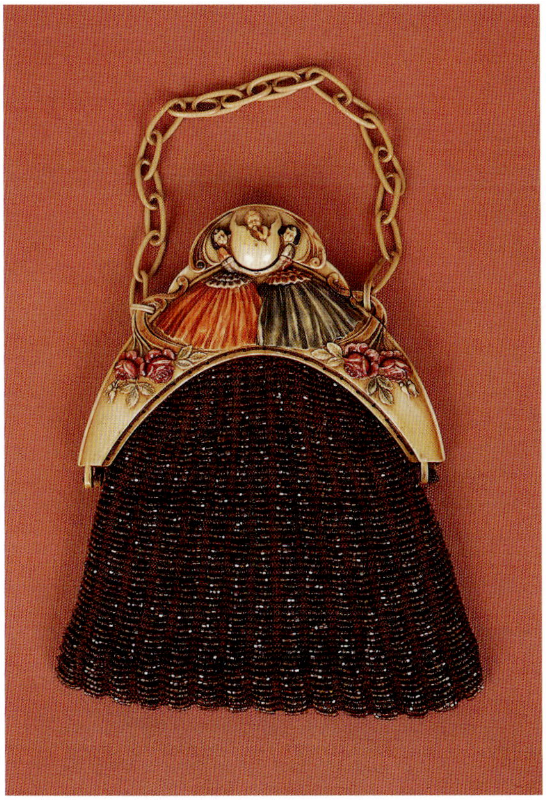

A wide celluloid frame of distinctive and rare design is attached to a beaded and crocheted purse. On this frame, two woman hold an egg, with a baby inside. Frame designers certainly didn't lack for imagination. 8 x 5.75 in. *Collection of Lori Blaser.* $850-950.

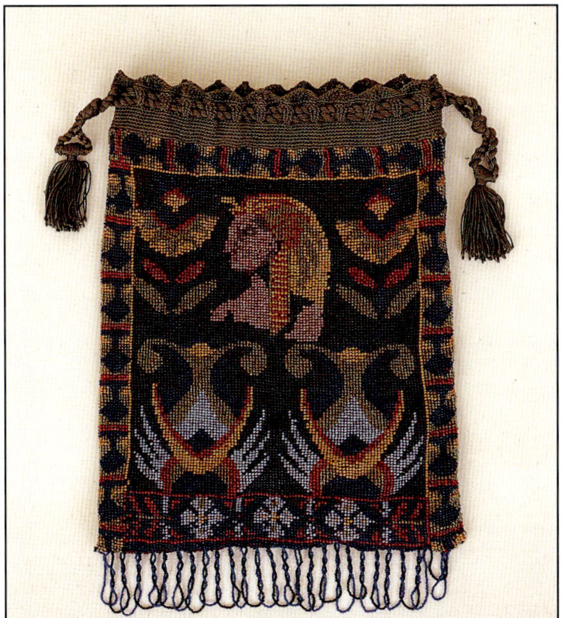

Egyptian motifs flank a Pharaoh's head on this fine beaded purse, dating to c.1922. Egyptian designs are often sought after by collectors looking for a specialized collecting niche. 10.5 x 7.5 in. *Collection of Melissa Overdorf.* $1,000-1,200.

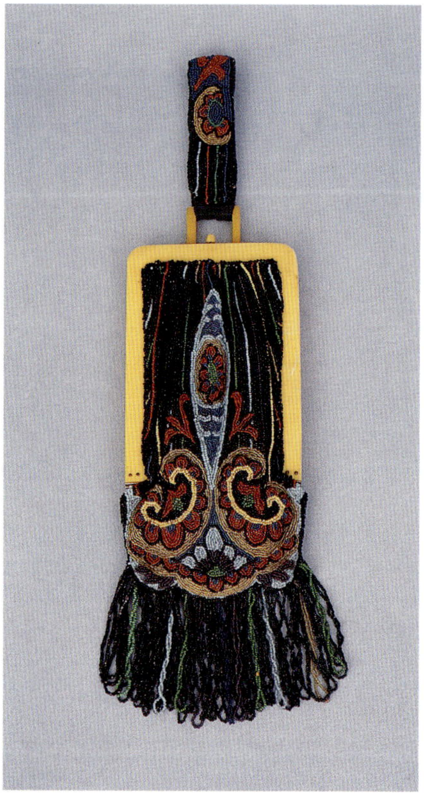

The unusual shape of this Art Deco purse lends itself to a long celluloid frame. A matching beaded strap adds length to an already linear design. 16.5 x 4.25 in. *Collection of Lori Blaser.* $650-750.

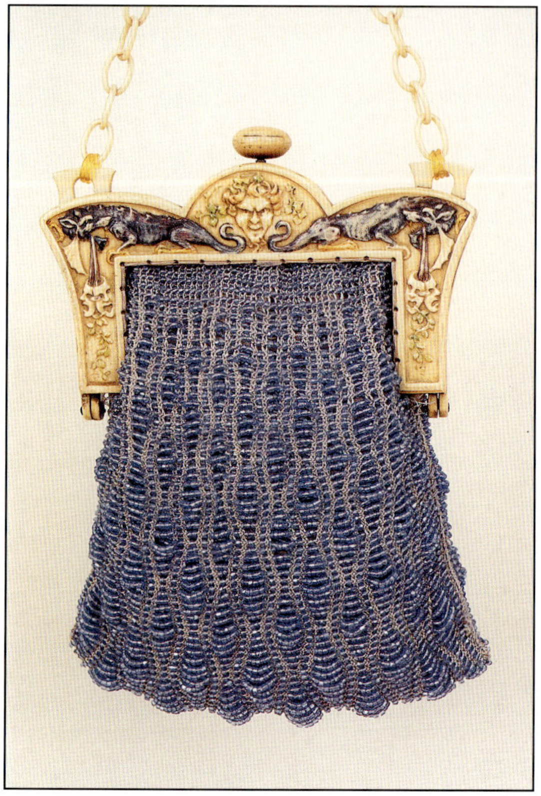

This swag beaded purse has a celluloid frame decorated with the head of Zeus or a devil. Flanking the head are mythological animals and face masks. The animals are colored in a matching shade of blue. 7.5 x 5.5 in. *Collection of Lori Blaser.* $750-850.

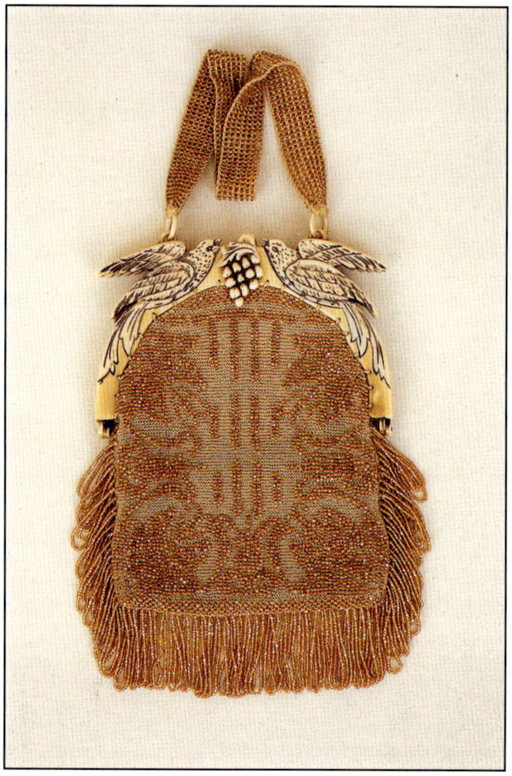

A figural carved, celluloid frame of uncommon beauty, is attached to a lovely gold beaded bag. The attached strap is in perfect condition. Celluloid frames of this quality are always worthy of any collection. It is important to make sure they are in good condition and not suffering from celluloid disease. While some problems can be repaired (cracks), others cannot. 9.5 x 6.5 in. *Collection of Lori Blaser.* $850-950.

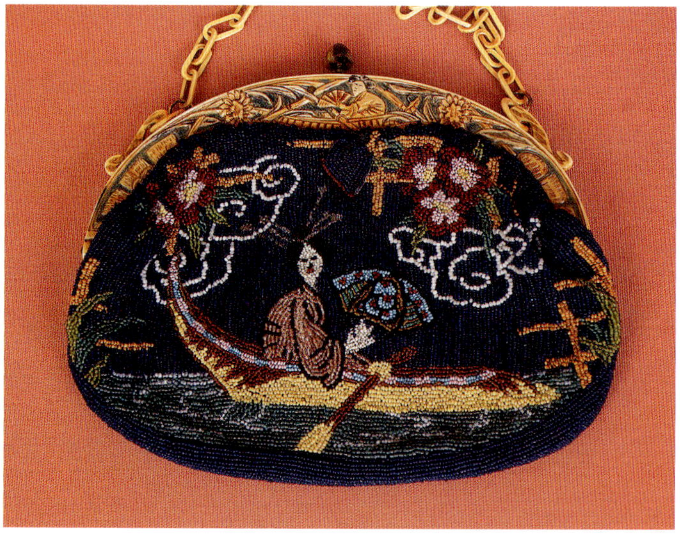

A beaded figural of a Geisha, sitting in a boat, matches the Geisha on the celluloid frame. A purse design that matches its frame design, adds value to the purse. 8.5 x 7.5 in. *Collection of Lori Blaser.* $950-1,200.

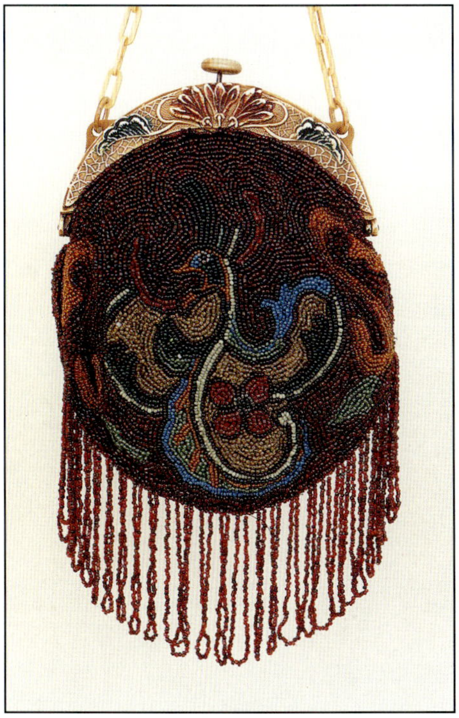

An abstract design of a Phoenix is attached to a colored celluloid frame. The frame design compliments the purse design. 10 x 6 in. *Collection of Lori Blaser.* $650-700.

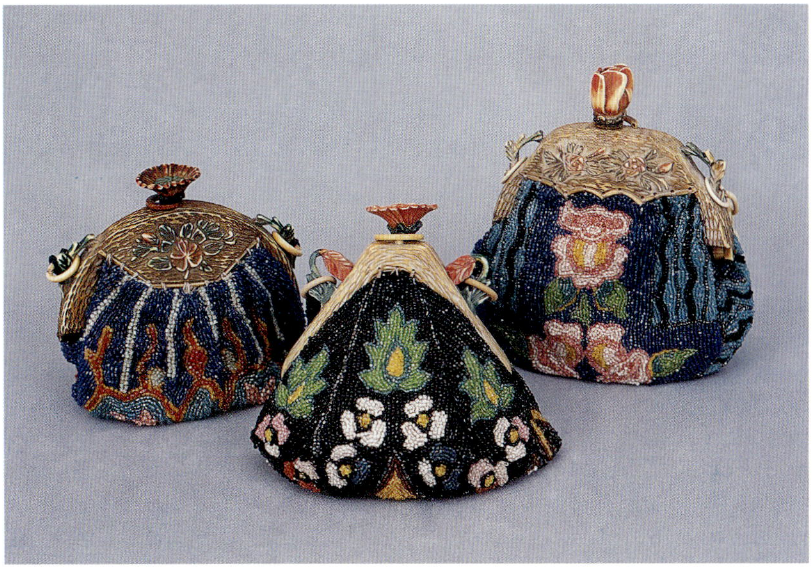

This trio of puffy beaded purses, with floral celluloid frames, makes a beautiful picture. Left: 7 x 6 in. Center: 6 x 6 in. Right: 6 x 5 in. *Collection of Lori Blaser.* $500-600.

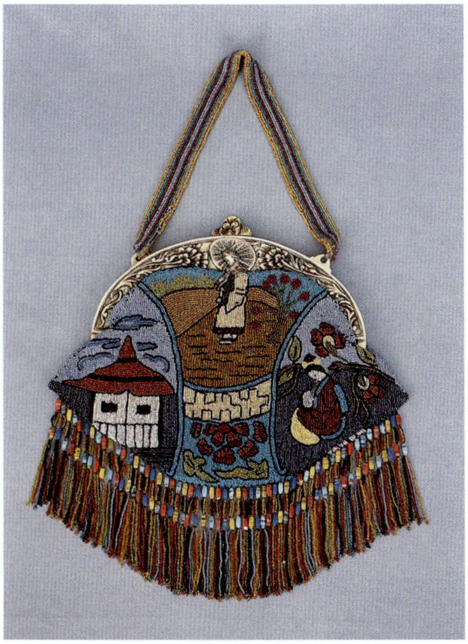

Beaded purses don't come more imaginative than this one. The Asian inspired design features a house on the left, a Japanese woman on the right, and a Japanese man in the middle. The man's body is beaded, but his head is part of the celluloid frame. In other words, the frame and purse designs are integrated. The fringe is also extraordinary. Cylindrical beads are interspersed with small seed beads, adding texture to the fringe. 11.5 x 11.25 in. *Collection of Ellen Foster.* Rare.

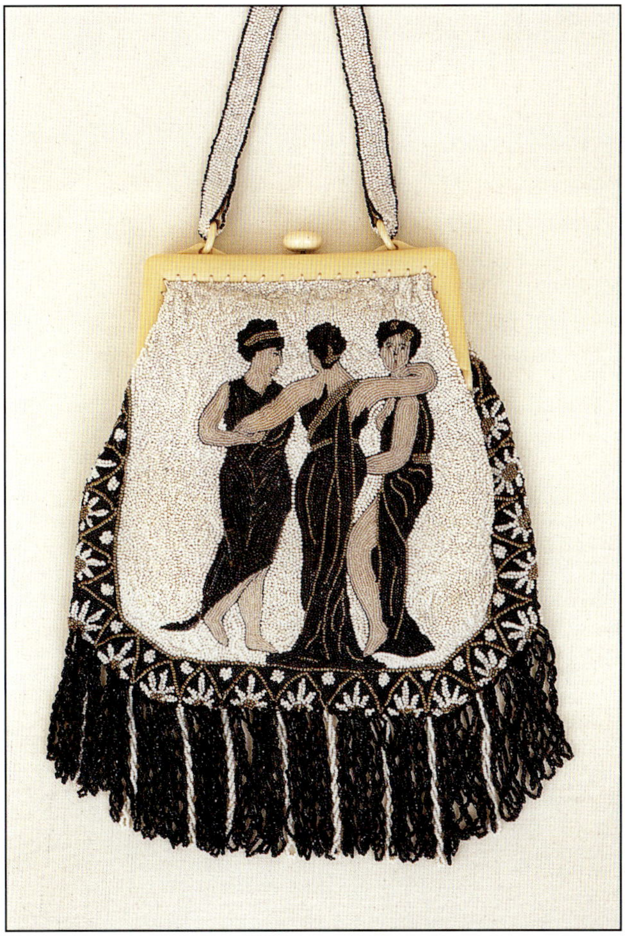

This purse is one of the more visually striking purses a collector could encounter. Black, white, and beige are effectively used to create Grecian figures, possibly the Three Graces. It is mounted on a cream celluloid frame. 12 x 9 in. *Collection of Ellen Foster.* Rare.

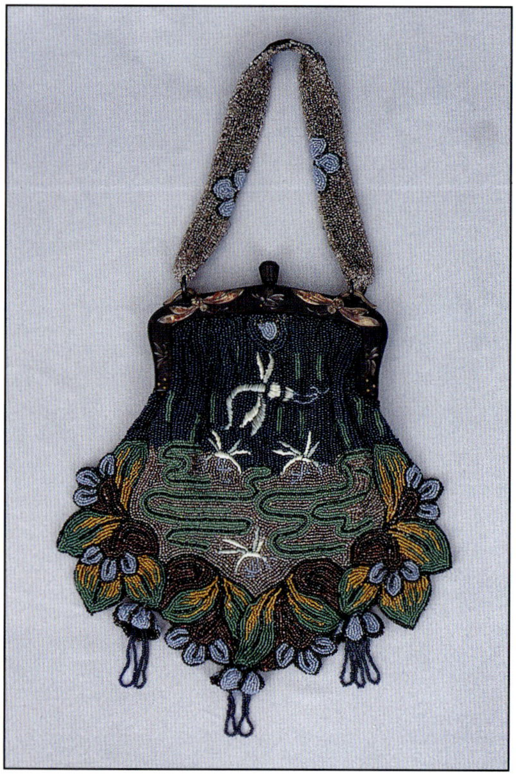

Purses with a "carved" edge are rare, but when you add in the dragonfly theme, which is repeated on the celluloid frame, you have a truly spectacular and innovative purse. 10.5 x 9 in. *Collection of Ellen Foster.* Rare.

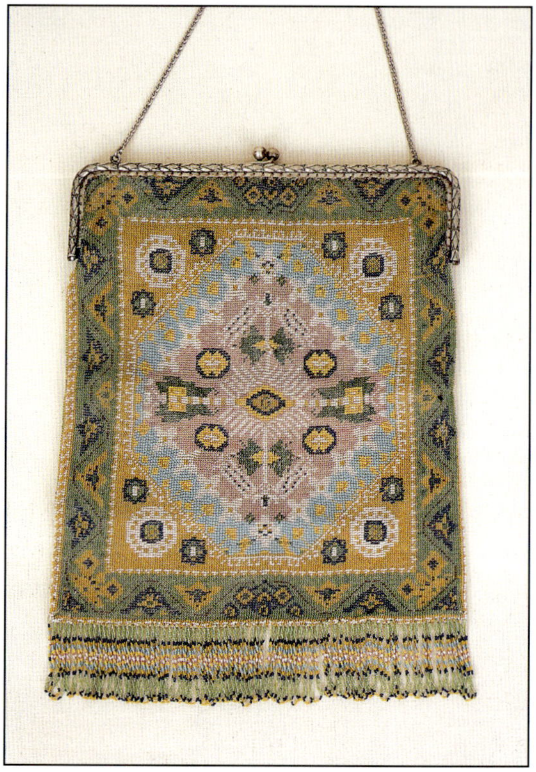

A green, peach, blue, and pink rug designed purse has considerable eye appeal, as well as fine beadwork and beautiful execution. 12 x 9 in. *Collection of Melissa Overdorf.* $750-850.

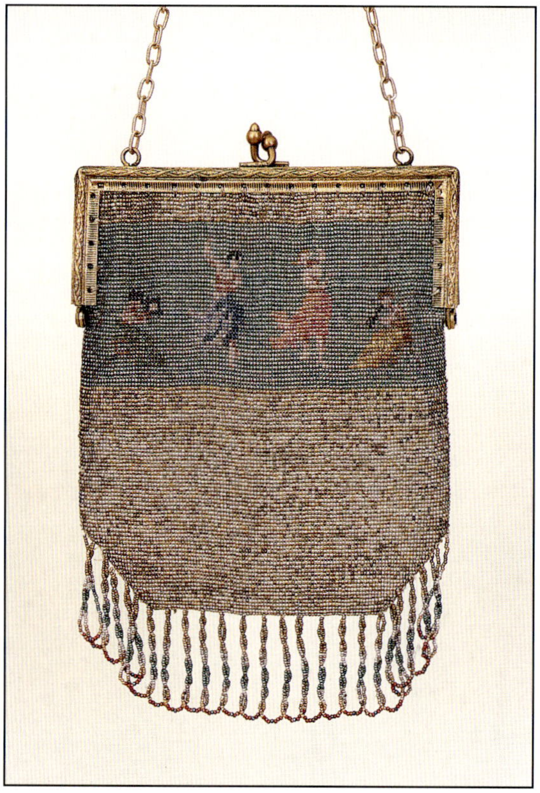

A loomed, steel beaded purse features Greek figures dancing at the top. This is an uncommon design, especially for a cut steel purse. Loomed purses should never be hung on walls because of their weight. Once a loomed purse breaks down, repair is possible but it is difficult and costly. 7 x 4.5 in. *Collection of Melissa Overdorf.* $400-450.

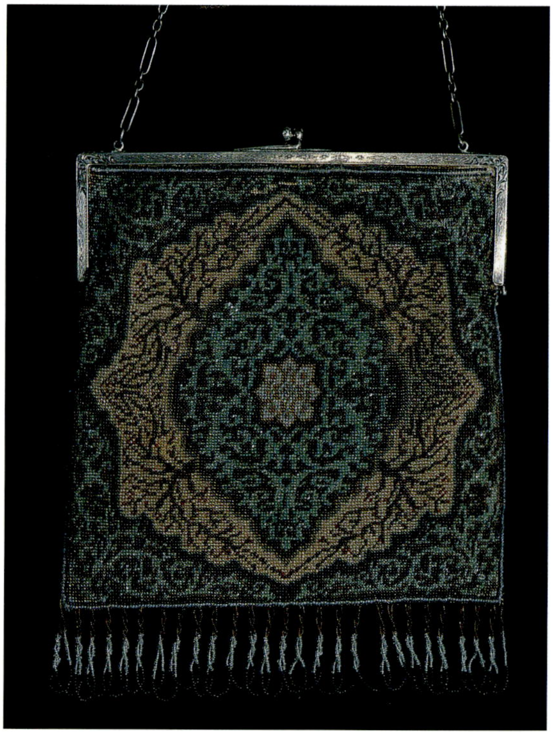

A very fine beaded geometric purse, made with cut black beads, glistens in the light. It is mounted on a sterling frame. 8.75 x 6.5 in. *Collection of Linda Marshall.* $700-750.

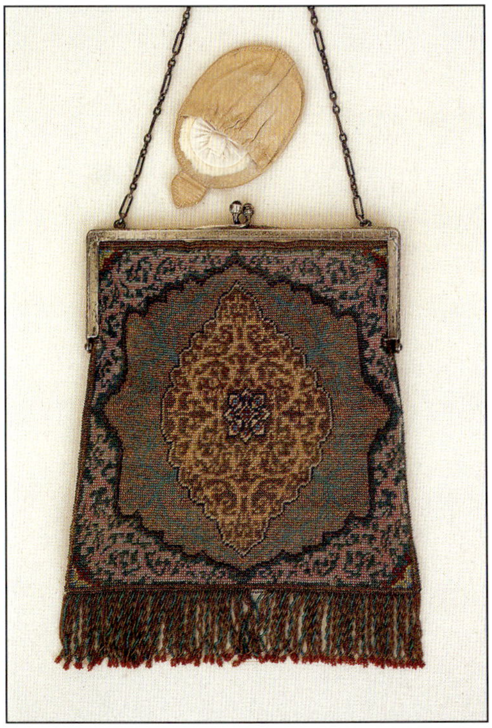

This purse has the same design as the one shown in the previous picture, but with a different color scheme. The beads are very fine and it is also mounted on a sterling frame. 8.75 x 6.5 in. *Collection of Lori Blaser.* $700-750.

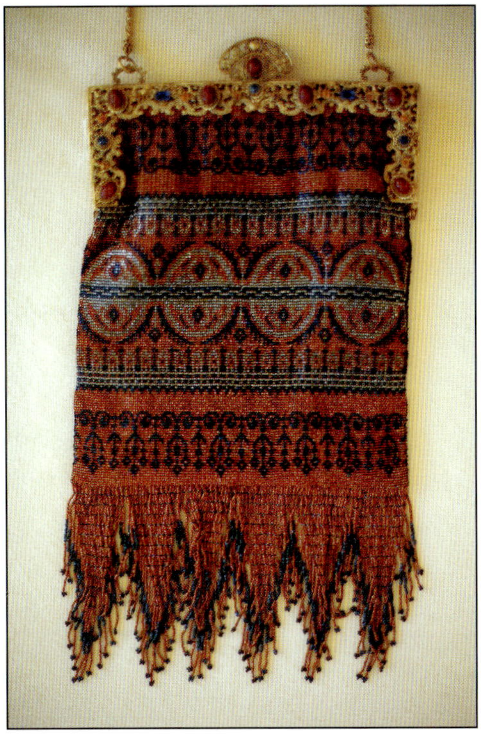

Steel beaded purses often suffer from oxidation, fading, and damaged fringe. This example is in mint condition. The colors are vibrant, the exceptional fringe is intact, and the jeweled frame compliments the design perfectly. 10 x 5.5 in. *Collection of Linda Marshall.* $600-650.

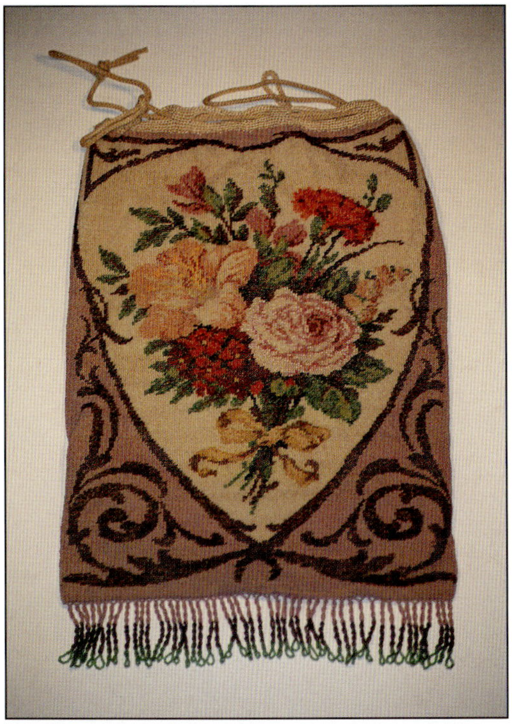

Floral purses don't have to be uninspired. Bead knitted, with very fine beads, the color scheme and the unusual heart shaped design add to its value. Some collectors might be tempted to add a jeweled frame to increase the value and embellish the purse. Others would prefer to maintain the purse's historical integrity whenever possible. 11.5 x 7.5 in. *Collection of Paula Higgins.* $750-850.

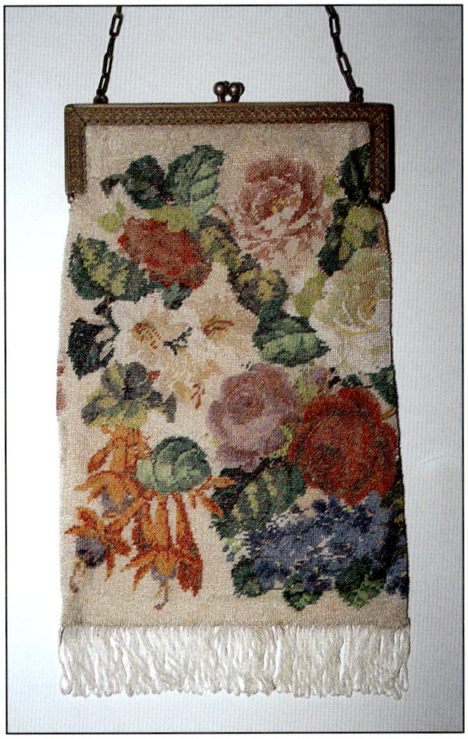

Another colorful floral purse, bead knitted with fine beads. This pattern covers the whole purse, which makes it more desirable. The flowers are also realistically rendered against the cream background. On the reverse side is a different floral design. 10 x 7 in. *Collection of Paula Higgins.* $650-700.

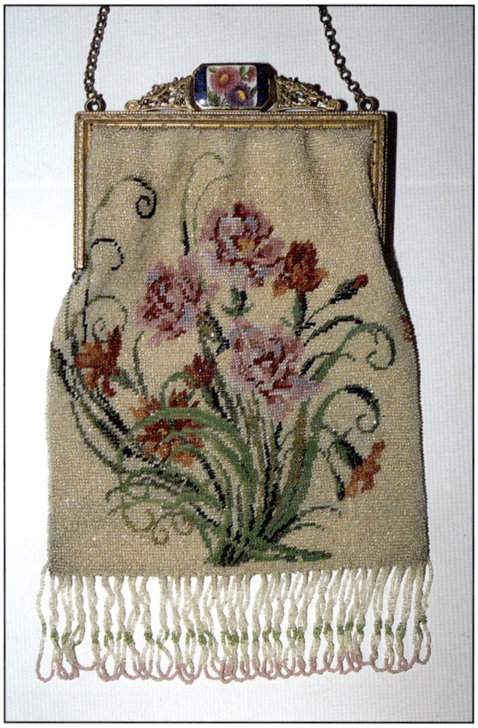

Bead embroidered on canvas, this purse has a matching enameled frame, which adds to its value and its appearance. 10 x 6.25 in. *Collection of Paula Higgins.* $500-600.

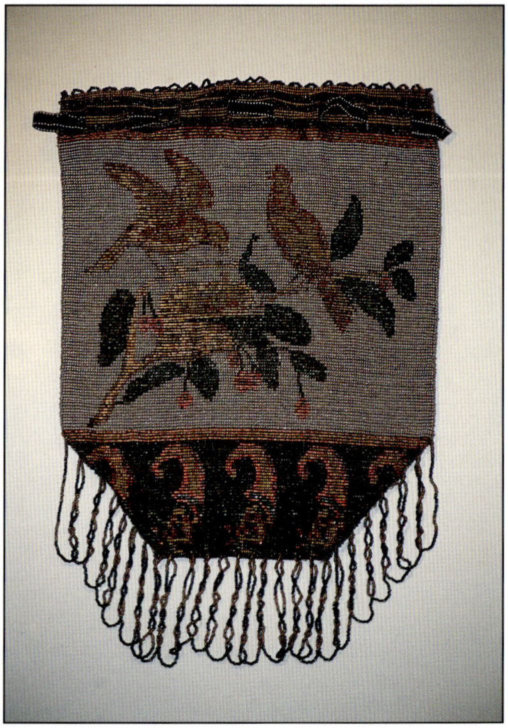

This c.1920 colored cut steel purse has a charming design of birds feeding their babies in a nest. It is woven with fine steel beads. The purse also has its original beaded strap. 8 x 6 in. *Collection of Paula Higgins.* $375-450.

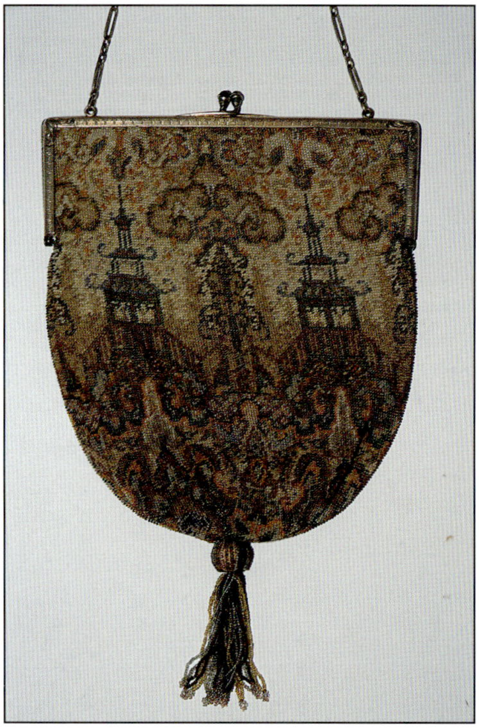

All things oriental were popular during the first third of the 20th century, especially Chinese and Japanese design influences. This very fine beaded purse was designed with Chinese pagodas and clouds. The pagoda was one of the most recognizable symbols of China. Dresses from c.1914 were actually designed in a pagoda style, with multiple tiers, which stood away from the body. This purse also would have worked well with the oriental inspired designs of Poiret, and the dresses of Callot Soeurs, who were heavily influenced by the designs on Chinese export shawls. 9.5 x 5.5 in. *Collection of Paula Higgins.* $600-700.

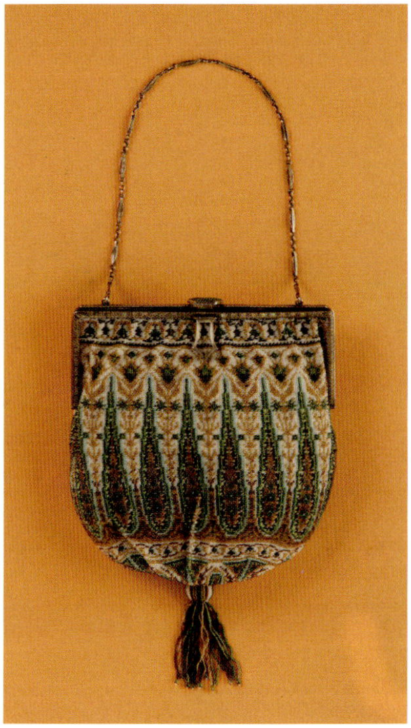

A high quality beaded purse, made with very fine beads in an oriental feather design. These bags were covered with detailed designs, typically geometric. They were made by professional beaders, mounted on sterling frames, and usually sold from jewelry stores. 9.5 x 6 in. *Collection of Sharon Lu-Visi.* $600-700.

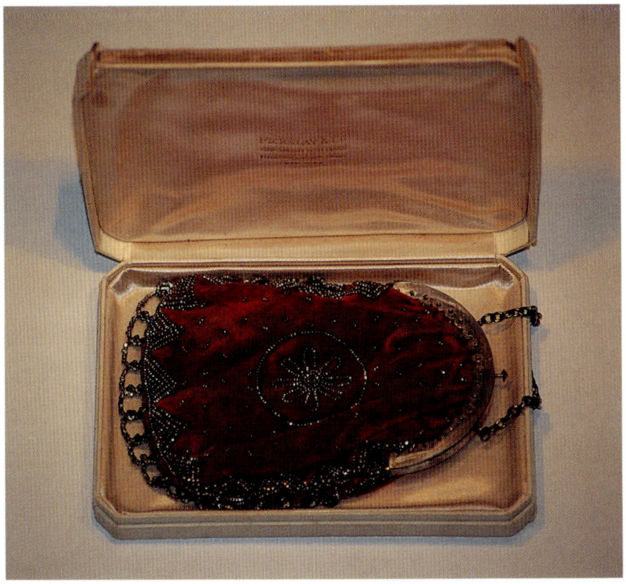

Children's purses have an undeniable appeal. This tiny replica of an adult's cut steel beaded purse was sold by Pickslay and Company from The Sherry-Netherland Hotel in the 1920s. Fuschia is a nice bright color that would have appealed to a child, unlike the black velvet versions sold to adults. The purse sits in its original box. 5 x 4 in. *Collection of Paula Higgins.* $300-350.

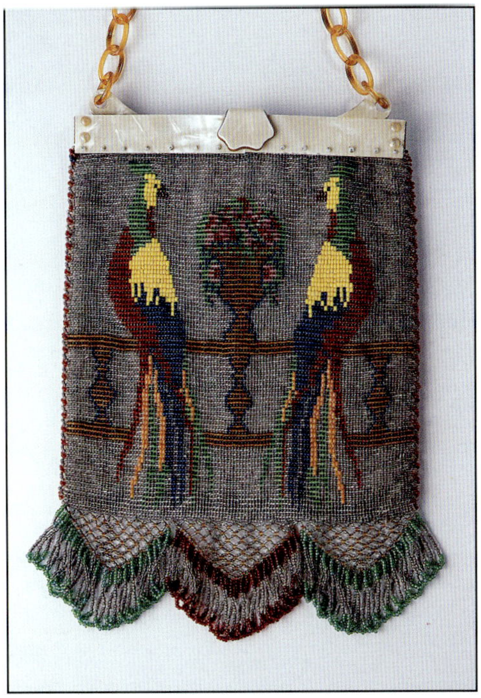

Two peacocks flank an urn in this well balanced design. The basketweave and looped fringe, in coordinating colors, is the perfect finish for this purse. It is attached to a celluloid frame with a pearl finish. 9 x 7 in. *Collection of Kim Stonecipher.* $525-575.

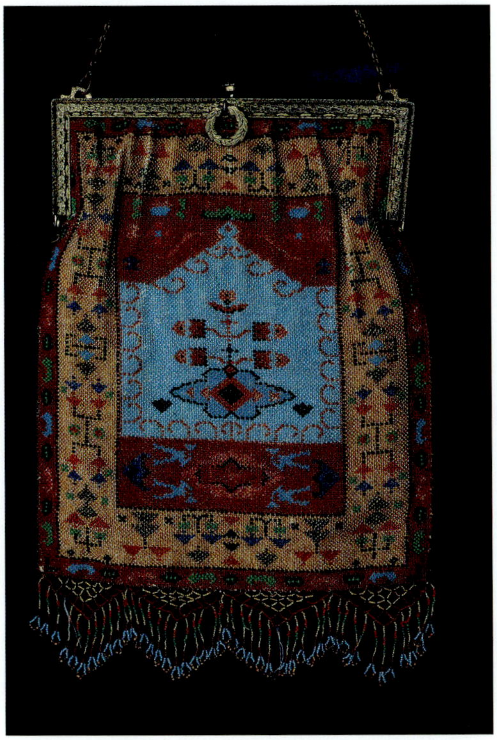

This colorful purse is bead embroidered on canvas. The vibrant color scheme of ruby red, turquoise, and gold is rich and adds value to the purse. The basketweave and stick and loop fringe are commonly seen on bead embroidered purses. 11 x 7 in. *Collection of Linda Marshall.* $600-650.

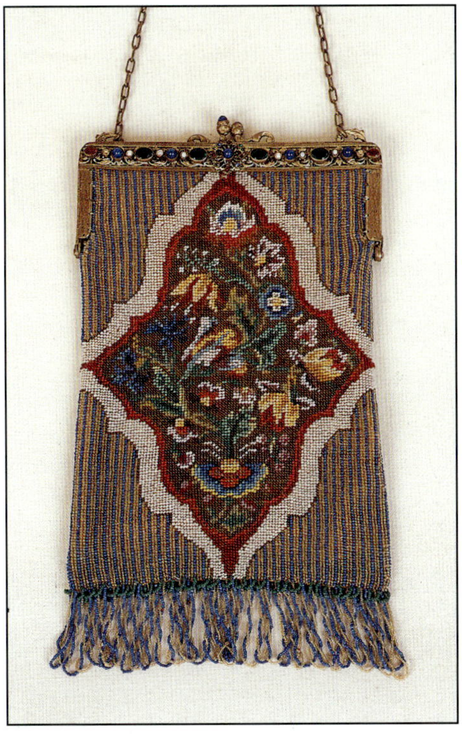

Atypical floral designs are always collectible. The colorful floral cartouche, set against a striped background, creates a visually interesting design. This bead knitted purse is mounted on a lovely jeweled frame. 11 x 6.5 in. *Collection of Lori Blaser.* $650-750.

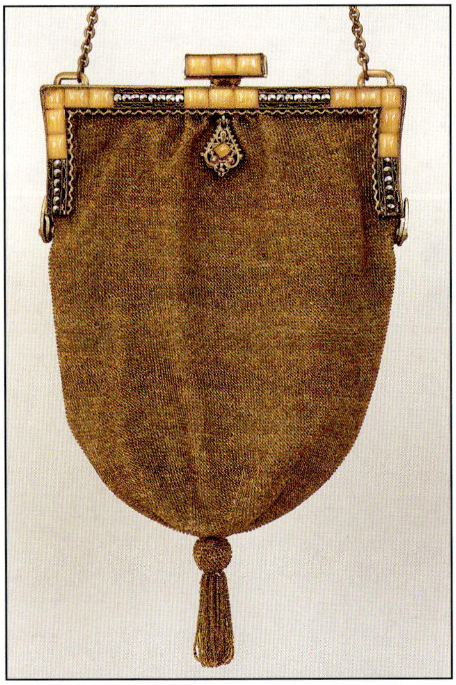

When all the best qualities come together in a geometric purse design, this is what you get: a gorgeous color scheme, very fine beading, a complex but balanced design, and an elegant sterling frame. The feather motif is commonly seen on fine geometric beaded purses. 9.5 x 8 in. *Collection of Lori Blaser.* $800-850.

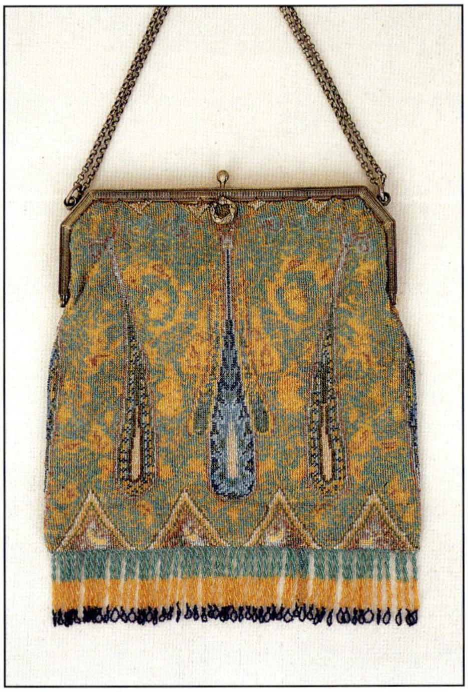

Here is proof that solid color beaded purses can be beautiful and elegant. This purse is knitted with very fine gold/amber colored beads. The frosted glass and marcasite frame is a sophisticated and perfect match. 7.75 x 4.75 in. *Collection of Lori Blaser.* $500-550.

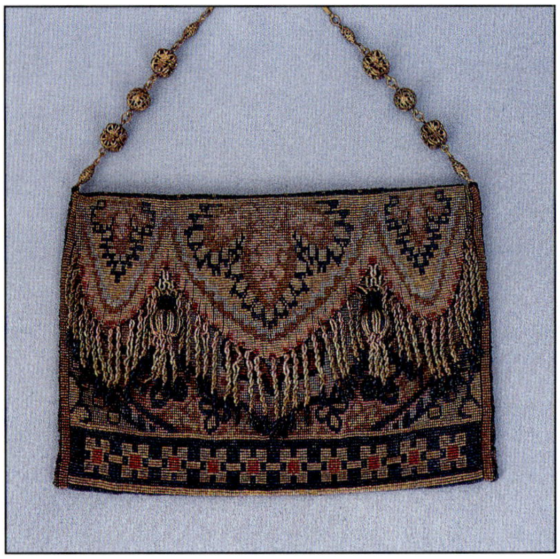

This steel beaded envelope purse is exceptional. The design, colors, the metal strap with the filigreed balls, all set this purse apart from most cut steel purses. There are also two beaded ball tassels that hang from the front flap. The majority of steel beaded envelope purses suffer some form of damage, making this a relatively rare survival. 7 x 5.25 in. *Collection of Lori Blaser.* Rare.

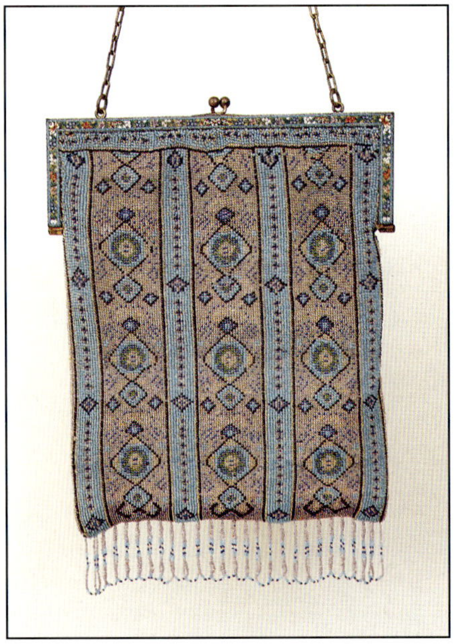

A pale lavender and blue geometric beaded purse is unusual. Bead knitted with very fine beads, it is attached to a floral micromosaic frame. The colors of the micromosaic frame blend well with the color scheme on the purse. 10 x 7.25 in. *Collection of Lori Blaser.* $700-800.

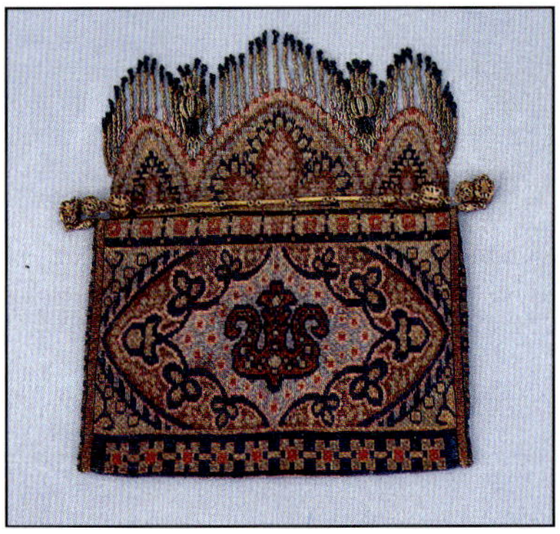

The inside of the steel beaded purse.

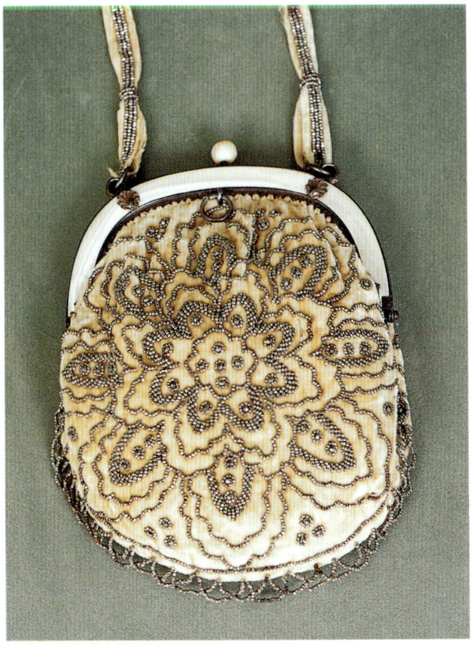

Cut steel beading on this cream velvet purse creates an elegant impression, but the addition of a genuine mother-of-pearl frame adds to its value and beauty. On the frame is the name: *E. Gauthier Hruedes Petits Champs Paris.* 8 x 6 in. *Collection of Lori Blaser.* $650-750.

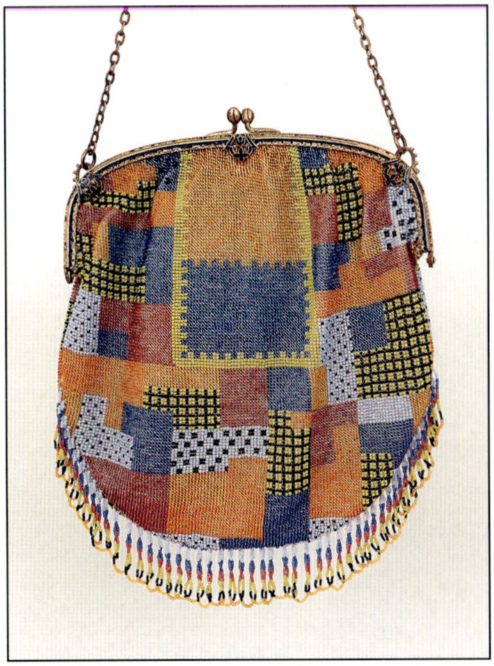

Beaded purses come in many styles and shapes, but this patchwork design has to qualify as one of the most unique. The blue patches almost look like denim. Knitted with very fine beads, it is mounted on an enameled and gold frame. 8 x 6.5 in. *Collection of Lori Blaser.* $700-750.

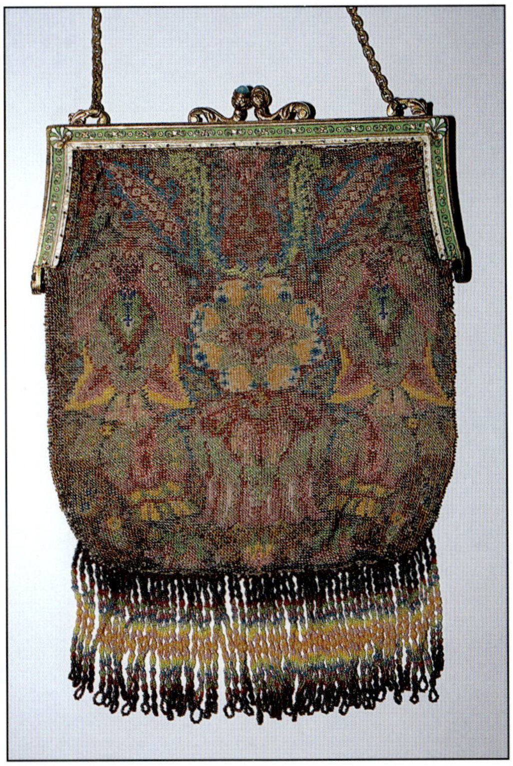

This paisley inspired design, with its jewel toned color scheme, is lovely. The beautiful enameled frame is original to the purse. 9 x 6.5 in. *Collection of Paula Higgins.* $650-750.

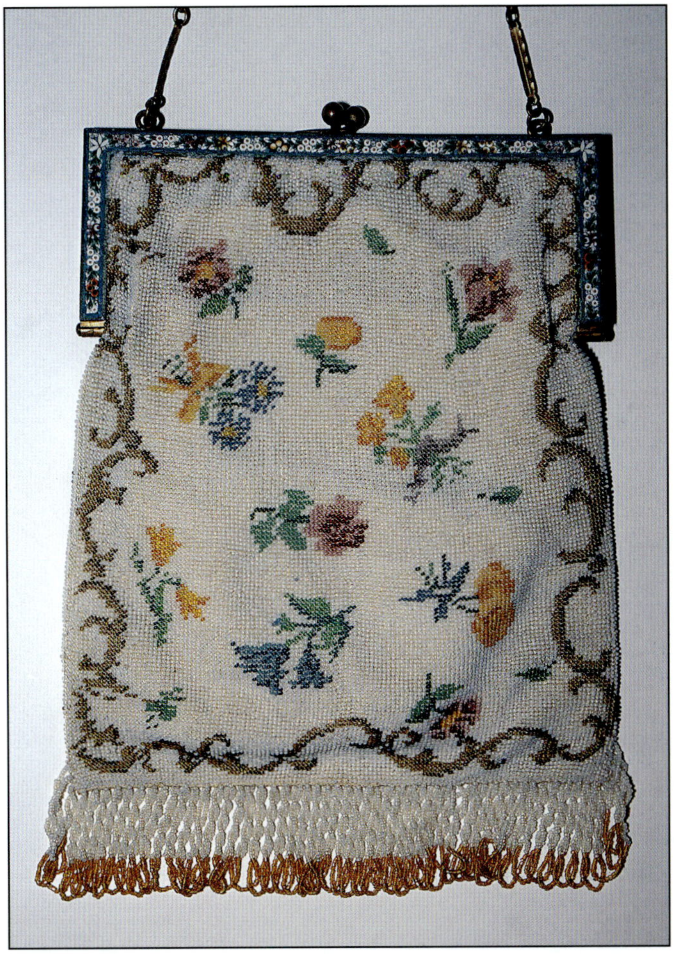

White beads are a perfect background for this floral beaded purse. The fringe is highlighted with gold beads and the frame is made from micromosaics. 9 x 6.5 in. *Collection of Paula Higgins.* $650-750.

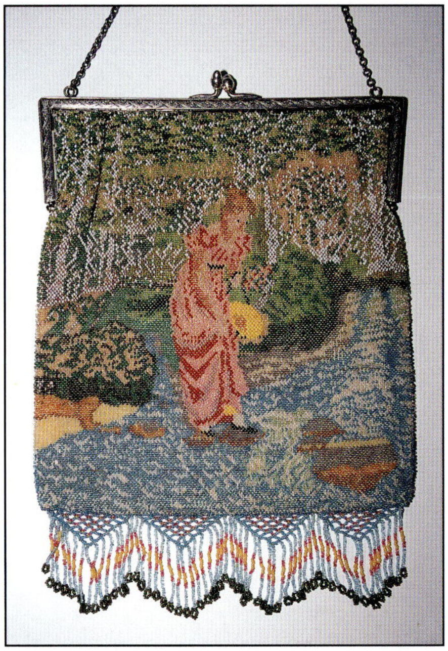

Bead embroidered purses, like this one, are impressive. Made with fine beads, it shows a woman gingerly walking on stones across a pond. Wearing a high waisted dress and flat shoes from the Empire Period, she is also carrying a purse. White birch trees form the scenic background. 10.5 x 8 in. *Collection of Paula Higgins.* $2,200-2,500.

This intricately designed geometric purse is knitted with very fine beads and mounted on an enameled and jeweled frame. Inside the bag is a silk lining with a tag that says: *George Goldwin, San Francisco.* 9 x 8 in. *Collection of Paula Higgins.* $700-750.

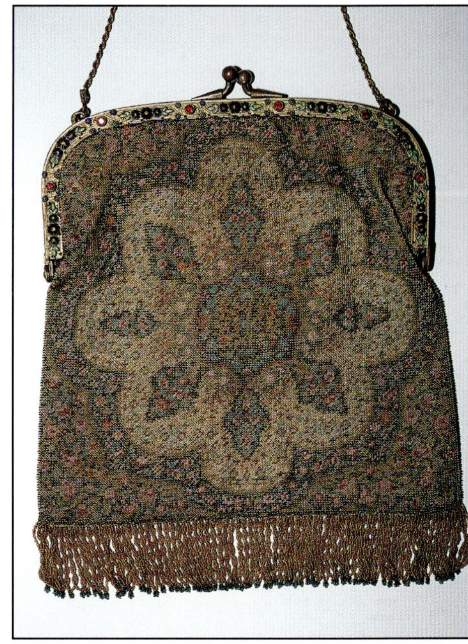

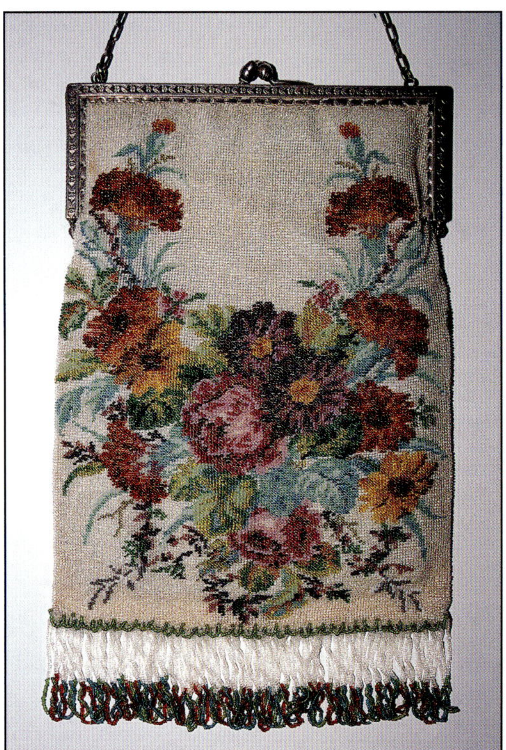

A beautiful spray of flowers is the focal point of this purse design. The color green is used artfully in several different shades. 11 x 6.5 in. *Collection of Paula Higgins.* $500-600.

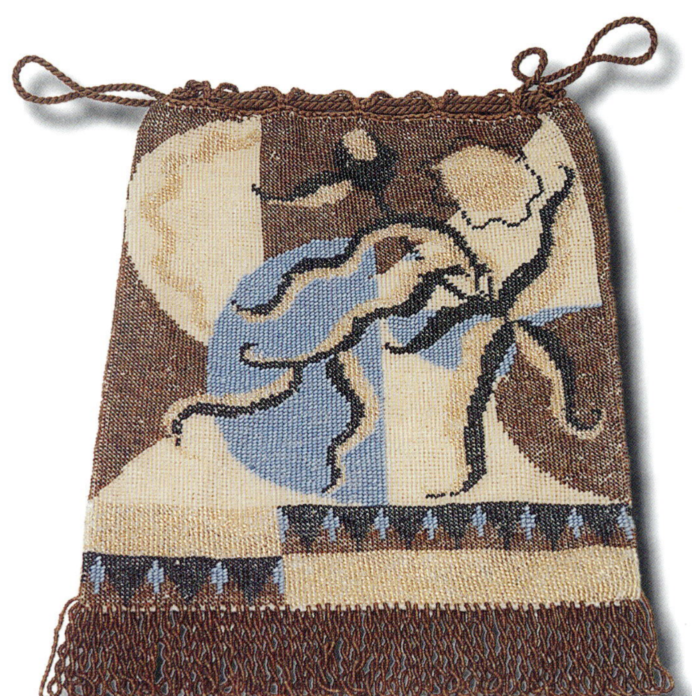

Purses reflecting the design aesthetic of the Wiener Werkstatte (The Vienna Workshop) are very desirable. In the early years of the 20th century, Josef Hoffman and Koloman Moser opened a workshop for artists in Vienna, Austria. Their goal was to produce art and objects in a linear and geometric form, in direct opposition to the more ornate Art Nouveau designs. Their work was also heavily influenced by the Arts and Crafts movement and Japanese design. The workshop operated until 1932. This purse is a classic representation of the Wiener Werkstatte style. 7.5 x 5.75 in. *Collection of Lori Blaser.* $700-750.

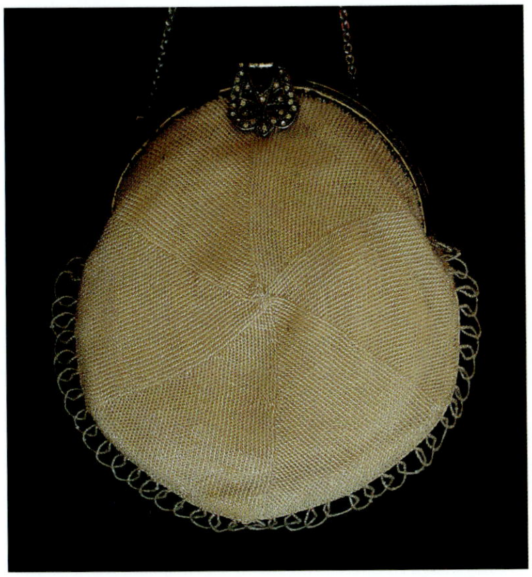

This c.1920 piecrust purse was knitted with fine white beads, and then fringed end to end. The clasp is set with rhinestones. 7.5 x 4.5 in. *Collection of Linda Marshall.* $350-450.

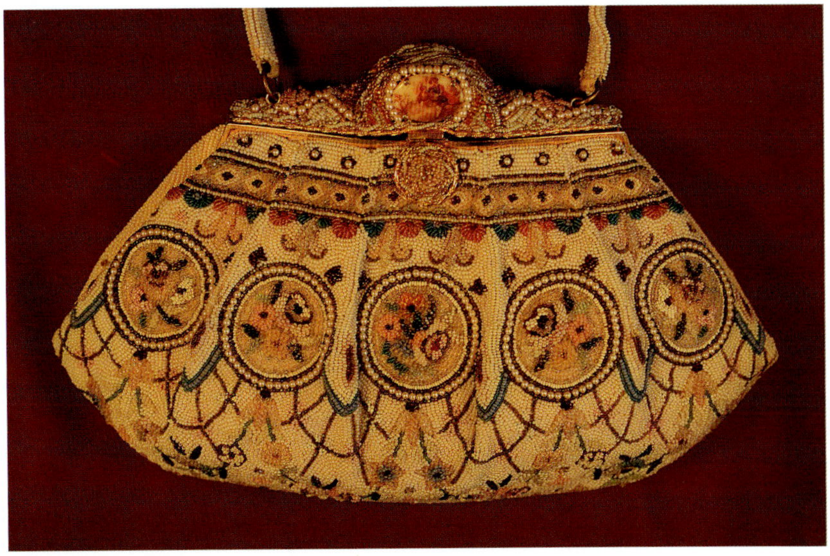

The French produced some of the most beautiful evening purses ever made. This c.1930 example is stunning. Floral designs are set into pearl medallions, which are centered on the purse. The frame is beaded, decorated with pearls, and set with hand painted medallions on both sides of the purse. 10 x 7 in. *Collection of Linda Marshall.* $550-650.

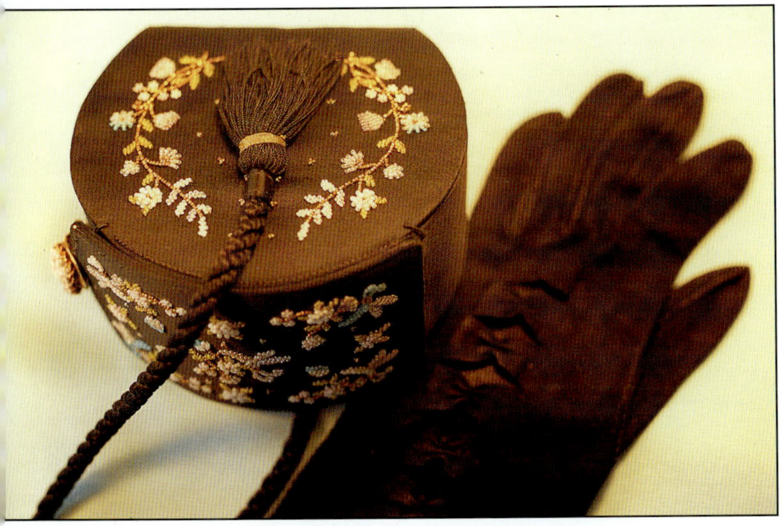

Beadwork decorates this black silk barrel purse in a delicate floral design. It is made with a silk carry cord, and tassels hang from the sides of the purse. Made in France. 5 x 5.5 in. *Collection of Linda Marshall.* $300-350.

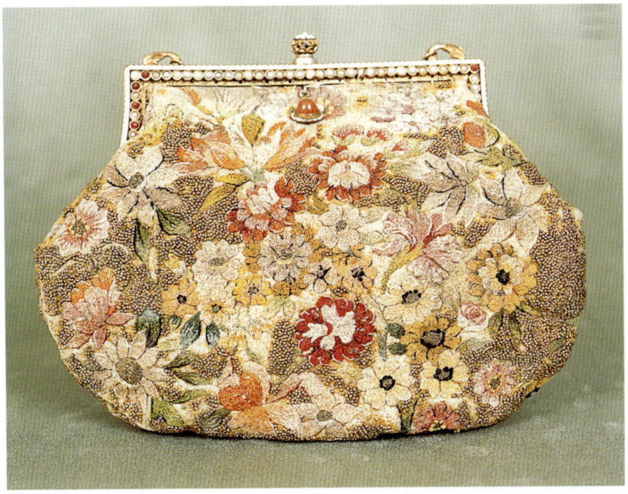

This is another example of French craftsmanship at its finest. Silk stitched flowers are interspersed with gold beadwork. The frame is set with seed pearls and coral. 8 x 6.5 in. *Collection of Lori Blaser.* $550-650.

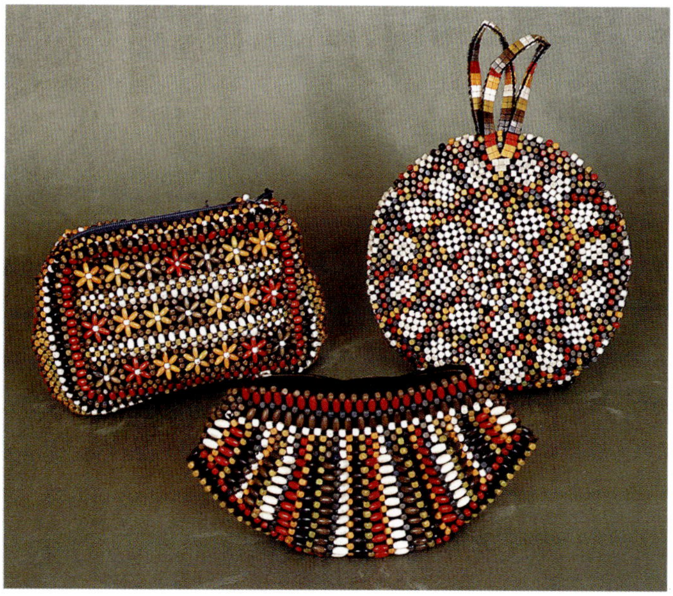

A trio of wooden beaded purses designed with flair. The purse on the upper right is especially stylish. C.1930s-1940s. Left: 10 x 7 in. Center: 10 x 6 in. Right: 9.5 x 9.5 in. *Collection of Ruth Penson.* $200-300.

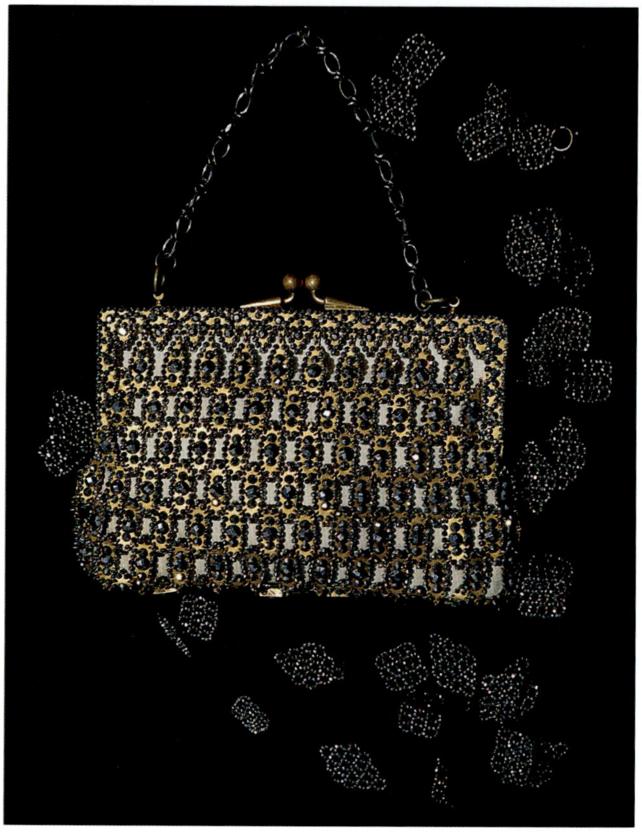

Difficult to categorize, this purse is not beaded but made with links which have faux marcasites attached to each link. So although this is not technically a beaded purse, it gives the impression of beading. This is a truly distinctive purse. 6 x 4 in. *Collection of Linda Marshall.* $300-350.

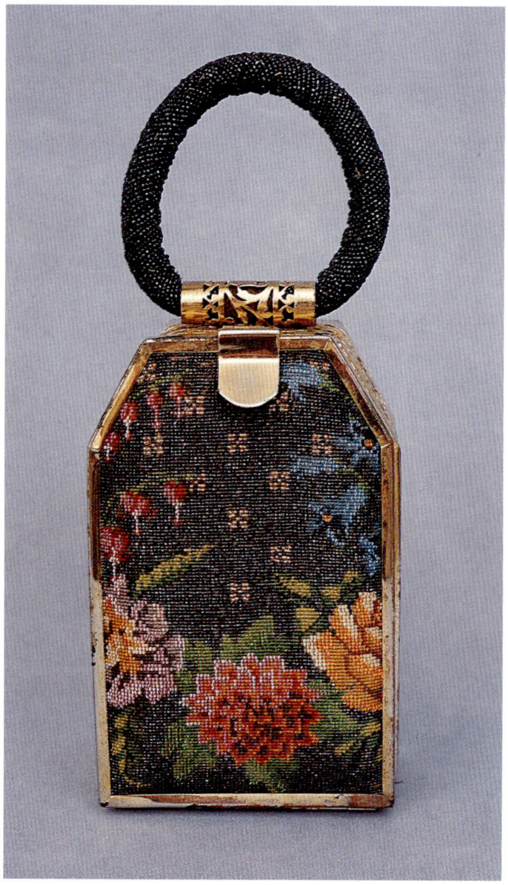

Made by Tyrolean of New York, this floral bead embroidered purse is encased in a filigreed frame. The round handle is also completely covered with beads. 8.5 x 5 in. *Collection of Marcy Rick.* $400-450.

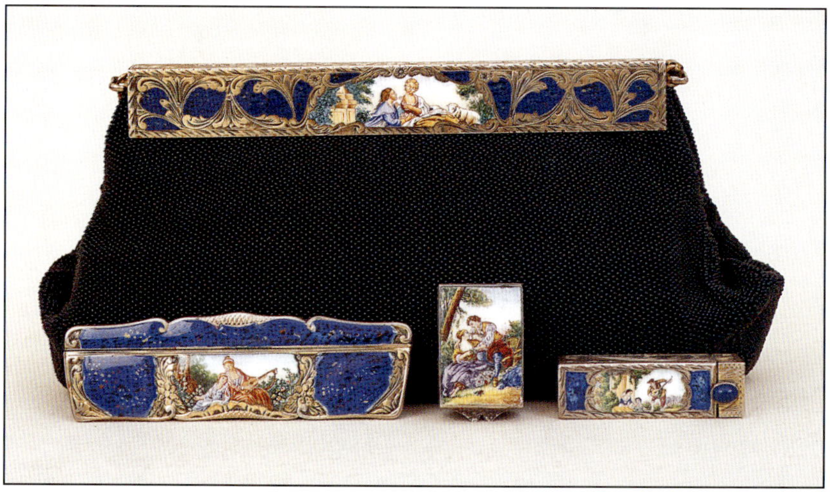

Navy blue beadwork is the perfect foil for the richly enameled, figural frame. The beadwork purse was made in France, but the enameled frame was most likely made in Italy, possibly by Ugo Bellini. Matching accessories include: a comb, pill box, and lipstick case. 9.5 x 5.75 in. *Collection of Lori Blaser.* Purse: $700-750.

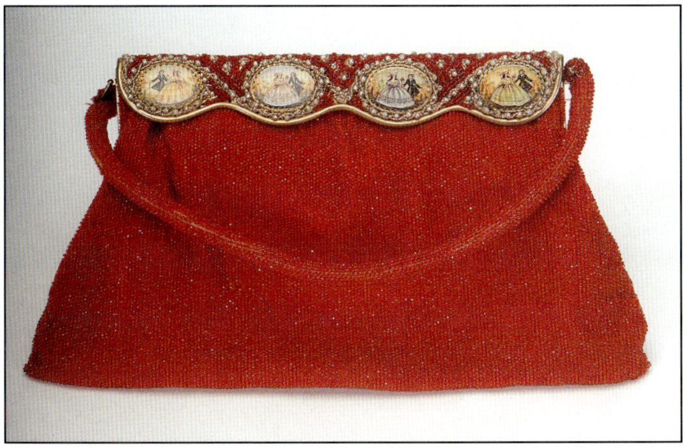

This mid-twentieth century, red beaded purse is bold and beautiful. The frame is set with hand painted medallions, surrounded by pearls, and covered by glass. 9 x 6 in. *Collection of Lori Blaser.* $500-550.

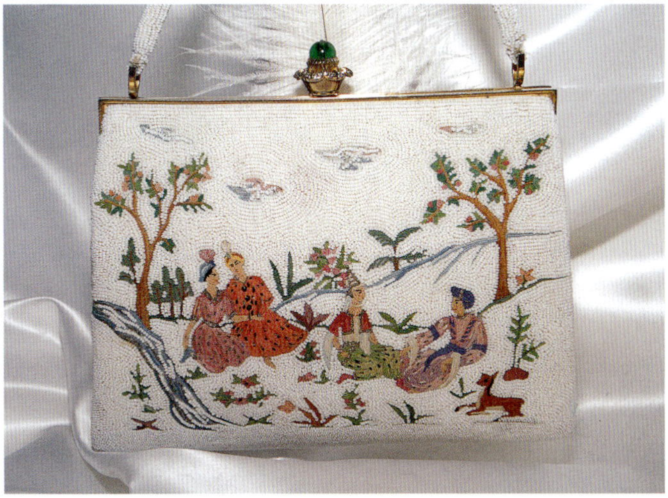

Tambour and bead embroidered purses from the mid-twentieth century typically featured floral designs, surrounded by beadwork. This example is a high end version of the tambour and bead embroidered purse. Made in France. 8 x 6 in. *Collection of Paula Higgins.* $500-550.

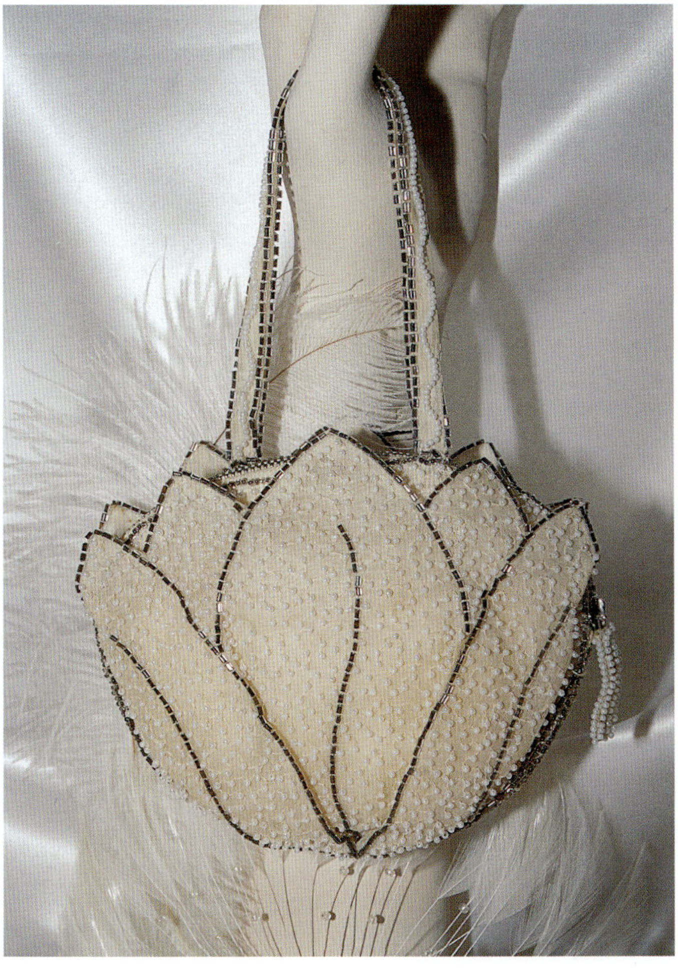

Tiny pearls decorate this tulip shaped purse from the mid-twentieth century. 6.5 x 6.5 in. *Collection of Paula Higgins.* $50-75.

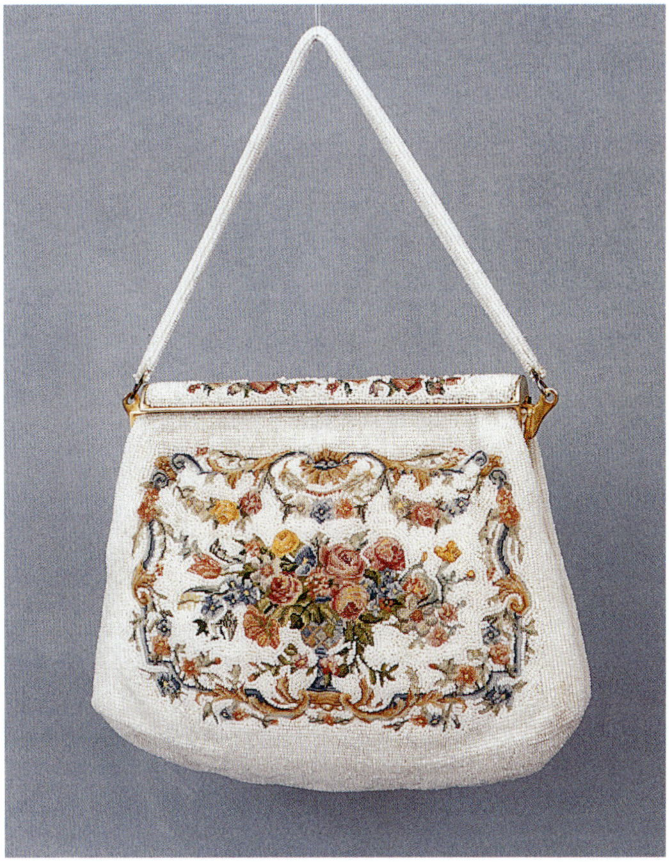

A lovely petit point vase of flowers is surrounded by hand beading. Made in France by Denise Francelle. C.1950s. 8 x 7 in. *Collection of Melissa Overdorf.* $300-350.

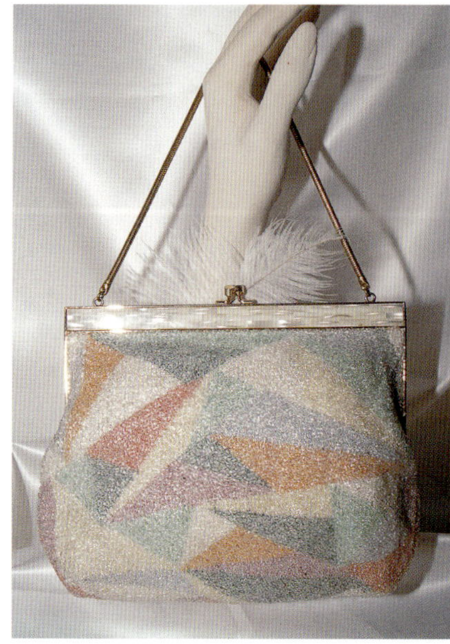

Made in Hong Kong, this sherbet colored purse is beaded in triangular shapes. The frame is made from mother-of-pearl. C.1950s. 9.5 x 6 in. *Collection of Paula Higgins.* $75-100.

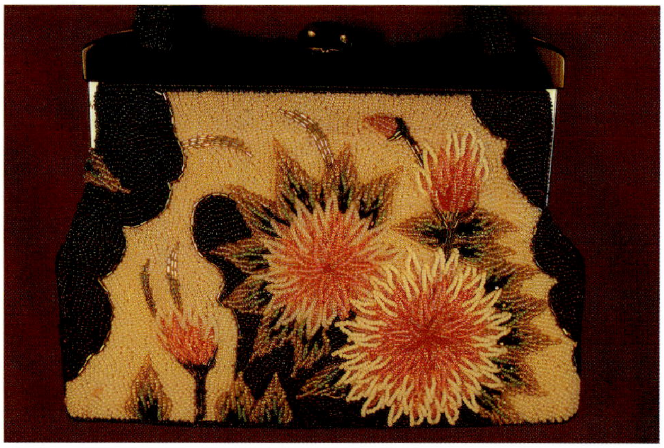

This purse is one of the owner's favorites. She says it never fails to impress people who have seen it. The flowers are beaded in a stunning coral color, in a three dimensional design, adding texture and impact. The frame is made from black plastic. C.1950s. 10 x 7 in. *Collection of Linda Marshall.* $300-350.

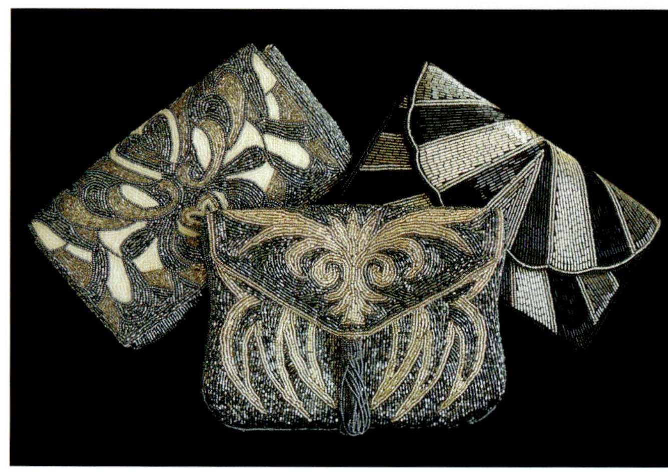

Three more mid-twentieth century purses beaded in silver, black, and beige color schemes. *Collection of Linda Marshall.* $75-100.

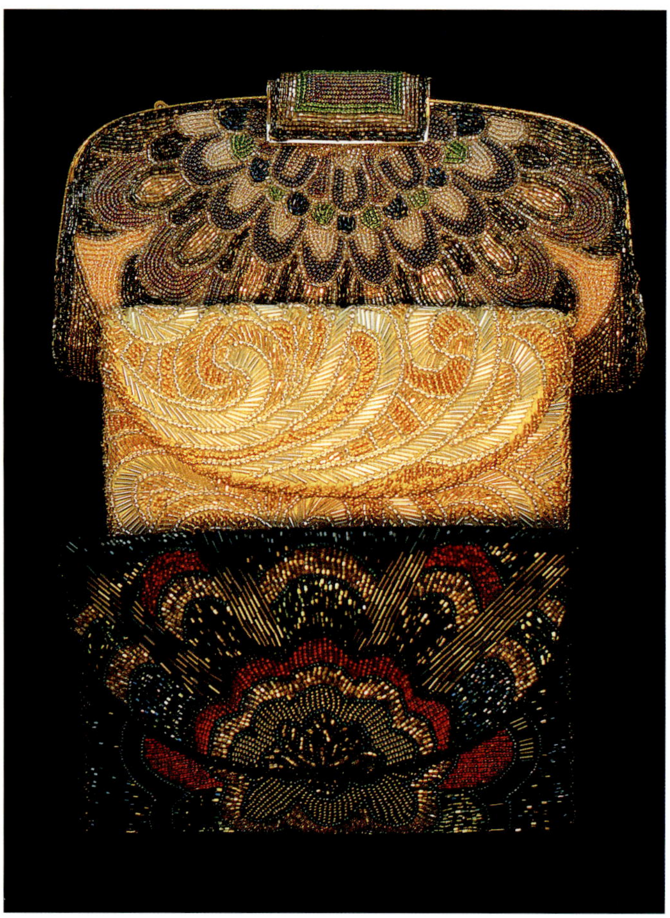

Three, hand beaded vintage purses from the mid-twentieth century. The purse at the top has a peacock feather design. *Collection of Linda Marshall.* $100-150.

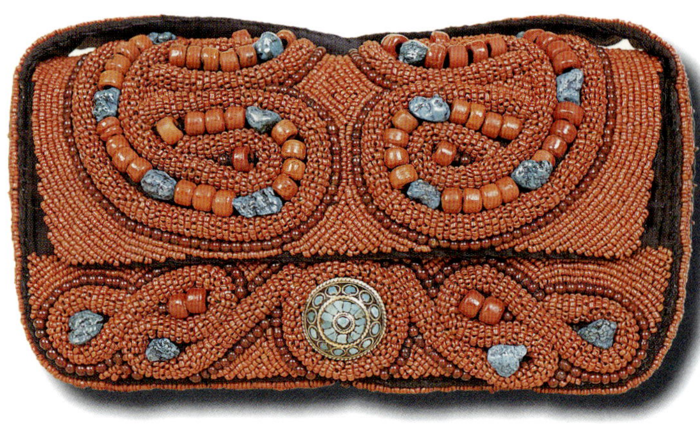

Made in 2004 in India, this purse is entirely beaded with genuine coral and turquoise stones. The effect is exotic and rich. 10 x 5 in. *Collection of Ruth Penson.* $300-350.

Chapter 10
Tortoiseshell, Shell, Ivory, Enamel, and Other Materials

During the first two decades of the 19th century, tortoiseshell and leather purses were made in France and Germany. They were beautifully crafted with polished plaques of tortoiseshell, set into gold embossed, leather bags. In Germany, the tortoiseshell was inlaid with mother-of-pearl, adding a truly lovely touch. The bags were finished with cut steel chains and lyre shaped clasps. The French versions had small, elliptical shaped, steel plaques on the back inscribed with the word "Souvenir" which translated means "Remember Me." Pauline Bonaparte, Napoleon's sister, owned a tortoiseshell and leather purse almost exactly like one pictured in this chapter. Her name was embossed in gold on the under side of the top flap. Another variation of this purse was made in Italy. It was also designed with embossed leather and set with composition plaques.

Tortoiseshell coin purses dating to the nineteenth century were decorated with glass covered painted scenes. Early styles depicted Chinese trade/harbor scenes and later versions pictured scenes from the Paris Exposition of 1867, the Crystal Palace, and the Great Exhibition. These purses were basically a type of souvenir purse. Other tortoiseshell coin purses were inset with small watches, paintings of women, arabesque designs in piqué work, shields, and mother-of-pearl.

Marine shells, especially bi-valve shells, were another popular medium for coin purses. Many were left plain and undecorated with brass hinges and hinged closures. But others were painted with flowers and seascapes. A bi-valve shell in this section was shell carved with a scene of a ship. Sailors carved these wonderful pieces of folk art during their free time while out at sea. After the design was carved, it was colored with berry juice or coal dust, and then set with wax. Shell carving was popular in Birmingham, England during the mid-nineteenth century.

Ivory, along with malachite, mother-of-pearl, and enamel work, was used as an alternative to tortoiseshell in the 19th century to make coin purses. They were decorated in the same manner as the tortoiseshell purses and inset with metals, watches, and paintings. In this chapter there is a carved and pierced ivory coin purse with an attached, carved ivory chain, shown on page 240. This little purse has considerable appeal and it is also rare. A very rare Dieppe tortoiseshell and ivory purse was recently auctioned on Ebay. Made in the early years of the 19th century, it featured finely carved, elliptical plaques of cherubs and flowers set on a curved tortoiseshell frame. A plain fabric bag was attached and the carry chain was made from alternating links of ivory and tortoiseshell. Dieppe, France was the center for fine ivory carving in Europe during the 18th and 19th centuries. Vegetable ivory, which comes from a palm plant, should not be confused with elephant or whale ivory.

During the early 20th century, ivory, enamel, and tortoiseshell were also used to decorate purses. Slim, envelope clutches were decorated with plaques of tortoiseshell and carved ivory scenes. One tortoiseshell example was inlaid with a diamond swag design. Other examples were made with enamel plaques inset with hand painted scenes. These purses bring high prices when offered for sale and are avidly sought after by collectors.

Buying, selling, importing, and exporting tortoiseshell and ivory is difficult because they are materials protected by international law. As of December 28, 1973, tortoiseshell and ivory acquired protected status and stiff penalties are incurred for failure to observe the law. Documentation of the age of the purse is necessary, especially if you are importing and exporting the item.

When buying a tortoiseshell or ivory purse be aware they can suffer condition issues not encountered with other purse materials. Tortoiseshell can become quite dry, which can result in chipping, shattering, cracking, and clouding. Dropping an old tortoiseshell purse on a hard surface can easily cause chipping and scratching. Oiling tortoiseshell with mineral oil will help preserve it. Ivory can also crack under the right conditions. They need to be handled with care.

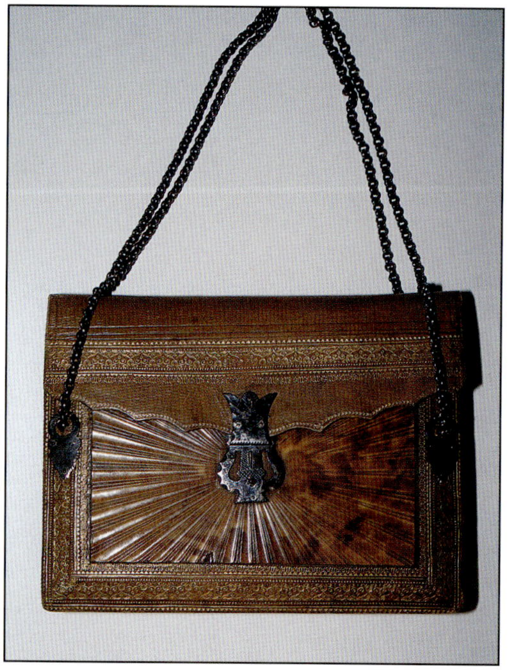

C.1810 French tortoiseshell and leather purse. The leather is embossed with gold and the clasp is made from steel in a lyre shape. On the back is an elliptical steel plaque inscribed with the word "*Souvenir*" which translates to "Remember Me." This was not a souvenir purse in the literal sense of the word. It was meant to be a sentimental expression. Other versions (Italian) were made with composition plaques instead of tortoiseshell. The Germans inlaid their tortoiseshell plaques with mother-of-pearl for an especially beautiful look. 6.25 x 5.25 in. *Collection of Paula Higgins.* Rare.

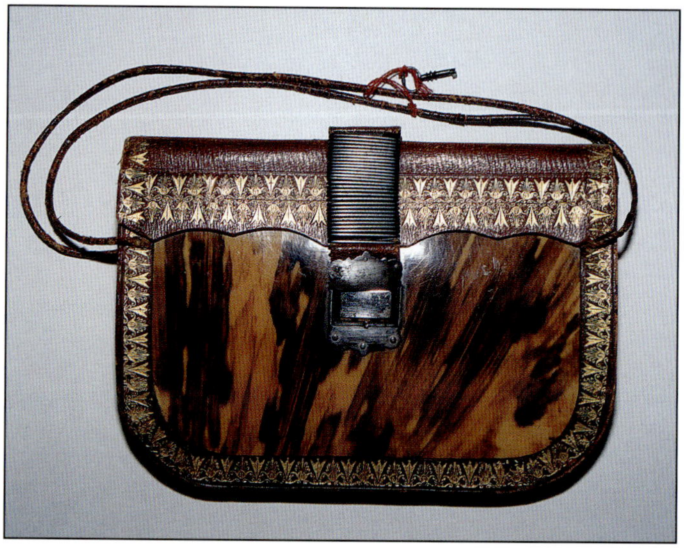

Another early 19th century tortoiseshell and leather purse, originally purchased in England. The original key, which inserts into a lock on the other side, still works. This plaque is polished smooth, rather than scribed like the French purse. 6.5 x 5 in. *Collection of Paula Higgins.* Rare.

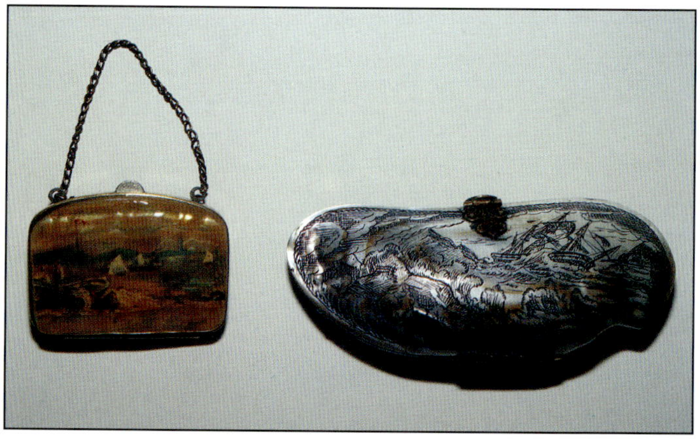

On the left is a small coin purse hand painted with a seascape, dating to the late 19th century. On the right is a rare, shell carved purse with a scene of a ship at sea. On the reverse is a nude. This purse dates to the mid-nineteenth century and was made in England. Sailors would carve shells while out at sea, color them with coal dust or berry juice, and then set the design with wax. Left: 3 x 2.5 in. Right: 4.5 x 2 in. *Collection of Paula Higgins.* Left: $75-100. Right: Rare.

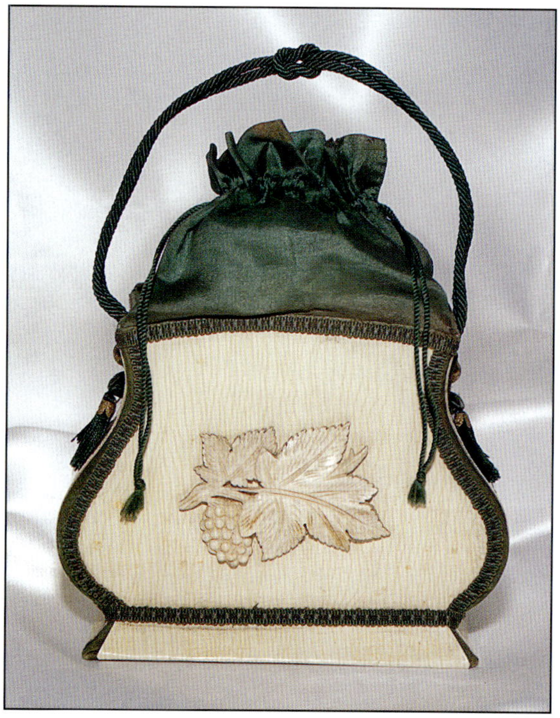

This c.1830, bombé-shaped purse was made of card, painted to look like ivory. The carved leaf is made from real ivory. There are two side tassels, which are barely visible. It is in completely original condition. 6.5 x 5 in. *Collection of Paula Higgins.* Rare.

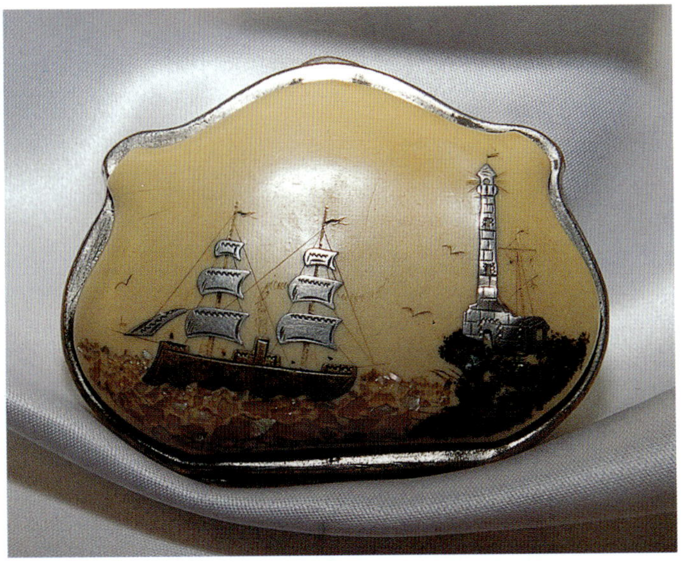

This mid-nineteenth century coin purse has considerable appeal. Made from ivory, mother-of-pearl, silver, and brass, it features a ship at sea and a lighthouse on the rocks. A few fine details are scrimshawed in. 2.75 x 2.75 in. *Collection of Paula Higgins.* $350-450.

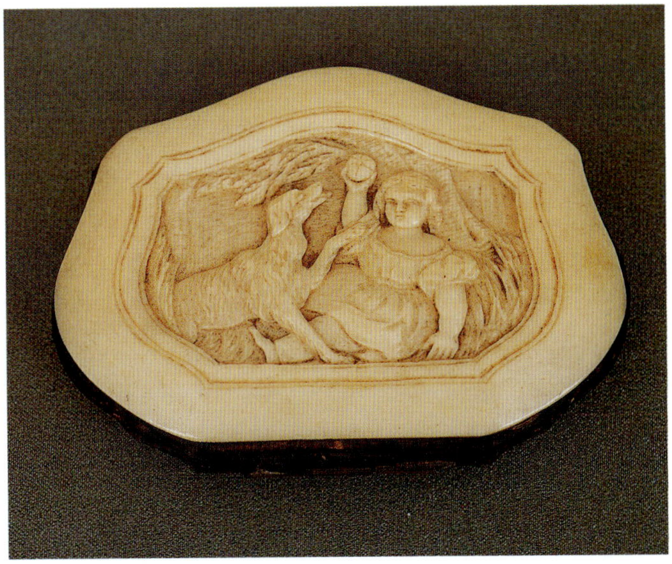

The small child carved on this ivory purse is dressed in mid-nineteenth century period clothing. She is playing ball with her dog in this particularly charming scene. The carving is of a very fine, three dimensional quality. 3 x 2.25 in. *Collection of Lori Blaser.* $350-375.

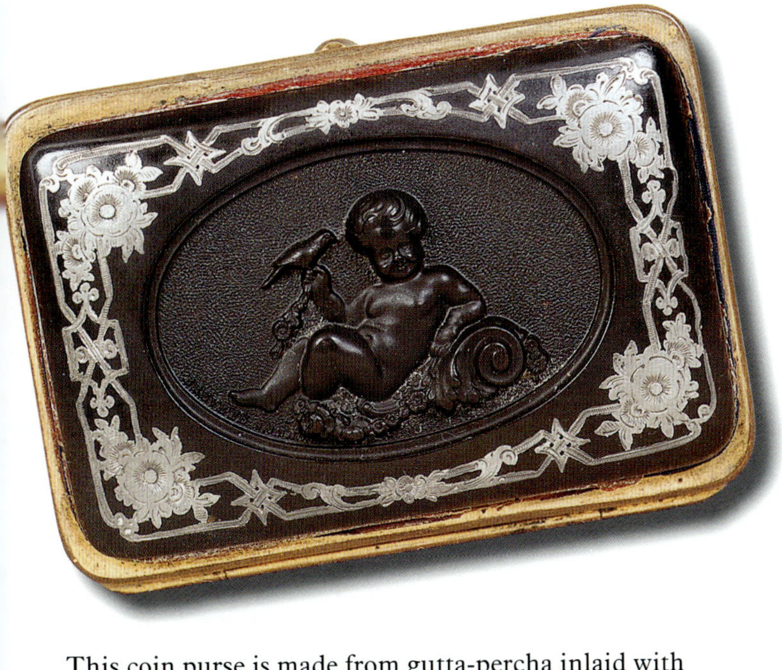

This coin purse is made from gutta-percha inlaid with silver. Gutta-percha was a latex type substance discovered in 1842. It was made from the sap of the gutta-percha tree in South East Asia. The cherub and bird design was very popular during the mid-nineteenth century. 4 x 3 in. *Collection of Lori Blaser.* $300-350.

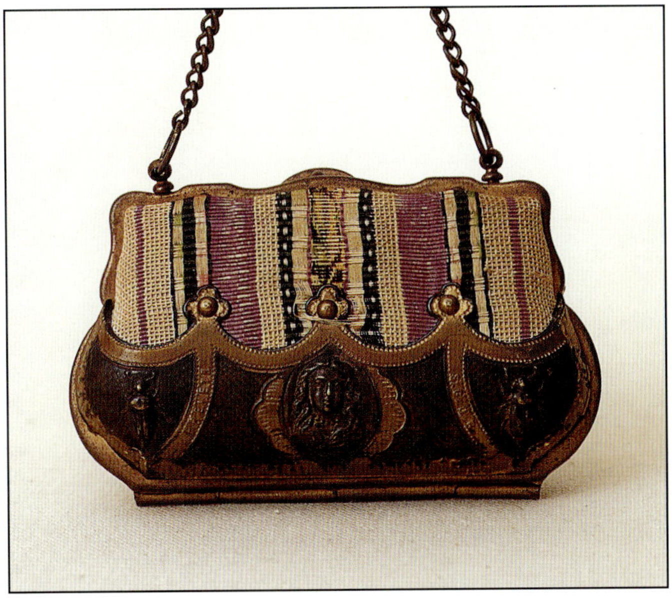

Made in France in the mid-nineteenth century, this silk striped coin purse has a solid bottom decorated with the head of a woman and scarabs. The shape of the purse resembles traveling bags from the same period. 3.5 x 2.5 in. *Collection of Lori Blaser.* $300-350.

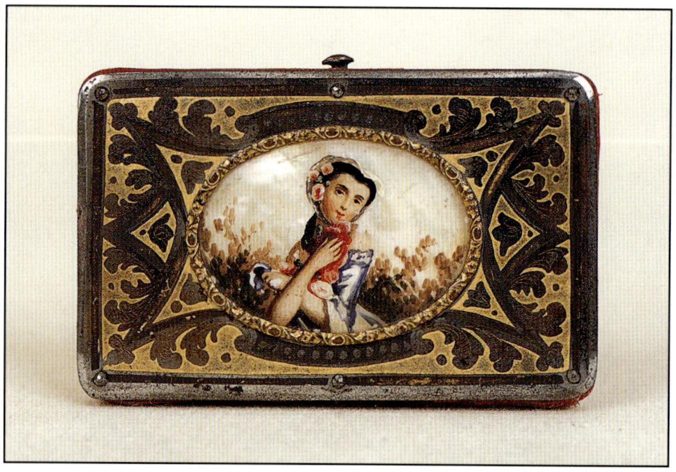

Fine coin purses from the mid-nineteenth century were often decorated with portraits. This 18th century figural is hand painted on a mother-of-pearl background. 3.5 x 2 in. *Collection of Lori Blaser.* $400-450.

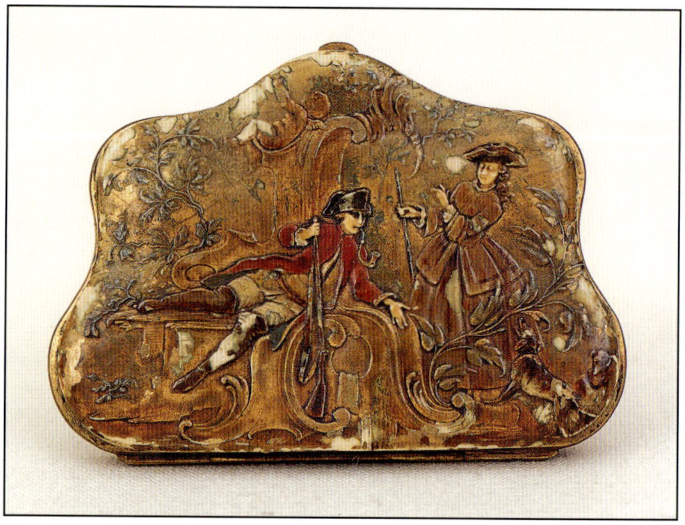

A lovely shape and beautiful enamel work distinguish this coin purse. Decorated with an 18th century hunting scene, it is dated "1888." It is also marked: *M. Klein. Graben 28. Wien. Paris. Carlsbad.* 3.75 x 2.75 in. *Collection of Lori Blaser.* $350-450.

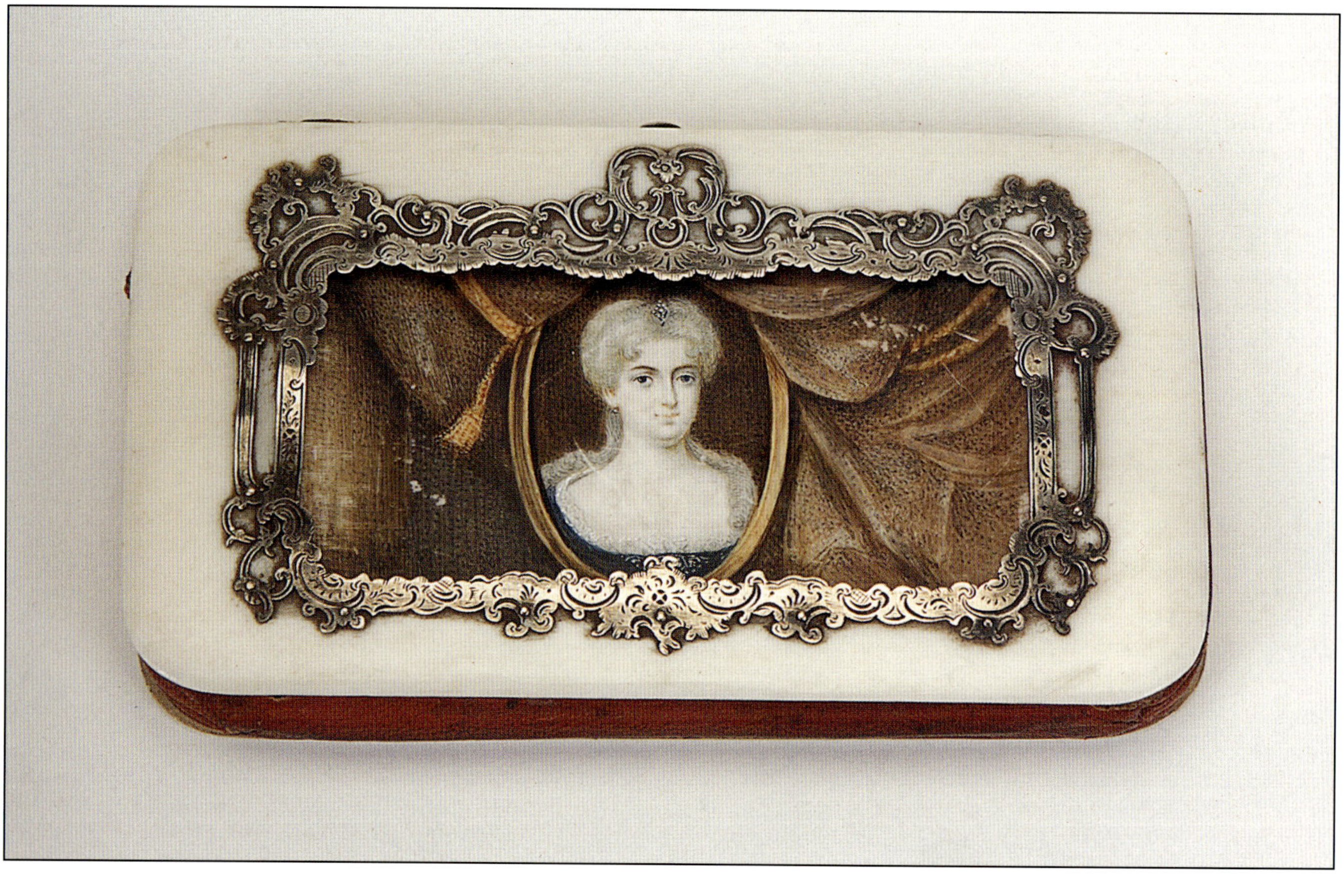

This late 19th century coin purse is spectacular. Made from ivory and silver, the center portrait is hand painted with a figure from the Queen Anne Period, surrounded by draped fabric. The silver frame is beautifully engraved and provides a nice contrast to the grisaille color scheme. The interior is lined with red silk. 4.5 x 2.5 in. *Collection of Lori Blaser.* $450-550.

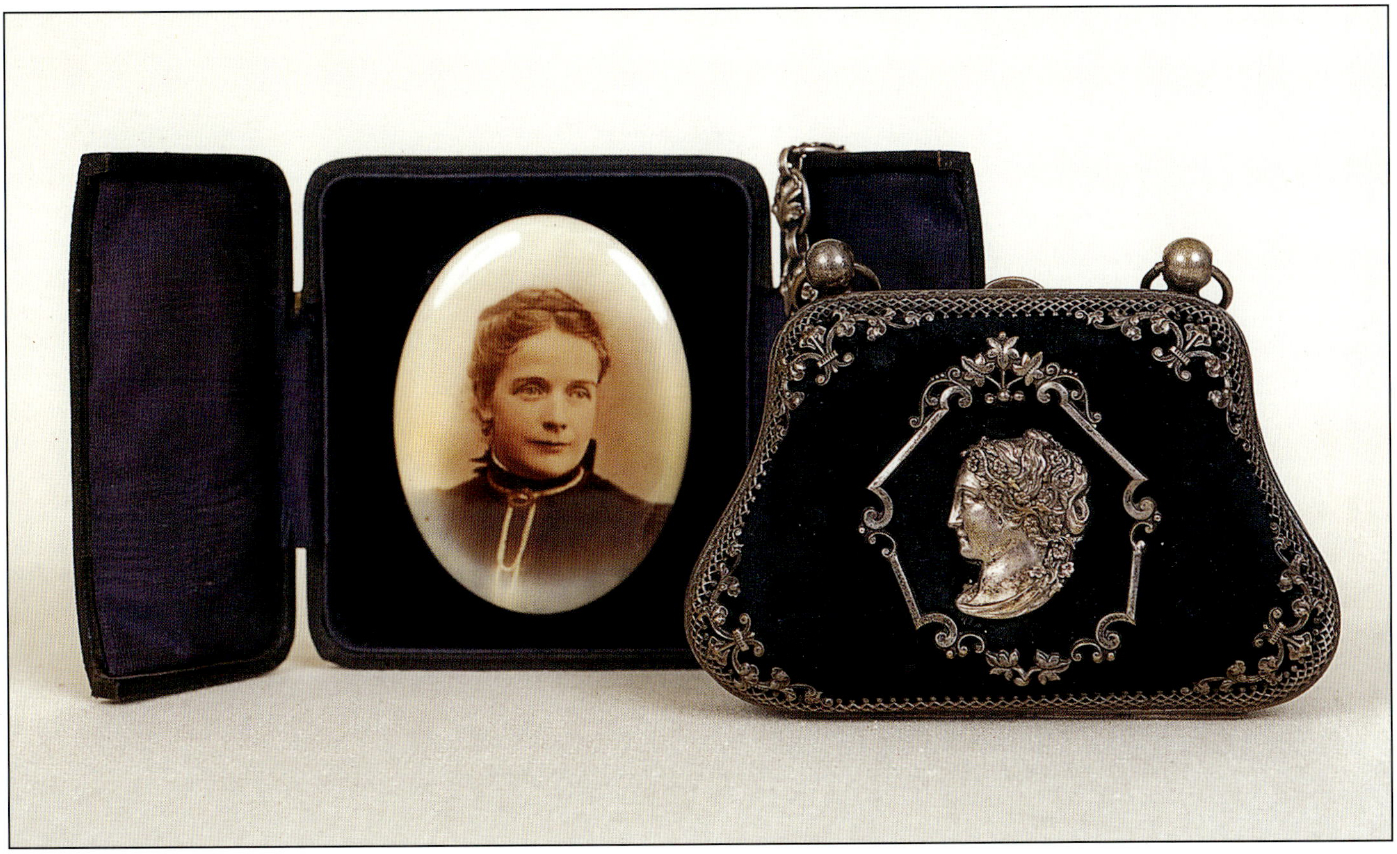

The lovely lady in this picture was a Scottish woman known as "Aunt Jenny" and the original owner of this purse. The velvet hard bodied purse is decorated with a silver Grecian head cameo. It is a very unusual and well preserved coin purse. 5 x 3.5 in. *Collection of Lori Blaser.* Rare.

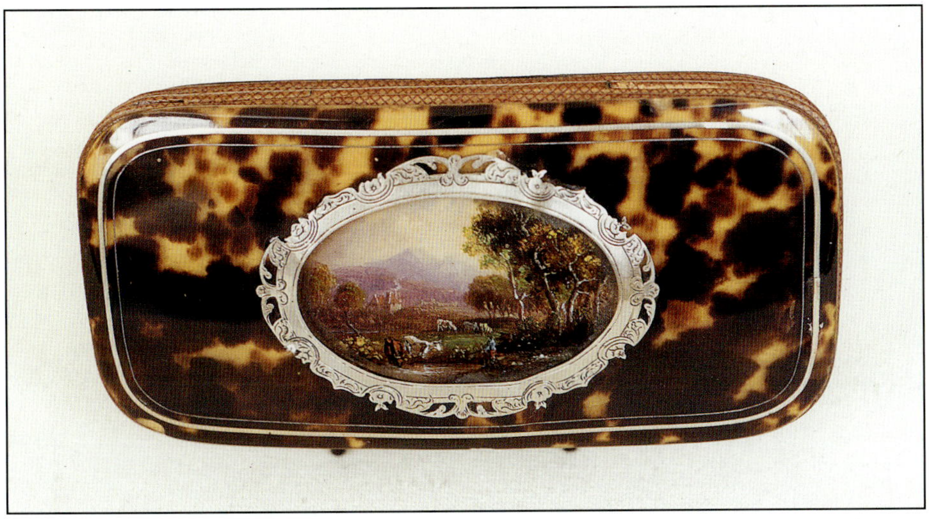

Many purses were decorated with hand painted scenes, but few resemble fine paintings like this one does. Reminiscent of a Turner landscape, the detail in this scene is exceptional. The tortoiseshell is in excellent condition as well. 5.5 x 3 in. *Collection of Lori Blaser.* Rare.

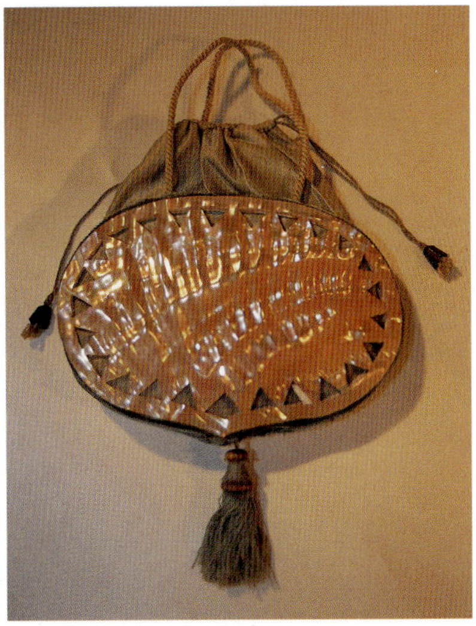

Two large shells were carved and polished to create the front and back for this late 19th century reticule. American. 7.5 x 6 in. *Collection of Paula Higgins.* $100-125.

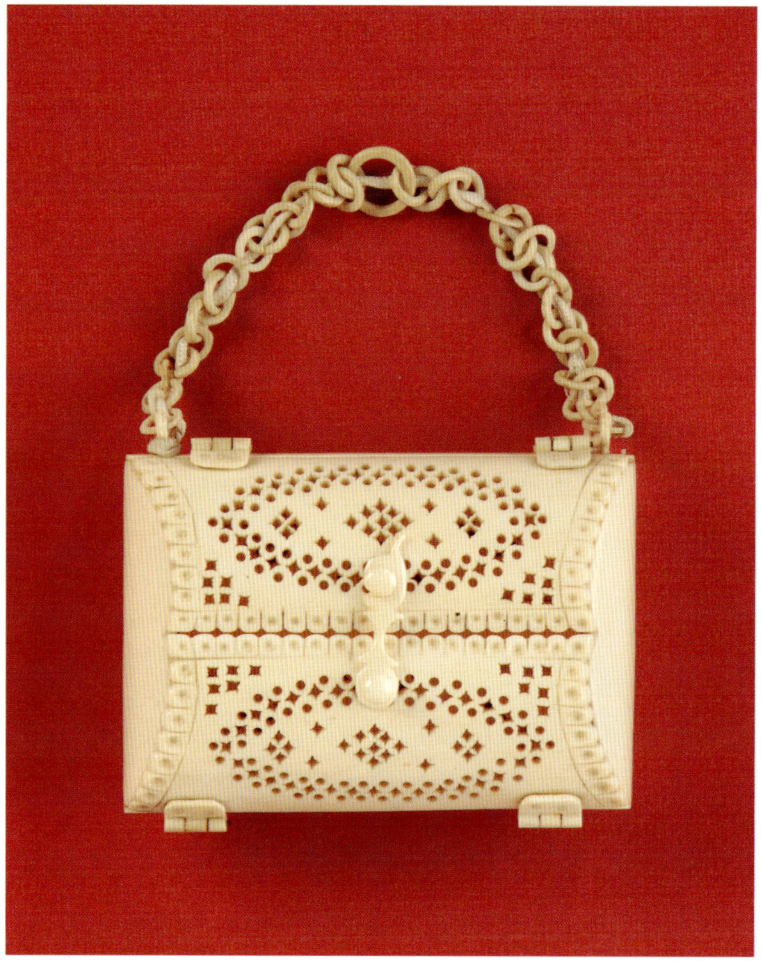

This rare purse is completely made from ivory, including its chain, hinges, and clasp. The design is carved and pierced. Made to hold only a few coins, it is delicate and precious. 4 x 3 in. *Collection of Sharon LuVisi.* Rare.

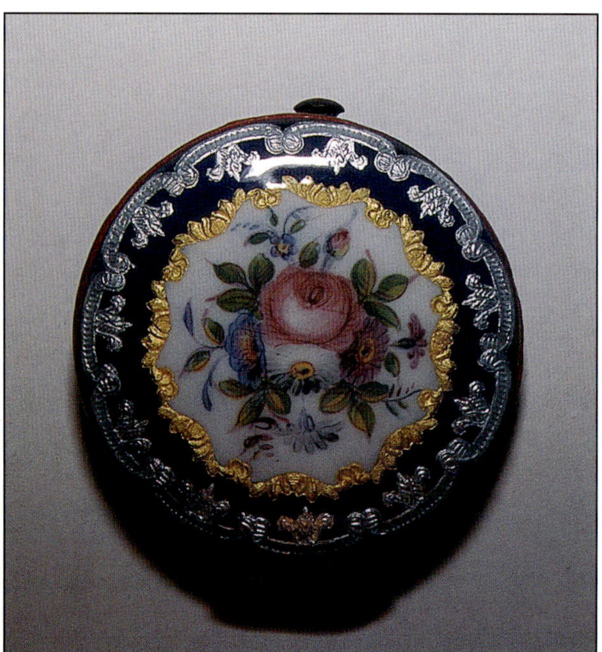

Beautifully enameled, this late 19th century coin purse is more decorative than functional. Because of its small size, it could hold only a few coins. The enamel work is in excellent condition. 3 x 3 in. *Collection of Paula Higgins.* $300-350.

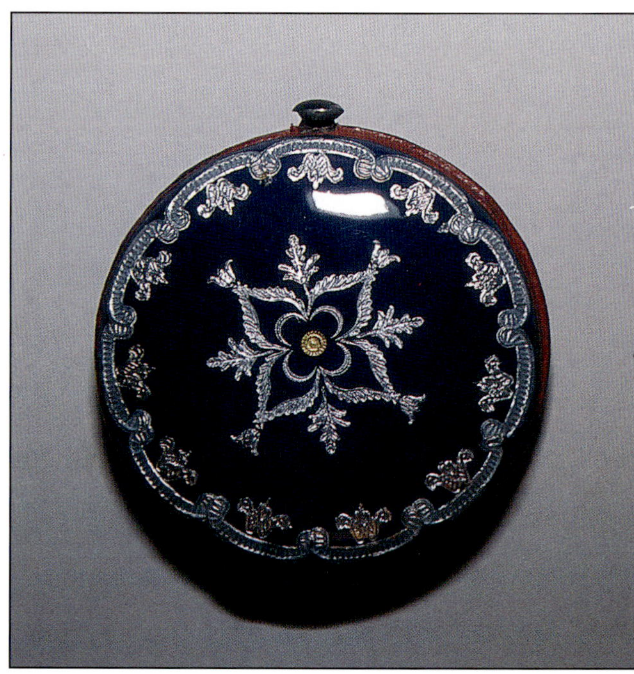

The reverse side of the enameled coin purse.

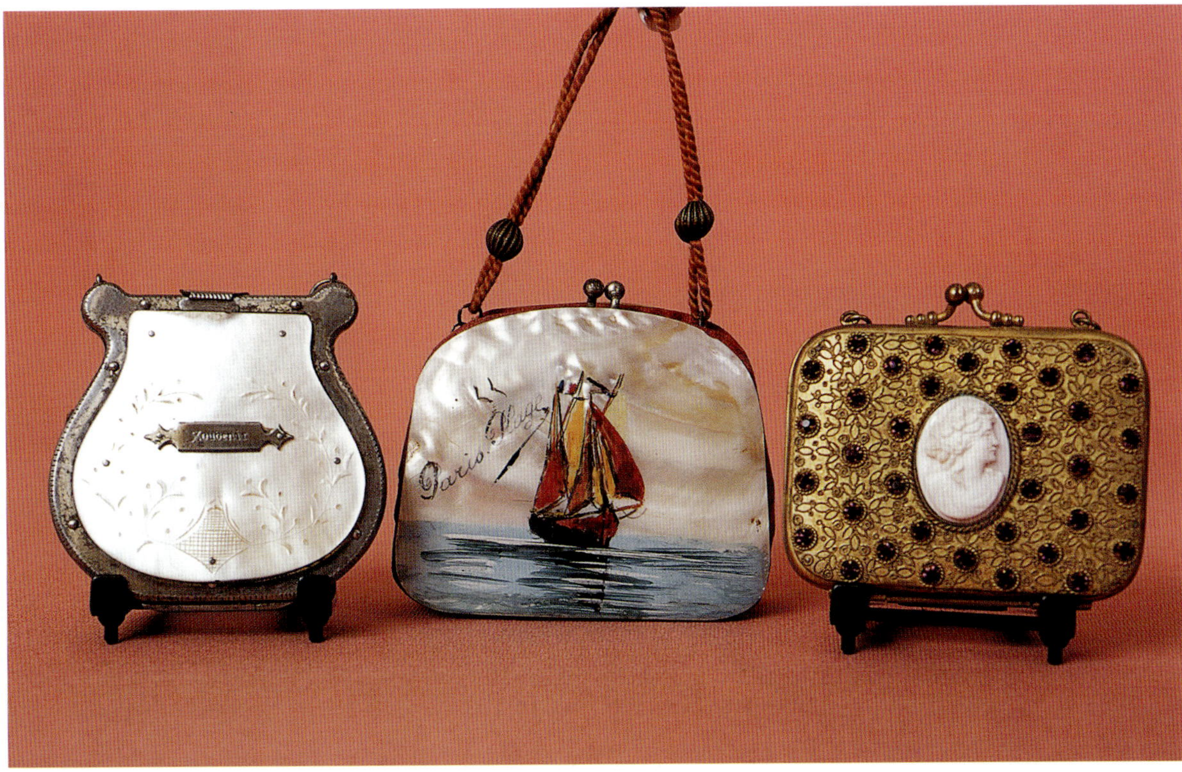

Three nineteenth century coin purses. On the left is a lyre shaped mother-of-pearl coin purse, with a small plate that says "*Souvenir*." In the center is a colorful seascape signed "*Paris Hugs.*" On the right is a coin purse set with a pink coral, carved cameo, surrounded by purple paste stones. Left: 3 x 3 in. Center: 4 x 3 in. Right: 3 x 2.5 in. *Collection of Lori Blaser.* $200-350.

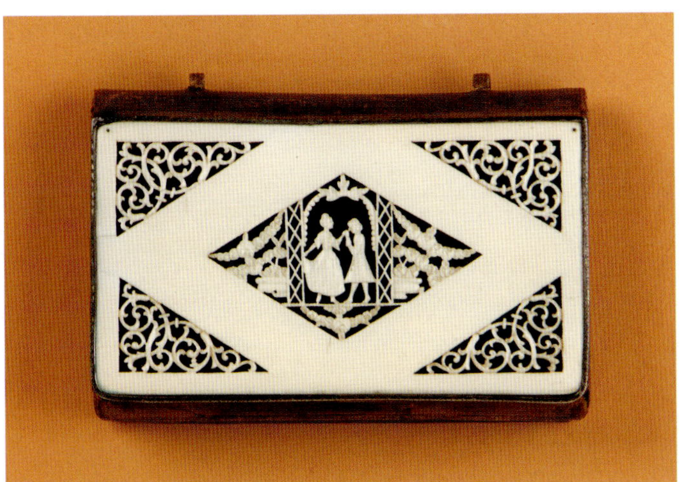

Leather handbags inset with carved ivory panels, real and faux, were popular c.1920. This scene of a woman and girl is flanked by beautiful arabesque designs. The ivory is in very good condition. 9 x 6 in. *Collection of Sharon LuVisi.* $450-600.

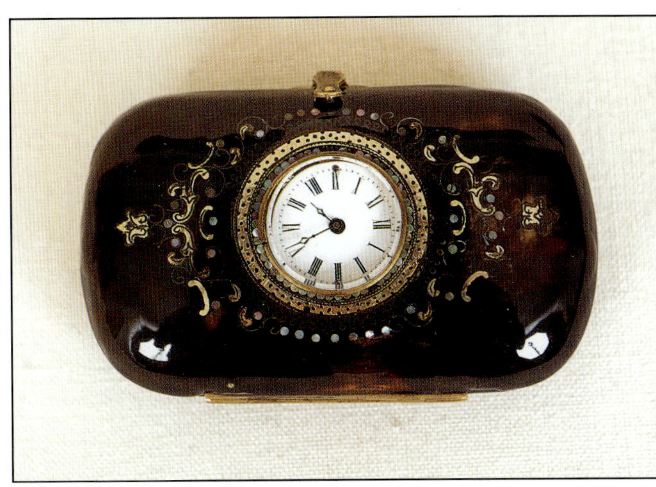

Clock set coin purses are uncommon, particularly in working order with its winding key. This late 19th century tortoiseshell example is also inlaid with mother-of-pearl and piqué work. 3.5 x 2.25 in. *Collection of Lori Blaser.* Rare.

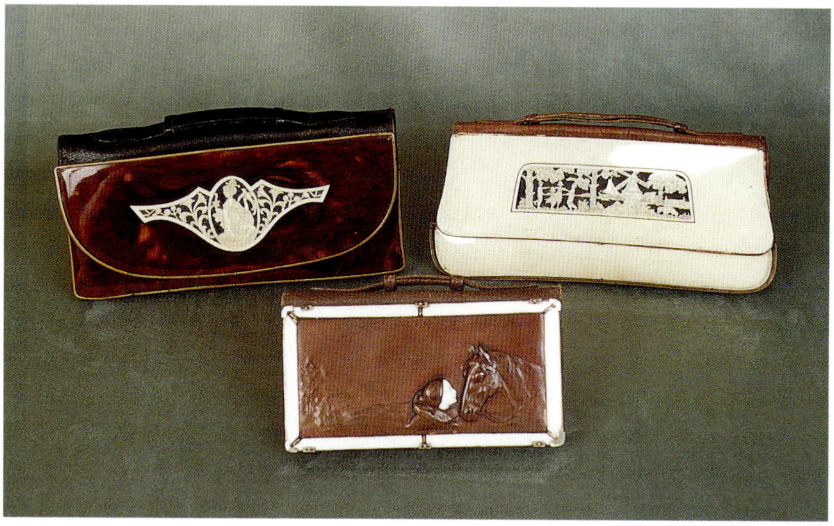

Three pocketbooks from the early 20th century. The purse on the left is made of tortoiseshell. On the front there is a carved, ivory figural design. In the center is a bronze and ivory wallet with a raised design of a Pierette and her horse. On the right is a purse with an ivory carved scene. All three purses have leather backs. Left: 7.75 x 3.75 in. Center: 7.75 x 3.75 in. Right: 5.75 x 3.5 in. *Collection of Lori Blaser.* Left and right: $450-600. Center: Rare.

This impressive c.1920 pocketbook has a guilloche enamel plaque on the front, which is inset with a hand painted medallion. The painted courting scene was made famous by the Rococo Era painter, Jean-Honore Fragonard. The back is made from suede. 8 x 5 in. *Collection of Lori Blaser.* $650-750.

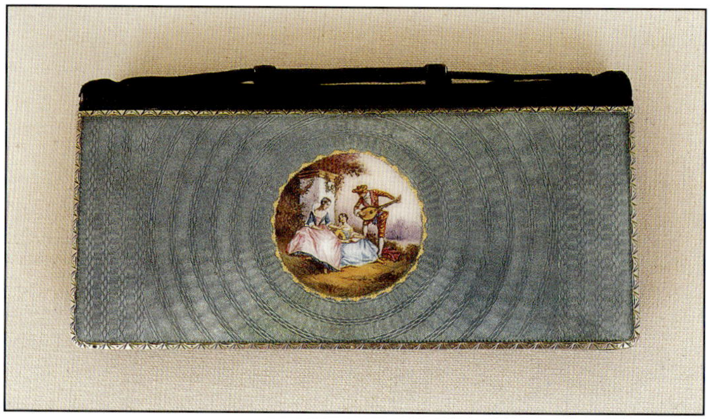

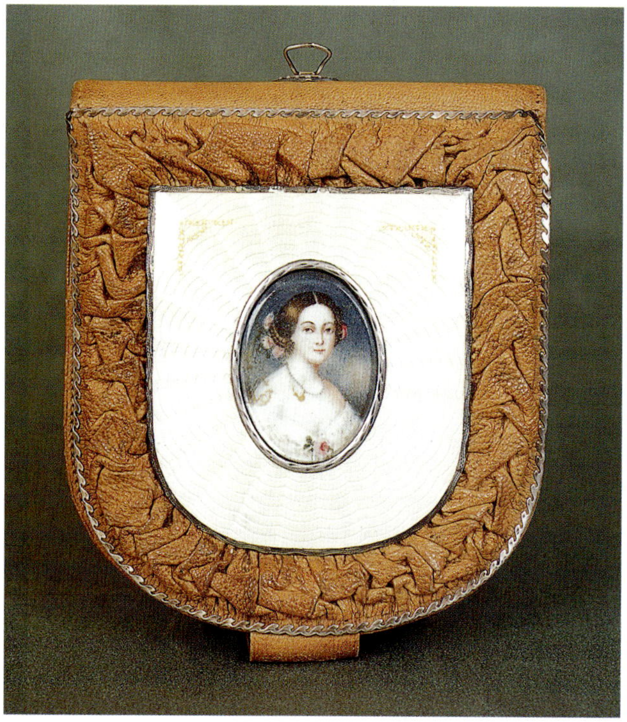

A purse with an unusual shape, is beautifully decorated with a guilloche enamel plaque, and inset with a hand painted portrait on ivory. The leather border is ruched. Purses like this have a universal appeal. 6.25 x 3.25 in. *Collection of Lori Blaser.* $650-750.

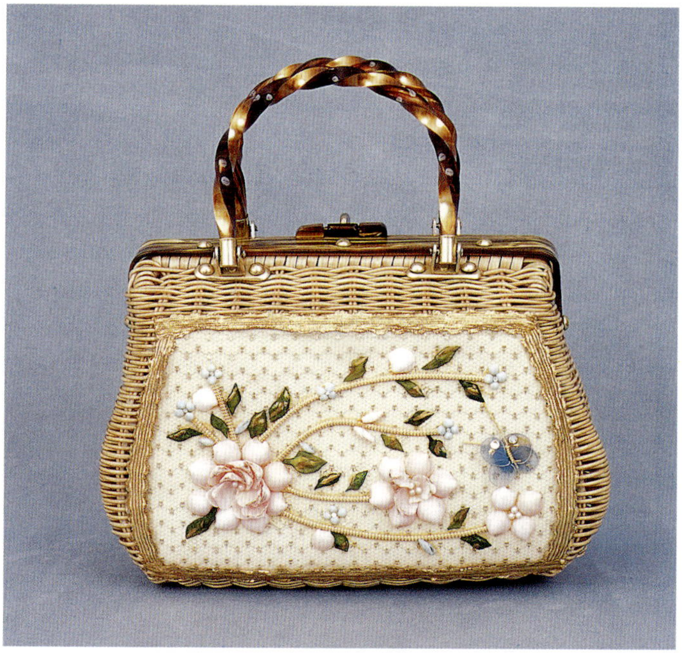

Shell purses were made well into the 20th century. The flowers on this wicker purse are made from sea shells. It was designed by Atlas Florida. 10 x 9 in. *Collection of Lori Blaser.* $100-150.

Chapter 11
Souvenir Purses

Among the earliest known souvenir purses are 18th century leather pocketbooks made in Turkey and embroidered with the name *Constantinople*. Some were dated as well, confirming not only their place of origin, but also their date in time.

By the mid-nineteenth century, small coin purses were inset with paintings and lithographs of great events such as the Great Exhibition, the Paris Exposition, the opening of the Crystal Palace, and the Columbian Exposition in Chicago. Others were made with scenes of the Rialto Bridge in Venice. All appealed to the sentimental side of the 19th century traveler. A very special type of souvenir purse was made in France during the mid-nineteenth century. An example is pictured in the following chapter made from blue velvet, a gilt basket, and painted ivory medallions. Besides being rare and costly, it is an exceptionally beautiful example.

Other purses were sold as souvenirs from the seaside, especially in England. Usually made from mother-of-pearl, they were hand painted with scenes or words. By the 20th century, souvenir purses were sold from Niagara Falls, the New Jersey shores, and the World Fair. Small, beaded box purses, made by American Indians, were also sold to tourists during the early 20th century.

During World War I, purses were made in France specifically to sell to allied soldiers. Men bought these purses to send to their wives and girlfriends back home. Decorated with the flags of France and America, or in some cases a complete set of allied flags, they appear for sale periodically. Others are embroidered with the words "Souvenir of France." Besides boosting support for the war, they provided badly needed income.

By the 1930s, people were traveling in ever increasing numbers, and to more exotic locations thanks to the airplane. Prior to World War II, the Japanese made leather clutches with embossed and painted Japanese scenes to sell to western consumers. Travelers to Egypt returned with leather bags decorated with hieroglyphics, sphinx, and pharaohs. Gold embossed Florentine bags from Italy were another popular tourist item.

The mid-twentieth century brought us novelty bags from Disneyland and leather worked bags from the southwest. All were made to sell to tourists. Traveling had become so popular by the mid-twentieth century that box handbags were decorated with the words "Paris," "London," and "Rome" and sold from retail stores. You didn't even have to leave America to own one. By the late 20th century, everyone was traveling, and what was once a special and rare event, had become commonplace. So while souvenir purses became a thing of the past, they also became a new collectible.

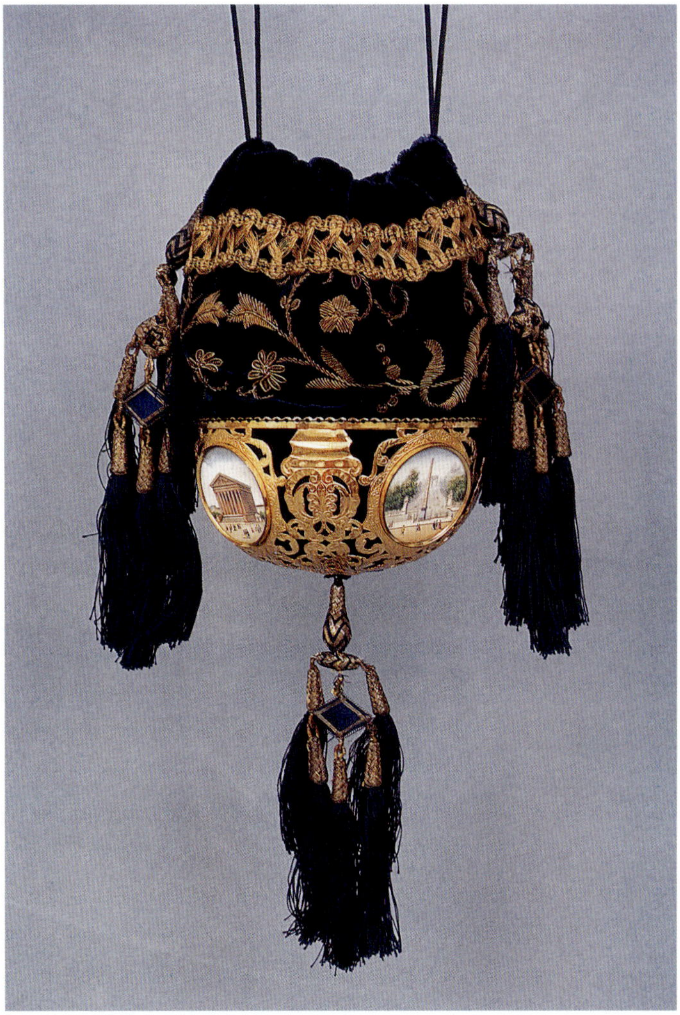

One of the most beautiful purses anyone will ever see is this mid-nineteenth century, Grand Tour souvenir purse from France. Made from blue velvet, embroidered with gold thread, the reticule is surrounded by a gilt metal basket. The basket is pierced and inset with ivory medallions, hand painted with scenes of Paris. Hanging from the bottom and sides are ornate tassels, wrapped with braided gold thread, and decorated with pieces of Venetian glass. The exceptional quality of this souvenir purse distinguishes it from other examples. 10 x 5.5 in. *Collection of Lori Blaser.* Very rare.

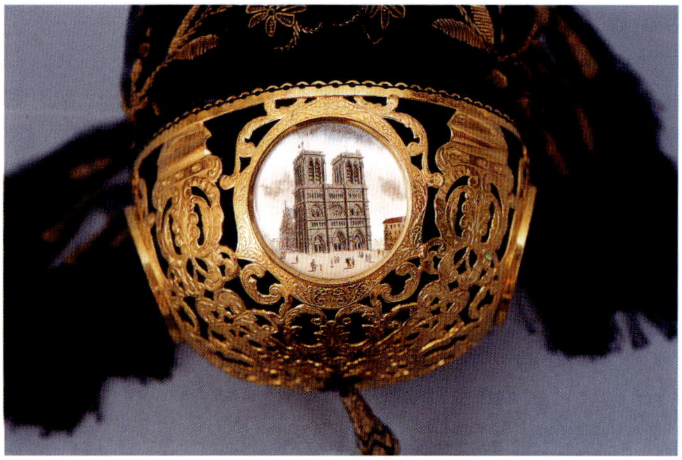

A view of Notre Dame Cathedral.

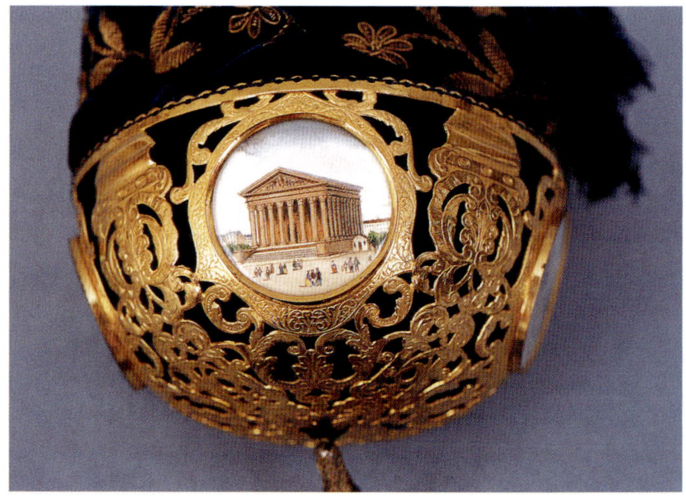

La Madeleine, a famous church built in the Greek temple style.

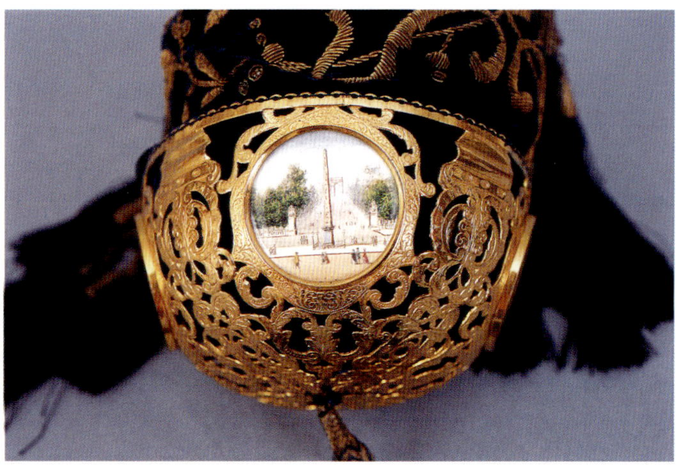

The Egyptian Obelisk in the Place de la Concorde.

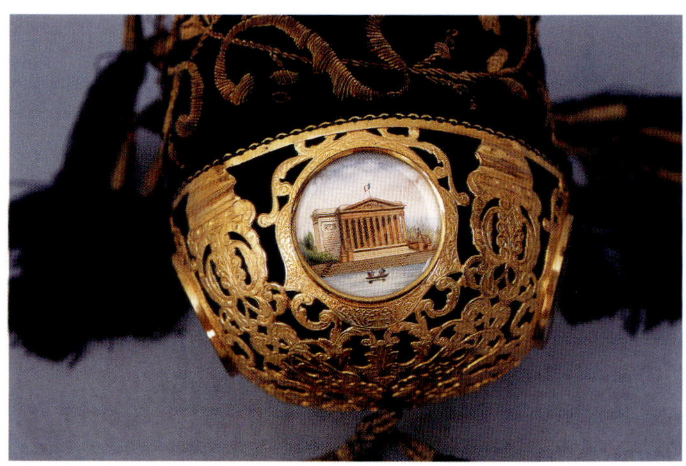

A Parisian building built in the Greek temple style, possibly the National Assembly building.

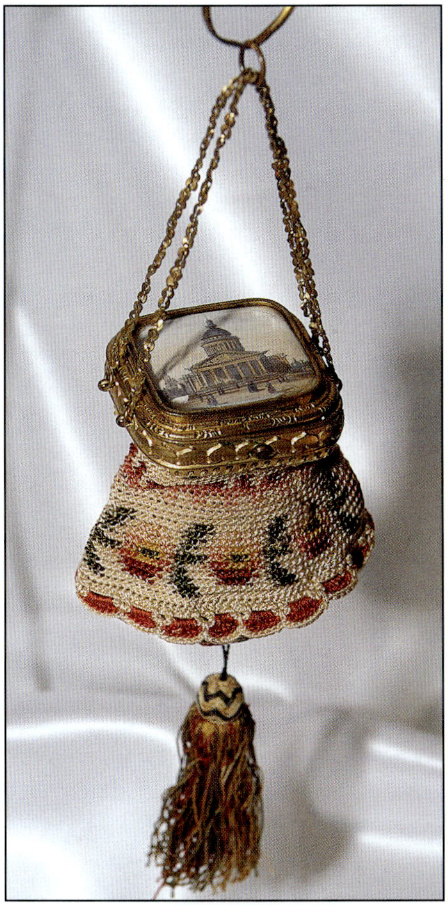

A gilt metal finger chatelaine, with a lithographed picture of the Pantheon in Paris. Many of the finger ring souvenir purses were made with vinaigrettes or calendars built into their tops, although this purse does not have either. Mid-nineteenth century. 4.5 x 1.75 in. *Collection of Paula Higgins.* $450-550.

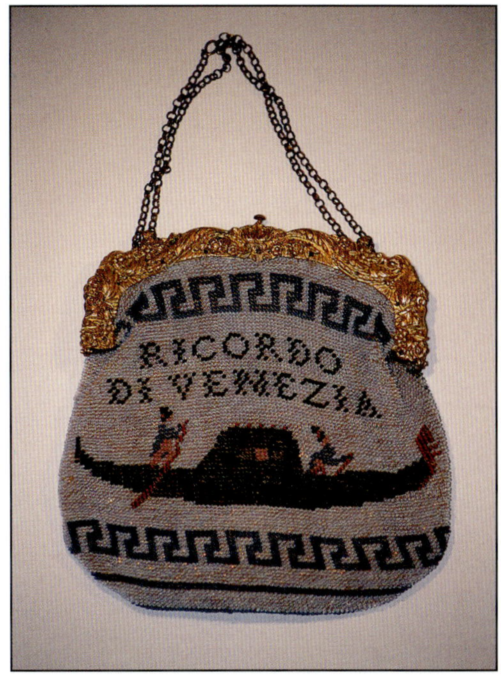

Mid-nineteenth century beaded purses from Venice were popular tourist items. The covered, 19th century gondola was a typical design on these souvenir purses. "Ricordo Di Venezia" translates to "Memory of Venice." The scrolling gilt frame is highly decorative. It dates to the mid-nineteenth century. 7 x 7 in. *Collection of Paula Higgins.* $350-450.

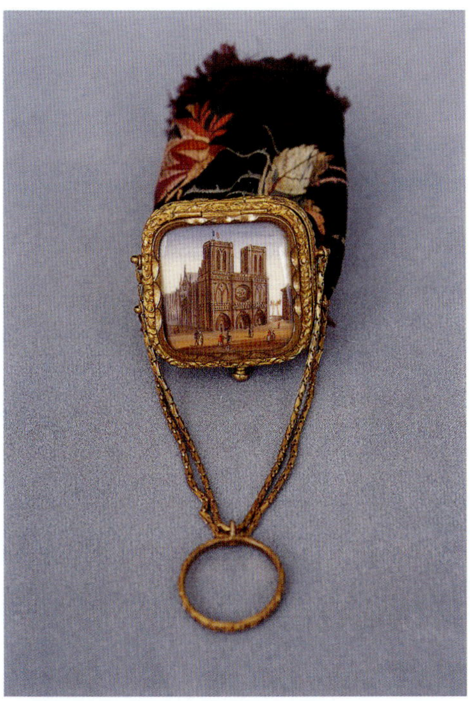

Another finger ring chatelaine made for the souvenir/tourist market. The scene is of Notre Dame Cathedral in Paris. The gilt metal frame and finger chain are attached to fabric, which has been silk stitched. Inside the top frame is a vinaigrette. Mid-nineteenth century. 3.75 x 1.75 in. *Collection of Lori Blaser.* $625-675.

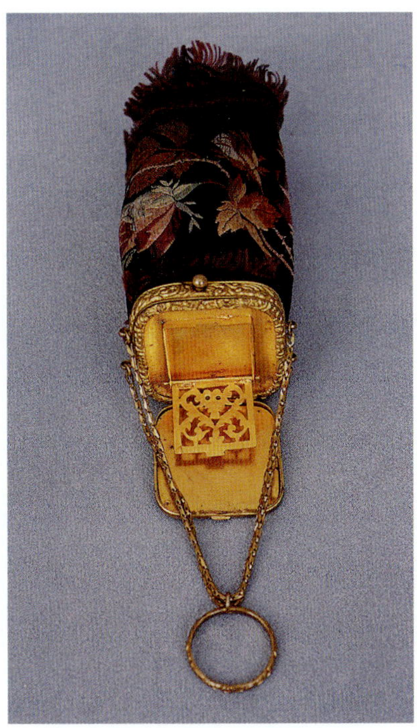

An interior view of the top of the finger ring chatelaine showing the vinaigrette.

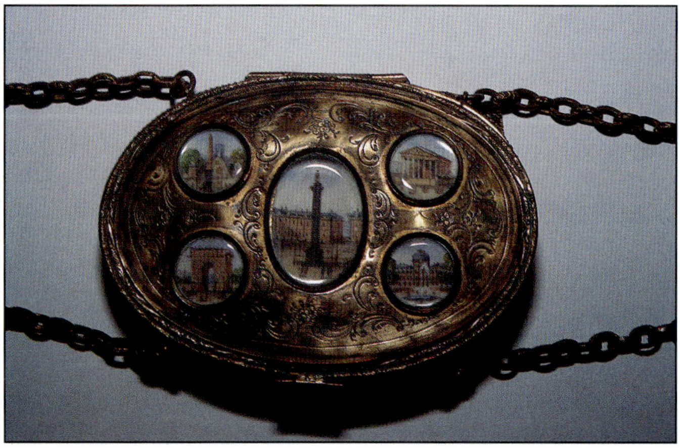

A close-up of the top shows scenes of Paris. Top left: the Egyptian Obelisk in the Place de la Concorde. Lower left: The Arch de Triomphe. Center: The July Column in the Place de la Bastille. Top right: La Madeleine (church). Bottom right: Probably the Tuileries Palace before it was burned down in the 1870s.

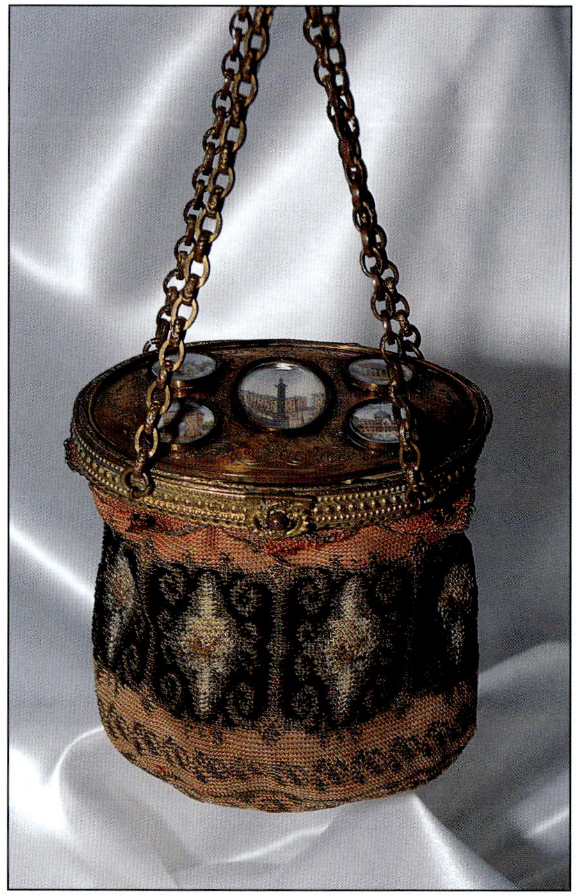

A French souvenir purse, with a silk and gold thread knitted bottom. The gilt metal top is set with hand painted ivory medallions, covered by glass. Mid-nineteenth century. 6 x 4.5 in. *Collection of Paula Higgins.* $650-750.

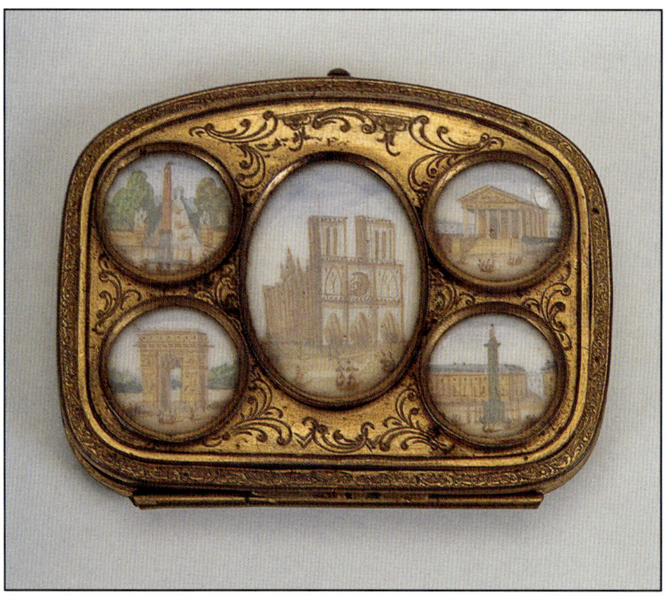

A Grand Tour souvenir coin purse with a gilt top, and ivory painted medallions of Paris scenes. Top left: The Egyptian Obelsik in the Place de la Concorde. Bottom left: The Arch de Triomphe. Center: Notre Dame Cathedral. Top right: La Madeleine (church). Bottom right: The July Column in the Place de la Bastille. Mid-nineteenth century. 2.75 x 2.25 in. *Collection of Lori Blaser.* $600-650.

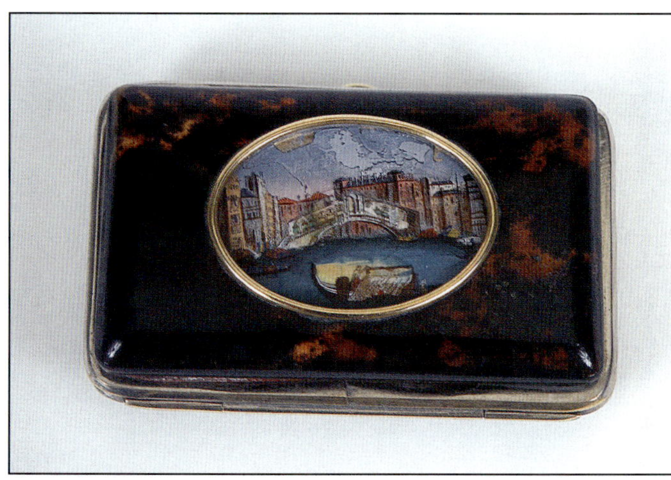

Italy also produced some lovely souvenir coin purses. This example is eglomise painted (reverse painted on glass) with a scene of the Rialto Bridge in Venice. Scenes of Venice are rarely seen on these coin purses. 3.5 x 2.5 in. Mid-nineteenth century. *Collection of Lori Blaser.* $500-600.

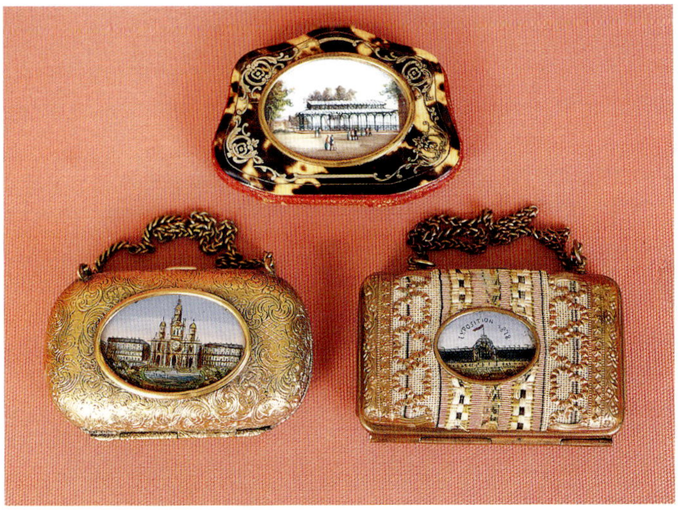

Starting from the mid-nineteenth century, Universal Exhibitions were held in Paris every eleven years. Coin purses were made to commemorate these exhibitions. There was also a World's Fair held in Paris in 1878, and again, more purses were made as souvenirs. In 1851, in England, The Great Exhibition at the Crystal Palace was held. Coin purses were made for this event as well. The purses pictured here, were made as souvenirs for these exhibitions. The purse on the right is marked "*Exposition 1878.*" Left: 3.25 x 2.25 in. Top: 3.25 x 2.25 in. Right: 3.25 x 2.25 in. *Collection of Lori Blaser.* $400-450.

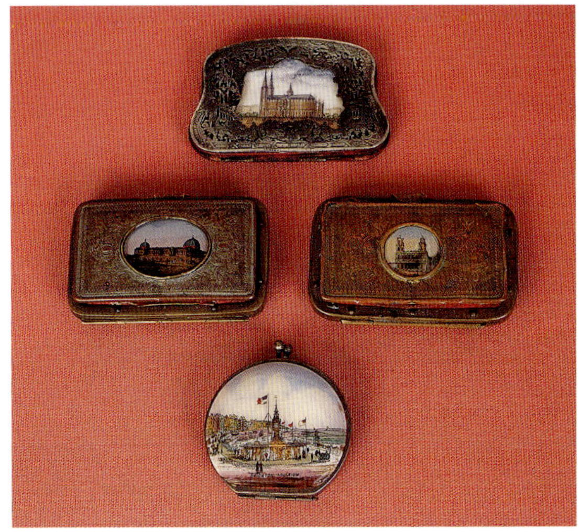

Four 19th century souvenir purses, three with hand painted scenes. The bottom purse has a painted scene of the Brighton Aquarium in England. Mid-nineteenth century. Top, Left, and Right: 3.25 x 2.25 in. Bottom: 2.25 x 2.25 in. *Collection of Lori Blaser.* $350-450.

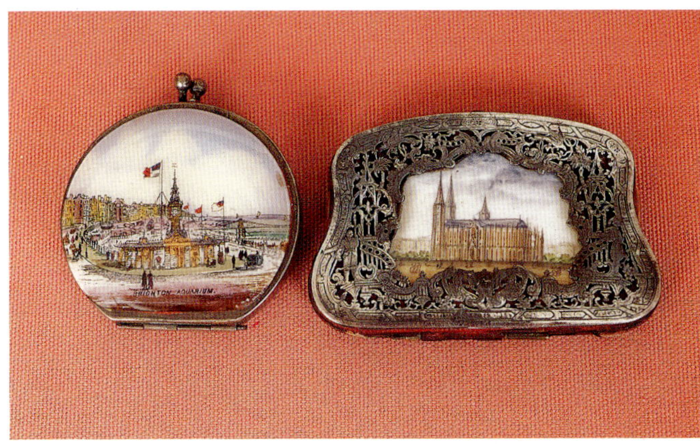

A close-up of two of coin purses from the previous picture.

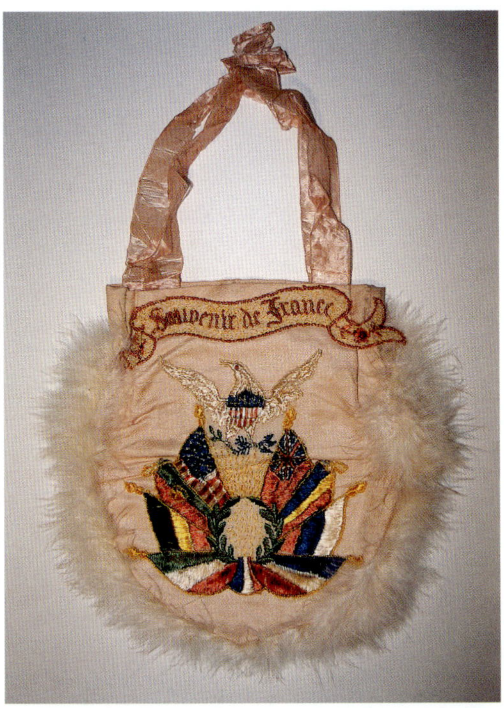

During World War I, the French made souvenir purses for American soldiers to send to their wives and girlfriends back home. This is an example of a purse designed to appeal to any soldier's sense of patriotism. The flags of the principal allies are appliquéd onto the pink silk background. Above the flags, "*Souvenir de France*" is embroidered. 8 x 8 in. *Collection of Paula Higgins.* $200-250.

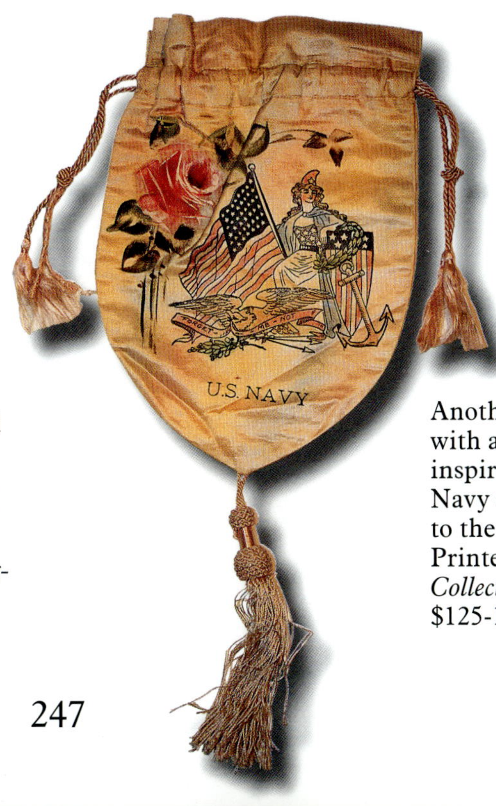

Another patriotic purse with a United States Navy inspired design. This U.S. Navy souvenir purse dates to the World War One era. Printed on silk. 11 x 7 in. *Collection of Paula Higgins.* $125-150.

Chapter 12
Plastic Purses

Early plastic purses were made from celluloid and Bakelite. By 1910, celluloid was used to make purse frames and fittings. Because it easily imitated the more costly ivory and tortoiseshell, it was widely used. But this early plastic was highly flammable, creating potentially dangerous situations. So Bakelite, made from phenol, carbolic acid, and formaldehyde, was used as an alternative prior to World War II. In the book *Bags*, by Hendrikje Ivo of the Tassenmuseum Hendrikje, are three Rodolac pochettes from the 1930s. Besides being rare, they are among the earliest purses made completely of plastic. An early Bakelite purse, pictured in this chapter, was inset with rhinestones and made for a child. Bakelite originally came in five colors, but after the patent was acquired by the Catalin Company in 1927, the process was modified to allow a wider range of colors. Fifteen more colors were added. Some experts feel that as much as 70% of all objects identified as Bakelite were actually made by the Catalin Company. The Bakelite Company was bought by Union Carbide in 1938.

Lucite first made its appearance in 1931, but it wasn't until after World War II that purse designers used it to combine inspiration with form and function. The plastic purses of the 1950s are not only accessories, but pieces of sculpture as well. Combined with rhinestone decoration, pearls, metals, shells, gold threads, and fabric they were highly decorative. Lucite purses were carved, molded, and twisted into a myriad of shapes and forms. It could be made opaque or translucent. A whole wall of these bags is an impressive sight and also an interesting way to decorate a room. Major designers of Lucite purses included: Wilardy, Llewellyn, Rialto, Kahn, Florida, Dorset Rex, Tyrolean, Myles Originals, Gilli Originals, and Patricia of Miami. Cheaper versions were made by other manufacturers, making them even more accessible.

Other bags were made in the clutch style out of small plastic tiles in the 1940s or from coiled plastic, like telephone cords, in the 1950s. Many of us remember the clear plastic, which covered the fabric flowers on the children's purses from the 1950s. By the last quarter of the 20th century, vinyl and acrylic had replaced Lucite in the purse world. Vinyl and acrylic were used by purse designers everywhere, even by couture designers like Coco Chanel. In the book *Handbags*, by Anna Johnson, there is a purse pictured made of acrylic, which has been completely hand painted on the inside with pink flowers. Made by Joyce Francis in 2002, it is a visual feast for the eyes. Purses like this one are true investment pieces for the future.

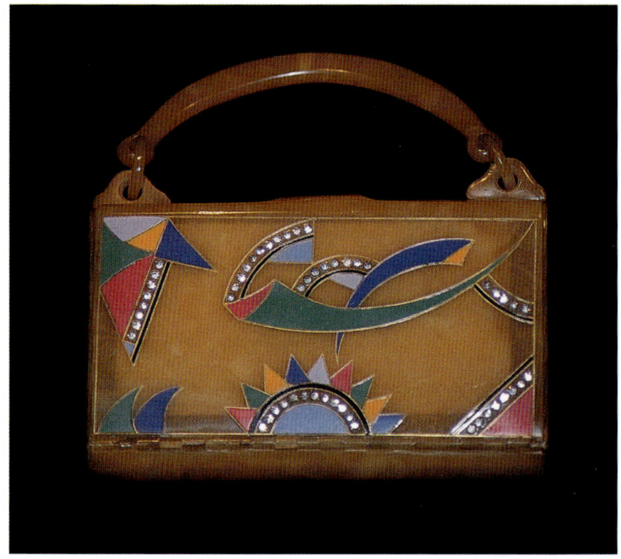

Bakelite was invented in 1907, but wasn't used in purse design until c.1920. This yellow Bakelite purse was made for a child, which accounts for the bright inlaid colors. Rhinestone set, like the adult versions, it provided plenty of sparkle to make any child happy. 5 x 3 in. *Collection of Paula Higgins.* $400-500.

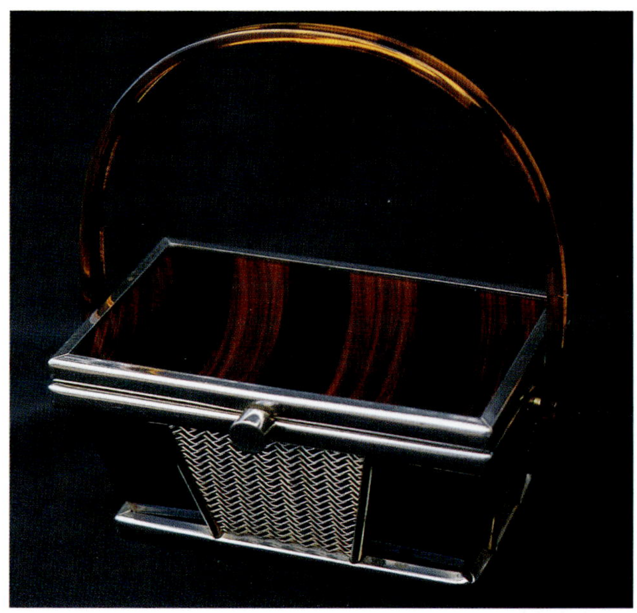

Tyrolean specialized in Lucite bags, made with metal filigreed panels. Faux tortoiseshell was one of their signature colors and their designers favored the box shape. Made in the 1950s. 7.5 x 4.0 in. *Collection of Linda Marshall.* $350-450.

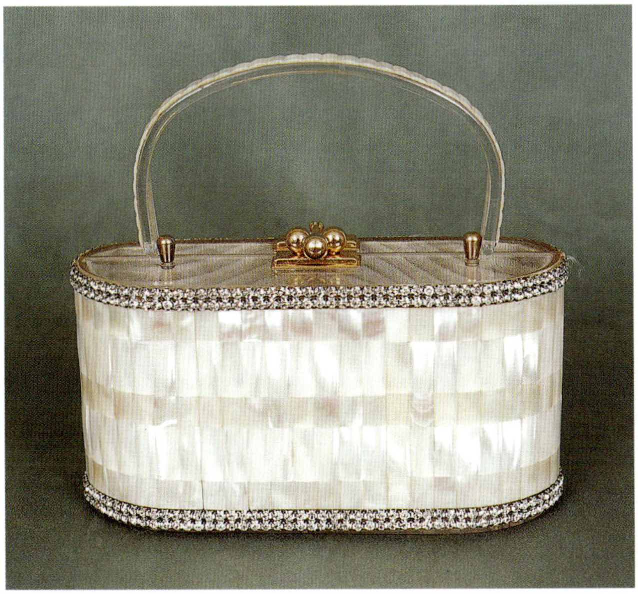

Lucite, made in a mother-of-pearl finish, makes for a stunning bag. Rows of rhinestones border the top and bottom. The exceptional finish and the rhinestones surrounding the whole bag, make this a very desirable Lucite purse. It is unmarked and dates to the 1950s. 8.5 x 7.5 in. *Collection of Ruth Penson.* $400-500.

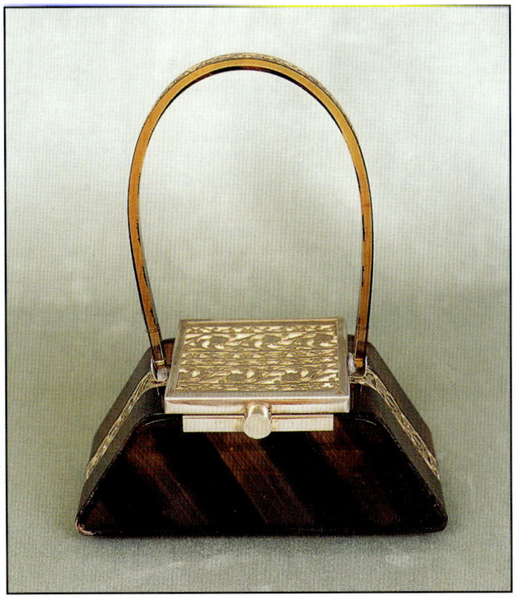

Another Tyrolean of New York faux tortoiseshell purse made with a brass filigreed top. The sides of the bag are also decorated with metal work banding. 8.5 x 4 in. *Collection of Ruth Penson.* $350-450.

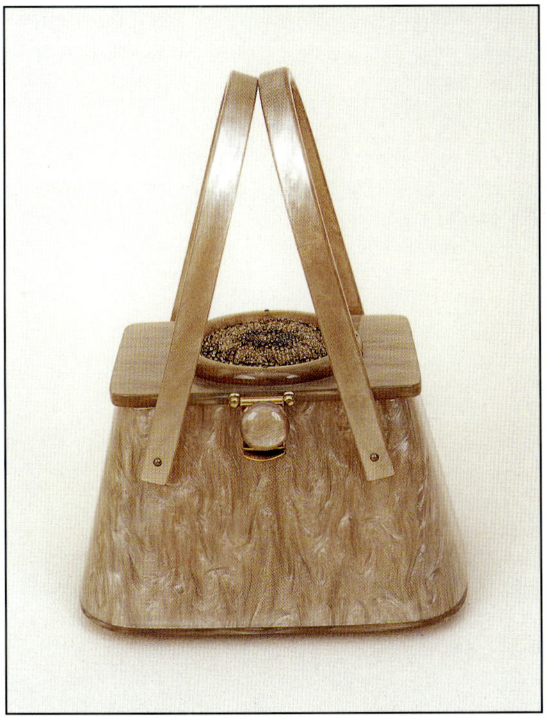

This marbleized Lucite purse has a beaded top, combining the best of both worlds. Made by Rialto in the 1950s. 6.5 x 5 in. *Collection of Marcy Rick.* $350-450.

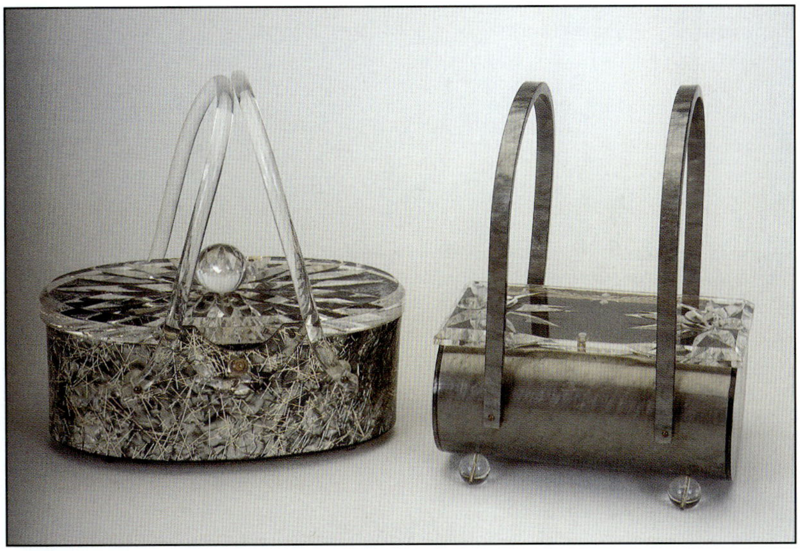

The purse on the left is made of marbleized gray Lucite. A confetti thread design decorates the body of the purse. The top is designed to look like cut crystal. Made by Gilli Originals of New York. On the right is a gray Lucite purse made with a clear cut top and clear ball feet. Marked "Original Rialto New York." Left: 9 x 5 in. Right: 7.25 x 4.5 in. *Collection of Marcy Rick.* $350-450.

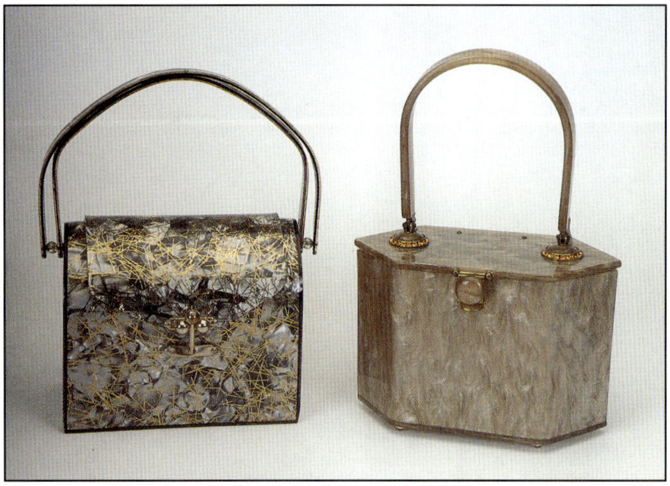

Left: This Lucite purse is made with a pearlized and marbleized finish, and decorated with gold threads. The handle is joined at the top. Made by Florida Handbags. Right: A purse made from swirled and pearlized Lucite, and decorated with gold rhinestones on the top, makes a sophisticated statement . Made by Rialto New York. Left: 7 x 6.5 in. Right: 8 x 5.5 in. *Collection of Marcy Rick.* $350-450.

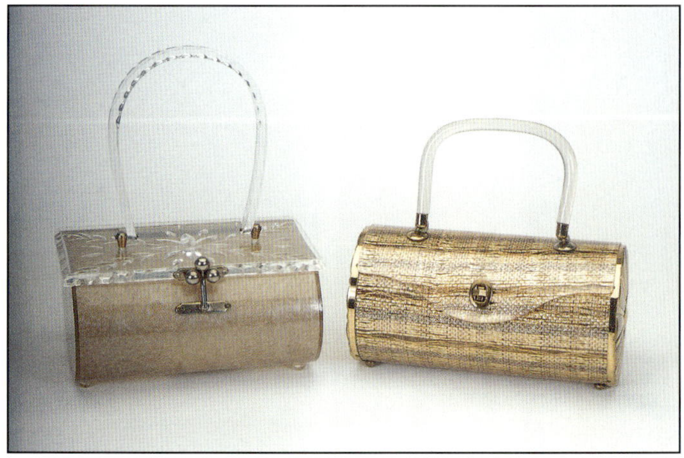

Left: Charles S. Kahn made this marbleized purse with the clear cut top and handle. Right: This cylindrical shaped Lucite bag is made from tri-color metal threads. The sides have metal panels. Made by Majestic. 7.5 x 5 in. *Collection of Marcy Rick.* $350-450.

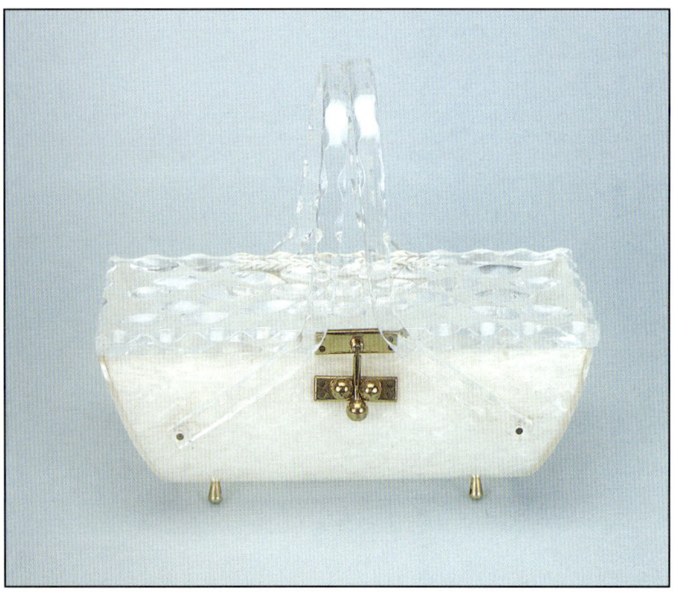

A classic, white marbleized Lucite purse, with a clear cut top and ball clasp, could be worn with anything. The bag is unmarked. It is important to check plastic purses for unusual odors, crazing, and discoloration. All of these are condition issues or signs of plastic disease, which should avoided. 10 x 4 in. *Collection of Marcy Rick.* $300-350.

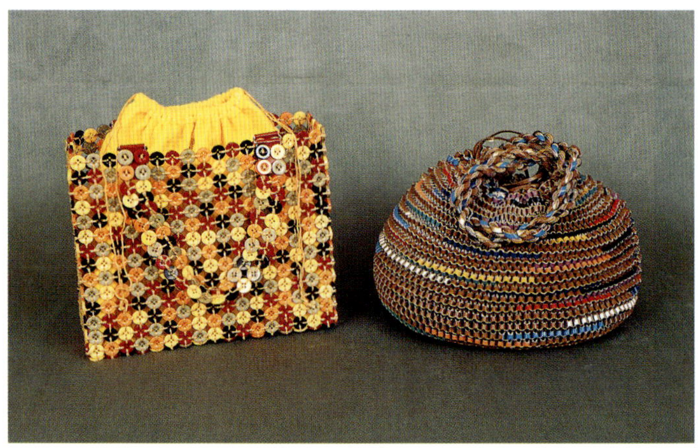

The purse on the left was made from plastic buttons sewn together. Even the straps are made from buttons. Inside the purse is a yellow reticule top. Made in 2004 by an unknown maker. The Italian purse on the right was made from knitted leather in the 1980s. The Italian textile industry has been known for their knitted items for centuries. Left: 10 x 9 in. Right: 11 x 10 in. *Collection of Ruth Penson.* $100-200.

Chapter 13
Unique, Unusual, and Rare Purses

Longtime purse collectors have learned and know instinctively what is unique, unusual, and rare in the purse world. The longer you collect, the more familiar you become with what is special and what is not. The purses in this chapter were chosen because they are either one of a kind, unusual, or rarely seen. It is worth noting that there are many purses in the earlier chapters that could have been included in this chapter.

As a purse form, sweet meat purses are very rare. The English sweet meat purse pictured in this chapter is extraordinary. Made from tent stitch on fine canvas with polychrome silk and silver metallic threads, it dates to 1600-1630. The tassels, drawstrings, and acorn tassels are all original. One side depicts a flowering tree, plants, a leopard, and a snake under a tree. The reverse side shows a fawn, and a stream with a duck. This exceptional purse was sold within the past two years by Cora Ginsburg LLC for $26,000.

Bebilla needle lace purses can be seen at The Museum of Fine Arts in Boston and collections in England, Armenia, and Turkey. Dating to the late 18th and early 19th centuries, they are a very rare type of purse. Bebilla needle lace, also known as Oya needle lace, is a very fine lace that dates back to 600 B.C. Because of its delicacy it was highly prized. Bebilla is a type of fine knot work produced with a needle and a thread. In its highest form, beautiful lace-like flowers were created, which were attached to network reticules. These purses were exported to Europe during the late 18th and early 19th centuries. In the 20th century, bebilla needle lace is used for edging textiles.

Knitted plant fiber purses from the late 18th and early 19th centuries were made in the Philippines for export to Europe and America. Some textile experts believe they were also made in Spain. The example pictured in this chapter was made in the Philippines and transported by ship to America. Its original shipping label with the name of the American ship *Eliza* is shown with the purse. This was an exciting discovery as other previously seen examples had been shipped to Europe. Now there is proof that this unusual type of purse was exported to the United States during the early 19th century as well. Made with vertical floral designs, from pear or pineapple fibers, most examples had basket bottoms. One recently seen version was made with three fiber tassels across the bottom instead of a basket.

Another basket purse pictured in this chapter was handmade by artists from Nantucket Island. It is a Nantucket Lightship Basket purse made by Alan SW Reed and scrimshawed by Lee Ann Papale. The workmanship is extraordinary and worthy of any museum collection. Made in the tradition of the 19th century lightship baskets, it is an investment quality piece. These purses are highly valued in New England and by knowledgeable collectors around the world. Nantucket Lightship baskets were made from oak and cane staves, and then typically decorated with scrimshawed ivory. Purses are often custom ordered from the artist, although ready-made purses are available.

Artist designed purses are very collectible and in many cases, unique works of art. In this chapter is an opera purse made from polymer clay, oil pigments, canes, foils, glitter, wirework, and beads by Katerina Musetti. Ms. Musetti is an award-winning artist in residence at Seton Hill University and an international opera singer. Highly decorative and compelling, her opera purses are made by a complex technique that involves layering and curing, sanding, and polishing. The end result is a finish that mimics fine Asian lacquer and a completed work of art.

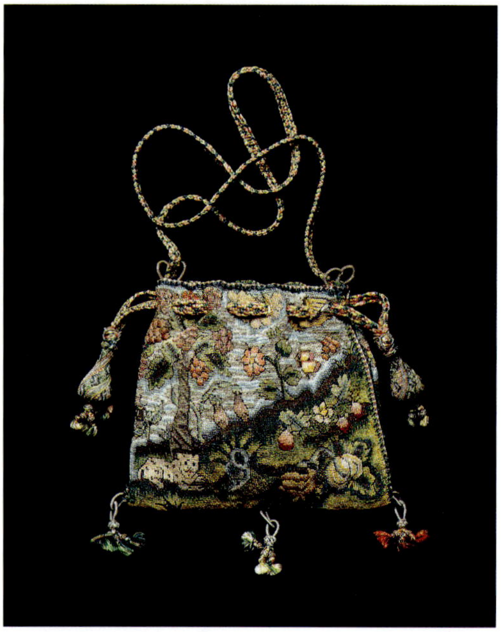

Early purses dating to before 1700 are very rare. The sweet meat purse pictured here is beyond rare; it is extraordinary. Made between 1600-1630, it was tent stitched in polychrome and silver metallic thread. This side shows a leopard and snake under a tree, surrounded by flowering trees and plants. Each side has a different design. The tassels and drawstrings are all original, as is the pink silk, taffeta lining. 4.5 x 5 in. *Courtesy of Cora Ginsburg LLC, New York.* Very rare.

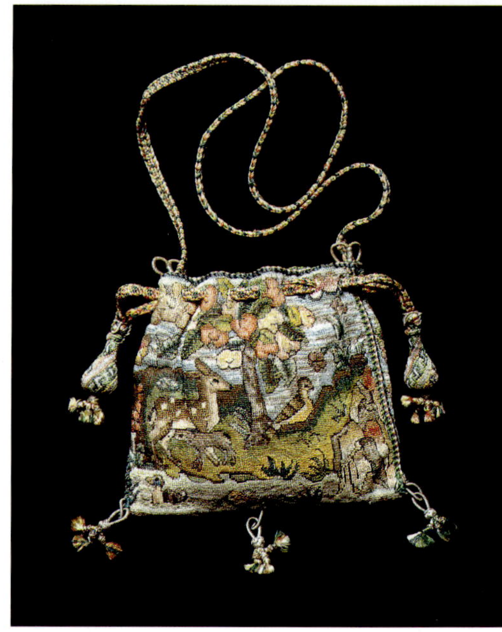

The reverse side of the tent stitched, sweet meat purse. A fawn, bird, and a duck in a stream decorate this side. *Courtesy of Cora Ginsburg, LLC, New York.*

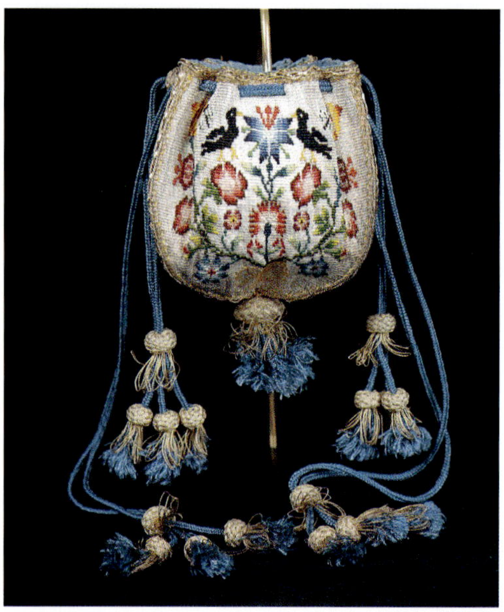

This late 17th century purse has four sides, and is made with polychrome silk and silver metallic thread. One side features two confronting blackbirds, and a small vase with blue, pink, and yellow flowers. The other side (not shown) shows a larger vase with a rose and pansies. The edges are trimmed with gold cord. The tassels have complex knots, which survive in extraordinary condition. It is lined with blue silk twill. English. *Courtesy of Cora Ginsburg LLC, New York.* Very rare.

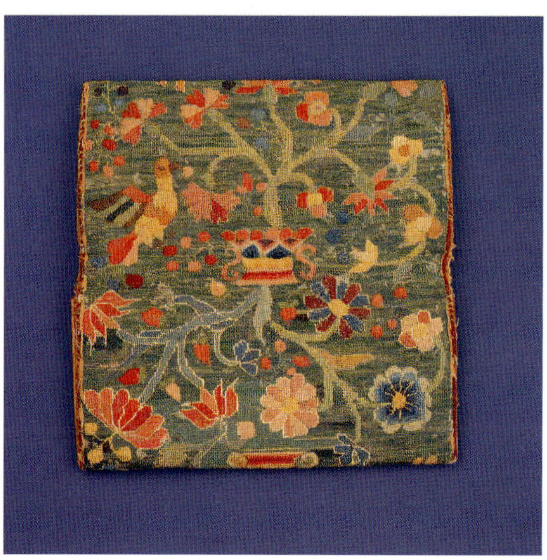

Early American pocketbooks like this one are in a separate class by themselves. The liveliness of the design and the liberal use of bright colors help to identify this exceptional purse as American. It also came with a note, if there was any doubt. It states: "Purse believed to have been worked by Lucy Palmer….." It is worked in tent stitch on an unusual green ground. The lining is made from salmon silk. Mid-eighteenth century. *Courtesy of Cora Ginsburg LLC, New York.* Very rare.

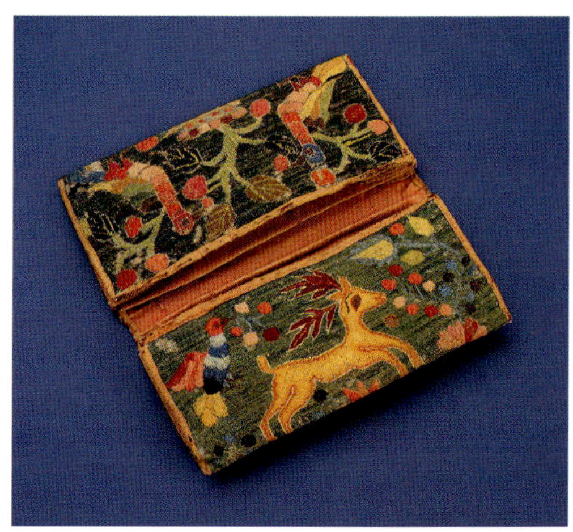

The inside of this beautiful and charming pocketbook. *Courtesy of Cora Ginsburg, LLC, New York.*

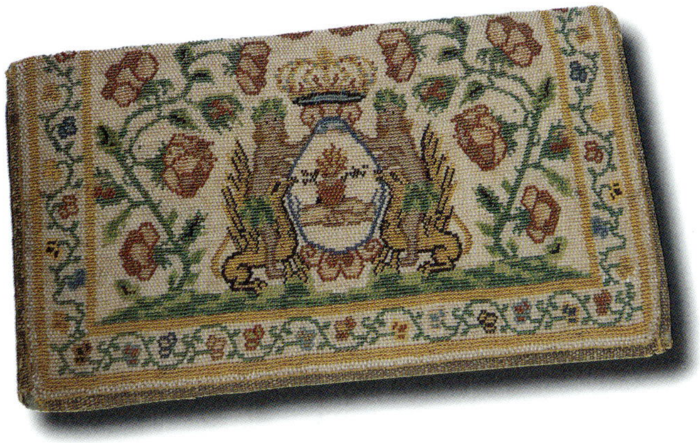

Sablé beaded pocketbooks with figural designs are rare. On one side of this French pocketbook is a scene of nymphs riding griffins, a burning heart, and crown. This wonderful piece was originally owned by the 18th century author and textile authority, Charles Germain de Saint-Aubin, the chief designer to Louis XV. 7 x 4.5 in. *Collection of Lori Blaser.* Rare.

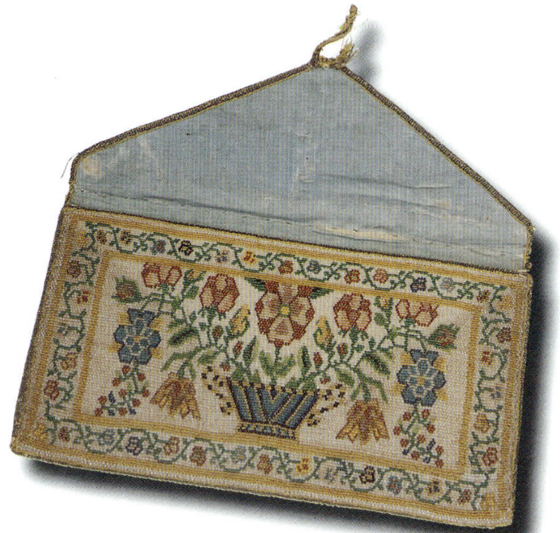

The front side of the sablé beaded purse, which shows a stylized basket of flowers.

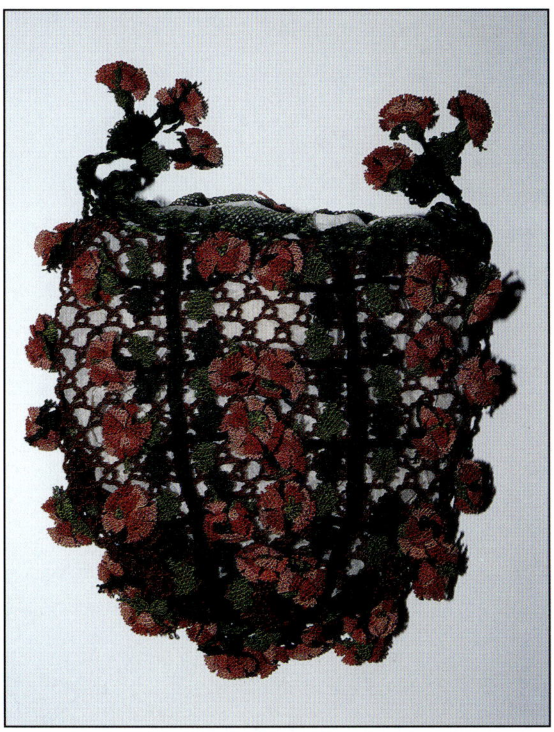

Bebilla needle lace purses were made in the 18th and early 19th centuries by the Turks and the Greeks. It was also made by the Armenians, who know it as Oya needle lace. The technique dates back to 600 B.C., and because of its delicacy, it is highly prized. Bebilla is a type of fine knot work, produced with a needle and a thread. Today it is only used to edge small textile items. This purse was formerly in the collection of the famous textile collector, Emma-Henriette Schiff von Suvero (1863-1924). It dates to the early 19th century. Each flower has 6-8 beautifully shaded petals, dark green stems, and lighter green leaves, set against a brown and green network. 5.5 x 5 in. *Collection of Paula Higgins.* Very rare.

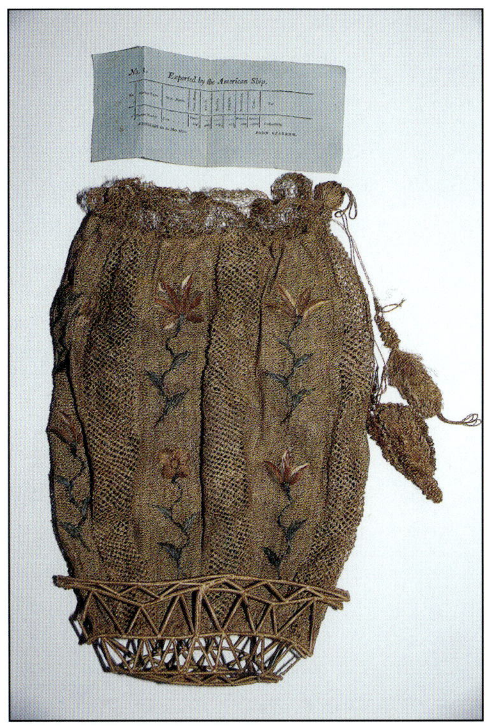

This early plant fiber purse was brought to America by the American ship *Eliza* in 1811. Prior to this, plant fiber purses were known to have been imported to Europe in the late 18th and early 19th centuries. They were made for export from pear or pineapple fibers, in the Philippines. Most examples have basket bottoms of varying designs, but one example has been seen with tassels instead of a basket. The original shipping slip from the *Eliza* has remained with the purse. This reticule has the typical linear floral design, embroidered on the outside over paper forms. The bag is knitted. 14 x 11 in. *Collection of Paula Higgins.* Rare.

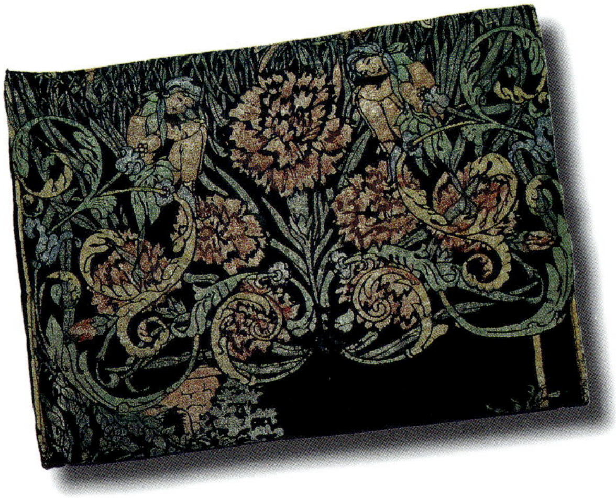

Art Nouveau purses decorated with faeries and Peter Pan figures are a rare type of purse. Made from felt, it is hand painted with an imaginative woodlands scene. It shows faeries, and a Peter Pan figure, sitting on a mushroom and playing a pan flute. In this picture, long faerie hair is intertwined with the flower design. In the next picture, the purse is completely open to show the full scene. Inside the purse is a castle scene.9.5 x 7 in. *Collection of Paula Higgins.* Rare.

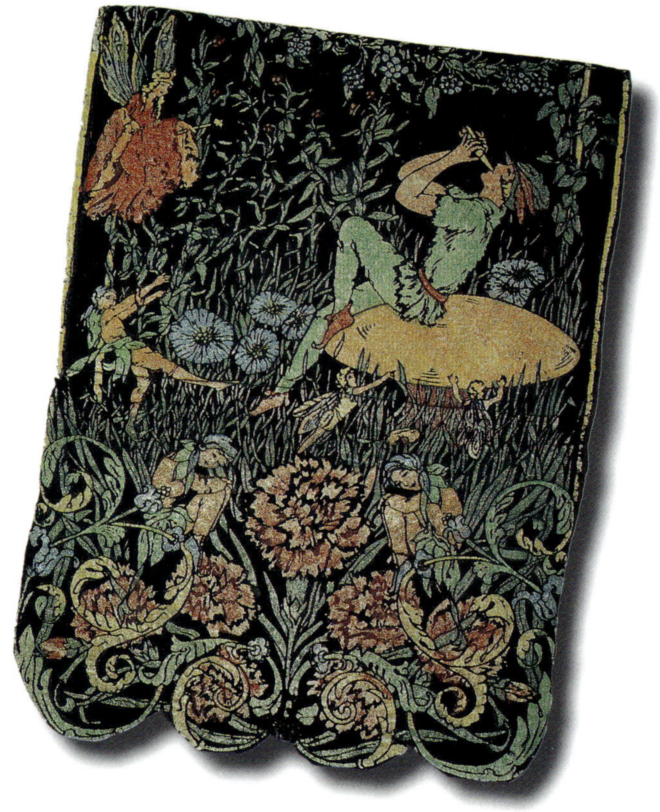

The faerie scene purse completely opened.

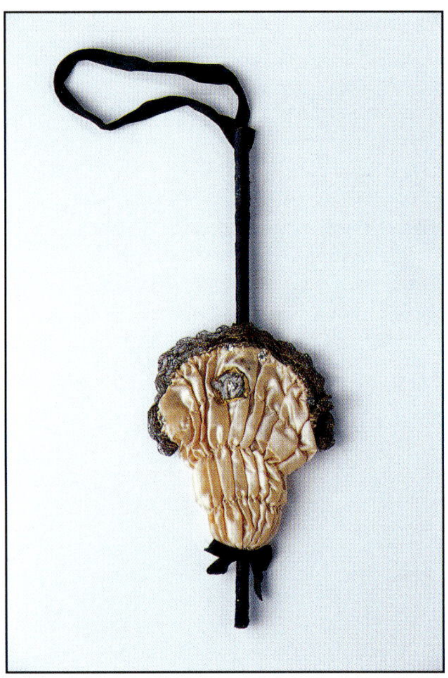

Umbrella purses from the mid-twentieth century are seen periodically (typically made from straw), but earlier examples, like this one, are less common. Pink silk is ruched to form the reticule part of the umbrella and it is edged with black lace. The pink silk closes with old snaps. The concept of a purse authentically designed and decorated like a period umbrella is unusual and charming. *Collection of Kim Stonecipher.* Rare.

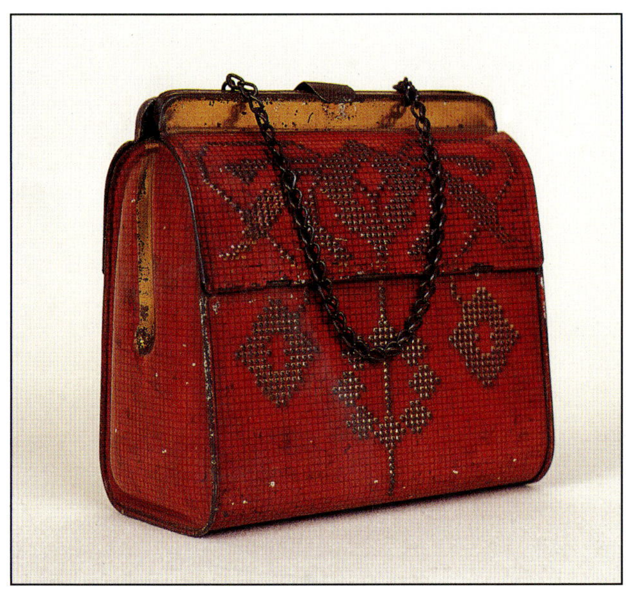

Tins designed as purses were made in Europe and America to hold biscuits. This purse tin was made in 1909 by MacFarlane, Lang and Co. The owner uses it as a functional purse. Because of its punched tin design, which resembles a piece of folk art, it never fails to evoke commentary. 5 x 4.75 in. *Collection of Lori Blaser.* Rare.

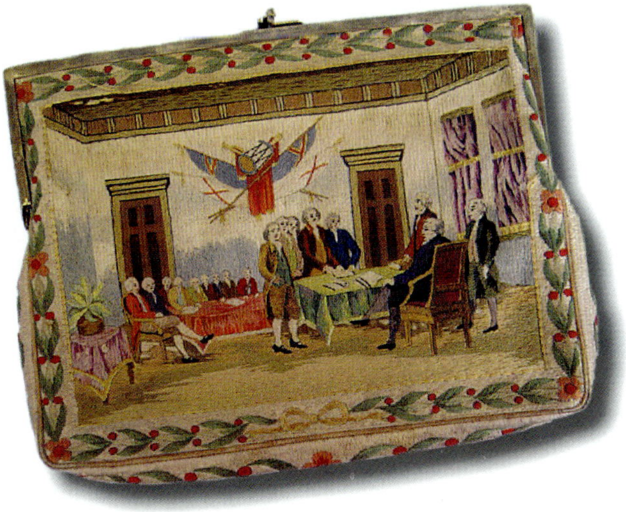

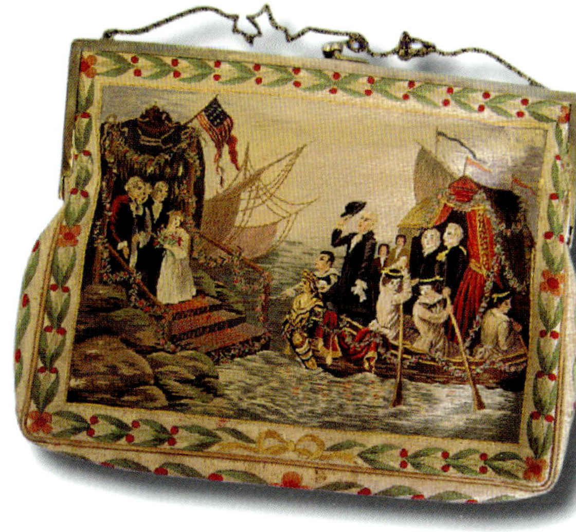

The famous painting by John Trumbull, entitled *The Declaration of Independence*, was the inspiration for this extraordinary silk stitched purse. It is possible that is was a commissioned, one of a kind piece, made for a wealthy and patriotic client. As in the painting, John Hancock is seen sitting in a chair, and standing from left to right are: John Adams, Roger Sherman, Robert Livingston, Thomas Jefferson, and Benjamin Franklin. Although this scene never actually took place, Trumbull captured the spirit of a series of events that led up to the signing of The Declaration of Independence. The embroiderer of the purse created a faithful and beautiful representation of this famous work of art. *Collection of Shara Stewart.* Very rare.

The reverse of the purse shows another famous scene. George Washington is shown arriving in New York for his presidential inauguration in 1789. The boat shown was made especially to transport him from Elizabeth Town, New Jersey, across the Hudson River, and to the New York shore. It was rowed by thirteen sailors dressed in white, and it was accompanied by escort ships firing guns in salute. Upon his arrival at the landing, he was greeted by New York Governor DeWitt Clinton, the mayor of New York, and other prominent citizens. This was a cause for great celebration in the new nation and his arrival was treated with pomp and glory. The quality of workmanship required to design and execute this embroidered scene was exceptional.

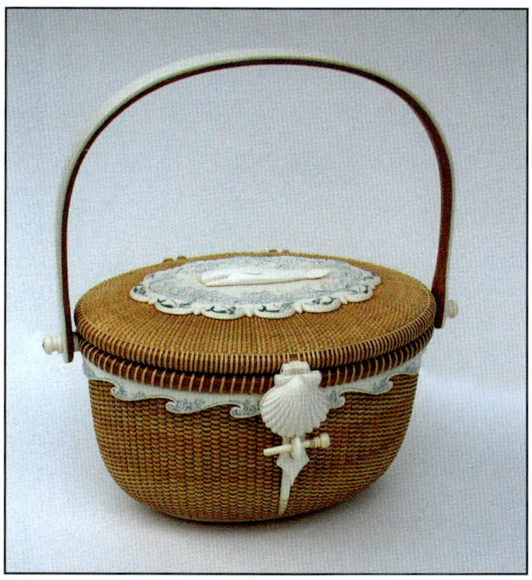

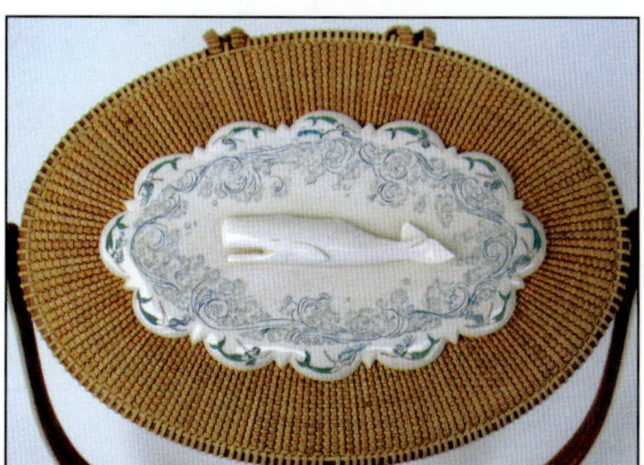

Nantucket Lightship Basket purses are a uniquely American purse form. This purse design is based on the baskets made by sailors on the Nantucket lightships during the mid-nineteenth century. In 1945, José Formoso Reyes, a native of the Philippines married to an American, came to Nantucket. With the help of Mitchell Ray, a native of Nantucket, he started to make baskets in the tradition of the early Nantucket lightship basket makers. By 1948, he had made his first covered basket and sold it as a purse. From there, the tradition evolved, and it continues to the present day. The Nantucket Lightship Basket purses made today on Nantucket Island are exquisite works of art, made to be handed down to future generations. The basket purse pictured here, entitled "*Wave*" was made in 2005 by Alan SW Reed. The scrimshawed ivory top, clasp, and wave design were made by Lee Ann Papale, a noted scrimshaw artist. This purse is beautifully worked, and the difference in quality is readily noticeable when compared to imported baskets. It is important to know, that baskets imported from Asia are mounted with scrimshaw plaques once they arrive in the United States. They are being sold as Nantucket Lightship Basket Purses, when they are in fact a pale imitation. Baskets can be made in a variety of shapes and with many different scrimshaw designs. *Courtesy of Alan SW Reed and Lee Ann Papale.* Rare.

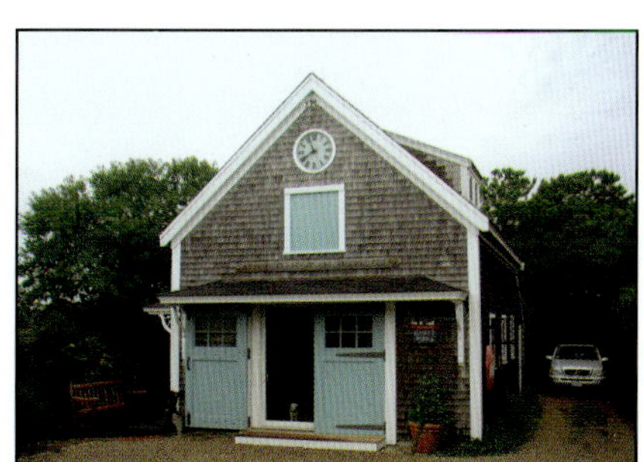

The Nantucket Basket Works.

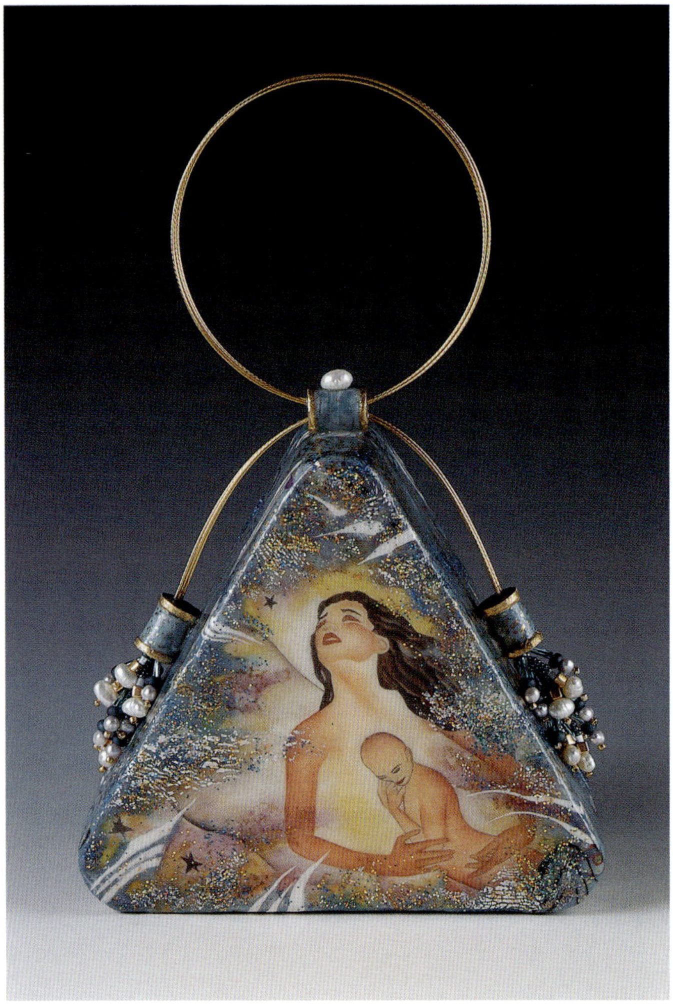

Unique, one of a kind purses are being made by artists around the world. The following two purses were made by award winning artist and professional opera singer, Katerina Musetti. Her polymer clay Opera purses have been worn by celebrities desiring the unique and beautiful. The purse pictured here is entitled "*Suor Angelica.*" Made on a wooden base, it is then layered with solid and liquid polymers. The process involves repeated layering of oil pigments, canes, and liquid polymer. This technique mimics Asian lacquer work, which layers lacquer with pigment. Many materials may be used on one purse such as: foil, glitter, canes, and semi-precious and precious stones. The end result is a unique and compelling piece of art in the form of a purse. *Courtesy of Katerina Musetti.* Rare.

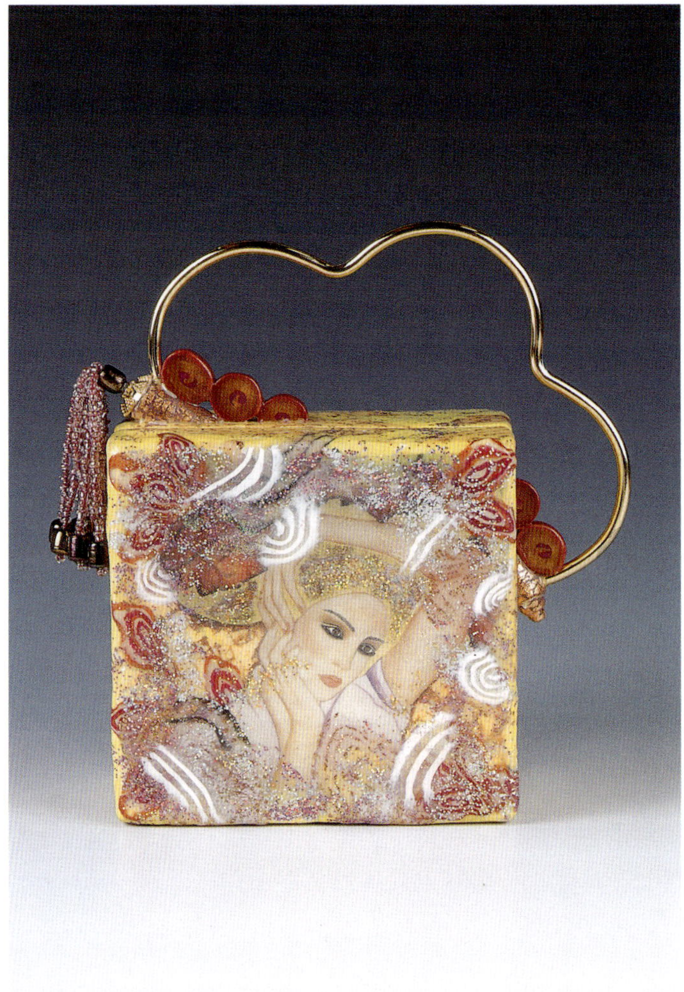

This lovely purse by Katerina Musetti is entitled "*Leonora.*" *Courtesy of Katerina Musetti.* Rare.

Chapter 14
Antique Beaded Purse Restoration

by Terri Lykins

Antique beaded purse restoration is a skill that requires artistic judgment, extreme patience, and resourcefulness. Most purse restorers are self-taught, through trial and error. Years of experience are needed to make the best decisions about supplies, bead sizes, bead colors, and techniques to repair various types of holes and damage. My personal "playbook" of strategies has taken almost twenty years to build, and I add to it constantly.

Purse repairs vary as much as the purses themselves. Each poses a different set of issues. In this chapter, we will evaluate purse construction and repair techniques for each category. We will consider factors such as converting a purse from a drawstring to a frame closure, adding fringes, linings and trim, and the effect of each on purse value. Finally, it helps to know when to walk away from a purse that is damaged beyond repair. We will evaluate conditions that may make a restoration too costly, or impossible to achieve.

Materials

The best repairs blend so well into the purse that they aren't detectable unless you know exactly where to look. Hole repairs using the wrong bead size or color, or fringes that don't match the purse, detract from the value of the purse itself. Once you develop an eye for spotting "McFringe" (my term for cheap, fast, and easy fringes made with shiny, modern craft store seed beads), you can quickly determine which purses need a complete fringe replacement to attain their true value. If you are shopping for a beaded bag, use this factor as a bargaining tool when negotiating price. Some dealers may not realize that a purse they are selling has been reworked with inferior beads, and may appreciate the quick lesson this offers for their future negotiations.

Beads

Having the right beads for repairs, such as correcting holes in knit bags, is essential. If the bead color does not match, and the hole is in a solid area of the design, the repair will show. It will stand out in contrast to the original bead color used in that area. If you have the correct color match, but a slightly smaller sized bead, this will blend well and the result will be good. But a larger bead will not blend well, even if the color is a good match.

In a colorful area of a purse, a few liberties may be taken. If I am missing a particular color to repair a hole in a purse, I variegate two or three beads in similar shades to fill in the missing beads. Usually, the mirror image of each purses' design is on the flip side, so I fold the corner over to see the area on the other side of the purse, as a guide in determining the missing pattern. The artistic component occurs when trying to recreate a pattern with the closest bead colors and sizes to the original, and creating the impression of accuracy if the bead colors are not as close, in some instances.

Most collectors are aware that the tiny seed beads, often called "micro beads", have been out of production since the 1940s. Although there are some modern Japanese and French reproduction beads labeled as 14/0-18/0, the actual size of these beads is much larger than the antique Czech or Italian seed beads. The colors are very limited too, and the finishes are inferior. These beads are more suitable for repairs on purses made with larger beads, such as the Art Deco Style, 1930-1940 abstract design purses with celluloid frames. Valuable scenic or figural bags deserve the best matching antique seed beads that can be obtained, for authenticity and value.

The only available sources for these antique beads are a few bead sellers/shops in the U.S. who have bought out old bead factory stock. Some secondary sellers are buying beads from these sources and reselling online for $7-13 a hank, or 3 grams. Steel beads can sell for as high as $15 per hank. One hank provides enough beads to make about six fringe loops on an average purse. As bead supplies become more limited, these prices will continue to rise, along with the cost of repairs, and of existing purses in excellent, original, or restored condition.

Purse collectors have asked me why I don't salvage beads from disintegrated bags. The biggest disadvantage is that most purses are multicolored, and it isn't helpful to have colorful bead mixes when trying to create patterned fringes. You have to plan ahead and know that there is enough of each bead color to execute a fringe design. Solid colored bags can be recycled for beads, or those with bands of color in large enough areas to yield significant amounts of each color. I find it hard to sacrifice even a small piece of ornate beadwork for scrap when it could be used to make a Christmas ornament, jewelry bauble, button cover, or pillow insert!

Needles and Thread

Tiny micro seed beads require a very thin needle to pass through their holes. When repairing a hole in a purse body, this situation is compounded by inserting the needle and thread through rows of micro beads that already have thick silk thread running through them. The English make the smallest beading needle that I have ever found, in a size 16. These needles vary in size within a package, also. They are the only needles I can use with beads sized below a 16/0.

You can find beading needles in sizes 10-12 at your local craft store. These work well with larger beads, size 11/0-14/0, which were often used in purses from the 1930s and 1940s.

There are only two thread types that I find will fit through a size 16 English beading needle: Nymo and Monocord. Both of these are available in very fine weights and many colors, and are not twisted, which allows them to pass through a tiny needle eye. They are both made of nylon, which is less desirable when restoring a primitive purse of historical significance. The benefit is that nylon doesn't break or rot, like antique silk or cotton thread. I have wooden spools of antique thread that can be used for historical restoration, but it is so fragile that I only use it if absolutely necessary. The old purse twist is very thick, and can only be passed through a size 10 beading needle, in most cases. It is nice to use when restoring crocheted or knit bags with swag designs, because it is the same thread that the purses were made of, originally.

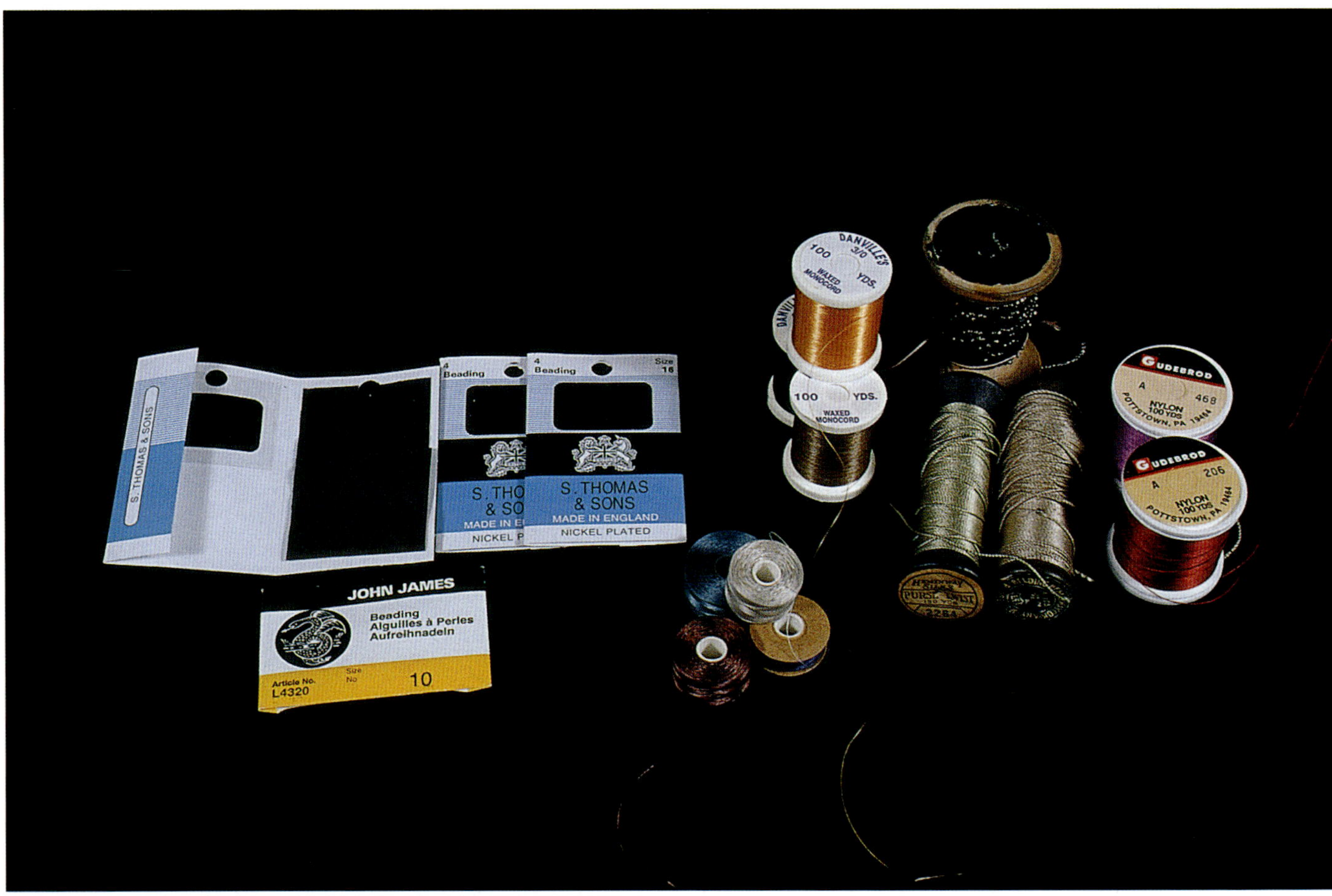

An assortment of needle and threads used to repair beaded purses.

Gudebrod ("rod-winding") thread is a twisted nylon plied thread that is ideal for making individually twisted strands of fringe, but it is hard to pass through a beading needle smaller than a size 12. I have recently discovered that Monocord will twist into tight fringes if the thread is wound enough, before sewing the fringe back into the purse body.

Here is an interesting fact: the thread color running inside a transparent bead will change the shade of the bead on the purse or in the fringe. Try threading some transparent light purple beads on white thread, then on dark brown thread. The bead will change tone, depending upon the thread. This is helpful information when repairing purses that were originally knit in colored silk thread. I am currently restoring a bag that was knitted with dark purple silk thread running through the beads. The predominant bead color looked like a dark olive green, until I examined a few beads that had fallen off the purse. They are actually a pale, clear green, so I used dark purple Nymo thread through transparent green beads to create an exact match and repair several holes.

Additional Tools Aiding Restoration

Lighted Magnifiers

I recommend the type of magnifier that clamps to a table and has a crane neck for raising and lowering. A fluorescent circular bulb provides excellent light that can be lowered close to the purse. I rarely have to use the magnifier itself to see the areas I repair, but in another ten years I will probably be thankful for this feature!

Ceramic Bead Trays

Shaped like flowers, these trays have nine compartments and are too heavy to tip over. A tiny metal scoop enables collection of beads from the compartments to return to their own tiny zip lock bags.

Tweezerman Tweezers

These very sharp-tipped, fine point tweezers enable you to grab your needle and pull through beads when they get stuck on the needle.

Purse Construction

Purse construction varied over the centuries. The general categories are:

Bead Knitted: Beads were strung onto silk thread in a counted design, and knitted into a fabric of beads. The reverse side of the piece will look like a fine gauge sock. Bead knitted purses are soft and pliable.

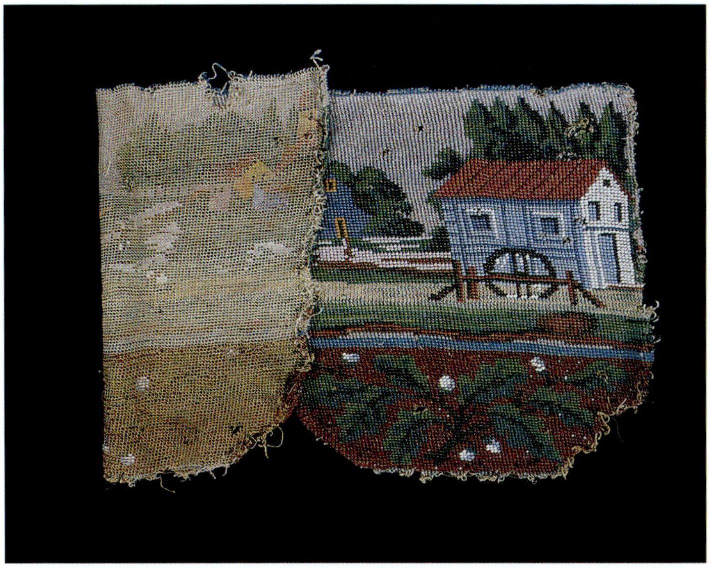

A continuous, bead knitted scenic design that was cut apart on a side seam. The folded edge shows the reverse side of the piece.

Bead Embroidered: Beads were embroidered onto a medium to heavy weight cotton canvas, similar to Aida cloth. The beads were sewn directly onto the cloth in rows, either vertically or horizontally.

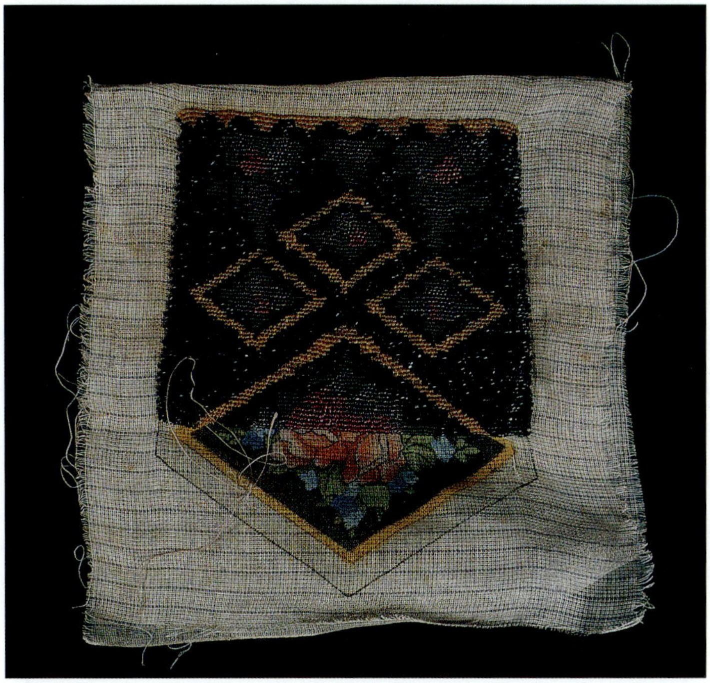

An original, unfinished bead embroidered purse panel with its original needle and thread. The pre-printed canvas resembles modern day needlepoint projects.

Some collectors believe that these bags don't have the same fine resolution qualities that bead knitted bags possess, but I disagree. For an example of a high quality bead embroidered purse, see the finely detailed figural that is bead embroidered on page 227.

Tambour Embroidered and Chain Stitched: The beads were tamboured onto very fine, thin netting in rows, with a hook, creating a chain stitch on the backside. Sadly, when the thread breaks in a row, the entire length of row can quickly unchain itself and become a loose thread of falling beads.

Crocheted: These bags tend to be thicker and heavier in weight, constructed with crochet hooks, large beads, and heavy gauge thread. This technique is seen in swag design bags, and in German drawstring reticules made in the late twenties and early thirties.

Loomed: The purse is constructed on a loom, with warp and weft threads. The beads are attached horizontally in rows. I have seen some stunning examples of loomed scenics and figurals. These purses often have very thick, elaborate fringes with wonderful designs.

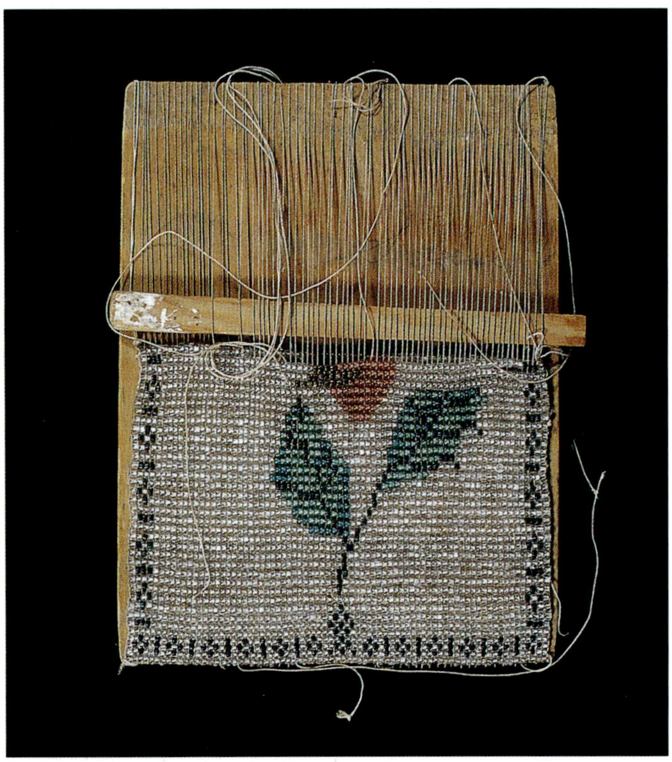

A handmade loom with an unfinished purse in its original state.

Restoration Projects

Bead Knitted Purses

A bead knitted purse may develop holes over time. As the silk deteriorates, the purse becomes weakened. Moths seem to enjoy knitted bags too, and will leave tiny chew holes. The successful repair of these holes depends primarily upon the purse being strong enough to allow a needle and thread to pass through its rows. I have had a few very old primitive bags, circa 1850, break off as I passed a needle and thread through the rows. This creates more holes and makes repair work impossible. A good test is to gently pick at the area around a hole. If it breaks off easily, it is dry rotted, and it should be considered for a display piece only.

The size of the hole determines which repair technique can be used. Some literature suggests that a hole of more than four beads in any direction should not be attempted by stringing the missing beads between the rows. There are a few techniques that can be employed to keep the rows flat and aligned if they exceed this number. If the area is much larger than 6-8 beads, it may require backing and tacking, or a treatment similar to bead embroidery. I have been able to achieve results that look like bead knitting, when in fact, I have really embroidered the beads into the area of loss.

Bead Embroidered Purses

Repairs on these bags are usually focused on replacing missing beads, in portions of rows. Most collectors understand that it is impractical to replace every missing bead, and the absence of a random bead or two around the purse body is acceptable. The most common areas to find loss are around the top of the purse, near the frame lines, on the side seams, and around the hinges. Purse beads were more likely to be rubbed in these areas, weakening the threads, and eventually causing breakage. Very old, historical bags will sometimes show missing beads in areas where a particular color of bead has crumbled and fallen off. This is symptomatic of glass disease, and it is often confined to one or two colors on a purse. The reason for this is the instability of the chemical composition of the glass bead.

When evaluating the time needed to replace missing beads on these purses, keep in mind that every missing bead in the bald area will be sewn on, one at a time, and the pattern will be replicated, too. You can look at the spacing and size of the beads as one indication of the time it will take to fill in the areas. Be sure to add all of the damaged areas together mentally, and you may realize that the hours of work and cost won't justify the repair. This is particularly true of large-bead

German bags. Many of us started out collecting these purses because they were easily attainable. They are bead-embroidered with big size 11/0-14/0 beads on thick canvas, and if you look at the canvas you will see a grid of heavy threads on the surface. Each of these grids, or squares, requires that a bead be sewn between it, usually in vertical rows. You cannot thread two or three beads in the row and then sew into the grid, because the beads will lie on top of the canvas and stand out as a repair. Instead, each bead must be added, one by one, and your needle must go beneath the next grid thread running up the row vertically. The time involved in filling in these missing beads on the grid can be enormous. A young woman once sent me a bead embroidered clutch style purse that had belonged to her grandmother. She wanted it returned to perfect condition. By the time I had finished, she spent close to $300 for a purse that could be purchased on the internet for $50, in near perfect condition. I generally shy away from buying the German large beaded purses that need repair, unless the design is usual or the purse is very inexpensive.

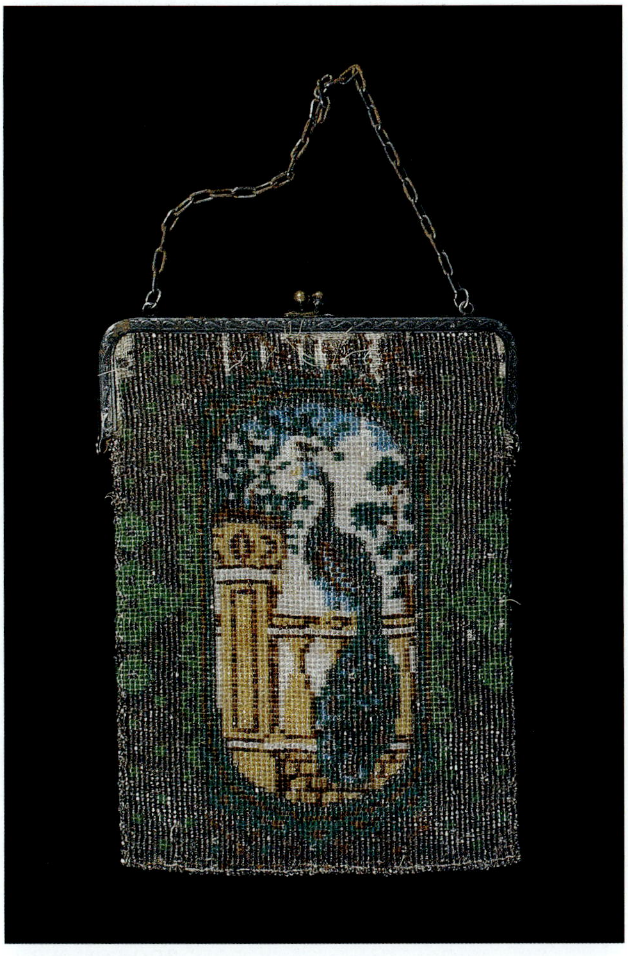

An unusual peacock design, in a large bead German construction, with a factory applied frame. Note the missing beads and the canvas beneath.

Purses created from the finer, thinner threaded cotton embroidery fabric tend to have much smaller beads in more complex designs. Remember, the smaller the bead, the more resolution you can obtain in the design itself, much like pixels in digital photography. I find it fascinating that beaded purses can be made using minutely tiny, colored glass beads, to create scenes and designs with shading, depth, and fine details. This artwork was cleverly crafted into purses, allowing the creator to wear and display her work. The science and mathematics involved in the creation of these designs allowed anyone with dexterity and patience to create visual artwork, with predictable results. It sure beats paint-by-numbers!

If a hole has developed in a bead embroidered purse, it can be patched with a piece of similar fabric, and the patched area embroidered in the same manner that the purse was constructed.

Tamboured and Chain-stitched Purses

Purses made with this technique are tricky to repair. First, secure loose rows back to the purse, by first tacking and sewing the end of the thread that is still attached to the purse with your own thread. This will keep the chained row from continuing to unravel. Next, carefully lay the loose, beaded part of the row back into place, and tack it down with your thread, securing every three or four beads down the line. You may need to tie off against the very end of the row, so save enough room and remove a few beads for this task. If you have to create a missing row, you can thread 2-3 beads and sew back into the net each time by going under one thread in the weave, and continuing in the direction of the design. It is important to push your threaded beads close to the last group you added, so there are no gaps in the rows. Think about all of this work when you see an Art Deco designed bag, chain stitched on fine mesh, with lots of loose, unraveled strands. This should help you decide if the purse requires more repair than it is worth. These types of purse bodies are seen frequently on fancy celluloid and Bakelite frames. They are often intricately patterned, with bright colors and long fringes. They tend to be beaded in size 12/0-14/0 beads. Some are very large purses, and can be astoundingly beautiful when executed in elegant patterns with exceptional frames. There seems to be a huge emphasis on bead knit bags being the most desirable, but there are examples of exceptional purses, considered very rare and valuable, in all construction types. See the picture of a Pharoah head purse, worked in chain stitching, and considered a very rare design. It is known to sell for over $2000.

Crocheted Purses

Crocheted purse repair usually requires re-threading of missing beads and reattachment into the crocheted design. The biggest challenge is to find the exact beads to match the missing ones. Many of these bags are monochromatic swag purses made with faceted cut beads, in iridescent finishes. The next concern is finding thread that is a very close match to the original purse twist, in color and texture. These repairs often require recreating portions of the crocheted pattern, so the thread choice must be appropriate. If purse twist is not available, you may find a shade of DMC embroidery floss that will work. Experiment with the number of strands you wish to use, to replicate the thickness of the purse body. Embroidery floss is also useful for creating customized crocheted drawstring headers for reticules. The variety of colors include many olive and hunter green shades that I prefer for primitive reticule headers.

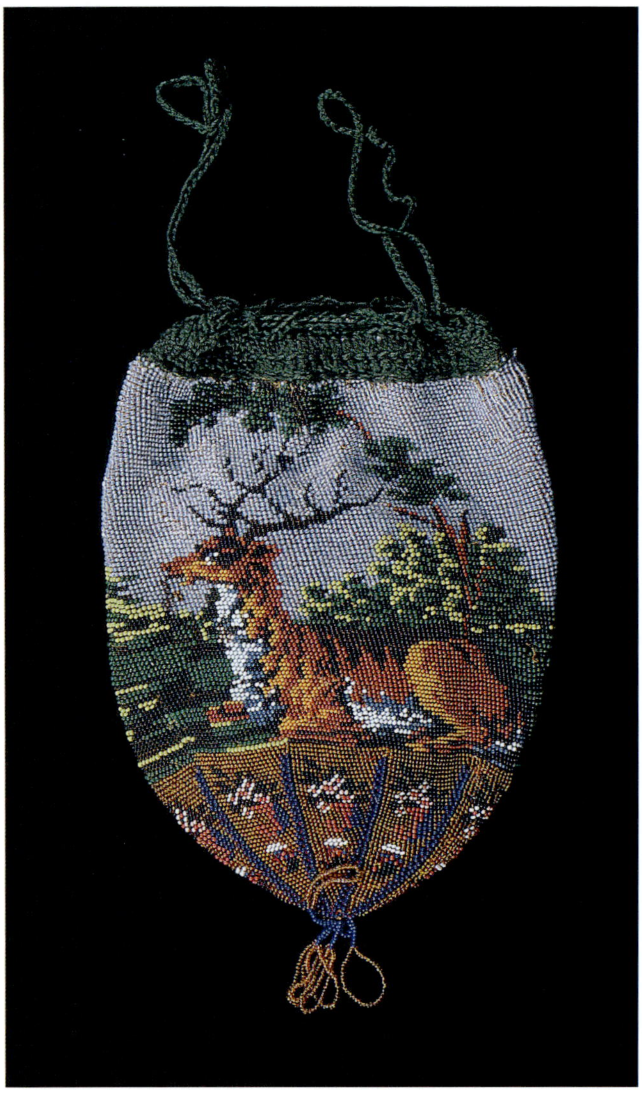

A crocheted header made from DMC floss.

Loomed Purses

Loomed purses are the most difficult purses to repair, particularly metal beaded, loomed bags. Now that the bags are 100 years old, and their original designers are gone, we can see the effects that gravity has waged upon their heavy metal beads when they are held together with delicate silk thread, which rots and deteriorates. Loomed purses often suffer "the splits", a condition of breakage that occurs when the structural warp (vertical) threads break from the weight of the bead rows. The breaks generally occur above or below a horizontal row (weft) of beads. It is common to see these splits at the hinge corners, frame lines, and sometimes along the bottom edges of metal beaded, woven bags.

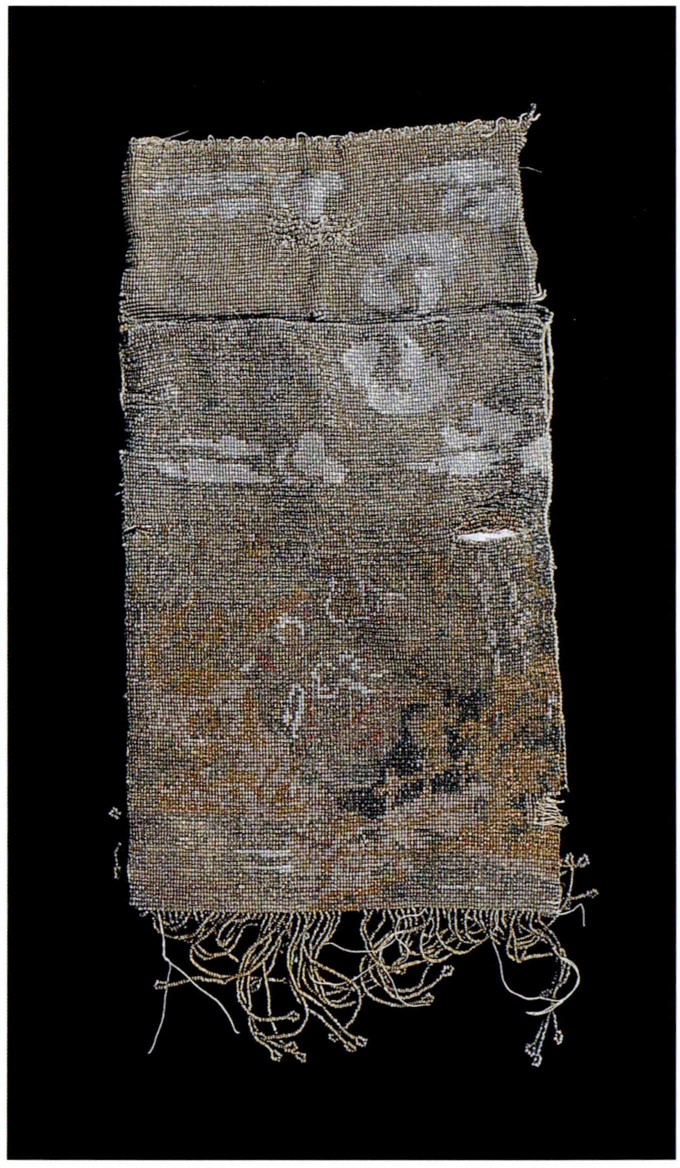

Horizontal splits in a metal beaded bag.

Repair of these bags is more tedious and time-consuming than other forms of purse work. I know of one woman who is completely re-weaving these bags for her own use, but the only technique I know for repairing metal beaded purses is as follows:

Push all of the beads over as far as they will go, until they are touching each other in the loose or broken horizontal row.

Add the missing beads to the row, if it is open at the end.

Using an appropriately colored, 000 mono-cord thread and a size 16 beading needle, sew into the bag several rows below the split area to anchor your thread, and run your needle and thread through the existing weft (horizontal) thread between each bead, running upward vertically. You are essentially splitting the existing thread with your thread. Sometimes a doubled thread was used to create the weft, and in that case, you would be running your thread between the two weft threads. In this way, you are actually recreating the warp thread with your own thread.

Go several rows past the split row(s), turn your needle and thread around and come down the next vertical row of beads, going several rows past the split rows, but do not keep turning around at the same level each time! You will add too much stress to the area where you are making the turns. Try to stagger your re-entry areas.

I recommend a magnifier with a fluorescent light, and a bottle of aspirin, when attempting these repairs.

Framing Considerations

To frame or not to frame, collectors are divided on this issue. Some feel that it is best to leave a purse in its authentic, original condition, while other collectors may change a purse frame several times in the course of owning the item. I believe it is best to leave historically significant purses intact. Altering them may decrease their value, while diminishing the integrity of a historically significant purse. If you are in doubt as to whether a purse should be altered or not, contact a purse restorer or member of the Antique Purse Collector's Society. Purses that are not in this category, to me, are fair game.

One justifying factor in converting a reticule/drawstring purse to a framed bag, or even upgrading a frame to a fancier one, is that the ladies of the past did this very thing. In the 1920s, women often updated their family heirloom purses with the addition of frames, and even lush fringes, and carried them with renewed flair. It is difficult to determine which purses were framed, or reframed, in more recent times, as opposed to seventy years ago. Most collectors don't insist on knowing the authenticity of a frame before they will purchase a purse. Replacing an old, unattractive frame with a truly attractive frame, can increase its value and appeal.

Fine quality frames have become highly sought after, and very expensive. Larger frames are harder to find, especially when they approach seven inches or more in width. An ornate, seven-inch jeweled frame may fetch upward of $350. Ornate, thick frames of various silver content, featuring angels or cherubs, are also popular and are ever-increasing in value. They remain more cost effective and attainable than large jeweled frames, however.

In general, I like to match purse styles, eras and constructions with appropriate frame types. Primitive reticules and unframed rug design (geometric) purses are well suited to the straight frames. Simple, straight frames are often original to early beaded purses. Straight frames that open into squares, do not require cutting into the purse, so the beadwork remains intact.

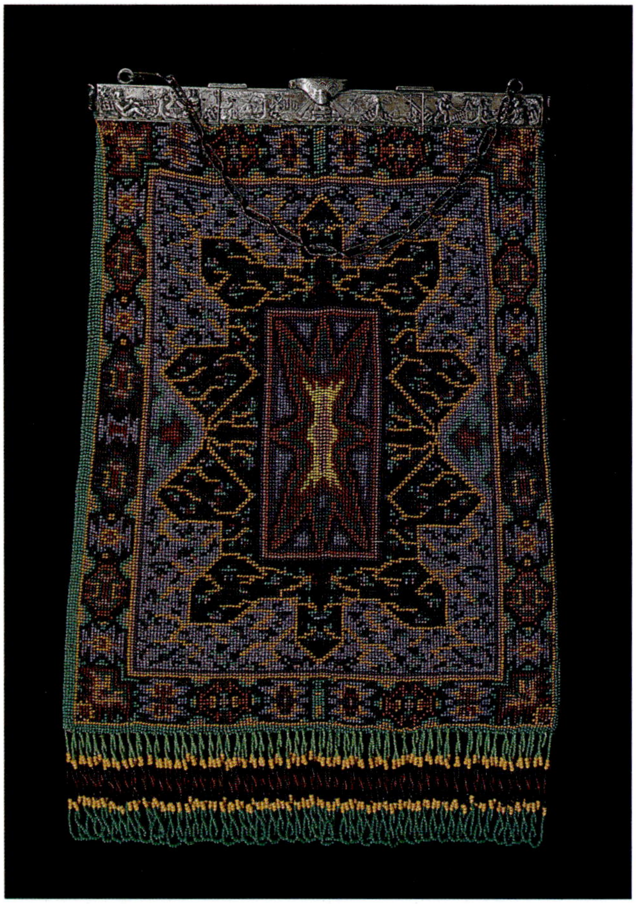

An intricate rug designed purse, framed on a straight frame that opens into a square.

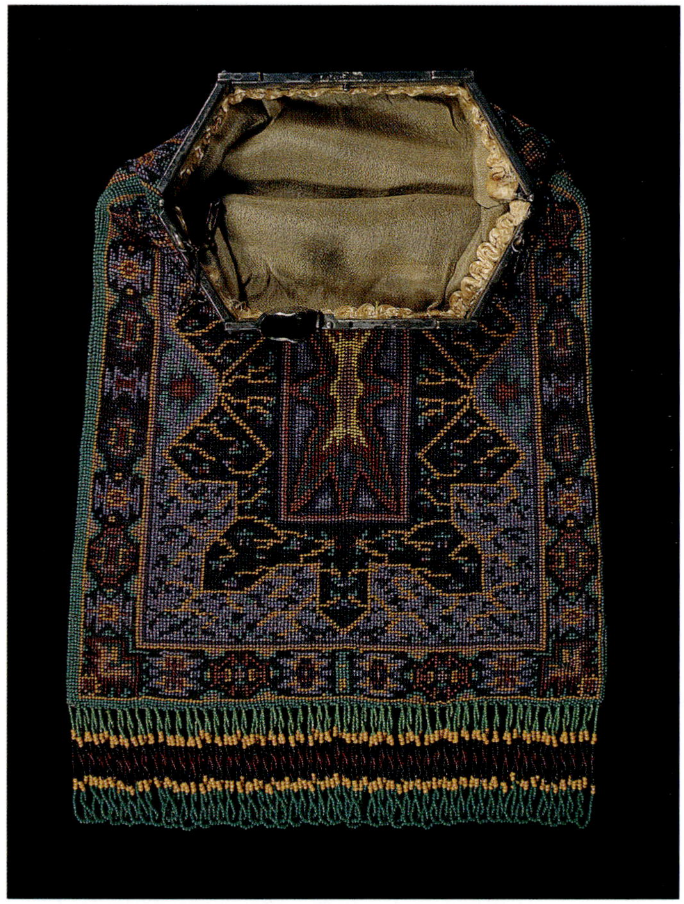

The square frame opened.

Although this is a late 19th century style frame, it allows for the preservation of the beadwork on very early purses, which may no longer have intact headers. Pre-1900 reticules are attractive when framed with ornate, curved or round edge square frames with chatelaine hooks atop their chains. I would strongly discourage the use of any type of plastic frame, such as celluloid, on a pre-1900 purse.

The celluloid and faux tortoiseshell frames are attractive when used on larger-bead purses, such as the Art Deco bags of the 1930s and 1940s. I have also used them on German floral and bead-embroidered scenic bags. Occasionally, a bead knitted purse will feature a design, such as an Egyptian theme, that looks stunning with an antique plastic frame.

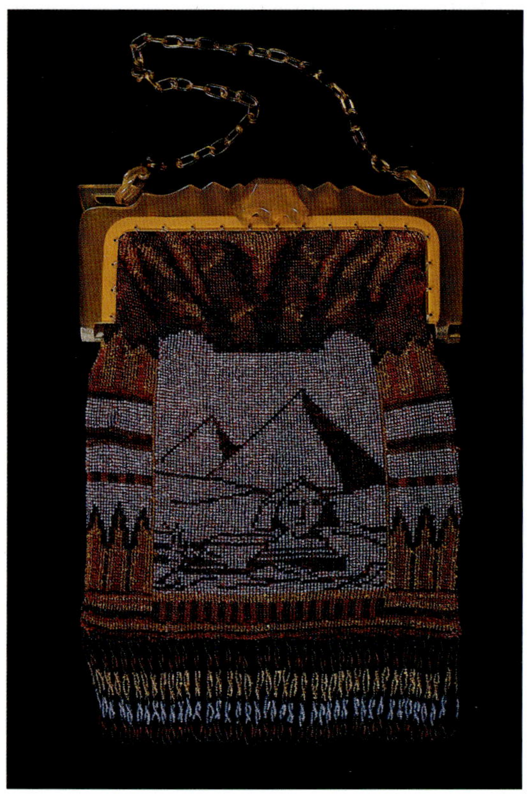

A fine bead knitted Egyptian scenic, mounted on an early plastic frame.

Delicate, finely bead knitted scenic and figural purses look best framed in the fancier, jeweled and enameled frames. These frames compliment the artistic value of the purse and elevate value substantially. It is important to try to match the stones and the style of the frame to the purse colors. If the frame is thick and chunky, consider using it on a heavier purse. A beaded bag with many opaque colors in the design is better suited to a frame adorned with marble or other solid stones. Purses with predominantly light, transparent colored beads are well suited to more delicate frames with sparkling glass rhinestones or semi-precious clear stones.

Loomed, glass-beaded purses generally look best in German silver, wide, square frames. I recently had a customer who wanted a gold finish, ornate frame with stones and a stand-up clasp applied to a loomed floral bag. I was skeptical, but the end result was beautiful. Generally, loomed purses seem more authentic to the eye when framed with German silver frames.

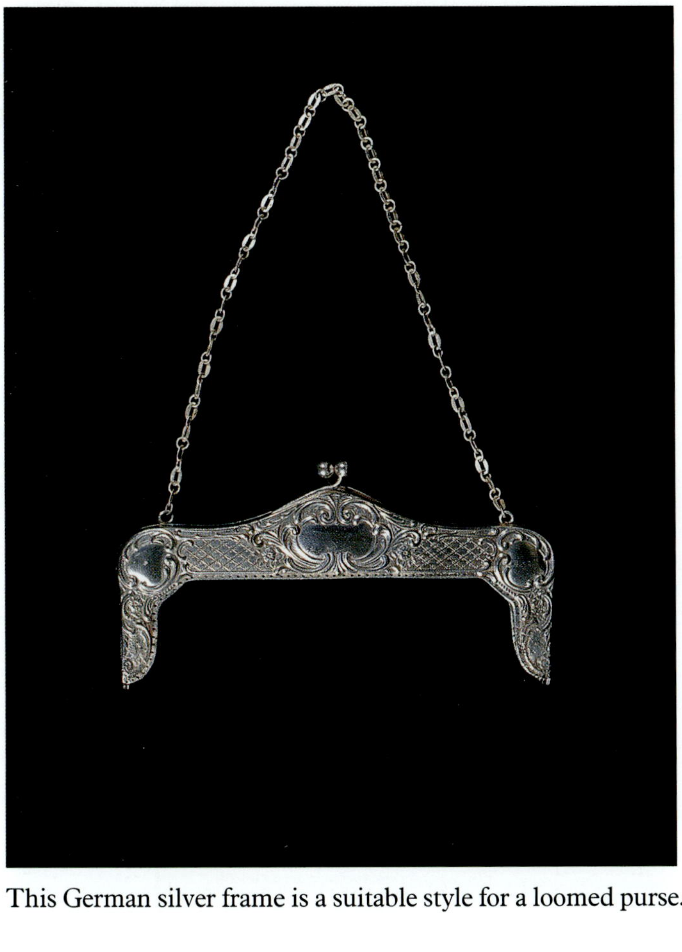

This German silver frame is a suitable style for a loomed purse.

Large, floral reticules were often framed in curved, heavy silver frames with repoussé designs. Many of these purses had kid leather linings that were actually glued to cardboard inserts, and then glued inside the frame! Glue is the four-letter word of the purse world. Never use glue to make purse repairs.

Linings and Trims

Fine beaded purses deserve high quality lining fabric. It is important to match the weight of the purse with an appropriate weight lining fabric, which means that not every purse is best lined in silk. Chain stitched purses were usually sewn onto thin netting, and require a heavier fabric lining to offer shape and support. This can be overlaid with a thin piece of silk if the owner desires, but polished black cotton can be used as the primary and only lining with a nice result, especially if trimmed with authentic Art Deco edging.

I have found lovely vintage silk, and other fine, delicate fabrics that are wonderful as linings, but the key is that the fabric must be strong enough to withstand sewing and that it shows no signs of dry rot. Test the fabric by scratching a small area with your fingernail, if it splits, it is showing signs of dry rot.

Fine vintage (1900-1940) and antique (pre-1900) trims are expensive, but produce the most authentic results when lining a purse. The only appropriate new trims that I have encountered are the "Buds and Bows" line that is offered by several online retailers. It ranges from $6.50-8.50 per yard. High quality antique trim often costs $6.50-11.00 per yard. Doll collectors are interested in the same antique and vintage trims for costumes, so prices reflect this demand.

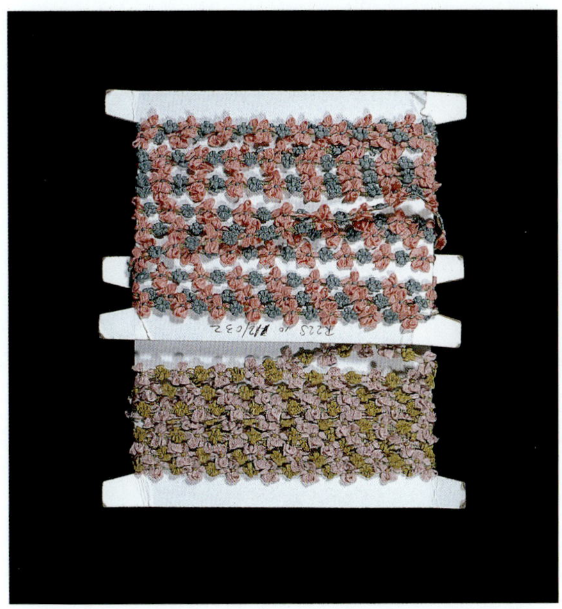

Selections from the Buds-N-Bows collection.

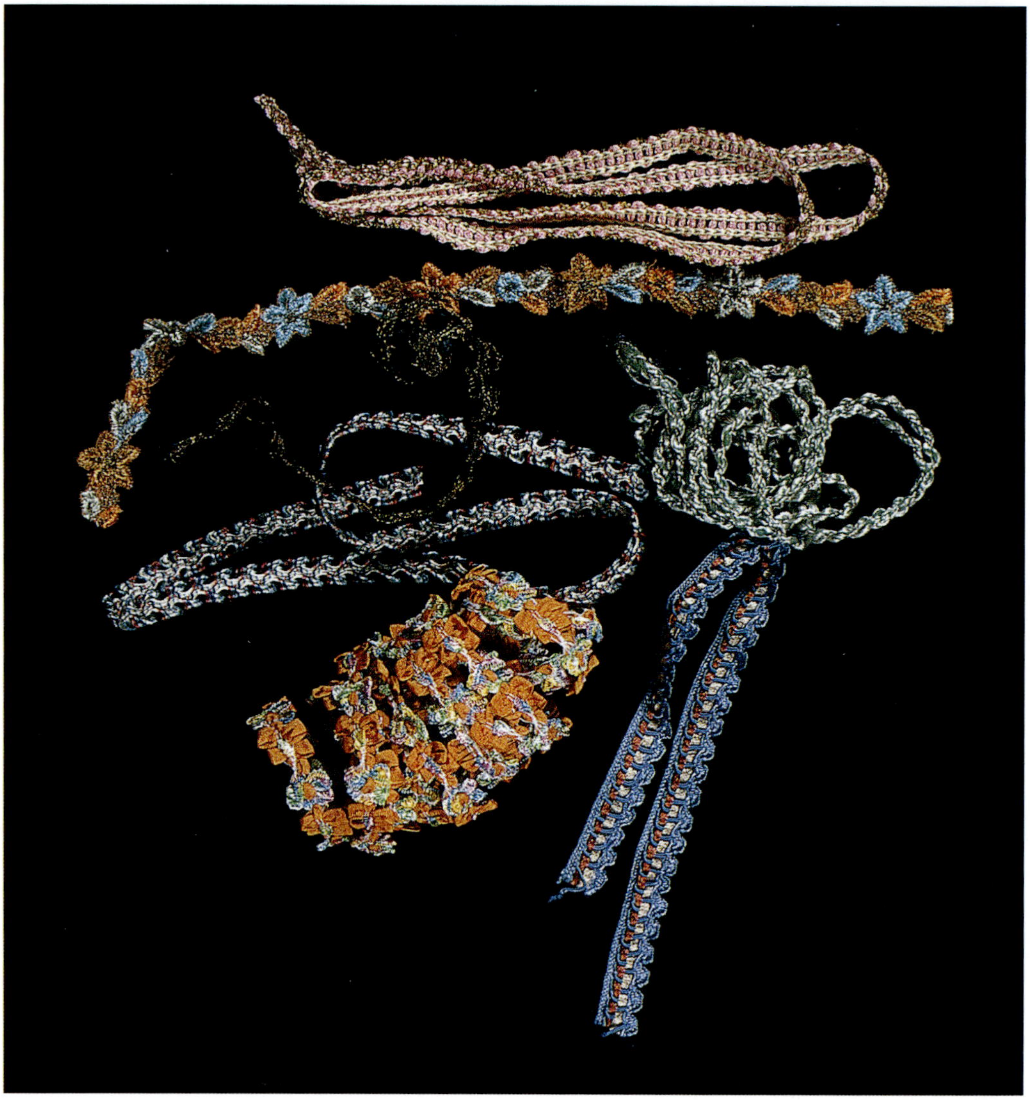

An assortment of antique trims.

Lining colors should be considered, because a dark or strong-colored lining will show through a pale purse. Even pink or yellow linings will alter the purse color, particularly if the background bead is clear or a pale transparent shade, and the body has been knitted in beige silk.

I like the trim selection to coordinate with the lining and with the colors in the purse. To this end, I have had to purchase many different types of trim, some costing over $10 per yard. It is wonderful to discover a vendor selling large quantities of suitable antique trim at a flea market. I try to stock up, whenever possible.

Fringes

Fringes are the finishing touch that can make a bland purse exciting, or create a visual foundation to make a colorful, garish purse more distinctive and cohesive. Fringes vary as much as the purse designs, which adds an enjoyable aspect to their restoration. I am always challenged by the creation of a fringe from scratch, and I will experiment with designs in various patterns and color changes, until I create the arrangement that I like best. Some fringe designs only really come to life after a substantial portion is filled in, which is worrisome until the true beauty begins to be revealed. Then the project is gratifying.

I try to keep my fringes as authentic and stylistically accurate as possible, to maximize the resale and aesthetic value of each purse. The following are several styles of fringes that are well suited to various purse constructions, although I have seen exceptions to these guidelines:

Twisted Interlocking Loop

The most common fringe, also known as a three twist, whereby each fringe is twisted three times around the one in front of it, then anchored into the purse. When positioned very closely together, the fringes can create a beautiful, rippled "wall" of beads.

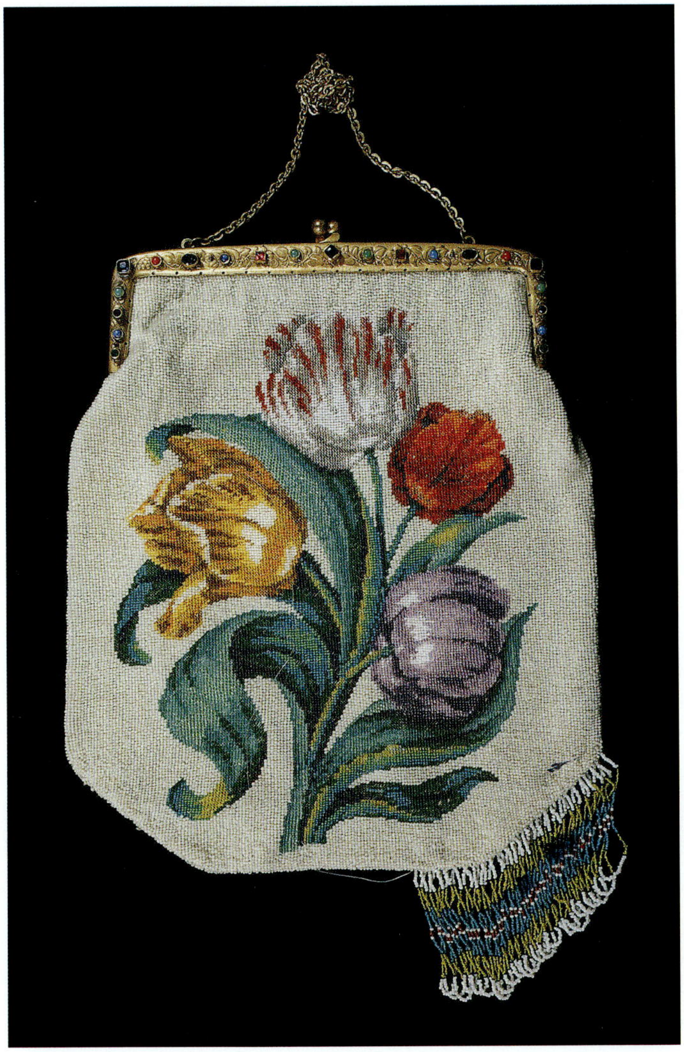

A floral purse with a twisted, interlocked loop fringe in progress.

Single Untwisted Loop

Each loop is formed and sewn back into the purse body without being interconnected to any other loop. Seen in larger beaded purses such as Art Deco designs, or in primitive reticules.

Individual Twisted Strands

These fringes eluded me for years. What little I had read about them indicated that they were formed by twisting the beaded fringe loop around a pencil or knitting needle, then somehow the whole beaded strand would magically twist into place. This sounds logical but doesn't work. The "a-ha" moment came when I realized that it is the thread that should be twisted, not the beads. Once the beads are all threaded onto the strand, twist the thread in the opposite direction of the fringe twist you desire. When the thread has been sufficiently twisted, pinch clamp the end near the beads to preserve the twist, and let the free end of the thread unwind, then sew the twist into the purse and anchor it into the purse body before going on to create the next twist. This style of twist is seen frequently on fine quality, knitted scenic and figural purses. This style is rarely seen on bead embroidered purses, although I have seen it used on tambour stitched bags.

Stick or Loop

Stick fringe is my term for long, straight fringes that are not interconnected. They are seen most often on large bead German floral and scenic bags. Another variation used on the same style of purse is the "stick and loop", which is a straight fringe with a loop at the end. This offers a more sophisticated look, particularly when the loop is done in a different color than the stick.

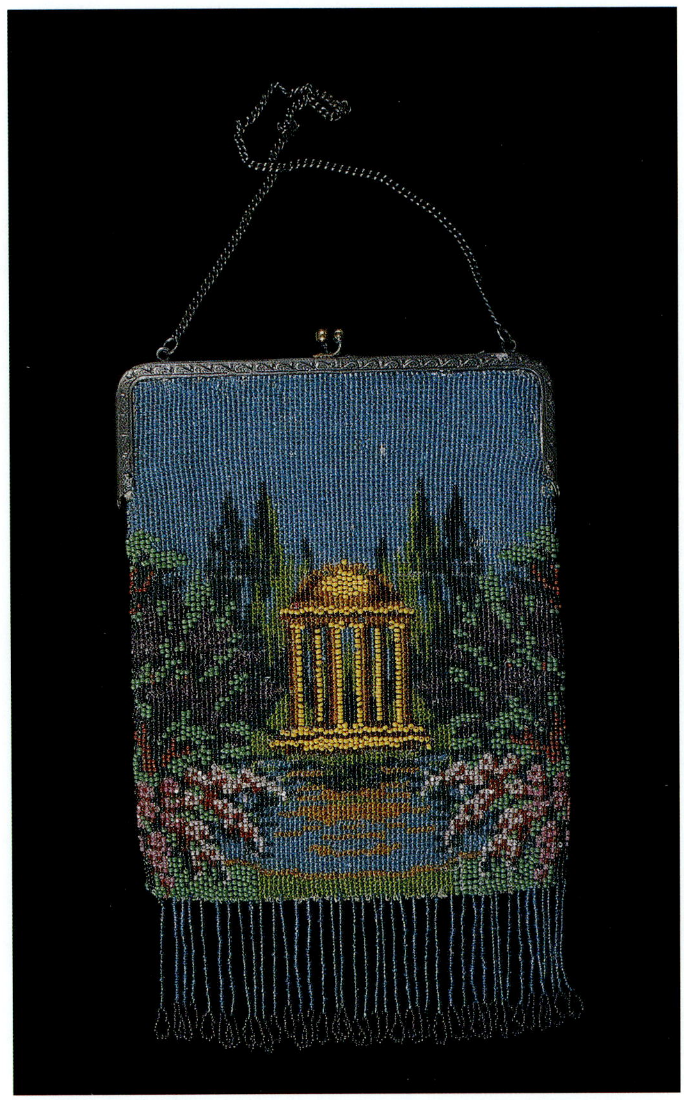

An example of a "stick and loop" fringe on a large beaded, German scenic purse.

Basket Weave Fringe

These are pointed triangular sections of latticework, with various styles of fringe adorning their outer edges. Occasionally, a basket weave may be created as a solid horizontal piece of latticework, in gradually shortened rows. The bottom hanging fringe may be stick and loop, or interlocking loop.

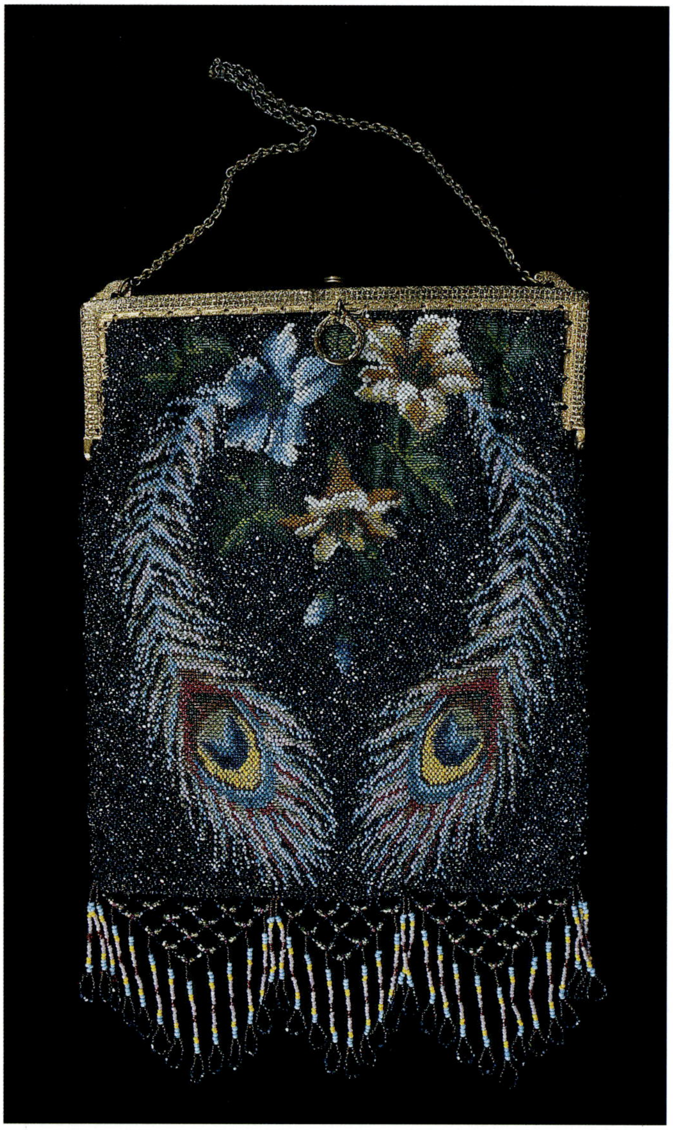

A basketweave design with a "stick and loop" fringe.

Tassel and Ball

These were typically placed at the bottom of large reticules, particularly floral-designed bags. Beaded balls were made by wrapping a wooden bead with strands of seed beads, then creating fringes through the far end of the ball.

McFringe

This is my term for reproduction fringes made with modern, inexpensive craft store beads, or sparsely made fringes with big loops. Nothing is easier than using large, perfectly uniform beads with huge holes to make multicolored, twisted interlocking looped fringes that are quickly strung with large needles, and appear thick and lush, even when spaced far apart. The problem with this inexpensive shortcut is that you have created the equivalent of a craft fair necklace at the bottom of a rare antique treasure. Always insist that your restorations be done with authentic antique seed beads, not reproductions, unless the original bead size used on the purse allows for it, and the color match is excellent. Usually, McFringes don't match the beads used in the body of the purse; the shades may be off, and the finishes of the beads are usually only transparent (clear) or flat opaque. The biggest tip off is the precise, uniform nature of these beads. There are times when I have had to alter bead counts due to sizing inconsistencies of antique seed beads, but the new beads are perfectly sized, and their fringes are too even and perfect to appear antique.

Cleaning Purses

Beaded purses become dirty and dusty over time, and tend to absorb airborne or contact pollution from the environment where they are stored. I have had purses that immediately turned the water black when they were soaked, and there were no dark elements in the color scheme to create this; it was grime. Most purses benefit from cleaning, and become more sparkling and brilliant afterward. The exception to this is a metal beaded purse. You absolutely cannot soak or wet a metal beaded bag. There is not a significantly effective cleaning method for these purses, and they tend to oxidize/rust and fade over time. However, it is possible to use the inside of a metal woven bag as the outside of the purse, if the inside is in good condition (often that is the case). The inside and the outside of a metal woven bag are exactly the same, which allows for this type of fix. It involves removing the frame, taking the bag apart, reversing the inside to the outside, and sewing the seams. This can only be done with a woven metal bag that is structurally sound. For very minor darkening of metal beads, an eraser used with a light touch, or a Hagerty's cleaning cloth for metal (also used with a light touch), can clean off surface grime and brighten the beads.

Because there are dangers to cleaning beaded purses, it is often best left to an expert. New holes can open in a purse with weak spots, particularly on bead knitted bags. Weak fringes may break in the water. A purse collector friend called at 11:00 PM recently, in a panic, and told me she had soaked a rare, knit beaded horse and carriage scenic bag, and fourteen new holes opened on one side of the purse. "Can you fix it?" she asked, in a trembling voice. I assured her it was repairable, since the holes were tiny despite being numerous. Most of the holes were in very colorful parts of the purse, which also helps.

Worst of all, if you are not careful with metal frames, they can rust or corrode the bag if left on the purse to soak. Must all frames be removed before cleaning, then reapplied afterward? No, but I absolutely refuse to soak a purse with a factory applied frame. The frame must be removed. Factory applied frames are actually pressed onto the purse by a machine, and have no sew holes. Once they are pried off, they cannot be reused. Most German large bead bags have factory-applied frames that are made of pot metal, and they rust.

Stained purses can occasionally be rescued by soaking in concentrated Biz and water. The balancing act is in deciding how long it is safe to soak a purse before risking weak threads, new holes, and breaking fringes. If I do the cleaning, my clients know I can fix any damage that occurs along the way.

What if glue has been used on a purse? I have tried removing glue with solvents, and I have had some limited success with nail polish remover, and with Goo Gone. If it is a really hard lump, it may have to be cut out and the resulting hole repaired.

When To Walk Away

As we discussed before, dry rot is a deal breaker in my book. Lightly pick and pluck at the edges of torn, frayed areas or holes and if it breaks easily, walk away, or accept that the purse should be laid flat, or framed in a display with other objects covering the damage.

Too many holes are a negative, especially if they are in solid colored areas of the purse. After repairing all of those holes, the texture of the bag may appear altered to the eye, and seem odd.

Too many missing beads on a bead embroidered bag are another difficult problem to deal with, especially if they are missing from a large bald area. The entire missing design would have to be recreated, which would require careful charting and planning, and consume many hours of time.

Purses that have been obviously shortened or inappropriately patched together ("Franken purses") are problematic. Unless you love the purse and can accept that it has been surgically altered, you should avoid such bags for investment purposes. The good news is that occasionally, a shortened purse will have the original remaining purse tucked inside itself, and can be let out and restored to its original dimensions. I had a gorgeous bag sent to me for repair by an unsuspecting customer, who was delighted when I told her the bag had three additional inches tucked inside, in perfect condition when I let it out! Some prior owner had shortened it, perhaps for style purposes.

Purses that have been cut and attached to hard, 1950s style handbag forms should be avoided. These are time consuming to remove from the forms, and are usually missing too many needed parts of the purse design to be authentically restored.

Knitted purses that have been cut apart and sewn together are another issue. A really good restoration expert might be able to disguise the seams, but knitted beaded bags usually do not have seams down the sides. It may be an indication that they have been altered.

Badly stained purses should be carefully considered before purchasing. It is impossible to determine in advance which stains will come out, and which will stay. It is a gamble to spend a great deal of money on stained purses, because the value is diminished substantially if the stains won't come out. If in desperation you want to switch from Biz to chlorine bleach, to really knock out a stain, you will find that the stain will disappear, and so will the rest of the purse thread.

Huge holes, which are larger than a quarter, may not be repairable, unless it is only one hole, and then the hole should be no larger than a silver dollar. Even within these guidelines, some large holes above 4-5 missing beads can result in noticeable repairs, depending upon the construction of the purse and the color scheme and design of the missing area.

Purses with numerous crumbling, breaking beads may indicate the purse has glass disease. There are some old beads of various colors, particularly brown beads that tend to break over time. Unless you are comfortable with a balding effect, be cautious about buying purses with this condition, because each time you handle the purse, more beads will break off.

Bibliography

Ashelford, Jane. *The Art of Dress: Clothes and Society 1500-1914,* New York, New York: Harry N. Abrams, 1996.

Beck, Thomasina. *The Embroiderer's Story,* England: A David and Charles Book, 1995.

Benn, Elizabeth. *Treasures From The Embroiderer's Guild,* England: A David and Charles Book, 1991.

Chenoune, Farid, editor. *Carried Away-All About Bags,* New York, New York: The Vendome Press, 2005.

Crabtree, Caroline and Stallebrass, Pam. *Beadwork-A World Guide,* New York, New York: Rizzoli International Publications, Inc., 2002.

Cummings, Valerie. *The Visual History of Costume Accessories,* London, England: BT Batsford Ltd. Press, 1998.

Cummins, Genevieve E. and Taunton, Nerylla D. *Chatelaines: Utility to Glorious Extravagance,* England: Antique Collector's Club.

Ettinger, Roseann. *Handbags,* West Chester, Pennsylvania: Schiffer Publishing, 1991.

Foster, Vanda. *Bags and Purses,* London, England: BT Batsford Ltd. Press, 1982.

Haertig, Evelyn. *Antique Combs and Purses,* Carmel, California: Gallery Press, 1990.

Haertig, Evelyn. *More Beautiful Purses,* Carmel, California: Gallery Press, 1990.

Himmelhefer, George. *Biedermeier 1815-1835,* Germany: Te Neus Publishing Company, 1989.

Ivo, Hendrikje-The Tassenmuseum. *Bags,* Amsterdam, the Netherlands, 2004.

Johnson, Anna. *Handbags—The Power of the Purse,* New York, New York: Workman Publishing, 2002.

Kyoto Costume Institute: Starobinski, Dubay, Fukai, Kanai, Horii, Arnold and Kamer. *Revolution In Fashion: European Clothing 1715-1815,* New York, New York: Abbeville Press, 1989.

Miller, Judith. *Handbags,* London, New York: Dorling Kindersley: A Penguin Company, 2006.

O'Neill, John P.-The Metropolitan Museum of Art. *Orientalism: Visions Of The East In Western Dress,* New York, New York: The Costume Institute and East Greenwich, Rhode Island: Meridian Printing Company.

Pina, Leslie and Johnson, Donald-Brian. *Whiting & Davis Purses-The Perfect Mesh,* Atglen, Pennsylvania: Schiffer Publishing Company, 2002.

Schurenburg, Sabina. *Glasperlarbeiten Taschen Und Beutel,* Germany: Hirmer Press, 1998.

Schwartz, Lynell. *Vintage Purses At Their Best,* Atglen, Pennsylvania: Schiffer Publishing, 1995.

Schwartz, Lynell. *Purse Masterpieces,* Paducah, Kentucky: Collector Books, 2004.

Smith, Desire. *Handbag Chic,* Atglen, Pennsylvania: Schiffer Publishing, 2005.

Swan, Susan Burrows. *Plain and Fancy—American Women and Their Needlework 1700-1850,* New York, New York: Holt, Rhinehart, and Winstar, 1977.

Van Der Krol, Yolanda., *"Ladies' Pockets," The Magazine ANITQUES,* New York, New York: Brant Publications, March 1996.

Wang, Loretta H. *The Chinese Purse,* Union City, California: Heian International, 1986.

Weissman, Judith and Lavitt, Wendy. *Labors of Love-American Textiles and Needlework 1650-1930,* New York, New York: Random House, 1987.

Wilcox, Claire. *Bags,* London, England: Victoria and Albert Museum Publications, 1999.

Yurova, Elena. *The Glorious Epoch Of Beads In Russia,* Moscow, Russia: Interbook Business Publishing, 2003.

Index